2008
Advanced
Biology AS

Student Workbook

Advanced *Biology AS* 2008

Student Workbook

Previous annual editions 1999-2007
Tenth edition 2008

ISBN 978-1-877329-96-8

Copyright © **2007** Richard Allan
Published by **BIOZONE International Ltd**

Printed by REPLIKA PRESS PVT LTD using paper
produced from renewable and waste materials

About the Writing Team

Tracey Greenwood joined the staff of Biozone at the beginning of 1993. She has a Ph.D in biology, specialising in lake ecology, and taught undergraduate and graduate biology at the University of Waikato for four years.

Lyn Shepherd joined as an author in 2003, bringing her 20 years experience as a secondary school biology teacher to Biozone.

Lissa Bainbridge-Smith joined Biozone as an author this year after working in industry for 8 years. Lissa has an MSc. from Waikato University, majoring in aquatic toxicology.

Richard Allan has had 11 years experience teaching senior biology at Hillcrest High School in Hamilton, New Zealand. He attained a Masters degree in biology at Waikato University, New Zealand.

As always, the authors acknowledge and thank our graphic artist Dan Butler for his continued dedication to the job at hand.

Purchases of this workbook may be made direct from the publisher:

BIOZONE

www.biozone.co.uk

UNITED KINGDOM:

BIOZONE Learning Media (UK) Ltd.
P.O. Box 23698, Edinburgh EH5 2WX, **Scotland**
Telephone: (131) 557 5060
FAX: (131) 557 5030
E-mail: sales@biozone.co.uk

AUSTRALIA:

BIOZONE Learning Media Australia
P.O. Box 7523, GCMC 4217 QLD, **Australia**
Telephone: +61 (7) 5575 4615
FAX: +61 (7) 5572 0161
E-mail: info@biozone.com.au

NEW ZEALAND:

BIOZONE International Ltd.
P.O. Box 13-034, Hamilton, **New Zealand**
Telephone: +64 (7) 856 8104
FAX: +64 (7) 856 9243
E-mail: sales@biozone.co.nz

Preface to the 2008 Edition

This tenth edition of the workbook is designed to meet the needs of students enrolled in biology courses for: **AQA specifications A and B**, **EDEXCEL**, **OCR**, Cambridge International Examinations (**CIE**), and Salters-Nuffield Advanced Biology (**SNAB**). It is also suitable for senior level biology courses in **Wales**, **Northern Ireland**, and **Scotland**. Previous editions of this workbook have received very favourable reviews (see our web site: **www.biozone.co.uk** for details). A new feature this year is the page tab identifying "**Related activities**" in the workbook and "**Web links**". These will help students to locate related material within the workbook and provides access to web links and activities (including animations) that will enhance their understanding of the topic. See page 11 to find out more about these. A further enhancement is the placement of two page activities back-to-back facilitating easier removal of discrete activities without upsetting the flow of information. Supplementary material and extension activities continue to be available with a limited photocopy licence on Biozone's **Teacher Resource CD-ROM**. A guide to using the Teacher Resource CD-ROM to best effect has been included in the introductory section of the workbook and can be used in conjunction with the revised course guides. As in previous years, we have updated the listed resources and include crosswords on the TRC as a student-friendly way in which to test vocabulary. Revised and new activities are indicated in the contents pages. These annual upgrades are in keeping with our ongoing commitment to providing up-to-date, relevant, interesting, and accurate information.

A Note to the Teacher

This workbook has been produced as a student-centred resource, and benefits students by facilitating independent learning and critical thinking. Biozone's workbooks motivate and challenge a wide range of students by providing a highly visual format, a clear map through the course, and a synopsis of supplementary resources. In modern biology, a single textbook may no longer provide all the information a student needs to grasp a topic. This workbook is a generic resource and **not a textbook**, and we make a point of referencing texts from other publishers. Above all, we are committed to continually revising and improving this resource **every year**. The price remains below £11 for students, as a reflection of our commitment to providing high-quality, cost effective resources for biology. Please **do not photocopy** from this workbook. We cannot afford to supply single copies to schools and still provide annual updates as we intend. If you think it is worth using, then we recommend that the students themselves own this resource and keep it for their own use. A free model answer book is supplied with your **first order** of 5 or more workbooks.

How Teachers May Use This Workbook

This workbook may be used in the classroom to guide students through each topic. Some activities may be used to introduce topics while others may be used to consolidate and test concepts already covered by other means. The workbook may be used as the primary tool in teaching some topics, but it should not be at the expense of good, 'hands-on' biology. Students may attempt the activities on their own or in groups. The latter provides opportunities for healthy discussion and peer-to-peer learning. Many of the activities may be set as homework exercises. Each page is perforated, allowing for easy removal of pages to be submitted for marking. This has been facilitated this year by the back-to-back format of two page activities. Teachers may prescribe the activities to be attempted by the students (using the check boxes next to the objectives for each topic), or they may allow students a degree of freedom with respect to the activities they attempt. The objectives for each topic will allow students to keep up to date even if they miss lessons and teachers who are away from class may set work easily in their absence. I thank you for your support.

Richard Allan

Acknowledgements

We would like to thank those who have contributed towards this edition:
• Joan and John Allan for kindly agreeing to pose for the photos on age related health issues • Joseph E. Armstrong, Professor of Botany, Head Curator at ISU Herbarium, USA for his permission to use the photo showing a child with kwashiorkor • Sam Banks and the Australian Broadcasting Corporation (www.abc.net.au/science/) for the photograph of wombat scat • Bio-Rad Laboratories, Inc. for allowing us to photograph the Helios gene gun • Daniel Butler for his photograph of a wounded finger • Corel Corporation, for use of their eps clipart of plants and animals from the Corel MEGAGALLERY collection • ©2002 EliLily and Co. for the photo of the human insulin product, humalog • Stacey Farmer and Greg Baillie, Waikato DNA Sequencing Facility, University of Waikato, for their assistance with material on PCR, DNA sequencing, and genetic profiling • Genesis Research and Development Corp. Auckland, for the photo used on the HGP activity • Charles Goldberg, University of California, San Diego School of Medicine, for the photograph of a patient with rheumatoid arthritis • Marc King for photographs of comb types in chickens • Kurchatov Institute for the photo of Chornobyl • Sue Fitzgerald and Mary McDougall for their efficient handling of the office • Stephen Moore for his photos of freshwater insects • Jan Morrison for her line diagrams • Liam Nolan, Leo Sanchez, and Burkhard Budel for photographs and information contributing to the activity on the genetic biodiversity of Antarctic springtails • Pharmacia (Aust) Pty Ltd. for the photographs of DNA gel sequencing • Roslin Institute, for photographs of Dolly • TechPool Studios, for their clipart collection of human anatomy: Copyright ©1994, TechPool Studios Corp. USA (some of these images were modified by Richard Allan and Tracey Greenwood) • Totem Graphics, for their clipart collection of plants and animals • ©1999 University of Kansas, for the photo of the incubator for culture of cell lines • Dr Roger Wagner, Dept of Biological Sciences, University of Delaware, for the LS of a capillary • Dr. David Wells, Agresearch, New Zealand, for information and photos on cloning. • The 3D modelling by Dan Butler using Poser IV, Curious Labs and Bryce.

Photo Credits

Royalty free images, purchased by Biozone International Ltd, are used throughout this workbook and have been obtained from the following sources: Corel Corporation from various titles in their Professional Photos CD-ROM collection; IMSI (International Microcomputer Software Inc.) images from IMSI's MasterClips® and MasterPhotosTM Collection, 1895 Francisco Blvd. East, San Rafael, CA 94901-5506, USA; ©1996 Digital Stock, Medicine and Health Care collection; ©Hemera Technologies Inc, 1997-2001; © 2005 JupiterImages Corporation www.clipart.com; ©Click Art, ©T/Maker Company; ©1994., ©Digital Vision; Gazelle Technologies Inc.; PhotoDisc®, Inc. USA, www.photodisc.com. Photos kindly provided by individuals or corporations have been indentified by way of coded credits as follows: **BF**: Brian Finerran (Uni. of Canterbury), **BH**: Brendan Hicks (Uni. of Waikato), **BOB**: Barry O'Brien (Uni. of Waikato), **CDC**: Centers for Disease Control and Prevention, Atlanta, USA, **DEQ**: Department of Environment Queensland Ltd., **DH**: Don Horne, **EII**: Education Interactive Imaging, **EW**: Environment Waikato, **Eyewire**: Eyewire, Inc © 1998-2001, www.eyewire.com **FRI**: Forest Research Institute, **GW**: Graham Walker, **HGSI**: Human Genome Sciences, Inc., **JDG**: John Green (Uni. of Waikato), **MPI**: Max Planck Institute for Developmental Biology, Germany; **NASA**: National Aeronautics and Space Administration, **RA**: Richard Allan, **RCN**: Ralph Cocklin, **TG**: Tracey Greenwood, **WBS**: Warwick Silvester (Uni. of Waikato), **WMU**: Waikato Microscope Unit.

Special thanks to all the partners of the Biozone team for their support.

Cover Photographs

Main photograph: The snowy owl (*Bubo scandiacus*) is a large, diurnal owl with a distinctive white plumage which is variably barred or speckled with thin, black, horizontal bars or spots. Females (pictured) are more heavily marked than males, which may be almost pure white. PHOTO: photos.com ©JUPITERIMAGES.

Background photograph: Autumn leaves, Image ©2005 JupiterImages Corporation www.clipart.com

Contents

Skills in Biology

Biological Molecules

Cell Structure

Cell Membranes and Transport

CODES: Δ   **Upgraded** this edition   ☆   **New** this edition   **Activity** is marked: ● to be done;   ✓ when completed

CONTENTS *(continued)*

CODES: △ **Upgraded** this edition ☆ **New** this edition **Activity** is marked: ⬛ to be done; ✔ when completed

CONTENTS (continued)

CODES: Δ   **Upgraded** this edition   ☆ **New** this edition   Activity is marked: ⦁ to be done; ☑ when completed

How to Use this Workbook

This workbook is designed to provide you with a resource that will make the subject of biology more enjoyable and fun to study. It is suitable for students in their AS year of the following biology courses: **AQA specifications A** and **B**, **Edexcel**, **CIE**, **OCR**, Cambridge International Examinations, and the new Salters-Nuffield Advanced Biology (**SNAB**). This workbook is also appropriate for senior level biology courses in **Northern** **Ireland**, **Wales**, and **Scotland (Biology Higher)**. The Syllabus Guides on pages 13-19 (or on the Teacher Resource CD-ROM) indicate where the material required by your syllabus is covered. This workbook will reinforce and extend the ideas developed by your teacher. It is **not a textbook**; its aim is to complement the texts written for your course. The workbook provides the following useful resources for each topic:

Guidance Provided for Each Topic

Learning objectives:

These provide a map of the topic content. Completing the relevant learning objectives will help you to satisfy the knowledge requirements of your course. Your teacher may add to or omit points from this list.

Topic outcomes:

This panel provides details of the learning objectives that need to be completed in order to satisfy the requirements (relevant to that topic) for each exam board. Attempt to meet the objectives relating to your exam board only. See pages 13-19 for a synopsis of the syllabus requirements for your course.

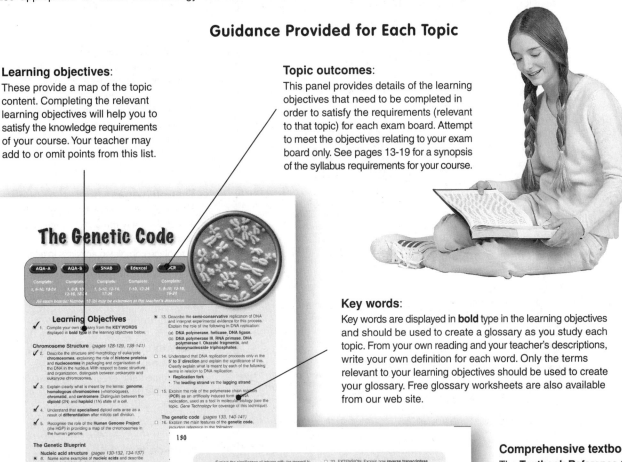

Key words:

Key words are displayed in **bold** type in the learning objectives and should be used to create a glossary as you study each topic. From your own reading and your teacher's descriptions, write your own definition for each word. Only the terms relevant to your learning objectives should be used to create your glossary. Free glossary worksheets are also available from our web site.

Use the check boxes to mark objectives to be completed.
Use a **dot** to be done (•).
Use a **tick** when completed (✓).

Comprehensive textbooks

The **Textbook Reference Grid** on pages 8-9 lists the major comprehensive textbooks available for your course (these are texts providing coverage of the majority of course topics). The grid provides the pages or chapters from each text relevant to each topic in the workbook.

Internet addresses:

Access our database of links to more than **800** web sites (updated regularly) relevant to topics covered in the manual. Go to Biozone's own web site: **www.biozone.co.uk** and link directly to listed sites using the *BioLinks* button.

Supplementary texts:

References to supplementary texts, which have only a restricted topic coverage, are provided as appropriate in each topic.

Periodical articles:

Ideal for those seeking more depth or the latest research on a specific topic. Articles are sorted according to their suitability for student or teacher reference. Visit your school, public, or university library for these articles.

Supplementary resources from Biozone Supporting Presentation MEDIA are noted where appropriate. Computer software and videos relevant to every topic in the workbook are provided on the **Teacher Resource CD-ROM** (which may be purchased separately). See page 12 for details.

Activity Pages

The activities and exercises make up most of the content of this book. They are designed to reinforce the concepts you have learned about in the topic. Your teacher may use the activity pages to introduce a topic for the first time, or you may use them to revise ideas already covered. They are excellent for use in the classroom, and as homework exercises and revision. In most cases, the activities should not be attempted until you have carried out the necessary background reading from your textbook. Your teacher should have a model answers book with the answers to each activity. Because this workbook caters for more than one exam board, you will find some activities that may not be relevant to your course. Although you will miss out these pages, our workbooks still represent exceptional value.

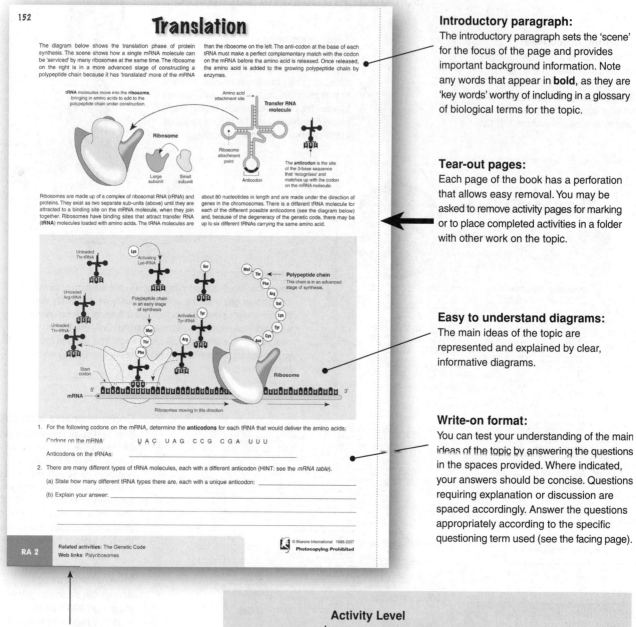

Introductory paragraph:
The introductory paragraph sets the 'scene' for the focus of the page and provides important background information. Note any words that appear in **bold**, as they are 'key words' worthy of including in a glossary of biological terms for the topic.

Tear-out pages:
Each page of the book has a perforation that allows easy removal. You may be asked to remove activity pages for marking or to place completed activities in a folder with other work on the topic.

Easy to understand diagrams:
The main ideas of the topic are represented and explained by clear, informative diagrams.

Write-on format:
You can test your understanding of the main ideas of the topic by answering the questions in the spaces provided. Where indicated, your answers should be concise. Questions requiring explanation or discussion are spaced accordingly. Answer the questions appropriately according to the specific questioning term used (see the facing page).

Activity code and links:
Activity codes (explained right) help to identify the type of activities and the skills they require. Most activities require knowledge recall as well as the application of knowledge to explain observations or predict outcomes.

Use the **Related activities** indicated to visit pages that may help you with understanding the material or answering the questions.

Web links indicate additional material of assistance or interest (either web pages or pdf activities). You can access these from: *www.biozone.co.uk/weblink/UK1-9968.html*

Activity Level

1 = Simple questions not requiring complex reasoning
2 = Some complex reasoning may be required
3 = More challenging, requiring integration of concepts

RA 2 | Related activities: The Genetic Code
Web links: Polyribosomes

Type of Activity

D = Includes some data handling and/or interpretation
P = includes a paper practical
R = May require research outside the page
A = Includes application of knowledge to solve a problem
E = Extension material

Explanation of Terms

Questions come in a variety of forms. Whether you are studying for an exam or writing an essay, it is important to understand exactly what the question is asking. A question has two parts to it: one part of the question will provide you with information, the second part of the question will provide you with instructions as to how to answer the question. Following these instructions is most important. Often students in examinations know the material but fail to follow instructions and do not answer the question appropriately. Examiners often use certain key words to introduce questions. Look out for them and be clear as to what they mean. Below is a description of terms commonly used when asking questions in biology.

Commonly used Terms in Biology

The following terms are frequently used when asking questions in examinations and assessments. Students should have a clear understanding of each of the following terms and use this understanding to answer questions appropriately.

Account for: Provide a satisfactory explanation or reason for an observation.

Analyse: Interpret data to reach stated conclusions.

Annotate: Add **brief** notes to a diagram, drawing or graph.

Apply: Use an idea, equation, principle, theory, or law in a new situation.

Appreciate: To understand the meaning or relevance of a particular situation.

Calculate: Find an answer using mathematical methods. Show the working unless instructed not to.

Compare: Give an account of similarities and differences between two or more items, referring to both (or all) of them throughout. Comparisons can be given using a table. Comparisons generally ask for similarities more than differences (see contrast).

Construct: Represent or develop in graphical form.

Contrast: Show differences. Set in opposition.

Deduce: Reach a conclusion from information given.

Define: Give the precise meaning of a word or phrase as concisely as possible.

Derive: Manipulate a mathematical equation to give a new equation or result.

Describe: Give a detailed account, including all the relevant information.

Design: Produce a plan, object, simulation or model.

Determine: Find the only possible answer.

Discuss: Give an account including, where possible, a range of arguments, assessments of the relative importance of various factors, or comparison of alternative hypotheses.

Distinguish: Give the difference(s) between two or more different items.

Draw: Represent by means of pencil lines. Add labels unless told not to do so.

Estimate: Find an approximate value for an unknown quantity, based on the information provided and application of scientific knowledge.

Evaluate: Assess the implications and limitations.

Explain: Give a clear account including causes, reasons, or mechanisms.

Identify: Find an answer from a number of possibilities.

Illustrate: Give concrete examples. Explain clearly by using comparisons or examples.

Interpret: Comment upon, give examples, describe relationships. Describe, then evaluate.

List: Give a sequence of names or other brief answers with no elaboration. Each one should be clearly distinguishable from the others.

Measure: Find a value for a quantity.

Outline: Give a brief account or summary. Include essential information only.

Predict: Give an expected result.

Solve: Obtain an answer using algebraic and/or numerical methods.

State: Give a specific name, value, or other answer. No supporting argument or calculation is necessary.

Suggest: Propose a hypothesis or other possible explanation.

Summarise: Give a brief, condensed account. Include conclusions and avoid unnecessary details.

In Conclusion

Students should familiarise themselves with this list of terms and, where necessary throughout the course, they should refer back to them when answering questions. The list of terms mentioned above is not exhaustive and students should compare this list with past examination papers / essays etc. and add any new terms (and their meaning) to the list above. The aim is to become familiar with interpreting the question and answering it appropriately.

Introduction

Resources Information

Your set textbook should always be a starting point for information. There are also many other resources available, including scientific journals, magazine and newspaper articles, supplementary texts covering restricted topic areas, dictionaries, computer software and videos, and the internet.

A synopsis of currently available resources is provided below. Access to the publishers of these resources can be made directly from Biozone's web site through our resources hub: **www. biozone.co.uk/resource-hub.html**, or by typing in the relevant addresses provided below. Most titles are also available through amazon.co.uk. Please note that our listing any product in this workbook does not, in any way, denote Biozone's endorsement of that product.

Comprehensive Biology Texts Referenced

Appropriate texts for this course are referenced in this workbook. Page or chapter references for each text are provided in the text reference grid on page 8. These will enable you to identify the relevant reading as you progress through the activities in this workbook. Publication details of texts referenced in the grid are provided below and opposite. For further details of text content, or to make purchases, link to the relevant publisher via Biozone's resources hub or by typing: **www.biozone.co.uk/resources/uk-comprehensive-pg1.html**

Bailey, M. and K. Hirst, 2000
Collins Advanced Modular-Biology AS, 2 ed.
Publisher: HarperCollins Publishers Ltd.
Pages: 224
ISBN: 0-00-327751-8
Comments: *Appropriate to AQA AS-level Biology (B) specification. Student support packs for AQA B and Edexcel specifications are available at extra cost.*

Boyle, M. and K. Senior, 2002
Collins Advanced Science: Biology, 2 ed.
Publisher: HarperCollins Publishers Ltd
Pages: approx. 630 (based on previous edn)
ISBN: 0-00-713600-5
Comments: *Fully revised to reflect some of the more changes in the specifications. Includes a new section on plant biology and a new chapter on biotechnology.*

Bradfield, P., J. Dodds, J. Dodds, and N. Taylor, 2001
AS Level Biology
Publisher: Longman
Pages: 566
ISBN: 0-582-42926-3
Comments: *Written to match all AS level specifications and at a level suitable for AS students progressing from GCSE.*

Clegg, C.J., 2000
Introduction to Advanced Biology
Publisher: John Murray
Pages: 528
ISBN: 0-7195-7671-7
Comments: *Matches new AS/A2 specifications but aims to provide a bridge from GCSE (grade C pass) to A level. Detailed specification matches are available on CD-ROM, FREE on request.*

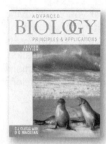

Clegg, C.J. and D.G. McKean, 2000
Advanced Biology: Principles and Applications 2 ed.
Publisher: John Murray
Pages: 712
ISBN: 0-7195-7670-9
Comments: *Student study guide also available. A general text with specific references for use by biology students of the AS and A2 curricula in the UK.*

Fullick, A., 2000
Heinemann Advanced Science: Biology, 2 ed.
Publisher: Heinemann Educational Publishers
Pages: 760
ISBN: 0-435-57095-1
Comments: *Suitable as a general text for use with all specifications.*

Indge, B, M. Rowland, and M. Baker, 2000
AQA Biology Specification A: A New Introduction to Biology (AS)
Publisher: Hodder & Stoughton
Pages: 240
ISBN: 0-340-78167-X
Comments: *Written specifically for the AQA biology specification A. AS content is covered in full, with assignments for each area to build skills and knowledge.*

Jones, M., R. Fosbery, and D. Taylor, 2000
Biology 1
Publisher: Cambridge University Press
Pages: 208
ISBN: 0-521-78719-X
Comments: *Provides coverage of the core material for the first year of advanced level biology (OCR). Contents: Foundation Biology, Transport, and Human Health & Disease.*

Jones, M., R, Fosbery, D. Taylor, and J. Gregory, 2007
CIE Biology AS and A Level, 2 ed.
Publisher: Cambridge University Press
Pages: 424
ISBN: 0-521-53674-X
Comments: *This text meets the new CIE requirements and covers the complete AS level syllabus, the core A level syllabus, and the new Applications of Biology section.*

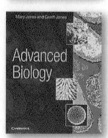

Jones, M. and G. Jones, 1997
Advanced Biology
Publisher: Cambridge University Press
Pages: 560
ISBN: 978-0-521703-06-2
Comments: *Provides full coverage of the core material included in all advanced biology syllabuses. Suitable for students studying for a range of qualifications.*

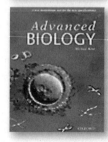

Kent, N. A. 2000
Advanced Biology
Publisher: Oxford University Press
Pages: 624
ISBN: 0-19-914195-9
Comments: *Each book comes with a free CD-ROM to help with specification planning. Book is formatted as a series of two page concept spreads.*

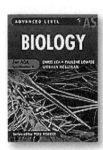

Lea, C, P. Lowrie, and S. McGuigan, (M. Hiscock, ed), 2000
Advanced Level Biology for AQA: AS
Publisher: Heinemann Educational Pubs
Pages: 267
ISBN: 0-435-58083-3
Comments: *Appropriate for AQA specification B. Accompanying Resource Pack, providing support material, and extra questions and tasks, is also available.*

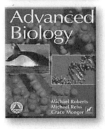

Roberts, M., G. Monger, M. Reiss, 2000
Advanced Biology
Publisher: NelsonThornes
Pages: approx. 781
ISBN: 0-17-438732-6
Comments: *Provides thorough coverage of the Advanced Level specifications within one volume.*

SNAB Project Team, 2005
Salters-Nuffield Advanced Biology AS Student Book
Publisher: Heinemann
Pages: 229
ISBN: 978-0-435628-57-4
Comments: *Developed for the SNAB AS specification. This new text takes a contextual approach to help develop a sound understanding of biological principles.*

SNAB Project Team, May 2006
Salters-Nuffield Advanced Biology A2 Student Book
Publisher: Heinemann
Pages: 260 approx
ISBN: 978-0-435628-58-1
Comments: *Developed for the SNAB A Level specification in which students explore biological concepts within relevant and high interest contexts. Although an A2 text, this volume contains reading for this workbook.*

Taylor D.J., N.P.O. Green, & G.W. Stout, 1997
Biological Science 1 & 2, 3 ed. (hardback)
Publisher: Cambridge University Press
Pages: 984
ISBN: 0-521-56178-7
Comments: *An older but comprehensive and accurate text, with clear line diagrams and photographs and methodical treatment of a wide range of topic areas.*

Toole G. and S. Toole, 2000
New Understanding Biology for Advanced Level, 4 ed.
Publisher: NelsonThornes
Pages: 672
ISBN: 0-7487-3964-5
Comments: *Fully revised to match AS and A2 specifications. Also available with Course Study Guide, which provides additional support material.*

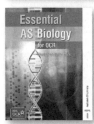

Toole G. and S. Toole, 2004
Essential AS Biology for OCR
Publisher: NelsonThornes
Pages: 280
ISBN: 0-7487-8511-6
Comments: *A text written to meet the AS specifications for OCR. The 2-page-spread format is appealing and student-friendly. A comprehensive glossary is included.*

Williams, G., 2000
Advanced Biology for You
Publisher: NelsonThornes
Pages: 464
ISBN: 0-7487-5298-6
Comments: *Covers the current AS-level specifications and the core topics of all A2 specifications.*

Supplementary Texts

For further details of text content, or to make purchases, link to the relevant publisher via Biozone's resources hub or by typing: **www.biozone.co.uk/resources/uk-supplementary-pg1.html**

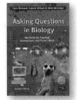

Barnard, C., F. Gilbert, F., and P. McGregor, 2007
Asking Questions in Biology: Key Skills for Practical Assessments & Project Work, 256 pp.
Publisher: Benjamin Cummings
ISBN: 978-0132224352
Comments: *Covers many aspects of design, analysis and presentation of practical work.*

Cadogan, A. and Ingram, M., 2002
Maths for Advanced Biology
Publisher: NelsonThornes
ISBN: 0-7487-6506-9
Comments: *Covers the maths requirements of AS/A2 biology. Includes worked examples.*

Chenn, P., 1997.
Microorganisms and Biotechnology, 176 pp.
Publisher: John Murray
ISBN: 0-71957-509-5
One of several titles in the Advanced Biology Reader series covering microbial diversity, the culture and growth of microbes, and the use of microorganisms in biotechnology.

Freeland, P., 1999
Hodder Advanced Science: Microbes, Medicine, and Commerce, 160 pp.
Publisher: Hodder and Stoughton
ISBN: 0-340-73103-6
Comments: *Combines biotechnology, pathology, microbiology, and immunity in a thorough text.*

Fullick, A., 1998
Human Health and Disease, 162 pp.
Publisher: Heinemann Educational Publishers
ISBN: 0435570919
Comments: *An excellent supplement for courses with modules in human health and disease. Includes infectious and non-infectious disease.*

Indge, B., 2003
Data and Data Handling for AS and A Level Biology, 128 pp.
Publisher: Hodder Arnold H&S
ISBN: 1340856475
Comments: *Examples and practice exercises to improve skills in data interpretation and analysis.*

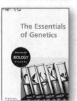

Jones, N., A. Karp., & G. Giddings, 2001.
Essentials of Genetics, 224 pp.
Publisher: John Murray
ISBN: 0-7195-8611-9
One of several titles in the Advanced Biology Reader series providing comprehensive coverage of genetics and evolution (including cell division, molecular genetics, and genetic engineering).

6

Jones, A., R. Reed, and J. Weyers, 4th ed. 2007
Practical Skills in Biology, approx. 300 pp.
Publisher: Pearson
ISBN: 978-0-131775-09-3
Comments: *Provides information on all aspects of experimental and field design, implementation, and data analysis. Contact www.amazon.co.uk*

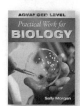
Morgan, S., 2002
Advanced Level Practical Work for Biology, 128 pp.
Publisher: Hodder and Stoughton
ISBN: 0-340-84712-3
Comments: *Caters for the investigative requirements of A level studies: experimental planning, techniques, observation and measurement, and interpretation and analysis.*

Cambridge Advanced Sciences (Cambridge UP)
Modular-style texts covering material for the A2 options for OCR, but suitable as student extension for core topics in other courses.

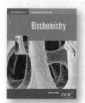
Harwood, R. 2002.
Biochemistry, 96 pp.
ISBN: 0521797519
Methodical coverage of the structure and role of the main groups of biological molecules. Questions and exercises are provided and each chapter includes an introduction and summary.

Jones, M. and G. Jones, 2002.
Mammalian Physiology and Behaviour, 104 pp.
ISBN: 0521797497
Covers mammalian nutrition, the structure and function of the liver, support and locomotion, the nervous system, and senses and behaviour. Each chapter includes an introduction and summary.

Lowrie, P. & S. Wells, 2000.
Microbiology and Biotechnology, 112 pp.
ISBN: 0521787238
This text covers the microbial groups important in biotechnology, basic microbiological techniques, and the various applications of microbes, including the industrial-scale production and use of microbial enzymes.

Reiss, M. & J. Chapman, 2000.
Environmental Biology, 104 pp.
ISBN: 0521787270
An introduction to environmental biology covering agriculture, pollution, resource conservation and conservation issues, and practical work in ecology. Questions and exercises are provided, and each chapter includes an introduction and summary.

Taylor, D. 2001.
Growth, Development and Reproduction, 120 pp.
ISBN: 0521787211
Includes coverage of asexual reproduction, sexual reproduction in flowering plants and mammals, and regulation of growth and development. Questions and exercises are provided, and each chapter includes an introduction and summary.

Collins Advanced Modular Sciences (HarperCollins)
Modular-style texts covering material for the A2 options for AQA specification B. Useful as extension reading for other courses.

Allen, D, M. Jones, and G. Williams, 2001.
Applied Ecology, 104 pp.
ISBN: 0-00-327741-0
Includes coverage of methods in practical ecology, the effects of pollution on diversity, adaptations, agricultural ecosystems and harvesting (including fisheries), and conservation issues. Local examples are emphasised throughout.

Hudson, T. and K. Mannion, 2001.
Microbes and Disease, 104 pp.
ISBN: 0-00-327742-9
Coverage of selected aspects of microbiology including the culture and applications of bacteria, and the role of bacteria and viruses in disease. Immunity, vaccination, and antimicrobial drug use are covered in the concluding chapter.

Murray, P. & N. Owens, 2001.
Behaviour and Populations, 82 pp.
ISBN: 0-00-327743-7
This text covers an eclectic range of topics including patterns of behaviour, reproduction and its control, human growth and development, human populations, aspects of infectious disease, and issues related to health and lifestyle.

Illustrated Advanced Biology (John Murray Publishers)
Modular-style supplements for AS and A2 level biology courses.

Clegg, C.J., 2002.
Microbes in Action, 92 pp.
ISBN: 0-71957-554-0
Microbes and their roles in disease and biotechnology. It includes material on the diversity of the microbial world, microbiological techniques, and a short, but useful, account of enzyme technology.

Clegg, C.J., 1999.
Genetics and Evolution, 96 pp.
ISBN: 0-7195-7552-4
Concise but thorough coverage of molecular genetics, genetic engineering, inheritance, and evolution. An historical perspective is included by way of introduction, and a glossary and a list of abbreviations used are included.

Clegg, C.J., 1998.
Mammals: Structure & Function, 96 pp.
ISBN: 0-7195-7551-6
An excellent, clearly written supplementary text covering most aspects of basic mammalian anatomy and physiology. Note: This text is now out of print from the publishers, but many schools will still have copies in their collections and it is still available from amazon: www.amazon.co.uk

Clegg, C.J., 2003
Green Plants: The Inside Story, approx. 96 pp.
ISBN: 0-7195-7553-2
The emphasis in this text is on flowering plants. Topics include leaf, stem, and root structure in relation to function, reproduction, economic botany, and sensitivity and adaptation.

Nelson Advanced Sciences (NelsonThornes)
Modular-style texts covering material for the A2 specifications for Edexcel, but are suitable as teacher reference and student extension reading for core topics in other AS/A2 biology courses.

Adds, J., E. Larkcom & R. Miller, 2004.
Exchange and Transport, Energy and Ecosystems, revised edition 240 pp.
ISBN: 0-7487-7487-4
Includes exchange processes (gas exchanges, digestion, absorption), transport systems, adaptation, sexual reproduction, energy and the environment, and human impact. Practical activities are included in several of the chapters.

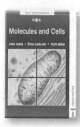
Adds, J., E. Larkcom & R. Miller, 2003.
Molecules and Cells, revised edition 112 pp.
ISBN: 0-7487-7484-X
Includes coverage of the basic types of biological molecules, with extra detail on the structure and function of nucleic acids and enzymes, cellular organisation, and cell division. Practical activities are provided for most chapters.

Adds, J., E. Larkcom & R. Miller, 2004.
Genetics, Evolution, and Biodiversity, revised edition, 200 pp.
ISBN: 0-7487-7492-0
A range of topics including photosynthesis and the control of growth in plants, classification and quantitative field ecology, populations and pest control, conservation, Mendelian genetics and evolution, gene technology and human evolution.

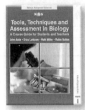

Adds, J., E. Larkcom, R. Miller, & R. Sutton, 1999. **Tools, Techniques and Assessment in Biology**, 160 pp.
ISBN: 0-17-448273-6
A course guide covering basic lab protocols, microscopy, quantitative lab and field techniques, advanced DNA techniques and tissue culture, data handling and statistical tests, and exam preparation.

Biology Dictionaries

Access to a good biology dictionary is valuable when dealing with biological terms. Some selected titles are listed below. All are available from www.amazon.co.uk. For further details, link to the relevant publisher via Biozone's resources hub or by typing:
www.biozone.co.uk/resources/dictionaries-pg1.html

Clamp, A.
AS/A-Level Biology. Essential Word Dictionary, 2000, 161 pp. Philip Allan Updates.
ISBN: 0-86003-372-4.
Carefully selected essential words for AS and A2. Concise definitions are supported by further explanation and illustrations where required.

Collin, P.H.
A Dictionary of Ecology and Environment 5 ed., 2001, 560 pp. Peter Collin Publishers Ltd
ISBN: 0747572011
A revised edition, with over 9000 definitions from all areas of ecology and environmental science, including climate and energy conservation.

Hale, W.G. **Collins: Dictionary of Biology** 4 ed., 2005, 528 pp. Collins.
ISBN: 0-00-720734-4.
Updated to take in the latest developments in biology and now internet-linked. This dictionary is specifically designed for advanced school students, and undergraduates in the life sciences.

Henderson, I.F, W.D. Henderson, and E. Lawrence.
Henderson's Dictionary of Biological Terms, 1999, 736 pp. Prentice Hall.
ISBN: 0582414989
This edition has been updated, rewritten for clarity, and reorganised for ease of use. An essential reference and the dictionary of choice for many.

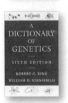

King, R.C. & W.D. Stansfield **A Dictionary of Genetics**, 6 ed., 2002, 544 pp. Oxford Uni. Press.
ISBN: 0-19-514325-6
A dictionary specifically addressing the needs of students and teachers for an up to date reference source for genetics and related fields. More than 7000 definitions and 395 illustrations.

McGraw-Hill (ed). **McGraw-Hill Dictionary of Bioscience**, 2 ed., 2002, 662 pp. McGraw-Hill.
ISBN: 0-07-141043-0
22 000 entries encompassing more than 20 areas of the life sciences. It includes synonyms, acronyms, abbreviations, and pronunciations for all terms. Accessible, yet comprehensive.

Thain, M. **Penguin Dictionary of Biology**, 2004, 750 pp. Penguin.
ISBN: 0-14-101396-6
Concise reference with definitions to more than 6000 terms. It covers fundamental concepts, core vocabulary, and new advances in the subject.

Rudin, N.
Dictionary of Modern Biology (1997), 504 pp.
Barron's Educational Series Inc
ISBN: 0812095162.
More than 6000 terms in biosciences defined for college level students. Includes extensive cross referencing and several useful appendices.

Periodicals, Magazines and Journals

Articles in *Biological Sciences Review (Biol. Sci. Rev.)*, *New Scientist*, and *Scientific American* can be of great value in providing current information on specific topics. Periodicals may be accessed in your school, local, public, and university libraries. Listed below are the periodicals referenced in this workbook. For general enquiries and further details regarding subscriptions, link to the relevant publisher via Biozone's resources hub or by typing:
www.biozone.co.uk/resources/resource-journal.html

Biological Sciences Review: *An informative and very readable quarterly publication for teachers and students of biology.* Enquiries: Philip Allan Publishers, Market Place, Deddington, Oxfordshire OX 15 OSE.
Tel: 01869 338652
Fax: 01869 338803
E-mail: sales@philipallan.co.uk
or subscribe from their web site.

New Scientist: *Widely available weekly magazine. Provides summaries of research in articles ranging from news releases to 3-5 page features on recent research.*
Subscription enquiries:
Reed Business Information Ltd
151 Wardour St. London WIV 4BN
Tel: (UK and intl):+44 (0) 1444 475636
E-mail: ns.subs@qss-uk.com
or subscribe from their web site.

Scientific American: *A monthly magazine containing mostly specialist feature articles. Articles range in level of reading difficulty and assumed knowledge.*
Subscription enquiries:
415 Madison Ave. New York. NY10017-1111
Tel: (outside North America): 515-247-7631
or subscribe from their web site.

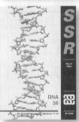

School Science Review: *A quarterly journal published by the ASE for science teachers in 11-19 education. SSR includes articles, reviews, and news on current research and curriculum development. Free to Ordinary Members of the ASE or available on subscription.* Subscription enquiries:
Tel: 01707 28300
Email: info@ase.org.uk *or visit their web site.*

Biologist: *Published five times a year, this journal from the IOB includes articles relevant to teachers of biology in the UK. Articles referenced in the workbook can be identified by title and volume number. The IOB also publish the Journal of Biological Education, which provides articles and reviews relevant to those in the teaching profession. Archived articles from both journals are available online at no cost to IOB members and subscribers. Visit their web site for more information.*

8

Textbook Reference Grid

Guide to use: Chapter or page numbers refer to the material provided in each text relevant to the stated topic in the workbook.

TOPIC IN WORKBOOK	Bailey & Hirst 2000	Boyle & Senior 2002	Bradfield et al. 2001	Clegg 2000
Skills in Biology	see A2 companion text: Chpt. 14-16	701-704	N/A*	485-490
Biological Molecules	11-12, 18-19, 54-67	37-66, 89-104 (in part)	62-96, 101-113	25-50, 75-96
Cell Structure	6-25	1-36	1-31	2-22
Cell Membranes and Transport	26-43	67-88	37-57	53-72
The Genetic Code	88-102	485-502	119-147	106-116
Cell Division and Cloning	106-120	445-460	155-177	98-118, 410-411
Gene Technology	130-145	547-566, but also 105-132 as required	481-504	120-136
Gas Exchange	43-50	227-244	231-267	207-233
Transport Systems	154-167, 184-197	245-268, 567-592 (in part)	271-305, 309-23, 343-70	225-249
Defence and the Immune System	N/A	125-6, 265-8, 313-330	324-335	335-341
Aspects of Human Health	68-69, 101-102, 160	195-210, 446	509-521	103, 322-326
Infectious Disease	N/A	2, 330	511-513, 521-533	326-335
Energy and Ecosystems	see A2 companion text: Chpt. 10 & 12	Chpt 11, 627-662	413-435, chpt. 13	140-166, 365-379
Sexual Reproduction	Chpt. 8	453-58, 464-82, 612-21	168-75, chpt. 7-8	100-102, chpt. 19

TOPIC IN WORKBOOK	Kent 2000	Lea et al. 2000	Roberts et al. 2000	SNAB AS 2005
Skills in Biology	12-15	N/A*	1-10, 778-780	Minimal (p. 24)
Biological Molecules	16-35, 40-53	6-11, 14-17, 58-75	11-39, 118-136	30-37, 57-59, 70-72, 148-152, 159, 186-187
Cell Structure	56-65, 80-81	4-5, 40-58	41-60, 62-77	98-102, 124, 147-148, 152
Cell Membranes and Transport	66-73	78-91, 104-107	103-116	54-55, 60-65
The Genetic Code	390-405, 415	116-133	602-618	74-81
Cell Division and Cloning	74-79, 302-305	136-151	455-468	104-117, 126, 131-134, 175-176
Gene Technology	406-411	154-171	628-633	88-95, 119-120, 143, 174-182
Gas Exchange	112-17, 130-31, 280-81	90-103, 190-195	157-176	52-56
Transport Systems	118-133, 268-287	180-191, 196-229	217-265	8-12, 16-19, 26-29, 153-158, 160
Defence and the Immune System	326-335, 342-343	N/A	320-328, 330-338	N/A
Aspects of Human Health	344-345, 348-359	N/A	35-36, 174-76, 240-42, 317-18, 341, 466-68	2-7, 12-16, 20-25, 30, 38-49, 69, 131-34, 139-40
Infectious Disease	318-325, 336-337	N/A	318-20, 328-9, 331-32	N/A
Energy and Ecosystems	160-79, 506-13, 526-35	N/A	178-196, 651-675	183, 190-210
Sexual Reproduction	78-79, 244-265, 290-301	Unit 8 as reqd	472-473, chpt. 28-29	73, 102-104, 166-169

*Figures refer to page numbers unless indicated otherwise   * Although questions are integrated throughout*

Clegg & McKean
2000

Fullick
2000

Indge *et al.*
2000

Jones *et al.*
2000

Jones *et al.*
2007

Jones & Jones
1997

Clegg & McKean 2000	Fullick 2000	Indge et al. 2000	Jones et al. 2000	Jones et al. 2007	Jones & Jones 1997
12-17	N/A*	N/A*	N/A*	Appendix 3	N/A*
124-145, 178-191	17-32, 63-71, 714	37-72	21-50	Chpt. 2 and 3	1-48
148-169, 212-227	4-15	7-20	2-20	Chpt. 1	49-72
158-159, 228-241	46-62	21-32	51-64	Chpt. 4	73-80, 241
200-211	34-44	133-146	65-75, 88-91	Chpt. 5	97-110
192-199, 578-579, 582	355-358, 368-370	147-154	79-91	Chpt. 6	81-96, 397-398
628-645	33, 450, 461-65, 725-35	159-168	75-78, 151-152	Chpt. 21-22	113-125
302-311, 492	110-111, 124-136	73-85	172-185	Chpt. 11	249-270
320-330, 337-363	92-109	91-108	102-146	Chpt. 8, 9 and 10	205-248
364-369, 371	76-85, 631-642	47-48, 173-180, 186-189	219-230, 232-234	Chpt. 14	482-495
354-357, 526-528, 538-540	361-362, 650-686	N/A	148-171, 179-184, 187-202	Chpt. 12	87, 374
354-356, 370, 526-538	612-631, 643-646	37	203-218, 230-232	Chpt. 13	294-295, 477-482
44-65, 72-75, 246, 270-301	198-203, 507-8, 514-521, 528-531	N/A	92-100	Chpt. 7	Chpt 13, 419-428
196-99, 569-76, 587-99	chpt. 5.2-5.5 as reqd	N/A	N/A	Chpt. 24	88-91, chpt. 17-18

SNAB A2
2006

Taylor *et al.*
1997

Toole & Toole
2000

Toole & Toole
2004

Williams
2000

SNAB A2 2006	Taylor et al. 1997	Toole & Toole 2000	Toole & Toole 2004	Williams 2000
N/A	349-373, 951-958	N/A*	244-245	446-458
N/A	77-126	10-46	26-54	6-27, 63-79
N/A	128-139, 147-193	2-9, 47-66	6-24	28-47
N/A	140-147	54-55, 66-70	56-64	48-62
N/A	790-805, 832-833	102-119	72-84	99-111, 124, 371
N/A	776-790	134-147, 216-218	90-98	113-127, 152-153
N/A	834-857, 869-878	119-129	86-87	143-159
N/A	277-294	392-409, 451-452	68-69, 182-196	164-180
N/A	427-485	412-421, 429-475	110-152	181-214
Chpt. 6	482-494, 498-500, 518-520	420-429, 437-440	224-238	255, 267-278
N/A	495-498, 520-531,	626-627, 638-644, 650-661	154-180, 198-210	124-125, 220-238, 246-251
Chpt. 8	500-516	628-667	212-222	255-266
Chpt. 5.5	196, 227-55, 298-317	266-268, 290-313, 333-348	100-108	80-92, 390-403
N/A	711-747, 783-789	139-142, 218-250	N/A	Chpt. 8

Using the Internet

The internet is a powerful resource for locating information. There are several key areas of Biozone's web site that may be of interest to you. Go to the **BioLinks** area to browse through the hundreds of web sites hosted by other organisations. These sites provide a supplement to the activities provided in our workbooks and have been selected on the basis of their accurate, current, and relevant content. We have also provided links to biology-related **podcasts** and **RSS newsfeeds**. These provide regularly updated information about new discoveries in biology; perfect for those wanting to keep abreast of changes in this dynamic field.

The BIOZONE website: www.biozone.co.uk

The current internet address (URL) for the web site is displayed here. You can type a new address directly into this space.

Use Google to search for web sites of interest. The more precise your search words are, the better the list of results. EXAMPLE: If you type in "biotechnology", your search will return an overwhelmingly large number of sites, many of which will not be useful to you. Be more specific, e.g. "biotechnology medicine DNA uses".

Find out about our superb **Presentation Media**. These slide shows are designed to provide in-depth, highly accessible illustrative material and notes on specific areas of biology.

Podcasts: Access the latest news as audio files (mp3) that may be downloaded to your ipod (mp3 player) or played directly off your computer.

RSS Newsfeeds: See breaking news and major new discoveries in biology directly from our web site.

The **Resource Hub** provides links to the supporting resources referenced in the workbook. These resources include comprehensive and supplementary texts, biology dictionaries, computer software, videos, and science supplies.

Access the **BioLinks** database of web sites related to each major area of biology.

News: Find out about product announcements, shipping dates, and workshops and trade displays by Biozone at teachers' conferences around the world.

Introduction

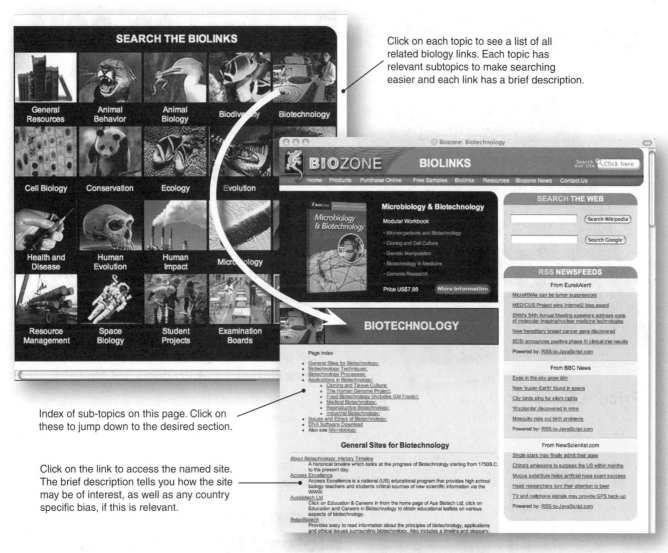

Click on each topic to see a list of all related biology links. Each topic has relevant subtopics to make searching easier and each link has a brief description.

Index of sub-topics on this page. Click on these to jump down to the desired section.

Click on the link to access the named site. The brief description tells you how the site may be of interest, as well as any country specific bias, if this is relevant.

Weblinks:

Go to: **www.biozone.co.uk/weblink/UK1-9968.html**

Throughout this workbook, some pages make reference to additional or alternative activities, as well as web sites that have particular relevance to the activity. See example of page reference below:

Related activities: Plant Cells, Animal Cells
Web links: Eukaryotic Cells Interactive Animation   **RA 2**

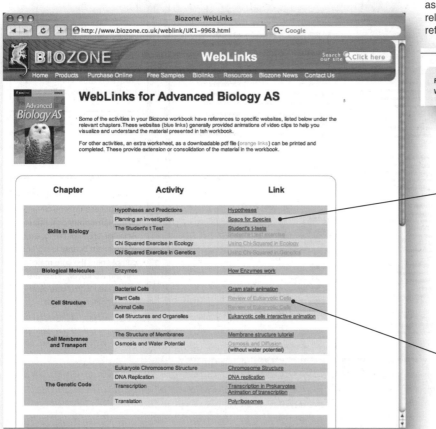

Web Link: provides a link to an **external web site** with supporting information for the activity

Web Link: provides a link to a downloadable **Acrobat (PDF) file** which may provide an additional activity or a different activity with an alternative set of features.

Using the Teacher Resource CD-ROM

Supporting resources for this workbook

Acrobat PDF files supplied on CD-ROM provide hyperlinks to an extensive collection of resources.

Details of this product can be viewed at:
www.biozone.co.uk/Products_UK.html

NOTE: Photocopy licence EXPIRES on **30 June 2008**

Price: £59.95

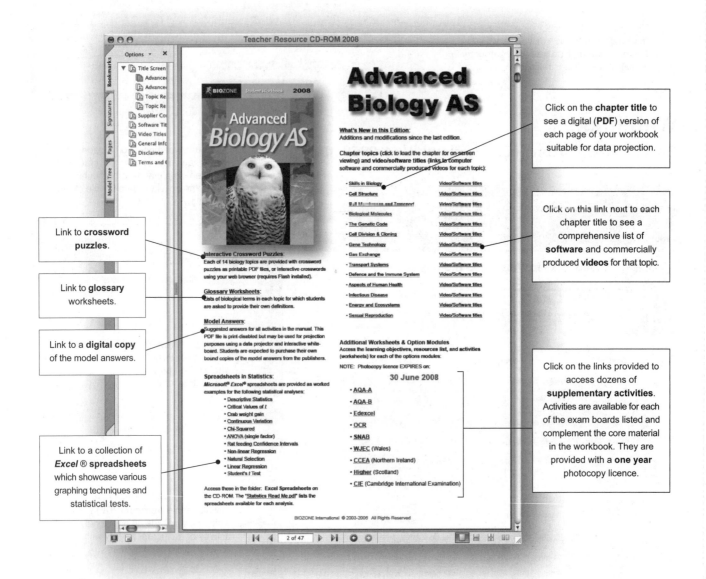

Link to **crossword puzzles**.

Link to **glossary** worksheets.

Link to a **digital copy** of the model answers.

Link to a collection of *Excel ®* **spreadsheets** which showcase various graphing techniques and statistical tests.

Click on the **chapter title** to see a digital (**PDF**) version of each page of your workbook suitable for data projection.

Click on this link next to each chapter title to see a comprehensive list of **software** and commercially produced **videos** for that topic.

Click on the links provided to access dozens of **supplementary activities**. Activities are available for each of the exam boards listed and complement the core material in the workbook. They are provided with a **one year** photocopy licence.

AQA Specification A for AS and A2

AQA-A offers a **Biology** or a **Human Biology** route. **AS** candidates must complete **three** assessment units. For Biology, modules 1, 2, and 4 and for Human Biology, modules 1, 3, and 4. Advanced Level candidates must complete the same 3 assessment units from the AS scheme and three units from the A2 scheme. For Biology, modules 5, 6, 8a and 8b and for Human Biology, 5, 6, 9a and 9b.

AS Module		Topics in AS workbook *(unless indicated)*
Module 1: Molecules, Cells and Systems		
10.1 10.2	Prokaryotic and eukaryotic cell structure. Electron microscopy. Cell organelles. Centrifugation.	Cell Structure
10.3	Cell membranes and cellular transport.	Cell Membranes and Transport
10.4 10.5	Biological molecules. Biochemical tests. Enzyme structure and function.	Biological Molecules
10.6	Cell specialisation and organisation. The structure and function of epithelial tissues and blood.	Cell Structure Transport Systems
10.7	Circulation and capillaries. Gas exchange and lung function.	Transport Systems Gas Exchange
10.8	Heart structure and function. The effects of exercise.	Transport Systems
Module 2: Making Use of Biology		*Biology only*
11.1	Isolation and applications of enzymes.	Biological Molecules
11.2	Mitosis and the cell cycle. The significance of meiosis.	Cell Division and Cloning
11.3	DNA structure and replication. The genetic code and protein synthesis.	The Genetic Code
11.4	Production and use of recombinant DNA. Production of human proteins.	Gene Technology
11.5	Principles of immunology (ABO blood grouping). Genetic fingerprinting and PCR.	Defence and the Immune System Gene Technology
11.6	Control of cereal crop plants. Fertilisers, pesticides, and pest management.	● TRC: Crop production
11.7	Reproductive hormones in mammals. Control of reproduction.	Sexual Reproduction ● TRC: Biotechnology and Reproduction
Module 3: Pathogens and Disease		*Human Biology only*
12.1	Pathogenic bacteria and viruses (HIV, *Salmonella*, and *M. tuberculosis*).	Infectious Disease ● TRC: Bacterial Growth
12.2	Adaptations and life cycle of parasites (includes malarial parasite).	Energy and Ecosystems Infectious Disease
12.3	The body's defence systems against disease. The immune system. Vaccinations and immunisation.	Transport Systems Defence and the Immune System
12.4	Mitosis, cell cycle., significance of meiosis.	Cell Division and Cloning
12.5	DNA structure and replication. The genetic code. Protein synthesis, gene expression.	The Genetic Code
12.6	Production and use of recombinant DNA. Production of human proteins.	Gene Technology
12.7	Non-communicable disease: basis and risk factors of heart disease and cancer.	Aspects of Human Health Cell Division and Cloning
12.8	Diagnosis of disease using DNA probes and enzymes as analytical reagents and biosensors.	Aspects of Human Health Biological Molecules ● TRC: Pre- and Post-Natal Testing
12.9	Control and treatment of diseases using drugs. Antibiotics. Monoclonal antibodies.	Infectious Disease Defence and the Immune System
Module 4: Centre Assessed Coursework		
	Assessment of planning and implementation of practical work, collection and presentation of raw data, data analysis and evaluation, ability to select and retrieve information and communication skills.	Skills in Biology

A2 Module		Topics in A2 workbook *(unless indicated)*
Module 5: Inheritance, Evolution and Ecosystems		
14.1 14.2	Meiosis, Mendelian inheritance, application of the chi-squared test. Sample variation. Causes of variation: meiosis, mutation, environment, polygeny.	Sources of Variation Inheritance
14.3	Hardy-Weinberg principle. Allele frequencies and selection. Speciation.	Population Genetics and Speciation
14.4	Species concept. The five kingdom classification.	Population Genetics and Speciation Biodiversity and Classification
14.5	Ecosystem numbers and distribution. Diversity indices. Succession.	Populations and Interactions Practical Ecology ● TRC: Ecosystems & Energy
14.6	Biochemistry of photosynthesis.	Cellular Metabolism
14.7	Ecological pyramids. Energy transfer between trophic levels.	Energy Flow and Nutrient Cycles ● TRC: Ecosystems & Energy
14.8	Respiration, respiratory quotient, ATP.	Cellular Metabolism
14.9	Carbon and nitrogen cycling and the role of microorganisms in these.	Energy Flow and Nutrient Cycles
14.10	Causes and effects of deforestation. Conservation and forest resources.	Populations and Interactions
Module 6: Physiology and the Environment		*Biology only*
15.1	Dicotyledon water uptake and transport. Potometers, Xeromorphic adaptations.	● TRC: Physiology & the Environment
15.2 15.3	Homeostasis, blood glucose control, thermoregulation Liver and kidney function. Nitrogenous waste and water balance.	Homeostasis
15.4 15.5 15.6 15.7	Fick's law and adaptation for gas exchange. Transport of respiratory gases. Digestion and absorption in mammals (including control of digestive secretion). Metamorphosis and insect nutrition.	● TRC: Physiology & the Environment
15.8 15.9 15.10	Components of the nervous system. Receptors and stimuli. Role of the nervous system in behaviour: reflexes, ANS, taxes, kineses.	Responses & Coordination
Module 7: The Human Life Span		*Human Biology only*
16.1 16.2 16.3 16.4	Sexual reproduction: gametogenesis & fertilisation. Foetal development. The placenta. The role of hormones in pregnancy. Growth and sexual development. Digestion and absorption in mammals (including control of digestive secretion).	● TRC: The Human Life Span
16.5	Nutrients and their role. Diet and BMR.	AS: Aspects of Human Health ● TRC: The Human Life Span
16.6	Transport of respiratory gases	● TRC: The Human Life Span
16.7 16.8	Components of the nervous system. Receptors and stimuli.	Responses & Coordination
16.9	Muscle structure and function	Muscles and Movement
16.10	Spinal reflexes and the ANS.	Responses & Coordination
16.11	Homeostasis: thermoregulation, control of blood glucose	Homeostasis ● TRC: The Human Life Span
Modules 8a/9a: Written synoptic papers		
Modules 8b/9b: Centre assessed coursework		
	Synoptic paper. Assessment of planning and implementation of practical work, statistical analysis, interpretation and evaluation of results, and communication skills.	Skills in Biology

AQA Specification B for AS and A2

AS candidates taking the AQA-B course must complete **three** compulsory assessment units. **Advanced Level (As+A2) candidates** must complete the same three compulsory assessment units from the AS scheme and **three** compulsory units from the A2 scheme, **plus one option unit** from the three offered (Option 6, or Option 7, or Option 8).

AS Module	Topics in AS workbook (unless indicated)
Module 1: Core Principles	
10.1 Biological molecules. Biochemical analyses.	Biological Molecules
10.2 Cell structure and organelles, microscopy, centrifugation, cell differentiation	Cell Structure
10.3 Cell membranes and cellular transport.	Cell Membranes & Transport
10.4 Surface area: volume ratios. Gas exchange and ventilation	Cell Membranes & Transport Gas Exchange
10.5 Enzyme structure and function	Biological Molecules
10.6 Human digestion and absorption.	● TRC: Digestion
Module 2: Genes and Genetic Engineering	
11.1 DNA structure and replication. The genetic code, transcription, and translation. Mutations and their consequences.	The Genetic Code ● TRC: Mutations
11.2 Mitosis and the cell cycle. Cloning.	Cell Division and Cloning
11.3 Gametogenesis and fertilisation. Meiosis	Sexual Reproduction
11.4 Principles and applications of gene technology. GMOs and gene therapy.	Gene Technology
Module 3a: Physiology and Transport	
12.1 Transport systems: heart structure and function. Role of blood and tissue fluid.	Transport Systems
12.2 Control of breathing and heart rate in humans. Physiological responses to exercise.	Gas Exchange Transport Systems
12.3 Energy and exercise: energy for muscle contraction. Muscle fatigue and blood lactate.	Gas Exchange A2: Muscles & Movement
12.4 Transport in plants (including root structure) Structural adaptations of xerophytes.	Transport Systems
Module 3b: Coursework	
Candidates undertake experiments and investigations. Skills include: planning and implementation of practical work, analysing evidence and drawing conclusions, and evaluating evidence and procedures.	Skills in Biology

A2 Module	Topics in A2 workbook (unless indicated)
Module 4: Energy, Control, and Continuity	
13.1 Photosynthesis, respiration, and ATP. 13.2 Biochemistry of photosynthesis. 13.3 Biochemistry of respiration.	Cellular Metabolism
13.4 Detecting stimuli: receptors and effectors. Reflex arc. Effects of hormones.	Homeostasis Responses & Coordination
13.5 Homeostasis.: thermoregulation, control of blood glucose, excretion, osmoregulation.	Homeostasis
13.6 The mammalian eye. Transmission of nerve impulses. Synapses. Effects of drugs. 13.7 Structure and function of the brain & ANS.	Responses & Coordination
13.8 Ultrastructure of skeletal muscle. Sliding filament theory of muscle contraction.	Muscles & Movement
13.9 Inheritance: genotype, meiosis & fertilisation, sex determination, mono- and dihybrid cross	Sources of Variation Inheritance
13.10 Continuous and discontinuous variation. Causes of genetic variation.	Sources of Variation
13.11 Natural selection and speciation	Population Genetics and Speciation
13.12 Principles and importance of taxonomy. The five kingdom classification.	Population Genetics and Speciation Principles of Classification
Module 5a: Environment	
14.1 Energy transfer and trophic levels. Ecological pyramids. 14.2 Carbon and nitrogen cycles, including the role of microorganisms in these.	AS: Energy & Ecosystems ... or ... ● TRC: Energy Flow and Nutrient cycles
14.3 Biological and physical sampling methods.	Practical Ecology
14.4 Features of populations. Population stability. Ecological succession.	Populations & Interactions
14.5 Human environmental impact: hedgerows, monocultures, pesticides, pollution.	Populations & Interactions ● TRC: Human Impact
Module 5b: Coursework	
Candidates will be assessed on planning, implementing, analysis, evaluation, and synthesis of principles and concepts.	AS: Skills in Biology A2: Practical Ecology
Option Module 6: Applied Ecology	
Ecosystem diversity, pollution, adaptations of organisms, agricultural ecosystems, harvesting, conservation.	● TRC: Option Module 6 *Applied Ecology*
Option Module 7: Microbes and Disease	
Features of bacteria, culture of microorganisms, commercial use of microorganisms, microbial pathogens.	● TRC: Option Module 7 *Microbes and Disease*
Option Module 8: Behaviour and Populations	
Innate and learned behaviours, reproductive behaviours, pregnancy, human growth and development, human population growth, effects of lifestyle on health.	● TRC: Option Module 8 *Behaviour and Populations*

Salters-Nuffield Advanced Biology

The SNAB Advanced GCE specification is divided into six units. The Advanced Subsidiary (AS) specification comprises Units 1, 2, and 3, with the practical assessment of Unit 3 consisting of two parts. The Advanced Level Specification comprises Units 1-6 and includes synoptic assessment. Practical skills are assessed in Unit 5 with submission of a written report of an experimental investigation that they have devised and carried out. Because of the contextual nature of the SNAB specification, it is recommended that students purchase both the AS and A2 volumes together and use them over the two-year duration of the course. This will enable the necessary scope of content to be covered as indicated below.

AS Unit

Topics in AS workbook
(unless indicated)

Unit 1: Topic 1 (1.1): Lifestyle, Health and Risk

Internal transport in animals: heart & blood	Transport Systems
Blood clotting	Defence & Immune system
Atherosclerosis, CVD, energy and diet, BMI	Aspects of Human Health
Simple carbohydrates and lipids	Biological Molecules

Unit 1: Topic 2 (1.2): Genes and Health

Gas exchange surfaces and lung structure	Gas Exchange
Membrane structure, cell transport processes	Cell Membranes & Transport
Nucleic acids, genetic code, protein synthesis	The Genetic Code
Amino acids and proteins, enzymes	Biological Molecules
DNA replication	The Genetic Code
Mutations: causes and consequences of CF	A2: Sources of Variation
Monohybrid inheritance, pedigree analysis	A2: Inheritance
Principles and applications of gene therapy	Gene Technology
Genetic profiling and screening.	Gene Technology
Prenatal testing: amniocentesis, CVS	Aspects of Human Health

Unit 2: Topic 3 (2.3): The Voice of the Genome

Ultrastructure of eukaryotic cells. Function of rER and Golgi. Prokaryotic v eukaryotic cells.	Cell Structure
Mitosis in the cell cycle.	Cell Division and Cloning
Mammalian gametes and fertilisation	Sexual Reproduction
Meiosis as a source of variation	Sources of Variation
Stem cell research	Cell Division and Cloning
Cell specialisation through gene switching	Cell Structure
Control of gene expression	A2: Cellular Metabolism
Effects of environment on genotype expression	A2: Sources of Variation
Polygenic inheritance	A2: Inheritance
Cancers as a result of uncontrolled cell division	Cell Division and Cloning
Genetic and environmental causes of cancer	Aspects of Human Health
HGP: principal outcomes and ethical issues	The Genetic Code

Unit 2: Topic 4 (2.4): Plants and Climate Change

Importance of water and inorganic ions to plants	Biological Molecules
Structure and function of polysaccharides	A2: Cellular Metabolism
Ultrastructure of plant cells v animal cells	Cell Structure
Structure and function of xylem. Transpiration.	Transport Systems
Seed structure and adaptations for dispersal	Sexual Reproduction
Uses of starch and plant oils by humans	Energy and Ecosystems
Genetic modification of plants (incl ethical issues)	Gene Technology
Role of the carbon cycle in regulating CO2	Energy and Ecosystems
Causes and consequences of global warming	TRC: Global warming
Reducing carbon emission: biofuels	TRC: Biofuels
Increased temperature: effect on enzyme activity	Biological Molecules

Unit 3: Report and Practical Review

Areas of practical work are: use of organisms, microscopy, lab techniques, and ecological methodology. Candidates are assessed on knowledge and experimental and investigative skills developed through the AS course.	Skills in Biology Cell Structure A2: Practical Ecology

A2 Unit

Topics in A2 workbook
(unless indicated)

Unit 4: Topic 5 (4.5): On the Wild Side

Taxonomy, biodiversity, and classification keys	Biodiversity & Classification
Genetic diversity: mutation, recombination	Sources of Variation
Dihybrid inheritance	Inheritance
Practical investigation of species ecology	Practical Ecology
Habitat, distribution, and adaptation	AS: Energy and Ecosystems
Photosynthesis in C3 plants	Cellular Metabolism
Primary productivity and ecological efficiency	AS: Energy and Ecosystems
Natural selection, gene mutation, and evolution	Popn Genetics & Speciation
Development of evolutionary theory	Popn Genetics & Speciation
Ecological succession	Populations and Interactions
Conservation of endangered species	TRC: Conservation Issues

Unit 4: Topic 6 (4.6): Infection, Immunity, and Forensics

Forensic pathology. Bacteria and viruses.	AS: Infectious Disease
Bacterial infection: TB. Viral infection: HIV.	AS: Infectious Disease
Non specific defence mechanisms. B cells, T cells and the immune response. Immunity.	AS Defence and the Immune System
Negative feedback and homeostasis	Homeostasis
Routes of infection. Immune system evasion.	AS: Infectious Disease
Antibiotics and their mode of action	AS: Infectious Disease
Development of antibiotic resistance	Sources of Variation
Evolution of pathogens	Popn Genetics & Speciation

Unit 5: Topic 7 (5.7): Run For Your Life

Movement and muscle physiology	Muscles and Movement
Role of ATP. Glycolysis and cellular respiration	Cellular Metabolism
Effects of exercise: variations in and control of ventilation rate and cardiac output.	AS: Gas Exchange AS: Transport Systems
Fast twitch v slow twitch muscle fibers	Muscles and Movement
Homeostasis: thermoregulation during exercise	Homeostasis
Exercise: too much v too little	AS: Aspects of Human Health

Unit 5: Topic 8 (5.8): Grey Matter

Nervous system structure and function. Vision.	Responses and Coordination
Nervous v hormonal regulatory systems	Homeostasis
Structure of the human brain	Responses and Coordination
Imaging: MRI, fMRI, CT scans	AS: Aspects of Human Health
Learning: habituation, conditioning, insight	Responses and Coordination
The effects of drugs at synaptic connections	Responses and Coordination
Continuous variation as a result of polygeny	Inheritance

Practical Assessment in Unit 5

Planning and implementing practicals: observations and recording, data interpretation and analysis, evaluation and communication of results.	AS: Skills in Biology A2: Practical Ecology

Unit 6: Synoptic Paper

Compulsory questions and an essay. This unit provides the chance to make connections between topics and to use skills and ideas in new contexts.	Integrated throughout

Edexcel AS and A2

Edexcel offers a **Biology** or **Biology (Human)** route for AS and A2 candidates. AS candidates must complete three compulsory assessment units: for 8040 Biology, units 6101, 6102, and 6103, and for 8042 Biology (Human) 6101, 6112, and 6103. A2 candidates must complete the same three units from the AS scheme, plus three compulsory units (including one option) from the A2 scheme.

AS Unit	Topics in AS workbook *(unless indicated)*
6101 Unit 1: Molecules and Cells	
1.1 Biological molecules and biochemical tests. DNA replication. Transcription & translation. Human Genome Project.	Biological Molecules The Genetic Code
1.2 Structure and function of enzymes (incl. immobilisation and commercial uses)	Biological Molecules
1.3 Cell structure and organisation. Microscopy. Cell membranes and transport. Tissues.	Cell Structure Cell Membranes & Transport
1.4 Chromosome structure and mitosis. Cloning in plants and animals.	The Genetic Code Cell Division and Cloning
6102 Unit 2: Exchange, Transport & Reproduction *Biology only*	
2B.1 Surface area to volume ratios. Gas exchanges. Use of a respirometer. Digestion and absorption in humans	Cell Membranes & Transport Gas Exchange ● TRC: Digestion & Absorption
2B.2 Transport in flowering plants (incl. root structure). Transport in mammals.	Transport Systems
2B.3 Structural and physiological adaptations in plants and animals.	Gas Exchange Transport Systems
2B.4 Sexual reproduction, meiosis, and variation. Reproductive systems.	Sexual Reproduction
6112 Unit 2H: Exchange, Transport & Reproduction in Humans *Human Biology only*	
2H.1 Structure & function of the breathing system Effects of smoking Digestion and absorption	Gas Exchange Aspects of Human Health ● TRC: Digestion & Absorption
2H.2 The circulatory system, blood, heart structure and function. Artificial pacemakers.	Transport Systems Aspects of Human Health
2H.3 Human adaptation to extreme environments. Homeostasis and thermoregulation.	Transport Systems A2: Homeostasis
2H.4 Human reproduction and development. Effects of ageing.	Sexual Reproduction Aspects of Human Health
6103 Unit 3: Energy and the Environment	
3.1 Modes of nutrition. Adaptations to diet. 3.2 Ecosystem structure and function. 3.3 Trophic relationships, energy transfers, ecological pyramids, productivity. 3.4 Carbon, nitrogen, and water cycles.	Energy and Ecosystems
3.5 Sustainable management of energy. 3.6 Human impact on the environment.	● TRC: Energy and the Environment
Paper 01: T1 Practical Assessment of Coursework	
Practical work is integrated into each unit as appropriate. Students carry out an investigation and present a report which will be teacher assessed.	Skills in Biology

A2 Unit	Topics in A2 workbook *(unless indicated)*
6104 Unit 4: Respiration and Coordination, and Options	
4.1 Enzymes and metabolic pathways. The biochemistry of cellular respiration.	Cellular Metabolism
4.2 Principles of homeostasis: kidney structure and function, blood glucose regulation. Photosensitivity: the eye, phytochrome. nervous and hormonal coordination.	Homeostasis Responses and Coordination
Option A: Microbiology and Biotechnology Diversity and classification of microbes, culture of bacteria, commercial use of microorganisms in biotechnology.	● TRC: Option A *Microbiology & Biotechnology*
Option B: Food Science Food and diet, additives and preservatives, food storage and spoilage, fermentation i in food biotechnology.	● TRC: Option B *Food Science*
Option C: Human Health and Fitness Physiology of cardiovascular, pulmonary, musculoskeletal, and lymphatic systems (including disorders). Effects of exercise.	● TRC: Option C *Human Health and Fitness*
6105 Unit 5B: Genetics, Evolution, & Biodiversity *Biology only*	
5B.1 Photosynthesis and plant mineral nutrition.	Cellular Metabolism
5B.2 Control of plant growth: plant hormones.	Responses and Coordination
5B.3 Taxonomy: the five kingdom classification. Population distribution and dynamics. Ecological succession. Predator-prey. Sampling to investigate distribution. Pest control, bioaccumulation, IPM, habitat management, farming and biodiversity.	Biodiversity and Classification Populations and Interactions Practical Ecology ● TRC: Farming and Conservation
5B.4 Continuous and discontinuous variation. Effect of environment on gene expression. Mendelian genetics, multiple alleles, sex determination, mutation. Natural selection, gene pools, reproductive isolating mechanisms, speciation. Gene technology, including applications of GMOs, PCR, genetic fingerprinting.	Sources of Variation ● Inheritance TRC: Chromosome mutations and aneuploidy Population Genetics and Speciation AS: Gene Technology ...or... ● TRC: Gene Technology
6115 Unit 5H: Genetics, Human Evolution & Biodiversity *Human Biology only*	
5H.1 Continuous and discontinuous variation. Effect of environment on gene expression. Mendelian genetics, multiple alleles, sex determination, mutation. Natural selection, gene pools, reproductive isolating mechanisms, speciation. Gene technology, including applications of GMOs, PCR, genetic fingerprinting.	Sources of Variation Inheritance TRC: Chromosome mutations and aneuploidy Population Genetics and Speciation AS: Gene Technology ...or ... ● TRC: Gene Technology
5H.2 Physical and cultural evolution of humans.	● TRC: Human Evolution
5H.3 Human population growth.	Populations and Interactions
5H.4 Biodiversity and conservation: population distribution. Ecological succession. Sampling to investigate distribution. Pest control, bioaccumulation, IPM, habitat management, farming and biodiversity.	Populations and Interactions Practical Ecology ● TRC: Farming and Conservation
Paper 01: T1 or Paper 02: W2. Paper 03 (Synoptic Paper)	
Practical work is integrated into each unit as appropriate. Students carry out an investigation and present a report which will be teacher assessed.	Skills in Biology

OCR AS and A2 Biology

Candidates taking the OCR AS course are required to complete the compulsory units 2801, 2802, plus 2803 (either components 01 and 02, or components 01 and 03). Candidates taking the OCR A2 course need to complete the requirements for the AS course, as well as 2804, 2805 (one of the five offered options), and 2806 (either components 01 and 02, or components 01 and 03).

Module	Topics in AS workbook (unless indicated)
5.1 Module 2801: Biology Foundation	
5.1.1 Cell structure: cell organisation, and characterisation, eukaryote and prokaryote cells, organelles, microscopy.	Cell Structure
5.1.2 Biological molecules, water and inorganic ions. Hydrolysis and condensation. 5.1.3 Enzyme structure and function.	Biological Molecules
5.1.4 Membrane structure and cell transport. Gas exchange in mammalian lungs. Root uptake systems.	Cell Membranes & Transport Gas Exchange Transport Systems
5.1.5 DNA structure & replication, protein synthesis. Gene manipulation: human insulin and factor VIII as examples.	The Genetic Code Gene Technology
5.1.6 Nuclei replication & division. Uncontrolled cell division (cancer). Chromosomes and mitosis. Meiosis in sexual reproduction.	Cell Division & Cloning Sexual Reproduction
5.1.7 Ecosystem structure and function. Energy transfer, nitrogen cycle.	Energy and Ecosystems
5.2 Module 2802: Human Health and Disease	
5.2.1 Health versus disease. Patterns of disease. Examples of diseases and disorders. The HGP and health and disease.	Aspects of Human Health Genetic Code
5.2.2 Balanced diet, energy and nutrient requirements. Malnutrition. Diet and CVD.	Aspects of Human Health
5.2.3 Human gas exchange system. The short and long term effects of exercise (incl. pulse and blood pressure).	Gas Exchange Transport Systems Aspects of Human Health
5.2.4 Health effects of smoking. Preventing & treating smoking-related diseases.	Aspects of Human Health
5.2.5 Causes, transmission, control and prevention of infectious disease: HIV/AIDS, TB, cholera and malaria.	Infectious Disease
5.2.6 The immune response, immunity and vaccination. Allergies.	Defence & Immune System
5.3 Module 2803: Transport/Experimental Skills 1	
5.3.1 Structure and function of the mammalian transport system. Adaptation to altitude. 5.3.2 Structure and function of the mammalian heart (incl. control of heart activity). 5.3.3 Transport in multicellular plants: xylem and phloem structure and distribution. Transpiration. Translocation. Xerophytes.	Transport Systems
Experimental Skills 1: *Option (candidates take either 02 or 03)*	
Component 02: Coursework 1: Internal assessment of experimental and investigative work. Planning and implementing a study, recording observations, measurements, data analysis and evaluation, drawing conclusions.	Skills in Biology
Component 03: Practical Examination 1: External assessment of experimental and investigative skills. Planning, implementing a study, recording observations, measurements, data analysis and evaluation, drawing conclusions. Components consist of a planning task, experimentation, and microscopy.	Skills in Biology Cell Structure

Module	Topics in A2 workbook (unless indicated)
5.4 Module 2804: Central Concepts	
5.4.1 Structure and role of ATP. Biochemistry of respiration. Respiratory quotients. 5.4.2 Dicot leaf structure. Chloroplasts. Biochemistry of photosynthesis. Limiting factors.	Cellular Metabolism
5.4.3 Population dynamics and species interactions. Ecological succession. Sampling distribution and abundance. Conservation v production. Sustainable management of forest ecosystems.	Populations & Interactions Practical Ecology Populations & Interactions
5.4.4 Meiosis. Genetic crosses, sex linkage, codominance, multiple alleles. Chi-squared. Mutation. Genes and environment Gene regulation in bacteria (*Lac* operon). Implications of the HGP.	Inheritance Sources of Variation Cellular metabolism Sources of Variation
5.4.5 Five kingdom classification system. Species & phylogeny. Natural selection. Factors affecting gene pools. Speciation. Adaptation to environment.	Biodiversity & Classification Popn Genetics & Speciation
5.4.6 Homeostasis. Kidney structure and function. Nervous system structure and function. Endocrine regulation (blood glucose). Role of hormones in flowering plants.	Homeostasis Responses & Coordination Homeostasis Responses & Coordination
5.5 Module 2805: Options in Biology	
01: Growth, Development & Reproduction Growth and development, asexual reproduction, sexual reproduction in humans and angiosperms. Role of hormones in growth and rreproduction.	TRC: Option 01 *Growth, Development, and Reproduction*
02: Applications of genetics Genetic variation, selective breeding, GE techniques, genetic screening and gene therapy, genetic fingerprinting, transplant compatibility. Ethical issues.	TRC: Option 02 *Applications of Genetics*
03: Environmental Biology Practical ecology, pollution, agricultural ecosystems, resource conservation (fisheries, land reclamation, recycling), nation and international conservation.	TRC: Option 03 *Environmental Biology*
04: Microbiology and Biotechnology Nature of microorganisms, culturing techniques, applications of biotechnology.	TRC: Option 04 *Microbiology and Biotechnology*
05: Mammalian Physiology & Behaviour Mammalian nutrition, the liver, locomotion, nervous system and sensory reception, principles of behaviour (innate and learned).	TRC: Option 05 *Mammalian Physiology and Behaviour*
5.10 Module 2806: Unifying Concepts in Biology Experimental Skills 2	
Component 01: Unifying concepts in Biology (compulsory) Exam questions based on concepts covered in the AS scheme, and module 2804 of A2.	
Experimental Skills 2: *Option (candidates take either 02 or 03)*	
Component 02: Coursework 2 Internal assessment of experimental and investigative work. Skills include planning and implementing a study, recording, analysing, and evaluating data, drawing conclusions.	AS Skills in Biology Practical Ecology
Component 03: Coursework 3 External assessment of experimental and investigative skills including planning and implementing a study, recording, analysing, and evaluating data, drawing conclusions. Components consist of planning a task, experimentation, and microscopy.	AS Skills in Biology AS Cell Structure Practical Ecology

CIE AS and A2 Biology

The subject content of the CIE programme is divided into AS and A2. The A2 includes a core and an Applications of Biology section, which is studied in its entirety, by all A2 candidates. Candidates taking the CIE AS will be assessed on the Learning Outcomes A-K.

A level candidates will be assessed on the Learning Outcomes L-U. The *Applications of Biology* section accounts for about 12% of the A level course. The acquisition of practical skills (and their assessment) underpins the course.

Module	Topics in AS workbook
Core Syllabus (*sections L-U are in Advanced biology A2*)	
A Light microscopy, electron microscopy, and cell structure. Eukaryote and prokaryote cells. Functions of organelles.	Cell Structure
B Structure and role of carbohydrates, lipids, and proteins. Water and inorganic ions. Hydrolysis and condensation reactions.	Biological Molecules
C Enzyme action, enzyme activity and enzyme inhibitors.	
D Fluid mosaic model of membrane structure. Transport across the membrane.	Cell Membranes and Transport
E Replication and division of nuclei and cells. Role of meiosis in sexual reproduction. Chromosome behaviour during mitosis. Uncontrolled cell division (cancer).	Cell Division and Cloning
F DNA structure and replication. The role of DNA in protein synthesis. Nucleotide base pairing.	The Genetic Code
G Transport in multicellular plants: structure and distribution of xylem and phloem in dicots. Transpiration. Translocation. Xerophytes. Structure and function of mammalian transport systems (including the heart). Haemoglobin and gas transport, gas exchange and altitude.	Transport Systems
H The structure and function of the human respiratory system. The effects of smoking on gas exchange. Smoking related diseases.	Gas Exchange Aspects of Human Health
I Causes and transmission of infectious diseases, their control and prevention. HIV/AIDS, TB, cholera and malaria. The use of antibiotics.	Infectious Disease
J Structure and function of the immune system. Types of immunity. Vaccinations.	Aspects of Human Health
K The ecosystem concept (habitat, niche, populations, communities). Energy transfer, ecological efficiency, the nitrogen cycle.	Energy and Ecosystems
Meeting Assessment Objectives	
A Knowledge with understanding, including the use of scientific vocabulary, understanding scientific ideas and concepts, using instruments and scientific measurements, applying of scientific and technological techniques.	Skills in Biology
B Handling information and solving problems: organising and extracting information. Manipulating and presenting data, and drawing conclusions. Applying knowledge to solve problems.	
C Experimental skills and investigations. Following detailed instructions, using techniques and apparatus correctly, making accurate observations, and interpreting the data to form predictions. Designing, planning and carrying out a scientific experiment or investigation.	

Module	Topics in A2 workbook (*unless indicated*)
Core Syllabus (*sections A-K are in Advanced biology AS*)	
L Energy requirements in living organisms. The structure and function of ATP. Cellular respiration, and energy transfer. Aerobic and anaerobic respiration. Respiratory quotient and the energy value of substrates. Respirometers.	Cellular Metabolism
M Photosynthesis and energy transfer. The biochemistry of photosynthesis. Limiting factors in photosynthesis. The structure of a dicot leaf.	Cellular Metabolism
N Homeostasis principles. Kidney function and structure. Nervous system: sensory receptors, neurones, action potential, and synapses. Endocrine glands (pancreas). Control of blood glucose (diabetes treatment). Role of hormones in flowering plants.	Homeostasis Responses & Coordination
O Genetic transfer. Meiosis. Genes and alleles. Monohybrid and dihybrid crosses, sex linkage, codominance, multiple alleles. Chi-squared. Mutations and environmental effects on phenotype.	Sources of Variation Inheritance
P Natural and artificial selection. The role of natural selection in evolution. The role of environmental factors and isolating mechanisms.The role of artificial selection on livestock improvement. Factors affecting allele frequencies (malaria and sickle cell anaemia).	Population Genetics and Speciation
Q The five kingdom classification system. The importance of biodiversity. Conservation issues: endangered species and strategies to protect them.	Biodiversity & Classification ● TRC: Conservation Issues
R Gene technology, techniques in gene technology. Uses of gene technology (insulin production, DNA sequencing, genetic fingerprinting, and genetic screening). Benefits and hazards of gene technology. Ethical issues	AS Gene Technology
S Biotechnology. Industrial use of microorganisms. Large scale production of microorganisms. Enzyme technology. The use of monoclonal antibodies.	● TRC: Biotechnology
T Crop plant reproduction and adaptations. Methods of improving crop production.	● TRC: Crop Plants
U Human reproduction. Gametogenesis (mitosis, growth, meiosis and maturation). The role of hormones in the menstrual cycle. Contraception. In-vitro fertilisation.	● TRC: Aspects of Human Reproduction
Meeting Assessment Objectives	
A Knowledge with understanding. Including the use of scientific vocabulary, understanding scientific ideas and concepts, using instruments and scientific measurements, the application of scientific and technological techniques.	Skills in Biology Practical Ecology
B Handling information and solving problems. Understand how to organise and extract information. Know how to manipulate and present data, and draw conclusions. Apply knowledge to problem solve.	
C Experimental skills and investigations. Following detailed instructions, using techniques and apparatus correctly, making accurate observations, and interpreting the data to form predictions. Designing, planning and carrying out a scientific experiment or investigation.	

WJEC AS and A2 Biology

WJEC candidates in the AS course are required to complete the three compulsory assessment units BI1, BI2, and BI3. A2 candidates are required to complete the same three units from the AS scheme, as well as three compulsory units (BI4, BI5, BI6) from the A2 scheme.

Module	Topics in AS workbook (unless indicated)
Module BI1: Fundamental Concepts and Organisation	
1.1 **Biological molecules**: (a-b) Carbohydrates, proteins, lipids, water. Condensation and hydrolysis reactions.	Biological Molecules
1.2 **Cell organisation**: (a-b) Eukaryotic cell structure & organelles. Prokaryotic cell structure. Viruses. Levels of organisation, tissues.	Cell Structure
1.3 **Cell membrane and transport**: (a-b) Cellular transport mechanisms.	Cell Membranes & Transport
1.4 Enzymes: (a-c) Nature of enzymes and activity. Enzyme inhibitors. 1.5 Application of enzymes: (a-b) Enzymes as biosensors. Immobilised enzymes.	Biological Molecules
1.6 **Nature of the genetic code**: (a-c) DNA and RNA structure. DNA replication. Transcription and translation. (d) DNA technology, HGP. Gene therapy for CF, genetic fingerprinting. Genetic engineering techniques, genetic fingerprinting. Ethical issues of GMOs.	The Genetic Code The Genetic Code Gene Technology
1.7 **Genetic information**: (a-b) Mitosis and meiosis. Cytokinesis. Meiosis and fertilisation. Asexual and sexual reproduction.	Cell Division & Cloning Sexual Reproduction ● TRC: Sexual Reproduction
Module BI2: Adaptations and Ecology	
2.1 **The need for transport systems**: (a) Unicellular organisms. Surface area to volume ratios. (b) Multicellular organisms. Transport systems and gas exchange.	Cell Membranes & Transport Gas Exchange Transport Systems
2.2 **Gas exchange**: (a-b) Gas exchange in plants and animals with respect to environment.	Gas Exchange
2.3 **Transport systems**: (a) Structure and function of a dicot root. Transpiration and translocation. Xerophyte adaptations. (b) Human circulatory system: blood, tissue fluid, lymph, gas transport.	Transport Systems
2.4 **Transfer of energy**: (a-b) Ecosystems & energy transfer. Heterotrophic nutrition. Food chains & webs, ecological pyramids, nutrient cycles.	Energy and Ecosystems
2.5 **Nutrition and population growth**: (a-b) Population growth and regulation. Ecological succession.	● TRC: Nutrition and Population Growth A2: Popns & Interactions
2.6 **Human Impact**: (a-b) Deforestation, overfishing. Pest control. Human impact on nutrient cycles.	● TRC: Human Impact
Module BI3: Practical Work	
Skills include: planning and implementing practical work (including microscopy), observations and recording, interpretation and analysis of results, evaluation and communication of results.	Skills in Biology

Module	Topics in A2 workbook (unless indicated)
Module BI4: Biochemistry and Health	
4.1 (a-c) The role and synthesis of ATP. 4.2 (a-d) The biochemistry of respiration. 4.3 (a-d) Pigments and light absorption. Biochemistry of photosynthesis. Factors influencing photosynthesis.	Cellular Metabolism
4.4 (a-b) Gut structure & function. Histology of the ileum. Digestion & absorption.	● TRC: Digestion & Absorption
4.5 (a-b) Bacterial classification. Microbiological techniques.	● TRC: Microbiology
4.6 (a-b) Causes and transmission of disease. Control and prevention of disease.	AS Infectious Disease
4.7 (a-b) Barriers to infection. The immune response and immunity, vaccination.	AS Defence & Immune System
4.8 (a) Industrial fermentation (penicillin). Monoclonal antibodies. Antibiotic resistance. (b) Drug use and antibiotic resistance. Vaccination programmes.	● TRC: Microbiology AS: Defence & Immune System Sources of Variation Popn Genetics & Speciation AS: Defence & Immune System
Module BI5: Variety and Control	
5.1 (a-b) Alleles, Mendelian inheritance, sex linkage, mutagens and mutation. Random assortment, fertilisation, and variation.	Sources of Variation Inheritance ● TRC: Chromosome Mutations & Aneuploidy
5.2 (a-b) Continuous variation (t-test). Gene pool, genetic drift, natural selection, reproductive isolation and speciation. (c) Evolutionary consequences of human impact on the environment. Artifical selection. Conservation.	● Inheritance Popn Genetics & Speciation TRC: Conservation of Biodiversity
5.3 (a-b) Angiosperm reproduction.	AS Sexual Reproduction ● TRC: Fruits and Seeds
5.4 (a-b) Human reproduction.	AS Sexual Reproduction
5.5 Plant and animal cloning.	AS Cell Division & Cloning
5.6 (a-b) Five kingdom classification. Binomial nomenclature. Species and phylogeny.	Biodiversity & Classification Popn Genetics & Speciation
5.7 (a-b) Homeostasis, the mammalian kidney, endocrine control.	Homeostasis
5.8 Response to stimuli. The ear.	Responses & Coordination
5.9 (a-c) The nervous system. Nerve impulses, the brain, reflexes. (d) Effectors, skeletal muscle structure, sliding filament hypothesis.	Responses & Coordination Muscles & Movement
Module BI6: Practical Work	
Practical work is integrated into each unit.	Practical Ecology AS Skills in Biology

Skills in Biology

AQA-A
Complete:
AS/A2: 1-30

AQA-B
Complete:
AS/A2: 1-30

SNAB
Complete:
AS/A2: 1-30

Edexcel
Complete:
AS/A2: 1-30

OCR
Complete:
AS/A2: 1-30

Descriptive statistics and statistical tests as appropriate for A2 students only

Learning Objectives

☐ 1. Compile your own glossary from the **KEY WORDS** displayed in **bold type** in the learning objectives below.

☐ 2. Demonstrate an understanding of the meaning of the following terms: **compare**, **contrast**, **define**, **describe**, **discuss**, **explain** (or account for), **evaluate**, **identify**, **illustrate**, **list**, **outline**, **state**, **suggest**, **summarise**. A correct understanding of these terms will enable you to answer questions appropriately *(see page 3 for help)*.

Planning an Investigation *(pages 22-32)*

☐ 3. Recall the role of **observation** as a prelude to forming a **hypothesis**. In your research, you will make observations, and use these to formulate a hypothesis, from which you can generate testable predictions. Guidelines for planning and executing practical studies in the field are provided in *Advanced Biology A2*.

☐ 4. Appreciate that your study design will be determined by the nature of the investigation, i.e. a controlled experiment vs a population study in the field. *Some of the following objectives apply specifically to controlled experiments. They will also apply, with modification if necessary, to field studies.*

☐ 5. Formulate a **hypothesis** from which you can generate **predictions** about the outcome of your investigation. Consider a **pilot study**, to test the experimental procedure you have in mind.

☐ 6. Define and explain the purpose of each of the following variables in a controlled experiment:
- **Independent variable** (manipulated variable)
- **Dependent variable** (response variable)
- **Controlled variables** (to control nuisance factors)

☐ 7. For your own investigation distinguish clearly between:
- A **data value** for a particular **variable**, e.g. height.
- The individual sampling unit, e.g. a test-tube with an enzyme at a particular pH.
- The sample size, e.g. the number of test-tubes in each treatment.

☐ 8. Determine the amount of data that you need to collect in order to reasonably test your hypothesis.
- For lab based investigations, determine the **sample size** (e.g. the number of samples within each treatment) and the number of **treatments** (the range of the independent variable).
- For field based investigations, determine the size of the sampling unit (it may be an individual organism or a quadrat size) and the sample size (e.g. the number of organisms or quadrats).

☐ 9. Determine the type of data that you will collect (e.g. counts, measurements) and how you will collect it. Have a clear idea about how you are going to analyse your data before you start and appreciate why this is important. Understand why it is desirable to collect **quantitative** rather than **qualitative** data.

☐ 10. Describe any **controls** in your investigation and identify any assumptions made in the investigation.

☐ 11. Identify different methods for systematically recording data: tables, spreadsheets, and software linked to **dataloggers**. Decide on the method by which you will **systematically record** the data as they are collected.

☐ 12. Identify **sources of error** in your experimental design and explain how you will minimise these.

☐ 13. Recognise that all biological investigations should be carried out with appropriate regard for safety and the well-being of living organisms and their environment.

Dealing with Data *(pages 29-42, 55-56)*

☐ 14. Collect and record data systematically according to your plan (#11). Critically evaluate the **accuracy** of your methods for data collection, any **measurement errors**, and the repeatability (**precision**) of any measurements.

☐ 15. Demonstrate an ability to perform simple and appropriate **data transformations**, e.g. totals, percentages, increments, reciprocals, rates, and log.

☐ 16. Demonstrate an ability to use **SI units** and an appropriate number of **significant figures**. Understand the relationship between the appropriate number of significant figures and the accuracy of a measurement.

☐ 17. Describe the benefits of graphing data. Recognise the **x axis** and **y axis** of graphs and identify which variable (dependent or independent) is plotted on each.

☐ 18. Demonstrate an ability to plot data in an appropriate way using different methods of graphical presentation: **scatter plots**, **line graphs**, **pie graphs**, **bar graphs** (and column graphs), **kite graphs**, and **histograms**.

☐ 19. Explain what is meant by a '**line of best fit**' and when it is appropriate to use it. Draw 'lines of best fit' to graphs with plotted points. Use error bars to place your line or try a computer generated fit (see #26).

☐ 20. Make good **biological drawings** as a way of recording information where appropriate to your investigation.

Descriptive Statistics *(pages 45-48)*

☐ 21. Distinguish between a **statistic** and a **parameter**. Demonstrate an understanding of the calculation and use of the following **descriptive statistics**:
(a) Sample **mean** and **standard deviation**. Identify when the use of these statistics is appropriate.
(b) **Median** and **mode** (calculated from your own, or second hand, data). Explain what each statistic summarises and when its use is appropriate.

☐ 22. Calculate measures of dispersion for your data, related to the true population parameters. Consider:
   (a) The **standard error** of the mean.
   (b) The **95% confidence intervals** and the **95% confidence limits**.

☐ 23. Identify **trends** in your data for further analysis and discussion. Evaluate unexpected results and outlying data points and be prepared to discuss them.

Statistical Tests (pages 43-44)

☐ 24. Use the flow chart provided in this topic to help you decide on the appropriate analysis for your data. Some further guidelines are provided below.

Tests for a trend (pages 49-51)
Recognise tests for trends (relationships) in data.

☐ 25. **Correlation**: Data are **correlated** when there is a relationship between the two variables in question, but neither is assumed to be dependent on the other. A test for correlation can demonstrate that two measures are associated; it cannot establish cause and effect.

☐ 26. **Regression**: A regression is appropriate when the magnitude of one variable (the dependent variable) is determined by the magnitude of the second variable (the independent variable). Recognise:

   Linear regression: This is the simplest functional relationship of one variable to another and is indicated by a straight line relationship on a scatter plot. Generate a **line of best fit** for plotted data and comment on the fit of the data to the line. Discuss the **predictive** nature of linear regression analyses.

   Non-linear regression: Many relationships between an independent variable and its corresponding biological response are not linear (e.g. change in respiration rate with changes in salinity). If your data plot in a non-linear scatter, consider a non-linear regression to test the relationship.

Tests for difference (pages 52-54)
Recognise tests for difference between groups.

☐ 27. **Chi-squared** is a test for difference between two groups where the observed result is compared to an expected outcome. It is often used in ecology and for testing the outcome of simple genetic crosses.

☐ 28. **Student's _t_ test** is a test for difference between two means, and can be used even when sample sizes are small. It is often used to test differences between densities of organisms in different habitats.

☐ 29. **ANOVA** (analysis of variance) is a test for difference between more than two means. ANOVA is an appropriate test for investigations involving a biological response to specific treatments, such as different fertilisers or soils. It is covered in _Advanced Biology A2_.

Writing a Report (pages 57-63)

☐ 30. Write up your report. Give it a concise, descriptive title, and organise it into the following sections:

   (a) **Introduction**: Explain the aim, outline your hypothesis, and summarise the current state of the knowledge in the topic area.

   (b) **Materials and methods**: Describe how you carried out your investigation in a way that allows the method to be reproduced by others.

   (c) **Results**: Use text, graphs, and tables to describe your results; do not discuss them at this stage.

   (d) **Discussion**: Discuss your results, including a critical evaluation of any discrepancies in your results. Include reference to published work.

   (e) **Conclusion**: Summarise your findings with respect to your original hypothesis. Draw conclusions _only_ about the variable that you planned to investigate.

   (f) **Reference list**: Distinguish between a bibliography and a reference list, and use whichever meets your requirements. List all sources of information, including personal communications.

Skills in Biology

See the 'Textbook Reference Grid' on pages 8-9 for textbook page references relating to material in this topic.

Supplementary Texts
See pages 5-7 for additional details of these texts:

■ Adds, J. _et al.,_ 1999. **Tools, Techniques and Assessment in Biology** (NelsonThornes).

■ Barnard, C., _et al.,_ 2007. **Asking Questions in Biology: Key Skills for Practical Assessments and Project Work**, 2 edn (Prentice Hall).

■ Cadogan, A. and Ingram, M., 2002. **Maths for Advanced Biology** (NelsonThornes).

■ Indge, B., 2003. **Data and Data Handling for AS and A Level Biology** (Hodder Arnold H&S).

■ Jones, A., _et al.,_ 2007. **Practical Skills in Biology** (Pearson).

■ Morgan, S., 2002. **Advanced Level Practical Work for Biology** (Hodder and Stoughton).

See pages 10-11 for details of how to access **Bio Links** from our web site: **www.biozone.co.uk**. From Bio Links, access sites under the topics:

STUDENT PROJECTS: • A scientific report • Scientific investigation • Study skills - biology • The scientific method • Tree lupins • Woodlice online ... _and others_

See page 7 for details of publishers of periodicals:

STUDENT'S REFERENCE

■ **AS: A Word at the Start?** Biol. Sci. Rev., 13(1) Sept. 2000, pp. 6-8. _A useful summary of the importance of understanding the facts, reading carefully, and accurately communicating your knowledge when answering examination questions._

■ **Size Does Matter** Biol. Sci. Rev., 17 (3) February 2005, pp. 10-13. _Measuring the size of organisms and calculating magnification and scale._

■ **Percentages** Biol. Sci. Rev., 17(2) Nov. 2004, pp. 28-29. _The calculation of percentage and the appropriate uses of this important transformation._

■ **The Variability of Samples** Biol. Sci. Rev., 13(4) March 2001, pp. 34-35. _The variability of sample data and the use of sample statistics as estimators for population parameters._

■ **Experiments** Biol. Sci. Rev., 14(3) February 2002, pp. 11-13. _The basics of experimental design and execution: determining variables, measuring them, and establishing a control._

■ **Descriptive Statistics** Biol. Sci. Rev., 13 (5) May 2001, pp. 36-37. _A synopsis of descriptive statistics. The appropriate use of standard error and standard deviation is discussed._

■ **Dealing with Data** Biol. Sci. Rev., 12 (4) March 2000, pp. 6-8. _A short account of the best ways in which to deal with the interpretation of graphically presented data in examinations._

■ **Describing the Normal Distribution** Biol. Sci. Rev., 13(2) Nov. 2000, pp. 40-41. _The normal distribution, with an introduction to data spread, mean, median, variance, and standard deviation._

■ **Statistical Modelling** New Scientist, 17 Sept. 1994 (Inside Science). _Useful presentation of data; distributions, normal curves, and histograms._

■ **The Truth is Out There** New Scientist, 26 Feb. 2000 (Inside Science). _The philosophy of scientific method explained clearly and with examples._

■ **Statistical Sampling** New Scientist, 10 June 1995 (Inside Science). _Hypotheses, sampling methodology, significance, & central limit theorem._

■ **Estimating the Mean and Standard Deviation** Biol. Sci. Rev., 13(3) January 2001, pp. 40-41. _Simple statistical analysis. Includes formulae for calculating sample mean and standard deviation._

■ **Correlation** Biol. Sci. Rev., 14(3) February 2002, pp. 38-41. _An examination of the relationship between variables. An excellent synopsis._

■ **Ecological Projects** Biol. Sci. Rev., 8(5) May 1996, pp. 24-26. _Planning and carrying out a field-based project (includes analysis and reporting)._

■ **Fieldwork - Sampling Animals** Biol. Sci. Rev., 10(4) March 1998, pp. 23-25. _The appropriate methodology for collecting animals in the field._

■ **Fieldwork Sampling - Plants** Biol. Sci. Rev., 10(5) May 1998, pp. 6-8. _Methods for sampling plant communities (transects and quadrats)._

TEACHER'S REFERENCE

■ **Biology Statistics made Simple using Excel** SSR 83(303), Dec. 2001, pp. 29-34. _An instructional account on the use of spreadsheets for statistics in A level science (excellent)._

Working spreadsheets support this topic:

Teacher Resource CD-ROM
• **Statistics spreadsheets**

Teacher Resource CD-ROM

Terms and Notation

The definitions for some commonly encountered terms related to making biological investigations are provided below. Use these as you would use a biology dictionary when planning your investigation and writing up your report. It is important to be consistent with the use of terms i.e. use the same term for the same procedure or unit throughout your study. Be sure, when using a term with a specific statistical meaning, such as sample, that you are using the term correctly.

General Terms

Data: Facts collected for analysis.

Qualitative: Not quantitative. Described in words or terms rather than by numbers. Includes subjective descriptions in terms of variables such as colour or shape.

Quantitative: Able to be expressed in numbers. Numerical values derived from counts or measurements.

The Design of Investigations

Hypothesis: A tentative explanation of an observation, capable of being tested by experimentation. Hypotheses are written as clear statements, not as questions.

Control treatment (control): A standard (reference) treatment that helps to ensure that responses to other treatments can be reliably interpreted. There may be more than one control in an investigation.

Dependent variable: A variable whose values are determined by another variable (the independent variable). In practice, the dependent variable is the variable representing the biological response.

Independent variable: A variable whose values are set, or systematically altered, by the investigator.

Controlled variables: Variables that may take on different values in different situations, but are controlled (fixed) as part of the design of the investigation.

Experiment: A contrived situation designed to test (one or more) hypotheses and their predictions. It is good practice to use sample sizes that are as large as possible for experiments.

Investigation: A very broad term applied to scientific studies; investigations may be controlled experiments or field based studies involving population sampling.

Parameter: A numerical value that describes a characteristic of a population (e.g. the mean height of all 17 year-old males).

Prediction: The prediction of the response (Y) variable on the basis of changes in the independent (X) variable.

Random sample: A method of choosing a sample from a population that avoids any subjective element. It is the equivalent to drawing numbers out of a hat, but using random number tables. For field based studies involving quadrats or transects, random numbers can be used to determine the positioning of the sampling unit.

Repeat / Trial: The entire investigation is carried out again at a different time. This ensures that the results are reproducible. Note that repeats or trials are not **replicates** in the true sense unless they are run at the same time.

Replicate: A duplication of the entire experimental design run at the same time.

Sample: A sub-set of a whole used to estimate the values that might have been obtained if every individual or response was measured. A sample is made up of **sampling units,** In lab based investigations, the sampling unit might be a test-tube, while in field based studies, the sampling unit might be an individual organism or a quadrat.

Sample size (n): The number of samples taken. In a field study, a typical sample size may involve 20-50 individuals or 20 quadrats. In a lab based investigation, a typical sample size may be two to three sampling units, e.g. two test-tubes held at 10°C.

Sampling unit: Sampling units make up the sample size. Examples of sampling units in different investigations are an individual organism, a test tube undergoing a particular treatment, an area (e.g. quadrat size), or a volume. The size of the sampling unit is an important consideration in studies where the area or volume of a habitat is being sampled.

Statistic: An estimate of a parameter obtained from a sample (e.g. the mean height of all 17 year-old males in your class). A precise (reliable) statistic will be close to the value of the parameter being estimated.

Treatments: Well defined conditions applied to the sample units. The response of sample units to a treatment is intended to shed light on the hypothesis under investigation. What is often of most interest is the comparison of the responses to different treatments.

Variable: A factor in an experiment that is subject to change. Variables may be controlled (fixed), manipulated (systematically altered), or represent a biological response.

Precision and Significance

Accuracy: The correctness of the measurement (the closeness of the measured value to the true value). Accuracy is often a function of the calibration of the instrument used for measuring.

Measurement errors: When measuring or setting the value of a variable, there may be some difference between your answer and the 'right' answer. These errors are often as a result of poor technique or poorly set up equipment.

Objective measurement: Measurement not significantly involving subjective (or personal) judgment. If a second person repeats the measurement they should get the same answer.

Precision (of a measurement): The repeatability of the measurement. As there is usually no reason to suspect that a piece of equipment is giving inaccurate measures, making precise measurements is usually the most important consideration. You can assess or quantify the precision of any measurement system by taking repeated measurements from individual samples.

Precision (of a statistic): How close the statistic is to the value of the parameter being estimated. Also called **reliability**.

The Expression of Units

The value of a variable must be written with its units where possible. Common ways of recording measurements in biology are: volume in litres, mass in grams, length in metres, time in seconds. The following example shows different ways to express the same term. Note that ml and cm³ are equivalent.

Oxygen consumption (millilitres per gram per hour)
Oxygen consumption ($mlg^{-1}h^{-1}$) or ($mLg^{-1}h^{-1}$)
Oxygen consumption (ml/g/h) or (mL/g/h)
Oxygen consumption/$cm^3g^{-1}h^{-1}$

Statistical significance: An assigned value that is used to establish the probability that an observed trend or difference represents a true difference that is not due to chance alone. If a level of significance is less than the chosen value (usually 1-10%), the difference is regarded as statistically significant. Remember that in rigorous science, it is the hypothesis of no difference or no effect (the null hypothesis, H_0) that is tested. The alternative hypothesis (your tentative explanation for an observation) can only be accepted through statistical rejection of H_0.

Validity: Whether or not you are truly measuring the right thing.

Hypotheses and Predictions

Scientific knowledge grows through a process called the **scientific method**. This process involves observation and measurement, hypothesising and predicting, and planning and executing investigations designed to test formulated **hypotheses**. A scientific hypothesis is a tentative explanation for an observation, which is capable of being tested by experimentation. Hypotheses lead to **predictions** about the system involved and they are accepted or rejected on the basis of findings arising from the investigation. Rejection of the hypothesis may lead to new, alternative explanations (hypotheses) for the observations. Acceptance of the hypothesis as a valid explanation is not necessarily permanent: explanations may be rejected at a later date in light of new findings. This process eventually leads to new knowledge (theory, laws, or models).

Making Observations

These may involve the observation of certain behaviours in wild populations, physiological measurements made during previous experiments, or 'accidental' results obtained when seeking answers to completely unrelated questions.

Asking Questions

The observations lead to the formation of questions about the system being studied.

Forming a Hypothesis

Features of a sound hypothesis:

- It is based on observations and prior knowledge of the system.
- It offers an explanation for an observation.
- It refers to only one independent variable.
- It is written as a definite statement and not as a question.
- It is testable by experimentation.
- It leads to predictions about the system.

Generating a Null Hypothesis

A hypothesis based on observations is used to generate the **null hypothesis** (H_0); the hypothesis of no difference or no effect. Hypotheses are expressed in the null form for the purposes of statistical testing. H_0 may be rejected in favour of accepting the alternative hypothesis, H_A.

Accept or reject the hypothesis

Testing the Predictions

The predictions are tested out in the practical part of an investigation.

Testing predictions may lead to new observations

Designing an Investigation

Investigations are planned so that the predictions about the system made in the hypothesis can be tested. Investigations may be laboratory or field based.

Making Predictions

Based on a hypothesis, **predictions** (expected, repeatable outcomes) can be generated about the behaviour of the system. Predictions may be made on any aspect of the material of interest, e.g. how different variables (factors) relate to each other.

Related activities: Experimental Method
Web links: Hypotheses

A 2

Useful Types of Hypotheses

A hypothesis offers a tentative explanation to questions generated by observations. Some examples are described below. Hypotheses are often constructed in a form that allows them to be tested statistically. For every hypothesis, there is a corresponding **null hypothesis**; a hypothesis against the prediction. Predictions are tested with laboratory and field experiments and carefully focused observations. For a hypothesis to be accepted it should be possible for anyone to test the predictions with the same methods and get a similar result each time.

Hypothesis involving manipulation
Used when the effect of manipulating a variable on a biological entity is being investigated. **Example**: The composition of applied fertiliser influences the rate of growth of plant A.

Hypothesis of choice
Used when species preference, e.g. for a particular habitat type or microclimate, is being investigated. **Example**: Woodpeckers (species A) show a preference for tree type when nesting.

Hypothesis involving observation
Used when organisms are being studied in their natural environment and conditions cannot be changed. **Example**: Fern abundance is influenced by the degree to which the canopy is established.

1. Generate a prediction for the hypothesis: *"Moisture level of the microhabitat influences woodlouse distribution"*:

   _____

2. During the course of any investigation, new information may arise as a result of observations unrelated to the original hypothesis. This can lead to the generation of further hypotheses about the system. For each of the incidental observations described below, formulate a prediction, and an outline of an investigation to test it. *The observation described in each case was not related to the hypothesis the experiment was designed to test:*

   (a) **Bacterial cultures**

   Prediction: _____

   _____

   Outline of the investigation: _____

   _____

   _____

   _____

   _____

   _____

Bacterial Cultures

Observation: During an experiment on bacterial growth, the girls noticed that the cultures grew at different rates when the dishes were left overnight in different parts of the laboratory.

   (b) **Plant cloning**

   Prediction: _____

   _____

   _____

   Outline of the investigation: _____

   _____

   _____

   _____

   _____

   _____

   _____

Plant Cloning

Observation: During an experiment on plant cloning, a scientist noticed that the root length of plant clones varied depending on the concentration of a hormone added to the agar.

Planning an Investigation

Investigations involve written stages (planning and reporting), at the start and end. The middle stage is the practical work when the data are collected. Practical work may be laboratory or field based. Typical lab based studies involve investigating how a biological response is affected by manipulating a particular **variable**, e.g. temperature. Field work often involves investigating features of a population or community. These may be interrelationships, such as competition, or patterns, such as zonation. Where quantitative information must be gathered from the population or community, particular techniques (such as quadrat sampling) and protocols (e.g. random placement of sampling units) apply. These aspects of practical work are covered in *Advanced Biology A2*. Investigations in the field are usually more complex than those in the laboratory because natural systems have many more variables that cannot easily be controlled or accounted for.

Skills in Biology

Planning

- Formulate your hypothesis from an observation.
- Use a checklist (see the next activity) or a template (above) to construct a plan.

Execution

- Spend time (as appropriate to your study) collecting the data.
- Record the data in a systematic format (e.g. a table or spreadsheet).

Analysis and Reporting

- Analyse the data using graphs, tables, or statistics to look for trends or patterns.
- Write up your report including all the necessary sections.

Identifying Variables

A variable is any characteristic or property able to take any one of a range of values. Investigations often look at the effect of changing one variable on another. It is important to identify all variables in an investigation: independent, dependent, and controlled, although there may be nuisance factors of which you are unaware. In all fair tests, only one variable is changed by the investigator.

Dependent variable
- Measured during the investigation.
- Recorded on the y axis of the graph.

Dependent variable (y axis) vs Independent variable (x axis)

Controlled variables
- Factors that are kept the same or controlled.
- List these in the method, as appropriate to your own investigation.

Independent variable
- Set by the person carrying out the investigation.
- Recorded on the x axis of the graph.

Assumptions

In any experimental work, you will make certain assumptions about the biological system you are working with.

Assumptions are features of the system (and your experiment) that you assume to be true but do not (or cannot) test.

Examples of Investigations

Aim		Variables	
Investigate the effect of varying ...	on the following ...	Independent variable	Dependent variable
Temperature	Leaf width	Temperature	Leaf width
Light intensity	Activity of woodlice	Light intensity	Woodlice activity
Soil pH	Plant height at age 6 months	pH	Plant height

Related activities: Variables and Data, Experimental Method
Web links: Space for Species

A 2

In order to write a sound method for your investigation, you need to determine how the independent, dependent, and controlled variables will be set and measured (or monitored). A good understanding of your methodology is crucial to a successful investigation. You need to be clear about how much data, and what type of data, you will collect. You should also have a good idea about how you will analyse the data. Use the example below to practise your skills in identifying this type of information.

Case Study: Catalase Activity

Catalase is an enzyme that converts hydrogen peroxide (H_2O_2) to oxygen and water. An experiment investigated the effect of temperature on the rate of the catalase reaction. Small (10 cm^3) test tubes were used for the reactions, each containing 0.5 cm^3 of enzyme and 4 cm^3 of hydrogen peroxide. Reaction rates were assessed at four temperatures (10°C, 20°C, 30°C, and 60°C). For each temperature, there were two reaction tubes (e.g. tubes 1 and 2 were both kept at 10°C). The height of oxygen bubbles present after one minute of reaction was used as a measure of the reaction rate; a faster reaction rate produced more bubbles. The entire experiment, involving eight tubes, was repeated on two separate days.

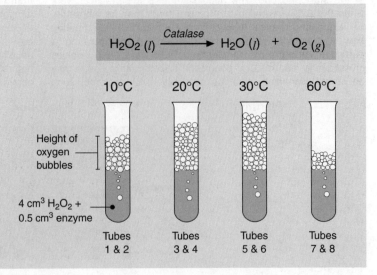

$$H_2O_2 \, (l) \xrightarrow{\text{Catalase}} H_2O \, (l) \; + \; O_2 \, (g)$$

10°C   20°C   30°C   60°C

Height of oxygen bubbles

4 cm^3 H_2O_2 + 0.5 cm^3 enzyme

Tubes 1 & 2   Tubes 3 & 4   Tubes 5 & 6   Tubes 7 & 8

1. Write a suitable aim for this experiment: _____

_____

2. Write a suitable hypothesis for this experiment: _____

_____

3. (a) Identify the **independent variable**: _____

   (b) State the range of values for the independent variable: _____

   (c) Name the unit for the independent variable: _____

   (d) List the equipment needed to set the independent variable, and describe how it was used: _____

   _____

4. (a) Identify the **dependent variable**: _____

   (b) Name the unit for the dependent variable: _____

   (c) List the equipment needed to measure the dependent variable, and describe how it was used: _____

   _____

5. (a) Each temperature represents a treatment/sample/trial (circle one):

   (b) State the number of tubes at each temperature: _____

   (c) State the sample size for each treatment: _____

   (d) State how many times the whole investigation was repeated: _____

6. Explain why it would have been desirable to have included an extra tube containing no enzyme: _____

   _____

7. Identify three variables that might have been controlled in this experiment, and how they could have been monitored:

   (a) _____

   (b) _____

   (c) _____

8. Explain why controlled variables should be monitored carefully: _____

   _____

Experimental Method

An aim, hypothesis, and method for an experiment are described below. Explanations of the types of variables for which data are collected, and methods of recording these, are provided in the next two activities. The method described below includes numbered steps and incorporates other features identified in the previous activity. The method can be thought of as a 'statement of intent' for the practical work, and it may need slight changes during execution. The investigation described below was based on the observation that plant species 'A' was found growing in soil with a low pH (pH 4-5). The investigators wondered whether plant species 'A' was adapted to grow more vigorously under acid conditions than under alkaline or neutral conditions.

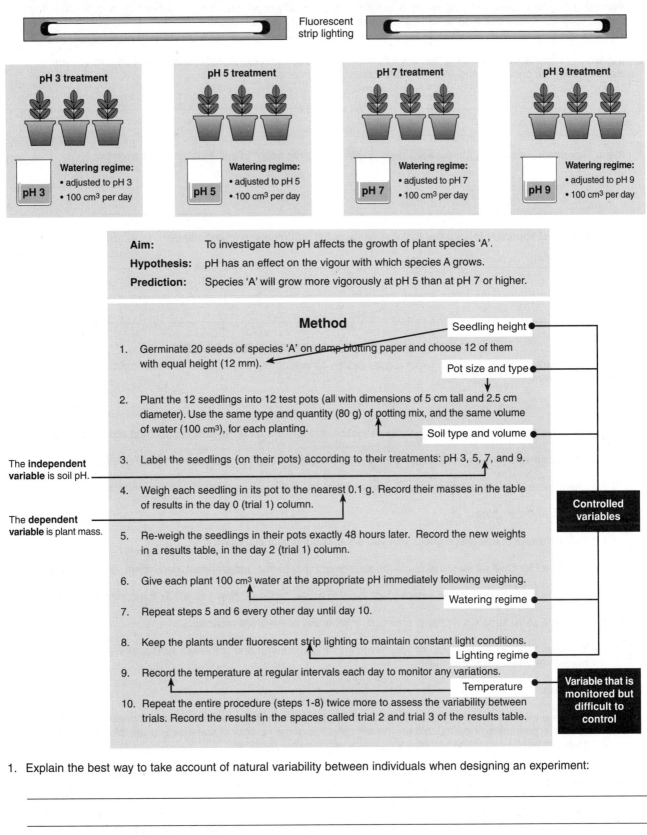

Fluorescent strip lighting

pH 3 treatment

Watering regime:
• adjusted to pH 3
• 100 cm³ per day

pH 3

pH 5 treatment

Watering regime:
• adjusted to pH 5
• 100 cm³ per day

pH 5

pH 7 treatment

Watering regime:
• adjusted to pH 7
• 100 cm³ per day

pH 7

pH 9 treatment

Watering regime:
• adjusted to pH 9
• 100 cm³ per day

pH 9

Aim: To investigate how pH affects the growth of plant species 'A'.

Hypothesis: pH has an effect on the vigour with which species A grows.

Prediction: Species 'A' will grow more vigorously at pH 5 than at pH 7 or higher.

Method

Seedling height

1. Germinate 20 seeds of species 'A' on damp blotting paper and choose 12 of them with equal height (12 mm).

Pot size and type

2. Plant the 12 seedlings into 12 test pots (all with dimensions of 5 cm tall and 2.5 cm diameter). Use the same type and quantity (80 g) of potting mix, and the same volume of water (100 cm³), for each planting.

Soil type and volume

3. Label the seedlings (on their pots) according to their treatments: pH 3, 5, 7, and 9.

The **independent variable** is soil pH.

4. Weigh each seedling in its pot to the nearest 0.1 g. Record their masses in the table of results in the day 0 (trial 1) column.

The **dependent variable** is plant mass.

5. Re-weigh the seedlings in their pots exactly 48 hours later. Record the new weights in a results table, in the day 2 (trial 1) column.

6. Give each plant 100 cm³ water at the appropriate pH immediately following weighing.

Watering regime

7. Repeat steps 5 and 6 every other day until day 10.

8. Keep the plants under fluorescent strip lighting to maintain constant light conditions.

Lighting regime

9. Record the temperature at regular intervals each day to monitor any variations.

Temperature

10. Repeat the entire procedure (steps 1-8) twice more to assess the variability between trials. Record the results in the spaces called trial 2 and trial 3 of the results table.

Controlled variables

Variable that is monitored but difficult to control

Skills in Biology

1. Explain the best way to take account of natural variability between individuals when designing an experiment:

_____

_____

_____

_____

Related activities: Variables and Data

Replication in experiments

Replication refers to the number of times you repeat your entire experimental design (including controls). True replication is not the same as increasing the sample size (*n*) although it is often used to mean the same thing. Replication accounts for any unusual and unforseen effects that may be operating in your set-up (e.g. field trials of plant varieties where soil type is variable). Replication is necessary when you expect that the response of treatments will vary because of factors outside your control. It is a feature of higher level experimental designs, and complex statistics are needed to separate differences between replicate treatments. For simple experiments, it is usually more valuable to increase the sample size than to worry about replicates.

2. Explain the importance of ensuring that any influencing variables in an experiment (except the one that you are manipulating) are controlled and kept constant across all treatments:

_____

_____

3. In the experiment outlined on the previous page, explain why only single plants were grown in each pot:

_____

_____

4. Suggest why it is important to consider the physical layout of treatments in an experiment: _____

_____

_____

_____

YOUR CHECKLIST FOR EXPERIMENTAL DESIGN

The following provides a checklist for an experimental design. Check off the points when you are confident that you have satisfied the requirements in each case:

1. **Preliminary:**

   ☐ (a) You have determined the aim of your investigation and formulated a hypothesis based on observation(s).

   ☐ (b) The hypothesis (and its predictions) are testable using the resources you have available (the study is feasible).

   ☐ (c) The organism you have chosen is suitable for the study and you have considered the ethics involved.

2. **Assumptions and variables:**

   ☐ (a) You are aware of any assumptions that you are making in your experiment.

   ☐ (b) You have identified all the variables in the experiment (controlled, independent, dependent, uncontrollable).

   ☐ (c) You have set the range of the independent variable and established how you will fix the controlled variables.

   ☐ (d) You have considered what (if any) preliminary treatment or trials are necessary.

   ☐ (e) You have considered the layout of your treatments to account for any unforseen variability in your set-up and you have established your control(s).

3. **Data collection:**

   ☐ (a) You have identified the units for all variables and determined how you will measure or monitor each variable. You have determined how much data you will collect, e.g. the number of samples you will take. The type of data collected will be determined by how you are measuring your variables.

   ☐ (b) You have considered how you will analyse the data you collect and made sure that your experimental design allows you to answer the questions you have asked.

   ☐ (c) You have designed a method for systematically recording your results and had this checked with a teacher. The format of your results table or spreadsheet accommodates all your raw results, any transformations you intend to make, and all trials and treatments.

   ☐ (d) You have recorded data from any preliminary trials and any necessary changes to your methodology.

Recording Results

Designing a table to record your results is part of planning your investigation. Once you have collected all your data, you will need to analyse and present it. To do this, it may be necessary to transform your data first, by calculating a mean or a rate. An example of a table for recording results is presented below. This example relates to the investigation described in the previous activity, but it represents a relatively standardised layout. The labels on the columns and rows are chosen to represent the design features of the investigation. The first column contains the entire range chosen for the independent variable. There are spaces for multiple sampling units, repeats (trials), and averages. A version of this table should be presented in your final report.

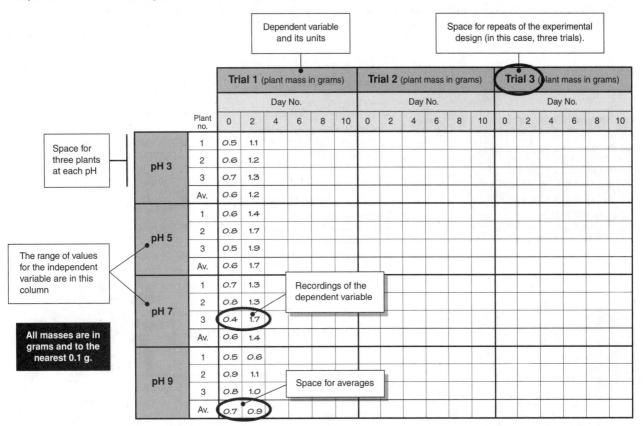

	Plant no.	Trial 1 (plant mass in grams)						Trial 2 (plant mass in grams)						Trial 3 (plant mass in grams)					
		Day No.						Day No.						Day No.					
		0	2	4	6	8	10	0	2	4	6	8	10	0	2	4	6	8	10
pH 3	1	0.5	1.1																
	2	0.6	1.2																
	3	0.7	1.3																
	Av.	0.6	1.2																
pH 5	1	0.6	1.4																
	2	0.8	1.7																
	3	0.5	1.9																
	Av.	0.6	1.7																
pH 7	1	0.7	1.3																
	2	0.8	1.3																
	3	0.4	1.7																
	Av.	0.6	1.4																
pH 9	1	0.5	0.6																
	2	0.9	1.1																
	3	0.8	1.0																
	Av.	0.7	0.9																

Dependent variable and its units

Space for repeats of the experimental design (in this case, three trials).

Space for three plants at each pH

The range of values for the independent variable are in this column

All masses are in grams and to the nearest 0.1 g.

Recordings of the dependent variable

Space for averages

1. In the space (below) design a table to collect data from the case study below. Include space for individual results and averages from the three set ups (use the table above as a guide).

Case Study
Carbon dioxide levels in a respiration chamber

A datalogger was used to monitor the concentrations of carbon dioxide (CO_2) in respiration chambers containing five green leaves from one plant species. The entire study was performed in conditions of full light (quantified) and involved three identical set-ups. The CO_2 concentrations were measured every minute, over a period of ten minutes, using a CO_2 sensor. A mean CO_2 concentration (for the three set-ups) was calculated. The study was carried out two more times, two days apart.

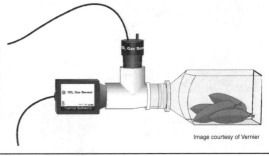

Image courtesy of Vernier

2. Next, the effect of various light intensities (low light, half-light, and full light) on CO_2 concentration was investigated. Describe how the results table for this investigation would differ from the one you have drawn above (for full light only):

_____

_____

Related activities: Transforming Raw Data, Data Presentation

DA 2

Skills in Biology

Variables and Data

When planning a biological investigation, it is important to consider the type of data that will be collected. It is best, whenever possible, to collect quantitative data, as these data lend themselves well to analysis and statistical testing. Recording data in a systematic way as you collect it, e.g. using a table or spreadsheet, is important, especially if data manipulation and transformation are required. It is important to calculate summary, **descriptive statistics** (e.g. mean) as you proceed. These will help you to recognise important trends or features in your data as they become apparent. The biggest hurdle in undertaking an experimental study will be in choosing a topic that lends itself to the aims of the investigation and is designed in such a way that analysis is straightforward and biologically meaningful. Guidelines are given below, together with a synopsis of types of variables. You should be familiar with the qualities of data before you start, as this will help you to develop a well designed investigation.

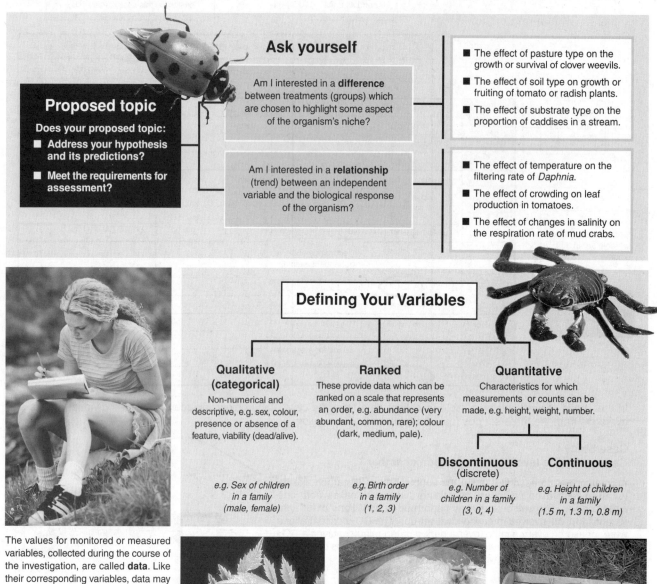

Ask yourself

Proposed topic

Does your proposed topic:
- Address your hypothesis and its predictions?
- Meet the requirements for assessment?

Am I interested in a **difference** between treatments (groups) which are chosen to highlight some aspect of the organism's niche?

- The effect of pasture type on the growth or survival of clover weevils.
- The effect of soil type on growth or fruiting of tomato or radish plants.
- The effect of substrate type on the proportion of caddises in a stream.

Am I interested in a **relationship** (trend) between an independent variable and the biological response of the organism?

- The effect of temperature on the filtering rate of *Daphnia*.
- The effect of crowding on leaf production in tomatoes.
- The effect of changes in salinity on the respiration rate of mud crabs.

Defining Your Variables

Qualitative (categorical)

Non-numerical and descriptive, e.g. sex, colour, presence or absence of a feature, viability (dead/alive).

e.g. Sex of children in a family (male, female)

Ranked

These provide data which can be ranked on a scale that represents an order, e.g. abundance (very abundant, common, rare); colour (dark, medium, pale).

e.g. Birth order in a family (1, 2, 3)

Quantitative

Characteristics for which measurements or counts can be made, e.g. height, weight, number.

Discontinuous (discrete)

e.g. Number of children in a family (3, 0, 4)

Continuous

e.g. Height of children in a family (1.5 m, 1.3 m, 0.8 m)

The values for monitored or measured variables, collected during the course of the investigation, are called **data**. Like their corresponding variables, data may be quantitative, qualitative, or ranked.

Leaf shape: qualitative

Number per litter: quantitative, discontinuous

Fish length: quantitative, continuous

1. Suggest how you might measure the colour of light (red, blue, green) quantitatively: _____

_____

_____

2. Sometimes, ranked data are given numerical values, e.g. rare = 1, occasional = 2, frequent = 3, common = 4, abundant = 5. Suggest why these data are sometimes called semi-quantitative:

_____

_____

Related activities: Descriptive Statistics

Transforming Raw Data

Data often have to be transformed as a first step in the initial analysis of results. Transforming data can make them more useful by helping to highlight trends and making important features more obvious. Data transformations may be quite simple (e.g. percentages, totals, and rates) or they may be more complex transformations used before statistical procedures (e.g. log transformations). Some of the simple transformations are outlined below.

Transformation	Rationale for transformation
Frequency table	A tally chart of the number of times a value occurs in a data set. It is a useful first step in data analysis as a neatly constructed tally chart can double as a simple histogram.
Total	The sum of all data values for a variable. Useful as an initial stage in data handling, especially in comparing replicates. Used in making other data transformations.
Percentages	Provide a clear expression of what proportion of data fall into any particular category. This relationship may not be obvious from the raw data values.
Rates	Expressed as a measure per unit time. Rates show how a variable changes over a standard time period (e.g. one second, one minute or one hour). Rates allow meaningful comparison of data that may have been recorded over different time periods.
Reciprocals	Reciprocals of time (1/data value) can provide a crude measure of rate in situations where the variable measured is the total time taken to complete a task, e.g. time taken for a colour change to occur in an enzyme reaction.
Relative values	These involve expression of data values relative to a standard value e.g. number of road deaths per 1000 cars or calorie consumption per gram of body weight. They allow data from different sample sizes or different organisms to be meaningfully compared. Sometimes they are expressed as a percentage (e.g. 35%) or as a proportion (e.g. 0.35).

Skills in Biology

1. (a) Explain what it means to **transform data**: _____

_____

(b) Briefly explain the general purpose of transforming data: _____

_____

_____

2. For each of the following examples, state a suitable transformation, together with a reason for your choice:

(a) Determining relative abundance from counts of four plant species in two different habitat areas:

Suitable transformation: _____

Reason: _____

(b) Making a meaningful comparison between animals of different size in the volume of oxygen each consumed:

Suitable transformation: _____

Reason: _____

(c) Making a meaningful comparison of the time taken for chemical precipitation to occur in a flask at different pH values:

Suitable transformation: _____

Reason: _____

(d) Determining the effect of temperature on the production of carbon dioxide by respiring seeds:

Suitable transformation: _____

Reason: _____

Related Activities: Data Presentation

DA 2

3. Complete the transformations for each of the tables on the right. The first value is provided in each case.

(a) TABLE: *Incidence of cyanogenic clover in different areas*

Working: 124 ÷ 159 = 0.78 = 78%

This is the number of cyanogenic clover out of the total.

Incidence of cyanogenic clover in different areas

Clover plant type	Frost free area		Frost prone area		Totals
	Number	%	Number	%	
Cyanogenic	124	78	26		
Acyanogenic	35		115		
Total	159				

(b) TABLE: *Plant transpiration loss using a bubble potometer*

Working: (9.0 – 8.0) ÷ 5 min = 0.2

This is the distance the bubble moved over the first 5 minutes. Note that there is no data entry possible for the first reading (0 min) because no difference can be calculated.

Plant transpiration loss using a bubble potometer

Time /min	Pipette arm reading /cm^3	Plant water loss /cm^3 min^{-1}
0	9.0	–
5	8.0	0.2
10	7.2	
15	6.2	
20	4.9	

(c) TABLE: *Photosynthetic rate at different light intensities*

Working: 1 ÷ 15 = 0.067

This is time taken for the leaf to float. A reciprocal gives a per minute rate (the variable measured is the time taken for an event to occur).

NOTE: In this experiment, the flotation time is used as a crude measure of photosynthetic rate. As oxygen bubbles are produced as a product of photosynthesis, they stick to the leaf disc and increase its buoyancy. The faster the rate, the sooner they come to the surface. The rates of photosynthesis should be measured over similar time intervals, so the rate is transformed to a 'per minute' basis (the reciprocal of time).

Photosynthetic rate at different light intensities

Light intensity /%	Average time for leaf disc to float / min	Reciprocal of time / min^{-1}
100	15	0.067
50	25	
25	50	
11	93	
6	187	

(d) TABLE: *Frequency of size classes in a sample of eels*

Working: (7 ÷ 270) x 100 = 2.6 %

This is the number of individuals out of the total that appear in the size class 0-50 mm. The relative frequency is rounded to one decimal place.

Frequency of size classes in a sample of eels

Size class /mm	Frequency	Relative frequency/ %
0-50	7	2.6
50-99	23	
100-149	59	
150-199	98	
200-249	50	
250-299	30	
300-349	3	
Total	270	

Data Presentation

Data can be presented in a number of ways. **Tables** provide an accurate record of numerical values and allow you to organise your data in a way that helps to identify trends and facilitate analysis. **Graphs** provide a visual representation of trends in the data that may not be evident from a table. It is useful to plot your data as soon as possible, even during your experiment, as this will help you to evaluate your results as you proceed and make adjustments as necessary (e.g. to the sampling interval). The choice between graphing or tabulation in the final report depends on the type and complexity of the data and the information that you are wanting to convey. Usually, both are appropriate. Some of the basic rules for constructing tables and graphs are outlined below. Note that values for standard deviation and 95% confidence intervals are provided in these examples. Calculating these will help you to understand your data better and critically evaluate your results. Always allow enough space for a graph, e.g. one third to one half of an A4 page. The examples in this workbook are usually reduced for reasons of space.

Presenting Data in Tables

Tables should have an accurate, descriptive title. Number tables consecutively through the report. →

Table 1: Length and growth of the third internode of bean plants receiving three different hormone treatments (data are given ± standard deviation).

Independent variable in left column.

Control values (if present) should be placed at the beginning of the table.

Each row should show a different experimental treatment, organism, sampling site etc.

Heading and subheadings identify each set of data and show units of measurement.

Tables can be used to show a calculated measure of spread of the values about the mean (e.g. standard deviation or 95% confidence interval).

Treatment	Sample size	Mean rate of internode growth / mm day^{-1}	Mean internode length / mm	Mean mass of tissue added / g day^{-1}
Control	50	0.60 ± 0.025	32.3 ± 2.3	0.36 ± 0.025
Hormone 1	46	1.52 ± 0.030	41.6 ± 3.4	0.51 ± 0.030
Hormone 2	98	0.82 ± 0.018	38.4 ± 0.9	0.56 ± 0.028
Hormone 3	85	2.06 ± 0.019	50.2 ± 1.4	0.68 ± 0.020

Show values only to the level of significance allowable by your measuring technique.

Columns that need to be compared should be placed alongside each other.

Organise the columns so that each category of like numbers or attributes is listed vertically.

Presenting Data in Graph Format

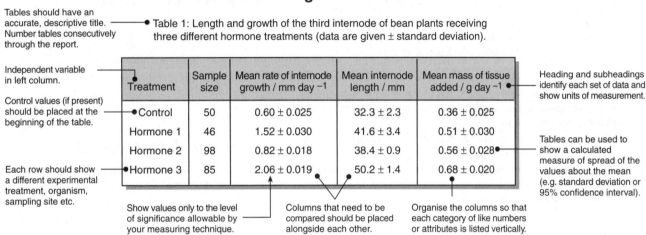

Fig. 1: Yield of two bacterial strains at different antibiotic levels (± 95% confidence intervals, $n= 6$)

Plot points accurately. Different responses can be distinguished using different symbols, lines or bar colours.

Label both axes (provide SI units of measurement if necessary).

Place the dependent variable, e.g. biological response, on the vertical (y) axis (if you are drawing a scatter graph it does not matter).

A break in an axis allows economical use of space if there is no data in the "broken" area. A floating axis (where zero points do not meet) allows data points to be plotted away from the vertical axis.

The 95% CIs between these means do not overlap. The means are significantly different.

Sensitive strain
Resistant strain

Graphs (called figures) should have a concise, explanatory title. If several graphs appear in your report they should be numbered consecutively.

Measures of spread about the plotted mean value can be shown on the graph. Such measures include standard deviation and the 95% confidence intervals (CI). The values are plotted as **error bars** and give an indication of the reliability of the mean value. If the 95% confidence intervals do not overlap between points, then these means will be significantly different.

A key identifies symbols. This information sometimes appears in the title or the legend.

Each axis should have an appropriate scale. Decide on the scale by finding the maximum and minimum values for each variable.

Place the independent variable, e.g. treatment, on the horizontal (x) axis.

1. What can you conclude about the difference (labelled **A**) between the two means plotted above? Explain your answer:

_____

2. Discuss the reasons for including both graphs and tables in a final report: _____

_____

_____

_____

_____

Drawing Bar Graphs

Guidelines for Bar Graphs

Bar graphs are appropriate for data that are non-numerical and **discrete** for at least one variable, i.e. they are grouped into separate categories. There are no dependent or independent variables. Important features of this type of graph include:

- Data are collected for discontinuous, non-numerical categories (e.g. place, colour, and species), so the bars do not touch.
- Data values may be entered on or above the bars if you wish.
- Multiple sets of data can be displayed side by side for direct comparison (e.g. males and females in the same age group).
- Axes may be reversed so that the categories are on the x axis, i.e. the bars can be vertical or horizontal. When they are vertical, these graphs are sometimes called column graphs.

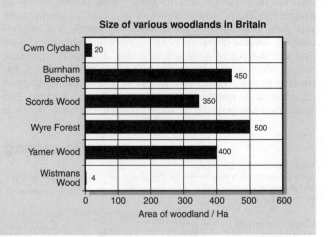

Size of various woodlands in Britain

1. Counts of eight mollusc species were made from a series of quadrat samples at two sites on a rocky shore. The summary data are presented here.

   (a) Tabulate the mean (**average**) numbers per square metre at each site in Table 1 (below left).

   (b) Plot a **bar graph** of the tabulated data on the grid below. For each species, plot the data from both sites side by side using different colours to distinguish the sites.

Average abundance of 8 mollusc species from two sites along a rocky shore.

Species	Average/ no m^{-2}	
	Site 1	Site 2

Field data notebook

Total counts at site 1 (11 quadrats) and site 2 (10 quadrats). Quadrats 1 sq m.

Species	Site 1		Site 2	
	No m^{-2} Total	Mean	No m^{-2} Total	Mean
Ornate limpet	232	21	299	30
Radiate limpet	68	6	344	34
Limpet sp. A	420	38	0	0
Cats-eye	68	6	16	2
Top shell	16	2	43	4
Limpet sp. B	628	57	389	39
Limpet sp. C	0	0	22	2
Chiton	12	1	30	3

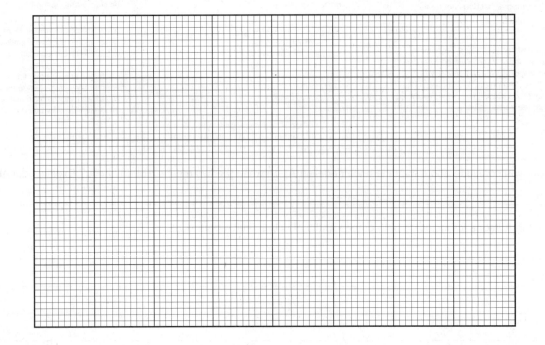

Drawing Histograms

Guidelines for Histograms

Histograms are plots of **continuous** data and are often used to represent frequency distributions, where the y-axis shows the number of times a particular measurement or value was obtained. For this reason, they are often called frequency histograms. Important features of this type of graph include:

- The data are numerical and continuous (e.g. height or weight), so the bars touch.

- The x-axis usually records the class interval. The y-axis usually records the number of individuals in each class interval (frequency).

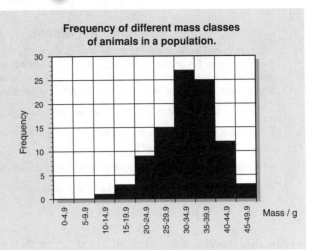

Frequency of different mass classes of animals in a population.

1. The weight data provided below were recorded from 95 individuals (male and female), older than 17 years.

   (a) Create a tally chart (frequency table) in the frame provided, organising the weight data into a form suitable for plotting. An example of the tally for the weight grouping 55-59.9 kg has been completed for you as an example. Note that the raw data values, once they are recorded as counts on the tally chart, are crossed off the data set in the notebook. It is important to do this in order to prevent data entry errors.

   (b) Plot a **frequency histogram** of the tallied data on the grid provided below.

Weight /kg	Tally	Total
45-49.9		
50-54.9		
55-59.9	LHT //	7
60-64.9		
65-69.9		
70-74.9		
75-79.9		
80-84.9		
85-89.9		
90-94.9		
95-99.9		
100-104.9		
105-109.9		

Lab notebook

Weight (in kg) of 95 individuals

63.4		
56.5	81.2	65
84	83.3	75.6
81.5	95	76.8
73.4	105.5	67.8
56	82	68.3
60.4	73.5	63.5
83.5	75.2	56
82	63	56.5
61	70.4	50
55.2	82.2	92
48	87.8	91.5
53.5	86.5	88.3
63.8	85.5	81
69	87	72
82.8	98	66.5
68.5	71	61.5
67.2	76	66
82.5	72.5	65.5
83	61	67.4
78.4	60.5	73
76.5	67	67
83.4	86	71
77.5	85	70.5
77	93.5	65.5
87	62	68
89	62.5	90
93.4	63	83.5
83	60	73
80	71.5	66
76	73.8	57.5
56	77.5	76
	74	

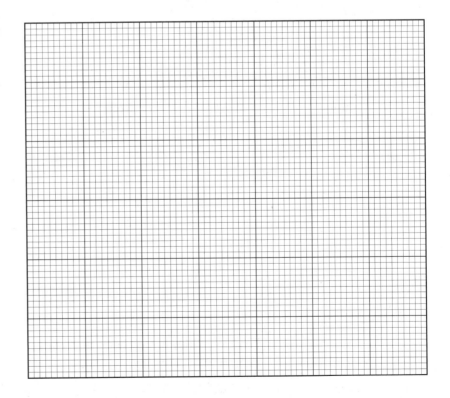

Skills in Biology

Related activities: Transforming Raw Data

DA 2

Drawing Pie Graphs

Guidelines for Pie Graphs

Pie graphs can be used instead of bar graphs, generally in cases where there are six or fewer categories involved. A pie graph provides strong visual impact of the relative proportions in each category, particularly where one of the categories is very dominant. Features of pie graphs include:

- The data for one variable are discontinuous (non-numerical or categories).

- The data for the dependent variable are usually in the form of counts, proportions, or percentages.

- Pie graphs are good for visual impact and showing relative proportions.

- They are not suitable for data sets with a large number of categories.

Average residential water use

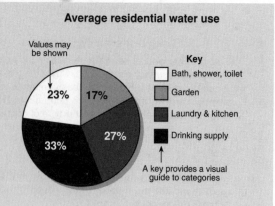

Values may be shown

Key
- Bath, shower, toilet
- Garden
- Laundry & kitchen
- Drinking supply

A key provides a visual guide to categories

1. The data provided below are from a study of the diets of three vertebrates.

   (a) Tabulate the data from the notebook in the frame provided. Calculate the angle for each percentage, given that each percentage point is equal to 3.6° (the first example is provided: 23.6 x 3.6 = 85).

   (b) Plot a pie graph for each animal in the circles provided. The circles have been marked at 5° intervals to enable you to do this exercise without a protractor. For the purposes of this exercise, begin your pie graphs at the 0° (= 360°) mark and work in a clockwise direction from the largest to the smallest percentage. Use one key for all three pie graphs.

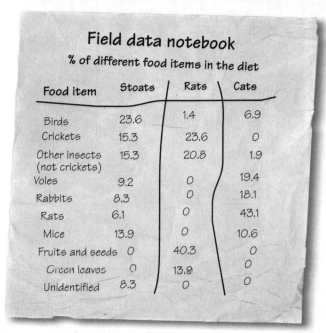

Field data notebook
% of different food items in the diet

Food item	Stoats	Rats	Cats
Birds	23.6	1.4	6.9
Crickets	15.3	23.6	0
Other insects (not crickets)	15.3	20.8	1.9
Voles	9.2	0	19.4
Rabbits	8.3	0	18.1
Rats	6.1	0	43.1
Mice	13.9	0	10.6
Fruits and seeds	0	40.3	0
Green leaves	0	13.8	0
Unidentified	8.3	0	0

Percentage occurrence of different foods in the diet of stoats, rats, and cats. Graph angle representing the % is shown to assist plotting.

Food item in diet	Stoats		Rats		Cats	
	% in diet	Angle / °	% in diet	Angle / °	% in diet	Angle / °
Birds	23.6	85				

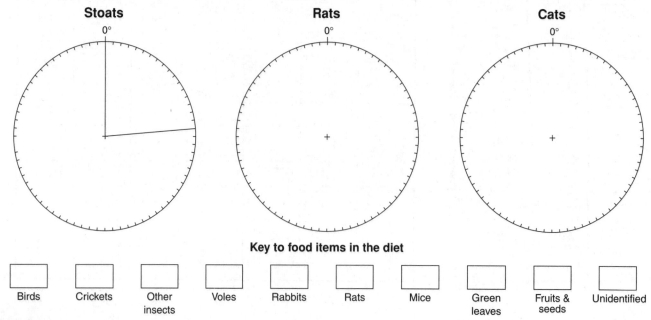

Stoats   0°

Rats   0°

Cats   0°

Key to food items in the diet

| Birds | Crickets | Other insects | Voles | Rabbits | Rats | Mice | Green leaves | Fruits & seeds | Unidentified |

DA 2

Drawing Kite Graphs

Guidelines for Kite Graphs

Kite graphs are ideal for representing distributional data, e.g. abundance along an environmental gradient. They are elongated figures drawn along a baseline. Important features of kite graphs include:

- Each kite represents changes in species abundance across a landscape. The abundance can be calculated from the kite width.

- They often involve plots for more than one species; this makes them good for highlighting probable differences in habitat preferences between species.

- A thin line on a kite graph represents species absence.

- The axes can be reversed depending on preference.

- Kite graphs may also be used to show changes in distribution with time, for example, with daily or seasonal cycles of movement.

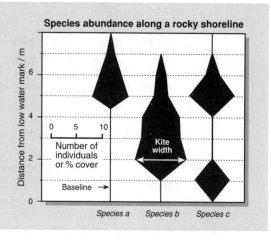

Species abundance along a rocky shoreline

1. The following data were collected from three streams of different lengths and flow rates. Invertebrates were collected at 0.5 km intervals from the headwaters (0 km) to the stream mouth. Their wet weight was measured and recorded (per m²).

   (a) Tabulate the data below for plotting.

   (b) Plot a **kite graph** of the data from all three streams on the grid provided below. Do not forget to include a scale so that the weight at each point on the kite can be calculated.

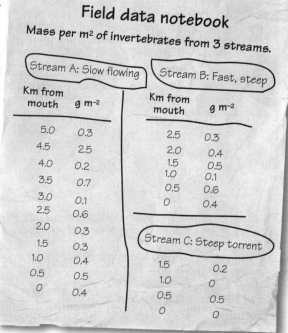

Field data notebook

Mass per m² of invertebrates from 3 streams.

Wet mass of invertebrates along three different streams

Distance from mouth/ km	Wet weight/ g m⁻²		
	Stream A	Stream B	Stream C

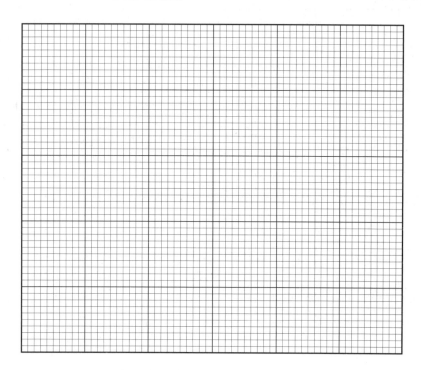

Skills in Biology

Drawing Line Graphs

Guidelines for Line Graphs

Line graphs are used when one variable (the independent variable) affects another, the dependent variable. Line graphs can be drawn without a measure of spread (top figure, right) or with some calculated measure of data variability (bottom figure, right). Important features of line graphs include:

- The data must be continuous for both variables.

- The dependent variable is usually the biological response.

- The independent variable is often time or the experimental treatment.

- In cases where there is an implied trend (e.g. one variable increases with the other), a line of best fit is usually plotted through the data points to show the relationship.

- If fluctuations in the data are likely to be important (e.g. with climate and other environmental data) the data points are usually connected directly (point to point).

- Line graphs may be drawn with measure of error. The data are presented as points (the calculated means), with bars above and below, indicating a measure of variability or spread in the data (e.g. standard error, standard deviation, or 95% confidence intervals).

- Where no error value has been calculated, the scatter can be shown by plotting the individual data points vertically above and below the mean. By convention, bars are not used to indicate the range of raw values in a data set.

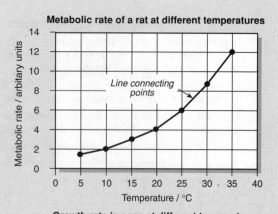

Metabolic rate of a rat at different temperatures

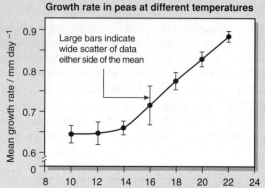

Growth rate in peas at different temperatures

---

1. The results (shown right) were collected in a study investigating the effect of temperature on the activity of an enzyme.

   (a) Using the results provided in the table (right), plot a line graph on the grid below:

   (b) Estimate the rate of reaction at 15°C: _____

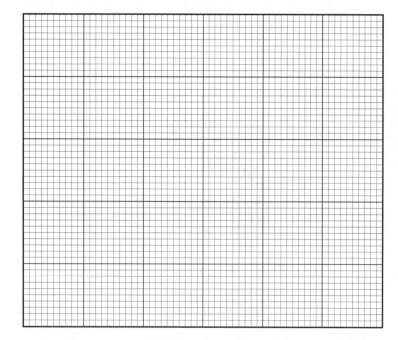

Lab Notebook

An enzyme's activity at different temperatures

Temperature /°C	Rate of reaction /mg of product formed per minute
10	1.0
20	2.1
30	3.2
35	3.7
40	4.1
45	3.7
50	2.7
60	0

Related activities: The Reliability of the Mean, Interpreting Line graphs

Plotting Multiple Data Sets

A single figure can be used to show two or more data sets, i.e. more than one curve can be plotted per set of axes. This type of presentation is useful when you want to visually compare the trends for two or more treatments, or the response of one species against the response of another. Important points regarding this format are:

- If the two data sets use the same measurement units and a similar range of values for the independent variable, one scale on the y axis is used.

- If the two data sets use different units and/or have a very different range of values for the independent variable, two scales for the y axis are used (see example provided). The scales can be adjusted if necessary to avoid overlapping plots

- The two curves must be distinguished with a key.

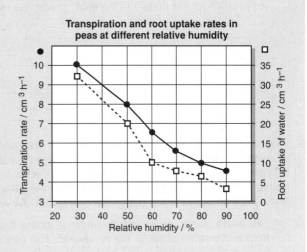

2. A census of a deer population on an island indicated a population of 2000 animals in 1960. In 1961, ten wolves (natural predators of deer) were brought to the island in an attempt to control deer numbers. Over the next nine years, the numbers of deer and wolves were monitored. The results of these population surveys are presented in the table, right.

Plot a line graph (joining the data points) for the tabulated results. Use one scale (on the left) for numbers of deer and another scale (on the right) for the number of wolves. Use different symbols or colours to distinguish the lines and include a key.

Field data notebook
Results of a population survey on an island

Time /yr	Wolf numbers	Deer numbers
1961	10	2000
1962	12	2300
1963	16	2500
1964	22	2360
1965	28	2244
1966	24	2094
1967	21	1968
1968	18	1916
1969	19	1952

Skills in Biology

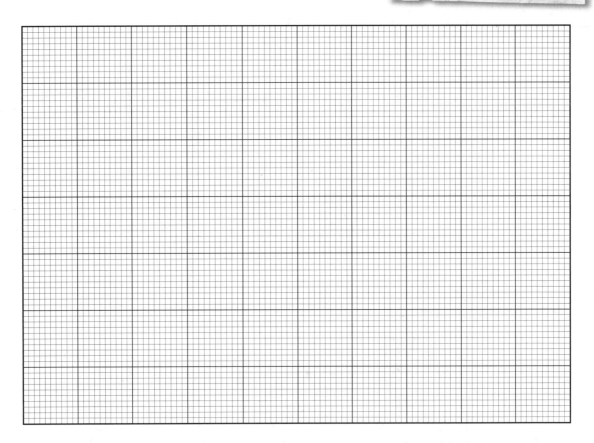

(b) Study the line graph that you plotted for the wolf and deer census on the previous page. Provide a plausible explanation for the pattern in the data, stating the evidence available to support your reasoning:

_____

_____

_____

_____

3. In a sampling programme, the number of perch and trout in a hydro-electric reservoir were monitored over a period of time. A colony of black shag was also present. Shags take large numbers of perch and (to a lesser extent) trout. In 1960-61, 424 shags were removed from the lake during the nesting season and nest counts were made every spring in subsequent years. In 1971, 60 shags were removed from the lake, and all existing nests dismantled. The results of the population survey are tabulated below (for reasons of space, the entire table format has been repeated to the right for 1970-1978).

(a) Plot a line graph (joining the data points) for the survey results. Use one scale (on the left) for numbers of perch and trout and another scale for the number of shag nests. Use different symbols to distinguish the lines and include a key.

(b) Use a vertical arrow to indicate the point at which shags and their nests were removed.

Results of population survey at reservoir

Time/ year	Fish number (average per haul)		Shag nest numbers	Time/ year continued	Fish number (average per haul)		Shag nest numbers
	Trout	Perch			Trout	Perch	
1960	–	–	16	1970	1.5	6	35
1961	–	–	4	1971	0.5	0.7	42
1962	1.5	11	5	1972	1	0.8	0
1963	0.8	9	10	1973	0.2	4	0
1964	0	5	22	1974	0.5	6.5	0
1965	1	1	25	1975	0.6	7.6	2
1966	1	2.9	35	1976	1	1.2	10
1967	2	5	40	1977	1.2	1.5	32
1968	1.5	4.6	26	1978	0.7	2	28
1969	1.5	6	32				

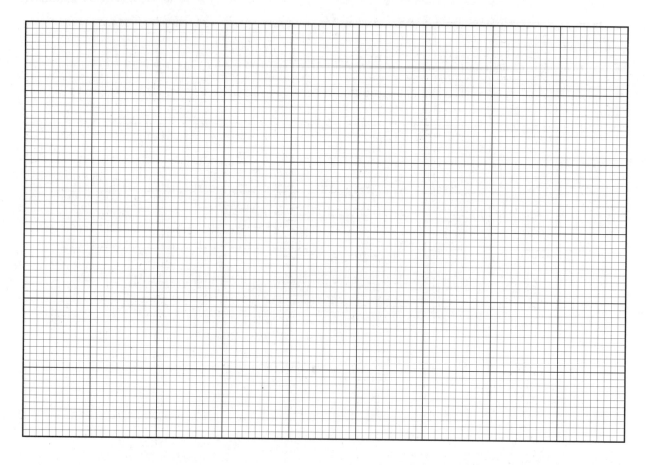

Interpreting Line Graphs

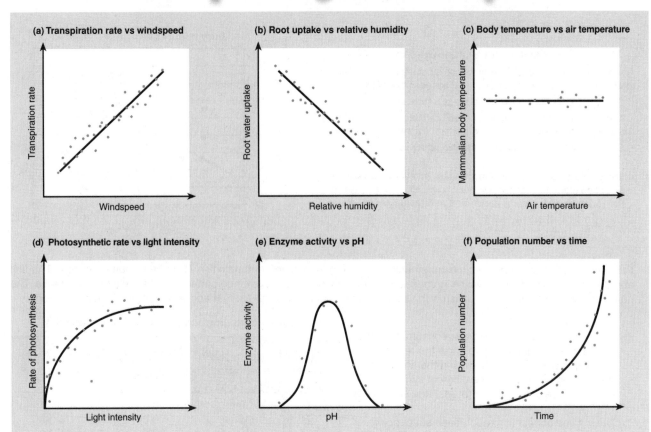

(a) Transpiration rate vs windspeed
Transpiration rate / Windspeed

(b) Root uptake vs relative humidity
Root water uptake / Relative humidity

(c) Body temperature vs air temperature
Mammalian body temperature / Air temperature

(d) Photosynthetic rate vs light intensity
Rate of photosynthesis / Light intensity

(e) Enzyme activity vs pH
Enzyme activity / pH

(f) Population number vs time
Population number / Time

Skills in Biology

1. For each of the graphs (b-f) above, give a description of the slope and an interpretation of how one variable changes with respect to the other. For the purposes of your description, call the independent variable (horizontal or x-axis) in each example "variable X" and the dependent variable (vertical or y-axis) "variable Y". Be aware that the existence of a relationship between two variables does not necessarily mean that the relationship is causative (although it may be).

(a) Slope: _Positive linear relationship, with constantly rising slope_

   Interpretation: _Variable Y (transpiration) increases regularly with increase in variable X (windspeed)_

(b) Slope: _____

   Interpretation: _____

(c) Slope: _____

   Interpretation: _____

(d) Slope: _____

   Interpretation: _____

(e) Slope: _____

   Interpretation: _____

(f) Slope: _____

   Interpretation: _____

2. Study the line graph that you plotted for the wolf and deer census on the previous page. Provide a plausible explanation for the pattern in the data, stating the evidence available to support your reasoning:

   _____

   _____

   _____

   _____

Related activities: Drawing Line Graphs, Linear Regression, Non-linear Regression

RDA 2

Drawing Scatter Plots

Guidelines for Scatter Graphs

A scatter graph is a common way to display continuous data where there is a relationship between two interdependent variables.

- The data for this graph must be continuous for both variables.
- There is no independent (manipulated) variable, but the variables are often correlated, i.e. they vary together in some predictable way.
- Scatter graphs are useful for determining the relationship between two variables.
- The points on the graph need not be connected, but a line of best fit is often drawn through the points to show the relationship between the variables (this may be drawn be eye or computer generated).

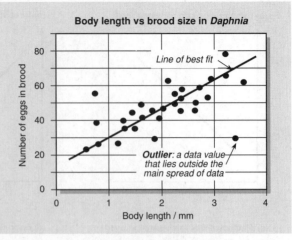

Body length vs brood size in *Daphnia*

1. In the example below, metabolic measurements were taken from seven Antarctic fish *Pagothenia borchgrevinski.* The fish are affected by a gill disease, which increases the thickness of the gas exchange surfaces and affects oxygen uptake. The results of oxygen consumption of fish with varying amounts of affected gill (at rest and swimming) are tabulated below.

   (a) Using **one** scale only for oxygen consumption, plot the data on the grid below to show the relationship between oxygen consumption and the amount of gill affected by disease. Use different symbols or colours for each set of data (at rest and swimming).

   (b) Draw a line of best fit through each set of points.

2. Describe the relationship between the amount of gill affected and oxygen consumption in the fish:

   (a) For the **at rest** data set:

   _____

   _____

   _____

   _____

   _____

   _____

   _____

   (b) For the **swimming** data set:

   _____

   _____

   _____

   _____

   _____

   _____

   _____

Oxygen consumption of fish with affected gills

Fish number	Percentage of gill affected	Oxygen consumption/ $cm^3\ g^{-1}\ h^{-1}$	
		At rest	Swimming
1	0	0.05	0.29
2	95	0.04	0.11
3	60	0.04	0.14
4	30	0.05	0.22
5	90	0.05	0.08
6	65	0.04	0.18
7	45	0.04	0.20

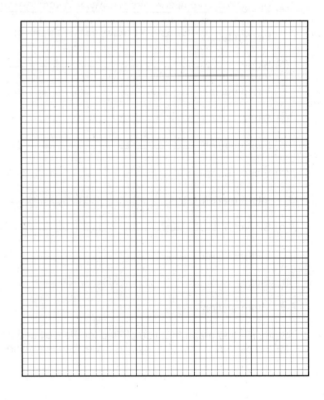

3. Describe how the gill disease affects oxygen uptake in resting fish: _____

   _____

Related activities: Interpreting Line Graphs, Linear Regression

Taking the Next Step

By this stage, you will have completed many of the early stages of your investigation. Now is a good time to review what you have done and reflect on the biological significance of what you are investigating. Review the first page of this flow chart in light of your findings so far. You are now ready to begin a more in-depth analysis of your results. Never under-estimate the value of plotting your data, even at a very early stage. This will help you decide on the best type of data analysis (see the next page).

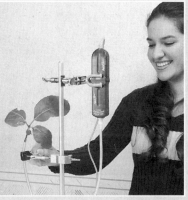

Photos courtesy of Pasco

Skills in Biology

Observation

Something ...

- Changes or affects something else.

- Is more abundant, etc. along a transect, at one site, temperature, concentration, etc. than others.

- Is bigger, taller, or grows more quickly.

Pilot study

Lets you check ...

- Equipment, sampling sites, sampling interval.

- How long it takes to collect data.

- Problems with identification or other unforeseen issues.

Research

To find out ...

- Basic biology and properties.

- What other biotic or abiotic factors may have an effect.

- Its place within the broader biological context.

Analysis

Are you looking for a ...

- **Difference**.

- **Trend** or relationship.

- **Goodness of fit** (to a theoretical outcome).

GO TO NEXT PAGE

Be prepared to revise your study design in the light of the results from your pilot study

Variables

Next you need to ...

- Identify the key variables likely to cause the effect.

- Identify variables to be controlled in order to give the best chance of showing the effect that you want to study.

Hypothesis

Must be ...

- Testable

- Able to generate predictions

so that in the end you can say whether your data supports or allows you to reject your hypothesis.

Related activities: The Reliability of the Mean, Linear Regression, Non-linear Regression, The Student's t Test, Chi-squared Exercise in Ecology and Genetics   **Web links**: ANOVA

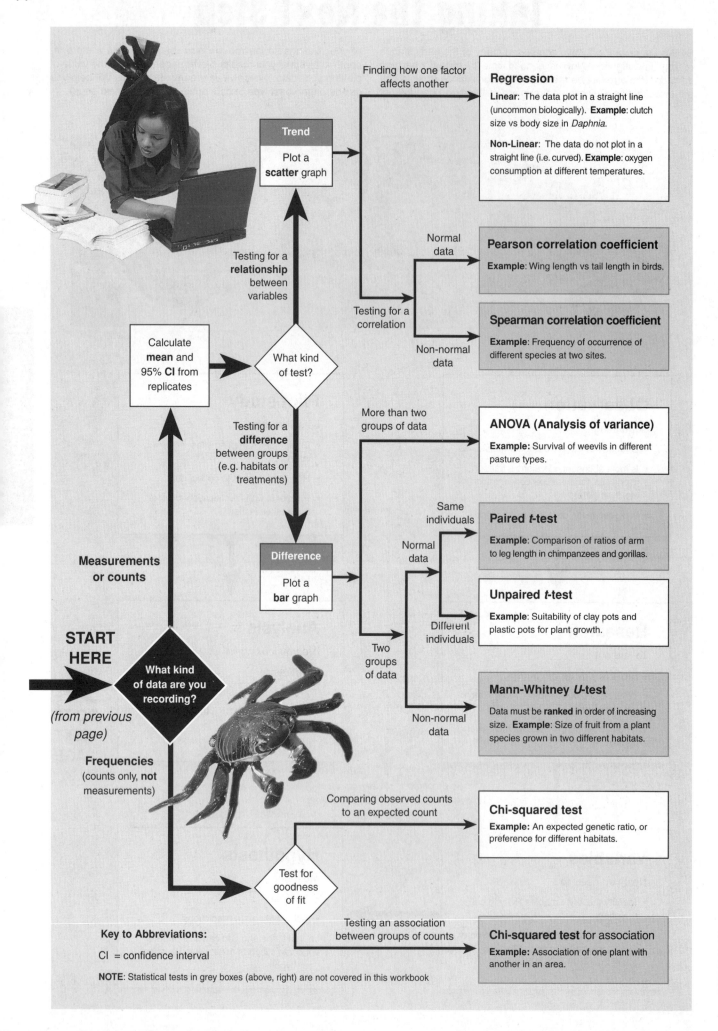

Trend

Plot a **scatter** graph

Finding how one factor affects another

Regression

Linear: The data plot in a straight line (uncommon biologically). **Example**: clutch size vs body size in *Daphnia*.

Non-Linear: The data do not plot in a straight line (i.e. curved). **Example**: oxygen consumption at different temperatures.

Testing for a **relationship** between variables

Testing for a correlation

Normal data

Pearson correlation coefficient

Example: Wing length vs tail length in birds.

Non-normal data

Spearman correlation coefficient

Example: Frequency of occurrence of different species at two sites.

Calculate **mean** and 95% **CI** from replicates

What kind of test?

Testing for a **difference** between groups (e.g. habitats or treatments)

More than two groups of data

ANOVA (Analysis of variance)

Example: Survival of weevils in different pasture types.

Difference

Plot a **bar** graph

Same individuals

Normal data

Paired *t*-test

Example: Comparison of ratios of arm to leg length in chimpanzees and gorillas.

Different individuals

Unpaired *t*-test

Example: Suitability of clay pots and plastic pots for plant growth.

Measurements or counts

Two groups of data

Non-normal data

Mann-Whitney *U*-test

Data must be **ranked** in order of increasing size. **Example**: Size of fruit from a plant species grown in two different habitats.

START HERE

(from previous page)

What kind of data are you recording?

Frequencies (counts only, **not** measurements)

Comparing observed counts to an expected count

Chi-squared test

Example: An expected genetic ratio, or preference for different habitats.

Test for goodness of fit

Key to Abbreviations:

CI = confidence interval

NOTE: Statistical tests in grey boxes (above, right) are not covered in this workbook

Testing an association between groups of counts

Chi-squared test for association

Example: Association of one plant with another in an area.

Descriptive Statistics

For most investigations, measures of the biological response are made from more than one sampling unit. The sample size (the number of sampling units) will vary depending on the resources available. In lab based investigations, the sample size may be as small as two or three (e.g. two test-tubes in each treatment). In field studies, each individual may be a sampling unit, and the sample size can be very large (e.g. 100 individuals). It is useful to summarise the data collected using **descriptive statistics**.

Descriptive statistics, such as mean, median, and mode, can help to highlight trends or patterns in the data. Each of these statistics is appropriate to certain types of data or distributions, e.g. a mean is not appropriate for data with a skewed distribution (see below). Frequency graphs are useful for indicating the distribution of data. Standard deviation and standard error are statistics used to quantify the amount of spread in the data and evaluate the reliability of estimates of the true (population) mean.

Variation in Data

Whether they are obtained from observation or experiments, most biological data show variability. In a set of data values, it is useful to know the value about which most of the data are grouped; the centre value. This value can be the mean, median, or mode depending on the type of variable involved (see schematic below). The main purpose of these statistics is to summarise important trends in your data and to provide the basis for statistical analyses.

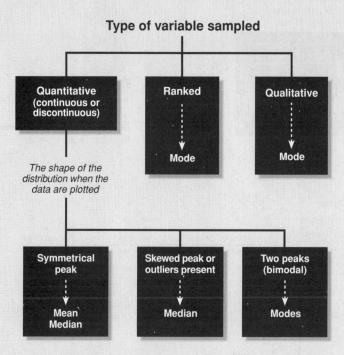

Variability in continuous data is often displayed as a **frequency distribution**. A frequency plot will indicate whether the data have a normal distribution (A), with a symmetrical spread of data about the mean, or whether the distribution is skewed (B), or bimodal (C). The shape of the distribution will determine which statistic (mean, median, or mode) best describes the central tendency of the sample data.

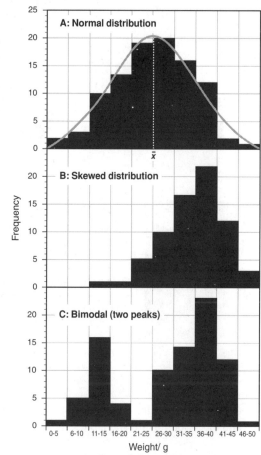

Statistic	Definition and use	Method of calculation
Mean	• The average of all data entries. • Measure of central tendency for normally distributed data.	• Add up all the data entries. • Divide by the total number of data entries.
Median	• The middle value when data entries are placed in rank order. • A good measure of central tendency for skewed distributions.	• Arrange the data in increasing rank order. • Identify the middle value. • For an even number of entries, find the mid point of the two middle values.
Mode	• The most common data value. • Suitable for bimodal distributions and qualitative data.	• Identify the category with the highest number of data entries using a tally chart or a bar graph.
Range	• The difference between the smallest and largest data values. • Provides a crude indication of data spread.	• Identify the smallest and largest values and find the difference between them.

When NOT to calculate a mean:

In certain situations, calculation of a simple arithmetic mean is inappropriate.

Remember:

• *DO NOT* calculate a mean from values that are already means (averages) themselves.

• *DO NOT* calculate a mean of ratios (e.g. percentages) for several groups of different sizes; go back to the raw values and recalculate.

• *DO NOT* calculate a mean when the measurement scale is not linear, e.g. pH units are not measured on a linear scale.

Skills in Biology

Related activities: The Reliability of the Mean

DA 2

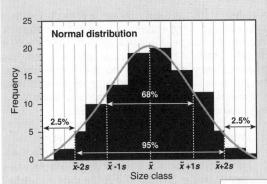

Normal distribution

68%

95%

2.5%   2.5%

$\bar{x}-2s$ $\bar{x}-1s$ $\bar{x}$ $\bar{x}+1s$ $\bar{x}+2s$

Size class

Measuring Spread

The **standard deviation** is a frequently used measure of the variability (spread) in a set of data. It is usually presented in the form $\bar{x} \pm s$. In a normally distributed set of data, 68% of all data values will lie within one standard deviation (s) of the mean ($\bar{x}$) and 95% of all data values will lie within two standard deviations of the mean (left).

Two different sets of data can have the same mean and range, yet the distribution of data within the range can be quite different. In both the data sets pictured in the histograms below, 68% of the values lie within the range $\bar{x} \pm 1s$ and 95% of the values lie within $\bar{x} \pm 2s$. However, in B, the data values are more tightly clustered around the mean.

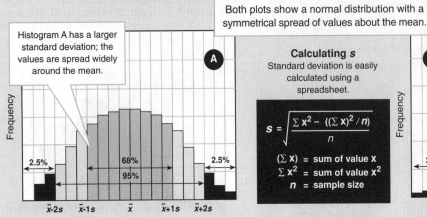

Histogram A has a larger standard deviation; the values are spread widely around the mean.

Both plots show a normal distribution with a symmetrical spread of values about the mean.

Histogram B has a smaller standard deviation; the values are clustered more tightly around the mean.

A

B

Calculating s
Standard deviation is easily calculated using a spreadsheet.

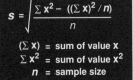

$$s = \sqrt{\frac{\sum x^2 - ((\sum x)^2 / n)}{n}}$$

$(\sum x)$ = sum of value x
$\sum x^2$ = sum of value x^2
n = sample size

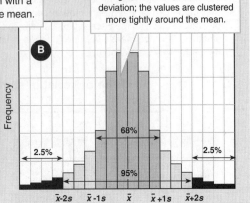

Case Study: Fern Reproduction

Raw data (below) and descriptive statistics (right) from a survey of the number of spores found on the fronds of a fern plant.

Fern spores

Raw data: Number of spores per frond

64	60	64	62	68	66	63
69	70	63	70	70	63	62
71	69	59	70	66	61	70
67	64	63	64

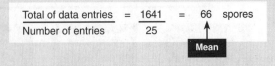

$$\frac{\text{Total of data entries}}{\text{Number of entries}} = \frac{1641}{25} = 66 \text{ spores}$$

Mean

Number of spores per frond (in rank order)	
59	66
60	66
61	67
62	68
62	69
63	69
63	70
63	70
63	70
64	70
64	70
64	71
64	

Median

Mode

Spores per frond	Tally	Total
59	✔	1
60	✔	1
61	✔	1
62	✔✔	2
63	✔✔✔✔	4
64	✔✔✔✔	4
65		0
66	✔✔	2
67	✔	1
68	✔	1
69	✔✔	2
70	✔✔✔✔✔	5
71	✔	1

1. Give a reason for the difference between the mean, median, and mode for the fern spore data:

_____

_____

_____

_____

2. Calculate the mean, median, and mode for the data on beetle masses below. Draw up a tally chart and show all calculations:

Beetle masses / g		
2.2	2.1	2.6
2.5	2.4	2.8
2.5	2.7	2.5
2.6	2.6	2.5
2.2	2.8	2.4

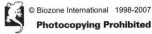

The Reliability of the Mean

You have already seen how to use the **standard deviation** (*s*) to quantify the spread or **dispersion** in your data. The **variance** (*s²*) is another such measure of dispersion, but the standard deviation is usually the preferred of these two measures because it is expressed in the original units. Usually, you will also want to know how good your sample mean ($\bar{x}$) is as an estimate of the true population mean (*μ*). This can be indicated by the standard error of the mean (or just **standard error** or SE). **SE** is often used as an error measurement simply because it is small, rather than for any good statistical reason. However, it is does allow you to calculate the **95% confidence interval (95% CI)**. The calculation and use of 95% CIs is outlined below and on the next page. By the end of this activity you should be able to:

- Enter data and calculate descriptive statistics using a spreadsheet programme such as *Microsoft Excel*. You can follow this procedure for any set of data.
- Calculate standard error and 95% confidence intervals for sample data and plot these data appropriately with error bars.
- Interpret the graphically presented data and reach tentative conclusions about the findings of the experiment.

Skills in Biology

Ladybird population

Sample

When we measure a particular attribute from a sample of a larger population and calculate a mean for that attribute, we can calculate how closely our sample mean (the statistic) is to the true population mean for that attribute (the parameter). **Example**: If we calculated the mean number of carapace spots from a sample of six ladybird beetles, how reliable is this statistic as an indicator of the mean number of carapace spots in the whole population? We can find out by calculating the **95% confidence interval**.

Reliability of the Sample Mean

When we take measurements from samples of a larger population, we are using those samples as indicators of the trends in the whole population. Therefore, when we calculate a sample mean, it is useful to know how close that value is to the true population mean (μ). This is not merely an academic exercise; it will enable you to make **inferences** about the aspect of the population in which you are interested. For this reason, statistics based on samples and used to estimate population parameters are called **inferential statistics.**

The Standard Error (SE)

The standard error (SE) is simple to calculate and is usually a small value. Standard error is given by:

$$SE = \frac{s}{\sqrt{n}}$$

where *s* = the standard deviation, and *n* = sample size.

Standard errors are sometimes plotted as error bars on graphs, but it is more meaningful to plot the **95% confidence intervals** (see box below). All calculations are easily made using a spreadsheet (see opposite).

The 95% Confidence Interval

SE is required to calculate the 95% confidence interval (CI) of the mean. This is given by:

$$95\% \text{ CI} = SE \times t_{P(n-1)}$$

Do not be alarmed by this calculation; once you have calculated the value of the SE, it is a simple matter to multiply this value by the value of *t* at *P* = 0.05 (from the *t* table) for the appropriate degrees of freedom (df) for your sample (*n* − 1).

For example: where the SE = 0.6 and the sample size is 10, the calculation of the 95% CI is:

$$95\% \text{ CI} = 0.6 \times 2.262 = \boxed{1.36}$$

Part of the *t* table is given to the right for *P* = 0.05. Note that, as the sample becomes very large, the value of *t* becomes smaller. For very large samples, *t* is fixed at 1.96, so the 95% CI is slightly less than twice the SE.

All these statistics, including a plot of the data with Y error bars, can be calculated using a programme such as *Microsoft Excel* (opposite).

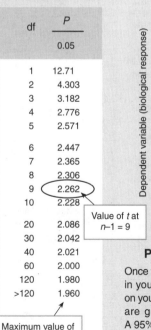

Critical values of Student's *t* distribution at *P* = 0.05.

df	*P* 0.05
1	12.71
2	4.303
3	3.182
4	2.776
5	2.571
6	2.447
7	2.365
8	2.306
9	2.262
10	2.228
20	2.086
30	2.042
40	2.021
60	2.000
120	1.980
>120	1.960

Value of *t* at *n*–1 = 9

Maximum value of *t* at this level of *P*

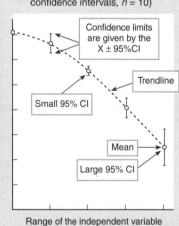

Relationship of Y against X (± 95% confidence intervals, *n* = 10)

Dependent variable (biological response)

Confidence limits are given by the X ± 95%CI

Trendline

Small 95% CI

Mean

Large 95% CI

Range of the independent variable

Plotting your confidence intervals

Once you have calculated the 95% CI for the means in your data set, you can plot them as error bars on your graph. Note that the **95% confidence limits** are given by the value of the **mean ± 95%CI**. A 95% confidence limit (i.e. *P* = 0.05) tells you that, on average, 95 times out of 100, the limits will contain the true population mean.

Comparing Treatments Using Descriptive Statistics

In an experiment, the growth of newborn rats on four different feeds was compared by weighing young rats after 28 days on each of four feeding regimes. The suitability of each food type for maximising growth in the first month of life was evaluated by comparing the means of the four experimental groups. Each group comprised 10 individual rats. All 40 newborns were born to sibling mothers with the same feeding history. For this activity, follow the steps outlined below and reproduce them yourself.

Calculating Descriptive Statistics

Entering your data and calculating descriptive statistics.

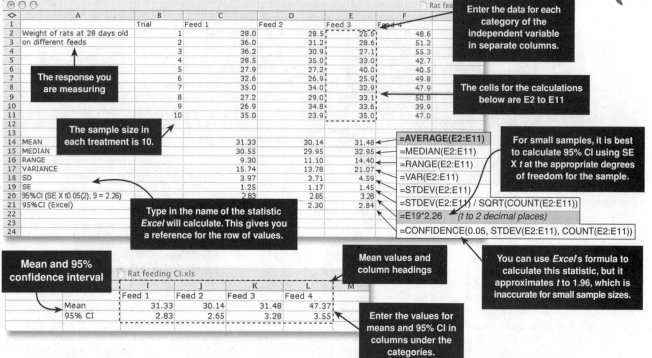

	A	B	C	D	E	F
1		Trial	Feed 1	Feed 2	Feed 3	Feed 4
2	Weight of rats at 28 days old	1	28.0	28.5	25.6	48.6
3	on different feeds	2	36.0	31.2	28.6	51.2
4		3	36.2	30.9	27.1	55.3
5		4	28.5	35.0	33.0	42.7
6		5	27.9	27.2	40.0	40.5
7		6	32.6	26.9	25.9	49.8
8		7	35.0	34.0	32.9	47.9
9		8	27.2	29.0	33.1	50.8
10		9	26.9	34.8	33.6	39.9
11		10	35.0	23.9	35.0	47.0
12						
13						
14	MEAN		31.33	30.14	31.48	
15	MEDIAN		30.55	29.95	32.95	
16	RANGE		9.30	11.10	14.40	
17	VARIANCE		15.74	13.78	21.07	
18	SD		3.97	3.71	4.59	
19	SE		1.25	1.17	1.45	
20	95%CI (SE X t0.05(2), 9 = 2.26)		2.83	2.65	3.28	
21	95%CI (Excel)			2.30	2.84	
22						
23						
24						

Enter the data for each category of the independent variable in separate columns.

The response you are measuring

The cells for the calculations below are E2 to E11

The sample size in each treatment is 10.

Type in the name of the statistic *Excel* **will calculate. This gives you a reference for the row of values.**

=AVERAGE(E2:E11)
=MEDIAN(E2:E11)
=RANGE(E2:E11)
=VAR(E2:E11)
=STDEV(E2:E11)
=STDEV(E2:E11) / SQRT(COUNT(E2:E11))
=E19*2.26 *(t to 2 decimal places)*
=CONFIDENCE(0.05, STDEV(E2:E11), COUNT(E2:E11))

For small samples, it is best to calculate 95% CI using SE X *t* at the appropriate degrees of freedom for the sample.

You can use *Excel*'s formula to calculate this statistic, but it approximates *t* to 1.96, which is inaccurate for small sample sizes.

Mean values and column headings

Rat feeding CI.xls

	I	J	K	L	M
		Feed 1	Feed 2	Feed 3	Feed 4
Mean		31.33	30.14	31.48	47.37
95% CI		2.83	2.65	3.28	3.55

Mean and 95% confidence interval

Enter the values for means and 95% CI in columns under the categories.

Drawing the Graph

To plot the graph, you will need to enter the data values you want to plot in a format that *Excel* can use (above). To do this, enter the values in columns under each category.

■ Each column will have two entries: mean and 95% CI. In this case, we want to plot the mean weight of 28 day rats fed on different foods and add the 95% confidence intervals as error bars.

■ The independent variable is categorical, so the correct graph type is a column chart. Select the row of mean values (including column headings)

1 From the menu bar choose: **Insert > Chart > Column**. This is **Step 1** in the Chart Wizard. Click **Next**.

2 At **Step 2**, click **Next**.

3 At **Step 3**, you have the option to add a title, labels for your X and Y axes, turn off gridlines, and add (or remove) a legend. When you have added all the information you want, click **Next**.

4 At **Step 4**, specify the chart location. It should appear "as object in" Sheet 1 by default. Click on the chart and move it to reveal the data.

5 A chart will appear on the screen. **Right click** (Ctrl-click on Mac) on any part of any column and choose **Format data series**. To add error bars, select the **Y error bars** tab, and click on the symbol that shows Display both. Click on Custom, and use the data selection window to select the row of 95% CI data for "+" and "−" fields.

6 Click on OK and your chart will plot with error bars.

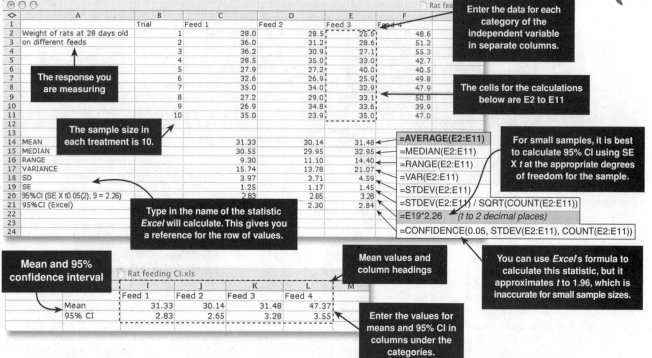

1

A column chart is the appropriate choice for these data.

2
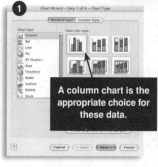
Add information for your graph in here ...

3
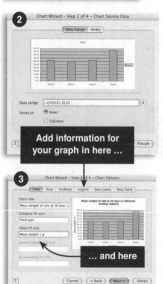
... and here

4

5
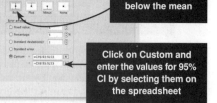
Select error bars for both above and below the mean

Click on Custom and enter the values for 95% CI by selecting them on the spreadsheet

6
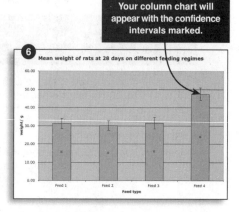
Your column chart will appear with the confidence intervals marked.

Mean weight of rats at 28 days on different feeding regimes

Linear Regression

Regression is a test for an association, relationship, or trend between two variables. It is suitable for continuous data when you have a reason to believe that the changes in one variable cause changes in the other, i.e. regression assumes a cause and effect. A regression is also predictive; the **regression equation** will be able to predict unknown values of the Y variable within the range covered by the data. Linear regression is the simplest

functional relationship of one variable to another. If your data are appropriate for this analysis, they will plot as a straight line spread on a scatter graph. It is best to perform your regression on the raw data, because information is lost when the calculation is performed on mean values. If your data plot is not linear, you have the choice of plotting a non-linear regression (see the next activity) or transforming your data to make them linear.

Linear regression is a simple relationship where the change in the independent variable causes a corresponding change in the dependent variable in a simple linear fashion. A line is fitted to the data and gives the values of the slope and intercept of the line (the computer does this for you).

Linear regressions are simple to perform using a computer programme such as *Microsoft Excel*. The steps for doing this are outlined here.

Clutch Size vs Body Size in *Daphnia*

Daphnia is a small, freshwater crustacean. In *Daphnia*, body size is a large determinant of the number of eggs they can carry (this female has none). The relationship between body size and clutch size can be described with a regression.

Skills in Biology

1 Clutch size (number of eggs per female) was estimated for 50 females, and body length was measured to the nearest 0.01 mm for the same individuals to give 50 paired values. These data values were entered directly into *Microsoft Excel*.

2 To draw the graph, highlight the data columns: "Body length" and "Clutch size".

- From the menu bar choose **Insert** > **Chart** > **XY (Scatter)**, and click on the option with no line. This is **Step 1** of 4 in the Chart Wizard. Click **Next**.

- At **Step 2**, click **Next**.

- At **Step 3**, you will have the option to add a title, labels for your X and Y axes, turn off gridlines, and add a legend. You may wish to do this in *Excel* (now or after drawing the graph), or add them yourself, by hand, later. Click **Next**.

- At **Step 4**, specify the chart location. It should appear "as object in" Sheet 1 by default. You can choose to have the chart appear in another worksheet if you wish. Click **Finish**.

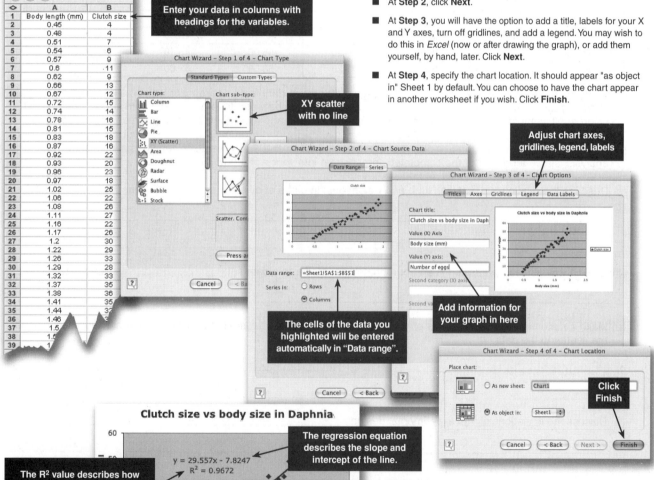

Enter your data in columns with headings for the variables.

XY scatter with no line

Adjust chart axes, gridlines, legend, labels

The cells of the data you highlighted will be entered automatically in "Data range".

Add information for your graph in here

Click Finish

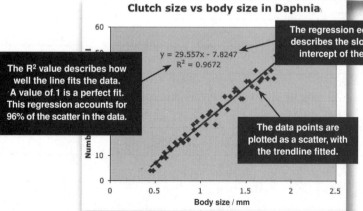

Clutch size vs body size in Daphnia

$y = 29.557x - 7.8247$
$R^2 = 0.9672$

The R² value describes how well the line fits the data. A value of 1 is a perfect fit. This regression accounts for 96% of the scatter in the data.

The regression equation describes the slope and intercept of the line.

The data points are plotted as a scatter, with the trendline fitted.

3 A chart will appear on the screen. If necessary, click on the chart and move it slightly to reveal the data. To add the trendline, **right click** (Ctrl-click on Mac) on any data point on the graph, choose **Add Trendline** and choose **Type > Linear**. Click on the Options tab and click on the check boxes for **Display equation on chart** and **Display R² value on chart**. **Click OK**. The equation is a text box that can be moved by clicking and dragging with the mouse.

Labels for the X and Y axes are added by right clicking within the plot area, and choosing Chart Options and the Titles tab.

Related activities: Transforming Raw Data, Drawing Scatter Plots, Descriptive Statistics, Non-linear Regression

DA 3

1. Explain why the data for clutch size and body size in *Daphnia* are appropriate for analysis with a linear regression:

_____

_____

_____

_____

2. A student's (hypothetical) experiment, investigated the effect of increasing seawater dilution on cumulative weight gain (as an indication of osmoregulatory ability) of a common shore crab. Six crabs in total were used in the experiment. Three were placed in seawater dilution of 75:25 (75% seawater) and three were placed in a seawater dilution of 50:50 (50% seawater). Cumulative weight gain in each of the six crabs was measured at regular intervals over a period of 30 minutes. The results are tabulated below:

Time / min	Crab weight gain at 75% seawater / mg			Crab weight gain at 50% seawater / mg		
	Crab number			Crab number		
	1	2	3	4	5	6
3	3.80	4.00	4.00	5.60	6.20	5.80
6	8.00	8.30	7.70	11.20	11.60	11.90
9	11.50	11.00	9.50	17.00	17.60	17.20
12	14.80	15.10	15.20	23.50	23.60	24.00
15	18.90	19.50	19.70	29.00	28.20	28.60
18	23.50	22.90	23.80	33.00	32.50	32.70
21	26.50	26.90	26.70	37.50	37.60	39.00
24	31.50	32.00	31.20	43.10	43.50	43.60
27	35.00	35.50	35.50	48.00	48.10	47.50
30	40.00	40.10	41.20	53.00	52.60	52.80

(a) Following the steps outlined on the previous page, enter these data in an appropriate way on a spreadsheet (e.g. *Microsoft Excel*) and plot a scatter plot to show the relationship between time and weight gain in crabs held at two different dilutions of seawater. Be sure to add appropriate titles and axis labels to your graph as you proceed.

(b) Fit a trendline to your plot, and display the regression equation and the R^2 value. When you have finished your analysis, staple a printout of the completed spreadsheet into your workbook.

(c) Describe the relationship between time and weight gain in crabs at different seawater dilutions: _____

_____

_____

(d) Explain why a linear regression is an appropriate analysis for this data set: _____

_____

(e) Make a statement about the results of your regression analysis with respect to how well the regression accounts for the scatter in the data:

_____

_____

(f) Discuss the limitations of this experimental design: _____

_____

_____

_____

(g) Suggest ways in which the experimental design could be improved: _____

_____

_____

_____

Non-linear Regression

The degree to which organisms respond physiologically to their environment depends on the type of organism and how tolerant they are of environmental changes. Biological responses are often not described by a simple linear relationship (although they may be linear when transformed). Many metabolic relationships are non-linear because organisms function most efficiently within certain environmental limits. When you plot the data for these kinds of relationships, they will plot out as something other than a straight line. An example of non-linear regression is described below for egg development time in *Daphnia*.

Egg Development Time in *Daphnia*

In *Daphnia*, the **egg development time** (EDT) is the time from egg deposition to release of the young from the brood pouch. From an experiment that measured EDT at controlled temperatures, means and 95% confidence intervals were calculated from a sample size of five animals at each of five temperatures between 9 and 25°C. The aim of this activity is to demonstrate an analysis of a non-linear metabolic relationship by:

- Plotting egg development time (in days) against water temperature (in °C).
- Adding error bars for the means.
- Fitting a nonlinear regression and showing the line equation and the R^2 value, which is a measure of appropriateness of the model describing the line. Here, we have used a power model, but if you have a non-linear relationship, you could also try a polynomial as a model (another choice in Chart Wizard).

1 Create a table in your spreadsheet with your summary data in columns, as shown below. Your raw data may already be entered in the spreadsheet and you can use the spreadsheet to calculate the **summary statistics**. See *Analysis of Variance (ANOVA)* for guidance on how to do this.

2 To perform this regression, follow the same sequence of steps to those in the earlier activity (linear regression).

- First, highlight the data columns: **Temperature** and **Mean days**. From the menu bar choose **Insert > Chart > XY (Scatter)**, and click on the option with no line. This is **Step 1** of 4 in the Chart Wizard. Click **Next**.
- At **Step 2**, click **Next**.
- At **Step 3**, you have the option to add a title, labels for your X and Y axes, turn off gridlines, and add (or remove) a legend. When you have added all the information you want, click **Next**.
- At **Step 4**, specify the chart location. It should appear "as object in" Sheet 1 by default. Click on the chart and move it to reveal the data.

3 A chart will appear on the screen. **Right click** (Ctrl-click on Mac) on any data point on the graph and choose **Format data series**. To add error bars, select the **Y error bars** tab, and click on the symbol that shows Display both. Click on Custom, and use the data selection window to select the data under the 95% CI column label. To add **trendline**, **right click** (Ctrl-click on Mac) on any data point on the graph, and choose **Add Trendline** and **Power**. Click on the Options tab to display the regression equation and the R^2 value.

	A	B	C	D	E	F
1	Temperature (°C)	Mean days	95% CI	Standard error	N	
2	9	8.6	0.56	0.20	5	
3	13	5.1	0.29	0.10	5	
4	17	3.7	0.37	0.13	5	
5	21	2.6	0.23	0.08	5	
6	25	1.9	0.21	0.07	5	
7						

Sample size

Independent variable = temperature

Mean number of days for eggs to develop.

95% confidence intervals

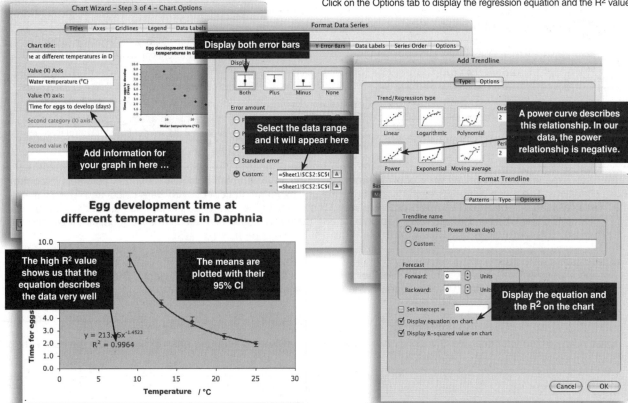

Skills in Biology

Chart Wizard – Step 3 of 4 – Chart Options

Titles | Axes | Gridlines | Legend | Data Labels

Chart title:
ne at different temperatures in D

Value (X) Axis
Water temperature (°C)

Value (Y) axis:
Time for eggs to develop (days)

Second category (X) axis:

Second value (Y

Add information for your graph in here ...

Display both error bars

Format Data Series

Y Error Bars | Data Labels | Series Order | Options

Display
Both | Plus | Minus | None

Error amount

Select the data range and it will appear here

Custom: + =Sheet1!$C$2:$C$6
− =Sheet1!$C$2:$C$6

Add Trendline

Type | Options

Trend/Regression type
Linear | Logarithmic | Polynomial
Power | Exponential | Moving average

A power curve describes this relationship. In our data, the power relationship is negative.

Format Trendline

Patterns | Type | Options

Trendline name
Automatic: Power (Mean days)
Custom:

Forecast
Forward: 0 Units
Backward: 0 Units

Set intercept = 0
☑ Display equation on chart
☑ Display R-squared value on chart

Display the equation and the R^2 on the chart

Cancel | OK

Egg development time at different temperatures in Daphnia

The high R^2 value shows us that the equation describes the data very well

The means are plotted with their 95% CI

$y = 213.95x^{-1.4523}$
$R^2 = 0.9964$

1. Describe the relationship between temperature and EDT in *Daphnia*: _____

_____

_____

Related activities: Descriptive Statistics, The Reliability of the Mean, Linear Regression **Web links**: ANOVA

DA 3

The Student's t Test

The Student's t test is a commonly used test when comparing two sample means e.g. means for a treatment and a control in an experiment, or the means of some measured characteristic between two animal or plant populations. The test is a powerful one, i.e. it is a good test for distinguishing real but marginal differences between samples. The t test is a simple test to apply, but it is only valid for certain situations. It is a two-group test and is not appropriate for multiple use i.e. sample 1 vs 2, then sample 1 vs 3. *You must have only two sample means to compare*. You are also assuming that the data have a normal (not skewed) distribution, and the scatter (standard deviations) of the data points is similar for both samples. You may wish to exclude obvious outliers from your data set for this reason. A simple outline of the general steps involved in a Student's t test is given below. It describes a simple example using a set of data from a fictitious experiment involving a treatment and a control (the units are not relevant in this case, only the values). A portion of the Student's t table of critical values is provided, sufficient to carry out the test. Follow the example through, making sure that you understand what is being done at each step.

Steps in performing a Student's t test	Explanatory notes
Step 1 *Calculate basic summary statistics for your two data sets* Control (A): 6.6, 5.5, 6.8, 5.8, 6.1, 5.9 $n_A = 6$, $\bar{x}_A = 6.12$, $s_A = 0.496$ Treatment (B): 6.3, 7.2, 6.5, 7.1, 7.5, 7.3 $n_B = 6$, $\bar{x}_B = 6.98$, $s_B = 0.475$	n_A and n_B are the number of values in the first and second data sets respectively (these need not be the same). $\bar{x}$ is the mean. s is the standard deviation (a measure of scatter in the data).
Step 2 *Set up and state your null hypothesis (H_0)* H_0: there is no treatment effect. The differences in the data sets are the result of chance variation only and they are not really different.	The alternative hypothesis is that there is a treatment effect and the two sets of data are truly different.
Step 3 *Decide if your test is one or two tailed* This tells you what section of the t table to consult. Most biological tests are two-tailed. Very few are one-tailed.	A one-tailed test looks for a difference only in one particular direction. A two-tailed test looks for any difference (+ or –).
Step 4 *Calculate the t statistic* For our sample data above the calculated value of t is –3.09. The degrees of freedom (df) are $n_1 + n_2 - 2 = 10$. Calculation of the t value uses the variance which is simply the square of the standard deviation (s^2). You may compute the t value by entering your data onto a computer and using a simple statistical programme.	It does not matter if your calculated t value is a positive or negative (the sign is irrelevant). If you do not have access to a statistical programme, computation of t is not difficult. Step 4 (calculating t) is detailed in the t test exercise following (both manual and spreadsheet versions).
Step 5 *Consult the t table of critical values* Selected critical values for Student's t statistic (two-tailed test) Critical value of t for 10 degrees of freedom. The calculated t value must exceed this to show a difference.	The absolute value of the t statistic (3.09) well exceeds the critical value for $P = 0.05$ at 10 degrees of freedom. *We can reject H_0 and conclude that the means are different at the 5% level of significance.* If the calculated absolute value of t had been less than 2.23, we could not have rejected H_0.

Degrees of freedom	$P = 0.05$	$P = 0.01$	$P = 0.001$
5	2.57	4.03	6.87
10	2.23	3.17	4.59
15	2.13	2.95	4.07
20	2.09	2.85	3.85

1. (a) In an experiment, data values were obtained from four plants in experimental conditions and three plants in control conditions. The mean values for each data set (control and experimental conditions) were calculated. The t value was calculated to be 2.16. The null hypothesis was: "The plants in the control and experimental conditions are not different". State whether the calculated t value supports the null hypothesis or its alternative (consult t table above):

   _____

   (b) The experiment was repeated, but this time using six control and six "experimental" plants. The new t value was 2.54. State whether the calculated t value supports the null hypothesis or its alternative now:

   _____

2. Explain why, in terms of applying Student's t test, extreme data values (outliers) are often excluded from the data set(s):

   _____

   _____

3. Explain what you understand by statistical significance (for any statistical test): _____

   _____

   _____

Related activities: Descriptive Statistics, The Reliability of the Mean
Web links: Student's t-Test, Student's t-Test Exercise

Using the Chi-Squared Test in Ecology

The **chi-squared test** (χ^2), like the student's t test, is a test for difference between data sets, but it is used when you are working with frequencies (counts) rather than measurements. It is a simple test to perform but the data must meet the requirements of the test. These are as follows:

- It can only be used for data that are raw counts (not measurements or derived data such as percentages).
- It is used to compare an experimental result with an expected theoretical outcome (e.g. an expected Mendelian ratio or a theoretical value indicating "no preference" or "no difference"

between groups in some sort of response such as habitat or microclimate preference).

- It is not a valid test when sample sizes are small (<20).

Like all statistical tests, it aims to test the null hypothesis; the hypothesis of no difference between groups of data. The following exercise is a worked example using chi-squared for testing an ecological study of habitat preference. As with most of these simple statistical tests, chi-squared is easily calculated using a spreadsheet. Guidelines for this are available on the Teacher Resource CD-ROM.

Skills in Biology

Using χ^2 in Ecology

Pneumatophores

In an investigation of the ecological niche of the mangrove, *Avicennia marina var. resinifera*, the density of pneumatophores was measured in regions with different substrate. The mangrove trees were selected from four different areas: mostly sand, some sand, mostly mud, and some mud. Note that the variable, substrate type, is categorical in this case. Quadrats (1 m by 1 m) were placed around a large number of trees in each of these four areas and the numbers of pneumatophores were counted. Chi-squared was used to compare the observed results for pneumatophore density (as follows) to an expected outcome of no difference in density between substrates.

Mangrove pneumatophore density in different substrate areas			
Mostly sand	85	Mostly mud	130
Some sand	102	Some mud	123

Using χ^2, the probability of this result being consistent with the expected result could be tested. Worked example as follows:

Step 1: Calculate the expected value (E)

In this case, this is the sum of the observed values divided by the number of categories.

$$\frac{440}{4} = 110$$

Step 2: Calculate O – E

The difference between the observed and expected values is calculated as a measure of the deviation from a predicted result. Since some deviations are negative, they are all squared to give positive values. This step is usually performed as part of a tabulation (right, darker grey column).

Step 3: Calculate the value of χ^2

$$\chi^2 = \sum \frac{(O-E)^2}{E}$$

Where: O = the observed result
E = the expected result
$\sum$ = sum of

The calculated χ^2 value is given at the bottom right of the last column in the tabulation.

Step 4: Calculating degrees of freedom

The probability that any particular χ^2 value could be exceeded by chance depends on the number of degrees of freedom. This is simply *one less than the total number of categories* (this is the number that could vary independently without affecting the last value). *In this case: 4–1 = 3.*

Category	O	E	O – E	$(O-E)^2$	$\frac{(O-E)^2}{E}$
Mostly sand	85	110	−25	625	5.68
Some sand	102	110	−8	64	0.58
Mostly mud	130	110	20	400	3.64
Some mud	123	110	13	169	1.54

Total = 440 χ^2 $\sum = 11.44$

Step 5a: Using the χ^2 table

On the χ^2 table (part reproduced in Table 1 below) with 3 degrees of freedom, the calculated value for χ^2 of 11.44 corresponds to a probability of between 0.01 and 0.001 (see arrow). *This means that by chance alone a χ^2 value of 11.44 could be expected between 1% and 0.1% of the time.*

Step 5b: Using the χ^2 table

The probability of between 0.1 and 0.01 is lower than the 0.05 value which is generally regarded as significant. The null hypothesis can be rejected and we have reason to believe that the observed results differ significantly from the expected (at $P = 0.05$).

Table 1: Critical values of χ^2 at different levels of probability. By convention, the critical probability for rejecting the null hypothesis (H_0) is 5%. If the test statistic is less than the tabulated critical value for $P = 0.05$ we cannot reject H_0 and the result is not significant. If the test statistic is greater than the tabulated value for $P = 0.05$ we reject H_0 in favour of the alternative hypothesis.

Degrees of freedom	Level of probability (P)									
	0.98	0.95	0.80	0.50	0.20	0.10	0.05	0.02	0.01	0.001
1	0.001	0.004	0.064	0.455	1.64	2.71	3.84	5.41	6.64 χ^2	10.83
2	0.040	0.103	0.466	1.386	3.22	4.61	5.99	7.82	9.21	13.82
3	0.185	0.352	1.005	2.366	4.64	6.25	7.82	9.84	11.35	16.27
4	0.429	0.711	1.649	3.357	5.99	7.78	9.49	11.67	13.28	18.47
5	0.752	0.145	2.343	4.351	7.29	9.24	11.07	13.39	15.09	20.52

← Do not reject H_0 Reject H_0 →

Related activities: Using the Chi-squared Test in Genetics
Web links: Chi-squared Exercise in Ecology

Using the Chi-Squared Test in Genetics

The **chi-squared test**, χ^2, is frequently used for testing the outcome of dihybrid crosses against an expected (predicted) Mendelian ratio, and it is appropriate for use in this way. When using the chi-squared test for this purpose, the null hypothesis predicts the ratio of offspring of different phenotypes according to the expected Mendelian ratio for the cross, assuming independent assortment of alleles (no linkage). Significant departures from the predicted Mendelian ratio indicate linkage of the alleles in question. Raw counts should be used and a large sample size is required for the test to be valid.

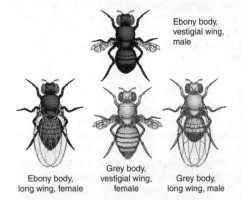

Ebony body, vestigial wing, male

Ebony body, long wing, female

Grey body, vestigial wing, female

Grey body, long wing, male

Images of *Drosophila* courtesy of **Newbyte Educational Software**: *Drosophila* Genetics Lab (**www.newbyte.com**)

Using χ^2 in Mendelian Genetics

In a *Drosophila* genetics experiment, two individuals were crossed (the details of the cross are not relevant here). The predicted Mendelian ratios for the offspring of this cross were 1:1:1:1 for each of the four following phenotypes: grey body-long wing, grey body-vestigial wing, ebony body-long wing, ebony body-vestigial wing. The observed results of the cross were not exactly as predicted. The following numbers for each phenotype were observed in the offspring of the cross:

Observed results of the example *Drosophila* cross

Grey body, long wing	98	Ebony body, long wing	102
Grey body, vestigial wing	88	Ebony body, vestigial wing	112

Using χ^2, the probability of this result being consistent with a 1:1:1:1 ratio could be tested. Worked example as follows:

Step 1: Calculate the expected value (E)

In this case, this is the sum of the observed values divided by the number of categories (see note below)

$$\frac{400}{4} = 100$$

Step 2: Calculate O – E

The difference between the observed and expected values is calculated as a measure of the deviation from a predicted result. Since some deviations are negative, they are all squared to give positive values. This step is usually performed as part of a tabulation (right, darker grey column).

Category	O	E	O – E	$(O-E)^2$	$\dfrac{(O-E)^2}{E}$
Grey, long wing	98	100	–2	4	0.04
Grey, vestigial wing	88	100	–12	144	1.44
Ebony, long wing	102	100	2	4	0.04
Ebony, vestigial wing	112	100	12	144	1.44

Total = 400 $\qquad \chi^2 \quad \Sigma = 2.96$

Step 3: Calculate the value of χ^2

$$\chi^2 = \sum \frac{(O-E)^2}{E}$$

Where: O = the observed result
E = the expected result
Σ = sum of

The calculated χ^2 value is given at the bottom right of the last column in the tabulation.

Step 5a: Using the χ^2 table

On the χ^2 table (part reproduced in Table 1 below) with 3 degrees of freedom, the calculated value for χ^2 of 2.96 corresponds to a probability of between 0.2 and 0.5 (see arrow). *This means that by chance alone a χ^2 value of 2.96 could be expected between 20% and 50% of the time.*

Step 4: Calculating degrees of freedom

The probability that any particular χ^2 value could be exceeded by chance depends on the number of degrees of freedom. This is simply *one less than the total number of categories* (this is the number that could vary independently without affecting the last value). *In this case: 4–1 = 3.*

Step 5b: Using the χ^2 table

The probability of between 0.2 and 0.5 is higher than the 0.05 value which is generally regarded as significant. The null hypothesis cannot be rejected and we have no reason to believe that the observed results differ significantly from the expected (at $P = 0.05$).

Footnote: Many Mendelian crosses involve ratios other than 1:1. For these, calculation of the expected values is not simply a division of the total by the number of categories. Instead, the total must be apportioned according to the ratio. For example, for a total of 400 as above, in a predicted 9:3:3:1 ratio, the total count must be divided by 16 (9+3+3+1) and the expected values will be 225: 75: 75: 25 in each category.

Table 1: Critical values of χ^2 at different levels of probability. By convention, the critical probability for rejecting the null hypothesis (H_0) is 5%. If the test statistic is less than the tabulated critical value for $P = 0.05$ we cannot reject H_0 and the result is not significant. If the test statistic is greater than the tabulated value for $P = 0.05$ we reject H_0 in favor of the alternative hypothesis.

Degrees of freedom	Level of probability (P)									
	0.98	0.95	0.80	0.50	0.20	0.10	0.05	0.02	0.01	0.001
1	0.001	0.004	0.064	0.455 χ^2	1.64	2.71	3.84	5.41	6.64	10.83
2	0.040	0.103	0.466	1.386	3.22	4.61	5.99	7.82	9.21	13.82
3	0.185	0.352	1.005	2.366	4.64	6.25	7.82	9.84	11.35	16.27
4	0.429	0.711	1.649	3.357	5.99	7.78	9.49	11.67	13.28	18.47
5	0.752	0.145	2.343	4.351	7.29	9.24	11.07	13.39	15.09	20.52

← Do not reject H_0 $\qquad$ Reject H_0 →

Related activities: Using the Chi-squared Test in Ecology
Web links: Chi-squared Exercise in Genetics

Biological Drawings

Microscopes are a powerful tool for examining cells and cell structures. In order to make a permanent record of what is seen when examining a specimen, it is useful to make a drawing. It is important to draw **what is actually seen**. This will depend on the **resolution** of the microscope being used. Resolution refers to the ability of a microscope to separate small objects that are very close together. Making drawings from mounted specimens is a skill. Drawing forces you to observe closely and accurately. While photographs are limited to representing appearance at a single moment in time, drawings can be composites of the observer's cumulative experience, with many different specimens of the same material. The total picture of an object thus represented can often communicate information much more effectively than a photograph. Your attention to the outline of suggestions below will help you to make more effective drawings. If you are careful to follow the suggestions at the beginning, the techniques will soon become habitual.

1. **Drawing materials**: All drawings should be done with a clear pencil line on good quality paper. A sharp HB pencil is recommended. A soft rubber of good quality is essential. Diagrams in ballpoint or fountain pen are unacceptable because they cannot be corrected.

2. **Positioning**: Centre your diagram on the page. Do not draw it in a corner. This will leave plenty of room for the addition of labels once the diagram is completed.

3. **Size**: A drawing should be large enough to easily represent all the details you see without crowding. Rarely, if ever, are drawings too large, but they are often too small. Show only as much as is necessary for an understanding of the structure; a small section shown in detail will often suffice. It is time consuming and unnecessary, for example, to reproduce accurately the entire contents of a microscope field.

4. **Accuracy**: Your drawing should be a complete, accurate representation of the material you have observed, and should communicate your understanding of the material to anyone who looks at it. Avoid making "idealised" drawings; your drawing should be a picture of what you actually see, not what you imagine should be there. Proportions should be accurate. If necessary, measure the lengths of various parts with a ruler. If viewing through a microscope, estimate them as a proportion of the field of view, then translate these proportions onto the page. When drawing shapes that indicate an outline, make sure the line is complete. Where two ends of a line do not meet (as in drawing a cell outline) then this would indicate that the structure has a hole in it.

5. **Technique**: Use only simple, narrow lines. Represent depth by stippling (dots close together). Indicate depth only when it is essential to your drawing (usually it is not). Do not use shading. Look at the specimen while you are drawing it.

6. **Labels**: Leave a good margin for labels. All parts of your diagram must be labelled accurately. Labelling lines should be drawn with a ruler and should not cross. Where possible, keep label lines vertical or horizontal. Label the drawing with:
   - A title, which should identify the material (organism, tissues or cells).
   - Magnification under which it was observed, or a scale to indicate the size of the object.
   - Names of structures.
   - In living materials, any movements you have seen.

Remember that drawings are intended as records for you, and as a means of encouraging close observation; artistic ability is not necessary. Before you turn in a drawing, ask yourself if you know what every line represents. If you do not, look more closely at the material. *Take into account the rules for biological drawings and draw what you see, not what you think you see!*

Examples of acceptable biological drawings: The diagrams below show two examples of biological drawings that are acceptable. The example on the left is of a whole organism and its size is indicated by a scale. The example on the right is of plant tissue: a group of cells that are essentially identical in the structure. It is not necessary to show many cells even though your view through the microscope may show them. As few as 2-4 will suffice to show their structure and how they are arranged. Scale is indicated by stating how many times larger it has been drawn. Do not confuse this with what magnification it was viewed at under the microscope. The abbreviation **T.S.** indicates that the specimen was a *cross* or *transverse section*.

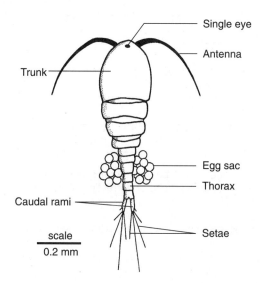

Cyclopoid copepod

- Single eye
- Antenna
- Trunk
- Egg sac
- Thorax
- Caudal rami
- Setae

scale
0.2 mm

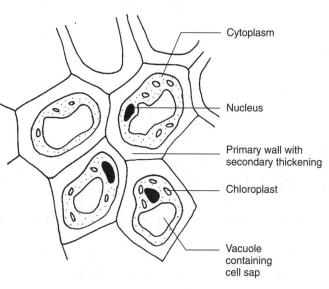

Collenchyma T.S. from Helianthus stem
Magnification x 450

- Cytoplasm
- Nucleus
- Primary wall with secondary thickening
- Chloroplast
- Vacuole containing cell sap

Related activities: Optical Microscopes

A 2

56

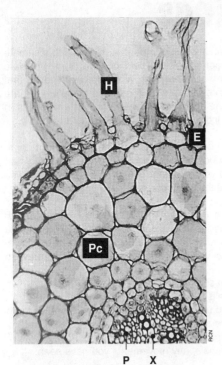

P   X

Specimen used for drawing

The photograph above is a light microscope view of a stained transverse section (cross section) of a root from a *Ranunculus* (buttercup) plant. It shows the arrangement of the different tissues in the root. The vascular bundle is at the centre of the root, with the larger, central xylem vessels (**X**) and smaller phloem vessels (**P**) grouped around them. The root hair cells (**H**) are arranged on the external surface and form part of the epidermal layer (**E**). Parenchyma cells (**Pc**) make up the bulk of the root's mass. The distance from point **X** to point **E** on the photograph (above) is about 0.15 mm (150 μm).

An Unacceptable Biological Drawing

The diagram below is an example of how *not* to produce a biological drawing; it is based on the photograph to the left. There are many aspects of the drawing that are unacceptable. The exercise below asks you to identify the errors in this student's attempt.

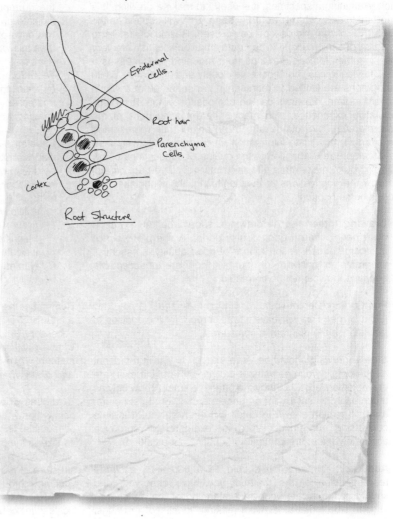

1. Identify and describe eight unacceptable features of the student's biological diagram above:

    (a) _____

    (b) _____

    (c) _____

    (d) _____

    (e) _____

    (f) _____

    (g) _____

    (h) _____

2. In the remaining space next to the 'poor example' (above) or on a blank piece of refill paper, attempt your own version of a biological drawing for the same material, based on the photograph above. Make a point of correcting all of the errors that you have identified in the sample student's attempt.

3. Explain why accurate biological drawings are more valuable to a scientific investigation than an 'artistic' approach:

    _____

    _____

    _____

The Structure of a Report

Once you have collected your data and analysed it, you can write your report. The structure of a scientific report is described below. The final order of the different sections of a report is not usually the order in which they are written. It is a good idea to write either the methods or the results sections first, followed by the discussion and conclusion. Although you should do some background reading in preparation, the introduction should be one of the last sections that you write. Writing the other sections first provides you with a better understanding of your investigation and enables you to be better able to make clear statements about the topic you investigated.

Section	Content	Purpose
Title	Provides a clear description of the project.	Provides the reader with a summary of the type and extent of the investigation.
Introduction	Includes the aim and hypothesis, and background information to the project.	Provides the reader with the relevant background to the topic and the rationale for the investigation.
Materials and method	A description of the materials used and the experimental procedures involved.	Important because it allows the procedures to be repeated and confirmed.
Results	A full description of the results including tables and graphs. This section should not discuss the results, but can state trends.	Provides the reader with the findings of the investigation and allows them to evaluate these for themselves.
Discussion	An interpretation of the results written in paragraph form. It includes a description of trends and a discussion of the findings in light of the biological concepts involved. It also includes comments on sources of error, limitations of the data, assumptions made by the investigator about the system, and ideas for further investigations.	Provides the reader with the investigator's evaluation of the investigation. It also informs the reader as to the limitations of the investigation, and ideas on how the design of the investigation could have been improved.
Conclusion	A clear statement describing whether or not the results of the investigation support the hypothesis. If a statistical conclusion is made, this sometimes appears before the discussion.	Provides the reader with the investigator's analysis of the results.
Acknowledgements / Bibliography	A list of sources of information, including citations of written material (e.g. journals, texts), web pages, and practical and advisory help. It is important that entries are consistent within your report. Your teacher will advise you as to the format preferred.	Acknowledging sources of information and assistance is part of scientific integrity. It acknowledges the work and expertise of others and allows your work to be assessed in the light of other work in the area.

Skills in Biology

As is often the case in science, after completing your investigation and discussing your results, you may conclude that your hypothesis is not supported. This does not necessarily mean that the science was flawed or of no value. However, it does present the opportunity to propose a new, tentative explanation (hypothesis) for the observations you made. The example below describes this type of situation. Completing the questions will develop your skills in evaluating your results even if your investigations do not turn out as you might expect:

1. A student found that a herbaceous plant species was found growing around, but not right up to, a stand of rhododendrons. In a controlled experiment, she investigated the effect of soil, taken from within the rhododendron stand, on the vigour with which the soft leaved species grew. She found no effect:

   (a) Propose a suitable prediction and conclusion for this investigation:

   Prediction: _____

   _____

   Conclusion: _____

   (b) The student then measured the water content of the soil immediately around the rhododendrons, and found it to be drier than the soil in which the herbaceous plants were growing. Revise your prediction in the light of this information:

   _____

   _____

Related activities: Hypotheses and Predictions, Writing the Methods & Results, Writing Your Discussion, Citing and Listing References, Report Checklist

RA 2

Writing the Methods

The materials and methods section of your report should be brief but informative. All essential details should be included but those not necessary for the repetition of the study should be omitted. The following diagram illustrates some of the important details that should be included in a methods section. Obviously, a complete list of all possible equipment and procedures is not possible because each experiment or study is different. However, the sort of information that is required for both lab and field based studies is provided.

Field Studies

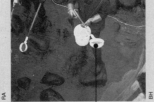

Study site & organisms
- Site location and features
- Why that site was chosen
- Species involved

Specialised equipment
- pH and oxygen meters
- Thermometers
- Nets and traps

Data collection
- Number and timing of observations/collections
- Time of day or year
- Sample sizes and size of the sampling unit
- Methods of preservation
- Temperature at time of sampling
- Weather conditions on the day(s) of sampling
- Methods of measurement/sampling
- Methods of recording

Laboratory Based Studies

Data collection
- Pre-treatment of material before experiments
- Details of treatments and controls
- Duration and timing of experimental observations
- Temperature
- Sample sizes and details of replication
- Methods of measurement or sampling
- Methods of recording

Experimental organisms
- Species or strain
- Age and sex
- Number of individuals used

Specialised equipment
- pH meters
- Water baths & incubators
- Spectrophotometers
- Centrifuges
- Aquaria & choice chambers
- Microscopes and videos

Special preparations
- Techniques for the preparation of material (staining, grinding)
- Indicators, salt solutions, buffers, special dilutions

General guidelines for writing a methods section

- Choose a suitable level of detail. *Too little detail and the study could not be repeated. Too much detail obscures important features.*
- Do NOT include the details of standard procedures (e.g. how to use a balance) or standard equipment (e.g. beakers and flasks).
- Include details of any statistical analyses and data transformations.
- Outline the reasons why procedures were done in a certain way or in a certain order, if this is not self-evident.
- If your methodology involves complicated preparations (e.g. culture media) then it is acceptable to refer just to the original information source (e.g. lab manual) or include the information as an appendix.

1. The following text is part of the methods section from a report. Using the information above and on the checklist on page 63, describe eight errors (there are ten) in the methods. The errors are concerned with a lack of explanation or detail that would be necessary to repeat the experiment (they are not typographical, nor are they associated with the use of the active voice, which is now considered preferable to the passive):

"We collected the worms for this study from a pond outside the school. We carried out the experiment at room temperature on April 16, 1997. First we added full strength seawater to each of three 200 cm³ glass jars; these were the controls. We filled another three jars with diluted seawater. We blotted the worms dry and weighed them to the nearest 0.1 g, then we added one worm to each jar. We reweighed the worms (after blotting) at various intervals over the next two hours."

(a) _____

(b) _____

(c) _____

(d) _____

(e) _____

(f) _____

(g) _____

(h) _____

© Biozone International 1998-2007

Related activities: The Structure of a Report, Report checklist

Writing Your Results

The results section is arguably the most important part of any research report; it is the place where you can bring together and present your findings. When properly constructed, this section will present your results clearly and in a way that shows you have organised your data and carefully considered the appropriate analysis. A portion of the results section from a scientific paper on the habitat preference of New Zealand black mudfish is presented below (Hicks, B. and Barrier, R. (1996), NZJMFR. 30, 135-151). It highlights some important features of the results section and shows you how you can present information concisely, even if your results are relatively lengthy. Use it as a guide for content when you write up this section.

Results

A total of 222 black mudfish were caught in the 400 traps set be[...] Mean total length (TL) was 67 mm (range 26-139 mm, $n = 214$) [...] had black mudfish. Mudfis[...] [...]ly amo[...] independence, $P < 0.001$: [...] at 8 out [...] at 20 out of 30 wetland sit[...] [...] at only [...] none of the 6 lake margin or 4 pond, dam, and lagoon sites. Categorical variables that distinguished [...] [...] x^2 tests of independence, $P < 0.05$: Table 4) were: [...]rate disturbance scale rating; presence of emergent [...]sed or peat bog substrate types; absence of fish [...]orphus cotidianus) and inanga (Galaxias maculatus):

> **Graphs (figures) illustrate trends in the data. Be sure to choose the correct type of graph and allocate enough space to it in the report.**

> **Keep your statement of important findings brief.**

> **Label figures and tables clearly and in sequence so that they can be referred to easily in the text.**

> **Scientific names are included if they are known.**

Table 4: χ^2 tests of association between presence or absence of black mudfish and categorical habitat variables at sites in the Waikato region.

Habitat variable	χ^2 statistic	df	Probability	
Absence of water in summer	31.84	1	<0.001	
Disturbance scale rating	23.92	4	<0.001	
Emergent vegetation	17.56	1	<0.001	
Overhanging vegetation	11.82	1	<0.001	Significant
Surface substrate type	16.51	2	<0.001	
Absence of bullies and inanga	6.17	1	0.013	
Tree roots	4.00	1	0.040	
Underlying soil type	8.05	4	0.090	Not significant

> **Tables summarise raw data, any transformations, and the results of statistical tests.**

> **Distinction is made between those statistical values that are significant and those that are not (at $P < 0.05$).**

Means of t[...] [...] depth, wint[...] water dept[...] [...]es with and [...] 5). Mean summer water depth was only 2.1 cm at sites with mudfish, compared to 22.6 cm at sites without. Winter and maximum water depths were also less at sites with mudfish than at sites without mudfish. M[...] [...]elometric turbidity units (NTU) at sites with mudfish, but 21.3 NTU at site[...] [...]ity, total dissolved solids, dissolved oxygen at the water surface, humic cond[...] [...]ocity were similar at all sites (t-test, $P > 0.153$: Table 5). Catch rates at site[...] [...] mudfish per trap per night (geometric mean 0.70: Table 5).

> **Only include results; this is not the place to discuss them.**

> **Any abbreviations are noted the first time they occur.**

> **Tables and figures are referred to in brackets.**

Table 5: Characteristics [...]

Variable	Sites with mudfish Mean ± CI	SD	Sites without mudfish Mean ± CI	SD	Proba[...]
Mudfish catch rate /fish per trap per night	0.70 ± 1.31	0.84	0.00		
Summer water depth /cm	2.1 ± 1.9	2.2	22.6 ± 7.8	24.7	<0.001
Winter water depth /cm	28.9 ± 4.3	5.8	40.2 ± 7.7	24.4	0.012
Turbidity /NTU	11.5 ± 2.5	13.3	21.3 ± 7.1	22.6	0.012

> **Any extra information for a figure can be shown by an asterisk and included elsewhere.**

Catch rates for classes within variables, and the habitat preference [...] that mudfish were virtually absent from water of > 30 cm depth in s[...] mudfish preferred water depths between 15 and 50 cm. Disturban[...] preferred, as were turbidities of < 15 NTU. Preference for the DSR of 1 was assumed to be the same as for the DSR of 2, as the small number of sites with DSR of 1 and 2 ($n = 5$ in each case) made their separate preferences unreliable.

Fig. 2 Relationship of winter catch rate to four habitat parameters

* All fish were caught at sites in winter. Summer water depth refers to water depth at those sites in summer (many sites dry out).

1. Explain why you should make reference to tables and figures in the body of the text: _____

_____

2. Explain why you might present the same data in a table and as a figure: _____

_____

_____

Writing Your Discussion

In the discussion section of your report, you must interpret your results in the context of the specific questions you set out to answer in the investigation. You should also place your findings in the context of any broader relevant issues. If your results coincide exactly with what you expected, then your discussion will be relatively brief. However, be prepared to discuss any unexpected or conflicting results and critically evaluate any problems with your study design. The Discussion section may (and should) refer to the findings in the Results section, but it is not the place to introduce new results. Try to work towards a point in your discussion where the reader is lead naturally to the conclusion. The conclusion may be presented within the discussion or it may be included separately after the discussion as a separate section.

Discussion:

Black mudfish habitat in the Waikato region can be ad···········ses by four variables that are easy to measure: summer water depth, winter wa······cated by vegetation), and turbidity. Catch rates of black mudfish can be extreme······es ranged from 0.2 to 8.4 mudfish per trap per night (mean 0.70) between May and October 1992, and were similar to those of Dean (1995) in September 1993 and October 1994 in the Whangamarino Wetland complex (0.0-2.0 mudfish per trap per night). The highest mean catch rate in our study, 8.4 mudfish per trap per night, was at Site 24 (Table 1, Figure 1). The second highest (6.4 mudfish per trap per night) was at Site 32, in a drain about 4 km east of Hamilton. Black mudfish in the Waikato region were most commonly found at sites in wetlands with absence of water in summer, moderate depth of water in winter, limited modification of the vegetation (low DSR), and low turbidity (Fig. 2). There are similarities between the habitat requirements of black mudfish and those of brown mudfish and the common river galaxias *(Galaxias vulgaris)*. Brown mudfish inhabited shallow water, sometimes at the edges of deeper water bodies, but were usually absent from water deeper than about 30-50 cm (Eldon 1978). The common river galaxias also has a preference for shallow water, occupying river margins < 20 cm deep (Jowett and Richardson 1995).

Support your statements with reference to Tables and Figures from the Results section.

The discussion describes the relevance of the results of the investigation.

Sites where black mudfish were found were not just shallow or dry in sum······al variation in water depth. A weakness of this study is the fact that sites were trap······ere spread relatively widely at each site to maximise the chance of catching any fish······nt for black mudfish, in the form of emergent or overhanging vegetation, or tree roots. The significance of cover in determining the pres······s predictable, considering the shallow nature of their habitats. Mudfish, though noc······require cover during the to protect them from avian predators, such as bitterns (Bo······fishers *(Halcyon sancta vagans)*. Predation of black mudfish by a swamp bittern has······1). Cover is also important for brown mudfish (Eldon 1978). Black mudfish were found at sites with the predatory mosquitofish and juvenile eels, and the seasonal drying of their habitats may be a key to the successful coexistence of mudfish with their predators. Mosquitofish are known predators of mudfish fry (Barrier & Hicks 1994), and eels would presumably also prey on black mudfish, as t······h (Eldon 1979b). If, however, black mudfish are relatively uncompetitive and vulnerable to pr······s as to how they manage to coexist with juvenile eels and mosquitofish. The habitat varia······can be used to classify the suitability of sites for black mudfish in future. The adaptability of black mudfish allows them to survive in some altered habitats, such as farm or roadside drains. From this study, we can conclude that the continued existence of suitable habitats appears to be more important to black mudfish than the presence of predators and competitors. This study has also improved methods of identifying suitable mudfish habitats in the Waikato region.

State any limitations of your approach in carrying out the investigation and what further studies might be appropriate.

Reference is made to the work of others.

Further research is suggested

A clear conclusion is made towards the end of the discussion.

1. Explain why it is important to discuss any weaknesses in your study design: _____

_____

_____

2. Explain why you should **critically evaluate** your results in the discussion: _____

_____

_____

_____

3. Describe the purpose of the conclusion: _____

_____

Related activities: The Structure of a Report, Report checklist

Citing and Listing References

Proper referencing of sources of information is an important aspect of report writing. It shows that you have explored the topic and recognise and respect the work of others. There are two aspects to consider: **citing sources** within the text (making reference to other work to support a statement or compare results) and **compiling a reference list** at the end of the report. A **bibliography** lists all sources of information, but these may not necessarily appear as citations in the report. In contrast, a reference list should contain only those texts cited in the report.

Citations in the main body of the report should include only the authors' surnames, publication date, and page numbers (or internet site), and the citation should be relevant to the statement it claims to support. Accepted methods for referencing vary, but your reference list should provide all the information necessary to locate the source material, it should be consistently presented, and it should contain only the references that you have yourself read (not those cited by others). A suggested format is described below.

Preparing a Reference List

When teachers ask students to write in "APA style", they are referring to the editorial style established by the **American Psychological Association** (APA). These guidelines for citing **electronic (online) resources** differ only slightly from the **print sources**.

For the Internet

Where you use information from the internet, you must provide the following:
• The website address (URL), the person or organisation who is in charge of the web site and the date you accessed the web page.
This is written in the form: URL (person or organisation's name, day, month, and year retrieved)
   This goes together as follows:
       http://www.scientificamerican.com (Scientific American, 17.12.03)

For Periodicals (or Journals)

This is written in the form: author(s), date of publication, article title, periodical title, and publication information.
Example: Author's family name, A. A. (author's initials only), Author, B. B., & Author, C. C. (xxxx = year of publication in brackets). Title of article. Title of Periodical, volume number, page numbers (Note, only use "pp." before the page numbers in newspapers and magazines).
   This goes together as follows:
       Bamshad M. J., & Olson S. E. (2003). Does Race Exist? Scientific American, 289(6), 50-57.

For Online Periodicals based on a Print Source

At present, the majority of periodicals retrieved from online publications are exact duplicates of those in their print versions and although they are unlikely to have additional analyses and data attached to them, this is likely to change in the future.

• If the article that is to be referenced has been viewed only in electronic form and not in print form, then you must add in brackets, "Electronic version", after the title.
   This goes together as follows:
       Bamshad M. J., & Olson S. E. (2003). Does Race Exist? (Electronic version). Scientific American, 289(6), 50-57.
• If you have reason to believe the article has changed in its electronic form, then you will need to add the date you retrieved the document and the URL.
   This goes together as follows:
       Bamshad M. J., & Olson S. E. (2003). Does Race Exist? (Electronic version). Scientific American, 289(6), 50-57. Retrieved December 17, 2003, from http://www.scientificamerican.com

For Books

This is written in the form: author(s), date of publication, title, and publication information.
Example: Author, A. A., Author, B. B., & Author, C. C. (xxxx). Title (any additional information to enable identification is given in brackets). City of publication: publishers name.
This goes together as follows:
       Martin, R.A. (2004). Missing Links Evolutionary Concepts & Transitions Through Time. Sudbury, MA: Jones and Bartlett

For Citation in the Text of References

This is written in the form: authors' surname(s), date of publication, page number(s) (abbreviated p.), chapter (abbreviated chap.), figure, table, equation, or internet site, in brackets at the appropriate point in text.
This goes together as follows:
       (Bamshad & Olson, 2003, p. 51) or (Bamshad & Olson, 2003, http://www.scientificamerican.com)

This can also be done in the form of footnotes. This involves the use of a superscripted number in the text next to your quoted material and the relevant information listed at the bottom of the page.
This goes together as follows:
       .... Bamshad & Olson reported that ....[1]

[1]Bamshad & Olson, 2003, p. 51

Related activities: The Structure of a Report, Report Checklist

A 3

Skills in Biology

62

Example of a Reference List

Lab notes can be listed according to title if the author is unknown.

→ Advanced biology laboratory manual (2000). Cell membranes. pp 16-18. Sunhigh College.

References are listed alphabetically according to the author's surname.

Cooper, G.M. (1997). *The cell: A molecular approach* (2nd ed.). Washington D.C.: ASM Press

Book title in italics (or underlined)   Place of publication: Publisher

Davis, P. (1996) Cellular factories. *New Scientist* 2057: Inside science supplement.

Publication date   Journal title in italics   A supplement may not need page references

If a single author appears more than once, then list the publications from oldest to most recent.

Indge, B. (2001). Diarrhoea, digestion and dehydration. *Biological Sciences Review*, 14(1), 7-9.

Indge, B. (2002). Experiments. *Biological Sciences Review*, 14(3), 11-13.

Article title follows date

Kingsland, J. (2000). Border control. *New Scientist* 2247: Inside science supplement.

Spell out only the last name of authors. Use initials for first and middle names.

Laver, H. (1995). Osmosis and water retention in plants. *Biological Sciences Review* 7(3), 14-18

Volume (Issue number), Pages

Steward, M. (1996). Water channels in the cell membrane. *Biological Sciences Review*, 9(2), 18-22.

Internet sites change often so the date accessed is included. The person or organisation in charge of the site is also included.

→ http://www.cbc.umn.edu/~mwd/cell_intro.html (Dalton, M. "Introduction to cell biology" 12.02.03)

1. Distinguish between a **reference list** and a **bibliography**: _____

_____

_____

_____

2. Explain why internet articles based on a print source are likely to have additional analyses and data attached in the future, and why this point should be noted in a reference list:

_____

_____

3. Following are the details of references and source material used by a student in preparing a report on enzymes and their uses in biotechnology. He provided his reference list in prose. From it, compile a correctly formatted reference list:

Pages 18-23 in the sixth edition of the textbook "Biology" by Neil Campbell. Published by Benjamin/Cummings in California (2002). New Scientist article by Peter Moore called "Fuelled for life" (January 1996, volume 2012, supplement). "Food biotechnology" published in the journal Biological Sciences Review, page 25, volume 8 (number 3) 1996, by Liam and Katherine O'Hare. An article called "Living factories" by Philip Ball in New Scientist, volume 2015 1996, pages 28-31. Pages 75-85 in the book "The cell: a molecular approach" by Geoffrey Cooper, published in 1997 by ASM Press, Washington D.C. An article called "Development of a procedure for purification of a recombinant therapeutic protein" in the journal "Australasian Biotechnology", by I Roberts and S. Taylor, pages 93-99 in volume 6, number 2, 1996.

REFERENCE LIST

_____

_____

_____

_____

_____

_____

_____

Report Checklist

A report of your findings at the completion of your investigation may take one of the following forms: a written document, seminar, poster, web page, or multimedia presentation. The following checklist identifies points to consider when writing each section of your report. Review the list before you write your report and then, on satisfactory completion of each section of your write-up, use the check boxes to tick off the points:

Title:

☐ (a) Gives a clear indication of what the study is about.

☐ (b) Includes the species name and a common name of all organisms used.

Introduction:

☐ (a) Includes a clear aim.

☐ (b) Includes a well written hypothesis.

☐ (c) Includes a synopsis of the current state of knowledge about the topic.

Materials and methods:

☐ (a) Written clearly. Numbered points are appropriate at this level.

☐ (b) Describes the final methods that were used.

☐ (c) Includes details of the how data for the dependent variable were collected.

☐ (d) Includes details of how all other variables were manipulated, controlled, measured, or monitored.

☐ (e) If appropriate, it includes an explanatory diagram of the design of the experimental set-up.

☐ (f) Written in the past tense, and in the active voice (We investigated ...) rather than the passive voice (An investigation was done ...).

Results:

☐ (a) Includes the raw data (e.g. in a table).

☐ (b) Where necessary, the raw data have been averaged or transformed.

☐ (c) Includes graphs (where appropriate).

☐ (d) Each figure (table, graph, drawing, or photo) has a title and is numbered in a way that makes it possible to refer to it in the text (Fig. 1 etc.).

☐ (e) Written in the past tense and, where appropriate, in the active voice.

Discussion:

☐ (a) Includes an analysis of the data in which the findings, including trends and patterns, are discussed in relation to the biological concepts involved.

☐ (b) Includes an evaluation of sources of error, assumptions, and possible improvements to design.

Conclusion:

☐ (a) Written as a clear statement, which relates directly to the hypothesis.

Bibliography or References:

☐ (a) Lists all sources of information and assistance.

☐ (b) Does not include references that were not used.

© Biozone International 1998-2007
Photocopying Prohibited

Related activities: The Structure of a Report, Writing the Methods, Writing Your Results and Discussion, Citing and Listing References

A 3

Biological Molecules

AQA-A	AQA-B	SNAB	Edexcel	OCR
Complete:	Complete:	Complete:	Complete:	Complete:
1-5, 9-15, 17-28, 30-36, 38-43	1-7, 9-10, 12-15, 17-31, 33-35, 38-40	1, 9-12, 14, 16, 18-24, 26-40	1-7, 9-16, 18-35, 38-41, 43	1-15, 17-40

Learning Objectives

The learning objectives relating to the structure and function of nucleic acids are provided in the topic "The Genetic Code".

☐ 1. Compile your own glossary from the **KEY WORDS** displayed in **bold type** in the learning objectives below.

Basic Organic Chemistry *(pages 66-68, 78)*

☐ 2. List the four most common elements found in living things. Provide examples of where these elements occur in cells. Explain what is meant by **organic chemistry** and explain its importance in biology.

☐ 3. Distinguish between ionic bonds and covalent bonds and understand the importance of **covalent bonds** in carbon-based compounds.

☐ 4. Distinguish between **monomers** and **polymers** and provide examples of each type. Explain clearly what is meant by a **macromolecule** and give examples.

☐ 5. Explain the basis of **chromatography** as a technique for separating and identifying biological molecules. Describe the calculation and use of **Rf values**.

Water and Inorganic Ions *(pages 66, 68)*

☐ 6. Describe the structure of water, including reference to the polar nature of the water molecule, the nature of the bonding within the molecule, and the importance of **hydrogen bonding** *between* water molecules.

☐ 7. Identify the physical properties of water that are important in biological systems. Explain why water is termed the *universal solvent* and describe its various roles: e.g. metabolic role, as a solvent, as a lubricant, and as a fluid in hydrostatic skeletons and cell turgor.

☐ 8. Provide a definition of an **inorganic** (mineral) **ion**. With reference to specific examples, describe the role of inorganic ions in biological systems. Examples could include: Na^+, K^+, Mg^{2+}, Cl^-, NO_3^-, and PO_4^{3-}. Distinguish between **macronutrients** and **trace elements** and provide examples of each.

Carbohydrates *(pages 69-70, 78)*

☐ 9. Describe the basic composition and general formula of carbohydrates. Explain the main roles of carbohydrates in both plants and animals.

☐ 10. Describe what is meant by a **monosaccharide** and give its general formula. Provide examples of **triose**, **pentose**, and **hexose sugars** (including fructose and galactose). For each, identify its biological role.

☐ 11. Distinguish between **structural** and **optical isomers** in monosaccharides, explaining the basis for the isomerism in each case. Describe structural isomers of glucose (α and β **glucose**) and their biological significance.

☐ 12. Describe what is meant by a **disaccharide**. Explain how disaccharides are formed by a **condensation** reaction and broken apart by **hydrolysis**. Identify the **glycosidic bond** formed and broken in each case. Give examples of disaccharides and their functions, and name the monosaccharides involved in each case.

☐ 13. Identify examples of **reducing** and **non-reducing sugars**, and describe the **Benedict's test** for distinguishing these. Explain the basis of the test and its result. Describe a test for a non-reducing sugar.

☐ 14. Explain what is meant by a **polysaccharide** and describe how polysaccharides are formed. Describe the molecular structure of the following examples of polysaccharides: *starch, glycogen, cellulose* and relate their structure to their function in biological systems.

☐ 15. Describe the **I₂/KI** (*iodine in potassium iodide solution*) **test** for starch. Explain its basis and result.

Lipids *(pages 71-72, 78)*

☐ 16. Describe the general properties of lipids. Recognise the diversity of lipids in biological systems (e.g. steroids, phospholipids, waxes, and fats and oils and describe their functional roles.

☐ 17. Describe the **emulsion test** for lipids. Explain the basis of the test and its result.

☐ 18. Recognise that most lipids are **triglycerides** (triacyl-glycerols). Describe how triglycerides are classified as *fats* or *oils* and explain the basis of the classification.

☐ 19. Describe the basic structure of a triglyceride. Explain their formation by **condensation** reactions between glycerol and three fatty acids. Identify the **ester bonds** that result from this. Distinguish between **saturated** and **unsaturated fatty acids** and relate this difference to the properties of the fat or oil that results.

☐ 20. Using a diagram, describe the basic structure of a **phospholipid** and explain how it differs from the structure of a triglyceride. Explain how the structure of phospholipids is important to their role in membranes.

Amino Acids and Proteins *(pages 73-77, 78)*

☐ 21. Draw or describe the general structure and formula of an **amino acid**. Explain the basis for the different properties of amino acids.

☐ 22. Recognise that, of over 170 amino acids, only 20 are commonly found in proteins. Distinguish between **essential** and **non-essential amino acids**.

☐ 23. Recognise the property of **optical isomerism** in amino acids and explain its basis. Distinguish L- and D- forms and identify which isomer is active in biological systems.

☐ 24. Using a diagram, describe how amino acids are joined together in a **condensation reaction** to form **dipeptides** and **polypeptides**. Describe the nature of **peptide bonds** that result. Describe how polypeptides are broken down by **hydrolysis**.

☐ 25. Describe the **biuret test** for proteins. Explain the basis of the test and its result.

☐ 26. Identify where (in the cell) proteins are made and recognise the ways in which they can be modified after production. Distinguish between the **primary structure** of a protein and its **secondary structure**.

☐ 27. Recognise the two main types of secondary structure found in proteins: alpha-helix and beta-pleated sheet.

☐ 28. Explain what is meant by the **tertiary structure** of a protein and explain how it arises. Describe the relationship between the tertiary structure of a **globular protein** and its biological function.

☐ 29. With reference to examples (e.g. collagen and insulin or haemoglobin), distinguish between **globular** and **fibrous proteins**. Consider the structure, properties, and biological functions of the protein.

☐ 30. With reference to specific examples (e.g. collagen, insulin, haemoglobin), describe the role of different types of bonds in proteins: *hydrogen bonds, ionic bonds, disulfide bonds, hydrophobic interactions*.

☐ 31. Explain what is meant by protein **denaturation** and explain why it destroys the activity of proteins. Describe how different agents denature proteins.

☐ 32. Explain what is meant by the **quaternary structure** of a protein. In a named example (e.g. *haemoglobin, a globular protein*) describe how the quaternary structure arises and relate it to the protein's function.

☐ 33. Recognise the ways in which proteins can be classified:
- By their structure (e.g. *globular* or *fibrous*)
- By their functional role: structural, protective (role in immunity), as enzymes, as hormones, as respiratory pigments, in transport, contractile, in storage.

Enzymes (pages 79-86)

☐ 34. Define: **enzyme, catalyst, active site,** and **substrate**. Describe the general properties of enzymes and explain their role in regulating cell metabolism.

☐ 35. Explain the mechanism by which enzymes work as catalysts to bring about reactions in cells. Define: **enzyme-substrate complex, activation energy**.

☐ 36. Contrast the **induced fit** and the **lock and key** models of enzyme function, clearly explaining how they differ.

☐ 37. Describe ways in which the time course of an enzyme-catalysed reaction can be followed: by measuring the rate of product formation (e.g. catalase) or by measuring the rate of substrate use (e.g. amylase).

☐ 38. Distinguish between **coenzymes** and **cofactors**. Explain how cofactors enable an enzyme to work.

☐ 39. Distinguish **reversible** from **irreversible** inhibition. Describe the effects of **competitive** and **non-competitive inhibitors** on enzyme activity.

☐ 40. Describe the effect of the following factors on enzyme activity: substrate concentration, enzyme concentration, pH, temperature. Identify the **optimum conditions** for some named enzymes. Recognise that enzymes (being proteins) can be **denatured**.

☐ 41. Appreciate some of the commercial applications of microbial enzymes, e.g. pectinases and rennin in the food industry and proteases in biological detergents.

☐ 42. Distinguish between **intracellular** and **extracellular** enzymes and outline the basic procedure for the production of enzymes from microorganisms (including growth in culture and **downstream processing**).

☐ 43. Explain the advantages of enzyme isolation and immobilisation in industry. Identify necessary properties of enzymes used in industry (e.g. thermostability).

Textbooks

See the 'Textbook Reference Grid' on pages 8-9 for textbook page references relating to material in this topic.

Supplementary Texts

See pages 5-7 for additional details of these texts:

■ Adds, J. *et al.*, 2003. **Molecules and Cells**, (NelsonThornes), chpt. 1 & 3.

■ Adds, J., E. Larkcom, R. Miller, & R. Sutton, 1999. **Tools, Techniques and Assessment in Biology**, (NelsonThornes), pp. 9-12, 45-47, 74-76.

■ Chenn, P. 1997. **Microorganisms and Biotechnology**, (John Murray), Chpt. 7.

■ Clegg, C.J., 2002. **Microbes in Action**, (John Murray), 50-53 (enzyme technology).

■ Harwood, R., 2002. **Biochemistry**, (Cambridge University Press), entire text.

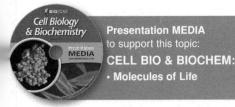

Presentation MEDIA
to support this topic:

CELL BIO & BIOCHEM:
• **Molecules of Life**

Periodicals

See page 7 for details of publishers of periodicals:

STUDENT'S REFERENCE
Water, ions, and carbon chemistry

■ **Water** Biol. Sci. Rev., 8(3) Jan. 1996, pp. 38-40. *The important properties and roles of water.*

■ **Of Hydrogen Bondage** Biol. Sci. Rev., 10(1) Sept. 1997, pp. 36-38. *The critical role of hydrogen bonding in biological molecules and water.*

■ **Why Life Chose Carbon** Biol. Sci. Rev., 10(2) November 1997, pp. 15-17. *The structure of the carbon atom and its role in biological chemistry.*

■ **D-Glucose: A Shapely, Stable Molecule** Biol. Sci. Rev., 16(2) Nov. 2003, pp. 15-20. *Properties of glucose: a small, six carbon sugar.*

■ **Designer Starches** Biol. Sci. Rev., 19(3) Feb. 2007, pp. 18-20. *The composition of starch, and an excellent account of its properties and functions.*

■ **Glucose & Glucose-Containing Carbohydrates** Biol. Sci. Rev., 19(1) Sept. 2006, pp. 12-15. *The structure of glucose and its polymers.*

■ **Stuck with Structures?** Biol. Sci. Rev., 15(2) Nov. 2002, pp. 28-29. *A guide to interpreting the structural formulae of common organic compounds.*

■ **Foetal Haemoglobin** Biol. Sci. Rev., 16(1) Sept. 2003, pp. 15-17. *The complex quaternary structure of haemoglobin molecules.*

■ **Making Proteins Work (I)** Biol. Sci. Rev., 15(1) Sept. 2002, pp. 22-25. *A synopsis of how a globular and a fibrous protein each become functional.*

■ **Making Proteins Work (II)** Biol. Sci. Rev., 15(2) Nov. 2002, pp. 24-27. *How carbohydrates are added to proteins to make them functional.*

■ **Exploring Proteins** Biol. Sci. Rev., 16(4) April 2004, pp. 32-36. *Understanding how proteins function as complexes within the cell. Chromatographic techniques are also described.*

■ **Universal Body Builder** New Scientist, 23 May 1998 (Inside Science). *The structure and role of collagen, the most common protein in animals.*

Enzymes and enzyme technology

■ **Enzymes** Biol. Sci. Rev., 15(1) Sept. 2002, pp. 2-5. *Enzymes as catalysts: how they work, models of enzyme function, and cofactors and inhibitors.*

■ **Enzymes: Fast and Flexible** Biol. Sci. Rev., 19(1) Sept. 2006, pp. 2-5. *The structure of enzymes and how they work so efficiently at relatively low temperatures.*

■ **Enzyme Technology** Biol. Sci. Rev., 12 (5) May 2000, pp. 26-27. *The range and importance of industrial enzymes in modern biotechnology.*

■ **Enzymes from Fungi** Biol. Sci. Rev., 13(3) Jan. 2001, pp. 19-21. *A discussion of the production and applications of fungal enzymes.*

Internet

See pages 10-11 for details of how to access **Bio Links** from our web site: **www.biozone.co.uk**. From Bio Links, access sites under the topics:

BIOTECHNOLOGY > Applications in Biotechnology > Industrial Biotechnology: • About industrial enzymes • Chapter 19: industrial microbiology • Discover enzymes ... *and others*
CELL BIOLOGY AND BIOCHEMISTRY:
• Cell & molecular biology online ... *and others*
> Biochemistry and Metabolic Pathways:
• Enzymes • Energy and enzymes • Energy, enzymes and catalysis problem set • Reactions and enzymes • The Biology project: Biochemistry

The Biochemical Nature of the Cell

The molecules that make up living things can be grouped into five classes: water, carbohydrates, lipids, proteins, and nucleic acids. Water is the main component of organisms and provides an environment in which metabolic reactions can occur. Water molecules attract each other, forming large numbers of hydrogen bonds. It is this feature that gives water many of its unique properties, including its low viscosity and its chemical behaviour as a **universal solvent**. Apart from water, most other substances in cells are compounds of carbon, hydrogen, oxygen, and nitrogen. The combination of carbon atoms with the atoms of other elements provides a huge variety of molecular structures. These are described on the following pages.

Important Properties of Water

Water is a liquid at room temperature and many substances dissolve in it. It is a medium inside cells and for aquatic life.

A lot of energy is required before water will change state so aquatic environments are thermally stable and sweating and transpiration cause rapid cooling.

Carbohydrates form the structural components of cells, they are important in energy storage, and they are involved in cellular recognition.

Proteins may be structural (e.g. collagen), catalytic (enzymes), or they may be involved in movement, message signalling, internal defence and transport, or storage.

Nucleotides and nucleic acids Nucleic acids encode information for the construction and functioning of an organism. The nucleotide, ATP, is the energy currency of the cell.

Lipids provide insulation and a concentrated source of energy. Phospholipids are a major component of cellular membranes.

Water is a major component of cells: many substances dissolve in it, metabolic reactions occur in it, and it provides support and turgor.

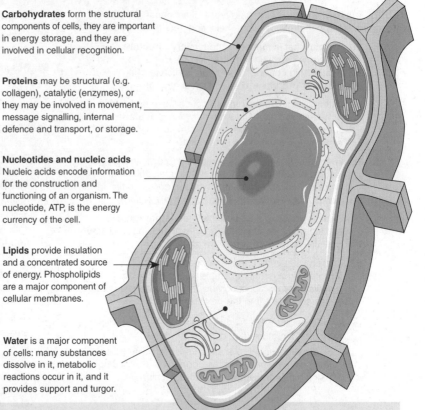

Ice is less dense than water. Consequently ice floats, insulating the underlying water and providing valuable habitat.

Water has a high surface tension and low viscosity. It forms droplets on surfaces and can flow freely through narrow vessels.

Water is colourless, with a high transmission of visible light, so light penetrates tissue and aquatic environments.

1. Explain the biological significance of each of the following physical properties of water:

   (a) Low viscosity: _____

   (b) Colourless and transparent: _____

   (c) Universal solvent: _____

   (d) Ice is less dense than water: _____

2. Identify the biologically important role of each of the following molecules:

   (a) Lipids: _____

   (b) Carbohydrates: _____

   (c) Proteins: _____

   (d) Nucleic acids: _____

A 1   **Related activities**: Organic Molecules, Water and Inorganic Ions

Organic Molecules

Organic molecules are those chemical compounds containing carbon that are found in living things. Specific groups of atoms, called **functional groups**, attach to a carbon-hydrogen core and confer specific chemical properties on the molecule. Some organic molecules in organisms are small and simple, containing only one or a few functional groups, while others are large complex assemblies called **macromolecules**. The macromolecules that make up living things can be grouped into four classes: carbohydrates, lipids, proteins, and nucleic acids. An understanding of the structure and function of these molecules is necessary to many branches of biology, especially biochemistry, physiology, and molecular genetics. The diagram below illustrates some of the common ways in which biological molecules are portrayed. Note that the **molecular formula** expresses the number of atoms in a molecule, but does not convey its structure; this is indicated by the **structural formula**. Molecules can also be represented as **models**. A ball and stick model shows the arrangement and type of bonds while a space filling model gives a more realistic appearance of a molecule, showing how close the atoms really are.

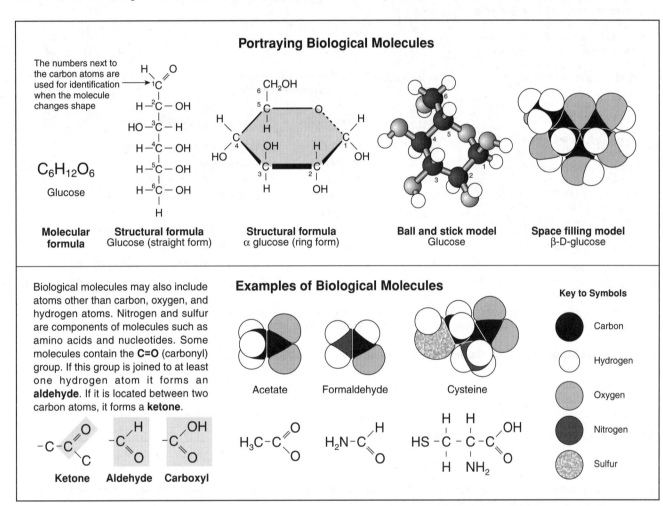

Portraying Biological Molecules

The numbers next to the carbon atoms are used for identification when the molecule changes shape

$C_6H_{12}O_6$
Glucose

| **Molecular formula** | **Structural formula** Glucose (straight form) | **Structural formula** α glucose (ring form) | **Ball and stick model** Glucose | **Space filling model** β-D-glucose |

Examples of Biological Molecules

Biological molecules may also include atoms other than carbon, oxygen, and hydrogen atoms. Nitrogen and sulfur are components of molecules such as amino acids and nucleotides. Some molecules contain the **C=O** (carbonyl) group. If this group is joined to at least one hydrogen atom it forms an **aldehyde**. If it is located between two carbon atoms, it forms a **ketone**.

Ketone **Aldehyde** **Carboxyl**

Acetate   Formaldehyde   Cysteine

Key to Symbols

- Carbon
- Hydrogen
- Oxygen
- Nitrogen
- Sulfur

1. Identify the three main elements comprising the structure of organic molecules: _____

2. Name two other elements that are also frequently part of organic molecules: _____

3. State how many covalent bonds a carbon atom can form with neighbouring atoms: _____

4. Distinguish between molecular and structural formulae for a given molecule: _____

_____

_____

5. Describe what is meant by a functional group: _____

_____

6. Classify formaldehyde according to the position of the C=O group: _____

7. Identify a functional group always present in amino acids: _____

8. Identify the significance of cysteine in its formation of disulfide bonds: _____

_____

Related activities: Biochemical Nature of the Cell, Amino Acids, Proteins

Biological Molecules

A 1

Water and Inorganic Ions

The Earth's crust contains approximately 100 elements but only 16 are essential for life (see the table of inorganic ions below). Of the smaller molecules making up living things water is the most abundant typically making up about two-thirds of any organism's body. Water has a simple molecular structure and the molecule is very polar, with ends that exhibit partial positive and negative charges. Water molecules have a weak attraction for each other and inorganic ions, forming weak hydrogen bonds.

Water and Inorganic Ions

Water provides an environment in which metabolic reactions can happen. Water takes part in, and is a common product of, many reactions. The most important feature of the chemical behaviour of water is its **dipole** nature. It has a small positive charge on each of the two hydrogens and a small negative charge on the oxygen.

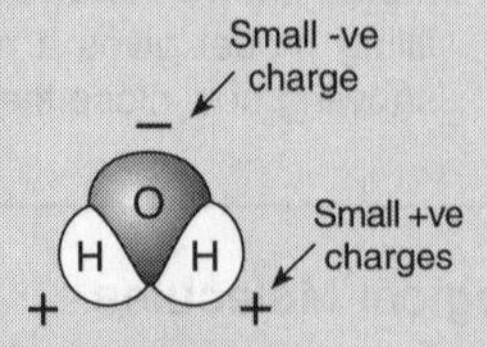

Small -ve charge

Small +ve charges

Water molecule
Formula: H_2O

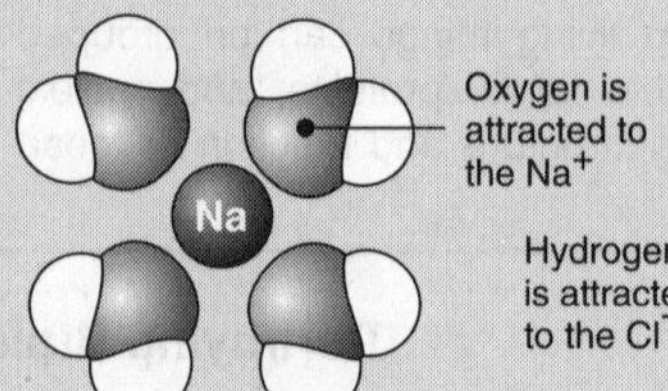

Oxygen is attracted to the Na^+

Water surrounding a positive ion (Na^+)

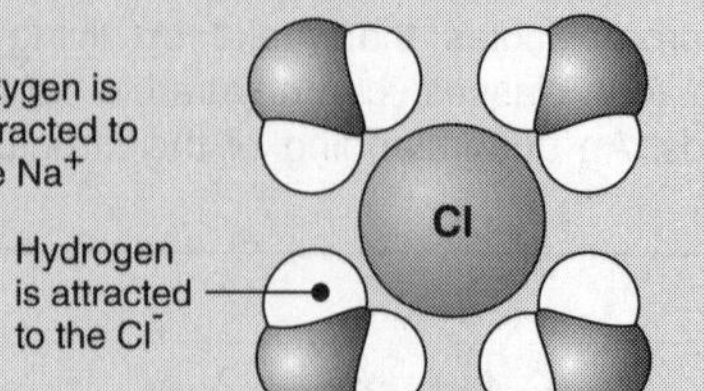

Hydrogen is attracted to the Cl^-

Water surrounding a negative ion (Cl^-)

Inorganic ions are important for the structure and metabolism of all living organisms. An ion is simply an atom (or group of atoms) that has gained or lost one or more electrons. Many of these ions are soluble in water. Some of the inorganic ions required by organisms and their biological roles are listed in the table on the right.

Ion	Name	Biological role
Ca^{2+}	Calcium	Component of bones and teeth
Mg^{2+}	Magnesium	Component of chlorophyll
Fe^{2+}	Iron (II)	Component of hemoglobin
NO_3^-	Nitrate	Component of amino acids
PO_4^{3-}	Phosphate	Component of nucleotides
Na^+	Sodium	Involved in the transmission of nerve impulses
K^+	Potassium	Involved in controlling plant water balance
Cl^-	Chloride	Involved in the removal of water from urine

1. On the diagram above, showing a positive and a negative ion surrounded by water molecules, draw the positive and negative charges on the water molecules (as shown in the example provided).

2. Explain the importance of the **dipole nature** of water molecules to the chemistry of life: _____

_____

_____

3. Distinguish between inorganic and organic compounds: _____

_____

4. Describe a role of the following elements in living organisms (plants, animals and prokaryotes) and a consequence of the element being deficient in an organism's diet:

(a) Calcium: _____

_____

(b) Iron: _____

_____

(c) Phosphorus: _____

_____

(d) Sodium: _____

_____

(e) Sulfur: _____

_____

(f) Nitrogen: _____

_____

Related activities: Biochemical Nature of the Cell, Organic Molecules

Carbohydrates

Carbohydrates are a family of organic molecules made up of carbon, hydrogen, and oxygen atoms with the general formula $(CH_2O)_x$. The most common arrangements found in sugars are hexose (6 sided) or pentose (5 sided) rings. Simple sugars, or monosaccharides, may join together to form compound sugars (disaccharides and polysaccharides), releasing water in the process (**condensation**). Compound sugars can be broken down into their constituent monosaccharides by the opposite reaction (**hydrolysis**). Sugars play a central role in cells, providing energy and, in some cells, contributing to support. They are the major component of most plants (60-90% of the dry weight) and are used by humans as a cheap food source, and a source of fuel, housing, and clothing. In all carbohydrates, the structure is closely related to their functional properties (below).

Monosaccharides

Monosaccharides are used as a primary energy source for fuelling cell metabolism. They are **single-sugar** molecules and include glucose (grape sugar and blood sugar) and fructose (honey and fruit juices). The commonly occurring monosaccharides contain between three and seven carbon atoms in their carbon chains and, of these, the 6C hexose sugars occur most frequently. All monosaccharides are classified as **reducing** sugars (i.e. they can participate in reduction reactions).

Single sugars (monosaccharides)

Triose

C-C-C

e.g. glyceraldehyde

Pentose

e.g. ribose, deoxyribose

Hexose

e.g. glucose, fructose, galactose

Disaccharides

Disaccharides are **double-sugar** molecules and are used as energy sources and as building blocks for larger molecules. The type of disaccharide formed depends on the monomers involved and whether they are in their α- or β- form. Only a few disaccharides (e.g. lactose) are classified as reducing sugars.

Sucrose = α-glucose + β-fructose (simple sugar found in plant sap)
Maltose = α-glucose + α-glucose (a product of starch hydrolysis)
Lactose = β-glucose + β-galactose (milk sugar)
Cellobiose = β-glucose + β-glucose (from cellulose hydrolysis)

Double sugars (disaccharides)

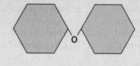

Examples
sucrose,
lactose,
maltose,
cellobiose

Polysaccharides

Cellulose: Cellulose is a structural material in plants and is made up of unbranched chains of β-**glucose** molecules held together by **1, 4 glycosidic links**. As many as 10 000 glucose molecules may be linked together to form a straight chain. Parallel chains become cross-linked with hydrogen bonds and form bundles of 60-70 molecules called microfibrils. Cellulose microfibrils are very strong and are a major component of the structural components of plants, such as the cell wall (photo, right).

Starch: Starch is also a polymer of glucose, but it is made up of long chains of α-**glucose** molecules linked together. It contains a mixture of 25-30% **amylose** (unbranched chains linked by α-1, 4 glycosidic bonds) and 70-75% **amylopectin** (branched chains with α-1, 6 glycosidic bonds every 24-30 glucose units). Starch is an energy storage molecule in plants and is found concentrated in insoluble **starch granules** within plant cells (see photo, right). Starch can be easily hydrolysed by enzymes to soluble sugars when required.

Glycogen: Glycogen, like starch, is a branched polysaccharide. It is chemically similar to amylopectin, being composed of α-**glucose** molecules, but there are more α-1,6 glycosidic links mixed with α-1,4 links. This makes it more highly branched and water-soluble than starch. Glycogen is a storage compound in animal tissues and is found mainly in **liver** and **muscle** cells (photo, right). It is readily hydrolysed by enzymes to form glucose.

Chitin: Chitin is a tough modified polysaccharide made up of chains of β-**glucose** molecules. It is chemically similar to cellulose but each glucose has an amine group (–NH_2) attached. After cellulose, chitin is the second most abundant carbohydrate. It is found in the cell walls of fungi and is the main component of the **exoskeleton** of insects (right) and other arthropods.

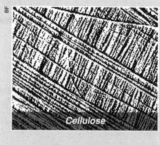

Cellulose

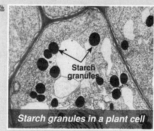

Starch granules

Starch granules in a plant cell

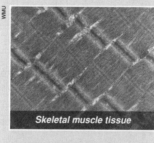

Skeletal muscle tissue

Chitinous insect exoskeleton

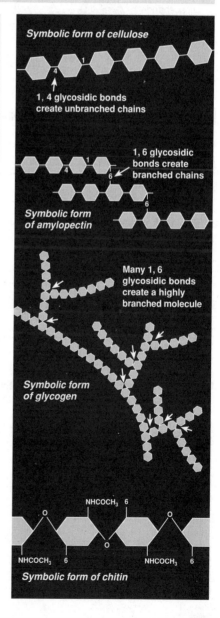

Symbolic form of cellulose

1, 4 glycosidic bonds create unbranched chains

1, 6 glycosidic bonds create branched chains

Symbolic form of amylopectin

Many 1, 6 glycosidic bonds create a highly branched molecule

Symbolic form of glycogen

NHCOCH₃

Symbolic form of chitin

Biological Molecules

Related activities: Organic Molecules, Biochemical Tests

A 2

Isomerism

Compounds with the same chemical formula (same types and numbers of atoms) may differ in the arrangement of their atoms. Such variations in the arrangement of atoms in molecules are called **isomers**. In **structural isomers** (such as fructose and glucose, and the α and β glucose, right), the atoms are linked in different sequences. **Optical isomers** are identical in every way but are mirror images of each other.

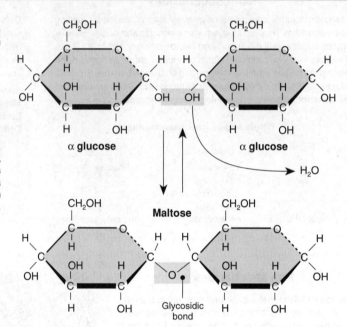

α glucose   β glucose

Condensation and Hydrolysis Reactions

Monosaccharides can combine to form compound sugars in what is called a **condensation** reaction. Compound sugars can be broken down by **hydrolysis** to simple monosaccharides.

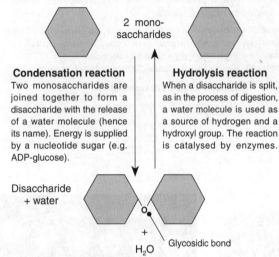

2 mono-saccharides

Condensation reaction
Two monosaccharides are joined together to form a disaccharide with the release of a water molecule (hence its name). Energy is supplied by a nucleotide sugar (e.g. ADP-glucose).

Hydrolysis reaction
When a disaccharide is split, as in the process of digestion, a water molecule is used as a source of hydrogen and a hydroxyl group. The reaction is catalysed by enzymes.

Disaccharide + water

+ H_2O Glycosidic bond

α glucose   α glucose

H_2O

Maltose

Glycosidic bond

1. Distinguish between structural and optical isomers in carbohydrates, describing examples of each:

_____

_____

_____

2. Explain how the isomeric structure of a carbohydrate may affect its chemical behaviour: _____

_____

_____

3. Explain briefly how compound sugars are formed and broken down: _____

_____

_____

4. Discuss the structural differences between the polysaccharides cellulose, starch, and glycogen, explaining how the differences in structure contribute to the functional properties of the molecule:

_____

_____

_____

_____

_____

_____

_____

Lipids

Lipids are a group of organic compounds with an oily, greasy, or waxy consistency. They are relatively insoluble in water and tend to be water-repelling (e.g. cuticle on leaf surfaces). Lipids are important biological fuels, some are hormones, and some serve as structural components in plasma membranes. Proteins and carbohydrates may be converted into fats by enzymes and stored within cells of adipose tissue. During times of plenty, this store is increased, to be used during times of food shortage.

Neutral Fats and Oils

The most abundant lipids in living things are **neutral fats**. They make up the fats and oils found in plants and animals. Fats are an economical way to store fuel reserves, since they yield more than twice as much energy as the same quantity of carbohydrate. Neutral fats are composed of a glycerol molecule attached to one (monoglyceride), two (diglyceride) or three (triglyceride) fatty acids. The fatty acid chains may be saturated or unsaturated (see below). **Waxes** are similar in structure to fats and oils, but they are formed with a complex alcohol instead of glycerol.

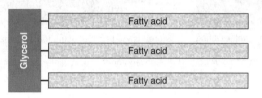

Triglyceride: an example of a neutral fat

Condensation

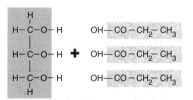

Glycerol   Fatty acids

Triglycerides form when glycerol bonds with three fatty acids. Glycerol is an alcohol containing three carbons. Each of these carbons is bonded to a hydroxyl (-OH) group.

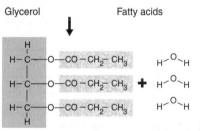

Triglyceride   Water

When glycerol bonds with the fatty acid, an **ester bond** is formed and water is released. Three separate condensation reactions are involved in producing a triglyceride.

Saturated and Unsaturated Fatty Acids

Fatty acids are a major component of neutral fats and phospholipids. About 30 different kinds are found in animal lipids. **Saturated fatty acids** contain the maximum number of hydrogen atoms. **Unsaturated fatty acids** contain some carbon atoms that are double-bonded with each other and are not fully saturated with hydrogens. Lipids containing a high proportion of saturated fatty acids tend to be solids at room temperature (e.g. butter). Lipids with a high proportion of unsaturated fatty acids are oils and tend to be liquid at room temperature. This is because the unsaturation causes kinks in the straight chains so that the fatty acids do not pack closely together. Regardless of their degree of saturation, fatty acids yield a large amount of energy when oxidised.

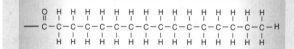

Formula (above) and molecular model (below) for **palmitic acid** (a saturated fatty acid)

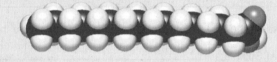

Formula (above) and molecular model (below) for **linoleic acid** (an unsaturated fatty acid)

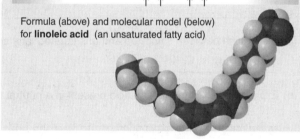

Phospholipids

Phospholipids are the main component of cellular membranes. They consist of a glycerol attached to two fatty acid chains and a phosphate (PO_4^{3-}) group. The phosphate end of the molecule is attracted to water (it is hydrophilic) while the fatty acid end is repelled (hydrophobic). The hydrophobic ends turn inwards in the membrane to form a **phospholipid bilayer**.

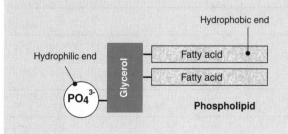

Steroids

Although steroids are classified as lipids, their structure is quite different from that of other lipids. Steroids have a basic structure of three rings made of 6 carbon atoms each and a fourth ring containing 5 carbon atoms. Examples of steroids include the male and female sex hormones (testosterone and oestrogen), and the hormones cortisol and aldosterone. Cholesterol, while not a steroid itself, is a sterol lipid and is a precursor to several steroid hormones.

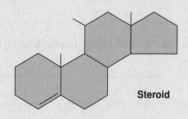

Steroid

Biological Molecules

Related activities: Organic Molecules, The Structure of Membranes, Biochemical Tests

A 2

Important Biological Functions of Lipids

Lipids are concentrated sources of energy and provide fuel for aerobic respiration.

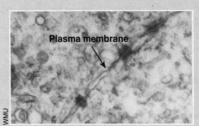

Plasma membrane

Phospholipids form the structural framework of cellular membranes.

Waxes and oils secreted on to surfaces provide waterproofing in plants and animals.

Fat absorbs shocks. Organs that are prone to bumps and shocks (e.g. kidneys) are cushioned with a relatively thick layer of fat.

Lipids are a source of metabolic water. During respiration, stored lipids are metabolised for energy, producing water and carbon dioxide.

Stored lipids provide insulation. Increased body fat reduces the amount of heat lost to the environment (e.g. in winter or in water).

1. Outline the key **chemical** difference between a phospholipid and a triglyceride: _____

_____

_____

2. Name the type of fatty acids found in lipids that form the following at room temperature:

(a) Solid fats: _____ (b) Oils: _____

3. Relate the structure of phospholipids to their chemical properties and their functional role in cellular membranes:

_____

_____

4 (a) Distinguish between saturated and unsaturated fatty acids. _____

_____

(b) Explain how the type of fatty acid present in a neutral fat or phospholipid is related to that molecule's properties:

_____

_____

(c) Suggest how the cell membrane structure of an Arctic fish might differ from that of tropical fish species:

_____

_____

5. Identify two examples of steroids. For each example, describe its physiological function:

(a) _____

(b) _____

6. Explain how fats can provide an animal with:

(a) Energy: _____

(b) Water: _____

(c) Insulation: _____

Amino Acids

Amino acids are the basic units from which proteins are made. Plants can manufacture all the amino acids they require from simpler molecules, but animals must obtain a certain number of ready-made amino acids (called **essential amino acids**) from their diet. All other amino acids can be constructed from these essential amino acids. The order in which the different amino acids are linked together to form proteins is controlled by genes on the chromosomes.

Structure of Amino Acids

There are over 150 amino acids found in cells, but only 20 occur commonly in proteins. The remaining, non-protein amino acids have specialised roles as intermediates in metabolic reactions, or as neurotransmitters and hormones. All amino acids have a common structure (see right). The only difference between the different types lies with the 'R' group in the general formula. This group is variable, which means that it is different in each kind of amino acid.

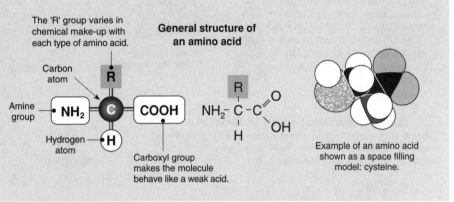

The 'R' group varies in chemical make-up with each type of amino acid.

General structure of an amino acid

Carbon atom — R

Amine group — NH$_2$ — C — COOH

Hydrogen atom — H

Carboxyl group makes the molecule behave like a weak acid.

NH$_2$— C — C $\lessgtr$ O / OH, H

Example of an amino acid shown as a space filling model: cysteine.

Properties of Amino Acids

Three examples of amino acids with different chemical properties are shown right, with their specific 'R' groups outlined. The 'R' groups can have quite diverse chemical properties.

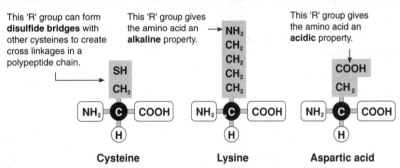

This 'R' group can form **disulfide bridges** with other cysteines to create cross linkages in a polypeptide chain.

SH / CH$_2$

NH$_2$ — C — COOH, H

Cysteine

This 'R' group gives the amino acid an **alkaline** property.

NH$_2$ / CH$_2$ / CH$_2$ / CH$_2$ / CH$_2$

NH$_2$ — C — COOH, H

Lysine

This 'R' group gives the amino acid an **acidic** property.

COOH / CH$_2$

NH$_2$ — C — COOH, H

Aspartic acid

A polypeptide chain

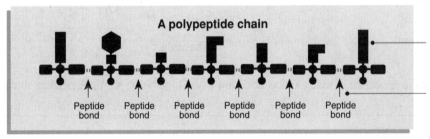

Peptide bond (×6)

The order of amino acids in a protein is directed by the order of nucleotides in DNA and mRNA.

Peptide bonds link amino acids together in long polymers called polypeptide chains. These may form part or all of a protein.

The amino acids are linked together by peptide bonds to form long chains of up to several hundred amino acids (called polypeptide chains). These chains may be functional units (complete by themselves) or they may need to be joined to other polypeptide chains before they can carry out their function. In humans, not all amino acids can be manufactured by our body: ten must be taken in with our diet (eight in adults). These are the 'essential amino acids' (indicated by the symbol ◆ on the right).

Amino acids occurring in proteins		
Alanine	Glycine	Proline
Arginine ◆	Histidine ◆	Serine
Asparagine	Isoleucine ◆	Threonine ◆
Aspartic acid	Leucine ◆	Tryptophan ◆
Cysteine	Lysine ◆	Tyrosine
Glutamine	Methionine ◆	Valine ◆
Glutamic acid	Phenylalanine ◆	

Biological Molecules

1. Describe the biological function of amino acids: _____

_____

_____

2. Describe what makes each of the 20 amino acids found in proteins unique: _____

_____

_____

Related activities: Organic Molecules, Proteins, Translation

A 2

Optical Isomers of Amino Acids

All amino acids, apart from the simplest one (glycine) show optical isomerism. The two forms that these optical isomers can take relate to the arrangement of the four bonding sites on the carbon atom. This can result in two different arrangements as shown on the diagrams on the right. With a very few minor exceptions, only the **L-forms** are found in living organisms.

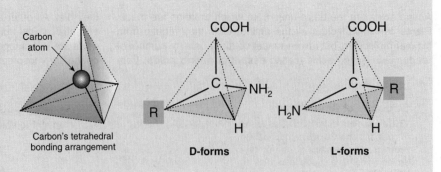

Carbon atom

Carbon's tetrahedral bonding arrangement

D-forms   **L-forms**

Condensation and Hydrolysis Reactions

Amino acids can combine to form peptide chains in what is called a **condensation** reaction. Peptide chains can be broken down by **hydrolysis** to simple amino acids.

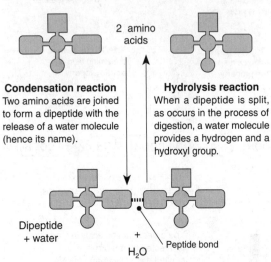

2 amino acids

Condensation reaction
Two amino acids are joined to form a dipeptide with the release of a water molecule (hence its name).

Hydrolysis reaction
When a dipeptide is split, as occurs in the process of digestion, a water molecule provides a hydrogen and a hydroxyl group.

Dipeptide + water

$+$
H_2O

Peptide bond

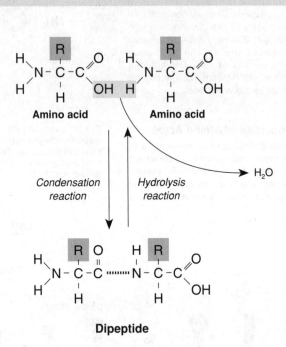

Amino acid   Amino acid

H_2O

Condensation reaction   *Hydrolysis reaction*

Dipeptide

3. Describe the process that determines the sequence in which amino acids are linked together to form polypeptide chains:

_____

_____

4. Explain what is meant by **essential amino acids**: _____

_____

_____

5. Describe briefly the process of the **condensation** reaction for amino acids: _____

_____

_____

_____

_____

6. Describe briefly the process of the **hydrolysis** reaction for amino acids: _____

_____

_____

_____

7. Name the optical isomeric form that occurs in nearly all amino acids in living things: _____

Proteins

The precise folding up of a protein into its **tertiary structure** creates a three dimensional arrangement of the active 'R' groups. The way each 'R' group faces with respect to the others gives the protein its unique chemical properties. If a protein loses this precise structure (denaturation), it is usually unable to carry out its biological function. Proteins are often classified on the basis of structure (globular vs fibrous). Some of the properties used for the basis of structural classification are outlined over the page.

Primary Structure - 1° *(amino acid sequence)*
Strings of hundreds of amino acids link together with peptide bonds to form molecules called polypeptide chains. There are 20 different kinds of amino acids that can be linked together in a vast number of different combinations. This sequence is called the **primary structure**. It is the arrangement of attraction and repulsion points in the amino acid chain that determines the higher levels of organisation in the protein and its biological function.

Secondary Structure - 2° *(α-helix or ß pleated sheet)*
Polypeptides become folded in various ways, referred to as the secondary (2°) structure. The most common types of 2° structures are a coiled α-**helix** and a β-**pleated sheet**. Secondary structures are maintained with hydrogen bonds between neighbouring CO and NH groups. H-bonds, although individually weak, provide considerable strength when there are a large number of them. The example, right, shows the two main types of secondary structure. In both, the **'R' side groups** (not shown) project out from the structure. Most globular proteins contain regions of α-helices together with β-sheets. Keratin (a fibrous protein) is composed almost entirely of α-helices. Fibroin (silk protein), is another fibrous protein, almost entirely in β-sheet form.

Tertiary Structure - 3° *(folding)*
Every protein has a precise structure formed by the folding of the secondary structure into a complex shape called the **tertiary structure**. The protein folds up because various points on the secondary structure are attracted to one another. The strongest links are caused by bonding between neighbouring **cysteine** amino acids which form disulfide bridges. Other interactions that are involved in folding include weak ionic and hydrogen bonds as well as hydrophobic interactions.

Quaternary Structure - 4°
Some proteins (such as enzymes) are complete and functional with a tertiary structure only. However, many complex proteins exist as aggregations of polypeptide chains. The arrangement of the polypeptide chains into a functional protein is termed the **quaternary structure**. The example (right) shows a molecule of haemoglobin, a globular protein composed of 4 polypeptide sub-units joined together; two identical **beta chains** and two identical **alpha chains**. Each has a haem (iron containing) group at the centre of the chain, which binds oxygen. Proteins containing non-protein material are **conjugated proteins**. The non-protein part is the **prosthetic group**.

Denaturation of Proteins
Denaturation refers to the loss of the three-dimensional structure (and usually also the biological function) of a protein. Denaturation is often, although not always, permanent. It results from an alteration of the bonds that maintain the secondary and tertiary structure of the protein, even though the sequence of amino acids remains unchanged. Agents that cause denaturation are:

- **Strong acids and alkalis**: Disrupt ionic bonds and result in coagulation of the protein. Long exposure also breaks down the primary structure of the protein.
- **Heavy metals**: May disrupt ionic bonds, form strong bonds with the carboxyl groups of the R groups, and reduce protein charge. The general effect is to cause the precipitation of the protein.
- **Heat and radiation** (e.g. UV): Cause disruption of the bonds in the protein through increased energy provided to the atoms.
- **Detergents and solvents**: Form bonds with the non-polar groups in the protein, thereby disrupting hydrogen bonding.

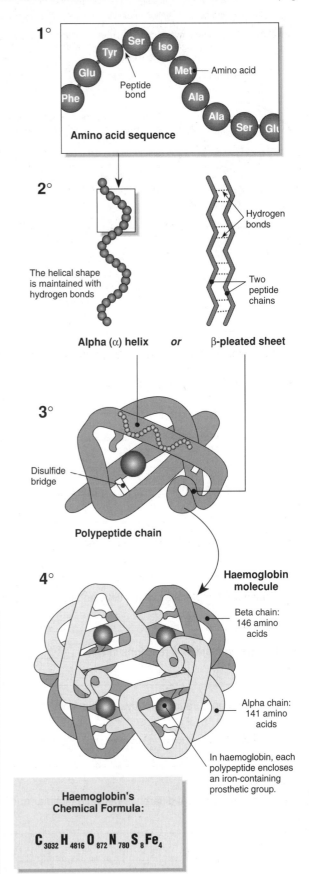

1°
Tyr — Ser — Iso
Glu
Phe — Peptide bond — Met — Amino acid
Ala
Ala — Ser — Glu

Amino acid sequence

2°

The helical shape is maintained with hydrogen bonds

Hydrogen bonds

Two peptide chains

Alpha (α) helix *or* **β-pleated sheet**

3°

Disulfide bridge

Polypeptide chain

4°

Haemoglobin molecule

Beta chain: 146 amino acids

Alpha chain: 141 amino acids

In haemoglobin, each polypeptide encloses an iron-containing prosthetic group.

Haemoglobin's Chemical Formula:

$$C_{3032}H_{4816}O_{872}N_{780}S_8Fe_4$$

Biological Molecules

Related activities: Organic Molecules, Amino Acids, Enzymes, Biochemical Tests, Modification of Proteins

RA 2

Structural Classification of Proteins

Fibrous Proteins

Properties • Water insoluble
• Very tough physically; may be supple or stretchy
• Parallel polypeptide chains in long fibres or sheets

Function • Structural role in cells and organisms *e.g. collagen found in connective tissue, cartilage, bones, tendons, and blood vessel walls.*
• Contractile *e.g. myosin, actin*

Globular Proteins

Properties • Easily water soluble
• Tertiary structure critical to function
• Polypeptide chains folded into a spherical shape

Function • Catalytic *e.g. enzymes*
• Regulatory *e.g. hormones (insulin)*
• Transport *e.g. haemoglobin*
• Protective *e.g. antibodies*

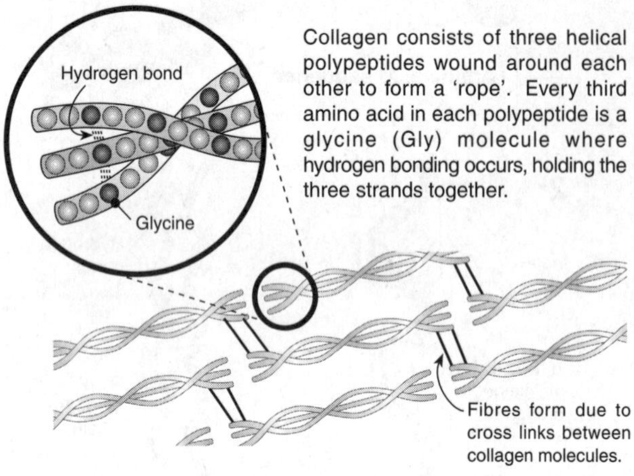

Collagen consists of three helical polypeptides wound around each other to form a 'rope'. Every third amino acid in each polypeptide is a glycine (Gly) molecule where hydrogen bonding occurs, holding the three strands together.

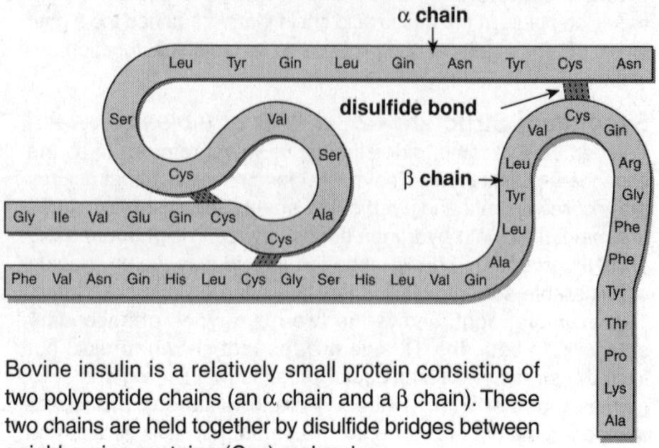

Hydrogen bond

Glycine

Fibres form due to cross links between collagen molecules.

α chain

disulfide bond

β chain

Leu Tyr Gin Leu Gin Asn Tyr Cys Asn
Ser Val Cys
Cys Ser Gin
Gly Ile Val Glu Gin Cys Ala
Cys
Phe Val Asn Gin His Leu Cys Gly Ser His Leu Val Gin
Val
Leu
Tyr
Leu
Ala
Arg
Gly
Phe
Phe
Tyr
Thr
Pro
Lys
Ala

Bovine insulin is a relatively small protein consisting of two polypeptide chains (an α chain and a β chain). These two chains are held together by disulfide bridges between neighbouring cysteine (Cys) molecules.

1. Giving examples, briefly explain how proteins are involved in the following functional roles:

   (a) Structural tissues of the body: _____

   _____

   (b) Regulating body processes: _____

   _____

   (c) Contractile elements: _____

   _____

   (d) Immunological response to pathogens: _____

   _____

   (e) Transporting molecules within cells and in the bloodstream: _____

   _____

   (f) Catalysing metabolic reactions in cells: _____

   _____

2. Explain how denaturation destroys protein function: _____

   _____

   _____

3. Describe one structural difference between globular and fibrous proteins: _____

   _____

   _____

4. Determine the total number of amino acids in the α and β chains of the insulin molecule illustrated above:

   (a) α chain: _____ (b) β chain: _____

Modification of Proteins

Proteins may be modified after they have been produced by ribosomes. After they pass into the interior of rough endoplasmic reticulum, some proteins may have carbohydrates added to them to form **glycoproteins**. Proteins may be further altered in the Golgi apparatus. The **Golgi apparatus** functions principally as a system for processing, sorting, and modifying proteins. Proteins that are to be secreted from the cell are synthesised by

ribosomes on the rough endoplasmic reticulum and transported to the Golgi apparatus. At this stage, carbohydrates may be removed or added in a step-wise process. Some of the possible functions of glycoproteins are illustrated below. Other proteins may have fatty acids added to them to form **lipoproteins**. These modified proteins transport lipids in the plasma between various organs in the body (e.g. gut, liver, and adipose tissue).

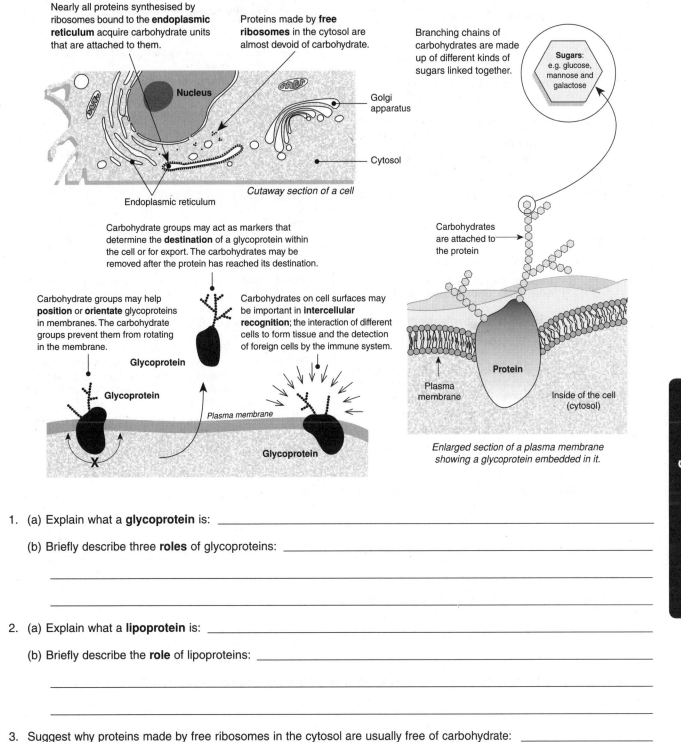

Nearly all proteins synthesised by ribosomes bound to the **endoplasmic reticulum** acquire carbohydrate units that are attached to them.

Proteins made by **free ribosomes** in the cytosol are almost devoid of carbohydrate.

Branching chains of carbohydrates are made up of different kinds of sugars linked together.

Sugars: e.g. glucose, mannose and galactose

Cutaway section of a cell

Carbohydrate groups may act as markers that determine the **destination** of a glycoprotein within the cell or for export. The carbohydrates may be removed after the protein has reached its destination.

Carbohydrate groups may help **position** or **orientate** glycoproteins in membranes. The carbohydrate groups prevent them from rotating in the membrane.

Carbohydrates on cell surfaces may be important in **intercellular recognition**; the interaction of different cells to form tissue and the detection of foreign cells by the immune system.

Carbohydrates are attached to the protein

Enlarged section of a plasma membrane showing a glycoprotein embedded in it.

1. (a) Explain what a **glycoprotein** is: _____

   (b) Briefly describe three **roles** of glycoproteins: _____

   _____

   _____

2. (a) Explain what a **lipoprotein** is: _____

   (b) Briefly describe the **role** of lipoproteins: _____

   _____

   _____

3. Suggest why proteins made by free ribosomes in the cytosol are usually free of carbohydrate: _____

   _____

4. Suggest why the orientation of a protein in the plasma membrane might be important: _____

   _____

   _____

Related activities: Proteins, The Structure of Membranes, The Role of Proteins in Cells

A 2

Biological Molecules

Biochemical Tests

Biochemical tests are used to detect the presence of nutrients such as lipids, proteins, and carbohydrates (sugar and starch) in various foods. These simple tests are useful for detecting nutrients when large quantities are present. A more accurate technique by which to separate a mixture of compounds involves chromatography. Chromatography is used when only a small sample is available or when you wish to distinguish between nutrients. Simple biochemical food tests will show whether sugar is present, whereas chromatography will distinguish between the different types of sugars (e.g. fructose or glucose).

Paper Chromatography

Set Up and Procedure

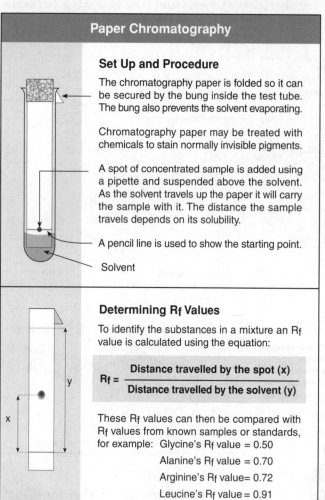

The chromatography paper is folded so it can be secured by the bung inside the test tube. The bung also prevents the solvent evaporating.

Chromatography paper may be treated with chemicals to stain normally invisible pigments.

A spot of concentrated sample is added using a pipette and suspended above the solvent. As the solvent travels up the paper it will carry the sample with it. The distance the sample travels depends on its solubility.

A pencil line is used to show the starting point.

Solvent

Determining Rf Values

To identify the substances in a mixture an R_f value is calculated using the equation:

$$R_f = \frac{\text{Distance travelled by the spot (x)}}{\text{Distance travelled by the solvent (y)}}$$

These R_f values can then be compared with R_f values from known samples or standards, for example: Glycine's R_f value = 0.50

Alanine's R_f value = 0.70

Arginine's R_f value= 0.72

Leucine's R_f value = 0.91

Simple Food Tests

Proteins: The Biuret Test

Reagent:	Biuret solution.
Procedure:	A sample is added to biuret solution and gently heated.
Positive result:	Solution turns from blue to lilac.

Starch: The Iodine Test

Reagent:	Iodine.
Procedure:	Iodine solution is added to the sample.
Positive result:	Blue-black staining occurs.

Lipids: The Emulsion Test

Reagent:	Ethanol.
Procedure:	The sample is shaken with ethanol. After settling, the liquid portion is distilled and mixed with water.
Positive result:	The solution turns into a cloudy-white emulsion of suspended lipid molecules.

Sugars: The Benedict's Test

Reagent:	Benedict's solution.
Procedure:	*Non reducing sugars*: The sample is boiled with dilute hydrochloric acid, then cooled and neutralised. A test for reducing sugars is then performed. *Reducing sugar*: Benedict's solution is added, and the sample is placed in a water bath.
Positive result:	Solution turns from blue to orange.

1. Calculate the Rf value for the example given above (show your working): _____

_____

2. Explain why the Rf value of a substance is always less than 1: _____

_____

3. Discuss when it is appropriate to use chromatography instead of a simple food test: _____

_____

_____

4. Predict what would happen if a sample was immersed in the chromatography solvent, instead of suspended above it:

_____

_____

5. With reference to their Rf values, rank the four amino acids (listed above) in terms of their solubility: _____

_____

6. Outline why lipids must be mixed in ethanol before they will form an emulsion in water: _____

_____

Enzymes

Most enzymes are proteins. They are capable of catalysing (speeding up) biochemical reactions and are therefore called biological **catalysts**. Enzymes act on one or more compounds (called the **substrate**). They may break a single substrate molecule down into simpler substances, or join two or more substrate molecules chemically together. The enzyme itself is unchanged in the reaction; its presence merely allows the reaction to take place more rapidly. When the substrate attains the required **activation energy** to enable it to change into the product, there is a 50% chance that it will proceed forward to form the product, otherwise it reverts back to a stable form of the reactant again. The part of the enzyme's surface into which the substrate is bound and undergoes reaction is known as the **active site**. This is made of different parts of polypeptide chain folded in a specific shape so they are closer together. For some enzymes, the complexity of the binding sites can be very precise, allowing only a single kind of substrate to bind to it. Some other enzymes have lower **specificity** and will accept a wide range of substrates of the same general type (e.g. lipases break up any fatty acid chain length of lipid). This is because the enzyme is specific for the type of chemical bond involved and not an exact substrate.

Enzyme Structure

The model on the right is of an enzyme called *Ribonuclease S*, that breaks up RNA molecules. It is a typical enzyme, being a globular protein and composed of up to several hundred atoms. The darkly shaded areas are called **active sites** and make up the **cleft**; the region into which the substrate molecule(s) are drawn. The correct positioning of these sites is critical for the catalytic reaction to occur. The substrate (RNA in this case) is drawn into the cleft by the active sites. By doing so, it puts the substrate molecule under stress, causing the reaction to proceed more readily.

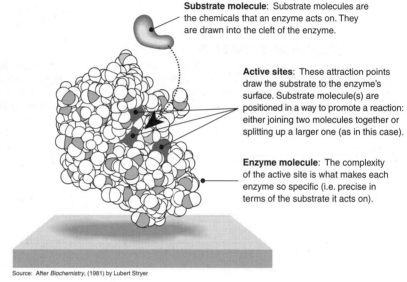

Substrate molecule: Substrate molecules are the chemicals that an enzyme acts on. They are drawn into the cleft of the enzyme.

Active sites: These attraction points draw the substrate to the enzyme's surface. Substrate molecule(s) are positioned in a way to promote a reaction: either joining two molecules together or splitting up a larger one (as in this case).

Enzyme molecule: The complexity of the active site is what makes each enzyme so specific (i.e. precise in terms of the substrate it acts on).

Source: After *Biochemistry*, (1981) by Lubert Stryer

How Enzymes Work

The **lock and key** model proposed earlier this century suggested that the substrate was simply drawn into a closely matching cleft on the enzyme molecule. More recent studies have revealed that the process more likely involves an **induced fit** (see diagram on the right), where the enzyme or the reactants change their shape slightly. The reactants become bound to enzymes by weak chemical bonds. This binding can weaken bonds within the reactants themselves, allowing the reaction to proceed more readily.

① Enzyme   **Substrate**   **②**   **③**   **Products**

The presence of an enzyme simply makes it easier for a reaction to take place. All **catalysts** speed up reactions by influencing the stability of bonds in the reactants. They may also provide an alternative reaction pathway, thus lowering the activation energy needed for a reaction to take place (see the graph below).

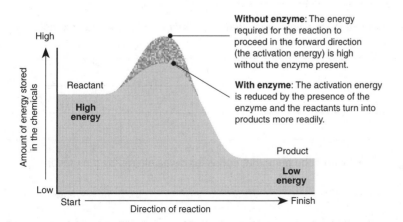

Without enzyme: The energy required for the reaction to proceed in the forward direction (the activation energy) is high without the enzyme present.

With enzyme: The activation energy is reduced by the presence of the enzyme and the reactants turn into products more readily.

Induced Fit Model

An enzyme fits to its substrate somewhat like a lock and key. The shape of the enzyme changes when the substrate fits into the cleft (called the **induced fit**):

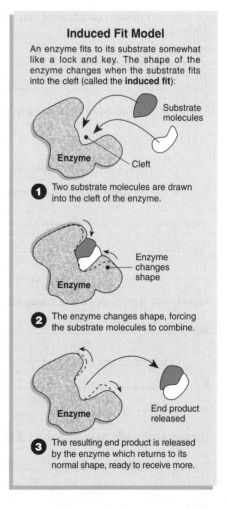

Substrate molecules

Enzyme   Cleft

① Two substrate molecules are drawn into the cleft of the enzyme.

Enzyme   Enzyme changes shape

② The enzyme changes shape, forcing the substrate molecules to combine.

Enzyme   End product released

③ The resulting end product is released by the enzyme which returns to its normal shape, ready to receive more.

Related activities: Enzyme Reaction Rates
Web links: How Enzymes Work

RA 2

Biological Molecules

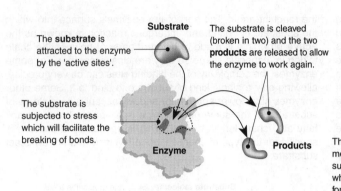

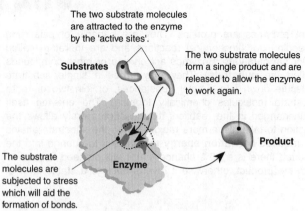

The **substrate** is attracted to the enzyme by the 'active sites'.

Substrate

The substrate is cleaved (broken in two) and the two **products** are released to allow the enzyme to work again.

The substrate is subjected to stress which will facilitate the breaking of bonds.

Enzyme

Products

The two substrate molecules are attracted to the enzyme by the 'active sites'.

Substrates

The two substrate molecules form a single product and are released to allow the enzyme to work again.

The substrate molecules are subjected to stress which will aid the formation of bonds.

Enzyme

Product

Catabolic reactions

Some enzymes can cause a single substrate molecule to be drawn into the active site. Chemical bonds are broken, causing the substrate molecule to break apart to become two separate molecules. **Examples**: *digestion, cellular respiration.*

Anabolic reactions

Some enzymes can cause two substrate molecules to be drawn into the active site. Chemical bonds are formed, causing the two substrate molecules to form bonds and become a single molecule. **Examples**: *protein synthesis, photosynthesis.*

1. Give a brief account of enzymes as **biological catalysts**, including reference to the role of the **active site**:

_____

_____

_____

_____

_____

2. Distinguish between **catabolism** and **anabolism**, giving an example of each and identifying each reaction as **endergonic** or **exergonic**:

_____

_____

3. Outline the key features of the '**lock and key**' model of enzyme action: _____

_____

_____

4. Outline the '**induced fit**' model of enzyme action, explaining how it differs from the lock and key model:

_____

_____

_____

5. Identify two factors that could cause enzyme denaturation, explaining how they exert their effects (see the next activity):

(a) _____

_____

(b) _____

_____

6. Explain what might happen to the functioning of an enzyme if the gene that codes for it was altered by a mutation:

_____

Industrial Production of Enzymes

Humans have used enzymes for thousands of years in food and beverage production, but the use of enzymes in industry is a comparatively recent development. Many industries now rely on the large scale production of microbial enzymes to catalyse a range of reactions. In the absence of enzymes, these reactions sometimes require high temperatures or pressures to proceed. Industrial enzymes must be relatively robust against denaturation and capable of maintaining activity over a wide temperature and pH range. Enzyme technology involves the production, isolation, purification, and application of useful enzymes. Commercial enzymes are produced from three main sources: plants, animals, and microorganisms (mainly bacteria and fungi). Most enzymes used in industrial processes today are microbial in origin and are produced in industrial-scale microbial fermentations using liquid or semi-solid growth media. Note that the term **fermentation**, when used in reference to industrial microbiology, applies to both aerobic and anaerobic microbial growth in **bioreactors**. Generalised plans for the industrial production of both extracellular and intracellular enzymes are illustrated below. Note that the isolation of intracellular enzymes (below, right) is more complex because the cells must first be disrupted to release the enzymes within.

1 **Growth of the microorganisms**:
A closed fermenter system is an enclosed, **sterile system** containing culture broth in which the microorganisms (bacteria or fungi) are grown until the extracellular products (or the cells themselves) have accumulated for harvesting. Conditions in the fermenter vessel are closely monitored and carefully regulated so that the conditions for maximal microbial growth are optimised.

The model (right) shows a cutaway section of a cylindrical fermentation chamber, typical of that used for continuous microbial cultures.

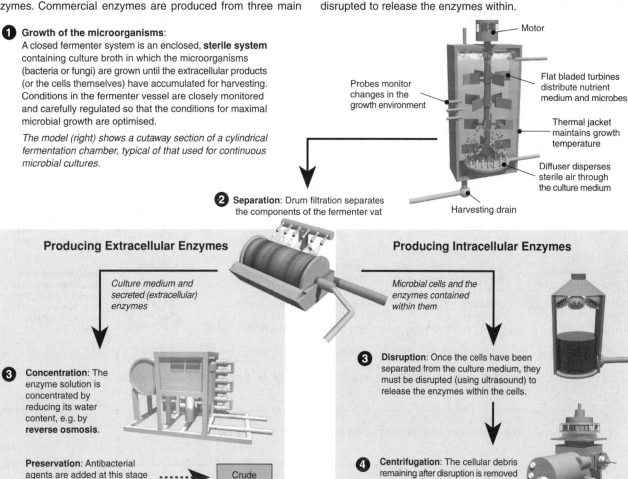

Motor

Flat bladed turbines distribute nutrient medium and microbes

Probes monitor changes in the growth environment

Thermal jacket maintains growth temperature

Diffuser disperses sterile air through the culture medium

2 **Separation**: Drum filtration separates the components of the fermenter vat

Harvesting drain

Producing Extracellular Enzymes

Culture medium and secreted (extracellular) enzymes

3 **Concentration**: The enzyme solution is concentrated by reducing its water content, e.g. by **reverse osmosis**.

Preservation: Antibacterial agents are added at this stage to prevent contamination.

3a → Crude product

4 **Purification and processing**: The crude enzyme product may be dried to produce a powder or further purified by precipitation, crystallisation or **adsorption** (e.g. on to clays).

Producing Intracellular Enzymes

Microbial cells and the enzymes contained within them

3 **Disruption**: Once the cells have been separated from the culture medium, they must be disrupted (using ultrasound) to release the enzymes within the cells.

4 **Centrifugation**: The cellular debris remaining after disruption is removed by centrifugation (or filtration).

5 **Purification and processing**: Initial purification involves precipitation with ammonium sulfate or organic solvents. Further purification occurs by **ion exchange chromatography** or gel electrophoresis.

Biological Molecules

1. The industrial production of microbial enzymes varies according to the enzyme involved and its desired end use. Compare the two flow diagrams, for intracellular and extracellular enzymes, above:

   (a) Explain the main way in which the two production methods differ: _____

   _____

   (b) Suggest the reason for this difference: _____

   _____

2. Enzyme solutions can be packaged and used as crude extracts without further purification (**3a**). State one benefit of this:

   _____

Related activities: Enzymes, Putting Enzymes to Use, Applications of Enzymes

A 3

Putting Enzymes to Use

Depending on the way in which the desired end-product is produced, enzymes may be used as crude whole cell preparations or as cell-free enzyme extracts. Whole cell preparations are cost effective, and appropriate when the processes involved in production of the end product are complex, as in waste treatment and the production of semi-synthetic antibiotics. Cell free enzyme extracts are more expensive to produce, but can be a more efficient option overall. To reduce costs and improve the efficiency of product production, enzymes are sometimes immobilised within a matrix of some kind and the reactants are passed over them. The various methods by which enzymes are put to work are compared in the diagram below.

Industrial enzymes

	Advantages	Disadvantages	Methods of Enzyme Immobilisation
Cell free enzyme extract Enzyme is used in solution	There is generally a high level of enzyme activity when the enzymes are free in solution.	The enzyme may be washed away after use. The end-product is not enzyme free and may require purification.	**Micro-encapsulation** The enzyme is held within a membrane, or within alginate or polyacrylamide capsules. Partially permeable membrane
Immobilised enzyme Enzyme is held in an inert material	The enzymes can be used repeatedly and recovered easily (this reduces costs). The enzyme-free end-product is easily harvested. The enzymes are more stable due to the protection of a matrix. The life of some enzymes, e.g. proteases, is extended by immobilisation.	The entrapment process may reduce the enzyme activity (more enzyme will be needed). Some methods offering high stability (e.g. covalent bonding) are harder to achieve. Immobilisation can be costly.	**Lattice entrapment** Enzyme is trapped in a gel lattice, e.g. silica gel. The substrate and reaction products diffuse in and out of the matrix. Enzymes trapped in a gel lattice. **Covalent attachment** Enzyme is covalently bonded to a solid surface e.g. collagen or a synthetic polymer. Enzyme Substrate, e.g. collagen
Whole cell preparation Whole cells may be immobilised	Useful for enzymes that are unstable or inactivated when outside the cell. Useful for complex processes utilising more than one intracellular enzyme.	Less expensive and more rapid than first producing a pure enzyme extract. Some of the substrate is used for microbial growth, so the process is less efficient overall.	**Direct cross-linking** Glutaraldehyde is used to cross-link the enzymes. They then precipitate out and are immobilised without support. Glutaraldehyde

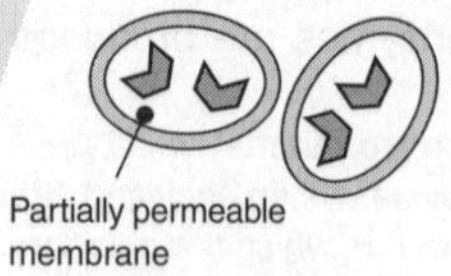

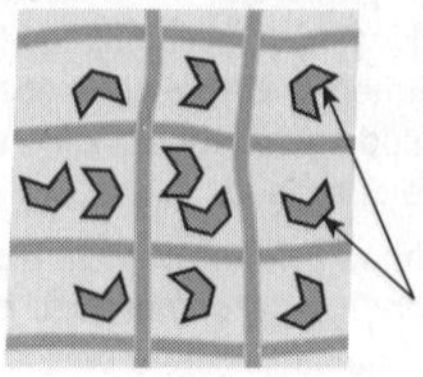

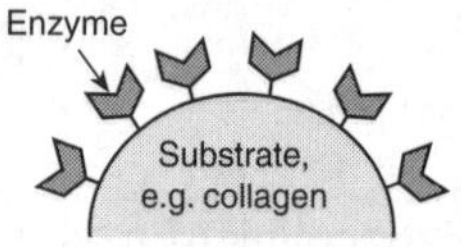

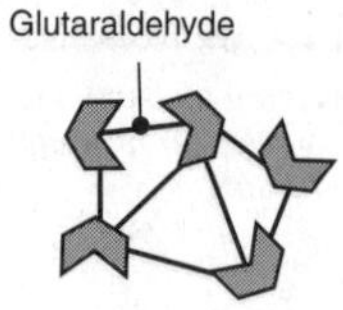

1. (a) Explain one benefit of using a cell free enzyme extract to produce a high-value end-product:

_____

(b) Identify one factor that might be important when deciding not to use a cell free extract:

_____

2. (a) Describe two benefits of using immobilised enzymes (rather than enzymes in solution) for industrial processes:

_____

_____

(b) Describe a disadvantage associated with the use of immobilised enzymes: _____

_____

(c) Describe a factor that would affect the rate of end-product harvest from immobilised enzymes:

_____

3. The useful life of protease enzymes is extended when they are immobilised (as opposed to being in solution). Using what you know of enzyme structure, explain why immobilisation has this effect in this case:

_____

_____

4. Suggest why immobilisation would reduce the activity of certain enzymes: _____

_____

_____

Related activities: Applications of Enzymes

Applications of Enzymes

Microbes are ideal organisms for the industrial production of enzymes because of their high productivity, ease of culture in industrial fermenters, and the ease with which they can be genetically modified to produce particular products. In addition, because there is an enormous diversity in microbial metabolism, the variety of enzymes available for exploitation is very large. Some of the microorganisms involved in industrial fermentations, and their enzymes and their applications are described below.

Enzymes are used in various stages of **cheese production**, e.g. chymosin from GE microbes now replaces the rennin previously obtained from calves.

In **beer brewing**, **proteases** (from bacteria) are added to prevent cloudiness. Amyloglucosidases are used to produce low calorie beers.

Citric acid is used in **jam production** and is synthesised by a mutant strain of the fungus *Aspergillus niger*, which produces the enzyme citrate synthase.

Biological detergents use **proteases**, **lipases**, and **amylases** extracted from fungi and thermophilic bacteria to break down organic material in stains.

Fungal ligninases are used in **pulp and paper industries** to remove lignin from wood pulp and treat wood waste.

Medical treatment of blood clots employs protease enzymes such as streptokinase from *Streptomyces* spp.

Some of the many applications of microbial enzymes in medicine, industry, and food manufacture.

In **soft centred chocolates**, **invertase** from yeast breaks down the solid filling to produce the soft centre.

Bacterial proteases are used to break down the wheat protein (gluten) in flour, to produce low gluten breads.

Cellulases and pectinases are used in the manufacture of packaged (as opposed to fresh) fruit juices to speed juice extraction and prevent cloudiness.

The silver residues from old photographs can be reclaimed for reuse when proteases are employed to digest the gelatin of old films.

The lactase from bacteria is used to convert lactose to glucose and galactose in the production of low-lactose and lactose free milk products.

Tanning industries now use proteases from *Bacillus subtilis* instead of toxic chemicals, such as sulfide pastes, to remove hairs and soften hides.

The enzyme, **glucose oxidase**, from *Aspergillus niger*, is immobilised in a semi-conducting silicon chip. It catalyses the conversion of glucose (from the blood sample) to gluconic acid.

Hydrogen ions from the gluconic acid cause a movement of electrons in the silicon, which is detected by a transducer. The strength of the electric current is directly proportional to the blood glucose concentration.

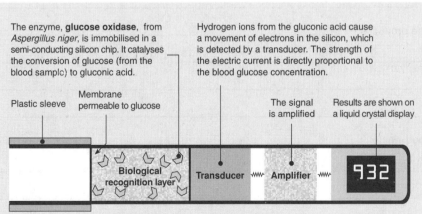

Plastic sleeve

Membrane permeable to glucose

Biological recognition layer

Transducer — Amplifier

The signal is amplified

Results are shown on a liquid crystal display

932

Biosensors are electronic monitoring devices that use biological material to detect the presence or concentration of a particular substance. Enzymes are ideally suited for use in biosensors because of their specificity and sensitivity. This example illustrates how **glucose oxidase** from the fungus *Aspergillus niger* is used in a biosensor to measure blood glucose level in diabetics.

Biological Molecules

Related activities: Putting Enzymes to Use

RA 3

1. Identify two probable consequences of the absence of enzymes from a chemical reaction that normally uses them:

   (a) _____

   (b) _____

2. Identify three properties of microbial enzymes that make them highly suitable as industrial catalysts. For each, explain why the property is important:

   (a) _____

   _____

   (b) _____

   _____

   (c) _____

   _____

3. Choose one example from those described in the diagram on the previous page and, in more detail, identify:

   (a) The enzyme and its specific microbial source: _____

   _____

   (b) The application of the enzyme in industry and the specific reaction it catalyses: _____

   _____

   _____

   _____

4. (a) Outline the basic principle of enzyme-based biosensors: _____

   _____

   (b) Suggest how a biosensor could be used to monitor blood alcohol level: _____

   _____

   _____

   _____

5. For each of the examples described below, suggest how the use of microbial enzymes has improved the efficiency, cost effectiveness, and/or safety of processing compared with traditional methods:

   (a) Use of microbial proteases to treat hides in the tanning industry: _____

   _____

   _____

   _____

   (b) Use of microbial chymosin in cheese production: _____

   _____

   _____

   _____

   (c) Use of fungal ligninases to treat wood waste: _____

   _____

   _____

   _____

Cell Structure

AQA-A	AQA-B	SNAB	Edexcel	OCR
Complete: 1-19, 21-24, 27	Complete: 1-25, 27	Complete: 1-11, 14-19	Complete: 1-19, 21-26	Complete: 1-11, 14-19, 21-26

Learning Objectives

☐ 1. Compile your own glossary from the **KEY WORDS** displayed in **bold type** in the learning objectives below.

Cell Theory *(page 89)*

☐ 2. Define the **cell theory**. Recognise the contribution of microscopy to the development of cell theory and our present knowledge of cell structure.

Features of Cells *(pages 90-99, 101-02, 107-08, 117)*

☐ 3. Define a **cell** and recognise it as the basic unit of living things. In simple terms, describe the main features of a cell (**plasma membrane**, **cytoplasm**, **organelles**). Identify the features that characterise living things and explain why cells are considered to be living entities.

☐ 4. Use different units of measurement (mm, µm, nm) to express cell sizes and to describe a range of cell sizes.

☐ 5. Contrast the generalised structure of **prokaryote** and **eukaryote** cells and provide examples of each type. If required, describe the specific features of protoctistan and fungal cells.

☐ 6. Recognise viruses as **non-cellular** minimal particles, specialised as intracellular parasites. Describe the basic structure of a virus identifying the features that distinguish them as non-cellular. Appreciate how our view of viruses is changing with the discovery of larger (bacterial-sized) viruses with relatively large genomes.

☐ 7. Describe the structure of a **bacterial cell** and its inclusions, as illustrated by a named example (e.g. *E. coli*). Identify the **bacterial cell wall** and the structures associated with it (**flagella**, pili), the **bacterial chromosome** and **plasmids**, the **plasma membrane**, glycogen granules, and lipid droplets. Recognise these structures in electron micrographs of bacterial cells and identify which of them are unique to prokaryotes.

☐ 8. Describe and interpret drawings and photographs of typical **plant** and **animal cells** (e.g. leaf palisade cell and liver cell) as seen using light microscopy.

☐ 9. Describe and interpret drawings and photographs of typical plant and animal cells (e.g. leaf palisade cell and liver cell) as seen using electron microscopy. Identify the following:
  • **nucleus**, **nuclear envelope**, **nucleolus**
  • **mitochondria**, **chloroplasts** (if present),
  • rough/smooth **endoplasmic reticulum**, **ribosomes**,
  • **plasma membrane**, **cell wall** (if present)
  • **Golgi apparatus**, **lysosomes**, **vacuoles** (if present),
  • **cytoplasm**, **cytoskeleton** (of **microtubules**), **centrioles**, **cilia** (if present)
  Outline the role of each of these cell components.

☐ 10. Identify which of the cellular structures above would be visible under light microscopy, transmission electron microscopy, and scanning electron microscopy.

☐ 11. List the differences between plant and animal cells, noting relative size and shape, and presence or absence of particular structures and organelles.

Separating Cellular Components *(page 100)*

☐ 12. Describe **cell fractionation** (differential centrifugation), explaining how it is achieved through homogenisation of a sample followed by **ultracentrifugation**.

☐ 13. Identify the components of the four fractions normally obtained from differential centrifugation: the **nuclear fraction**, the **mitochondrial fraction**, the **microsomal fraction**, and the **soluble fraction**. Explain the role of speed of centrifugation in separating these fractions.

Microscopy *(pages 103-106)*

☐ 14. Distinguish between **optical** and **electron microscopes**, outlining the structure of each. With respect to light and electron microscopy, explain and distinguish between: **magnification** and **resolution**.

☐ 15. With respect to the basic microscope structure and operation, and type of image produced, distinguish between TEM (**transmission electron microscopy**) and SEM (**scanning electron microscopy**). Recognise electron microscopy as an important tool in investigating cell structure and function.

☐ 16. Distinguish between **compound** and **stereo light microscopes**. Identify the situations in which these different microscopes would be used.

☐ 17. Familiarise yourself with the use of a light microscope. Demonstrate an ability to correctly use a microscope to locate material and focus images.

☐ 18. Demonstrate an ability to correctly use a microscope to locate material and focus images. Identify the steps required for preparing a **temporary mount** for viewing with a compound light microscope.

☐ 19. Demonstrate an ability to use simple **staining techniques** to show specific features of cells. Understand why **stains** are useful in the preparation of specimens. Demonstrate a knowledge of some specific stains, identifying the purpose of each named example.

Tissues and Organs *(pages 109-114)*

Also see the examples of tissues and organs described in the topics Gas Exchange and Transport Systems.

☐ 20. Summarise how the **zygote** (fertilised egg) undergoes division to produce an adult. Define the terms: **cellular differentiation**, **specialised cell**. Comment on the basic similarity of cells early in development.

□ 21. Recognise the hierarchy of organisation in multicellular organisms: molecular, organelle, cell, **tissue**, **organ**. With respect to the function of specialised cells, outline the benefits of being multicellular.

□ 22. EXTENSION: Appreciate that each step in the hierarchy of biological order is associated with the emergence of properties not present at simpler levels of organisation. Explain how these **emergent properties** (e.g. metabolism) result from the interactions of component parts.

□ 23. With reference to specific examples (e.g. epithelial tissues, blood, xylem, and/or phloem), explain how cells are organised into **tissues**.

□ 24. Identify and describe the structural adaptations and function of some specialised cells in humans, e.g. blood cells, liver cells, or intestinal epithelial cells. For each cell type, identify the tissue where it occurs.

□ 25. Identify and describe the structural adaptations and function of some of the specialised cell types found in angiosperm plant tissues, including the leaf palisade (mesophyll) cell. Categorise these into cells associated with the stem, roots, leaves, or reproductive structures.

□ 26. Describe examples of tissues (e.g. xylem) and organs (e.g. leaves) in plants, identifying their functional role in each case. Illustrate your examples and calculate the linear magnification of your drawing in each case.

□ 27. Describe examples of tissues (e.g. blood, epithelium) and organs (e.g. blood vessels, lung, small intestine, liver) in animals, identifying their functional role in each case. Illustrate your examples and calculate the linear magnification of your drawing in each case.

 See the 'Textbook Reference Grid' on pages 8-9 for textbook page references relating to material in this topic.

Supplementary Texts

See pages 5-7 for additional details of these texts:

■ Adds, J., *et al.,* 2003. **Molecules and Cells**, (NelsonThornes), chpt. 4.

■ Adds, J., *et al.,* 1999. **Tools, Techniques and Assessment in Biology**, (NelsonThornes), pp. 13-26.

■ Clegg, C.J., 1998. **Mammals: Structure and Function**, (John Murray), pp. 4-7, 10-11.

See page 7 for details of publishers of periodicals:

STUDENT'S REFERENCE
Cell structure and organelles

■ **Bacteria** National Geographic, 184(2) August 1993, pp. 36-61. *Structure and diversity of bacteria: the most abundant and useful organisms on Earth.*

■ **Cellular Factories** New Scientist, 23 November 1996 (Inside Science). *The structure and role of organelles in plant and animal cells.*

■ **Control Centre** New Scientist, 17 July 1999 (Inside Science). *The nucleus: the organisation of DNA in eukaryotic cells, how genes code for proteins, and the function of ribosomes and RNA.*

■ **The Beat Goes On: Cilia and Flagella** Biol. Sci. Rev., 18(4) April 2006, pp. 2-6. *The structure and function of cilia and flagella and their important roles in biological systems.*

■ **Border Control** New Scientist, 15 July 2000 (Inside Science). *The role of the plasma membrane in cell function: membrane structure and transport, and the role of membrane receptors.*

■ **Lysosomes: The Cell's Recycling Centres** Biol. Sci. Rev., 17(2) Nov. 2004, pp. 21-23. *This account covers the nature and role of lysosomes: small membrane-bound organelles found in all eukaryotic cells.*

■ **Lysosomes and their Versatile and Potentially Fatal Membranes** Biol. Sci. Rev., 17(3) Feb. 2005, pp. 14-16. *This article discusses the critical importance of the lysosome membrane and considers the effects of lysosomes in disease.*

■ **No Visible Means of Support** Biol. Sci. Rev., 8(4) March 1996, pp. 6-10. *The role of the cell cytoskeleton in plant & animal growth and support.*

■ **Water Channels in the Cell Membrane** Biol. Sci. Rev., 9(2) November 1996, pp. 18-22. *The role of proteins in membrane transport, including mechanisms involved in physiological processes.*

■ **The Force** New Scientist, 26 February 2000, pp. 30-35. *An account of mitochondria and how they can exercise control over reproduction.*

Microscopy

■ **The Power behind an Electron Microscopist** Biol. Sci. Rev., 18(1) Sept. 2005, pp. 16-20. *The principles of electron microscopy: how to recognise structures, magnification and scale, and the importance of 3D in interpreting cellular features.*

■ **Transmission Electron Microscopy** Biol. Sci. Rev., 13(2) November 2000, pp. 32-35. *An excellent account of the techniques and applications of TEM. Includes an excellent diagram comparing features of TEM and light microscopy.*

■ **X-Ray Microscopy** Biol. Sci. Rev., 14(2) November 2001, pp. 38-40. *A short account of the technique and application of X-ray microscopy. Its advantages over EM are explained, particularly with respect to specimen preparation.*

■ **Scanning Electron Microscopy** Biol. Sci. Rev., 13(3) January 2001, pp. 6-9. *An excellent account of the techniques and applications of SEM. Includes details of specimen preparation and recent advancements in the technology.*

■ **Light Microscopy** Biol. Sci. Rev., 13(1) Sept. 2000, pp. 36-38. *An excellent account of the basis and various techniques of light microscopy.*

■ **Size Does Matter** Biol. Sci. Rev., 17 (3) Feb. 2005, pp. 10-13. *Measuring the size of organisms and calculating magnification and scale.*

Cell differentiation and tissues

■ **Connective Tissues** Biol. Sci. Rev., 8(1) September 1995, pp. 27-30. *The varied and numerous roles of connective tissues in the body (includes histological details).*

■ **Surface Epithelial Tissue** Biol. Sci. Rev., 7(1) September 1994, pp. 23-27. *The structure and function epithelial tissues (excellent).*

■ **Basement Membranes** Biol. Sci. Rev., 13(4) March 2001, pp. 36-39. *The structure, function, and diversity of basement membranes (including their pivotal role in the structure of tissues).*

TEACHER'S REFERENCE

■ **Are Viruses Alive?** Scientific American, Dec. 2004, pp. 77-81. *Although viruses challenge our concept of what "living" means, they are vital members of the web of life. An excellent account.*

■ **Secret Language of Cells** New Scientist, 16 Feb 2002 (Inside Science). *An article about* communication between cells, including the role of gap junctions, hormones, ligands and receptors. It leads onto a discussion of how cell division is disrupted in cancer and following thalidomide use.

■ **Cells by Design** New Scientist, 3 June 1989, pp. 24-26. *Artificially produced cells have been made by simulating the plasma membrane and enclosing materials within.*

■ **The Birth of Complex Cells** Scientific American, April 1996, pp. 38-45. *An excellent article covering the evolution of cell structure and the functions of various organelles.*

■ **The Architecture of Life** Scientific American, January 1998, pp. 30-39. *The cytoskeleton within cells and the universal patterns of design.*

■ **Budding Vesicles in Living Cells** Scientific American, March 1996, pp. 50-55. *The function of the Golgi apparatus in cell transport.*

See pages 10-11 for details of how to access **Bio Links** from our web site: **www.biozone.co.uk**. From Bio Links, access sites under the topics:

GENERAL BIOLOGY ONLINE RESOURCES > Online Textbooks and Lecture Notes: • S-Cool! A level biology revision guide Learn. co.uk ... *and others* > **General online biology resources:** • Access Excellence • Biology I: Interactive animations • Ken's bio-web resources ... *and others* > **Glossaries:** • Cellular biology: Glossary of terms • Kimball's biology glossary

CELL BIOLOGY AND BIOCHEMISTRY: • Cell and molecular biology online • Cell structure and function web links • MIT biology hypertextbook > **Microscopy:** • A guide to microscopy and microanalysis • Biological applications of electron and light microscopy • Histology • Microscopy UK • Scanning Electron Microscope ... *and others* > **Cell Structure and Transport:** • Animal cells • CELLS alive! • Cell breakage and fractionation - Part 1 • Nanoworld • Talksaver cell biology • The virtual cell • Techniques of cell fractionation

Presentation MEDIA to support this topic:

CELL BIO & BIOCHEM:
• **Introduction to Cells**
• **Cell Structure**

Cell Biology & Biochemistry

The Cell Theory

The idea that all living things are composed of cells developed over many years and is strongly linked to the invention and refinement of the microscope. Early microscopes in the 1600s (such as Leeuwenhoek's below) opened up a whole new field of biology; the study of cell biology and microorganisms. The cell theory is a fundamental idea of biology.

Early Microscopes

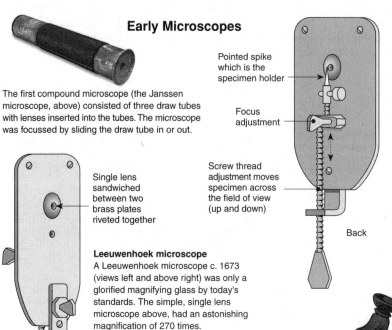

The first compound microscope (the Janssen microscope, above) consisted of three draw tubes with lenses inserted into the tubes. The microscope was focussed by sliding the draw tube in or out.

Single lens sandwiched between two brass plates riveted together

Pointed spike which is the specimen holder

Focus adjustment

Screw thread adjustment moves specimen across the field of view (up and down)

Back

Leeuwenhoek microscope
A Leeuwenhoek microscope c. 1673 (views left and above right) was only a glorified magnifying glass by today's standards. The simple, single lens microscope above, had an astonishing magnification of 270 times.

Front

Microscope

Lamp

Mirror

Robert Hooke c. 1665
Hooke was fascinated by microscopy, and in his book *Micrographia* (1665) he described the use of the compound microscope that he had devised (**right**). He was the first to coin the name cell after he observed the angular spaces that he saw in a thin section of cork.

Milestones in Cell Biology

1500s	Convex lenses with a magnification greater than x5 became available.
1595	Zacharias Janssen of Holland has been credited with the first compound microscope (more than one lens).
Early 1600s	First compound microscopes used in Europe (used two convex lenses to make objects look larger). Suffered badly from colour distortion; an effect called 'spherical aberration'.
1632-1723	**Antoni van Leeuwenhoek** of Holland produced over 500 single lens microscopes, discovering bacteria, human blood cells, spermatozoa, and protozoa. Friend of Robert Hooke.
1661	**Marcello Malpighi** used lenses to study insects. Discovered capillaries and may have described cells in writing of 'globules' and 'saccules'.
1662	**Robert Hooke** of England used the term 'cell' in describing the microscopic structure of cork. He believed that the cell walls were the important part of otherwise empty structures. Published *Micrographia* in 1665.
1672	**Nehemlah Grew** wrote the first of two well-illustrated books on the microscopic anatomy of plants.
1838-1839	Botanist **Matthias Schleiden** and zoologist **Theodor Schwann** proposed the cell theory based on their observations of plant and animal cells.
1855	**Rudolph Virchow** extended the cell theory by stating that "new cells are formed only by the division of previously existing cells".
1880	**August Weismann** added to Virchow's idea by pointing out that "all the cells living today can trace their ancestry back to ancient times", thus making the link between cell theory and evolution.

The Cell Theory

The idea that cells are fundamental units of life is part of the cell theory. The basic principles of the theory (as developed by early biologists) are:

▶ All living things are composed of cells and cell products.

▶ New cells are formed only by the division of preexisting cells.

▶ The cell contains inherited information (genes) that are used as instructions for growth, functioning, and development.

▶ The cell is the functioning unit of life; the chemical reactions of life take place within cells.

1. Briefly describe the impact the invention of microscopes has had on biology: _____

_____

_____

2. Before the development of the cell theory, it was commonly believed that living organisms could arise by spontaneous generation. Explain what this term means and why it has been discredited as a theory:

_____

_____

_____

Cell Structure

Related activities: Optical Microscopes, Electron Microscopes

A 2

Characteristics of Life

With each step in the hierarchy of biological order, new properties emerge that were not present at simpler levels of organisation. Life itself is associated with numerous **emergent properties**, including **metabolism** and growth. The cell is the site of life; it is the functioning unit structure from which living organisms are made. Viruses and cells are profoundly different. Viruses are non-cellular, lack the complex structures found in cells, and show only some of the properties we associate with living things. The traditional view of viruses is as a minimal particle, although the identification in 2004 of a new family of viruses, called mimiviruses, is forcing a rethink of this conservative view. Note the different scale to which the examples below are drawn. Refer to the scale bars for the comparative sizes (1000 nm = 1 µm = 0.001 mm).

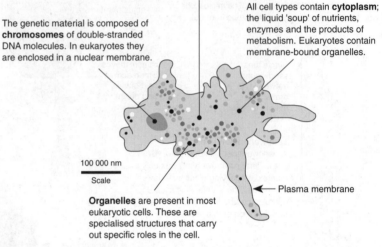

Although some viruses may contain an **enzyme**, it is incapable of working until it is inside a host cell's cytoplasm.

Single or double stranded molecule of **RNA** or **DNA**.

A **protein coat** surrounds the viral genetic material and enzyme (if present). There is no cellular membrane.

50 nm
Scale

No metabolism: The absence of cytoplasm means that a virus can not carry out any chemical reactions on its own; it is dependent upon parasitising a cell and using the cell's own machinery.

Metabolism: The total of all the chemical reactions occurring in the cell. Many take place in the cytoplasm.

The genetic material is composed of **chromosomes** of double-stranded DNA molecules. In eukaryotes they are enclosed in a nuclear membrane.

All cell types contain **cytoplasm**; the liquid 'soup' of nutrients, enzymes and the products of metabolism. Eukaryotes contain membrane-bound organelles.

100 000 nm
Scale

Plasma membrane

Organelles are present in most eukaryotic cells. These are specialised structures that carry out specific roles in the cell.

Virus
(e.g. HIV)

Viruses cannot become active outside a living host cell. They simply exist as inert virus particles called **virions**. Only when they invade a cell and take over the cell's metabolic machinery, can the virus carry out its 'living programme'.

Cell
(e.g. Amoeba)

Cells remain alive so long as their metabolic reactions in the cytoplasm are maintained. With a few rare exceptions (that involve freezing certain types of cells) if metabolism is halted, the cell dies.

1. Identify three features that all cells have in common: _____

_____

2. Describe how cells differ from viruses in the following aspects:

(a) Size: _____

_____

(b) Metabolism: _____

_____

(c) Organelles: _____

_____

(d) Genetic material: _____

_____

(e) Life cycle: _____

_____

3. Explain why multicellular organisms are said to show emergent properties: _____

_____

_____

Related activities: Types of Living Things, The Structure of Viruses

Types of Living Things

Living things are called organisms and **cells** are the functioning unit structure from which organisms are made. Under the five kingdom system, cells can be divided into two basic kinds: the **prokaryotes**, which are simple cells without a distinct, membrane-bound nucleus, and the more complex **eukaryotes**. The eukaryotes can be further organised into broad groups according to their basic cell type: the protoctists, fungi, plants, and animals. Viruses are non-cellular and have no cellular machinery of their own. All cells must secure a source of energy if they are to survive and carry out metabolic processes. **Autotrophs** can meet their energy requirements using light or chemical energy from the physical environment. Other types of cell, called **heterotrophs**, obtain their energy from other living organisms or their dead remains.

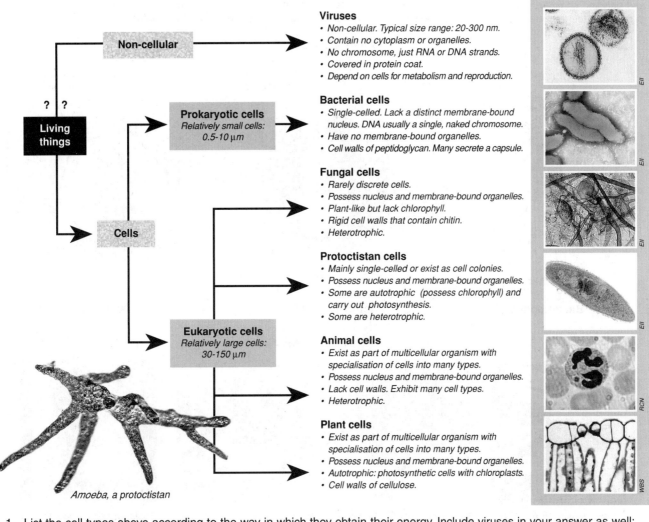

Non-cellular

Viruses
- Non-cellular. Typical size range: 20-300 nm.
- Contain no cytoplasm or organelles.
- No chromosome, just RNA or DNA strands.
- Covered in protein coat.
- Depend on cells for metabolism and reproduction.

? ?

Living things

Prokaryotic cells
Relatively small cells: 0.5-10 μm

Bacterial cells
- Single-celled. Lack a distinct membrane-bound nucleus. DNA usually a single, naked chromosome.
- Have no membrane-bound organelles.
- Cell walls of peptidoglycan. Many secrete a capsule.

Cells

Fungal cells
- Rarely discrete cells.
- Possess nucleus and membrane-bound organelles.
- Plant-like but lack chlorophyll.
- Rigid cell walls that contain chitin.
- Heterotrophic.

Protoctistan cells
- Mainly single-celled or exist as cell colonies.
- Possess nucleus and membrane-bound organelles.
- Some are autotrophic (possess chlorophyll) and carry out photosynthesis.
- Some are heterotrophic.

Eukaryotic cells
Relatively large cells: 30-150 μm

Animal cells
- Exist as part of multicellular organism with specialisation of cells into many types.
- Possess nucleus and membrane-bound organelles.
- Lack cell walls. Exhibit many cell types.
- Heterotrophic.

Plant cells
- Exist as part of multicellular organism with specialisation of cells into many types.
- Possess nucleus and membrane-bound organelles.
- Autotrophic: photosynthetic cells with chloroplasts.
- Cell walls of cellulose.

Amoeba, a protoctistan

1. List the cell types above according to the way in which they obtain their energy. Include viruses in your answer as well:

   (a) Autotrophic: _____

   (b) Heterotrophic: _____

2. Consult the diagram above and determine the two main features distinguishing **eukaryotic** cells from **prokaryotic** cells:

   (a) _____

   (b) _____

3. (a) Suggest why fungi were once classified as belonging to the plant kingdom: _____

   _____

   (b) Explain why, in terms of the distinguishing features of fungi, this classification was erroneous: _____

   _____

   _____

4. Suggest why the Protoctista have traditionally been a difficult group to classify: _____

   _____

Related activities: The Structure of Viruses, Bacteria Cells, Plant Cells, Animal Cells, Unicellular Eukaryotes

Cell Structure

A 1

The Structure of Viruses

Viruses are non-cellular **obligate intracellular parasites**, requiring a living host cell in order to reproduce. The traditional view of viruses is as a minimal particle, containing just enough genetic information to infect a host and highjack the host's machinery into replicating more viral particles. The recent discovery of a new family of viruses, called **mimiviruses**, is forcing a rethink of this conservative view. Mimiviruses overlap with parasitic cellular organisms in terms of both size (400 nm) and genome complexity (over 1000 genes) and their existence suggests a fourth domain of life. A typical, fully developed viral particle (**virion**) lacks the metabolic machinery of cells, containing just a single type of nucleic acid (DNA or RNA) encased in a protein coat or **capsid**. Being non-cellular, they do not conform to the existing criteria upon which a five or six kingdom classification system is based. Viruses can be distinguished by their structure (see below) and by the nature of their genetic material (single or double stranded DNA or RNA). Those that use bacterial cells as a host (**bacteriophages**) can be grown on bacterial cultures, but other viruses are more difficult to study because they require living animals, embryos, or cell cultures in order to replicate.

Viral Structure

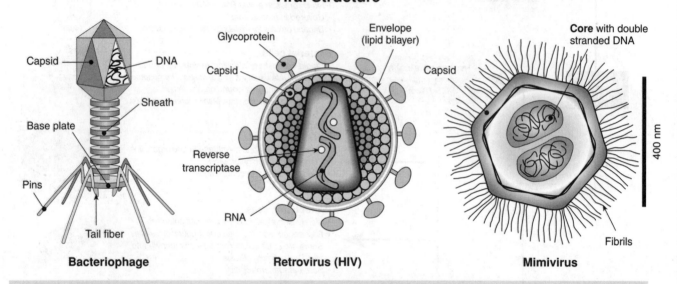

Bacteriophage — Capsid, DNA, Sheath, Base plate, Pins, Tail fiber

Retrovirus (HIV) — Glycoprotein, Capsid, Envelope (lipid bilayer), Reverse transcriptase, RNA

Mimivirus — Core with double stranded DNA, Capsid, 400 nm, Fibrils

Viral Diversity

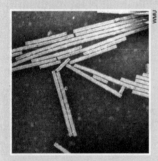

Tobacco Mosaic Virus (TMV): A single stranded RNA plant virus, with a helical capsid.

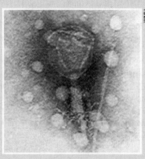

Bacteriophage T4: A complex virus that uses its contractile tail region to inject DNA into its host.

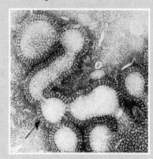

Influenzavirus has a flexible helical capsid and many glycoprotein spikes (arrowed).

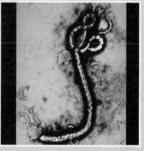

Ebola virus: A helical shaped, RNA filovirus. *Ebola* causes severe haemorrhagic disease (Ebola).

1. Describe the basic structure of a generalised virus particle (virion): _____

   _____

   _____

2. Explain why viruses are such a difficult group to classify conventionally: _____

   _____

3. State whether you regard viruses as living or non-living. Give a reason for your answer: _____

   _____

4. Outline why viruses are classified as obligate intracellular parasites: _____

   _____

5. Explain why viruses are difficult to culture: _____

   _____

Types of Cells

Cells come in a wide range of types and forms. The diagram below shows a selection of cell types from the five kingdoms. The variety that results from specialisation of undifferentiated cells is enormous. In the following exercise, identify which of the cell types belongs to each of the kingdoms and list the major distinguishing characteristics of their cells.

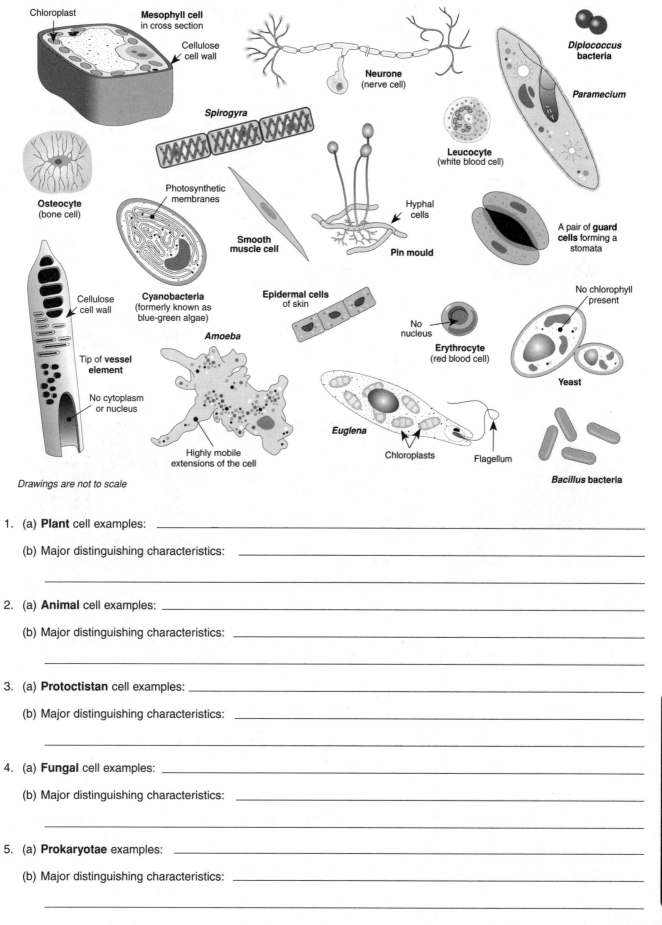

Drawings are not to scale

1. (a) **Plant** cell examples: _____

   (b) Major distinguishing characteristics: _____

   _____

2. (a) **Animal** cell examples: _____

   (b) Major distinguishing characteristics: _____

   _____

3. (a) **Protoctistan** cell examples: _____

   (b) Major distinguishing characteristics: _____

   _____

4. (a) **Fungal** cell examples: _____

   (b) Major distinguishing characteristics: _____

   _____

5. (a) **Prokaryotae** examples: _____

   (b) Major distinguishing characteristics: _____

   _____

Cell Structure

Related activities: Bacteria Cells, Plant Cells, Animal Cells, Unicellular Eukaryotes

RA 1

Cell Sizes

Cells are extremely small and can only be seen properly when viewed through the magnifying lenses of a microscope. The diagrams below show a variety of cell types, together with a virus and a microscopic animal for comparison. For each of these images, note the scale and relate this to the type of microscopy used.

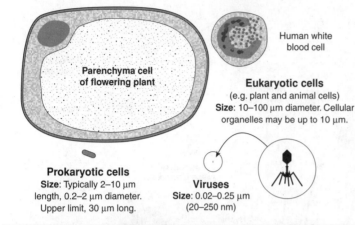

Human white blood cell

Parenchyma cell of flowering plant

Eukaryotic cells
(e.g. plant and animal cells)
Size: 10–100 µm diameter. Cellular organelles may be up to 10 µm.

Prokaryotic cells
Size: Typically 2–10 µm length, 0.2–2 µm diameter. Upper limit, 30 µm long.

Viruses
Size: 0.02–0.25 µm (20–250 nm)

Units of length (International System)

Unit	Metres	Equivalent
1 metre (m)	1 m	= 1000 millimetres
1 millimetre (mm)	10^{-3} m	= 1000 micrometres
1 micrometre (µm)	10^{-6} m	= 1000 nanometres
1 nanometre (nm)	10^{-9} m	= 1000 picometres

Micrometres are sometime referred to as **microns**. Smaller structures are usually measured in nanometres (nm) e.g. molecules (1 nm) and plasma membrane thickness (10 nm).

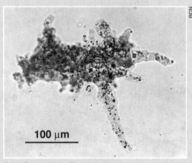

100 µm

An **Amoeba** showing extensions of the cytoplasm called pseudopodia. This protoctist changes its shape, exploring its environment.

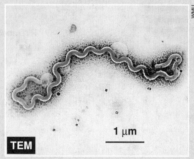

TEM

1 µm

A long thin cell of the spirochete bacterium **Leptospira pomona**, which causes the disease leptospirosis.

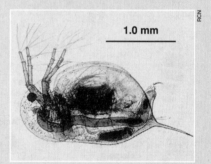

1.0 mm

Daphnia showing its internal organs. These freshwater microcrustaceans are part of the zooplankton found in lakes and ponds.

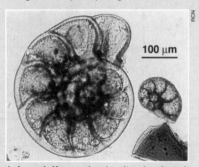

100 µm

A **foraminiferan** showing its chambered, calcified shell. These single-celled protozoans are marine planktonic amoebae.

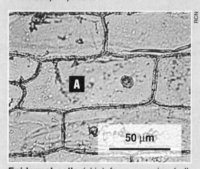

A

50 µm

Epidermal cells (skin) from an onion bulb showing the nucleus, cell walls and cytoplasm. Organelles are not visible at this resolution.

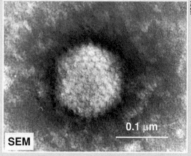

0.1 µm

SEM

Papillomavirus (human wart virus) showing its polyhedral protein coat (20 triangular faces, 12 corners) made of ball-shaped structures.

1. Using the measurement scales provided on each of the photographs above, determine the longest dimension (length or diameter) of the cell/animal/virus in µm and mm (choose the cell marked **A** for epidermal cells):

   (a) *Amoeba*: _____ µm _____ mm   (d) Epidermis: _____ µm _____ mm

   (b) Foraminiferan: _____ µm _____ mm   (e) *Daphnia*: _____ µm _____ mm

   (c) *Leptospira*: _____ µm _____ mm   (f) *Papillomavirus*: _____ µm _____ mm

2. List these six organisms in order of size, from the smallest to the largest: _____

_____

3. Study the scale of your ruler and state which of these six organisms you would be able to see with your unaided eye:

_____

4. Calculate the equivalent length in millimetres (mm) of the following measurements:

   (a) 0.25 µm: _____   (b) 450 µm: _____   (c) 200 nm: _____

Related activities: Optical Microscopes, Electron Microscopes

Bacterial Cells

Bacterial (prokaryotic) cells are much smaller and simpler than the cells of eukaryotes. They lack many eukaryotic features (e.g. a distinct nucleus and membrane-bound cellular organelles). The bacterial cell wall is an important feature. It is a complex, multi-layered structure and often has a role in virulence. These pages illustrate some features of bacterial structure and diversity.

Structure of a Generalised Bacterial Cell

Plasmids: Small, circular DNA molecules (accessory chromosomes) which can reproduce independently of the main chromosome. They can move between cells, and even between species, by **conjugation**. This property accounts for the transmission of antibiotic resistance between bacteria. Plasmids are also used as vectors in recombinant DNA technology.

Single, circular main chromosome: Makes them haploid for most genes. It is possible for some genes to be found on both the plasmid and chromosome and there may be several copies of a gene on a group of plasmids.

The cell lacks a nuclear membrane, so there is no distinct nucleus and the chromosomes are in direct contact with the cytoplasm. It is possible for free ribosomes to attach to mRNA while the mRNA is still in the process of being transcribed from the DNA.

Fimbriae: Hairlike structures that are shorter, straighter, and thinner than flagella. They are used for attachment, not movement. Pili are similar to fimbriae, but are longer and less numerous. They are involved in bacterial conjugation (below) and as phage receptors (opposite).

Cell surface membrane: Similar in composition to eukaryotic membranes, although less rigid.

1 µm

Cytoplasm

Glycocalyx. A viscous, gelatinous layer outside the cell wall. It is composed of polysaccharide and/or polypeptide. If it is firmly attached to the wall, it is called a **capsule**. If loosely attached, it is called a **slime layer**. Capsules may contribute to virulence in pathogenic species, e.g. by protecting the bacteria from the host's immune attack. In some species, the glycocalyx allows attachment to substrates.

Cell wall. A complex, semi-rigid structure that gives the cell shape, prevents rupture, and serves as an anchorage point for flagella. The cell wall is composed of a macromolecule called **peptidoglycan**; repeating disaccharides attached by polypeptides to form a lattice. The wall also contains varying amounts of lipopolysaccharides and lipoproteins. The amount of peptidoglycan present in the wall forms the basis of the diagnostic **gram stain**. In many species, the cell wall contributes to their virulence (disease-causing ability).

Flagellum (pl. flagella). Some bacteria have long, filamentous appendages, called flagella, that are used for locomotion. There may be a single polar flagellum (monotrichous), one or more flagella at each end of the cell, or the flagella may be distributed over the entire cell (peritrichous).

Bacterial cell shapes

Most bacterial cells range between 0.20-2.0 µm in diameter and 2-10 µm length. Although they are a very diverse group, much of this diversity is in their metabolism. In terms of gross morphology, there are only a few basic shapes found (illustrated below). The way in which members of each group aggregate after division is often characteristic and is helpful in identifying certain species.

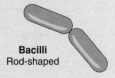

Bacilli
Rod-shaped

Bacilli: Rod-shaped bacteria that divide only across their short axis. Most occur as single rods, although pairs and chains are also found. The term bacillus can refer (as here) to shape. It may also denote a genus.

Cocci
Ball-shaped

Cocci: usually round, but sometimes oval or elongated. When they divide, the cells stay attached to each other and remain in aggregates e.g. pairs (diplococci) or clusters (staphylococci), that are usually a feature of the genus.

Spirilla
Spiral-shaped

Spirilla and vibrio: Bacteria with one or more twists. Spirilla bacteria have a helical (corkscrew) shape which may be rigid or flexible (as in spirochetes). Bacteria that look like curved rods (comma shaped) are called vibrios.

Bacterial conjugation

The two bacteria below are involved in conjugation: a one-way exchange of genetic information from a donor cell to a recipient cell. The plasmid, which must be of the 'conjugative' type, passes through a tube called a **sex pilus** to the other cell. Which is donor and which is recipient appears to be genetically determined. Conjugation should not be confused with sexual reproduction, as it does not involve the fusion of gametes or formation of a zygote.

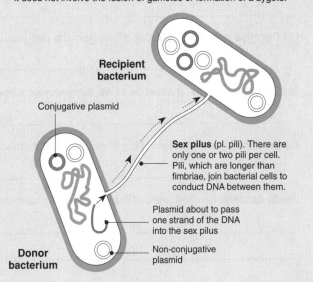

Recipient bacterium

Conjugative plasmid

Donor bacterium

Sex pilus (pl. pili). There are only one or two pili per cell. Pili, which are longer than fimbriae, join bacterial cells to conduct DNA between them.

Plasmid about to pass one strand of the DNA into the sex pilus

Non-conjugative plasmid

Cell Structure

Related activities: Restriction Enzymes, Ligation, Bacterial Diseases
Web links: Gram Stain Animation

RA 2

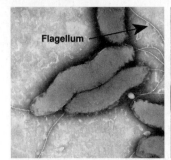

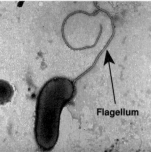

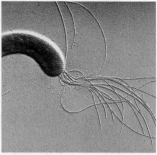

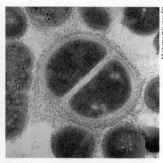

Campylobacter jejuni, a spiral bacterium responsible for foodborne intestinal disease. Note the single flagellum at each end (amphitrichous arrangement).

Helicobacter pylori, a comma-shaped vibrio bacterium that causes stomach ulcers in humans. This bacterium moves by means of multiple polar flagella.

A species of *Spirillum*, a spiral shaped bacterium with a tuft of polar flagella. Most of the species in this genus are harmless aquatic organisms.

Bacteria usually divide by binary fission. During this process, DNA is copied and the cell splits into two cells, as in these gram positive cocci.

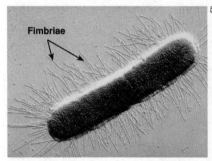

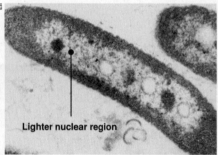

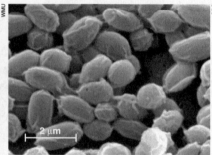

Escherichia coli, a common gut bacterium with **peritrichous** (around the entire cell) **fimbriae**. *E. coli* is a gram negative rod; it does not take up the gram stain but can be counter stained with safranin.

TEM showing *Enterobacter* bacteria, which belong to the family of gut bacteria commonly known as enterics. They are widely distributed in water, sewage, and soil. The family includes motile and non-motile species.

SEM of endospores of *Bacillus anthracis* bacteria, which cause the disease anthrax. These heat-resistant spores remain viable for many years and enable the bacteria to survive in a dormant state.

1. Describe three features distinguishing prokaryotic cells from eukaryotic cells:

   (a) _____

   (b) _____

   (c) _____

2. (a) Describe the function of flagella in bacteria: _____

   _____

   (b) Explain how fimbriae differ structurally and functionally from flagella: _____

   _____

   _____

3. (a) Describe the location and general composition of the bacterial cell wall: _____

   _____

   _____

   (b) Describe how the glycocalyx differs from the cell wall: _____

   _____

4. (a) Describe the main method by which bacteria reproduce: _____

   _____

   (b) Explain how conjugation differs from this usual method: _____

   _____

5. Briefly describe how the artificial manipulation of plasmids has been used for technological applications:

   _____

   _____

   _____

Plant Cells

Plant cells are enclosed in a cellulose cell wall. The cell wall protects the cell, maintains its shape, and prevents excessive water uptake. It does not interfere with the passage of materials into and out of the cell. The diagram below shows the structure and function of a typical plant cell and its organelles. Also see pages 101-102, where further information is provided on the organelles listed here but not described.

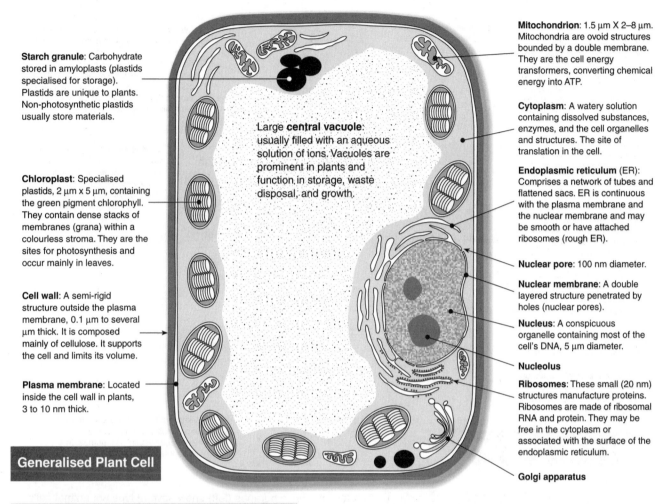

Starch granule: Carbohydrate stored in amyloplasts (plastids specialised for storage). Plastids are unique to plants. Non-photosynthetic plastids usually store materials.

Chloroplast: Specialised plastids, 2 μm x 5 μm, containing the green pigment chlorophyll. They contain dense stacks of membranes (grana) within a colourless stroma. They are the sites for photosynthesis and occur mainly in leaves.

Cell wall: A semi-rigid structure outside the plasma membrane, 0.1 μm to several μm thick. It is composed mainly of cellulose. It supports the cell and limits its volume.

Plasma membrane: Located inside the cell wall in plants, 3 to 10 nm thick.

Large **central vacuole**: usually filled with an aqueous solution of ions. Vacuoles are prominent in plants and function in storage, waste disposal, and growth.

Mitochondrion: 1.5 μm X 2–8 μm. Mitochondria are ovoid structures bounded by a double membrane. They are the cell energy transformers, converting chemical energy into ATP.

Cytoplasm: A watery solution containing dissolved substances, enzymes, and the cell organelles and structures. The site of translation in the cell.

Endoplasmic reticulum (ER): Comprises a network of tubes and flattened sacs. ER is continuous with the plasma membrane and the nuclear membrane and may be smooth or have attached ribosomes (rough ER).

Nuclear pore: 100 nm diameter.

Nuclear membrane: A double layered structure penetrated by holes (nuclear pores).

Nucleus: A conspicuous organelle containing most of the cell's DNA, 5 μm diameter.

Nucleolus

Ribosomes: These small (20 nm) structures manufacture proteins. Ribosomes are made of ribosomal RNA and protein. They may be free in the cytoplasm or associated with the surface of the endoplasmic reticulum.

Golgi apparatus

Generalised Plant Cell

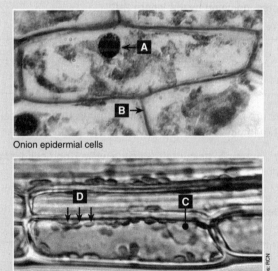

Onion epidermial cells

Elodea cells

Photos: RCN

1. The two photographs (left) show plant cells as seen by a light microscope. Identify the basic features labelled **A-D**:

   A: _____

   B: _____

   C: _____

   D: _____

2. Cytoplasmic streaming is a feature of eukaryotic cells, often clearly visible with a light microscope in plant (and algal) cells.

   (a) Explain what is meant by cytoplasmic streaming:

   _____

   _____

   (b) For the *Elodea* cell (lower, left), draw arrows to indicate cytoplasmic streaming movements.

3. Describe three structures/organelles present in generalised plant cells but absent from animal cells (also see page 98):

   (a) _____

   (b) _____

   (c) _____

Cell Structure

Related activities: Animal Cells, Cell Structure and Organelles, Plant Cells Specialisation **Web links**: Review of Eukaryotic Cells

RA 2

Animal Cells

Animal cells, unlike plant cells, do not have a regular shape. In fact, some animal cells (such as phagocytes) are able to alter their shape for various purposes (e.g. engulfment of foreign material). The diagram below shows the structure and function of a typical animal cell and its organelles. Note the differences between this cell and the generalised plant cell. Also see pages 101-102, where further information is provided on the organelles listed here but not described.

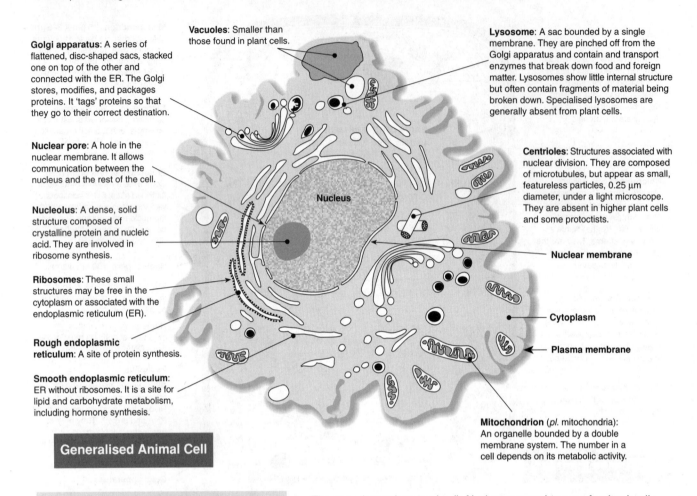

Golgi apparatus: A series of flattened, disc-shaped sacs, stacked one on top of the other and connected with the ER. The Golgi stores, modifies, and packages proteins. It 'tags' proteins so that they go to their correct destination.

Nuclear pore: A hole in the nuclear membrane. It allows communication between the nucleus and the rest of the cell.

Nucleolus: A dense, solid structure composed of crystalline protein and nucleic acid. They are involved in ribosome synthesis.

Ribosomes: These small structures may be free in the cytoplasm or associated with the endoplasmic reticulum (ER).

Rough endoplasmic reticulum: A site of protein synthesis.

Smooth endoplasmic reticulum: ER without ribosomes. It is a site for lipid and carbohydrate metabolism, including hormone synthesis.

Vacuoles: Smaller than those found in plant cells.

Lysosome: A sac bounded by a single membrane. They are pinched off from the Golgi apparatus and contain and transport enzymes that break down food and foreign matter. Lysosomes show little internal structure but often contain fragments of material being broken down. Specialised lysosomes are generally absent from plant cells.

Centrioles: Structures associated with nuclear division. They are composed of microtubules, but appear as small, featureless particles, 0.25 μm diameter, under a light microscope. They are absent in higher plant cells and some protoctists.

Nuclear membrane

Cytoplasm

Plasma membrane

Mitochondrion (*pl.* mitochondria): An organelle bounded by a double membrane system. The number in a cell depends on its metabolic activity.

Nucleus

Generalised Animal Cell

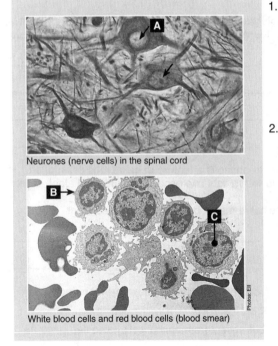

Neurones (nerve cells) in the spinal cord

White blood cells and red blood cells (blood smear)

1. The two photomicrographs (left) show several types of animal cells. Identify the features indicated by the letters **A-C**:

A: _____

B: _____

C: _____

2. White blood cells are mobile, phagocytic cells, whereas red blood cells are smaller than white blood cells and, in humans, lack a nucleus.

(a) In the photomicrograph (below, left), circle a white blood cell and a red blood cell:

(b) With respect to the features that you can see, explain how you made your decision.

_____

_____

_____

_____

3. Name and describe one structure or organelle present in generalised animal cells but absent from plant cells:

_____

_____

Related activities: Plant Cells, Cell Structure and Organelles, Differentiation and Specialisation of Human Cells **Web links**: Review of Eukaryotic Cells

© Biozone International 1998-2007
Photocopying Prohibited

Unicellular Eukaryotes

Unicellular (single-celled) **eukaryotes** comprise the majority of the diverse kingdom, Protoctista. They are found almost anywhere there is water, including within larger organisms (as parasites or symbionts). The protoctists are a very diverse group, exhibiting some features typical of generalised eukaryotic cells, as well as specialised features, which may be specific to one genus. Note that even within the genera below there is considerable variation in size and appearance. *Amoeba* and *Paramecium* are both **heterotrophic**, ingesting food, which accumulates inside a **vacuole**. *Euglena* and *Chlamydomonas* are autotrophic algae, although *Euglena* is heterotrophic when deprived of light. Other protoctists include the marine foraminiferans and radiolarians, specialised intracellular parasites such as *Plasmodium*, and zooflagellates such as the parasites *Trypanosoma* and *Giardia*.

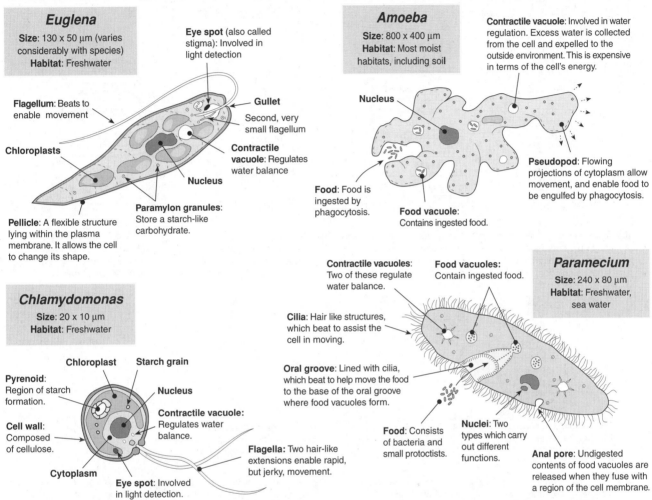

Euglena

Size: 130 x 50 μm (varies considerably with species)
Habitat: Freshwater

Eye spot (also called stigma): Involved in light detection

Flagellum: Beats to enable movement

Gullet Second, very small flagellum

Chloroplasts

Contractile vacuole: Regulates water balance

Nucleus

Paramylon granules: Store a starch-like carbohydrate.

Pellicle: A flexible structure lying within the plasma membrane. It allows the cell to change its shape.

Amoeba

Size: 800 x 400 μm
Habitat: Most moist habitats, including soil

Contractile vacuole: Involved in water regulation. Excess water is collected from the cell and expelled to the outside environment. This is expensive in terms of the cell's energy.

Nucleus

Pseudopod: Flowing projections of cytoplasm allow movement, and enable food to be engulfed by phagocytosis.

Food: Food is ingested by phagocytosis.

Food vacuole: Contains ingested food.

Chlamydomonas

Size: 20 x 10 μm
Habitat: Freshwater

Chloroplast **Starch grain**

Pyrenoid: Region of starch formation.

Nucleus

Cell wall: Composed of cellulose.

Contractile vacuole: Regulates water balance.

Cytoplasm

Eye spot: Involved in light detection.

Flagella: Two hair-like extensions enable rapid, but jerky, movement.

Paramecium

Size: 240 x 80 μm
Habitat: Freshwater, sea water

Contractile vacuoles: Two of these regulate water balance.

Food vacuoles: Contain ingested food.

Cilia: Hair like structures, which beat to assist the cell in moving.

Oral groove: Lined with cilia, which beat to help move the food to the base of the oral groove where food vacuoles form.

Food: Consists of bacteria and small protoctists.

Nuclei: Two types which carry out different functions.

Anal pore: Undigested contents of food vacuoles are released when they fuse with a region of the cell membrane.

1. Fill in the table below to summarise differences in some of the features and life functions of the protoctists shown above:

Organism	Nutrition	Movement	Osmoregulation	Eye spot present / absent	Cell wall present / absent
Amoeba					
Paramecium					
Euglena					
Chlamydomonas					

2. List the four organisms shown above in order of size (largest first): _____

_____

3. Suggest why an autotroph would have an eye spot: _____

_____

Related activities: Cell Structure and Organelles

EA 1

Cell Structure

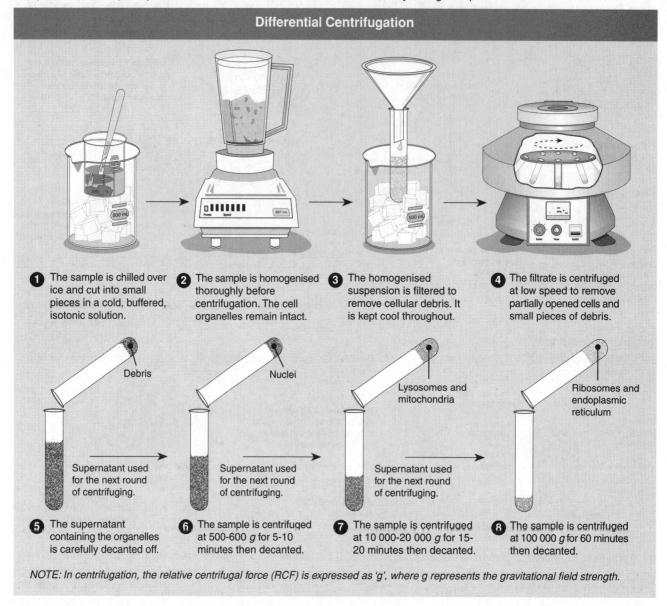

Differential Centrifugation

Differential centrifugation (also called cell fractionation) is a technique used to extract organelles from cells so that they can be studied. The aim is to extract undamaged intact organelles. Samples must be kept very cool so that metabolism is slowed and self digestion of the organelles is prevented. The samples must also be kept in a buffered, isotonic solution so that the organelles do not change volume and the enzymes are not denatured by changes in pH.

Differential Centrifugation

1 The sample is chilled over ice and cut into small pieces in a cold, buffered, isotonic solution.

2 The sample is homogenised thoroughly before centrifugation. The cell organelles remain intact.

3 The homogenised suspension is filtered to remove cellular debris. It is kept cool throughout.

4 The filtrate is centrifuged at low speed to remove partially opened cells and small pieces of debris.

Debris

Nuclei

Lysosomes and mitochondria

Ribosomes and endoplasmic reticulum

Supernatant used for the next round of centrifuging.

Supernatant used for the next round of centrifuging.

Supernatant used for the next round of centrifuging.

5 The supernatant containing the organelles is carefully decanted off.

6 The sample is centrifuged at 500-600 *g* for 5-10 minutes then decanted.

7 The sample is centrifuged at 10 000-20 000 *g* for 15-20 minutes then decanted.

8 The sample is centrifuged at 100 000 *g* for 60 minutes then decanted.

NOTE: In centrifugation, the relative centrifugal force (RCF) is expressed as 'g', where g represents the gravitational field strength.

1. Explain why it is possible to separate cell organelles using centrifugation: _____

_____

_____

2. Suggest why the sample is homogenised before centrifugation: _____

_____

3. Explain why the sample must be kept in a solution that is:

(a) Isotonic: _____

(b) Cool: _____

(c) Buffered: _____

4. **Density gradient centrifugation** is another method of cell fractionation. Sucrose is added to the sample, which is then centrifuged at high speed. The organelles will form layers according to their specific densities. Using the information above, label the centrifuge tube on the right with the organelles you would find in each layer.

Density gradient centrifugation

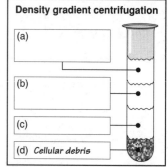

(a)

(b)

(c)

(d) *Cellular debris*

Cell Structures and Organelles

The table below provides a format to summarise information about structures and organelles of typical eukaryotic cells. Complete the table using the list provided and by referring to a textbook and to other pages in this topic. Fill in the final three columns by writing either 'YES' or 'NO'. The first cell component has been completed

for you as a guide and the log scale of measurements (top of next page) illustrates the relative sizes of some cellular structures. **List of structures and organelles**: cell wall, mitochondrion, chloroplast, centrioles, ribosome, endoplasmic reticulum, Golgi apparatus.

Cell Component	Details	Present in Plant cells	Animal cells	Visible under light microscope
(a) 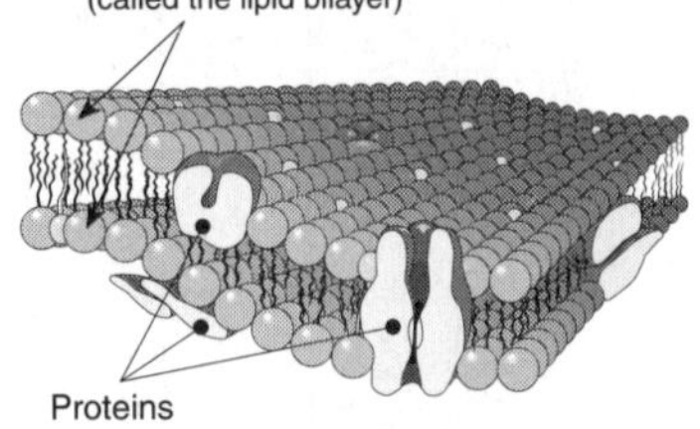 Double layer of phospholipids (called the lipid bilayer) / Proteins	Name: Plasma (cell surface) membrane Location: Surrounding the cell Function: Gives the cell shape and protection. It also regulates the movement of substances into and out of the cell.	YES	YES	YES (but not at the level of detail shown in the diagram)
(b) 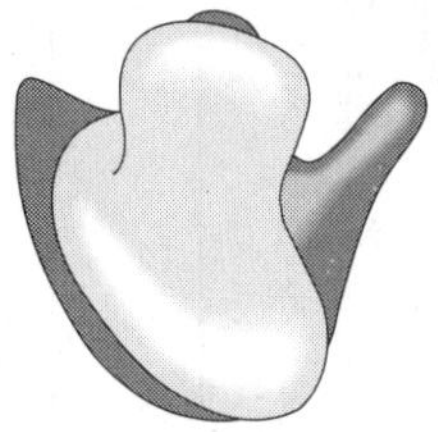	Name: Location: Function:			
(c) 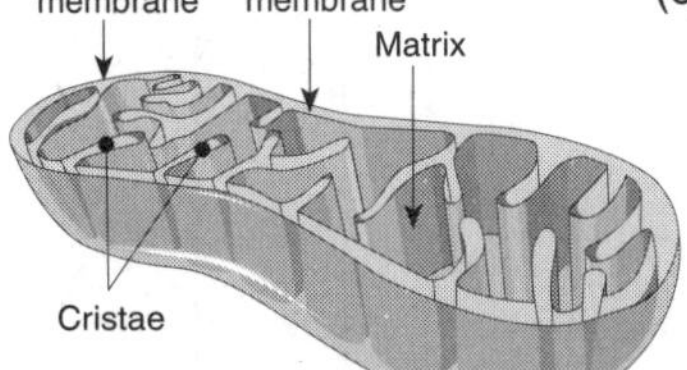 Outer membrane / Inner membrane / Matrix / Cristae	Name: Location: Function:			
(d) 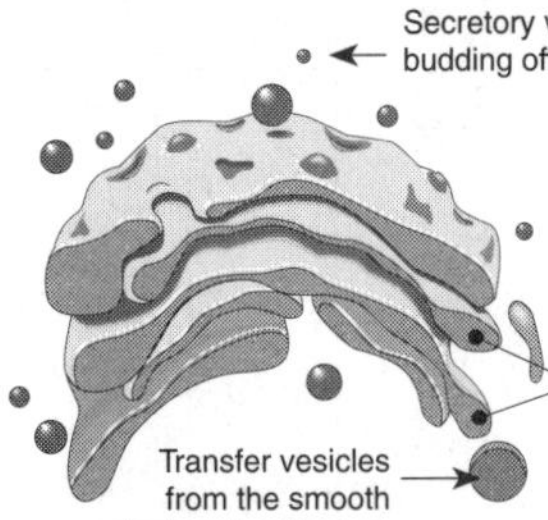 Secretory vesicles budding off / Cisternae / Transfer vesicles from the smooth endoplasmic reticulum	Name: Location: Function:			
(e) 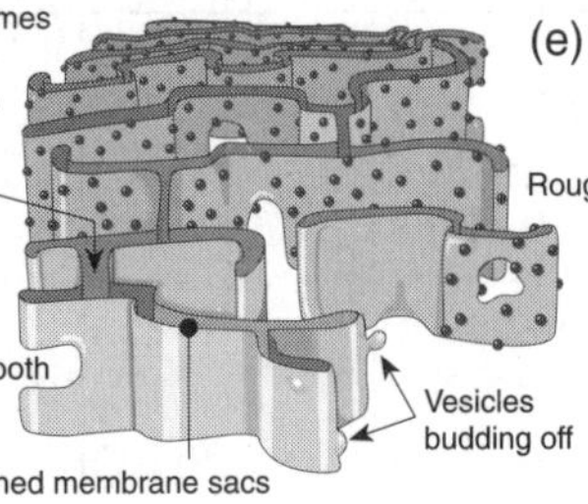 Ribosomes / Transport pathway / Rough / Smooth / Vesicles budding off / Flattened membrane sacs	Name: Location: Function:			
(f) 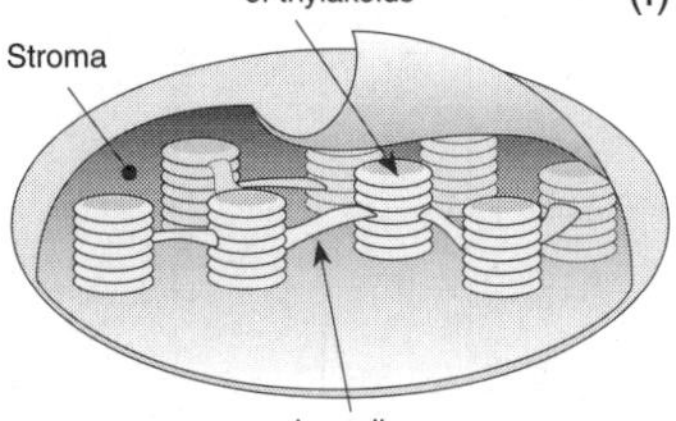 Grana comprise stacks of thylakoids / Stroma / Lamellae	Name: Location: Function:			

Related Activities: Plant Cells, Animal Cells, Unicellular Eukaryotes
Web links: Eukaryotic Cells Interactive Animation

RA 2

Cell Structure

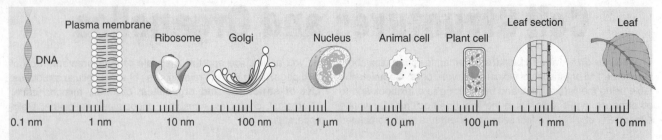

DNA	Plasma membrane	Ribosome	Golgi	Nucleus	Animal cell	Plant cell	Leaf section	Leaf

| 0.1 nm | 1 nm | 10 nm | 100 nm | 1 μm | 10 μm | 100 μm | 1 mm | 10 mm |

Cell Component	Details	Present in		Visible under light microscope
		Plant cells	Animal cells	
(g) Microtubules	Name: Location: Function:			
(h) Two central, single microtubules / 9 doublets of microtubules in an outer ring / Extension of plasma membrane surrounding a core of microtubules in a 9+2 pattern / Basal body anchors the cilium	Name: Cilia and flagella (some eukaryotic cells) Location: Function:			
(i) Cross-layering of cellulose	Name: Location: Function:			
(j) Lysosome	Name: Lysosome Location: Function:			
(k) Food Vacuole / Phagocytosis	Name: Vacuole (a food vacuole is shown) Location: Function:			
(l) Nuclear membrane / Nuclear pores / Nucleolus / Genetic material	Name: Nucleus Location: Function:			

Optical Microscopes

The light microscope is one of the most important instruments used in biology practicals, and its correct use is a basic and essential skill of biology. High power light microscopes use a combination of lenses to magnify objects up to several hundred times. They are called **compound microscopes** because there are two or more separate lenses involved. A typical compound light microscope (bright field) is shown below (top photograph). The specimens viewed with these microscopes must be thin and mostly transparent. Light is focused up through the condenser and specimen; if the specimen is thick or opaque,

little or no detail will be visible. The microscope below has two eyepieces (**binocular**), although monocular microscopes, with a mirror rather than an internal light source, may still be encountered. Dissecting microscopes (lower photograph) are a type of binocular microscope used for observations at low total magnification (x4 to x50), where a large working distance between objective lenses and stage is required. A dissecting microscope has two separate lens systems, one for each eye. Such microscopes produce a 3-D view of the specimen and are sometimes called stereo microscopes for this reason.

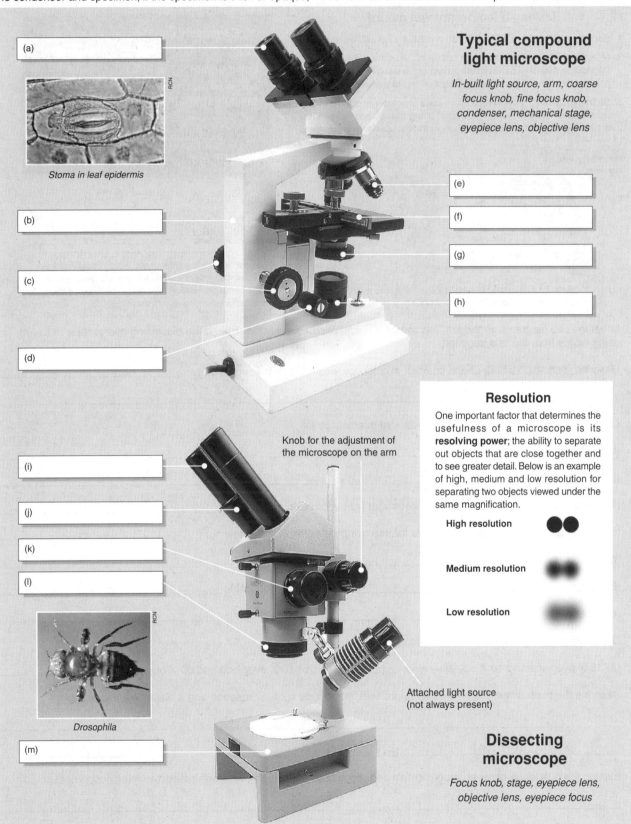

(a)

Stoma in leaf epidermis

(b)

(c)

(d)

Typical compound light microscope

In-built light source, arm, coarse focus knob, fine focus knob, condenser, mechanical stage, eyepiece lens, objective lens

(e)

(f)

(g)

(h)

(i)

(j)

(k)

(l)

Knob for the adjustment of the microscope on the arm

Resolution

One important factor that determines the usefulness of a microscope is its **resolving power**; the ability to separate out objects that are close together and to see greater detail. Below is an example of high, medium and low resolution for separating two objects viewed under the same magnification.

High resolution

Medium resolution

Low resolution

Attached light source (not always present)

Drosophila

(m)

Dissecting microscope

Focus knob, stage, eyepiece lens, objective lens, eyepiece focus

Cell Structure

Related Activities: Plant Cells, Animal Cells, Unicellular Eukaryotes

RDA 2

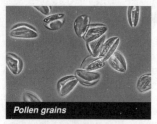

Pollen grains

Phase contrast illumination increases contrast of transparent specimens by producing interference effects.

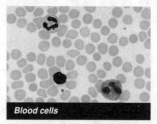

Blood cells

Leishman's stain is used to show red blood cells as red/pink, while staining the nucleus of white blood cells blue.

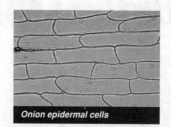

Onion epidermal cells

Standard **bright field** lighting shows cells with little detail; only cell walls, with the cell nuclei barely visible.

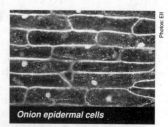

Onion epidermal cells

Dark field illumination is excellent for viewing near transparent specimens. The nucleus of each cell is visible.

Making a temporary wet mount

1. **Sectioning:** Very thin sections of fresh material are cut with a razorblade.

2. **Mounting:** The thin section(s) are placed in the centre of a clean glass microscope slide and covered with a drop of mounting liquid (e.g. water, glycerol or stain). A coverslip is placed on top to exclude air (below).

3. **Staining:** Dyes can be applied to stain some structures and leave others unaffected. The stains used in dyeing living tissues are called **vital stains** and they can be applied before or after the specimen is mounted.

Commonly used temporary stains

Stain	Final colour	Used for
Iodine solution	blue-black	Starch
Aniline sulfate	yellow	Lignin
Schultz's solution	blue	Starch
	blue or violet	Cellulose
	yellow	Protein, cutin, lignin, suberin
Methylene blue	blue	Nuclei

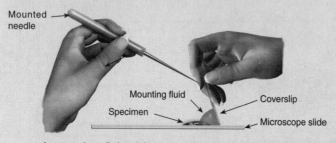

Mounted needle

Mounting fluid

Specimen

Coverslip

Microscope slide

A mounted needle is used to support the coverslip and lower it gently over the specimen. This avoids including air in the mount.

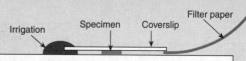

Irrigation   Specimen   Coverslip   Filter paper

If a specimen is already mounted, a drop of stain can be placed at one end of the coverslip and drawn through using filter paper (above). Water can be drawn through in the same way to remove excess stain.

1. Label the two diagrams on the left, the compound light microscope (a) to (h) and the dissecting microscope (i) to (m), using words from the lists supplied.

2. Describe a situation where phase contrast microscopy would improve image quality: _____
   _____

3. List two structures that could be seen with light microscopy in:

   (a) A plant cell: _____

   (b) An animal cell: _____

4. Name one cell structure that cannot be seen with light microscopy: _____

5. Identify a stain that would be appropriate for improving definition of the following:

   (a) Blood cells: _____   (d) Lignin: _____

   (b) Starch: _____   (e) Nuclei and DNA: _____

   (c) Protein: _____   (f) Cellulose: _____

6. Determine the magnification of a microscope using:

   (a) 15 X eyepiece and 40 X objective lens: _____   (b) 10 X eyepiece and 60 X objective lens: _____

7. Describe the main difference between a bright field, compound light microscope and a dissecting microscope:
   _____
   _____

8. Explain the difference between magnification and resolution (resolving power) with respect to microscope use:
   _____
   _____

Electron Microscopes

Electron microscopes (EMs) use a beam of electrons, instead of light, to produce an image. The higher resolution of EMs is due to the shorter wavelengths of electrons. There are two basic types of electron microscope: **scanning electron microscopes** (SEMs) and **transmission electron microscopes** (TEMs). In SEMs, the electrons are bounced off the surface of an object to produce detailed images of the external appearance. TEMs produce very clear images of specially prepared thin sections.

Transmission Electron Microscope (TEM)

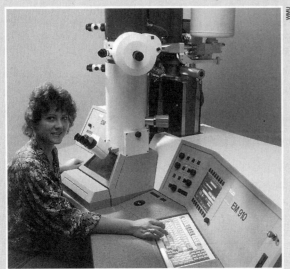

The transmission electron microscope is used to view extremely thin sections of material. Electrons pass through the specimen and are scattered. Magnetic lenses focus the image onto a fluorescent screen or photographic plate. The sections are so thin that they have to be prepared with a special machine, called an **ultramicrotome**, that can cut wafers to just 30 thousandths of a millimetre thick. It can magnify several hundred thousand times.

TEM diagram labels:
- Electron gun
- Electron beam
- Electromagnetic condenser lens
- Specimen
- Vacuum pump
- Electromagnetic objective lens
- Electromagnetic projector lens
- **TEM**
- Eyepiece
- Fluorescent screen or photographic plate

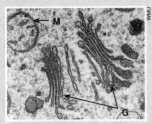

TEM photo showing the Golgi (**G**) and a mitochondrion (**M**).

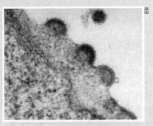

Three HIV viruses budding out of a human lymphocyte (TEM).

Scanning Electron Microscope (SEM)

The scanning electron microscope scans a sample with a beam of primary electrons that knock electrons from its surface. These secondary electrons are picked up by a collector, amplified, and transmitted onto a viewing screen or photographic plate, producing a superb 3-D image. A microscope of this power can easily obtain clear pictures of organisms as small as bacteria and viruses. The image produced is of the outside surface only.

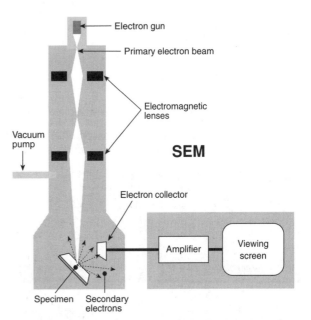

SEM diagram labels:
- Electron gun
- Primary electron beam
- Electromagnetic lenses
- Vacuum pump
- **SEM**
- Electron collector
- Amplifier
- Viewing screen
- Specimen
- Secondary electrons

SEM photo of stoma and epidermal cells on the upper surface of a leaf.

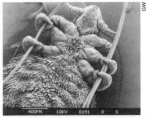

Image of hair louse clinging to two hairs on a Hooker's sealion (SEM).

Cell Structure

Related activities: Optical Microscopes, Interpreting Electron Micrographs

RA 2

	Light Microscope	Transmission Electron Microscope (TEM)	Scanning Electron Microscope (SEM)
Radiation source:	light	electrons	electrons
Wavelength:	400-700 nm	0.005 nm	0.005 nm
Lenses:	glass	electromagnetic	electromagnetic
Specimen:	living or non-living supported on glass slide	non-living supported on a small copper grid in a vacuum	non-living supported on a metal disc in a vacuum
Maximum resolution:	200 nm	1 nm	10 nm
Maximum magnification:	1500 x	250 000 x	100 000 x
Stains:	coloured dyes	impregnated with heavy metals	coated with carbon or gold
Type of image:	coloured	monochrome (black & white)	monochrome (black & white)

1. Explain why electron microscopes are able to resolve much greater detail than a light microscope:

   _____

   _____

   _____

2. Describe two typical applications for each of the following types of microscope:

   (a) Transmission electron microscope (TEM): _____

   _____

   (b) Scanning electron microscope (SEM): _____

   _____

   (c) Bright field, compound light microscope (thin section): _____

   _____

   (d) Dissecting microscope: _____

   _____

3. Identify which type of electron microscope (SEM or TEM) or optical microscope (bright field, compound light microscope or dissecting microscope) was used to produce each of the images in the photos below (A-H):

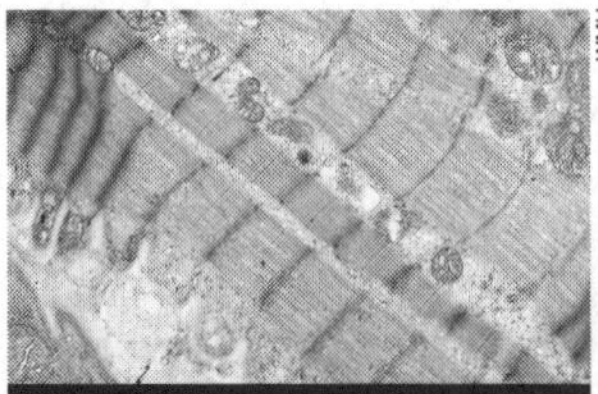

Cardiac muscle

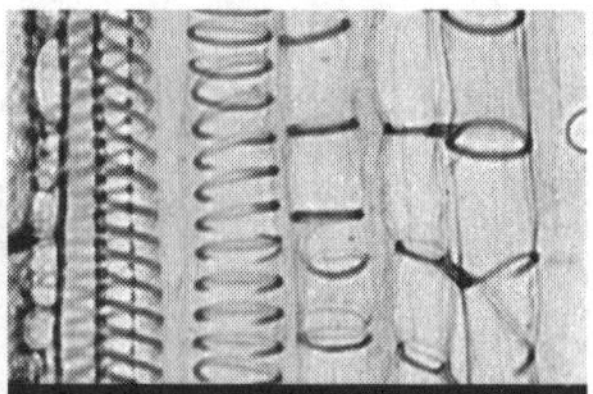

Plant vascular tissue

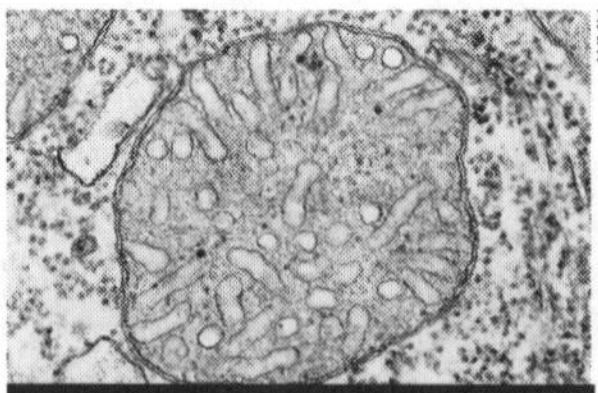

Mitochondrion

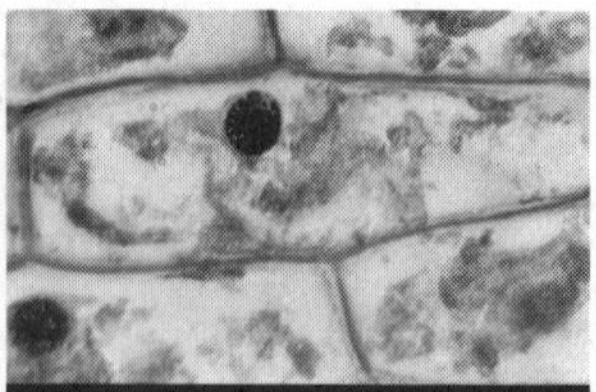

Plant epidermal cells

A _____   B _____   C _____   D _____

Head louse

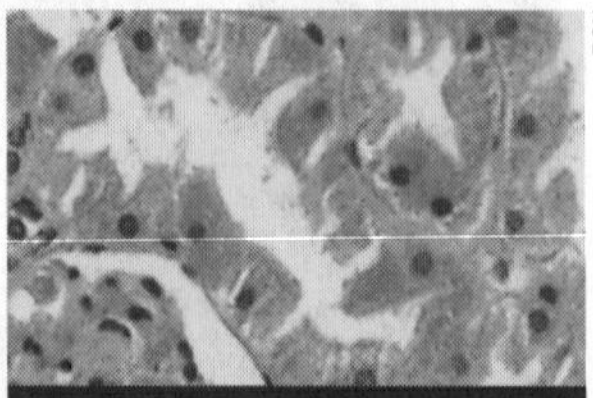

Kidney cells

Alderfly larva

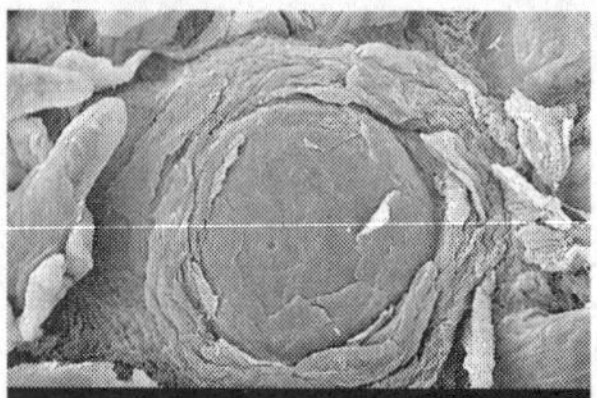

Tongue papilla

E _____   F _____   G _____   H _____

Interpreting Electron Micrographs

The photographs below were taken using a transmission electron microscope (TEM). They show some of the cell organelles in great detail. Remember that these photos are showing only **parts of cells, not whole cells**. Some of the photographs show more than one type of organelle. The questions refer to the main organelle in the centre of the photo.

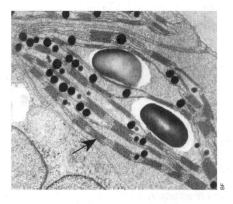

1. (a) Name this organelle (arrowed): _____

    (b) State which kind of cell(s) this organelle would be found in:

    _____

    (c) Describe the function of this organelle: _____

    _____

    _____

    (d) Label two structures that can be seen inside this organelle.

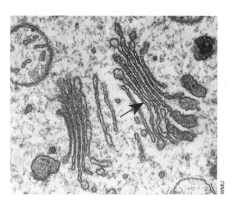

2. (a) Name this organelle (arrowed): _____

    (b) State which kind of cell(s) this organelle would be found in:

    _____

    (c) Describe the function of this organelle: _____

    _____

    _____

    _____

    _____

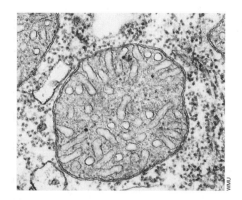

3. (a) Name the large, circular organelle: _____

    (b) State which kind of cell(s) this organelle would be found in:

    _____

    (c) Describe the function of this organelle: _____

    _____

    _____

    (d) Label two regions that can be seen inside this organelle.

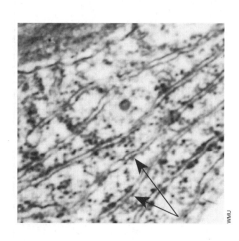

4. (a) Name and label the ribbon-like organelle in this photograph (arrowed):

    _____

    (b) State which kind of cell(s) this organelle is found in:

    _____

    (c) Describe the function of these organelles: _____

    _____

    _____

    (d) Name the dark 'blobs' attached to the organelle you have labelled:

    _____

Cell Structure

Related activities: Electron Microscopes, Plant Cells, Animal Cells, Cell Structures and Organelles

RA 2

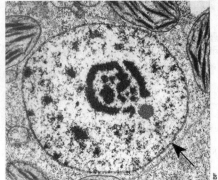

5. (a) Name this large circular structure (arrowed): _____

(b) State which kind of cell(s) this structure would be found in:

_____

(c) Describe the function of this structure: _____

_____

_____

(d) Label three features relating to this structure in the photograph.

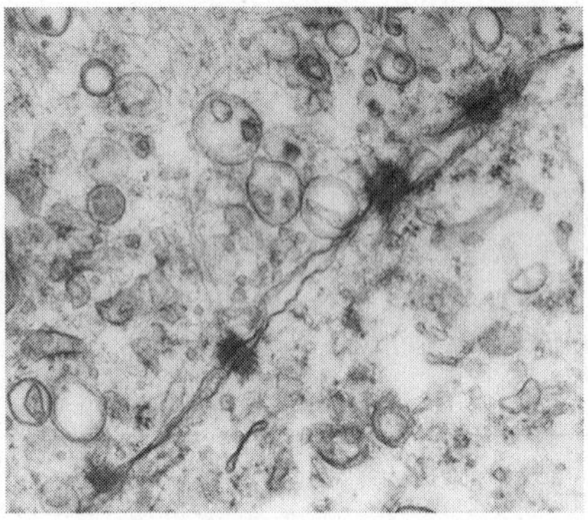

6. The four dark structures shown in this photograph are called **desmosomes**. They cause the plasma membranes of neighbouring cells to stick together. Without desmosomes, animal cells would not combine together to form tissues.

(a) Describe the functions of the plasma membrane:

_____

_____

_____

(b) Label the plasma membrane and the four desmosomes in the photograph.

7. In the space below, draw a simple, labelled diagram of a **generalised cell** to show the **relative size** and **location** of these six structures and organelles (simple outlines of the organelles will do):

Levels of Organisation

Organisation and the emergence of novel properties in complex systems are two of the defining features of living organisms. Organisms are organised according to a hierarchy of structural levels (below), each level building on the one below it. At each level, novel properties emerge that were not present at the simpler level. Hierarchical organisation allows specialised cells to group together into tissues and organs to perform a particular function. This improves efficiency of function in the organism.

In the spaces provided for each question below, assign each of the examples listed to one of the levels of organisation as indicated.

1. **Animals**: *adrenaline, blood, bone, brain, cardiac muscle, cartilage, collagen, DNA, heart, leucocyte, lysosome, mast cell, nervous system, neurone, phospholipid, reproductive system, ribosomes, Schwann cell, spleen, squamous epithelium.*

(a) Organ system: _____
_____

(b) Organs: _____
_____

(c) Tissues: _____
_____

(d) Cells: _____
_____

(e) Organelles: _____
_____

(f) Molecular level: _____
_____
_____

2. **Plants**: *cellulose, chloroplasts, collenchyma, companion cells, DNA, epidermal cell, fibres, flowers, leaf, mesophyll, parenchyma, pectin, phloem, phospholipid, ribosomes, roots, sclerenchyma, tracheid.*

(a) Organs: _____
_____

(b) Tissues: _____
_____

(c) Cells: _____
_____

(d) Organelles: _____
_____

(e) Molecular level: _____
_____
_____

The Organism
A complex, functioning whole that is the sum of all its component parts.

Organ System Level
In animals, organs form parts of even larger units known as organ systems. An organ system is an association of organs with a common function e.g. digestive system, cardiovascular system, and the urinogenital system.

Organ Level
Organs are structures of definite form and structure, comprising two or more tissues.

Animal examples *include: heart, lungs, brain, stomach, kidney.*

Plant examples *include: leaves, roots, storage organs, ovary.*

Tissue Level
Tissues are composed of groups of cells of similar structure that perform a particular, related function.

Animal examples *include: epithelial tissue, bone, muscle.*

Plant examples *include: phloem, chlorenchyma, endodermis, xylem.*

Cellular Level
Cells are the basic structural and functional units of an organism. Each cell type has a different structure and function; the result of cellular differentiation during development.

Animal examples *include: epithelial cells, osteoblasts, muscle fibres.*

Plant examples *include: sclereids, xylem vessels, sieve tubes.*

Organelle Level
Many diverse molecules may associate together to form complex, highly specialised structures within cells called cellular organelles e.g. mitochondria, Golgi apparatus, endoplasmic reticulum, chloroplasts.

Chemical and Molecular Level
Atoms and molecules form the most basic, level of organisation. This level includes all the chemicals essential for maintaining life e.g. water, ions, fats, carbohydrates, amino acids, proteins, and nucleic acids.

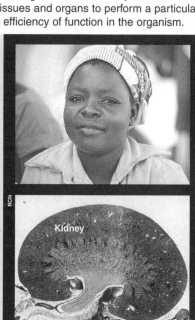

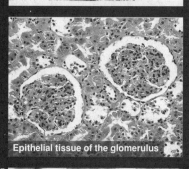
Kidney

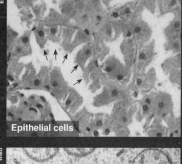
Epithelial tissue of the glomerulus

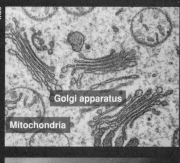
Epithelial cells

Golgi apparatus
Mitochondria

Cell Structure

Related activities: Cell Structure and Organelles

RA 2

The study of tissues is called **histology**. The cells of a tissue, and their associated intracellular substances e.g. collagen, are grouped together to perform particular functions. Tissues improve the efficiency of operation because they enable tasks to be shared amongst various specialised cells. **Animal tissues** can be divided into four broad groups: **epithelial tissues**, **connective tissues**, **muscle**, and **nervous tissues**. Some features of animal tissues are described below. Plant tissues are divided into two groups: simple and complex. Simple tissues contain only one cell type and form packing and support tissues (e.g. parenchyma). Complex tissues contain more than one cell type and form the conducting and support tissues of plants (periderm, xylem, phloem). Examples of these are illustrated elsewhere (see topics *Transport Systems, Gas Exchange*).

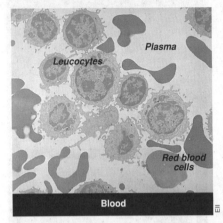

Blood

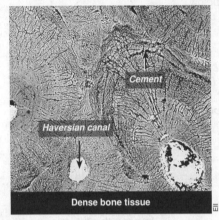

Dense bone tissue

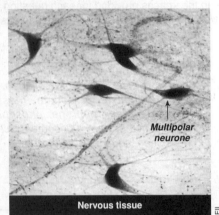

Nervous tissue

Connective tissue is the major supporting tissue of the animal body. It comprises cells, widely dispersed in a semi-fluid matrix. Connective tissues bind other structures together and provide support, and protection against damage, infection, or heat loss. Connective tissues include dentine (teeth), adipose (fat) tissue, bone (above) and cartilage, and the tissues around the body's organs and blood vessels. Blood (above, left) is a special type of liquid tissue, comprising cells floating in a liquid matrix.

Nervous tissue contains densely packed nerve cells (neurones) which are specialised for the transmission of nerve impulses. Associated with the neurones there may also be supporting cells and connective tissue containing blood vessels.

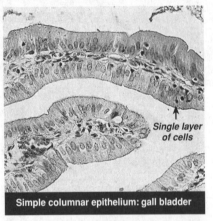

Simple columnar epithelium: gall bladder

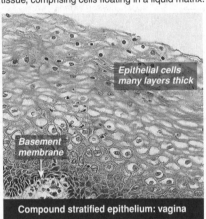

Compound stratified epithelium: vagina

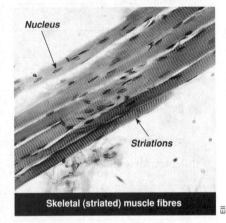

Skeletal (striated) muscle fibres

Epithelial tissue is organised into single (above, left) or layered (above) sheets. It lines internal and external surfaces (e.g. blood vessels, ducts, gut lining) and protects the underlying structures from wear, infection, and/or pressure. Epithelial cells rest on a basement membrane of fibres and collagen and are held together by a carbohydrate-based "glue". The cells may also be specialised for absorption, secretion, or excretion. Examples: stratified (compound) epithelium of vagina, ciliated epithelium of respiratory tract, cuboidal epithelium of kidney ducts, and the columnar epithelium of the intestine.

Muscle tissue consists of very highly specialised cells called fibres, held together by connective tissue. The three types of muscle in the body are cardiac muscle, skeletal muscle (above), and smooth muscle. Muscles bring about both voluntary and involuntary (unconscious) body movements.

3. Explain the advantage of the organisation seen in living things: _____

    _____

    _____

4. Give an example of an organ system in an animal, stating the organs, tissues, and specialised cells comprising it:

    Organ system: _____ Organs: _____

    Tissues: _____

    Specialised cells: _____

5. Describe the main features of the following animal tissues:

    (a) Epithelial tissues: _____

    (b) Connective tissues: _____

    (c) Muscle tissue: _____

    (d) Nervous tissue: _____

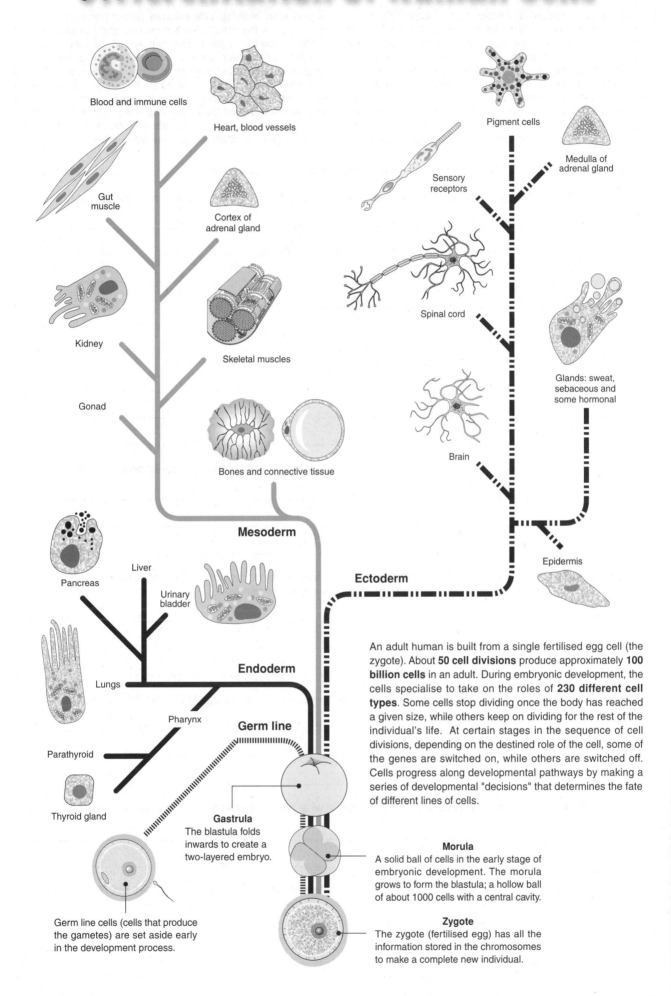

Differentiation of Human Cells

Blood and immune cells

Heart, blood vessels

Pigment cells

Medulla of adrenal gland

Sensory receptors

Gut muscle

Cortex of adrenal gland

Kidney

Skeletal muscles

Spinal cord

Glands: sweat, sebaceous and some hormonal

Gonad

Bones and connective tissue

Brain

Mesoderm

Epidermis

Liver

Urinary bladder

Ectoderm

Pancreas

Endoderm

An adult human is built from a single fertilised egg cell (the zygote). About **50 cell divisions** produce approximately **100 billion cells** in an adult. During embryonic development, the cells specialise to take on the roles of **230 different cell types**. Some cells stop dividing once the body has reached a given size, while others keep on dividing for the rest of the individual's life. At certain stages in the sequence of cell divisions, depending on the destined role of the cell, some of the genes are switched on, while others are switched off. Cells progress along developmental pathways by making a series of developmental "decisions" that determines the fate of different lines of cells.

Lungs

Pharynx

Germ line

Parathyroid

Thyroid gland

Gastrula
The blastula folds inwards to create a two-layered embryo.

Morula
A solid ball of cells in the early stage of embryonic development. The morula grows to form the blastula; a hollow ball of about 1000 cells with a central cavity.

Germ line cells (cells that produce the gametes) are set aside early in the development process.

Zygote
The zygote (fertilised egg) has all the information stored in the chromosomes to make a complete new individual.

Cell Structure

Related activities: Animal Cells, Differentiation of Human Cells, The Genetic Origins of Cancer, Cloning by Nuclear Transfer

ERA 2

Development is the process of progressive change through the lifetime of an organism. Part of this process involves growth (increase in size) and cell division (to generate the multicellular body). Cellular **differentiation** (the generation of specialised cells) and morphogenesis (the creation of the shape and form of the body) are also part of development. Differentiation defines the specific structure and function of a cell. As development proceeds, the possibilities available to individual cells become fewer, until each cell's **fate** is determined. The tissues and organs making up the body form from the aggregation and organisation of these differentiated cells. In animals, the final body form is the result of cell migration and the programmed death of certain cells during embryonic development. The diagram on the previous page shows how a single fertilised egg (zygote) gives rise to the large number of specialised cell types that make up the adult human body. The morula, blastula, and gastrula stages mentioned at the bottom of the diagram show the early development of the embryo from the zygote. The gastrula gives rise to the three layers of cells (ectoderm, mesoderm, and endoderm), from which specific cell types develop.

1. State how many different types of cell are found in the human body: _____

2. State approximately how many cell divisions take place from fertilised egg (zygote) to produce an adult: _____

3. State approximately how many cells make up an adult human body: _____

4. Name one cell type that continues to divide throughout a person's lifetime: _____

_____

5. Name one cell type that does not continue to divide throughout a person's lifetime: _____

_____

6. Germ line cells diverge (become isolated) from other cells at a very early stage in embryonic development.

   (a) Explain what the **germ line** is: _____

   _____

   _____

   (b) Explain why it is necessary for the germ line to become separated at such an early stage of development:

   _____

   _____

   _____

7. Cloning whole new organisms is possible by taking a nucleus from a cell during the blastula stage of embryonic development and placing it into an egg cell that has had its own nucleus removed.

   (a) Explain what a **clone** is: _____

   _____

   _____

   (b) Explain why the cell required for cloning needs to be taken at such an early stage of embryonic development:

   _____

   _____

   _____

8. Cancer cells are particularly damaging to organisms. Explain what has happened to a cell that has become cancerous:

   _____

   _____

9. Explain the genetic events that enable so many different cell types to arise from one unspecialised cell (the zygote):

   _____

   _____

   _____

Human Cell Specialisation

Animal cells are often specialised to perform particular functions. The eight specialised cell types shown below are representative of some 230 different cell types in humans. Each has specialised features that suit it to performing a specific role.

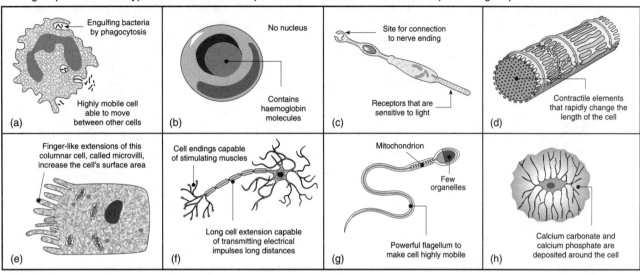

(a) Engulfing bacteria by phagocytosis — Highly mobile cell able to move between other cells

(b) No nucleus — Contains haemoglobin molecules

(c) Site for connection to nerve ending — Receptors that are sensitive to light

(d) Contractile elements that rapidly change the length of the cell

(e) Finger-like extensions of this columnar cell, called microvilli, increase the cell's surface area

(f) Cell endings capable of stimulating muscles — Long cell extension capable of transmitting electrical impulses long distances

(g) Mitochondrion — Few organelles — Powerful flagellum to make cell highly mobile

(h) Calcium carbonate and calcium phosphate are deposited around the cell

1. Identify each of the cells (b) to (h) pictured above, and describe their **specialised features** and **role** in the body:

   (a) Type of cell: _Phagocytic white blood cell (neutrophil)_

   Specialised features: _Engulfs bacteria and other foreign material by phagocytosis_

   Role of cell within body: _Destroys pathogens and other foreign material as well as cellular debris_

   (b) Type of cell: _____

   Specialised features: _____

   Role of cell within body: _____

   (c) Type of cell: _____

   Specialised features: _____

   Role of cell within body: _____

   (d) Type of cell: _____

   Specialised features: _____

   Role of cell within body: _____

   (e) Type of cell: _____

   Specialised features: _____

   Role of cell within body: _____

   (f) Type of cell: _____

   Specialised features: _____

   Role of cell within body: _____

   (g) Type of cell: _____

   Specialised features: _____

   Role of cell within body: _____

   (h) Type of cell: _____

   Specialised features: _____

   Role of cell within body: _____

Related activities: Animal Cells, Differentiation of Human Cells

RA 2

Cell Structure

Plant Cell Specialisation

Plants show a wide variety of cell types. The vegetative plant body consists of three organs: stems, leaves, and roots. Flowers, fruits, and seeds comprise additional organs that are concerned with reproduction. The eight cell types illustrated below are representatives of these plant organ systems. Each has structural or physiological features that set it apart from the other cell types. The differentiation of cells enables each specialised type to fulfil a specific role in the plant.

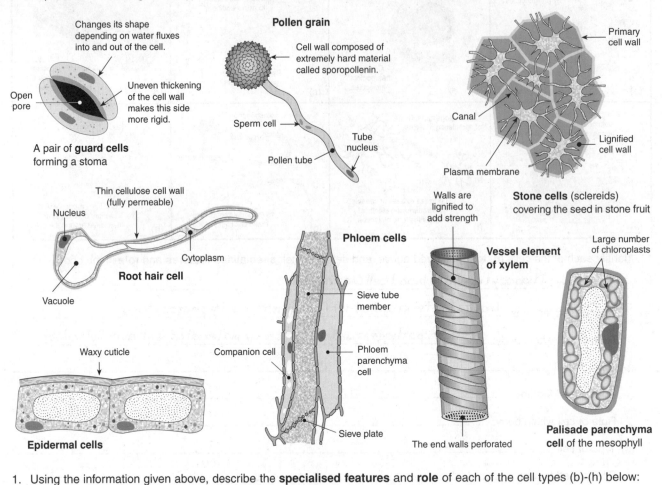

Changes its shape depending on water fluxes into and out of the cell.

Open pore

Uneven thickening of the cell wall makes this side more rigid.

A pair of guard cells forming a stoma

Pollen grain

Cell wall composed of extremely hard material called sporopollenin.

Sperm cell

Pollen tube

Tube nucleus

Primary cell wall

Canal

Plasma membrane

Lignified cell wall

Stone cells (sclereids) covering the seed in stone fruit

Thin cellulose cell wall (fully permeable)

Nucleus

Cytoplasm

Root hair cell

Vacuole

Waxy cuticle

Epidermal cells

Phloem cells

Sieve tube member

Companion cell

Phloem parenchyma cell

Sieve plate

Walls are lignified to add strength

Vessel element of xylem

The end walls perforated

Large number of chloroplasts

Palisade parenchyma cell of the mesophyll

1. Using the information given above, describe the **specialised features** and **role** of each of the cell types (b)-(h) below:

(a) **Guard cell**: Features: _Curved, sausage shaped cell, unevenly thickened._

Role in plant: _Turgor changes alter the cell shape to open or close the stoma._

(b) **Pollen grain**: Features: _____

Role in plant: _____

(c) **Palisade parenchyma cell**: Features: _____

Role in plant: _____

(d) **Epidermal cell**: Features: _____

Role in plant: _____

(e) **Vessel element**: Features: _____

Role in plant: _____

(f) **Stone cell**: Features: _____

Role in plant: _____

(g) **Sieve tube member**: Features: _____

Role in plant: _____

(h) **Root hair cell**: Features: _____

Role in plant: _____

Related activities: Plant Cells, Root Cell Development

Cell Membranes and Transport

AQA-A	AQA-B	SNAB	Edexcel	OCR
Complete:	Complete:	Complete:	Complete:	Complete:
1-16	1-16	1-10, 13-16	1-16	1-16

Learning Objectives

☐ 1. Compile your own glossary from the **KEY WORDS** displayed in **bold type** in the learning objectives below.

Cell Membranes *(pages 77, 117-120)*

☐ 2. Draw a simple labelled diagram of the structure of the **plasma membrane** (cell surface membrane), clearly identifying the arrangement of the lipids and proteins.

☐ 3. Describe and explain the current **fluid-mosaic model** of membrane structure, including the terms **lipid bilayer** and **partially permeable membrane**. Explain the roles of **phospholipids**, **cholesterol**, **glycolipids**, **proteins**, and **glycoproteins** in membrane structure. Recognise that the plasma membrane is essentially no different to the membranes of cellular organelles.

☐ 4. EXTENSION: Outline the evidence from freeze-fracture studies in support of the current model of membrane structure. Contrast this currently accepted model with the earlier Davson-Danielli model.

☐ 5. Describe the general functions of membranes (including the plasma membrane) in the cell, identifying their role in the structure of cellular organelles and their role in regulating the transport of materials within cells, as well as into and out of cells.

Cellular Transport *(pages 116, 121-128)*

☐ 6. Summarise the types of movements that occur across membranes. Outline the role of proteins in membranes as receptors and carriers in membrane transport.

☐ 7. Define: **passive transport**, **concentration gradient**. Describe the processes of **diffusion** and **osmosis**, identifying the types of substances moving in each case.

☐ 8. Describe **facilitated diffusion** (also called facilitated transport). Identify when and where this process might occur in a cell.

☐ 9. Identify factors determining the rate of diffusion. Explain how **Fick's law** provides a framework for determining maximum diffusion rates across cell surfaces.

☐ 10. Suggest why cell size is limited by the rate of diffusion. Discuss the significance of **surface area to volume ratio** to cells. Explain why organisms without efficient transport mechanisms remain small.

☐ 11. Explain what is meant by **water potential** (ψ) and identify its significance to the net movement of water in cells. Define the components of water potential: **solute potential** and **pressure potential**.

☐ 12. EXTENSION: Determine the net direction of water movement between solutions of different ψ.

☐ 13. With respect to plant cells, define the terms: **turgor** and **plasmolysis**. With respect to solutions of differing solute concentration, distinguish between: **hypotonic**, **isotonic**, **hypertonic**. Comment on the importance of ion concentrations in maintaining cell turgor.

☐ 14. Distinguish between passive and **active transport** mechanisms. Understand the principles involved in active transport, clearly identifying the involvement of protein molecules and energy.

☐ 15. Describe the following active transport mechanisms: **ion-exchange pumps**, **exocytosis**, **endocytosis**, **phagocytosis**, and **pinocytosis**. Give examples of when and where (in the plant or animal body) each type of transport mechanism occurs.

☐ 16. EXTENSION: Identify the mechanisms involved in the transport water, fatty acids, glucose, amino acids, O_2, CO_2, ions (e.g. mineral ions), and sucrose (in plants).

 **Textbooks**

 See the 'Textbook Reference Grid' on pages 8-9 for textbook page references relating to material in this topic.

Supplementary Texts

See pages 5-7 for additional details of these texts:

■ Adds, J., *et al.*, 2003. **Molecules and Cells**, (NelsonThornes), chpt. 4 as reqd.

■ Harwood, R., 2002. **Biochemistry**, (Cambridge University Press), chpt. 5.

 Cell Biology & Biochemistry

Presentation MEDIA to support this topic:

CELL BIO & BIOCHEM:
• Cell Membranes & Transport

 **Periodicals**

See page 7 for details of publishers of periodicals:

STUDENT'S REFERENCE

■ **Cellular Factories** New Scientist, 23 Nov. 1996 (Inside Science). *An overview of cellular processes and the role of organelles in plant and animal cells.*

■ **Osmosis and Water Retention in Plants** Biol. Sci. Rev., 7(3) January 1995, pp. 14-16. *A good explanation of osmosis, water and solute potential and water movement in and around plant cells.*

■ **Water Channels in the Cell Membrane** Biol. Sci. Rev., 9(2) November 1996, pp. 18-22. *The role of proteins in membrane transport, including the mechanisms involved in physiological processes.*

■ **Water, Water, Everywhere...** Biol. Sci. Rev., 7(5) May 1995, pp. 6-9. *The transport of water in plants (turgor, bulk flow and water potential).*

 **Internet**

See pages 10-11 for details of how to access **Bio Links** from our web site: **www.biozone.co.uk**. From Bio Links, access sites under the topics:

GENERAL BIOLOGY ONLINE RESOURCES
• Biology I interactive animations • Instructional multimedia, University of Alberta • HowStuffWorks • Biointeractive ... *and others* > **Online Textbooks and Lecture Notes**: • S-Cool! A level biology revision guide Learn.co.uk ... *and others* > **Glossaries**: • Cellular biology: Glossary of terms • Kimball's biology glossary ... *and others*

CELL BIOLOGY AND BIOCHEMISTRY: • Cell and molecular biology online • MIT biology hypertextbook > **Cell Structure and Transport**: • Aquaporins • CELLS alive! • The virtual cell • Transport in and out of cells

Cell Processes

All of the organelles and other structures in the cell have functions. The cell can be compared to a factory with an assembly line. Organelles in the cell provide the equivalent of the power supply, assembly line, packaging department, repair and maintenance, transport system, and the control centre. The sum total of all the processes occurring in a cell is known as **metabolism**. Some of these processes store energy in molecules (anabolism) while others release that stored energy (catabolism). Below is a summary of the major processes that take place in a cell.

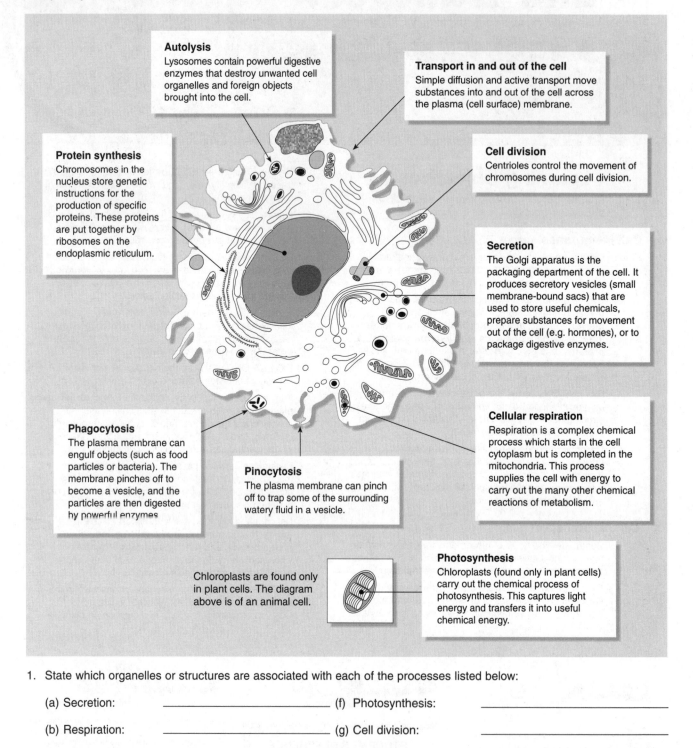

Autolysis
Lysosomes contain powerful digestive enzymes that destroy unwanted cell organelles and foreign objects brought into the cell.

Transport in and out of the cell
Simple diffusion and active transport move substances into and out of the cell across the plasma (cell surface) membrane.

Protein synthesis
Chromosomes in the nucleus store genetic instructions for the production of specific proteins. These proteins are put together by ribosomes on the endoplasmic reticulum.

Cell division
Centrioles control the movement of chromosomes during cell division.

Secretion
The Golgi apparatus is the packaging department of the cell. It produces secretory vesicles (small membrane-bound sacs) that are used to store useful chemicals, prepare substances for movement out of the cell (e.g. hormones), or to package digestive enzymes.

Phagocytosis
The plasma membrane can engulf objects (such as food particles or bacteria). The membrane pinches off to become a vesicle, and the particles are then digested by powerful enzymes

Pinocytosis
The plasma membrane can pinch off to trap some of the surrounding watery fluid in a vesicle.

Cellular respiration
Respiration is a complex chemical process which starts in the cell cytoplasm but is completed in the mitochondria. This process supplies the cell with energy to carry out the many other chemical reactions of metabolism.

Chloroplasts are found only in plant cells. The diagram above is of an animal cell.

Photosynthesis
Chloroplasts (found only in plant cells) carry out the chemical process of photosynthesis. This captures light energy and transfers it into useful chemical energy.

1. State which organelles or structures are associated with each of the processes listed below:

   (a) Secretion: _____

   (b) Respiration: _____

   (c) Pinocytosis: _____

   (d) Phagocytosis: _____

   (e) Protein synthesis: _____

   (f) Photosynthesis: _____

   (g) Cell division: _____

   (h) Autolysis: _____

   (i) Transport in/out of cell: _____

2. Explain what is meant by **metabolism** and describe an example of a metabolic process: _____
   _____
   _____

Related activities: Cell Structures and Organelles, Active and Passive Transport, The Roll of Membranes in Cells

© Biozone International 1998-2007
Photocopying Prohibited

The Structure of Membranes

All cells have a plasma membrane that forms the outer limit of the cell. Bacteria, fungi, and plant cells have a cell wall outside this, but it is quite distinct and outside the cell. Membranes are also found inside eukaryotic cells as part of membranous **organelles**. Present day knowledge of membrane structure has been built up as a result of many observations and experiments. The original model of membrane structure, proposed by Davson and Danielli, was the unit membrane; a lipid bilayer coated with protein. This model was later modified after the discovery that the protein molecules were embedded within the bilayer rather than coating the outside. The now-accepted model of membrane structure is the **fluid-mosaic model** described below.

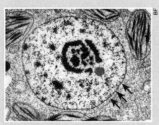
The **nuclear membrane** that surrounds the nucleus helps to control the passage of genetic information to the cytoplasm. It may also serve to protect the DNA.

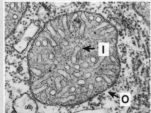
Mitochondria have an outer membrane (O) which controls the entry and exit of materials involved in aerobic respiration. Inner membranes (I) provide attachment sites for enzyme activity.

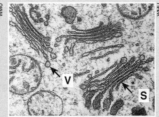
The **Golgi apparatus** comprises stacks of membrane-bound sacs (S). It is involved in packaging materials for transport or export from the cell as secretory vesicles (V).

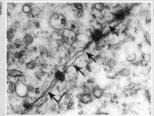
The cell is surrounded by a **plasma membrane** which controls the movement of most substances into and out of the cell. This photo shows two neighbouring cells (arrows).

The Fluid Mosaic Model

The currently accepted model for the structure of membranes is called the **fluid mosaic model**. In this model there is a double layer of lipids (fats) which are arranged with their 'tails' facing inwards. The double layer of lipids is thought to be quite fluid, with proteins 'floating' in this layer. The mobile proteins are thought to have a number of functions, including a role in active transport.

Glycoproteins (proteins with attached carbohydrate chains) play an important role in cellular recognition and the immune response, and act as receptors for hormones and neurotransmitters. Together with glycolipids, they stabilise membrane structure.

Some proteins completely penetrate the lipid layer. These proteins may control the entry and removal of specific molecules from the cell.

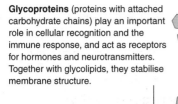
Generalised animal cell

Glycolipids, like glycoproteins, act as surface receptors and stabilise the membrane.

Double layer of phospholipids (the lipid bilayer).

Cholesterol disturbs the close packing of the phospholipids. It helps to regulate membrane fluidity and is important for membrane stability.

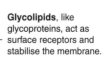
Phospholipid molecule

Hydrophilic end (water attracting)

Hydrophobic end (water repelling)

Some proteins are stuck to the surface of the membrane

Some substances, particularly ions and carbohydrates, are transported across the membrane via the channel proteins.

Some substances, including water, are transported directly through the lipid layer

1. (a) Describe the modern fluid mosaic model of membrane structure: _____

_____

_____

_____

_____

Related activities: Cell Membranes and Organelles, Modification of Proteins
The Role of Membranes in Cells   **Web links**: Membrane Structure Tutorial

RA 2

(b) Explain how the modern fluid mosaic model of membrane structure differs from the earlier Davson-Danielli model:

_____

_____

_____

2. Discuss the various functional roles of membranes in cells: _____

_____

_____

_____

3. (a) Name a cellular organelle that possesses a membrane: _____

(b) Describe the membrane's purpose in this organelle: _____

_____

4. Identify three other cell organelles that are made up of membrane systems:

(a) _____

(b) _____

(c) _____

5. (a) Describe the purpose of cholesterol in plasma membranes: _____

_____

(b) Suggest why marine organisms living in polar regions have a very high proportion of cholesterol in their membranes:

_____

_____

6. List three substances that need to be transported **into** all kinds of animal cells, in order for them to survive:

(a) _____ (b) _____ (c) _____

7. List two substances that need to be transported **out** of all kinds of animal cells, in order for them to survive:

(a) _____ (b) _____

8. Use the symbol for a phospholipid molecule (below) to draw a **simple labelled diagram** to show the structure of a plasma membrane (include features such as lipid bilayer and various kinds of proteins):

Symbol for phospholipid

The Role of Membranes in Cells

Many of the important structures and organelles in cells are composed of, or are enclosed by, membranes. These include: the endoplasmic reticulum, mitochondria, nucleus, Golgi apparatus, chloroplasts, lysosomes, vesicles and the plasma membrane itself. All membranes within eukaryotic cells share the same basic structure as the plasma membrane that encloses the entire cell.

They perform a number of critical functions in the cell: serving to compartmentalise regions of different function within the cell, controlling the entry and exit of substances, and fulfilling a role in recognition and communication between cells. Some of these roles are described below. The role of membranes in the production of macromolecules (e.g. proteins) is shown on the next page:

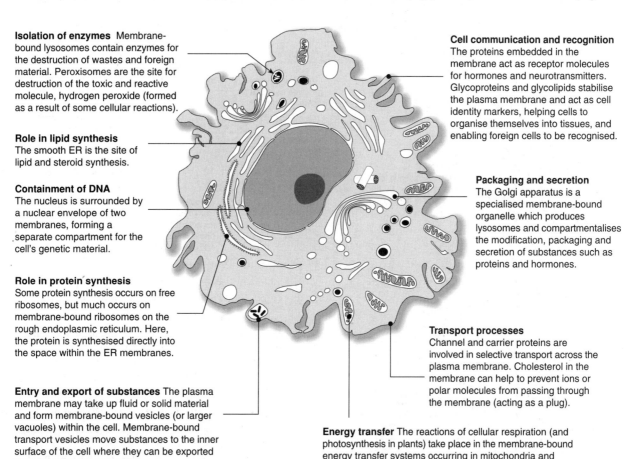

Isolation of enzymes Membrane-bound lysosomes contain enzymes for the destruction of wastes and foreign material. Peroxisomes are the site for destruction of the toxic and reactive molecule, hydrogen peroxide (formed as a result of some cellular reactions).

Role in lipid synthesis
The smooth ER is the site of lipid and steroid synthesis.

Containment of DNA
The nucleus is surrounded by a nuclear envelope of two membranes, forming a separate compartment for the cell's genetic material.

Role in protein synthesis
Some protein synthesis occurs on free ribosomes, but much occurs on membrane-bound ribosomes on the rough endoplasmic reticulum. Here, the protein is synthesised directly into the space within the ER membranes.

Entry and export of substances The plasma membrane may take up fluid or solid material and form membrane-bound vesicles (or larger vacuoles) within the cell. Membrane-bound transport vesicles move substances to the inner surface of the cell where they can be exported from the cell by exocytosis.

Cell communication and recognition
The proteins embedded in the membrane act as receptor molecules for hormones and neurotransmitters. Glycoproteins and glycolipids stabilise the plasma membrane and act as cell identity markers, helping cells to organise themselves into tissues, and enabling foreign cells to be recognised.

Packaging and secretion
The Golgi apparatus is a specialised membrane-bound organelle which produces lysosomes and compartmentalises the modification, packaging and secretion of substances such as proteins and hormones.

Transport processes
Channel and carrier proteins are involved in selective transport across the plasma membrane. Cholesterol in the membrane can help to prevent ions or polar molecules from passing through the membrane (acting as a plug).

Energy transfer The reactions of cellular respiration (and photosynthesis in plants) take place in the membrane-bound energy transfer systems occurring in mitochondria and chloroplasts respectively. See the example explained below.

Compartmentation within Membranes

Membranes play an important role in separating regions within the cell (and within organelles) where particular reactions occur. Specific enzymes are therefore often located in particular organelles. The reaction rate is controlled by controlling the rate at which substrates enter the organelle and therefore the availability of the raw materials required for the reactions.

Example (right): *The enzymes involved in cellular respiration are arranged in different parts of the mitochondria. Reactions are localised and separated by membrane systems.*

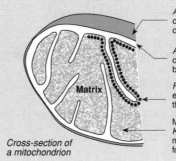

Cross-section of a mitochondrion

Matrix

Amine oxidases and other enzymes on the outer membrane surface

Adenylate kinase and other *phosphorylases* between the membranes

Respiratory assembly enzymes embedded in the membrane (ATPase)

Many soluble enzymes of the *Krebs cycle* floating in the matrix, as well as enzymes for fatty acid degradation.

1. Explain the crucial role of membrane systems and organelles in the following:

(a) Providing compartments within the cell: _____

_____

_____

(b) Increasing the total membrane surface area within the cell: _____

_____

_____

_____

Cells produce a range of **macromolecules**; organic polymers made up of repeating units of smaller molecules. The synthesis, packaging and movement of these molecules inside the cell involves a number of membrane bound organelles, as indicated below. These organelles provide compartments where the enzyme systems involved can be isolated.

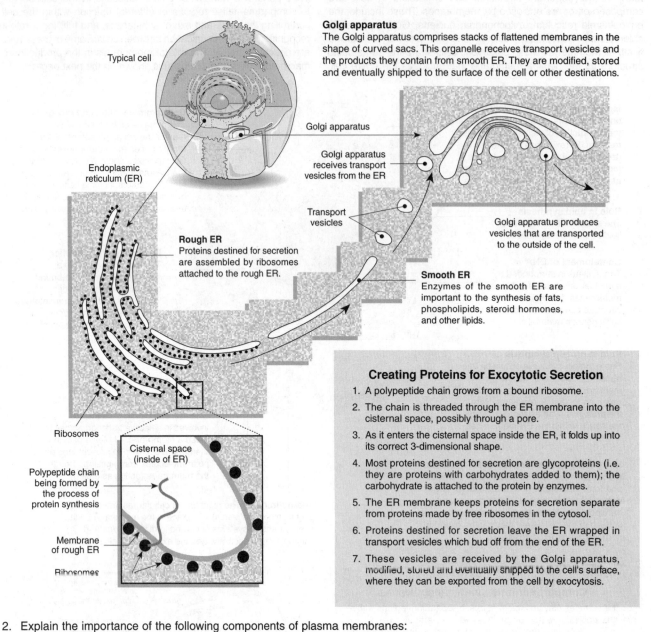

Typical cell

Endoplasmic reticulum (ER)

Golgi apparatus
The Golgi apparatus comprises stacks of flattened membranes in the shape of curved sacs. This organelle receives transport vesicles and the products they contain from smooth ER. They are modified, stored and eventually shipped to the surface of the cell or other destinations.

Golgi apparatus

Golgi apparatus receives transport vesicles from the ER

Transport vesicles

Golgi apparatus produces vesicles that are transported to the outside of the cell.

Rough ER
Proteins destined for secretion are assembled by ribosomes attached to the rough ER.

Smooth ER
Enzymes of the smooth ER are important to the synthesis of fats, phospholipids, steroid hormones, and other lipids.

Ribosomes

Cisternal space (inside of ER)

Polypeptide chain being formed by the process of protein synthesis

Membrane of rough ER

Ribosomes

Creating Proteins for Exocytotic Secretion

1. A polypeptide chain grows from a bound ribosome.

2. The chain is threaded through the ER membrane into the cisternal space, possibly through a pore.

3. As it enters the cisternal space inside the ER, it folds up into its correct 3-dimensional shape.

4. Most proteins destined for secretion are glycoproteins (i.e. they are proteins with carbohydrates added to them); the carbohydrate is attached to the protein by enzymes.

5. The ER membrane keeps proteins for secretion separate from proteins made by free ribosomes in the cytosol.

6. Proteins destined for secretion leave the ER wrapped in transport vesicles which bud off from the end of the ER.

7. These vesicles are received by the Golgi apparatus, modified, stored and eventually snipped to the cell's surface, where they can be exported from the cell by exocytosis.

2. Explain the importance of the following components of plasma membranes:

(a) Glycoproteins and glycolipids: _____

_____

(b) Channel proteins and carrier proteins: _____

_____

3. Explain how cholesterol can play a role in membrane transport: _____

_____

4. Non-polar (lipid-soluble) molecules diffuse more rapidly through membranes than polar (lipid-insoluble) molecules:

(a) Explain the reason for this: _____

_____

(b) Discuss the implications of this to the transport of substances into the cell through the plasma membrane:

_____

_____

Active and Passive Transport

Cells have a need to move materials both into and out of the cell. Raw materials and other molecules necessary for metabolism must be accumulated from outside the cell. Some of these substances are scarce outside of the cell and some effort is required to accumulate them. Waste products and molecules for use in other parts of the body must be 'exported' out of the cell.

Some materials (e.g. gases and water) move into and out of the cell by **passive transport** processes, without the expenditure of energy on the part of the cell. Other molecules (e.g. sucrose) are moved into and out of the cell using **active transport**. Active transport processes involve the expenditure of energy in the form of ATP, and therefore use oxygen.

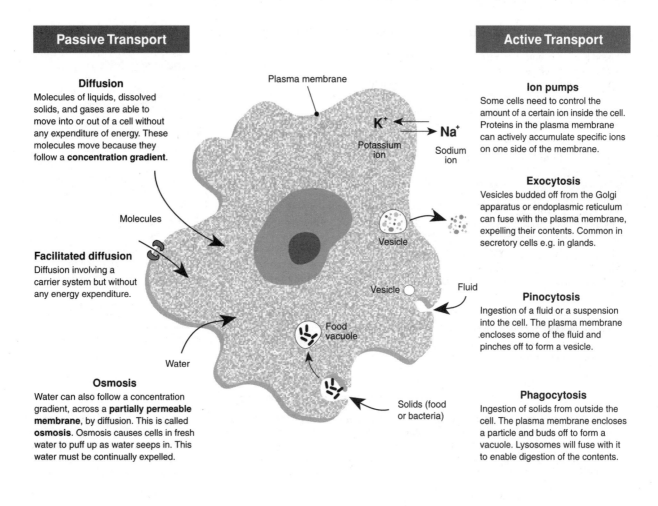

Passive Transport

Diffusion
Molecules of liquids, dissolved solids, and gases are able to move into or out of a cell without any expenditure of energy. These molecules move because they follow a **concentration gradient**.

Facilitated diffusion
Diffusion involving a carrier system but without any energy expenditure.

Osmosis
Water can also follow a concentration gradient, across a **partially permeable membrane**, by diffusion. This is called **osmosis**. Osmosis causes cells in fresh water to puff up as water seeps in. This water must be continually expelled.

Active Transport

Ion pumps
Some cells need to control the amount of a certain ion inside the cell. Proteins in the plasma membrane can actively accumulate specific ions on one side of the membrane.

Exocytosis
Vesicles budded off from the Golgi apparatus or endoplasmic reticulum can fuse with the plasma membrane, expelling their contents. Common in secretory cells e.g. in glands.

Pinocytosis
Ingestion of a fluid or a suspension into the cell. The plasma membrane encloses some of the fluid and pinches off to form a vesicle.

Phagocytosis
Ingestion of solids from outside the cell. The plasma membrane encloses a particle and buds off to form a vacuole. Lysosomes will fuse with it to enable digestion of the contents.

1. In general terms, describe the energy requirements of **passive** and **active** transport: _____

_____

_____

_____

2. Name two gases that move into or out of our bodies by **diffusion**: _____

_____

3. Name a gland which has cells where **exocytosis** takes place for the purpose of secretion:

_____

4. **Phagocytosis** is a process where solid particles are enveloped by the plasma membrane and drawn inside the cell.

(a) Name a protozoan (single-celled protoctist) that would use this technique for feeding: _____

(b) Describe how it uses the technique: _____

_____

(c) Name a type of cell found in human blood that uses this technique for capturing and destroying bacteria:

_____

Related activities: Diffusion, Osmosis and Water Potential, Ion Pumps, Exocytosis and Endocytosis, Unicellular Eukaryotes

RA 1

Diffusion

The molecules that make up substances are constantly moving about in a random way. This random motion causes molecules to disperse from areas of high to low concentration; a process called **diffusion**. The molecules move along a **concentration gradient**. Diffusion and osmosis (diffusion of water molecules across a partially permeable membrane) are **passive** processes, and use no energy. Diffusion occurs freely across membranes, as long as the membrane is permeable to that molecule (partially permeable membranes allow the passage of some molecules but not others). Each type of molecule diffuses along its own concentration gradient. Diffusion of molecules in one direction does not hinder the movement of other molecules. Diffusion is important in allowing exchanges with the environment and in the regulation of cell water content.

Diffusion of Molecules Along Concentration Gradients

Diffusion is the movement of particles from regions of high to low concentration (the **concentration gradient**), with the end result being that the molecules become evenly distributed. In biological systems, diffusion often occurs across partially permeable membranes. Various factors determine the rate at which this occurs (see right).

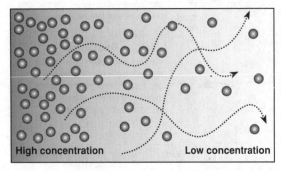

High concentration   **Low concentration**

Concentration gradient

If molecules are free to move, they move from high to low concentration until they are evenly dispersed.

Factors affecting rates of diffusion	
Concentration gradient:	Diffusion rates will be higher when there is a greater difference in concentration between two regions.
The distance involved:	Diffusion over shorter distances occurs at a greater rate than diffusion over larger distances.
The area involved:	The larger the area across which diffusion occurs, the greater the rate of diffusion.
Barriers to diffusion:	Thicker barriers slow diffusion rate. Pores in a barrier enhance diffusion.

These factors are expressed in **Fick's law**, which governs the rate of diffusion of substances within a system. It is described by:

$$\frac{\text{Surface area of membrane} \quad \text{X} \quad \text{Difference in concentration across the membrane}}{\text{Length of the diffusion path (thickness of the membrane)}}$$

Diffusion through Membranes

Each type of diffusing molecule (gas, solvent, solute) moves **along its own concentration gradient**. Two-way diffusion (below) is common in biological systems, e.g. at the lung surface, carbon dioxide diffuses out and oxygen diffuses into the blood. Facilitated diffusion (below, right) increases the diffusion rate selectively and is important for larger molecules (e.g. glucose, amino acids) where a higher diffusion rate is desirable (e.g. transport of glucose into skeletal muscle fibres, transport of ADP into mitochondria). Neither type of diffusion requires energy expenditure because the molecules are not moving against their concentration gradient.

Unaided diffusion

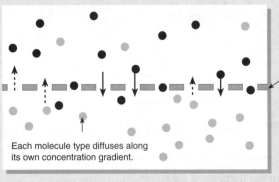

Each molecule type diffuses along its own concentration gradient.

Partially permeable membrane

Facilitated diffusion

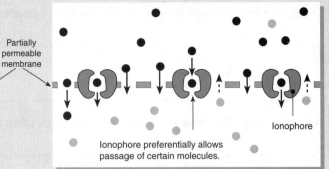

Ionophore

Ionophore preferentially allows passage of certain molecules.

Diffusion rates depend on the concentration gradient. Diffusion can occur in either direction but **net** movement is in the direction of the concentration gradient. An equilibrium is reached when concentrations are equal.

Facilitated diffusion occurs when a substance is aided across a membrane by a special molecule called an **ionophore**. Ionophores allow some molecules to diffuse but not others, effectively speeding up the rate of diffusion of that molecule.

1. Describe two properties of an exchange surface that would facilitate rapid diffusion rates:

   (a) _____ (b) _____

2. Identify one way in which organisms maintain concentration gradients across membranes: _____

   _____

3. State how facilitated diffusion is achieved: _____

Related activities: Active and Passive Transport, Osmosis & Water Potential
Web links: Osmosis and Diffusion

Osmosis and Water Potential

Osmosis is the term describing the diffusion of water along its concentration gradient across a partially permeable membrane. It is the principal mechanism by which water enters and leaves cells in living organisms. As it is a type of diffusion, the rate at which osmosis occurs is affected by the same factors that affect all diffusion rates (see earlier). The tendency for water to move in any particular direction can be calculated on the basis of the water potential of the cell sap relative to its surrounding environment. The use of water potential to express the water relations of cells has replaced the terms osmotic potential and osmotic pressure although these are still frequently used in areas of animal physiology and medicine. The concepts of osmosis, water potential, cell turgor, and plasmolysis are explained below and on the next page.

Osmosis and the Water Potential of Cells

Osmosis is simply the diffusion of water molecules from high concentration to lower concentration, across a partially permeable membrane. The direction of this movement can be predicted on the basis of the water potential of the solutions involved. The **water potential** of a solution (denoted with the symbol Ψ) is the term given to the tendency for water molecules to enter or leave a solution by osmosis. Pure water has the highest water potential, set at zero. Dissolving any solute into pure water lowers the water potential (makes it more negative). *Water always diffuses from regions of less negative to more negative water potential.* Water potential is determined by two components: the **solute potential**, Ψs (of the cell sap) and the **pressure potential**, Ψp. This is expressed as a simple equation:

$$\Psi cell = \Psi s + \Psi p$$

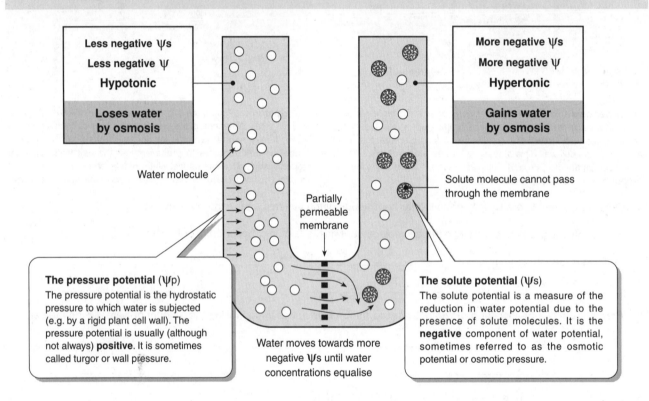

Less negative Ψs
Less negative Ψ
Hypotonic

Loses water by osmosis

Water molecule

Partially permeable membrane

More negative Ψs
More negative Ψ
Hypertonic

Gains water by osmosis

Solute molecule cannot pass through the membrane

The pressure potential (Ψp)
The pressure potential is the hydrostatic pressure to which water is subjected (e.g. by a rigid plant cell wall). The pressure potential is usually (although not always) **positive**. It is sometimes called turgor or wall pressure.

Water moves towards more negative Ψs until water concentrations equalise

The solute potential (Ψs)
The solute potential is a measure of the reduction in water potential due to the presence of solute molecules. It is the **negative** component of water potential, sometimes referred to as the osmotic potential or osmotic pressure.

1. State the water potential of pure water at standard temperature and pressure: _____

2. The three diagrams below show the solute and pressure potential values for three hypothetical situations where two solutions are separated by a selectively permeable membrane. For each example (a) - (c) calculate ψ for the solutions on each side of the membrane, as indicated:

3. Draw arrows on each diagram to indicate the direction of net flow of water:

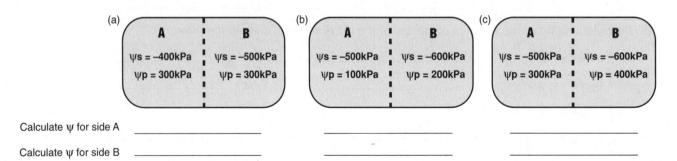

(a)

A	B
ψs = –400kPa	ψs = –500kPa
ψp = 300kPa	ψp = 300kPa

(b)

A	B
ψs = –500kPa	ψs = –600kPa
ψp = 100kPa	ψp = 200kPa

(c)

A	B
ψs = –500kPa	ψs = –600kPa
ψp = 300kPa	ψp = 400kPa

Calculate ψ for side A _____   _____   _____

Calculate ψ for side B _____   _____   _____

Related activities: Diffusion, Unicellular Eukaryotes
Web links: Osmosis and Diffusion

Water Relations in Plant Cells

The plasma membrane of cells is a partially permeable membrane and osmosis is the principal mechanism by which water enters and leaves the cell. When the external water potential is the same as that of the cell there is no net movement of water. Two systems (cell and environment) with the same water potential are termed **isotonic**. The diagram below illustrates two different situations: when the external water potential is less negative than the cell (**hypotonic**) and when it is more negative than the cell (**hypertonic**).

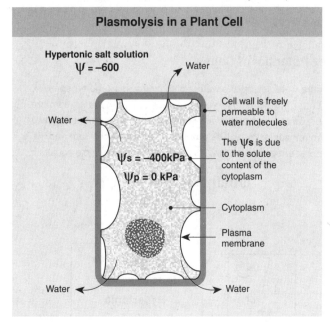

Plasmolysis in a Plant Cell

Hypertonic salt solution
$\Psi = -600$

Water

Cell wall is freely permeable to water molecules

The Ψs is due to the solute content of the cytoplasm

$\Psi s = -400kPa$

$\Psi p = 0$ kPa

Cytoplasm

Plasma membrane

Water

Water

Water

Turgor in a Plant Cell

Pure water (Hypotonic)
$\Psi = 0$

Water

Cell wall bulges outward

Water

$\Psi s = -400kPa$

$\Psi p = 200$ kPa

Cytoplasm takes on water, putting pressure on the plasma membrane and cell wall. Ψp rises (offsetting Ψs at full turgor)

Water

Water

In a **hypertonic** solution, the external water potential is more negative than the water potential of the cell ($\Psi cell = \Psi s + \Psi p$). Water leaves the cell and, because the cell wall is rigid, the plasma membrane shrinks away from the cell wall. This process is termed **plasmolysis** and the cell becomes **flaccid** ($\Psi p = 0$). Full plasmolysis is irreversible; the cell cannot recover by taking up water.

In a **hypotonic** solution, the external water potential is less negative than the $\Psi cell$. Water enters the cell causing it to swell tight. A pressure potential is generated when sufficient water has been taken up to cause the cell contents to press against the cell wall. Ψp rises progressively until it offsets Ψs. Water uptake stops when $\Psi cell = 0$. The rigid cell wall prevents cell rupture. Cells in this state are **turgid**.

4. Fluid replacements are usually provided for heavily perspiring athletes after endurance events.

   (a) Identify the preferable tonicity of these replacement drinks (isotonic, hypertonic, or hypotonic): _____

   (b) Give a reason for your answer: _____

   _____

5. *Paramecium* is a freshwater protozoan. Describe the problem it has in controlling the amount of water inside the cell:

   _____

   _____

6. (a) Explain the role of pressure potential in generating cell turgor in plants: _____

   _____

   (b) Explain the purpose of cell turgor to plants: _____

   _____

7. Explain how animal cells differ from plant cells with respect to the effects of net water movements: _____

   _____

8. Describe what would happen to an animal cell (e.g. a red blood cell) if it was placed into:

   (a) Pure water: _____

   (b) A hypertonic solution: _____

   (c) A hypotonic solution: _____

9. The malarial parasite lives in human blood. Relative to the tonicity of the blood, the parasite's cell contents would be hypotonic / isotonic / hypertonic (circle the correct answer).

Surface Area and Volume

When an object (e.g. a cell) is small it has a large surface area in comparison to its volume. In this case diffusion will be an effective way to transport materials (e.g. gases) into the cell. As an object becomes larger, its surface area compared to its volume is smaller. Diffusion is no longer an effective way to transport materials to the inside. For this reason, there is a physical limit for the size of a cell, with the effectiveness of diffusion being the controlling factor.

Diffusion in Organisms of Different Sizes

Respiratory gases and some other substances are exchanged with the surroundings by diffusion or active transport across the plasma membrane.

The **plasma membrane**, which surrounds every cell, functions as a selective barrier that regulates the cell's chemical composition. For each square micrometer of membrane, only so much of a particular substance can cross per second.

The surface area of an elephant is increased, for radiating body heat, by large flat ears.

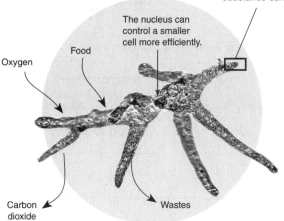

The nucleus can control a smaller cell more efficiently.

Food

Oxygen

Carbon dioxide

Wastes

A specialised gas exchange surface (lungs) and circulatory (blood) system are required to speed up the movement of substances through the body.

Respiratory gases cannot reach body tissues by diffusion alone.

Amoeba: The small size of single-celled protoctists, such as *Amoeba*, provides a large surface area relative to the cell's volume. This is adequate for many materials to be moved into and out of the cell by diffusion or active transport.

Multicellular organisms: To overcome the problems of small cell size, plants and animals became multicellular. They provide a small surface area compared to their volume but have evolved various adaptive features to improve their effective surface area.

Smaller is Better for Diffusion

One large cube

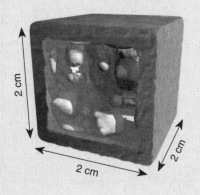

2 cm

2 cm

2 cm

Volume: = 8 cm³
Surface area: = 24 cm²

Eight small cubes

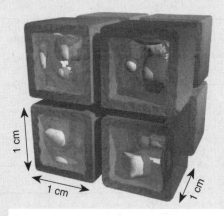

1 cm

1 cm

1 cm

Volume: = 8 cm³ for 8 cubes
Surface area: = 6 cm² for 1 cube
= 48 cm² for 8 cubes

The eight small cells and the single large cell have the same total volume, but their surface areas are different. The small cells together have twice the total surface area of the large cell, because there are more exposed (inner) surfaces. Real organisms have complex shapes, but the same principles apply.

The surface-area volume relationship has important implications for processes involving transport into and out of cells across membranes. For activities such as gas exchange, the surface area available for diffusion is a major factor limiting the rate at which oxygen can be supplied to tissues.

The diagram below shows four hypothetical cells of different sizes (cells do not actually grow to this size, their large size is for the sake of the exercise). They range from a small 2 cm cube to a larger 5 cm cube. This exercise investigates the effect of cell size on the efficiency of diffusion.

2 cm cube　　**3 cm cube**　　**4 cm cube**　　**5 cm cube**

1. Calculate the volume, surface area and the ratio of surface area to volume for each of the four cubes above (the first has been done for you). When completing the table below, show your calculations.

Cube size	Surface area	Volume	Surface area to volume ratio
2 cm cube	$2 \times 2 \times 6 = 24\,cm^2$ (2 cm x 2 cm x 6 sides)	$2 \times 2 \times 2 = 8\,cm^3$ (height x width x depth)	$24\ to\ 8 = 3{:}1$
3 cm cube			
4 cm cube			
5 cm cube			

2. Create a graph, plotting the surface area against the volume of each cube, on the grid on the right. Draw a line connecting the points and label axes and units.

3. State which increases the fastest with increasing size, the **volume** or **surface area**.

_____

4. Explain what happens to the ratio of surface area to volume with increasing size:

_____

_____

_____

_____

5. Diffusion of substances into and out of a cell occurs across the cell surface. Describe how increasing the size of a cell will affect the ability of diffusion to transport materials into and out of a cell:

_____

_____

_____

_____

Ion Pumps

Diffusion alone cannot supply the cell's entire requirements for molecules (and ions). Some molecules (e.g. glucose) are required by the cell in higher concentrations than occur outside the cell. Others (e.g. sodium) must be removed from the cell in order to maintain cell fluid balance. These molecules must be moved across the plasma membrane by active transport mechanisms. **Active transport** requires the expenditure of energy because the molecules (or ions) must be moved **against** their concentration gradient. The work of active transport is performed by specific carrier proteins in the membrane. These transport proteins harness the energy of ATP to pump molecules from a low to a high concentration. When ATP transfers a phosphate group to the carrier protein, the protein changes its shape in such a way as to move the bound molecule across the membrane. Three types of membrane pump are illustrated below. The sodium-potassium pump (below, left) is almost universal in animal cells and is common in plant cells also. The concentration gradient created by ion pumps such as this and the proton pump (centre) is frequently coupled to the transport of other molecules such as glucose and sucrose (below, right).

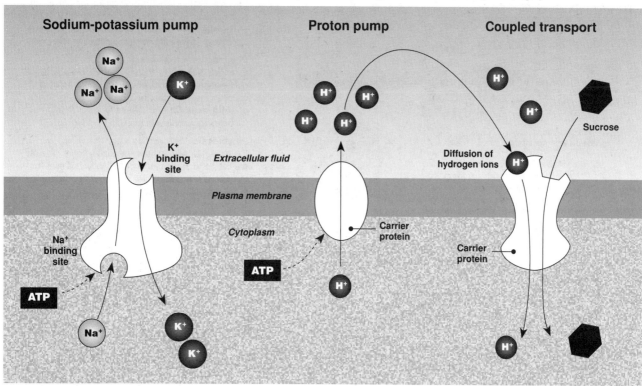

Sodium-potassium pump
The sodium-potassium pump is a specific protein in the membrane that uses energy in the form of ATP to exchange sodium ions (Na⁺) for potassium ions (K⁺) across the membrane. The unequal balance of Na⁺ and K⁺ across the membrane creates large concentration gradients that can be used to drive other active transport mechanisms.

Proton pumps
ATP driven proton pumps use energy to remove hydrogen ions (H⁺) from inside the cell to the outside. This creates a large difference in the proton concentration either side of the membrane, with the inside of the plasma membrane being negatively charged. This potential difference can be coupled to the transport of other molecules.

Coupled transport (cotransport)
Plant cells use the gradient in hydrogen ions created by proton pumps to drive the active transport of nutrients into the cell. The specific transport protein couples the return of H⁺ to the transport of sucrose into the phloem cells. The sucrose rides with the H⁺ as it diffuses down the concentration gradient maintained by the proton pump.

1. The sodium-potassium pump plays an important role in the water balance of cells. In terms of osmosis, explain the consequences of the sodium-potassium pumps not working:

_____

_____

2. Explain how the transport of molecules such as sucrose can be coupled to the activity of an ion exchange pump:

_____

_____

_____

3. Explain why the ATP is required for membrane pump systems to operate: _____

_____

_____

4. Name a type of cell that relies on coupled transport to perform its function: _____

Exocytosis and Endocytosis

Most cells carry out **cytosis**: a form of **active transport** involving the in- or outfolding of the plasma membrane. The ability of cells to do this is a function of the flexibility of the plasma membrane. Cytosis results in the bulk transport into or out of the cell and is achieved through the localised activity of microfilaments and microtubules in the cell cytoskeleton. Engulfment of material is termed **endocytosis.** Endocytosis typically occurs in protozoans and certain white blood cells of the mammalian defence system (e.g. neutrophils, macrophages). **Exocytosis** is the reverse of endocytosis and involves the release of material from vesicles or vacuoles that have fused with the plasma membrane. Exocytosis is typical of cells that export material (secretory cells).

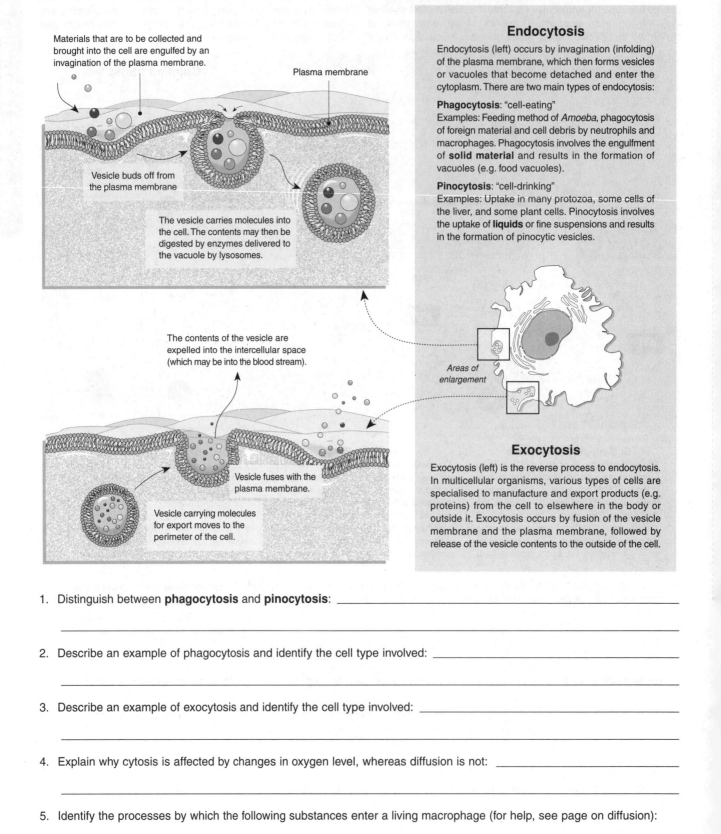

Materials that are to be collected and brought into the cell are engulfed by an invagination of the plasma membrane.

Plasma membrane

Vesicle buds off from the plasma membrane

The vesicle carries molecules into the cell. The contents may then be digested by enzymes delivered to the vacuole by lysosomes.

The contents of the vesicle are expelled into the intercellular space (which may be into the blood stream).

Vesicle fuses with the plasma membrane.

Vesicle carrying molecules for export moves to the perimeter of the cell.

Endocytosis

Endocytosis (left) occurs by invagination (infolding) of the plasma membrane, which then forms vesicles or vacuoles that become detached and enter the cytoplasm. There are two main types of endocytosis:

Phagocytosis: "cell-eating"
Examples: Feeding method of *Amoeba*, phagocytosis of foreign material and cell debris by neutrophils and macrophages. Phagocytosis involves the engulfment of **solid material** and results in the formation of vacuoles (e.g. food vacuoles).

Pinocytosis: "cell-drinking"
Examples: Uptake in many protozoa, some cells of the liver, and some plant cells. Pinocytosis involves the uptake of **liquids** or fine suspensions and results in the formation of pinocytic vesicles.

Areas of enlargement

Exocytosis

Exocytosis (left) is the reverse process to endocytosis. In multicellular organisms, various types of cells are specialised to manufacture and export products (e.g. proteins) from the cell to elsewhere in the body or outside it. Exocytosis occurs by fusion of the vesicle membrane and the plasma membrane, followed by release of the vesicle contents to the outside of the cell.

1. Distinguish between **phagocytosis** and **pinocytosis**: _____

_____

2. Describe an example of phagocytosis and identify the cell type involved: _____

_____

3. Describe an example of exocytosis and identify the cell type involved: _____

_____

4. Explain why cytosis is affected by changes in oxygen level, whereas diffusion is not: _____

_____

5. Identify the processes by which the following substances enter a living macrophage (for help, see page on diffusion):

(a) Oxygen: _____ (c) Water: _____

(b) Cellular debris: _____ (d) Glucose: _____

Related activities: Active and Passive Transport, Diffusion

The Genetic Code

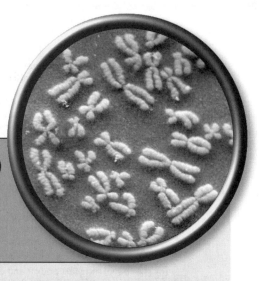

AQA-A	AQA-B	SNAB	Edexcel	OCR
Complete:	Complete:	Complete:	Complete:	Complete:
1, 6-16, 18-24	1, 6-8, 10, 12-16, 18-24	1, 5-10, 12-14, 17-24	1-10, 12-24	1, 6-10, 12-16, 18-24

All exam boards: Number 13 (b) may be extension at the teacher's discretion

Learning Objectives

☐ 1. Compile your own glossary from the **KEY WORDS** displayed in **bold type** in the learning objectives below.

Chromosome Structure *(pages 131-132, 141-144)*

☐ 2. Describe the structure and morphology of eukaryote **chromosomes**, explaining the role of **histone proteins** and **nucleosomes** in packaging and organisation of the DNA in the nucleus. With respect to basic structure and organization, distinguish between prokaryote and eukaryote chromosomes.

☐ 3. Explain clearly what is meant by the terms: **genome**, **homologous chromosomes** (=homologues), **chromatid**, and **centromere**. Distinguish between the **diploid** (2N) and **haploid** (1N) state of a cell.

☐ 4. Understand that **specialised** diploid cells arise as a result of **differentiation** after mitotic cell division.

☐ 5. Recognise the role of the **Human Genome Project** (the HGP) in providing a map of the chromosomes in the human genome.

The Genetic Blueprint

Nucleic acid structure *(pages 133-135, 137-140)*

☐ 6. Name some examples of **nucleic acids** and describe their role in biological systems.

☐ 7. Describe the components of a (mono)**nucleotide**: a 5C sugar (**ribose** or **deoxyribose**), a nitrogenous base (**purine** or **pyrimidine**), and a phosphate. Identify the purines and pyrimidines that form nucleotides.

☐ 8. Understand the role of **condensation** reactions in joining the components of nucleotides and in the formation of dinucleotides and **polynucleotides** (nucleic acids).

☐ 9. EXTENSION: Understand that DNA contains **repetitive sequences** and that only a small proportion constitutes **genes**. Appreciate the role of repetitive sequences in DNA technologies such as **DNA profiling**.

☐ 10. Describe the Watson-Crick **double-helix** model of DNA structure. Include reference to the **base pairing rule**, the **antiparallel strands**, and the role of **hydrogen bonding** between **purines** and **pyrimidines**. Contrast the structure and function of **DNA** and **RNA**.

☐ 11. Interpret evidence that DNA is the genetic material.

DNA replication *(pages 145-146)*

☐ 12. Demonstrate an understanding of the **base-pairing rule** for creating a **complementary strand** from a single strand of DNA.

☐ 13. Describe the **semi-conservative** replication of DNA and interpret experimental evidence for this process. Explain the role of the following in DNA replication:

(a) **DNA polymerase, helicase, DNA ligase**.

(b) **DNA polymerase III, RNA primase, DNA polymerase I, Okazaki fragments**, and **deoxynucleoside triphosphates**.

☐ 14. Understand that DNA replication proceeds only in the **5' to 3' direction** and explain the significance of this. Clearly explain what is meant by each of the following terms in relation to DNA replication:
- **Replication fork**
- The **leading strand** vs the **lagging strand**

☐ 15. Explain the role of the polymerase chain reaction (**PCR**) as an artificially induced form of DNA replication, used as a tool in molecular biology (see the topic, *Gene Technology* for coverage of this technique).

The genetic code *(pages 136, 143-144)*

☐ 16. Explain the main features of the **genetic code**, including reference to the following:
- The 4-letter alphabet and the 3-letter **triplet code** (**codon**) of base sequences.
- The **non-overlapping**, linear nature of the code which is read from a start point to a finish point in one direction.
- Specific punctuation codons (START, STOP codons) and their significance.
- The **universal nature** of the code.
- The **degeneracy** of the code.

☐ 17. Appreciate the **Human Genome Project** in the light of nucleic acid structure and consider the spiritual, moral, ethical, social, and cultural issues associated with it.

Gene expression *(pages 147-153)*

☐ 18. Outline the basis by which information is transferred from DNA to protein. Distinguish clearly between **allele** and **gene**. Explain what is meant by **gene expression** and define its two distinct stages: **transcription** and **translation**. *NOTE: Gene expression is often used to refer only to transcription, i.e. expression of the gene as its mRNA product.*

☐ 19. Recall the structure and role of messenger RNA (**mRNA**). Describe the process of **transcription**. In your description, demonstrate an understanding of the direction of transcription (5' → 3' direction) and explain the role of **RNA polymerase** in the process. Explain clearly what is meant by each of the following:
- **Coding (sense) strand**
- **Template (antisense) strand**
- **Introns** (sometimes called intronic DNA)
- **Exons** (sometimes called exonic DNA)

Explain the significance of introns with the respect to the production of a functional mRNA molecule.

☐ 20. Recall the structure of **proteins** as **polypeptides** with a complex (post-translational) structure. Explain how the 4-letter alphabet of bases provides the code for the 20 amino acids needed to assemble proteins.

☐ 21. Recognise translation as a process involving **initiation**, **elongation**, and **termination**, occurring in a 5' → 3' direction. Describe the process of **translation**, including reference to:
(a) The role of transfer RNA (**tRNA**) molecules, the reason for the large number of these, and the significance of the **anticodons**.
(b) The structure and role of ribosomes.
(c) The role of the **start codon** and **stop codons**.

☐ 22. EXTENSION: Explain how **reverse transcriptase** catalyses the production of DNA from RNA and describe how this enzyme is used by retroviruses. Appreciate the use of reverse transcriptase in molecular biology (see the topic, *Gene Technology*).

☐ 23. Recognise **enzymes** as proteins whose synthesis is controlled by DNA. Understand the role of enzymes in the control of metabolic pathways and in determining the phenotype of an organism.

☐ 24. EXTENSION: Contrast gene expression in prokaryotic and eukaryotic cells. Identify differences in mRNA processing after transcription, movement of mRNA to the translation site, and the speed of translation.

 See the 'Textbook Reference Grid' on pages 8-9 for textbook page references relating to material in this topic.

Supplementary Texts
See pages 5-7 for additional details of these texts:

■ Adds, J., *et al.*, 2003. **Molecules and Cells**, (NelsonThornes), chpt. 2.

■ Jones, N., *et al.*, 2001. **The Essentials of Genetics**, (John Murray), pp. 123-188, 257.

See page 7 for details of publishers of periodicals:

STUDENT'S REFERENCE
Gene structure and expression

■ **Gene Structure and Expression** Biol. Sci. Rev., 12 (5) May 2000, pp. 22-25. *An account of gene function, including a comparison of gene regulation in pro- and eukaryotes.*

■ **What is a Gene?** Biol. Sci. Rev., 15(2) Nov. 2002, pp. 9-11. *A good synopsis of genes and their role in heredity, mutations, and transcriptional control of gene expression.*

■ **Transfer RNA** Biol. Sci. Rev., 15(3) Feb. 2003, pp. 26-29. *A good account of the structure and role of tRNA in protein synthesis.*

■ **Control Centre** New Scientist, 17 July 1999, (Inside Science). *Easy to read account covering the organisation of DNA in eukaryotic cells, the origin of the nucleus, how genes code for proteins, and the role of ribosomes and RNA in translation.*

■ **DNA in a Spin** Biol. Sci. Rev., 11(3) Jan. 1999, pp. 15-17. *A short account of the methods used to establish the mechanism for DNA replication.*

■ **Stuff or Nonsense** New Scientist, 1 April 2000, pp. 38-41. *The functional and evolutionary role of introns (junk DNA) in the genomes of organisms.*

Genome analysis

■ **Bioinformatics** Biol. Sci. Rev., 15(3), February 2003, pp. 13-15 . *This account explores the bioinformation revolution. Bioinformatics is a branch of biology arising from the advancements in genome sequencing and development of the world wide web. A useful glossary of terms is provided.*

■ **Bioinformatics** Biol. Sci. Rev., 15(4) April 2003, pp. 2-6. *A follow up to the earlier account on the bioinformation revolution. This article looks at applications of bioinformatics in areas of basic biological and medical research.*

■ **Genes, the Genome, and Disease** New Scientist, 17 Feb. 2001, (Inside Science). *Understanding the human genome: producing genome maps, the role of introns in gene regulation, and the future of genomic research.*

■ **The Business of the Human Genome** Sci. American, July 2000, pp. 38-57. *The HGP: where will the research progress from here?*

■ **Sequence Me!** New Scientist, 21 Dec. 2002, pp. 44-47. *Which organisms have had their genomes sequenced and why? Which are next?*

■ **Mother Nature's DNA** Time, 20 June 2005, pp. 50-51. *The value of decoding different genomes and understanding what different genes do.*

TEACHER'S REFERENCE

■ **Ancient DNA** Scientific American, Nov. 1993, pp. 60-66. *Reconstituted DNA fragments allow comparisons between existing and ancient species.*

■ **Evolution Encoded** Scientific American, April 2004, pp. 56-63. *Genetic instructions for the manufacture of proteins are written in 3-letter codons, each specifying one of 20 amino acids or a 'stop translating' sign. Their arrangement indicates that natural selection has maintained an order that is good at minimising errors.*

■ **The Unseen Genome: Gems Among the Junk** Scientific American, Nov. 2003, pp. 26-33. *98% of the DNA in humans was once dismissed as junk, but the discovery of many hidden genes that work through RNA, rather than protein, has overturned this assumption.*

■ **DNA 50** SSR, 84(308), March 2003, pp. 17-80. *A special issue celebrating 50 years since the discovery of DNA. There are various articles examining the practical and theoretical aspects of teaching molecular genetics and inheritance.*

■ **DNA: 50 Years of the Double Helix** New Scientist, 15 March 2003, pp. 35-51. *A special issue on DNA: structure and function, repair, the new-found role of histones, and the functional significance of chromosome position in the nucleus.*

■ **The Hidden Genetic Program** Scientific American, Oct. 2004, pp. 30-37. *Large portions of the DNA of complex organisms may encode RNA molecules with important regulatory functions.*

■ **Wonderful Spam** New Scientist, 29 May 2004, pp. 42-45. *Much of the so-called junk DNA is in the form of transposons. It now appears that this DNA, once dismissed as repeating trash, could have directed evolution and even helped to invent sex.*

■ **RNA to the Rescue** Scientific American, June 2005, pp. 8-10. *The discovery that a species of plant can summon up genes its parents have lost highlights increasing recognition of RNA as a more versatile and important molecule in its own right.*

Genome analysis

■ **Proteins Rule** Scientific American, April 2002, pp. 27-33. *After the HGP, the race is on to catalogue human proteins and their functions.*

■ **Beyond the Genome** New Scientist, 4 Nov. 2000, pp. 28-55. *A series of articles examining the future directions of genome analysis.*

■ **Proteomics** Biologist 49(2) April 2002. *To really understand cellular functions, it is the proteome you need to analyse. What is involved in this?*

■ **The Genome has Landed** New Scientist, 20 May 2000, pp. 14-21. *Special section covering the status of the Human Genome Project.*

■ **Chimp Genome Review: What makes Us Human?** New Scientist, 21 Feb. 2004, pp. 36-39. *The chimp genome is complete, but a simple gene-for-gene comparison is only the first step to finding out what makes humans so special.*

■ **Genomes for All** Scientific American, Jan. 2006, pp. 32-40. *New approaches to reading DNA and ethical issues involved in use of personal information.*

See pages 10-11 for details of how to access **Bio Links** from our web site: **www.biozone.co.uk**. From Bio Links, access sites under the topics:

GENERAL BIOLOGY ONLINE RESOURCES
• Biointeractive • Biology I interactive animations • HowStuffWorks • Ken's bioweb resources ... *and others* > **Online Textbooks and Lecture Notes:** • S-Cool! A level biology revision guide • An on-line biology book • Learn.co.uk ... *and others* > **Glossaries:** • Genetic glossary • Genome glossary • Glossary of molecular biology terms • Kimball's biology glossary ... *and others*

CELL BIOLOGY AND BIOCHEMISTRY: • Cell & molecular biology online • MIT biology hypertextbook • Molecular biology web book

GENETICS: • DNA glossary • Gene almanac • MIT biology hypertextbook • Populations to molecules • Virtual library on genetics ... *and others* > **Molecular Genetics (DNA):** • Beginners guide to molecular biology • Center for Biomolecular Modeling • DNA interactive • DNA and molecular genetics • DNA workshop • Molecular genetics • Primer on molecular genetics • Protein synthesis ... *and others*

BIOTECHNOLOGY > **Applications in Biotechnology** > **Genome Projects:** • Genomes Online Database • A quick guide to sequenced genomes > **The Human Genome Project:** • A user's guide to the human genome • Genome FAQs file ... *and others*

Presentation MEDIA to support this topic:
GENES AND INHERITANCE
• The Genetic Code
• Gene Technology

Eukaryote Chromosome Structure

The chromosomes of eukaryote cells (such as those from plants and animals) are complex in their structure compared to those of prokaryotes. The illustration below shows a chromosome during the early stage of meiosis. Here it exists as a chromosome consisting of two chromatids. A non-dividing cell would have chromosomes with the 'equivalent' of a single chromatid only. The chromosome consists of a protein coated strand which coils in three ways during the time when the cell prepares to divide.

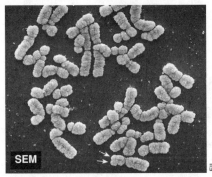

A cluster of human chromosomes seen during metaphase of cell division. Individual chromatids (arrowed) are difficult to discern on these double chromatid chromosomes.

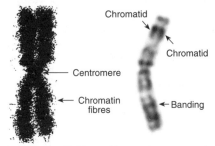

Chromosome TEM Human chromosome 3

A human chromosome from a dividing white blood cell (above left). Note the compact organisation of the chromatin in the two chromatids. The LM photograph (above right) shows the banding visible on human chromosome 3.

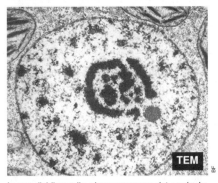

In non-dividing cells, chromosomes exist as single-armed structures. They are not visible as coiled structures, but are 'unwound' to make the genes accessible for transcription (above).

The evidence for the existence of looped domains comes from the study of giant lampbrush chromosomes in amphibian oocytes (above). Under electron microscopy, the lateral loops of the DNA-protein complex have a brushlike appearance.

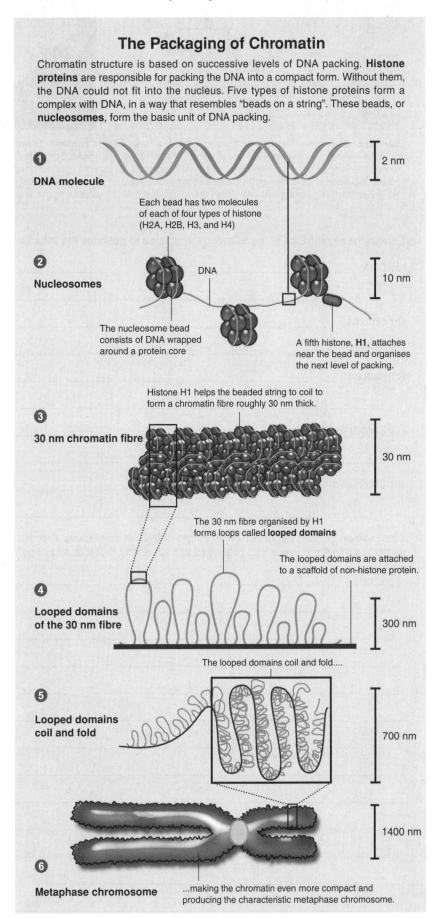

The Packaging of Chromatin

Chromatin structure is based on successive levels of DNA packing. **Histone proteins** are responsible for packing the DNA into a compact form. Without them, the DNA could not fit into the nucleus. Five types of histone proteins form a complex with DNA, in a way that resembles "beads on a string". These beads, or **nucleosomes**, form the basic unit of DNA packing.

① DNA molecule — 2 nm

Each bead has two molecules of each of four types of histone (H2A, H2B, H3, and H4)

② Nucleosomes — 10 nm

DNA

The nucleosome bead consists of DNA wrapped around a protein core

A fifth histone, **H1**, attaches near the bead and organises the next level of packing.

Histone H1 helps the beaded string to coil to form a chromatin fibre roughly 30 nm thick.

③ 30 nm chromatin fibre — 30 nm

The 30 nm fibre organised by H1 forms loops called **looped domains**

The looped domains are attached to a scaffold of non-histone protein.

④ Looped domains of the 30 nm fibre — 300 nm

The looped domains coil and fold....

⑤ Looped domains coil and fold — 700 nm

⑥ Metaphase chromosome — 1400 nm

...making the chromatin even more compact and producing the characteristic metaphase chromosome.

The Genetic Code

Related activities: DNA Molecules
Web links: Chromosome Structure

A 2

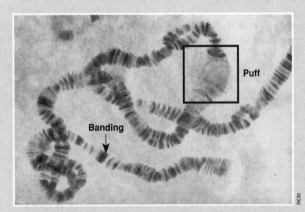

Banded chromosome: This light microscope photo is a view of the polytene chromosomes in a salivary gland cell of a sandfly. It shows a banding pattern that is thought to correspond to groups of genes. Regions of chromosome **puffing** are thought to occur where the genes are being transcribed into mRNA (see SEM on right).

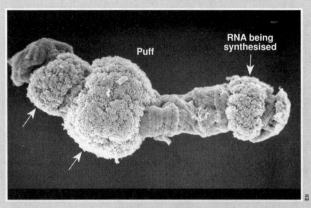

A **polytene chromosome** viewed with a scanning electron microscope (SEM). The arrows indicate localised regions of the chromosome that are uncoiling to expose their genes (puffing) to allow transcription of those regions. Polytene chromosomes are a special type of chromosome consisting of a large bundle of chromatids bound tightly together.

1. Explain the significance of the following terms used to describe the structure of chromosomes:

   (a) DNA: _____

   _____

   (b) Chromatin: _____

   _____

   (c) Histone: _____

   _____

   (d) Centromere: _____

   _____

   (e) Chromatid: _____

   _____

2. Each human cell has about a 1 metre length of DNA in its nucleus. Discuss the mechanisms by which this DNA is packaged into the nucleus and organised in such a way that it does not get ripped apart during cell division:

   _____

   _____

   _____

   _____

   _____

   _____

   _____

   _____

   _____

   _____

   _____

   _____

   _____

Nucleic Acids

Nucleic acids are a special group of chemicals in cells concerned with the transmission of inherited information. They have the capacity to store the information that controls cellular activity. The central nucleic acid is called **deoxyribonucleic acid** (DNA). DNA is a major component of chromosomes and is found primarily in the nucleus, although a small amount is found in mitochondria and chloroplasts. Other **ribonucleic acids** (RNA) are involved in the 'reading' of the DNA information. All nucleic acids are made up of simple repeating units called **nucleotides**, linked together to form chains or strands, often of great length (see the activity *DNA Molecules*). The strands vary in the sequence of the bases found on each nucleotide. It is this sequence which provides the 'genetic code' for the cell. In addition to nucleic acids, certain nucleotides and their derivatives are also important as suppliers of energy (**ATP**) or as hydrogen ion and electron carriers in respiration and photosynthesis (NAD, NADP, and FAD).

Chemical Structure of a Nucleotide

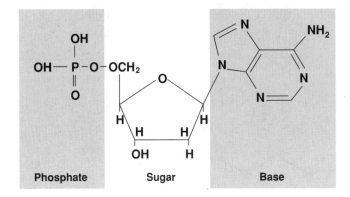

Phosphate   Sugar   Base

Symbolic Form of a Nucleotide

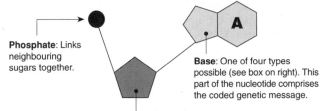

Phosphate: Links neighbouring sugars together.

Base: One of four types possible (see box on right). This part of the nucleotide comprises the coded genetic message.

Sugar: One of two types possible: ribose in RNA and deoxyribose in DNA.

Nucleotides are the building blocks of DNA. Their precise sequence in a DNA molecule provides the genetic instructions for the organism to which it governs. Accidental changes in nucleotide sequences are a cause of mutations, usually harming the organism, but occasionally providing benefits.

Bases

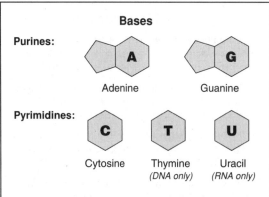

Purines:
   A — Adenine
   G — Guanine

Pyrimidines:
   C — Cytosine
   T — Thymine *(DNA only)*
   U — Uracil *(RNA only)*

The two-ringed bases above are **purines** and make up the longer bases. The single-ringed bases are **pyrimidines**. Although only one of four kinds of base can be used in a nucleotide, **uracil** is found only in RNA, replacing **thymine**. DNA contains: A, T, G, and C, while RNA contains A, U, G, and C.

Sugars

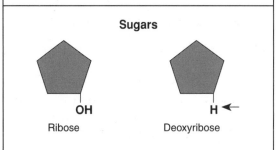

Ribose   Deoxyribose

Deoxyribose sugar is found only in DNA. It differs from **ribose** sugar, found in RNA, by the lack of a single oxygen atom (arrowed).

The Genetic Code

RNA Molecule

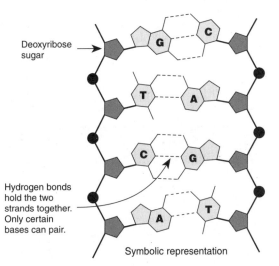

In RNA, uracil replaces thymine in the code.

Ribose sugar

Ribonucleic acid (RNA) comprises a *single strand* of nucleotides linked together.

DNA Molecule

Deoxyribose sugar

Hydrogen bonds hold the two strands together. Only certain bases can pair.

Symbolic representation

DNA Molecule

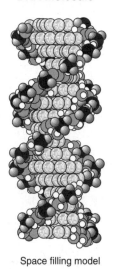

Space filling model

Deoxyribonucleic acid (DNA) comprises a *double strand* of nucleotides linked together. It is shown unwound in the symbolic representation (left). The DNA molecule takes on a twisted, double helix shape as shown in the space filling model on the right.

Related activities: DNA Molecules, Creating a DNA Molecule

A 1

Formation of a nucleotide

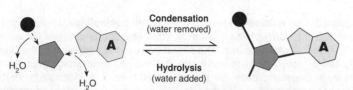

Condensation
(water removed)

Hydrolysis
(water added)

A nucleotide is formed when phosphoric acid and a base are chemically bonded to a sugar molecule. In both cases, water is given off, and they are therefore condensation reactions.

Formation of a dinucleotide

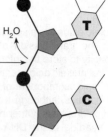

Two nucleotides are linked together by a condensation reaction between the phosphate of one nucleotide and the sugar of another.

Double-Stranded DNA

The **double-helix** structure of DNA is like a ladder twisted into a corkscrew shape around its longitudinal axis. It is 'unwound' here to show the relationships between the bases.

- The way the correct pairs of bases are attracted to each other to form hydrogen bonds is determined by the number of bonds they can form and the shape (length) of the base.

- The **template strand** the side of the DNA molecule that stores the information that is transcribed into mRNA. The template strand is also called the **antisense strand**.

- The other side (often called the **coding strand**) has the same nucleotide sequence as the mRNA except that T in DNA substitutes for U in mRNA. The coding strand is also called the **sense strand**.

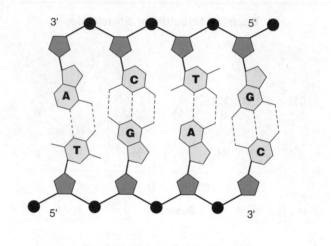

1. The diagram above depicts a double-stranded DNA molecule. Label the following parts on the diagram:
   (a) **Sugar** (deoxyribose)
   (b) **Phosphate**
   (c) **Hydrogen bonds** (between bases)
   (d) **Purine** bases
   (e) **Pyrimidine** bases

2. (a) Explain the **base-pairing rule** that applies in double-stranded DNA: _____

   _____

   (b) Explain how this differs in mRNA: _____

   (c) Describe the purpose of the hydrogen bonds in double-stranded DNA: _____

   _____

3. Describe the functional role of nucleotides: _____

   _____

4. Distinguish between the **template strand** and **coding strand** of DNA, identifying the functional role of each:

   _____

   _____

   _____

5. Complete the following table summarising the differences between DNA and RNA molecules:

	DNA	RNA
Sugar present		
Bases present		
Number of strands		
Relative length		

DNA Molecules

Even the smallest DNA molecules are extremely long. The DNA from the small *Polyoma* virus, for example, is 1.7 μm long; about three times longer than the longest proteins. The DNA comprising a bacterial chromosome is 1000 times longer than the cell into which it has to fit. The amount of DNA present in the nucleus of the cells of eukaryotic organisms varies widely from one species to another. In vertebrate sex cells, the quantity of DNA ranges from 40 000 **kb** to 80 000 000 **kb**, with humans about in the middle of the range. The traditional focus of DNA research has been on those DNA sequences that code for proteins, yet protein-coding DNA accounts for less than 2% of the DNA in human chromosomes. The rest of the DNA, once dismissed as non-coding 'evolutionary junk', is now recognised as giving rise to functional RNA molecules, many of which have already been identified as having important regulatory functions. While there is no clear correspondence between the complexity of an organism and the number of protein-coding genes in its genome, this is not the case for non-protein-coding DNA. The genomes of more complex organisms contain much more of this so-called "non-coding" DNA. These RNA-only 'hidden' genes tend to be short and difficult to identify, but the sequences are highly conserved and clearly have a role in inheritance, development, and health.

Sizes of DNA Molecules

Group	Organism	Base pairs (in 1000s, or kb)	Length
Viruses	Polyoma or SV40	5.1	1.7 μm
	Lambda phage	48.6	17 μm
	T2 phage	166	56 μm
	Vaccinia	190	65 μm
Bacteria	Mycoplasma	760	260 μm
	E. coli (from human gut)	4600	1.56 mm
Eukaryotes	Yeast	13 500	4.6 mm
	Drosophila (fruit fly)	165 000	5.6 cm
	Human	2 900 000	99 cm

Kilobase (kb)

A kilobase is unit of length equal to 1000 base pairs of a double-stranded nucleic acid molecule (or 1000 bases of a single-stranded molecule). One kb of double stranded DNA has a length of 0.34 μm. (1 μm = 1/1000 mm)

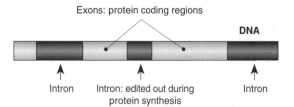

Exons: protein coding regions

DNA

Intron   Intron: edited out during protein synthesis   Intron

Most protein-coding genes in eukaryotic DNA are not continuous and may be interrupted by 'intrusions' of other pieces of DNA. Protein-coding regions (**exons**) are interrupted by non-protein-coding regions called **introns**. Introns range in frequency from 1 to over 30 in a single 'gene' and also in size (100 to more than 10 000 bases). Introns are edited out of the protein-coding sequence during protein synthesis, but probably, after processing, go on to serve a regulatory function.

Giant lampbrush chromosomes

Lampbrush chromosomes are large chromosomes found in amphibian eggs, with lateral loops of DNA that produce a brushlike appearance under the microscope. The two scanning electron micrographs (below and right) show minute strands of DNA giving a fuzzy appearance in the high power view.

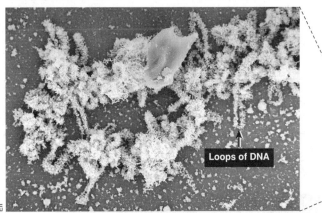

Loops of DNA

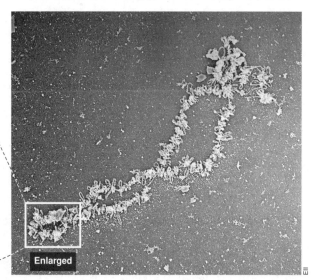

Enlarged

1. Consult the table above and make the following comparisons. Determine how much more DNA is present in:

   (a) The bacterium *E. coli* compared to the Lambda Phage virus: _____

   (b) Human cells compared to the bacteria *E. coli:* _____

2. State what proportion of DNA in a eukaryotic cell is used to code for proteins or structural RNA: _____

3. Describe two reasons why geneticists have reevaluated their traditional view that one gene codes for one polypeptide:

   (a) _____

   _____

   (b) _____

   _____

Related activities: Genomes, The Simplest Case: Genes to Proteins, Gene Expression

DA 2

The Genetic Code

The Genetic Code

The genetic information that codes for the assembly of amino acids is stored as three-letter codes, called **codons**. Each codon represents one of 20 amino acids used in the construction of polypeptide chains. The **mRNA-amino acid table** (bottom of page) can be used to identify the amino acid encoded by each of the mRNA codons. Note that the code is **degenerate** in that for each amino acid, there may be more than one codon. Most of this degeneracy involves the third nucleotide of a codon. The genetic code is **universal**; all living organisms on Earth, from viruses and bacteria, to plants and humans, share the same genetic code (with a few minor exceptions representing mutations that have occurred over the long history of evolution).

Amino acid		Codons that code for this amino acid	No.	Amino acid		Codons that code for this amino acid	No.
Ala	Alanine	GCU, GCC, GCA, GCG	4	**Leu**	Leucine		
Arg	Arginine			**Lys**	Lysine		
Asn	Asparagine			**Met**	Methionine		
Asp	Aspartic acid			**Phe**	Phenylalanine		
Cys	Cysteine			**Pro**	Proline		
Gln	Glutamine			**Ser**	Serine		
Glu	Glutamic acid			**Thr**	Threonine		
Gly	Glycine			**Try**	Tryptophan		
His	Histidine			**Tyr**	Tyrosine		
Iso	Isoleucine			**Val**	Valine		

1. Use the **mRNA-amino acid table** (below) to list in the table above all the **codons** that code for each of the amino acids and the number of different codons that can code for each amino acid (the first amino acid has been done for you).

2. (a) State how many amino acids could be coded for if a codon consisted of just two bases: _____

   (b) Explain why this number of bases is inadequate to code for the 20 amino acids required to make proteins:

   _____

   _____

3. Describe the consequence of the degeneracy of the genetic code to the likely effect of a change to one base in a triplet:

   _____

   _____

mRNA-Amino Acid Table

How to read the table: The table on the right is used to 'decode' the genetic code as a sequence of amino acids in a polypeptide chain, from a given mRNA sequence. To work out which amino acid is coded for by a codon (triplet of bases) look for the first letter of the codon in the row label on the left hand side. Then look for the column that intersects the same row from above that matches the second base. Finally, locate the third base in the codon by looking along the row from the right hand end that matches your codon.

Example: Determine **CAG**

C on the left row, A on the top column, G on the right row
CAG is Gln (**glutamine**)

Read second letter here · Read first letter here · Read third letter here

Second Letter				
First Letter	**U**	**C**	**A**	**G**	Third Letter
U	UUU Phe / UUC Phe / UUA Leu / UUG Leu	UCU Ser / UCC Ser / UCA Ser / UCG Ser	UAU Tyr / UAC Tyr / UAA STOP / UAG STOP	UGU Cys / UGC Cys / UGA STOP / UGG Try	U C A G
C	CUU Leu / CUC Leu / CUA Leu / CUG Leu	CCU Pro / CCC Pro / CCA Pro / CCG Pro	CAU His / CAC His / CAA Gln / CAG Gln	CGU Arg / CGC Arg / CGA Arg / CGG Arg	U C A G
A	AUU Iso / AUC Iso / AUA Iso / AUG Met	ACU Thr / ACC Thr / ACA Thr / ACG Thr	AAU Asn / AAC Asn / AAA Lys / AAG Lys	AGU Ser / AGC Ser / AGA Arg / AGG Arg	U C A G
G	GUU Val / GUC Val / GUA Val / GUG Val	GCU Ala / GCC Ala / GCA Ala / GCG Ala	GAU Asp / GAC Asp / GAA Glu / GAG Glu	GGU Gly / GGC Gly / GGA Gly / GGG Gly	U C A G

Related activities: Amino Acids, The Simplest Case: Genes to Proteins

Creating a DNA Model

Although DNA molecules can be enormous in terms of their molecular size, they are made up of simple repeating units called **nucleotides**. A number of factors control the way in which these nucleotide building blocks are linked together. These factors cause the nucleotides to join together in a predictable way. This is referred to as the **base pairing rule** and can be used to construct a complementary DNA strand from a template strand, as illustrated in the exercise below:

DNA Base Pairing Rule			
Adenine	is always attracted to	**Thymine**	A ⟷ T
Thymine	is always attracted to	**Adenine**	T ⟷ A
Cytosine	is always attracted to	**Guanine**	C ⟷ G
Guanine	is always attracted to	**Cytosine**	G ⟷ C

1. Cut around the nucleotides on page 139 and separate each of the 24 nucleotides by cutting along the columns and rows (see arrows indicating two such cutting points). Although drawn as geometric shapes, these symbols represent chemical structures.

2. Place one of each of the four kinds of nucleotide on their correct spaces below:

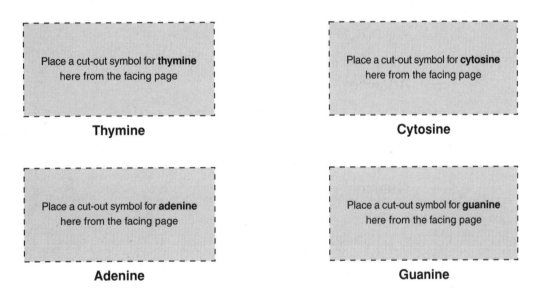

Place a cut-out symbol for **thymine** here from the facing page

Thymine

Place a cut-out symbol for **cytosine** here from the facing page

Cytosine

Place a cut-out symbol for **adenine** here from the facing page

Adenine

Place a cut-out symbol for **guanine** here from the facing page

Guanine

3. Identify and **label** each of the following features on the *adenine* nucleotide immediately above:
   phosphate, **sugar**, **base**, **hydrogen bonds**

4. Create one strand of the DNA molecule by placing the 9 correct 'cut out' nucleotides in the labelled spaces on the following page (DNA molecule). Make sure these are the right way up (with the **P** on the left) and are aligned with the left hand edge of each box. Begin with thymine and end with guanine.

5. Create the complementary strand of DNA by using the base pairing rule above. Note that the nucleotides have to be arranged upside down.

6. Under normal circumstances, it is not possible for adenine to pair up with guanine or cytosine, nor for any other mismatches to occur. Describe the two factors that prevent a mismatch from occurring:

   (a) Factor 1: _____

   _____

   (b) Factor 2: _____

   _____

7. Once you have checked that the arrangement is correct, you may glue, paste or tape these nucleotides in place.

NOTE:	There may be some value in keeping these pieces loose in order to practise the base pairing rule. For this purpose, *removable tape* would be best.

The Genetic Code

138

DNA Molecule

Put the named
nucleotides on the left
hand side to create
the template strand

Put the matching
complementary
nucleotides opposite
the template strand

Thymine

Cytosine

Adenine

Adenine

Guanine

Thymine

Thymine

Cytosine

Guanine

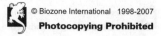

Nucleotides

Tear out this page along the perforation and separate each of the 24 nucleotides
by cutting along the columns and rows (see arrows indicating the cutting points).

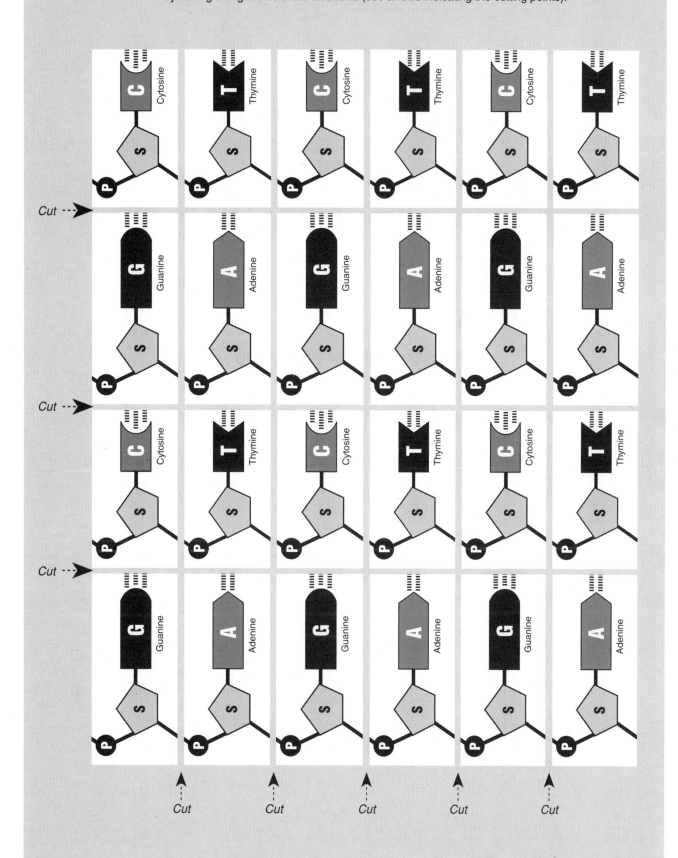

Cut

Cut

Cut

Cut   *Cut*   *Cut*   *Cut*   *Cut*

The Genetic Code

This page is left blank deliberately

Related activities: XXXXXXXX
Web links: XXXX

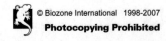

Genomes

Genome research has become an important field of genetics. A **genome** is the entire haploid complement of genetic material of a cell or organism. Each species has a unique genome, although there is a small amount of genetic variation between individuals within a species. For example, in humans the average genetic difference is one in every 500-1000 bases. Every cell in an individual has a complete copy of the genome. The base

sequence shown below is the total DNA sequence for the genome of a virus. There are nine genes in the sequence, coding for nine different proteins. At least 2000 times this amount of DNA would be found in a single bacterial cell. Half a million times the quantity of DNA would be found in the genome of a single human cell. The first gene has been highlighted grey, while the start and stop codes are in black rectangles.

Genome for the φX174 bacterial virus

Start

The grey area represents the nucleotide sequence for a single gene

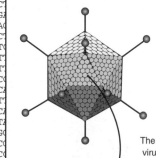

φX174 bacterial virus

This virus consists of a protein coat made up of a 20-sided polyhedron. Spikes made of protein at each of the 12 corners are used to attach itself to a bacterial cell.

The entire DNA sequence for the virus is made up of just 9 genes

1. Explain what is meant by the **genome** of an organism: _____

_____

2. Determine the number of bases, kilobases, and megabases in this genome (100 bases in each row, except the last):

   1 kb = 1 kilobase = 1000 bases   **1 Mb** = 1 megabase = 1 000 000 bases

   (a) Bases: _____   (b) Kilobases: _____   (c) Megabases: _____

3. Determine how many bases are present in the gene shown above (in the grey area): _____

4. State whether the genome of the virus above is **small, average** or **large** in size compared to those viruses listed in the table on the earlier page *DNA Molecules*:

_____

Related activities: DNA Molecules, Genome Projects, The Human Genome Project

RD 2

Genome Projects

There are many genome projects underway around the world, including the Human Genome Project. The aim of most genome projects is to determine the DNA sequence of the organism's entire genome. Over one hundred bacterial and viral genomes, as well as a number of larger genomes (including honeybee, nematode worm, African clawed frog, pufferfish, zebra fish, rice, cow, dog, and rat) have already been sequenced. Genomes that are, for a variety of reasons, high priority for DNA sequencing include the sea urchin, kangaroo, pig, cat, baboon, silkworm, rhesus monkey,

turkey and even Neanderthals (prehumans). Genome sequencing is costly, so candidates are carefully chosen. Important factors in this choice include the value of the knowledge to practical applications, the degree of technical difficulty involved, and the size of the genome (very large genomes are generally avoided). Genome sizes and the number of genes per genome vary, and are not necessarily correlated with the size and structural complexity of the organism itself. Once completed, genome sequences are analysed by computer to identify genes.

Artist's impression

Yeast (*Saccharomyces cerevisiae*)

Status: Completed in 1996
Number of genes: 6000
Genome size: 13 Mb

The first eukaryotic genome to be completely sequenced. Yeast is used as a model organism to study human cancer.

Bacteria (*Escherichia coli*)

Status: Completed in 1997
Number of genes: 4403
Genome size: 4.6 Mb

E. coli has been used as a laboratory organism for over 70 years. Various strains of *E. coli* are responsible for several human diseases.

Fruit fly (*Drosophila melanogaster*)

Status: Completed in 2000
Number of genes: 14 000
Genome size: 150 Mb

Drosophila has been used extensively for genetic studies for many years. About 50% of all fly proteins show similarities to mammalian proteins.

Mouse (*Mus musculus*)

Status: Completed in 2002
Number of genes: 30 000
Genome size: 2500 Mb

New drugs destined for human use are often tested on mice because more than 90% of their proteins show similarities to human proteins.

  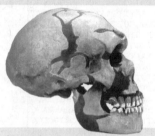 

Chimpanzee (*Pan troglodytes*)

Status: Draft, Dec. 2003, Completed, Sept. 2005
Genome size: 3000 Mb

Chimp and human genomes differ by <2%. Identifying differences could provide clues to the genetics of diseases such as cancer, to which chimps are less prone.

Banana (*Musa acuminata*)

Status: In progress. Due 2006
Genome size: 500-600 Mb

The first tropical crop to be sequenced. Bananas have high economic importance. Knowledge of the genome will assist in producing disease resistant varieties of banana.

Neanderthal
(*H. neanderthalensis*)

Status: In progress
Genome size: 3000 Mb

This ambitious project is attempting to reconstruct the genome of a Neanderthal. Already more than 1 000 000 base pairs have been sequenced from fossil remains.

Chicken (*Gallus gallus*)

Status: Completed in Feb. 2004
Genome size: 1200 Mb

Various human viruses were first found in chickens making this species important for the study of human disease and cross-species transfers. It was the first bird genome to be sequenced.

1. Calculate the number of genes per megabase (Mb) of DNA for the organisms above:

   (a) Yeast: _____ (b) *E. coli*: _____ (c) Fruit fly: _____ (d) Mouse: _____

2. Suggest why the number of genes per Mb of DNA varies between organisms (hint: consider relative sizes of introns):

   _____

   _____

3. Suggest why researchers want to sequence the genomes of plants such as wheat, rice, and maize:

   _____

   _____

4. Using a web engine search (or other research tool), find the following:

   (a) **First multicellular animal genome** to be sequenced: _____ Year: _____

   (b) **First plant genome** to be sequenced: _____ Year: _____

The Human Genome Project

The **Human Genome Project** (HGP) is a publicly funded venture involving many different organisations throughout the world. In 1998, Celera Genomics in the USA began a competing project, as a commercial venture, in a race to be the first to determine the human genome sequence. In 2000, both organisations reached the first draft stage, and the entire genome is now available as a high quality (golden standard) sequence. In addition to determining the order of bases in the human genome, genes are being identified, sequenced, and mapped (their specific chromosomal location identified). The next challenge is to assign functions to the identified genes. By identifying and studying the protein products of genes (a field known as **proteomics**),

scientists can develop a better understanding of genetic disorders. Long term benefits of the HGP are both medical and non-medical (see next page). Many biotechnology companies have taken out patents on gene sequences. This practice is controversial because it restricts the use of the sequence information to the patent holders. Other genome sequencing projects have arisen as a result of the initiative to sequence the human one. In 2002 the International HapMap Project was started with the aim of developing a haplotype map (HapMap) of the human genome. Initially data was gathered from four populations with African, Asian and European ancestry and additional populations may be included as analysis of human genetic variation continues.

Gene Mapping

This process involves determining the precise position of a gene on a chromosome. Once the position is known, it can be shown on a diagram.

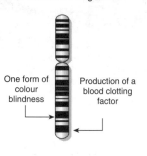

One form of colour blindness

Production of a blood clotting factor

X chromosome

Equipment used for DNA Sequencing

Banks of PCR machines prepare DNA for the sequencing gel stage. The DNA is amplified and chemically tagged (to make the DNA fluoresce and enable visualisation on a gel).

Banks of DNA sequencing gels and powerful computers are used to determine the base order in DNA.

Count of Mapped Genes

The length and number of mapped genes to date for each chromosome are tabulated below. The entire human genome contains approximately 20 000-25 000 genes.

Chromosome	Length (Mb)	No. of Mapped Genes
1	263	1873
2	255	1113
3	214	964
4	203	614
5	194	782
6	183	1217
7	171	995
8	155	591
9	145	803
10	144	872
11	144	1162
12	143	894
13	114	290
14	109	1013
15	106	510
16	98	658
17	92	1034
18	85	302
19	67	1129
20	72	599
21	50	386
22	56	501
X	164	1021
Y	59	122
Total:		**19 445**

As at: 18 February 2007 For an update see:
http://gdbwww.gdb.org/gdbreports/CountGeneByChromosome.html

Composition of the Genome

About 97% of the genome does not code for protein and its function was largely unknown. Recent genomic analyses have revealed that some this DNA (the intronic DNA) codes for functional RNA molecules with important regulatory roles. Some of it is repeat sequence DNA, which means the same section (the repeating unit) of DNA sequence is present many times, often in close proximity. The length of a repeating unit varies from two to many hundred bases and may be present hundreds of times. Some repeat DNA can be difficult, or impossible, to sequence; a consequence of technical difficulties of working with sections of DNA with unusual chemistry. As a result of this, 8-10% of the human genome will probably remain unsequenced.

Long repeats: repeating unit can be up to a few hundred bases.

Introns

Exons: protein coding regions make up 1.5% of the entire genome.

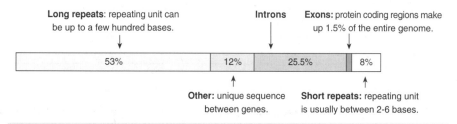

| 53% | 12% | 25.5% | 8% |

Other: unique sequence between genes.

Short repeats: repeating unit is usually between 2-6 bases.

Qualities of DNA Sequence Data

The aim of the HGP was to produce a continuous block of sequence information for each chromosome. Initially the sequence information was obtained to draft quality, with an error rate of 1 in 1000 bases. The **Gold Standard sequence**, with an error rate of <1 per 100 000 bases, was completed in October 2004. Key results of the research are:

- The analysis suggests that there are perhaps only 20 000-25 000 protein-coding genes in our human genome.
- The number of gaps has been reduced 400-fold to only 341
- It covers 99% of the gene containing parts of the genome and is 99.999% accurate.
- The new sequence correctly identifies almost all known genes (99.74%).
- Its accuracy and completeness allows systematic searches for causes of disease.

The Genetic Code

Benefits and ethical issues arising from the Human Genome Project

Medical benefits

- Improved **diagnosis** of disease and predisposition to disease by genetic testing.
- Better identification of disease carriers, through genetic testing.
- Better **drugs** can be designed using knowledge of protein structure (from gene sequence information) rather than by trial and error.
- Greater possibility of successfully using **gene therapy** to correct genetic disorders.

Non-medical benefits

- Greater knowledge of **family relationships** through genetic testing, e.g. paternity testing in family courts.
- Advances **forensic science** through analysis of DNA at crime scenes.
- Improved knowledge of the evolutionary relationships between humans and other organisms, which will help to develop better, more accurate classification systems.

Possible ethical issues

- It is unclear whether third parties, e.g. health insurers, have rights to genetic test results.
- If treatment is unavailable for a disease, genetic knowledge about it may have no use.
- Genetic tests are costly, and there is no easy answer as to who should pay for them.
- Genetic information is hereditary so knowledge of an individual's own genome has implications for members of their family.

Couples can already have a limited range of genetic tests to determine the risk of having offspring with some disease-causing mutations.

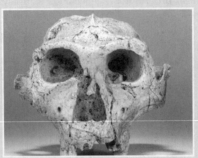

When DNA sequences are available for humans and their ancestors, comparative analysis may provide clues about human evolution.

Legislation is needed to ensure that there is no discrimination on the basis of genetic information, e.g. at work or for health insurance.

1. Briefly describe the objectives of the Human Genome Project (HGP): _____

   _____

   _____

   _____

2. Suggest a reason for developing a HapMap of the human genome: _____

   _____

   _____

3. Describe two possible **benefits** of Human Genome Project (HGP):

   (a) Medical: _____

   _____

   (b) Non-medical: _____

   _____

4. Explain what is meant by **proteomics** and explain its significance to the HGP and the ongoing benefits arising from it:

   _____

   _____

   _____

   _____

5. Suggest two possible points of view for one of the **ethical issues** described in the list above (top right):

   (a) _____

   _____

   (b) _____

   _____

DNA Replication

The replication of DNA is a necessary preliminary step for cell division (both mitosis and meiosis). This process creates the **two chromatids** that are found in chromosomes that are preparing to divide. By this process, the whole chromosome is essentially duplicated, but is still held together by a common centromere. Enzymes are responsible for all of the key events. The diagram below shows the essential steps in the process. The diagram on the next page shows how enzymes are involved at each stage.

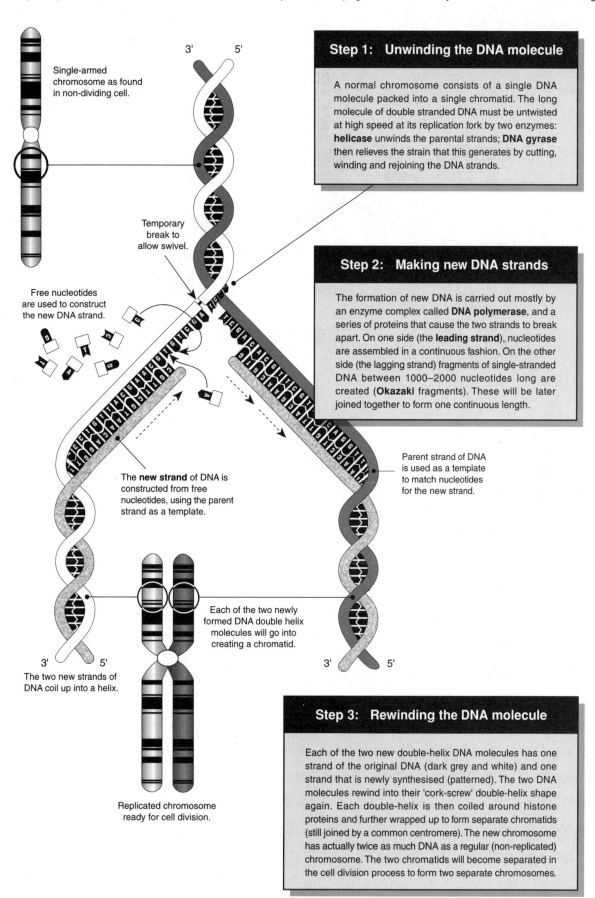

Single-armed chromosome as found in non-dividing cell.

3' 5'

Temporary break to allow swivel.

Free nucleotides are used to construct the new DNA strand.

The **new strand** of DNA is constructed from free nucleotides, using the parent strand as a template.

Parent strand of DNA is used as a template to match nucleotides for the new strand.

Each of the two newly formed DNA double helix molecules will go into creating a chromatid.

3' 5'

The two new strands of DNA coil up into a helix.

3' 5'

Replicated chromosome ready for cell division.

Step 1: Unwinding the DNA molecule

A normal chromosome consists of a single DNA molecule packed into a single chromatid. The long molecule of double stranded DNA must be untwisted at high speed at its replication fork by two enzymes: **helicase** unwinds the parental strands; **DNA gyrase** then relieves the strain that this generates by cutting, winding and rejoining the DNA strands.

Step 2: Making new DNA strands

The formation of new DNA is carried out mostly by an enzyme complex called **DNA polymerase**, and a series of proteins that cause the two strands to break apart. On one side (the **leading strand**), nucleotides are assembled in a continuous fashion. On the other side (the lagging strand) fragments of single-stranded DNA between 1000–2000 nucleotides long are created (**Okazaki** fragments). These will be later joined together to form one continuous length.

Step 3: Rewinding the DNA molecule

Each of the two new double-helix DNA molecules has one strand of the original DNA (dark grey and white) and one strand that is newly synthesised (patterned). The two DNA molecules rewind into their 'cork-screw' double-helix shape again. Each double-helix is then coiled around histone proteins and further wrapped up to form separate chromatids (still joined by a common centromere). The new chromosome has actually twice as much DNA as a regular (non-replicated) chromosome. The two chromatids will become separated in the cell division process to form two separate chromosomes.

The Genetic Code

Related activities: Mitosis and the Cell Cycle, Polymerase Chain Reaction
Web links: DNA Replication

DA 3

Enzyme Control of DNA Replication

This process of DNA replication occurs at an astounding rate. As many as 4000 nucleotides per second are replicated. This explains how under ideal conditions, bacterial cells with as many as 4 million nucleotides, can complete a cell cycle in about 20 minutes. See the section on **polymerase chain reaction** for a useful application of this process.

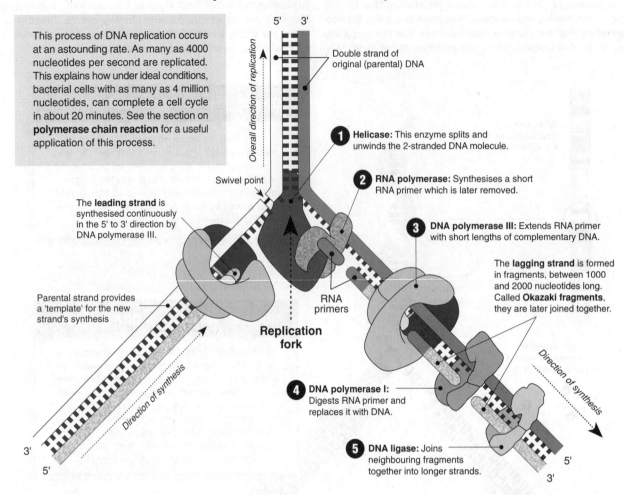

Overall direction of replication

5' 3'

Double strand of original (parental) DNA

Swivel point

The **leading strand** is synthesised continuously in the 5' to 3' direction by DNA polymerase III.

Parental strand provides a 'template' for the new strand's synthesis

1 Helicase: This enzyme splits and unwinds the 2-stranded DNA molecule.

2 RNA polymerase: Synthesises a short RNA primer which is later removed.

3 DNA polymerase III: Extends RNA primer with short lengths of complementary DNA.

The **lagging strand** is formed in fragments, between 1000 and 2000 nucleotides long. Called **Okazaki fragments**, they are later joined together.

RNA primers

Replication fork

Direction of synthesis

4 DNA polymerase I: Digests RNA primer and replaces it with DNA.

5 DNA ligase: Joins neighbouring fragments together into longer strands.

Direction of synthesis

3'

5'

5'

3'

The sequence of enzyme controlled events in DNA replication is shown above. Although shown as separate, many of the enzymes are found clustered together as enzyme complexes. These enzymes are also able to 'proof-read' the new DNA strand as it is made and correct mistakes. The polymerase enzyme can only work in one direction, so that one new strand is constructed as a continuous length (the leading strand) while the other new strand is made in short segments to be later joined together (the lagging strand). **NOTE** that the nucleotides are present as deoxynucleoside triphosphates. When hydrolysed, these provide the energy for incorporating the nucleotide into the strand.

1. Briefly explain the purpose of DNA replication: _____

_____

2. Summarise the steps involved in DNA replication (on the previous page):

(a) Step 1: _____

_____

(b) Step 2: _____

_____

(c) Step 3: _____

_____

3. Explain the role of the following enzymes in DNA replication: _____

(a) Helicase: _____

(b) DNA polymerase I: _____

(c) DNA polymerase III: _____

(d) Ligase: _____

4. Determine the time it would take for a bacteria to replicate its DNA (see note in diagram above): _____

The Simplest Case: Genes to Proteins

The traditionally held view of genes was as sections of DNA coding only for protein. This view has been revised in recent years with the discovery that much of the nonprotein-coding DNA encodes functional RNAs; it is not all non-coding "junk" DNA as was previously assumed. In fact, our concept of what constitutes a gene is changing rapidly and now encompasses all those segments of DNA that are transcribed (to RNA). This activity considers only the simplest scenario: one in which the gene codes for a functional protein. **Nucleotides**, the basic unit

of genetic information, are read in groups of three (**triplets**). Some triplets have a special controlling function in the making of a polypeptide chain. The equivalent of the triplet on the mRNA molecule is the **codon**. Three codons can signify termination of the amino acid chain (UAG, UAA and UGA in the mRNA code). The codon AUG is found at the beginning of every gene (on mRNA) and marks the starting point for reading the gene. The genes required to form a functional end-product (in this case, a functional protein) are collectively called a **transcription unit**.

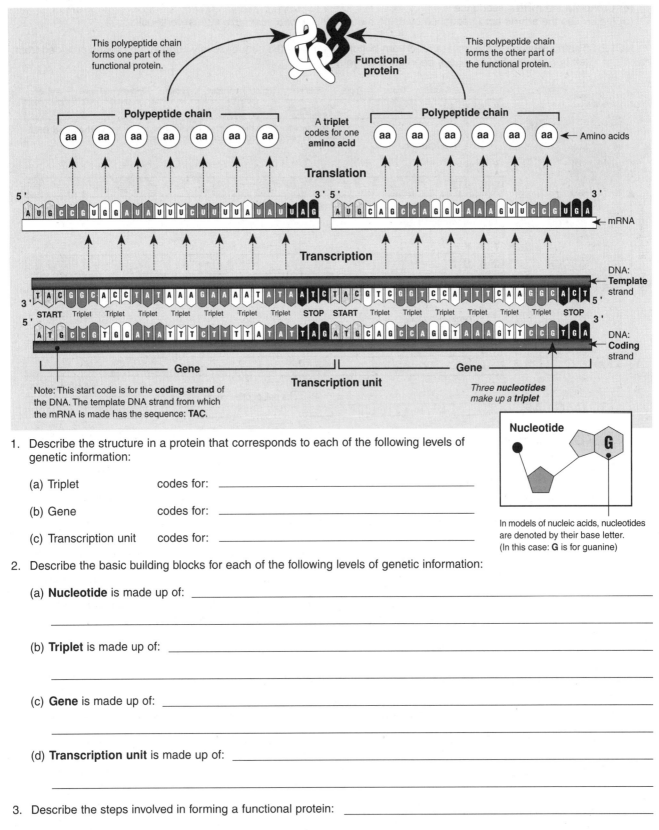

The Genetic Code

1. Describe the structure in a protein that corresponds to each of the following levels of genetic information:

    (a) Triplet   codes for: _____

    (b) Gene   codes for: _____

    (c) Transcription unit   codes for: _____

In models of nucleic acids, nucleotides are denoted by their base letter.
(In this case: **G** is for guanine)

2. Describe the basic building blocks for each of the following levels of genetic information:

    (a) **Nucleotide** is made up of: _____

    _____

    (b) **Triplet** is made up of: _____

    _____

    (c) **Gene** is made up of: _____

    _____

    (d) **Transcription unit** is made up of: _____

    _____

3. Describe the steps involved in forming a functional protein: _____

    _____

Related activities: Gene Expression   A 2

Analysing a DNA Sample

The nucleotide (base sequence) of a section of DNA can be determined using DNA sequencing techniques (see the topic *Gene Technology* later in this workbook for a description of this technology). The base sequence determines the amino acid sequence of the resultant protein therefore the DNA tells us what type of protein that gene encodes. This exercise reviews the areas of DNA replication, transcription, and translation using an analysis of a gel electrophoresis column. **Attempt it after you have completed the rest of this topic**. Remember that the gel pattern represents the sequence in the synthesised strand.

1. Determine the amino acid sequence of a protein from the nucleotide sequence of its DNA, with the following steps:

   (a) Determine the sequence of **synthesised DNA** in the gel
   (b) Convert it to the complementary sequence of the **sample DNA**
   (c) Complete the **mRNA** sequence
   (d) Determine the **amino acid** sequence by using the *mRNA - amino acid table* in this workbook.

   NOTE: The nucleotides in the gel are read from bottom to top and the sequence is written in the spaces provided from left to right (the first four have been done for you).

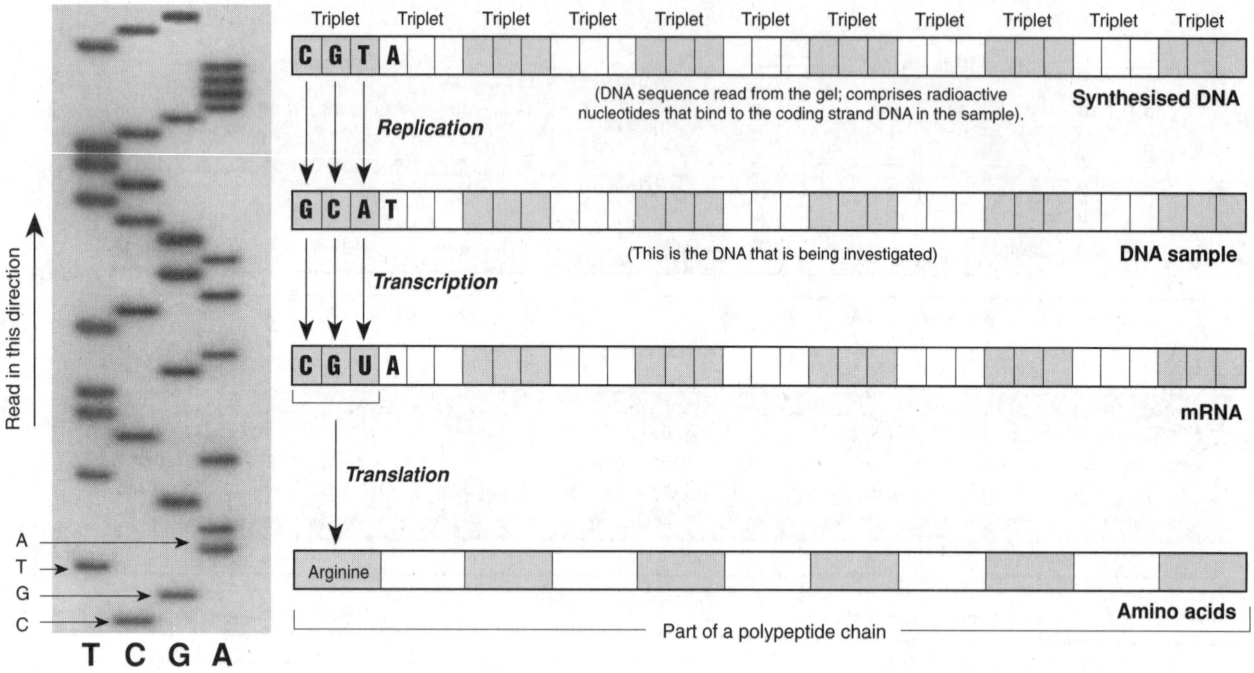

Part of a polypeptide chain

2. For each single strand DNA sequence below, write the base sequence for the **complementary DNA** strand:

   (a) DNA: T A C   T A G   C C G   C G A   T T T   A C A   A T T

   DNA: _____

   (b) DNA: T A C   G C C   T T A   A A G   G G C   C G A   A T C

   DNA: _____

   (c) Identify the cell process that this exercise represents: _____

3. For each single strand DNA sequence below, write the base sequence for the **mRNA** strand and the **amino acid** that it codes for (refer to the mRNA-amino acid table to determine the amino acid sequence):

   (a) DNA: T A C   T A G   C C G   C G A   T T T   A C A   A T T

   mRNA: _____

   Amino
   acids: _____

   (b) DNA: T A C   G C C   T T A   A A G   G G C   C G A   A T C

   mRNA: _____

   Amino
   acids: _____

   (c) Identify the cell process that this exercise represents: _____

Gene Expression

The process of transferring the information encoded in a gene to its functional gene product is called **gene expression**. The central dogma of molecular biology for the past 50 years or so has stated that genetic information, encoded in DNA, is transcribed as molecules of RNA, which are then translated into the amino acid sequences that make up proteins. The established opinion was often stated as "one gene-one protein" and proteins were assumed to be the main regulatory agents for the cell (including its gene expression). The one gene-one protein model is supported by studies of prokaryotic genomes, where the DNA consists almost entirely of protein-coding genes and their regulatory sequences.

Genes and Gene Expression in Prokaryotes

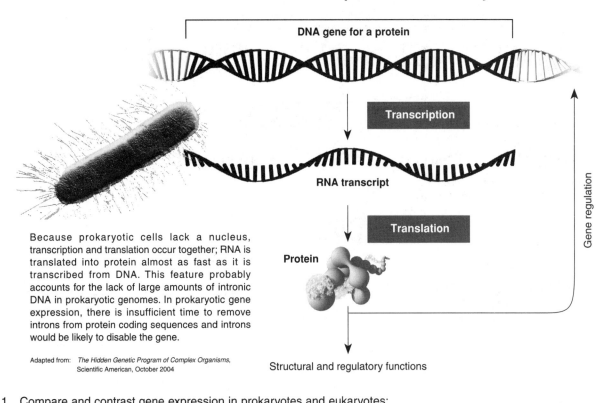

Because prokaryotic cells lack a nucleus, transcription and translation occur together; RNA is translated into protein almost as fast as it is transcribed from DNA. This feature probably accounts for the lack of large amounts of intronic DNA in prokaryotic genomes. In prokaryotic gene expression, there is insufficient time to remove introns from protein coding sequences and introns would be likely to disable the gene.

Adapted from: *The Hidden Genetic Program of Complex Organisms,* Scientific American, October 2004

1. Compare and contrast gene expression in prokaryotes and eukaryotes: _____

_____

_____

_____

_____

_____

_____

2. Study the table (right) summarising the traditional (old) and revised (new) views of gene expression in eukaryotes. Describe how the two models differ:

_____

_____

_____

_____

_____

_____

_____

_____

Gene Expression in Eukaryotes

The Old View	The New View
• Introns are spliced out of a primary RNA transcript.	• Introns are spliced out of a primary RNA transcript.
• All of the exon RNA (mRNA) is translated into proteins.	• Not all of the exon RNA (mRNA) is translated into proteins. Nonprotein-coding exonic RNA may contribute to microRNAs or has a function on its own.
• Introns are "junk DNA" with no assigned function; they are degraded and recycled.	• Many introns are processed into microRNAs which appear to be involved in regulating development.

The Genetic Code

Related activities: The Simplest Case: Genes to Proteins

A 3

In contrast to prokaryotes, eukaryotic genomes contain a large amount of DNA that does not code for proteins. These DNA sequences, called **introns** or intronic DNA, were termed "junk DNA", and were assumed to have no function. However new evidence, arising as more and more diverse genomes are sequenced, suggests that this DNA may encode a vast number of RNA molecules with regulatory functions. Among the eukaryotes, an increase in complexity is associated with an increase in the proportion of nonprotein-coding DNA. This makes sense if the nonprotein-coding DNA has a role in regulating genomic function. These pages contrast gene expression in prokaryotes, where there is very little nonprotein-coding DNA, with the new view of eukaryotic gene expression, where a high proportion of the genomic DNA does not code directly for proteins.

The New View of Gene Expression in Eukaryotes

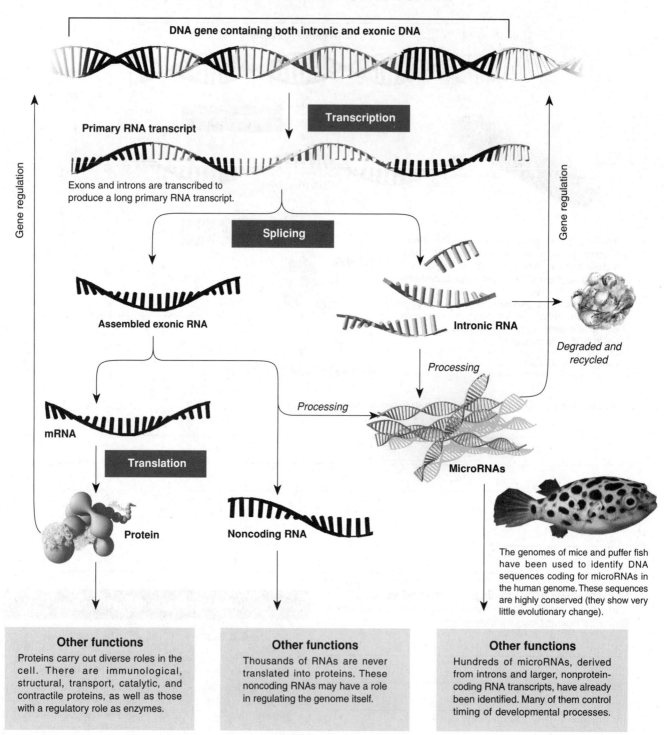

DNA gene containing both intronic and exonic DNA

Transcription

Primary RNA transcript

Exons and introns are transcribed to produce a long primary RNA transcript.

Splicing

Assembled exonic RNA

Intronic RNA

Processing

Degraded and recycled

mRNA

Processing

Processing

MicroRNAs

Translation

Protein

Noncoding RNA

Gene regulation

Gene regulation

The genomes of mice and puffer fish have been used to identify DNA sequences coding for microRNAs in the human genome. These sequences are highly conserved (they show very little evolutionary change).

Other functions
Proteins carry out diverse roles in the cell. There are immunological, structural, transport, catalytic, and contractile proteins, as well as those with a regulatory role as enzymes.

Other functions
Thousands of RNAs are never translated into proteins. These noncoding RNAs may have a role in regulating the genome itself.

Other functions
Hundreds of microRNAs, derived from introns and larger, nonprotein-coding RNA transcripts, have already been identified. Many of them control timing of developmental processes.

3. The one gene-one protein model does not seem to adequately explain gene expression in eukaryotes, but it is probably still appropriate for prokaryotes. Suggest why:

_____

_____

_____

Transcription is the process by which the code contained in the DNA molecule is transcribed (rewritten) into a **mRNA** molecule. Transcription is under the control of the cell's metabolic processes which must activate a gene before this process can begin. The enzyme that directly controls the process is RNA polymerase, which makes a strand of mRNA using the single strand of DNA (the **template strand**) as a template (hence the

term). The enzyme transcribes only a gene length of DNA at a time and therefore recognises start and stop signals (codes) at the beginning and end of the gene. Only RNA polymerase is involved in mRNA synthesis; it causes the unwinding of the DNA as well. It is common to find several RNA polymerase enzyme molecules on the same gene at any one time, allowing a high rate of mRNA synthesis to occur.

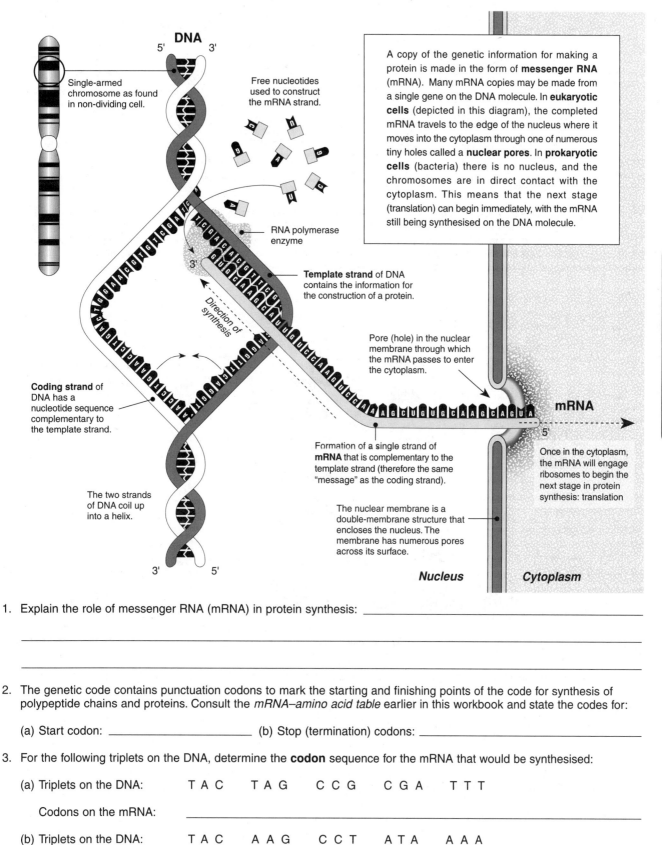

The Genetic Code

1. Explain the role of messenger RNA (mRNA) in protein synthesis: _____

_____

_____

2. The genetic code contains punctuation codons to mark the starting and finishing points of the code for synthesis of polypeptide chains and proteins. Consult the *mRNA–amino acid table* earlier in this workbook and state the codes for:

(a) Start codon: _____ (b) Stop (termination) codons: _____

3. For the following triplets on the DNA, determine the **codon** sequence for the mRNA that would be synthesised:

(a) Triplets on the DNA: T A C   T A G   C C G   C G A   T T T

   Codons on the mRNA: _____

(b) Triplets on the DNA: T A C   A A G   C C T   A T A   A A A

   Codons on the mRNA: _____

Related activities: The Genetic Code, Gene Expression
Web links: Transcription in Prokaryotes, Transcription Animation

RA 2

Translation

The diagram below shows the translation phase of protein synthesis. The scene shows how a single mRNA molecule can be 'serviced' by many ribosomes at the same time. The ribosome on the right is in a more advanced stage of constructing a polypeptide chain because it has 'translated' more of the mRNA than the ribosome on the left. The anti-codon at the base of each tRNA must make a perfect complementary match with the codon on the mRNA before the amino acid is released. Once released, the amino acid is added to the growing polypeptide chain by enzymes.

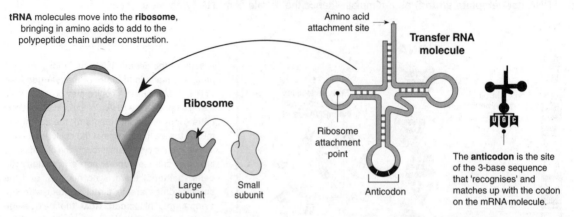

tRNA molecules move into the **ribosome**, bringing in amino acids to add to the polypeptide chain under construction.

Ribosome

Large subunit   Small subunit

Amino acid attachment site

Transfer RNA molecule

Ribosome attachment point

Anticodon

The **anticodon** is the site of the 3-base sequence that 'recognises' and matches up with the codon on the mRNA molecule.

Ribosomes are made up of a complex of ribosomal RNA (rRNA) and proteins. They exist as two separate sub-units (above) until they are attracted to a binding site on the mRNA molecule, when they join together. Ribosomes have binding sites that attract transfer RNA (**tRNA**) molecules loaded with amino acids. The tRNA molecules are about 80 nucleotides in length and are made under the direction of genes in the chromosomes. There is a different tRNA molecule for each of the different possible anticodons (see the diagram below) and, because of the degeneracy of the genetic code, there may be up to six different tRNAs carrying the same amino acid.

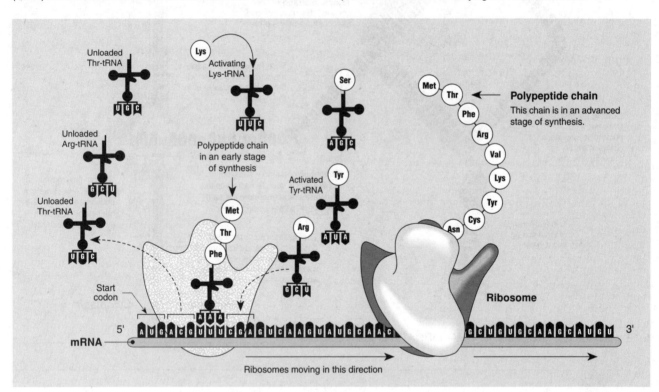

Unloaded Thr-tRNA

Lys
Activating Lys-tRNA

Ser

Met — Thr — Phe — Arg — Val — Lys — Tyr — Cys — Asn

Polypeptide chain
This chain is in an advanced stage of synthesis.

Unloaded Arg-tRNA

Polypeptide chain in an early stage of synthesis

Tyr
Activated Tyr-tRNA

Unloaded Thr-tRNA

Met
Thr
Phe

Arg

Start codon

Ribosome

5' mRNA   A U G A C G U U U C G A G U C A A G U A U G C A A C   G C U G U G C A A G C A U G U   3'

Ribosomes moving in this direction

1. For the following codons on the mRNA, determine the **anticodons** for each tRNA that would deliver the amino acids:

   Codons on the mRNA: U A C   U A G   C C G   C G A   U U U

   Anticodons on the tRNAs: _____

2. There are many different types of tRNA molecules, each with a different anticodon (HINT: see the *mRNA table*).

   (a) State how many different tRNA types there are, each with a unique anticodon: _____

   (b) Explain your answer: _____

   _____

   _____

Related activities: The Genetic Code
Web links: Polyribosomes

Review of Protein Synthesis

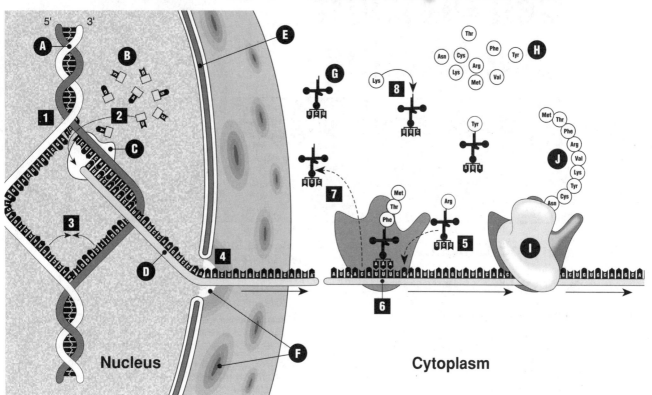

Nucleus

Cytoplasm

The diagram above shows an overview of the process of protein synthesis. It is a combination of the diagrams from the previous two pages. Each of the major steps in the process are numbered, while structures are labelled with letters.

1. Briefly describe each of the numbered processes in the diagram above:

   (a) Process 1: _____

   (b) Process 2: _____

   (c) Process 3: _____

   (d) Process 4: _____

   (e) Process 5: _____

   (f) Process 6: _____

   (g) Process 7: _____

   (h) Process 8: _____

2. Identify each of the structures marked with a letter and write their names below in the spaces provided:

   (a) Structure A: _____   (f) Structure F: _____

   (b) Structure B: _____   (g) Structure G: _____

   (c) Structure C: _____   (h) Structure H: _____

   (d) Structure D: _____   (i) Structure I: _____

   (e) Structure E: _____   (j) Structure J: _____

3. Describe two factors that would determine whether or not a particular protein is produced in the cell:

   (a) _____

   _____

   (b) _____

   _____

Related activities: Transcription, Translation

RA 2

Cell Division and Cloning

AQA-A	AQA-B	SNAB	Edexcel	OCR
Complete:	Complete:	Complete:	Complete:	Complete:
1-6, 12-13	1-6, 9-13	1-13	1-6, 9-13	1-7, 12-13

Learning Objectives

☐ 1. Compile your own glossary from the **KEY WORDS** displayed in **bold type** in the learning objectives below.

Mitosis and the Cell Cycle (pages 156, 159, 163)

☐ 2. Using diagrams, describe the behaviour of **chromosomes** during a mitotic **cell cycle** in eukaryotes. Include reference to: **mitosis**, **growth** (G₁ and G₂), and DNA replication (S).

☐ 3. Recognise and describe the following events in mitosis: **prophase**, **metaphase**, **anaphase**, and **telophase**.

☐ 4. EXTENSION: With respect to both plant and animal cells, understand the term **cytokinesis**, and distinguish between nuclear division and division of the cytoplasm.

☐ 5. Understand the role of mitosis in growth and repair, and asexual reproduction. Recognise the importance of **daughter nuclei** with chromosomes identical in number and type. Recognise cell division as a prelude to **cellular differentiation**.

☐ 6. Demonstrate appropriate staining techniques in the study of mitosis in plant material, e.g. root tip squash.

☐ 7. Explain how **carcinogens** can upset the normal controls regulating cell division. Define the terms: **cancer, tumour suppressor genes, oncogenes**. List factors that increase the chances of cancerous growth.

Cloning and Stem Cell Research (pages 157-158, 160-162, 164-166)

☐ 8. Explain how stem cells can be used in research and medicine and discuss the ethics involved in their use. Explain the terms: **totipotent** and **pluripotent**.

☐ 9. Recognise the role of mitosis in **cloning**. Describe the current and potential uses of cloning technology, including the use of stem cells in therapeutic cloning.

☐ 10. Explain the principles involved in reproducing plants by **vegetative propagation**. Describe methods of vegetative propagation including plant tissue culture (micropropagation). Recognise some of the benefits and disadvantages involved in plant cloning technology.

☐ 11. Explain the principles involved in **embryo splitting** and **nuclear transfer**. Contrast the two techniques and describe the benefits and disadvantages of each.

The Role of Meiosis (page 155)

☐ 12. Contrast the final products of **mitosis** and **meiosis**. Explain what is meant by the terms: **homologous pairs** (of chromosomes), **haploid, diploid, reduction division**. Explain why a reduction division is necessary before fertilisation in sexual reproduction.

☐ 13. Distinguish between the two divisions of meiosis: **Meiosis I (reduction division)** and **Meiosis II**. Recognise the main features of these stages.

 See the 'Textbook Reference Grid' on pages 8-9 for textbook page references relating to material in this topic.

Supplementary Texts

See pages 5-7 for additional details of these texts:

■ Adds, J. *et al.*, 2003. **Molecules and Cells**, (NelsonThornes), chpt. 5.

■ Jones, N., *et al.*, 2001. **The Essentials of Genetics**, (John Murray), pp. 9-25.

See page 7 for details of publishers of periodicals:

STUDENT'S REFERENCE

■ **To Divide or Not to Divide** Biol. Sci. Rev., 11(4) March 1999, pp. 2-5. *The cell cycle: cell growth and stages of cell division and their control.*

■ **The Cell Cycle and Mitosis** Biol. Sci. Rev., 14(4) April 2002, pp. 37-41. *Cell growth and division, key stages in the cell cycle, and the complex control over different stages of mitosis.*

■ **Rebels without a Cause** New Scientist, 13 July 2002, (Inside Science). *The causes of cancer: the uncontrolled division of cells that results in tumour formation. Breast cancer is a case example.*

■ **New Cells for Old** Biol. Sci. Rev., 18(3) Feb. 2006, pp. 6-9. *Embryo cloning and the issues associated with the use of cloned blastocysts as a source of embryonic stem cells for therapy.*

■ **Dance of the Chromosomes** Biol. Sci. Rev., 11(2) Nov. 1998, pp. 11-14. *Techniques to explore the role of chromosomes in the cell cycle help us to find out what happens when steps go wrong.*

■ **What is a Stem Cell?** Biol. Sci. Rev., 16(2) Nov. 2003, pp. 22-23. *The nature of stem cells and their therapeutic applications.*

■ **The Stem Cell Challenge** Scientific American, June 2004, pp. 60-67. *The scientific and political hurdles in the quest to understand and control embryonic stem cells.*

■ **Fast Tissue Culture** Biol. Sci. Rev., 10(3) Jan. 1998, pp. 2-6. *Techniques for plant propagation (includes design for a tissue culture project).*

■ **Human Cloning** Biol. Sci. Rev. 11(3) Jan. 1999, pp. 7-9. *Nuclear transfer and the ethics of the issues surrounding human and livestock cloning.*

■ **The Power to Divide** National Geographic, July 2005, pp. 2-27. *A series of case studies on different illnesses treated with therapeutic cloning.*

■ **Out of Control - Unlocking the Genetic Secrets of Cancer** Biol. Sci. Rev. 11(3) Jan. 1999, pp. 36-39. *The control of cell division: oncogenes and their role in the development of cancer.*

TEACHER'S REFERENCE

■ **Cloning for Medicine** Scientific American, December 1998, pp. 30-35. *The techniques and applications of cloning, including nuclear transfer.*

See pages 10-11 for details of how to access **Bio Links** from our web site: **www.biozone.co.uk**. From Bio Links, access sites under the topics:

GENERAL BIOLOGY ONLINE RESOURCES • Biology I interactive animations ... *and others*

CELL BIOLOGY AND BIOCHEMISTRY: • Cell & molecular biology online > **Cell Division**: • Cell division: Binary fission and mitosis ... *and others*

BIOTECHNOLOGY > Applications > **Cloning and Tissue Culture**: • Conceiving a clone • Tissue culture in the classroom ... *and others*

Presentation MEDIA to support this topic:

CELL BIO & BIOCHEM:
• **Processes in the Nucleus**

Cell Biology & Biochemist.

Cell Division

The life cycle of **diploid sexually reproducing organisms** (such as humans) is illustrated in the diagram below. **Gametogenesis** is the process responsible for the production of male and female gametes for the purpose of ...ual reproduction. The difference between meiosis in males ? in females should be noted (see spermatogenesis and ooge ..sis in the box below).

Human embryos have cells which are rapidly dividing by **mitosis**. The term **somatic** means 'body', so the cell divisions are creating new body cells (as opposed to gametes or sex cells). The **2N** number refers to how many whole sets of chromosomes are present in each body cell. For a normal human embryo, all cells will have a 2N number of 46.

Adults still continue to produce somatic cells by mitosis for cell replacement and growth. Blood cells are replaced by the body at the astonishing rate of two million per second, and a layer of skin cells is constantly lost and replaced about every 28 days.

Gamete production begins at puberty, and lasts until menopause for women, and indefinitely for men. Gametes are produced by the special type of cell division, called **meiosis**, which reduces the chromosome number to half. Human males produce about 200 million sperm per day (whether they are used or not), while females usually release a single egg only once a month.

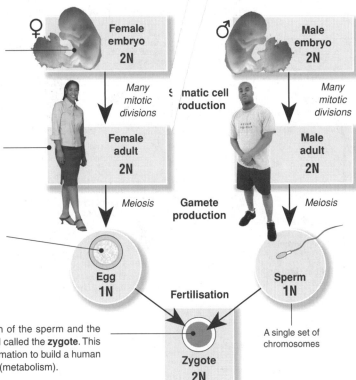

Fertilisation involves fusion of the sperm and the egg to produce a single cell called the **zygote**. This cell has all the genetic information to build a human body as well as maintain it (metabolism).

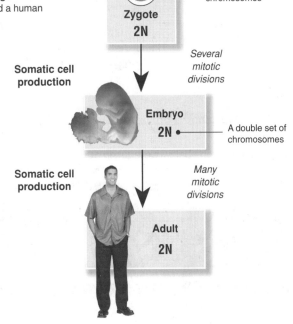

Spermatogenesis

Sperm production: Meiotic division of spermatogonia produces the male gametes. This process is called spermatogenesis. The nucleus of the **germ cell** in the male divides twice to produce four similar-sized sperm cells. Many organisms produce vast quantities of male gametes in this way (e.g. pollen and sperm).

Oogenesis

Egg production: In females, meiosis in the oogonium produces the egg cell or ovum. Unlike gamete production in males, the divison of the cytoplasm during oogenesis is unequal. Most of the cytoplasm and one of the four nuclei form the egg cell or **ovum**. The remainder of the cytoplasm, plus the other three nuclei, form much smaller **polar bodies** and are abortive (i.e. do not take part in fertilisation and formation of the zygote).

1. Describe the **purpose** of the following types of cell division:

   (a) Mitosis: _____

   _____

   (b) Meiosis: _____

   _____

2. Explain the significance of the **zygote**: _____

3. Describe the basic difference between the cell divisions involved in spermatogenesis and oogenesis:

   _____

   _____

Related activities: Mitosis and the Cell Cycle, Meiosis, Sexual Reproduction

A 1

Cell Division and Cloning

Mitosis and the Cell Cycle

Mitosis is part of the 'cell cycle' in which an existing cell (the parent cell) divides into two new ones (the daughter cells). Mitosis does not result in a change of chromosome numbers (unlike meiosis): the daughter cells are identical to the parent cell. Although mitosis is part of a continuous cell cycle, it is divided into stages (below). In plants and animals mitosis is associated with growth and repair of tissue, and it is the method by which some organisms reproduce asexually. The example below illustrates the cell cycle in a plant cell. Note that in animal cells, **cytokinesis** involves the formation of a constriction that divides the cell in two. It is usually well underway by the end of telophase and does not involve the formation of a cell plate.

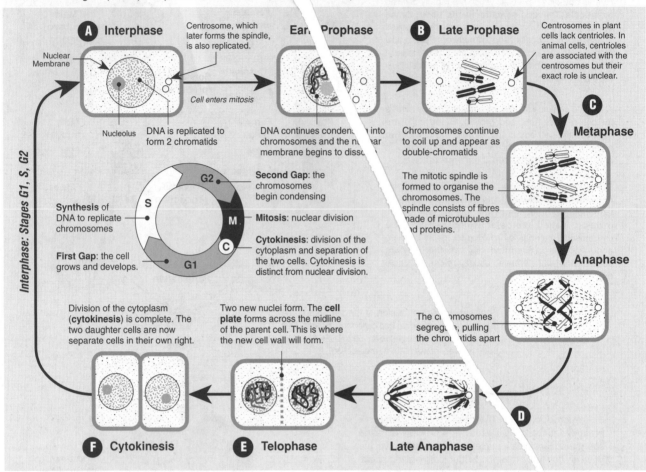

1. The five photographs below were taken at various stages through the process of mitosis in a plant cell. They are not in any particular order. Study the diagram above and determine the stage that each photograph represents (e.g. anaphase).

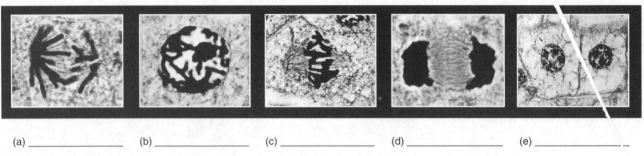

Photos: RCN

(a) _____   (b) _____   (c) _____   (d) _____   (e) _____

2. State two important changes that chromosomes must undergo before cell division can take place:

    _____

3. Briefly summarise the stages of the cell cycle by describing what is happening at the points (**A-F**) in the diagram above:

    A. _____

    B. _____

    C. _____

    D. _____

    E. _____

    F. _____

A 1   **Related activities**: The Genetic Origins of Cancer, Root Cell Development

Stem Cells and Tissue Engineering

Cell cultures have been used for many years for medical and research purposes, e.g. for the culture of viruses for vaccine production and in the production of monoclonal antibodies. Reliable techniques in cell culturing have paved the way for new technologies such as **cell replacement therapy** and **tissue engineering**. These technologies require a disease-free and plentiful supply of cells of specific types. Tissue engineering, for example, involves inducing living cells to grow on a scaffold of natural or synthetic material to produce a three-dimensional tissue such as bone or skin. In 1998, an artificial skin called Apligraf became the first product of this type to be approved for use as a biomedical device. It is now widely used in place of skin grafts. The applications of tissue engineering range from blood vessel replacement and skin, bone, tendon, and cartilage repair, to the treatment of degenerative nerve diseases. A key to the future of this technology will be the developments in **stem cell** research. Stem cells have the ability to develop and form all the tissues of the body. The best source of these is from very early embryos, but some adult tissues (e.g. bone marrow) also contain stem cells. Therapeutic **stem cell cloning** is still in its very early stages and, despite its enormous medical potential, research with human embryonic cells is still banned in some countries.

Engineering a Living Skin

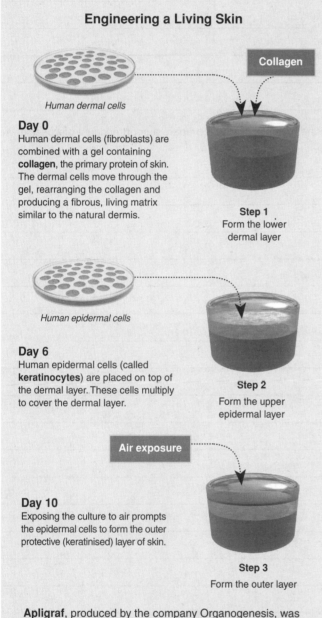

Day 0
Human dermal cells (fibroblasts) are combined with a gel containing **collagen**, the primary protein of skin. The dermal cells move through the gel, rearranging the collagen and producing a fibrous, living matrix similar to the natural dermis.

Step 1
Form the lower dermal layer

Day 6
Human epidermal cells (called **keratinocytes**) are placed on top of the dermal layer. These cells multiply to cover the dermal layer.

Step 2
Form the upper epidermal layer

Day 10
Exposing the culture to air prompts the epidermal cells to form the outer protective (keratinised) layer of skin.

Step 3
Form the outer layer

Apligraf, produced by the company Organogenesis, was the first living, tissue-engineered skin product to be commercially available. It is used to treat diabetic ulcers and burns, with the patient's own cells and tissues helping to complete the biological repair. Producing Apligraf is a three stage process (above), which results in a bilayered, living structure capable of stimulating wound repair through its own growth factors and proteins. The final size of the Apligraf product is about 75 mm and, from this, tens of thousands of pieces can be made. The cells used to start the culture are usually obtained from discarded neonatal foreskins collected after circumcision.

The Future? Embryonic Stem Cell Cloning

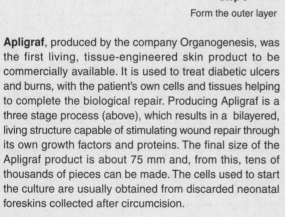

Adult cell from patient

Remove nucleus to produce an empty ovum

Human ovum

Patient who needs new organ or tissue

Remove nucleus

Transfer

A mild electric shock induces the development of a new pre-embryo cell containing the patient's DNA.

After 5 days development, the inner cell mass of about 30 stem cells is removed.

Isolated stem cells are cultured with the appropriate **growth factors** to grow into the required organ or tissue.

Heart   Kidney   Spinal cord   Insulin producing cells

Researchers still need to find out more about how to induce the stem cells to mature into different tissues. Engineering entire organs is still some time away.

Organ or tissue is transplanted into the patient with no rejection problems.

Cell Division and Cloning

Related activities: Differentiation of Human Cells, Human Cell Specialisation
Web links: Stem Cells in the Spotlight

RA 3

1. Outline the benefits of using a tissue engineered skin product, such as Apligraf, to treat wounds that require grafts:

_____

_____

2. Describe one potential advantage of embryonic stem cell cloning for tissue engineering technology:

_____

_____

3. Discuss the present and potential medical applications of tissue engineering: _____

_____

_____

_____

_____

4. Investigate the techniques or the applications of therapeutic stem cell cloning and prepare a short account discussing the technical or ethical issues involved.

_____

_____

_____

_____

_____

_____

_____

_____

_____

_____

_____

_____

_____

_____

_____

_____

_____

_____

_____

_____

_____

The Genetic Origins of Cancer

Normal cells do not live forever. Under certain circumstances, cells are programmed to die, particularly during development. Cells that become damaged beyond repair will normally undergo this programmed cell death (called **apoptosis** or **cell suicide**). Cancer cells evade this control and become immortal, continuing to divide regardless of any damage incurred. **Carcinogens** are agents capable of causing cancer. Roughly 90% of carcinogens are also mutagens, i.e. they damage DNA. Chronic exposure to carcinogens accelerates the rate at which dividing cells make errors. Susceptibility to cancer is also influenced by genetic make-up. Any one or a number of cancer-causing factors (including defective genes) may interact to induce cancer.

Cancer: Cells out of Control

Cancerous transformation results from changes in the genes controlling normal cell growth and division. The resulting cells become immortal and no longer carry out their functional role. Two types of gene are normally involved in controlling the cell cycle: proto-oncogenes, which start the cell division process and are essential for normal cell development, and **tumour-suppressor** genes, which switch off cell division. In their normal form, both kinds of genes work as a team, enabling the body to perform vital tasks such as repairing defective cells and replacing dead ones. But mutations in these genes can disrupt these finely tuned checks and balances. Proto-oncogenes, through mutation, can give rise to **oncogenes**; genes that lead to uncontrollable cell division. Mutations to tumour-suppressor genes initiate most human cancers. The best studied tumour-suppressor gene is **p53**, which encodes a protein that halts the cell cycle so that DNA can be repaired before division.

The panel, right, shows the mutagenic action of some selected carcinogens on four of five codons of the **p53 gene**.

Features of Cancer Cells

The diagram right shows a single **lung cell** that has become cancerous. It no longer carries out the role of a lung cell, and instead takes on a parasitic lifestyle, taking from the body what it needs in the way of nutrients and contributing nothing in return. The rate of cell division is greater than in normal cells in the same tissue because there is no *resting phase* between divisions.

A mutation in one or two of the controlling genes causes a **benign** (nonmalignant) **tumour**. As the number of controlling genes with mutations increases, so too does the loss of control until the cell becomes cancerous.

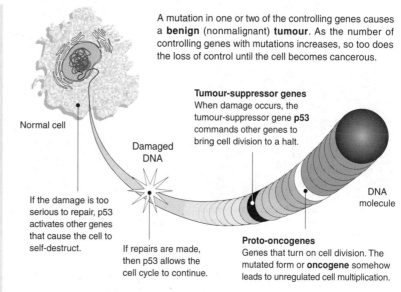

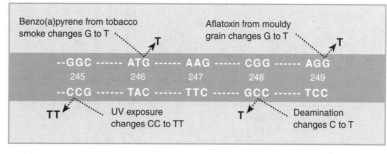

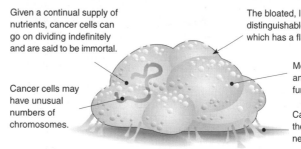

1. Explain how cancerous cells differ from normal cells: _____

2. Explain how the cell cycle is normally controlled, including reference to the role of **tumour-suppressor genes**:

3. With reference to the role of **oncogenes**, explain how the normal controls over the cell cycle can be lost:

Related activities: Mitosis and the Cell Cycle, Cancer, Breast Cancer

A 2

Cell Division and Cloning

Cloning by Embryo Splitting

Livestock breeds frequently produce only one individual per pregnancy and all individuals in a herd will have different traits. Cloning (by embryo splitting or other means) makes it possible to produce high value herds with identical traits more quickly. Developed in the 1980s, and adopted by livestock breeders, embryo splitting, or artificial twinning, is the simplest way in which to create a clone. Embryo splitting simply replicates the natural twinning process. A fertilised egg is grown into eight cells before being split into four individual embryos, each consisting of just two cells. The four genetically identical embryos are then implanted into surrogate mothers. While this technique produces multiple clones, the clones are derived from an embryo whose physical characteristics are not completely known. This represents a serious limitation for practical applications when the purpose of the procedure is to produce high value livestock. In 2000, a rhesus macaque was cloned in this manner, with the goal of producing identical individuals that could be used to perfect new therapies for human disease. Cloning technology can also be used to produce early embryos from which undifferentiated stem cells can be isolated for use in tissue and cell engineering.

Livestock are selected for cloning on the basis of desirable qualities such as wool, meat, or milk productivity.

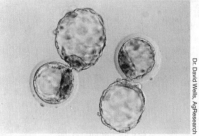

Cloned embryos immediately prior to implantation into a surrogate. These are at the blastocyst stage (a mass of cells that have begun to differentiate).

The individuals produced by embryo splitting have the same characteristics as the parents.

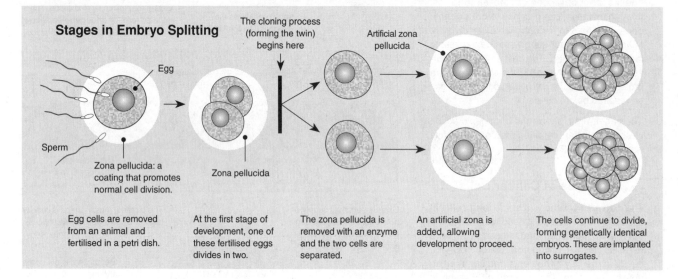

Stages in Embryo Splitting

Egg

Sperm

Zona pellucida: a coating that promotes normal cell division.

The cloning process (forming the twin) begins here

Zona pellucida

Artificial zona pellucida

Egg cells are removed from an animal and fertilised in a petri dish.

At the first stage of development, one of these fertilised eggs divides in two.

The zona pellucida is removed with an enzyme and the two cells are separated.

An artificial zona is added, allowing development to proceed.

The cells continue to divide, forming genetically identical embryos. These are implanted into surrogates.

1. Explain how **embryo splitting** differs from adult cloning: _____

_____

2. Briefly describe the possible benefits to be gained from cloning the following:

   (a) Stem cells for medical use: _____

   _____

   _____

   _____

   (b) High milk yielding cows: _____

   _____

   _____

   _____

3. Suggest one reason why it would be undesirable to produce all livestock using embryo splitting: _____

_____

Related activities: Cloning by Nuclear Transfer, Stem Cells & Tissue Engineering
Web links: What is Cloning?

Cloning by Nuclear Transfer

Clones are genetically identical individuals produced from one parent. Cloning is not new; it has been used in plant breeding for years. In recent years clones have been produced from both embryonic and non-embryonic cells using standard **nuclear transfer techniques** (below). In 2004, Australian genetic researchers successfully cloned a cow (called Brandy) using **serial nuclear transfer** (SNT) which involves an extra round of nuclear transfer to improve the reprogramming of the fused donor cells. In animal reproductive technology, cloning has facilitated the rapid production of genetically superior stock. These animals may then be dispersed among commercial herds. The **primary focus** of the new cloning technologies is to provide an economically viable way to rapidly produce transgenic animals with very precise genetic modifications.

Creating Dolly Using Standard Nuclear Transfer

Dolly, the Finn Dorset lamb born at the Roslin Institute (near Edinburgh) in July 1996, was the first mammal to be cloned from **non-embryonic cells**. Nuclear transfer has been used successfully to clone cells from embryonic tissue, but Dolly was created from a fully differentiated udder cell from a six year old ewe. This cell was made quiescent and then 'tricked' into re-entering an embryonic state. Dolly's birth was a breakthrough, because it showed that the processes leading to cell specialisation are not irreversible; even specialised cells can be 'reprogrammed' into an embryonic state. The steps involved in creating Dolly are outlined below. While cloning seems relatively easy to achieve using this method, Dolly's early death (right) has raised concerns that the techniques could have caused premature ageing. Although there is, as yet, no evidence for this, the long term viability of animals cloned from non-embryonic cells has still to be established.

Dolly Dies

Dolly the sheep was euthanased on **February 14th, 2003** after examinations showed she had developed progressive lung disease. Dolly was six years old; half the normal life expectancy of sheep. A post mortem examination showed that she succumbed to a viral infection, not uncommon in older sheep, especially those housed inside. Despite the concerns of some scientists, there is no evidence that cloning was a factor in Dolly contracting the disease.

1 Donor cells taken from udder: Cells from the udder of a Finn Dorset ewe were cultured in low nutrient medium for a week. The nutrient deprived cells stopped dividing, switched off their active genes, and became dormant.

2 Unfertilised egg has nucleus removed: In preparation for the nuclear transfer, an **unfertilised** egg cell was taken from a Scottish blackface ewe. Using micromanipulation techniques, the nucleus containing the DNA, was removed. This left a recipient egg cell with no nucleus, but an intact cytoplasm and the cellular machinery for producing an embryo.

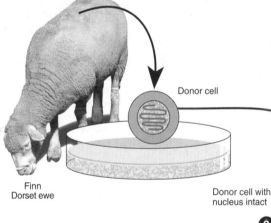

Finn Dorset ewe — Donor cell — Donor cell with nucleus intact

Nucleus is sucked up micropipette — Egg cell — Blunt "holding pipette" — micropipette — Nucleus of egg cell

First electric pulse

Cells are fused: The two cells (the dormant donor cell and the recipient egg cell) were placed next to each other and a gentle electric pulse causes them to fuse together (like soap bubbles). **3**

Egg cell without nucleus

A time delay improves the process by allowing as yet unknown factors in the cytoplasm to activate the chromatin.

Second electric pulse — Fused cells

4 Cell division is triggered: A second electric pulse triggers cellular activity and cell division, effectively jump-starting the cell into production of an embryo. This reaction can also be triggered by chemical means.

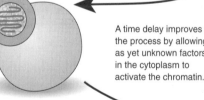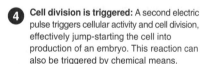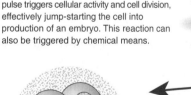

Blackface ewe

Dolly

5 After six days, the resulting embryo was surgically implanted into the uterus of the surrogate mother; another Scottish blackface ewe. Of the hundreds of reconstructed eggs, only 29 successfully formed embryos, and only Dolly survived to birth.

6 Birth: After a gestation of 148 days, the pregnant blackface ewe gave birth to Dolly, the Finn Dorset lamb that is genetically identical to the original donor.

Cell Division and Cloning

Related activities: Cloning by Embryo Splitting, Transgenic Organisms
Web links: Click and Clone

RA 2

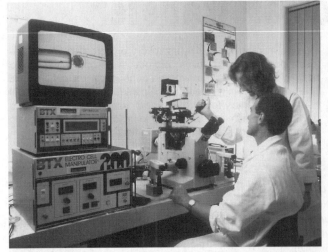

Embryo micromanipulation laboratory in Hamilton, New Zealand. Such labs use sophisticated equipment to manipulate ova (monitor's image is enlarged, right).

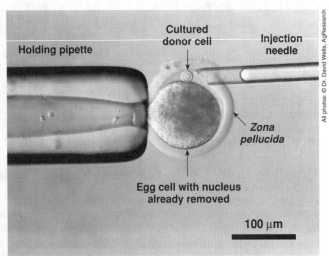

A single cultured cell is injected underneath the *zona pellucida* (the outer membrane) and positioned next to the egg cell (step 3 of diagram on the left).

Adult cloning heralds a new chapter in the breeding of livestock. Traditional breeding methods are slow, unpredictable, and suffer from a time delay in waiting to see what the phenotype is like before breeding the next generation. Adult cloning methods now allow a rapid spread of valuable livestock into commercial use among farmers. It will also allow the livestock industry to respond rapidly to market changes in the demand for certain traits in livestock products. In New Zealand, 10 healthy clones were produced from a single cow (the differences in coat colour patterns arise from the random migration of pigment cells in early embryonic development).

Lady is the last surviving cow of the rare Enderby Island (south of NZ) cattle breed. Adult cloning was used to produce her genetic duplicate, Elsie (born 31 July 1998). This result represents the first demonstration of the use of adult cloning in animal conservation.

1. Explain how cloning using **nuclear transfer** techniques differs from **embryo splitting**:

   _____

   _____

   _____

   _____

2. Explain how each of the following events is controlled in the **nuclear transfer** process:

   (a) The switching off of all genes in the donor cell: _____

   _____

   (b) The fusion (combining) of donor cell with enucleated egg cell: _____

   _____

   (c) The activation of the cloned cell into producing an embryo: _____

   _____

3. Describe a potential application of nuclear transfer technology for the cloning of animals: _____

   _____

   _____

Root Cell Development

In plants, cell division for growth (mitosis) is restricted to growing tips called **meristematic** tissue. These are located at the tips of every stem and root. This is unlike mitosis in a growing animal where cell divisions can occur all over the body. The diagram below illustrates the position and appearance of developing and growing cells in a plant root. Similar zones of development occur in the growing stem tips, which may give rise to specialised structures such as leaves and flowers.

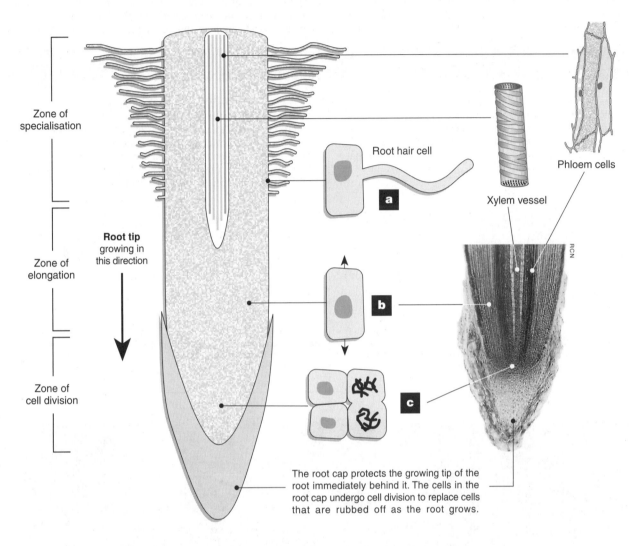

The root cap protects the growing tip of the root immediately behind it. The cells in the root cap undergo cell division to replace cells that are rubbed off as the root grows.

1. Briefly describe what is happening to the plant cells at each of the points labelled (**a**) to (**c**) in the diagram above:

   (a) _____

   (b) _____

   (c) _____

2. The light micrograph (below) shows a section of the cells of an onion root tip, stained to show up the chromosomes.

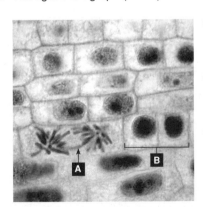

   (a) State the mitotic stage of the cell labelled A and explain your answer:

   _____

   (b) State the mitotic stage just completed in the cells labelled B and explain:

   _____

   (c) If, in this example, 250 cells were examined and 25 were found to be in the process of mitosis, state the proportion of the cell cycle occupied by mitosis:

   _____

   _____

3. Identify the cells that divide and specialise when a tree increases its girth (diameter): _____

Related activities: Mitosis and the Cell Cycle, Plant Cell Specialisation

RDA 2

Cell Division and Cloning

Vegetative Propagation of Plants

Many flowering plants are able to reproduce asexually and spread quickly through **vegetative** means (e.g. through runners and suckers). Humans exploit this ability in the vegetative propagation of plants by methods such as cutting and grafting. Such methods result in genetically identical plants (clones) year after year. Clones are produced for several reasons, e.g. to obtain a uniform plant performance (as in fruit trees), to multiply sterile or seedless species, or to propagate species with flowers in which the stamens have changed to petals and there is no pollen produced. In general, artificial propagation is a more efficient way to multiply certain kinds of plants because it produces a larger plant faster than one raised from seed and it avoids seed dormancy. New varieties can be developed by grafting, which combines the favourable characteristics of two existing varieties.

Artificial Vegetative Propagation

Cutting

Cutting is a method of propagation where a vegetative structure is removed from a parent plant and grown as a new individual. Cuttings are successfully used to propagate herbaceous plants, but can be used on woody plants with the use of hormones that promote root growth.

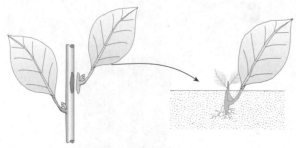

1 A leaf and axial bud is cut from the parent stock

2 The cutting is placed in a growth medium containing rooting hormones.

Grafting *(see photo series below)*

Grafting is a procedure by which the structures of two or more plants are joined. Typically a twig section (scion) from one plant is joined to the shoot of another (the rootstock). Grafting is used for many fruit and landscape trees because it avoids juvenility, and the special properties of the rootstock and the scion are able to be incorporated in the same plant.

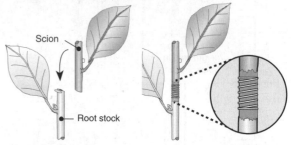
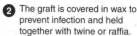

1 A **scion** is prepared by taking a cutting. The scion is then grafted to another plant (root stock).

2 The graft is covered in wax to prevent infection and held together with twine or raffia.

A scion is removed from the parent plant prior to grafting.

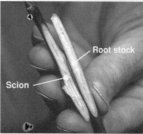

Scion being grafted onto the stem of the root stock.

The graft is sealed and covered to prevent water loss and infection.

The graft is then labelled for future reference and monitoring.

1. Discuss how humans have benefited from the vegetative propagation of plants by artificial means. Include reference to both biological and economic benefits:

_____

_____

_____

_____

2. Distinguish between **cutting** and **grafting** and suggest when each might be used: _____

_____

_____

_____

_____

_____

Related activities: Plant Tissue Culture

Plant Tissue Culture

Plant tissue culture, or **micropropagation**, is a method used for **cloning** plants. It is used widely for the rapid multiplication of commercially important plant species with superior genotypes, as well as in the recovery programmes for endangered plant species. Plant productivity and quality may be rapidly improved, and resistance to disease, pollutants, and insects increased. Continued culture of a limited number of cloned varieties leads to a change in the genetic composition of the population (genetic variation is reduced). New genetic stock may be introduced into cloned lines periodically to prevent this reduction in genetic diversity.

Micro-propagation is possible because differentiated plant cells have the potential to give rise to all the cells of an adult plant. It has considerable advantages over traditional methods of plant propagation (see table below), but it is very labour intensive. In addition, the optimal conditions for growth and regeneration must be determined and plants propagated in this way may be genetically unstable or infertile, with chromosomes structurally altered or in unusual numbers. The success of tissue culture is affected by factors such as selection of **explant** material, the composition of the culturing media, plant hormone levels, lighting, and temperature.

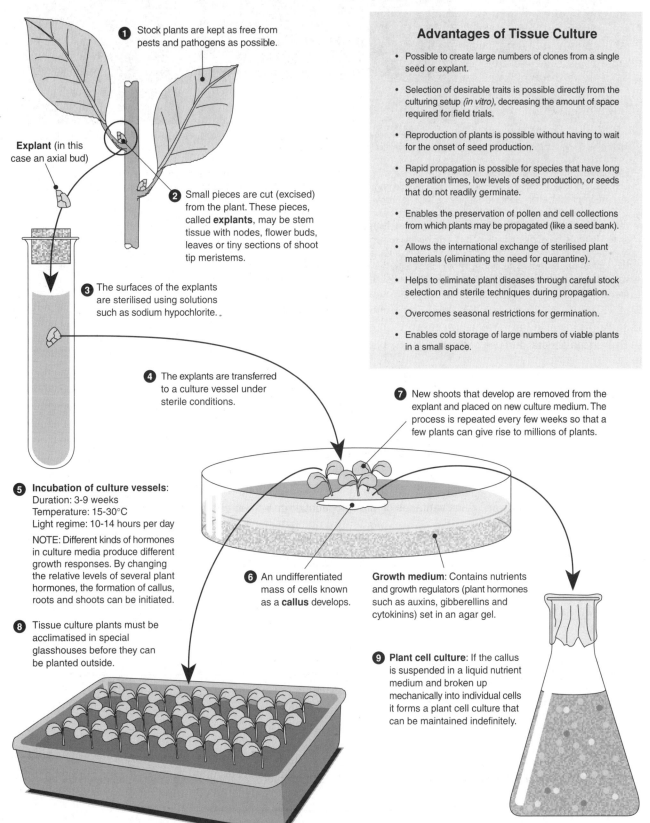

1 Stock plants are kept as free from pests and pathogens as possible.

Explant (in this case an axial bud)

2 Small pieces are cut (excised) from the plant. These pieces, called **explants**, may be stem tissue with nodes, flower buds, leaves or tiny sections of shoot tip meristems.

3 The surfaces of the explants are sterilised using solutions such as sodium hypochlorite.

4 The explants are transferred to a culture vessel under sterile conditions.

5 **Incubation of culture vessels**:
Duration: 3-9 weeks
Temperature: 15-30°C
Light regime: 10-14 hours per day

NOTE: Different kinds of hormones in culture media produce different growth responses. By changing the relative levels of several plant hormones, the formation of callus, roots and shoots can be initiated.

8 Tissue culture plants must be acclimatised in special glasshouses before they can be planted outside.

6 An undifferentiated mass of cells known as a **callus** develops.

Growth medium: Contains nutrients and growth regulators (plant hormones such as auxins, gibberellins and cytokinins) set in an agar gel.

7 New shoots that develop are removed from the explant and placed on new culture medium. The process is repeated every few weeks so that a few plants can give rise to millions of plants.

9 **Plant cell culture**: If the callus is suspended in a liquid nutrient medium and broken up mechanically into individual cells it forms a plant cell culture that can be maintained indefinitely.

Advantages of Tissue Culture

- Possible to create large numbers of clones from a single seed or explant.

- Selection of desirable traits is possible directly from the culturing setup *(in vitro)*, decreasing the amount of space required for field trials.

- Reproduction of plants is possible without having to wait for the onset of seed production.

- Rapid propagation is possible for species that have long generation times, low levels of seed production, or seeds that do not readily germinate.

- Enables the preservation of pollen and cell collections from which plants may be propagated (like a seed bank).

- Allows the international exchange of sterilised plant materials (eliminating the need for quarantine).

- Helps to eliminate plant diseases through careful stock selection and sterile techniques during propagation.

- Overcomes seasonal restrictions for germination.

- Enables cold storage of large numbers of viable plants in a small space.

Cell Division and Cloning

Related activities: Vegetative Propagation of Plants, Root Cell Development

RA 2

Micropropagation of the Tasmanian blackwood tree *(Acacia melanoxylon)*

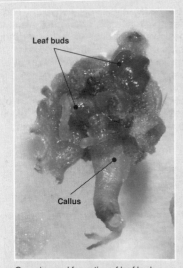

Greening and formation of leaf buds on a callus growing on culturing medium.

Normal shoots with juvenile leaves growing from a callus on media. They appear identical to those produced directly from seeds.

Seedling with juvenile foliage 6 months after transfer to greenhouse.

Photos: BOB

Micropropagation is increasingly used in conjunction with genetic engineering to propagate transgenic plants. Genetic engineering and micropropagation achieve similar results to conventional selective breeding but more precisely, quickly, and independently of growing season. The **Tasmanian blackwood** (above) is well suited to this type of manipulation. It is a versatile hardwood tree now being extensively trialled in some countries as a replacement for tropical hardwoods. The timber is of high quality, but genetic variations between individual trees lead to differences in timber quality and colour. Tissue culture allows the multiple propagation of trees with desirable traits (e.g. uniform timber colour). Tissue culture could also help to find solutions to problems that cannot be easily solved by forestry management. When combined with genetic engineering (introduction of new genes into the plant) problems of pest and herbicide susceptibility may be resolved. Genetic engineering may also be used to introduce a gene for male sterility, thereby stopping pollen production. This would improve the efficiency of conventional breeding programmes by preventing self-pollination of flowers (the manual removal of stamens is difficult and very labour intensive).

Information courtesy of Raewyn Poole, University of Waikato (Unpublished Msc. thesis).

1. Explain the general purpose of tissue culturing plants: _____

_____

2. (a) Explain what a **callus** is: _____

_____

(b) Explain how a callus may be stimulated to initiate root and shoot formation: _____

_____

3. Discuss the **advantages** and **disadvantages** of micropropagation compared with traditional propagation methods:

_____

_____

_____

_____

_____

_____

_____

_____

_____

4. Describe a potential problem with micropropagation in terms of long term ability to adapt to environmental changes:

_____

_____

Gene Technology

Learning Objectives

☐ 1. Compile your own glossary from the **KEY WORDS** displayed in **bold type** in the learning objectives below.

Introduction to Gene Technology *(pages 169-170)*

☐ 2. Explain what is meant by **gene technology** and distinguish it from the more general term, **biotechnology**. Distinguish between **genetic engineering** and **genetic modification** in general. Recognise one as a subset of the other.

☐ 3. Recognise that a small number of basic techniques (restriction digestion, DNA ligation, gel electrophoresis, and PCR) are used in a number of different processes (e.g. gene cloning, transgenesis, DNA profiling). Appreciate that these processes have wide application.

☐ 4. Provide an outline of the various applications of gene technology in modern medicine, agriculture, and industry. Appreciate the pivotal role of microorganisms in the development and application of this technology.

Techniques in Gene Technology *(pages 171-182)*

☐ 5. Explain the terms **restriction enzyme**, **plasmid**, and **recognition site**. Describe the basis by which restriction enzymes work, distinguishing between **sticky end** and **blunt end** DNA fragments produced by different types of restriction enzymes.

☐ 6. Identify the role of restriction enzymes in **recombinant DNA technology**. Identify some commonly used restriction enzymes and give their recognition sites.

☐ 7. Explain the technique and purpose of **DNA ligation** and **annealing**, including the role of **DNA ligase**.

☐ 8. Understand how **recombinant DNA** is produced by the ligation of DNA from different sources.

☐ 9. Explain the role of **gel electrophoresis** (of DNA) in gene technology. Outline the basic principles, including the role of **restriction digestion**. Identify properties of the **gel** that facilitate the separation of DNA fragments.

☐ 10. Explain how the DNA fragments on a gel are made visible. Describe the role of **DNA markers** in identifying fragments of different size.

☐ 11. Explain the role of **polymerase chain reaction** (PCR) in **DNA amplification**. Explain why PCR is an essential tool for many procedures in gene technology. Describe the basic technique of PCR, including the role of **primers**, **nucleotides**, and **DNA polymerase**.

☐ 12. Describe the use of **PCR**, **radioactive labelling**, and **gel electrophoresis** in **DNA sequencing**. Distinguish between **manual** and **automated** sequencing. Discuss how sequencing technology is used in **genome analysis** and identify some of its wider applications.

☐ 13. Describe the construction of a **DNA chip** (**microarray**), identifying the principles by which the chip operates.

Discuss some of the current and potential applications of this relatively new technology in gene research.

Processes & Applications in Gene Technology
(also see Review of Gene Technology on the TRC)

DNA profiling *(pages 183-190)*

☐ 14. Explain what is meant by **DNA profiling** (also called genetic profiling or DNA fingerprinting). Distinguish clearly between DNA profiling and sequencing.

☐ 15. Describe the process of DNA profiling using **PCR**, including reference to the role of **microsatellites**, **PCR**, and **gel electrophoresis**.

☐ 16. Describe DNA profiling using a **Southern blot**, including reference to the role of **gel electrophoresis**, the **blot**, and the **radioactively labelled probes**.

☐ 17. Describe applications of DNA profiling, e.g. in **forensic** analysis, in establishing paternity or pedigree, and as a tool in diagnostic medicine.

Gene cloning *(pages 189-190)*

☐ 18. Describe applications of **gene cloning** and recognise the stages involved, including preparation of the clone (#19) and the actual cloning of the gene itself (#20).

☐ 19. Outline the steps in preparing a gene for cloning:
　(a) Explain how the gene is **isolated** from cells.
　(b) Describe the role of **reverse transcriptase** in creating the gene to be inserted into the vector.
　(c) The creation of a **molecular clone**.

☐ 20. Explain how the prepared molecular clone is introduced into the host cells. Describe how bacterial colonies with the desired gene are identified, isolated, and grown in culture (to produce multiple copies of the gene).

☐ 21. Explain how gene expression is achieved in the organism that receives the molecular clone, e.g. in a crop plant where a gene of interest is introduced using the bacterium *Agrobacterium tumefaciens*.

Transgenesis *(pages 191-192)*

☐ 22. Explain clearly what is meant by a **transgenic organism**. Note the use of the term **transformation**, which is used specifically for the acquisition of genetic material by the uptake of **naked DNA** by the recipient. Transformation is a term most often used with respect to bacteria, but increasingly applied to other organisms.

☐ 23. Describe the techniques involved in transgenesis, including the role of viral or **plasmid vectors** in integrating foreign DNA into the genome of another organism. Explain how **recombinant vectors** are made using **restriction enzymes** and **DNA ligation**.

☐ 24. Explain the role of **marker genes** (also called genetic markers) in identifying transformed cells.

☐ 25. Review and summarise techniques used in gene technology, including transgenesis and profiling.

Meeting Human Needs and Demands

Valuable commodities *(pages 193-194, 197-198)*

☐ 26. Describe the role of **gene cloning** and **industrial-scale fermentation** technology in the mass production of valuable commodities such as:
   (a) Human proteins, including hormones, e.g. human **insulin**, **factor VIII**, and human growth hormone.
   (b) Vitamins, enzymes, and dietary supplements.
   (c) Pharmaceuticals such as **antibiotics** and **vaccines**.

☐ 27. Describe the use of transgenic livestock to produce human proteins, such as **alpha-1-antitrypsin** and **interferon**, which are used in treating human disease. Discuss the use of these proteins, explaining how they meet a human need and outlining the advantages and disadvantages of alternatives.

☐ 28. Describe the production of **chymosin** (rennin) from genetically modified (GM) microbes (yeast or bacteria) and describe its use. Discuss any benefits and disadvantages of using enzymes from a GM source (as opposed to traditional methods).

☐ 29. Explain how the application of recombinant DNA technology can meet human needs safely, and at relatively low cost. Identify any disadvantages and evaluate them with reference to traditional methods.

Improving crops & livestock *(pages 195-196)*

☐ 30. Discuss the potential of **genetically modified organisms** (GMOs) to meet human needs and demands. In your discussion, identify any techniques, such as the use of **DNA chips** (**microarrays**), that are important in the application of the technology.

Consider one or more of the following:
   (a) Crop resistance to herbicides and/or insect pests.
   (b) Changes in environmental tolerance.
   (c) Improved storage or crop quality (e.g. amino acid composition, protein content, or yield).
   (d) Use of transgenic livestock for vaccine, protein, or pharmaceutical production.
   (e) Use of transgenic livestock with properties for increased production (e.g. of wool or lean meat).

Gene therapy and DNA vaccines *(pages 199-202)*

☐ 31. Explain the production and application of **recombinant DNA vaccines**, identifying existing and future benefits of these over vaccines produced by traditional methods.

☐ 32. Using an appropriate example (e.g. SCIDS, Parkinson's disease, or **cystic fibrosis**), explain the basis of **gene therapy**, identifying the techniques involved, the **vectors** used, and delivery systems for these vectors. Discuss the current difficulties associated with gene therapy and explain why successful gene therapy has proved very difficult and, to date, largely unsuccessful.

Case study: Cystic fibrosis

☐ 33. Describe the genetic basis of **cystic fibrosis** (CF) and the symptoms of the disease that arise as a result of this defect. In terms of its genetic basis, explain the potential for CF to be treated/cured using gene therapy.

Ethics of Gene Technology *(pages 203-204)*

☐ 34. Discuss (in a balanced way) the relevant ethical, social, and economic issues associated with the production and use of genetically engineered organisms.

 See the 'Textbook Reference Grid' on pages 8-9 for textbook page references relating to material in this topic.

Supplementary Texts

See pages 5-7 for additional details of these texts:

■ Adds, J. *et al.,* 1999. **Tools, Techniques and Assessment in Biology** (NelsonThornes), pp. 56-71.

■ Adds, J., *et al.,* 2004. **Genetics, Evolution and Biodiversity**, (NelsonThornes), chpt. 9.

■ Clegg, C.J., 1999. **Genetics and Evolution** (John Murray), pp. 48-59.

■ Freeland, P., 1999. **Microbes, Medicine and Commerce** (Hodder and Stoughton), pp. 55-62.

■ Jones, N., *et al.,* 2001. **Essentials of Genetics** (John Murray), pp. 235-260.

See page 7 for details of publishers of periodicals:

STUDENT'S REFERENCE

■ **The Polymerase Chain Reaction** Biol. Sci. Rev., 16(3) Feb. 2004, pp. 10-13. *This account explains the techniques and applications of PCR.*

■ **Genetic Manipulation of Plants** Biol. Sci. Rev., 15(1) Sept. 2002, pp. 10-13. *The aims, methods, and applications of GM plants.*

■ **Food / How Altered?** National Geographic, May 2002, pp. 32-50. *An excellent account of the issue of "biotech foods". What are they, how altered are they, and how safe are they?*

■ **Tailor-Made Proteins** Biol. Sci. Rev., 13(4) March 2001, pp. 2-6. *Recombinant proteins and their uses in industry and medicine.*

■ **Birds, Bees, and Superweeds** Biol. Sci. Rev., 17(2) Nov. 2004, pp. 24-27. *Genetically modified crops: their advantages and commercial applications, as well as some of the risks and concerns associated with their use.*

■ **Agro-Biotech** Biol. Sci. Rev., 16(1) Sept. 2003, pp. 21-24. *Genetic engineering provides a tool to improving crops and meeting consumer demand. What is being developed and what are the risks?*

■ **Back to the Future of Cereals** Scientific American, Aug. 2004, pp. 26-33. *An excellent, up-to-date account of the state of crop technology. Fuelled by genomic studies, a new green revolution is predicted to increase crop yields ever further.*

■ **Recombinant Protein Production in Milk** Biol. Sci. Rev., 15(2) Nov. 2002, pp. 39-41. *A useful synopsis of the development and uses of transgenic livestock, including historical milestones.*

■ **Defensive Eating** Scientific American, May 2005, pp. 13-14. *Food vaccines developed as pills.*

■ **Food for All** New Scientist, 31 October 1998, pp. 50-52. *Crops that resist drought and disease could transform the lives of the poor. What problems are inherent in the dissemination of GM crops?*

TEACHER'S REFERENCE

■ **The Business of the Human Genome** Scientific American, July 2000, pp. 38-57. *A comprehensive account of the HGP.*

■ **Make me a Hipporoo** New Scientist, 11 Feb. 2006, pp. 25-38. *In the future, designing genomes with do-it-yourself kits could become a very personal thing, even an art form. What is the changing role of evolution as a result of this?*

■ **The Magic of Microarrays** Scientific American, Feb. 2002, pp. 34-41. *DNA chips (microarrays) and their use in identifying health and disease, along with implications for drug treatment.*

■ **The Land of Milk and Honey** Scientific American, Nov. 2005, pp. 72-75. *Alternative forms of protein manufacture are nearing completion, including an animal genetically engineered to produce a therapeutic protein in its milk.*

■ **Genomes for All** Scientific American, Jan. 2006, pp. 32-40. *New approaches such as genome-reading technology, and ethical issues involved in using personal genetic information.*

■ **Live and Let Live** New Scientist, 31 Oct. 1998, pp. 46-49. *Scientific and ethical arguments for and against genetically engineered crops.*

■ **GM Food Safety Special Report** Scientific American, April 2001. *Special issue examining aspects of the GM food debate (excellent).*

See pages 10-11 for details of how to access **Bio Links** from our web site: **www.biozone.co.uk** From Bio Links, access sites under the topics: **BIOTECHNOLOGY** > **General Biotechnology Sites:** • ABelgoBiotech • Molecular genetics *... and others* > **Biotechnology Techniques:** • Interactive biotechnology • Principle of the PCR • Recombinant DNA • Restriction enzymes *... and others* > **Biotechnology Processes:** • Animal and plant transformation • Basics of DNA fingerprinting • DNA workshop • Transgenic organisms *... and others* > **Applications in Biotechnology:** access sites under > *Food biotechnology* > *Medical biotechnology* > *Industrial biotechnology* > **Cloning and Tissue Culture:** • Conceiving a clone • Cloning and stem cell technology *... and others* > **The Human Genome Project:** • A users guide to the human genome • Genome FAQs file • Primer on molecular genetics *... and others* > **Genome Projects:** • Genomes OnLine • Genome News Network *... and others* **Issues & Ethics in Biotechnology:** • Bioethics for beginners • Genetic engineering and its dangers *... and others* > **DNA Software Download:** • Chromas DNA sequence viewer

Presentation MEDIA to support this topic: **GENES AND INHERITANCE** • Gene Technology

What is Genetic Modification?

The genetic modification of organisms is a vast industry, and the applications of the technology are exciting and far reaching. It brings new hope for medical cures, promises to increase yields in agriculture, and has the potential to help solve the world's pollution and resource crises. Organisms with artificially altered DNA are referred to as **genetically modified organisms** or **GMOs**. They may be modified in one of three ways (outlined below). Some of the current and proposed applications of gene technology raise complex ethical and safety issues, where the benefits of their use must be carefully weighed against the risks to human health, as well as the health and well-being of other organisms and the environment as a whole.

Producing Genetically Modified Organisms (GMOs)

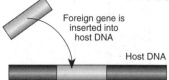

Foreign gene is inserted into host DNA

Host DNA

Add a foreign gene

A novel (foreign) gene is inserted from another species. This will enable the GMO to express the trait coded by the new gene. Organisms genetically altered in this way are referred to as **transgenic**.

Human insulin, used to treat diabetic patients, is now produced using transgenic bacteria.

Existing gene is altered

Host DNA

Alter an existing gene

An existing gene may be altered to make it express at a higher level (e.g. growth hormone) or in a different way (in tissue that would not normally express it). This method is also used for gene therapy.

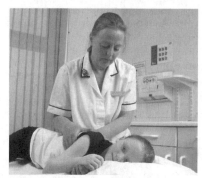

Gene therapy could be used treat genetic disorders, such as cystic fibrosis.

Gene is deleted or deactivated

Host DNA

Delete or 'turn off' a gene

An existing gene may be deleted or deactivated (switched off) to prevent the expression of a trait (e.g. the deactivation of the ripening gene in tomatoes produced the Flavr-Savr tomato).

Manipulating gene action is one way in which to control processes such as ripening in fruit.

1. Using examples, discuss the ways in which an organism may be genetically modified (to produce a GMO):

   _____

   _____

   _____

   _____

   _____

   _____

2. Explain how human needs or desires have provided a stimulus for the development of the following biotechnologies:

   (a) Gene therapy: _____

   _____

   _____

   (b) The production and use of transgenic organisms: _____

   _____

   _____

   (c) Plant micropropagation (tissue culture): _____

   _____

   _____

Related activities: Gene Therapy, Transgenic Organisms, Plant Tissue Culture
Web links: Landmarks in Biotechnology

RA 2

Gene Technology

Applications of GMOs

Techniques for genetic manipulation are now widely applied throughout modern biotechnology: in food and enzyme technology, in industry and medicine, and in agriculture and horticulture. Microorganisms are among the most widely used GMOs, with applications ranging from pharmaceutical production and vaccine development to environmental clean-up. Crop plants are also popular candidates for genetic modification although their use, as with much of genetic engineering of higher organisms, is controversial and sometimes problematic.

Applications of GMOs

Extending shelf life
Some fresh produce (e.g. tomatoes) have been engineered to have an extended keeping quality. In the case of tomatoes, the gene for ripening has been switched off, delaying the natural process of softening in the fruit.

Pest or herbicide resistance
Plants can be engineered to produce their own insecticide and become pest resistant. Genetically engineered herbicide resistance is also common. In this case, chemical weed killers can be used freely without crop damage.

Crop improvement
Gene technology is now an integral part of the development of new crop varieties. Crops can be engineered to produce higher protein levels or to grow in inhospitable conditions (e.g. salty or arid conditions).

Environmental clean-up
Some bacteria have been engineered to thrive on waste products, such as liquefied newspaper pulp or oil. As well as degrading pollutants and wastes, the bacteria may be harvested as a commercial protein source.

Biofactories
Transgenic bacteria are widely used to produce desirable products: often hormones or proteins. Large quantities of a product can be produced using bioreactors (above). Examples: insulin production by recombinant yeast, production of bovine growth hormone.

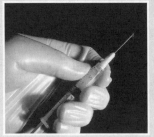

Vaccine development
The potential exists for multipurpose vaccines to be made using gene technology. Genes coding for vaccine components (e.g. viral protein coat) are inserted into an unrelated live vaccine (e.g. polio vaccine), and deliver proteins to stimulate an immune response.

Livestock improvement using transgenic animals
Transgenic sheep have been used to enhance wool production in flocks (above, left). The keratin protein of wool is largely made of a single amino acid, cysteine. Injecting developing sheep with the genes for the enzymes that generate cysteine produces woollier transgenic sheep. In some cases, transgenic animals have been used as biofactories. Transgenic sheep carrying the human gene for a protein, α-1-antitrypsin produce the protein in their milk. The antitrypsin is extracted from the milk and used to treat hereditary emphysema.

1. In a short account discuss one of the applications of GMOs described above: _____

_____

_____

_____

_____

_____

_____

_____

_____

_____

_____

_____

_____

Related activities: Transgenic Organisms, Genetically Modified Plants, Production of Human Proteins,

Restriction Enzymes

One of the essential tools of genetic engineering is a group of special **restriction enzymes** (also known as restriction endonucleases). These have the ability to cut DNA molecules at very precise sequences of 4 to 8 base pairs called **recognition sites**. These enzymes are the "molecular scalpels" that allow genetic engineers to cut up DNA in a controlled way. Although first isolated in 1970, these enzymes were discovered earlier in many bacteria (see panel on the next page). The purified forms of these bacterial restriction enzymes are used today as tools to cut DNA

(see table on the next page page for examples). Enzymes are named according to the bacterial species from which they were first isolated. By using a 'tool kit' of over 400 restriction enzymes recognising about 100 recognition sites, genetic engineers can isolate, sequence, and manipulate individual genes derived from any type of organism. The sites at which the fragments of DNA are cut may result in overhanging "sticky ends" or non-overhanging "blunt ends". Pieces may later be joined together using an enzyme called **DNA ligase** in a process called **ligation**.

Sticky End Restriction Enzymes

1 A **restriction enzyme** cuts the double-stranded DNA molecule at its specific **recognition site** (see the table opposite for a representative list of restriction enzymes and their recognition sites).

2 The cuts produce a DNA fragment with two **sticky ends** (ends with exposed nucleotide bases at each end). The piece it is removed from is also left with sticky ends.

Restriction enzymes may cut DNA leaving an overhang or sticky end, without its complementary sequence opposite. DNA cut in such a way is able to be joined to other exposed end fragments of DNA with matching sticky ends. Such joins are specific to their recognition sites.

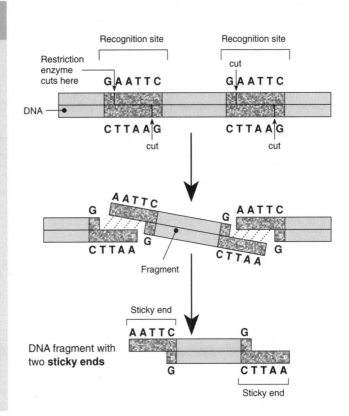

Blunt End Restriction Enzymes

1 A **restriction enzyme** cuts the double-stranded DNA molecule at its specific **recognition site** (see the table opposite for a representative list of restriction enzymes and their recognition sites).

2 The cuts produce a DNA fragment with two **blunt ends** (ends with no exposed nucleotide bases at each end). The piece it is removed from is also left with blunt ends.

It is possible to use restriction enzymes that cut leaving no overhang. DNA cut in such a way is able to be joined to any other blunt end fragment, but tends to be nonspecific because there are no sticky ends as recognition sites.

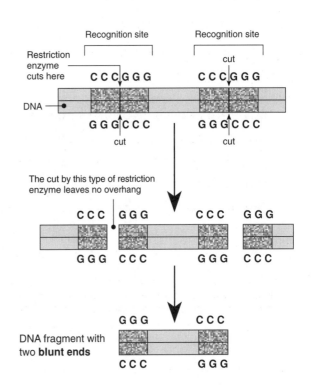

© Biozone International 1998-2007
Photocopying Prohibited

Related activities: Ligation
Web links: Review of Gene Technology

A 3

Gene Technology

Origin of Restriction Enzymes

Restriction enzymes have been isolated from many bacteria. It was observed that certain *bacteriophages* (viruses that infect bacteria) could not infect bacteria other than their usual hosts. The reason was found to be that other potential hosts could destroy almost all of the phage DNA using *restriction enzymes* present naturally in their cells; a defence mechanism against the entry of foreign DNA. Restriction enzymes are named according to the species they were first isolated from, followed by a number to distinguish different enzymes isolated from the same organism.

Recognition sites for selected restriction enzymes

Enzyme	Source	Recognition sites
*Eco*RI	*Escherichia coli* RY13	G A A T T C
*Bam*HI	*Bacillus amyloliquefaciens* H	G G A T C C
*Hae*III	*Haemophilus aegyptius*	G G C C
*Hind*III	*Haemophilus influenzae* Rd	A A G C T T
*Hpa*I	*Haemophilus parainfluenzae*	G T T A A C
*Hpa*II	*Haemophilus parainfluenzae*	C C G G
*Mbo*I	*Moraxella bovis*	G A T C
*Not*I	*Norcardia otitidis-caviarum*	G C G G C C G C
*Taq*I	*Thermus aquaticus*	T C G A

1. Explain the following terms, identifying their role in recombinant DNA technology:

   (a) Restriction enzyme: _____

   _____

   (b) Recognition site: _____

   _____

   (c) Sticky end: _____

   _____

   (d) Blunt end: _____

   _____

2. The action of a specific sticky end restriction enzyme is illustrated on the previous page (top). Use the table above to:

   (a) Identify the **restriction enzyme** used: _____

   (b) Name the organism from which it was first isolated: _____

   (c) State the **base sequence** for this restriction enzyme's recognition site: _____

3. A genetic engineer wants to use the restriction enzyme *Bam*HI to cut the DNA sequence below:

   (a) Consult the table above and state the recognition site for this enzyme: _____

   (b) Circle every **recognition site** on the DNA sequence below that could be cut by the enzyme *Bam*HI:

   ```
              10            20            30            40            50            60
   |AATGGGTACG|CACAGTGGAT|CCACGTAGTA|TGCGATGCGT|AGTGTTTATG|GAGAGAAGAA|
              70            80            90           100           110           120
   |AACGCGTCGC|CTTTTATCGA|TGCTGTACGG|ATGCGGAAGT|GGCGATGAGG|ATCCATGCAA|
             130           140           150           160           170           180
   |TCGCGGCCGA|TCGXGTAATA|TATCGTGGCT|GCGTTTATTA|TCGTGACTAG|TAGCAGTATG|
             190           200           210           220           230           240
   |CGATGTGACT|GATGCTATGC|TGACTATGCT|ATGTTTTTAT|GCTGGATCCA|GCGTAAGCAT|
             250           260           270           280           290           300
   |TTCGCTGCGT|GGATCCCATA|TCCTTATATG|CATATATTCT|TATACGGATC|GCGCACGTTT|
   ```

   (c) State how many fragments of DNA were created by this action: _____

4. When restriction enzymes were first isolated in 1970, there were not many applications to which they could be put to use. Now, they are an important tool in genetic engineering. Describe the human needs and demands that have driven the development and use of restriction enzymes in genetic engineering:

   _____

   _____

   _____

Ligation

DNA fragments produced using restriction enzymes may be reassembled by a process called **ligation**. Pieces are joined together using an enzyme called **DNA ligase**. DNA of different origins produced in this way is called **recombinant DNA** (because it is DNA that has been recombined from different sources). The combined techniques of using restriction enzymes and ligation are the basic tools of genetic engineering (also known as recombinant DNA technology).

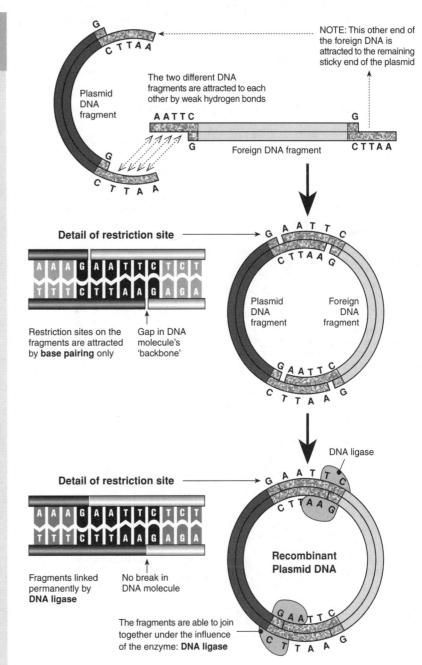

Creating a Recombinant DNA Plasmid

1. If two pieces of DNA are cut by the same restriction enzyme, they will produce fragments with matching **sticky ends** (ends with exposed nucleotide bases at each end).

2. When two such matching sticky ends come together, they can join by base-pairing. This process is called **annealing**. This can allow DNA fragments from a different source, perhaps a **plasmid**, to be joined to the DNA fragment.

3. The joined fragments will usually form either a linear molecule or a circular one, as shown here for a **plasmid**. However, other combinations of fragments can occur.

4. The fragments of DNA are joined together by the enzyme **DNA ligase**, producing a molecule of **recombinant DNA**.

NOTE: This other end of the foreign DNA is attracted to the remaining sticky end of the plasmid

The two different DNA fragments are attracted to each other by weak hydrogen bonds

Plasmid DNA fragment

Foreign DNA fragment

Detail of restriction site

Restriction sites on the fragments are attracted by **base pairing** only

Gap in DNA molecule's 'backbone'

Plasmid DNA fragment

Foreign DNA fragment

Detail of restriction site

Fragments linked permanently by **DNA ligase**

No break in DNA molecule

DNA ligase

Recombinant Plasmid DNA

The fragments are able to join together under the influence of the enzyme: **DNA ligase**

---

1. Explain in your own words the two main steps in the process of joining two DNA fragments together:

   (a) Annealing: _____

   _____

   (b) DNA ligase: _____

   _____

2. Refer to the activity, *DNA Replication*, and briefly state the **usual role** of DNA ligase in a cell:

   _____

3. Explain why **ligation** can be considered the reverse of the **restriction enzyme** process: _____

   _____

© Biozone International 1998-2007
Photocopying Prohibited

Related activities: Restriction Enzymes, DNA Replication
Web links: Review of Gene Technology

RA 3

Gene Technology

Gel Electrophoresis

Gel electrophoresis is a method that separates large molecules (including nucleic acids or proteins) on the basis of size, electric charge, and other physical properties. Such molecules possess a slight electric charge (see DNA below). To prepare DNA for gel electrophoresis the DNA is often cut up into smaller pieces. This is done by mixing DNA with restriction enzymes in controlled conditions for about an hour. Called **restriction digestion**, it produces a range of DNA fragments of different lengths. During electrophoresis, molecules are forced to move through the pores of a **gel** (a jelly-like material), when the electrical current is applied. Active electrodes at each end of the gel provide the driving force. The electrical current from one electrode repels the molecules while the other electrode simultaneously attracts the molecules. The frictional force of the gel resists the flow of the molecules, separating them by size. Their rate of migration through the gel depends on the strength of the electric field, size and shape of the molecules, and on the ionic strength and temperature of the buffer in which the molecules are moving. After staining, the separated molecules in each lane can be seen as a series of bands spread from one end of the gel to the other.

Analysing DNA using Gel Electrophoresis

DNA solutions: Mixtures of different sizes of DNA fragments are loaded in each well in the gel.

DNA markers, a mixture of DNA molecules with known molecular weights (size) are often run in one lane. They are used to estimate the sizes of the DNA fragments in the sample lanes. The figures below are hypothetical markers (bp = base pairs).

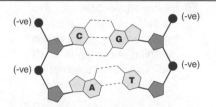

DNA is negatively charged because the phosphates (black) that form part of the backbone of a DNA molecule have a negative charge.

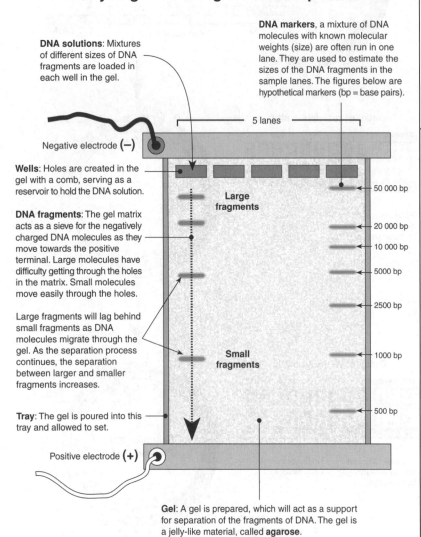

Wells: Holes are created in the gel with a comb, serving as a reservoir to hold the DNA solution.

DNA fragments: The gel matrix acts as a sieve for the negatively charged DNA molecules as they move towards the positive terminal. Large molecules have difficulty getting through the holes in the matrix. Small molecules move easily through the holes.

Large fragments will lag behind small fragments as DNA molecules migrate through the gel. As the separation process continues, the separation between larger and smaller fragments increases.

Tray: The gel is poured into this tray and allowed to set.

Negative electrode (–)

Positive electrode (+)

5 lanes

Large fragments

Small fragments

50 000 bp
20 000 bp
10 000 bp
5000 bp
2500 bp
1000 bp
500 bp

Gel: A gel is prepared, which will act as a support for separation of the fragments of DNA. The gel is a jelly-like material, called **agarose**.

Steps in the process of gel electrophoresis of DNA

1. A tray is prepared to hold the gel matrix.

2. A gel comb is used to create holes in the gel. The gel comb is placed in the tray.

3. Agarose gel powder is mixed with a buffer solution (the liquid used to carry the DNA in a stable form). The solution is heated until dissolved and poured into the tray and allowed to cool.

4. The gel tray is placed in an electrophoresis chamber and the chamber is filled with buffer, covering the gel. This allows the electric current from electrodes at either end of the gel to flow through the gel.

5. DNA samples are mixed with a "loading dye" to make the DNA sample visible. The dye also contains glycerol or sucrose to make the DNA sample heavy so that it will sink to the bottom of the well.

6. A safety cover is placed over the gel, electrodes are attached to a power supply and turned on.

7. When the dye marker has moved through the gel, the current is turned off and the gel is removed from the tray.

8. DNA molecules are made visible by staining the gel with **methylene blue** or ethidium bromide (which binds to DNA and fluoresces in UV light).

1. Explain the purpose of gel electrophoresis: _____

_____

_____

2. Describe the two forces that control the speed at which fragments pass through the gel:

   (a) _____

   (b) _____

3. Explain why the smallest fragments travel through the gel the fastest: _____

_____

_____

© Biozone International 1998-2007

Related activities: Nucleic Acids, Analysing a DNA Sample
Web links: DNA Extraction, Gel Electrophoresis, Review of Gene Technology

A 3

Polymerase Chain Reaction

Many procedures in DNA technology (such as DNA sequencing and DNA profiling) require substantial amounts of DNA to work with. Some samples, such as those from a crime scene or fragments of DNA from a long extinct organism, may be difficult to get in any quantity. The diagram below describes the laboratory technique called **polymerase chain reaction** (**PCR**). Using this technique, vast quantities of DNA identical to trace samples can be created. This process is often termed **DNA amplification**. Although only one cycle of replication is shown below, following cycles replicate DNA at an exponential rate. PCR can be used to make literally billions of copies in only a few hours. **Linear PCR** differs from regular PCR in that the same original DNA templates are used repeatedly. It is used to make many radio-labelled DNA fragments for DNA sequencing.

A Single Cycle of the Polymerase Chain Reaction

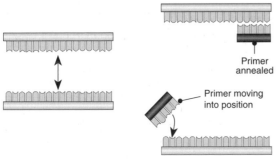

Primer annealed

Primer moving into position

DNA polymerase: A thermally stable form of the enzyme is used (e.g. *Taq* polymerase). This is extracted from thermophilic bacteria.

Nucleotides

Direction of synthesis

1 A DNA sample (called target DNA) is obtained. It is **denatured** (DNA strands are separated) by heating at 98°C for 5 minutes.

2 The sample is cooled to 60°C. Primers are **annealed** (bonded) to each DNA strand. In PCR, the primers are short strands of DNA; they provide the starting sequence for DNA extension.

3 Free nucleotides and the enzyme DNA polymerase are added. DNA polymerase binds to the primers and, using the free nucleotides, synthesises complementary strands of DNA.

4 After one cycle, there are now two copies of the original DNA.

Repeat for about 25 cycles

Repeat cycle of heating and cooling until enough copies of the target DNA have been produced

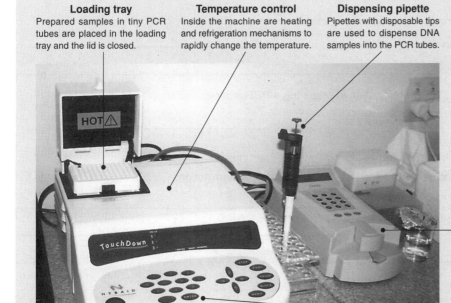

Loading tray
Prepared samples in tiny PCR tubes are placed in the loading tray and the lid is closed.

Temperature control
Inside the machine are heating and refrigeration mechanisms to rapidly change the temperature.

Dispensing pipette
Pipettes with disposable tips are used to dispense DNA samples into the PCR tubes.

HOT ⚠

TouchDown

Thermal Cycler

Amplification of DNA can be carried out with simple-to-use machines called **thermal cyclers**. Once a DNA sample has been prepared, in just a few hours the amount of DNA can be increased billions of times. Thermal cyclers are in common use in the biology departments of universities, as well as other kinds of research and analytical laboratories. The one pictured on the left is typical of this modern piece of equipment.

DNA quantitation
The amount of DNA in a sample can be determined by placing a known volume in this quantitation machine. For many genetic engineering processes, a minimum amount of DNA is required.

Controls
The control panel allows a number of different PCR programmes to be stored in the machine's memory. Carrying out a PCR run usually just involves starting one of the stored programmes.

Gene Technology

1. Explain the purpose of PCR: _____

   _____

   _____

   _____

Related activities: Restriction Enzymes, DNA Sequencing, DNA Profiling, Gene Cloning Using Plasmids   **Web links**: Review of Gene Technology

RDA 3

176

2. Briefly describe how the **polymerase chain reaction** (PCR) works: _____

_____

_____

_____

_____

_____

_____

_____

3. Describe three situations where only very small DNA samples may be available for sampling and PCR could be used:

(a) _____

_____

(b) _____

_____

(c) _____

_____

4. After only two cycles of replication, four copies of the double-stranded DNA exist. Calculate how much a DNA sample will have increased after:

(a) 10 cycles: _____   (b) 25 cycles: _____

5. The risk of contamination in the preparation for PCR is considerable.

(a) Explain what the effect would be of having a single molecule of unwanted DNA in the sample prior to PCR:

_____

_____

_____

(b) Describe two possible sources of DNA contamination in preparing a PCR sample:

Source 1: _____

Source 2: _____

(c) Describe two precautions that could be taken to reduce the risk of DNA contamination:

Precaution 1: _____

_____

Precaution 2: _____

_____

6. Describe two other genetic engineering/genetic manipulation procedures that require PCR amplification of DNA:

(a) _____

_____

(b) _____

_____

_____

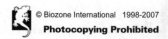

Manual DNA Sequencing

DNA sequencing techniques are used to determine the nucleotide (base) sequence of DNA. Two manual methods are in current use: the **Maxim-Gilbert** procedure and the most common method, the **Sanger** procedure (illustrated below). Both methods use a procedure called **electrophoresis**. The Sanger method is based on the premature termination of DNA synthesis resulting from the inclusion of specially modified nucleotides. DNA synthesis is initiated from a **primer** which is **radio-labelled** (contains a radioactive isotope that will appear on a photographic film called an **autoradiograph**). Four separate reactions are run, each containing a modified nucleotide mixed with its normal counterpart, as well as the three other normal nucleotides. When a modified nucleotide is added to the growing complementary DNA, synthesis stops. Each reaction yields a series of different sized fragments extending from the radioactive primer. The fragments from the four reactions are separated by electrophoresis and analysed by autoradiography to determine the DNA sequence.

The Sanger Method for DNA Sequencing

Four sequencing reactions

Using the same DNA sample to be sequenced (example used: **A C T G G T C T A G**), a separate sequencing reaction is carried out for each of the 4 bases: T, C, G, and A. In addition to the DNA sample, each reaction has normal (unaltered) copies of nucleotides: **T**, **C**, **G**, and **A**, plus a small quantity of one of the modified nucleotides:

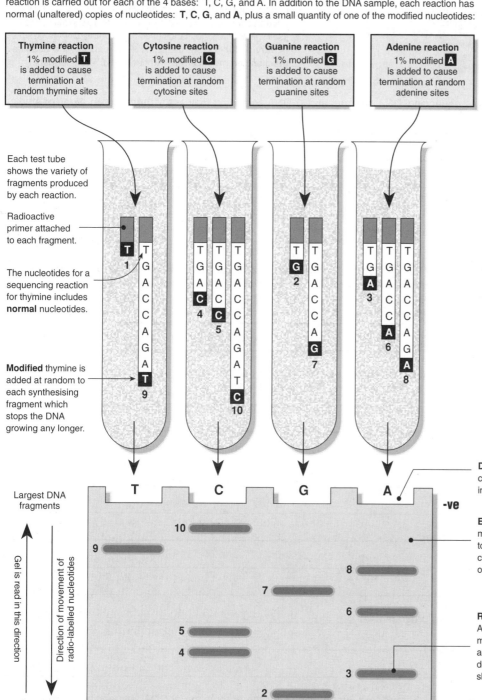

Thymine reaction
1% modified **T** is added to cause termination at random thymine sites

Cytosine reaction
1% modified **C** is added to cause termination at random cytosine sites

Guanine reaction
1% modified **G** is added to cause termination at random guanine sites

Adenine reaction
1% modified **A** is added to cause termination at random adenine sites

Each test tube shows the variety of fragments produced by each reaction.

Radioactive primer attached to each fragment.

The nucleotides for a sequencing reaction for thymine includes **normal** nucleotides.

Modified thymine is added at random to each synthesising fragment which stops the DNA growing any longer.

A typical **autoradiograph** showing a DNA sequence. The unexposed film is laid in contact with the gel after it has run. Radioactivity from the clustered DNA fragments create the dark shadows (blobs). Each blob contains millions of fragments.

Pharmacia (Aust) Pty Ltd

DNA samples: The four reactions containing DNA fragments are placed in separate wells at the top of the gel.

Electrophoresis gel: A jelly-like material that allows DNA fragments to move through it when an electric charge is applied. It is usually made of a material called *acrylamide*.

Radio-labelled DNA fragments: Attracted to the positive terminal, millions of DNA fragments of similar size and sequence move as a dark shadow down the gel. Larger pieces move more slowly and therefore do not travel as far.

Positive terminal: Attracts the fragments of DNA that are negatively charged.

Largest DNA fragments

Smallest DNA fragments

Gel is read in this direction

Direction of movement of radio-labelled nucleotides

-ve

+ve

Related activities: DNA Profiling, Polymerase Chain Reaction, The Human Genome Project **Web links**: Review of Gene Technology

Gene Technology

RA 3

How Fragments Are Formed

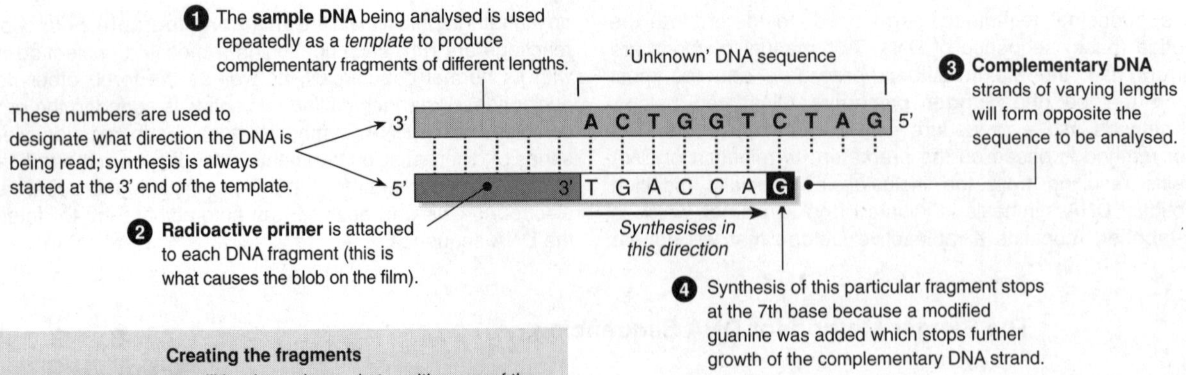

1 The **sample DNA** being analysed is used repeatedly as a *template* to produce complementary fragments of different lengths.

'Unknown' DNA sequence

3 **Complementary DNA** strands of varying lengths will form opposite the sequence to be analysed.

These numbers are used to designate what direction the DNA is being read; synthesis is always started at the 3' end of the template.

3' A C T G G T C T A G 5'

5' 3' T G A C C A G

Synthesises in this direction

2 **Radioactive primer** is attached to each DNA fragment (this is what causes the blob on the film).

4 Synthesis of this particular fragment stops at the 7th base because a modified guanine was added which stops further growth of the complementary DNA strand.

Creating the fragments

How long each fragment will be depends on what position one of the *chemically altered nucleotides* is incorporated into the sequence:

T Thymine
C Cytosine
G Guanine
A Adenine

Chemically altered so that they prevent further synthesis of the complementary DNA

What must be realised is that the DNA sample being analysed consists of many millions of individual molecules, each being used as a template to make fragments. Each template molecule itself will produce thousands of complementary DNA fragments of varying lengths. In the sample DNA above, the guanine reaction can produce two fragments of different lengths.

1. Briefly describe how PCR, DNA sequencing, DNA profiling, and/or DNA screening may assist the following areas of study:

(a) Forensic science:

(b) Legal disputes:

(c) Medical applications:

(d) Investigations into evolutionary relationships and taxonomy:

(e) Archaeology and anthropology:

(f) Conservation of endangered species:

(g) Management of livestock breeding programmes:

2. Explain why the Human Genome Project provided a large stimulus for the automation of DNA sequencing technology:

Automated DNA Sequencing

The process of DNA sequencing can be automated using **gel electrophoresis** machines that can sequence up to 600 bases at a time. Automation improves the speed at which samples can be sequenced and has made large scale sequencing projects (such as the **Human Genome Project**) possible. Instead of using radio-labelled DNA fragments, automated sequencing uses nucleotides labelled with **fluorescent dyes**; a different colour is used for each of the four types of bases. Another advantage is that the entire base sequence for a sample can be determined from a single lane on the gel (not four lanes as with the manual method). Computer software automatically interprets the data from the gel and produces a base sequence.

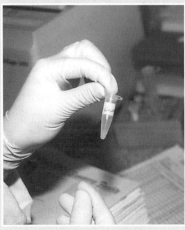

1. DNA sample arrives

Purified DNA samples may contain linear DNA or plasmids. The sample should contain about 1×10^{11} DNA molecules. The sample is checked to ensure that there is enough DNA present in the sample to work with.

2. Primer and reaction mix added

A **DNA primer** is added to the sample which provides a starting sequence for synthesis. Also added is the **sequencing reaction mix** containing the *polymerase enzyme* and free nucleotides, some which are labelled with dye.

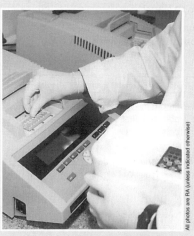

3. Create dye-labelled fragments

A **PCR** machine creates fragments of DNA complementary to the original template DNA. Each fragment is tagged with a fluorescent dye-labelled nucleotide. Running for 25 cycles, it creates 25×10^{11} single-stranded DNA molecules.

4. Centrifuge to create DNA pellet

The sample is chemically precipitated and centrifuged to settle the DNA fragments as a solid pellet at the bottom of the tube. Unused nucleotides, still in the liquid, are discarded.

5. DNA pellet washed, buffer added

The pellet is washed with ethanol, dried, and a gel loading buffer is added. All that remains now is single stranded DNA with one dye-labelled nucleotide at the end of each molecule.

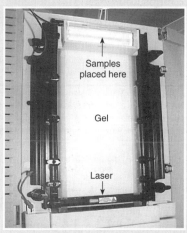

6. Acrylamide gel is loaded

The DNA sequencer is prepared by placing the gel (sandwiched between two sheets of glass) into position. A 36 channel 'comb' for receiving the samples is placed at the top of the gel.

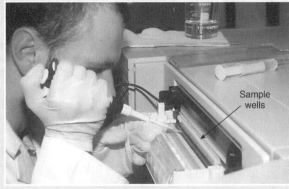

7. Loading DNA samples onto gel

Different samples can be placed in each of the 36 wells (funnel shaped receptacles) above the gel. A control DNA sample of known sequence is applied to the first lane of the sequencer. If there are problems with the control sequence then results for all other lanes are considered invalid.

8. Running the DNA sequencer

Powerful computer software controls the activity of the DNA sequencer. The gel is left to run for up to 10 hours. During this time an argon laser is constantly scanning across the bottom of the gel to detect the passing of dye-labelled nucleotides attached to DNA fragments.

Related activities: Manual DNA Sequencing, Gel Electrophoresis, Polymerase Chain Reaction, The Human Genome Project   **Web links**: Review of Gene Technology

Gene Technology

How a DNA Sequencer Operates

The gel is loaded following preparation of the samples and the gel (see steps 1-7 opposite and box, right).

Comb with 36 lanes into which different samples can be placed.

DNA fragments with dye-labelled nucleotides move down the gel over a period of 10 hours.

The smallest fragments move fastest down the gel and reach the argon laser first. Larger fragments arrive later.

DNA fragments separate into bands (see box below).

Argon laser excites fluorescent dye labels on nucleotides.

Lenses collect the emitted light and focus it into a spectrograph. An attached digital camera detects the light. See 'data collection' (below, right).

Negative terminal repels DNA fragments

Acrylamide gel

2400 volts 50 mA

Positive terminal attracts DNA fragments

Creating the dye labelled fragments

for gel electrophoresis is outlined in step 3, opposite. Key ingredients are:

(a) Original DNA template (the sample)

A C C G T A T G A T T C

(b) Many normal unlabelled nucleotides:

A   T   G   C

(c) Terminal nucleotides labelled with fluorescent dye (a different colour for each of the 4 bases). The structure of the nucleotides is altered so they act as terminators to stop further synthesis of the strand:

A○ T● G○ C●

Two examples of synthesised DNA fragments are shown below. One is relatively short, the other is longer:

Normal nucleotides   Terminal nucleotide labelled with dye

T G G○
A C C G T A T G A T T C

T G G C A T A C T○
A C C G T A T G A T T C

DNA fragments of different sizes are drawn down through the gel, separating into distinct bands of colour as they are illuminated by the laser:

Large fragments travel slowly down the gel

T G G C A T A C T A A G○ Yellow

T G G C A T A C T A A○ Green

T G G C A T A C T A○ Green

T G G C A T A C T○ Red

T G G C A T A C○ Blue

T G G C A T A○ Green

T G G C A T○ Red

T G G C A○ Green

T G G C○ Blue

T G G○ Yellow

T G○ Yellow

T○ Red

Small fragments travel quickly down the gel

Laser scans across the gel to detect the passing of each coloured dye

Data collection: The data from the digital camera are collected by computer software. The first of 23 samples is highlighted below in lane 1 with base sequences appearing on the far left.

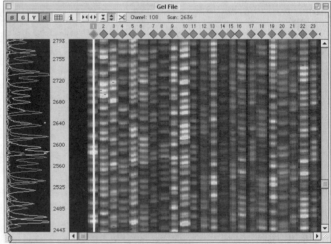

Data analysis: The data can be saved as a computer file which can then be analysed by other computer software. Such software can provide a printout of the base sequence as well as carry out comparisons with other DNA sequences (such as when looking for mutations).

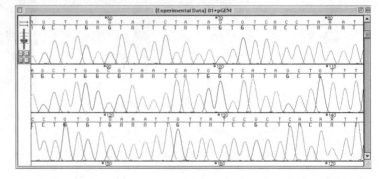

DNA Chips

Microarrays (DNA chips or gene chips) are relatively recent tools in gene research. Their development a decade ago built on earlier DNA probe technology and provided a tool to quickly compare the (known) DNA on a chip with (unknown) DNA to determine which genes were present in a sample or to determine the code of an unsequenced string of DNA. Microarrays have also provided a tool which, increasingly, is being used to investigate the activity level (the expression) of those genes. Microarrays rely on **nucleic acid hybridisation**, in which a known DNA fragment is used as a **probe** to find complementary sequences. In a microarray, DNA fragments, corresponding to known genes, are fixed to a solid support in an orderly pattern, usually as a series of dots. The fragments are tested for hybridisation with samples of labelled cDNA molecules. Computer analysis then reveals which genes are active in different tissues, in different stages of development, or in tissues in different states of health.

What is a DNA Chip?

A **microarray** (DNA chip) consists of DNA probes fixed to a small solid support such as a glass slide or a nylon filter. Each spot on the microarray has thousands to millions of copies of a different **DNA probe**. The probes are single stranded DNA molecules, each representing a gene.

Microarray (chip)

Segment of a chip

Spot containing copies of a single DNA molecule

Part of one DNA strand

How DNA Chips Work

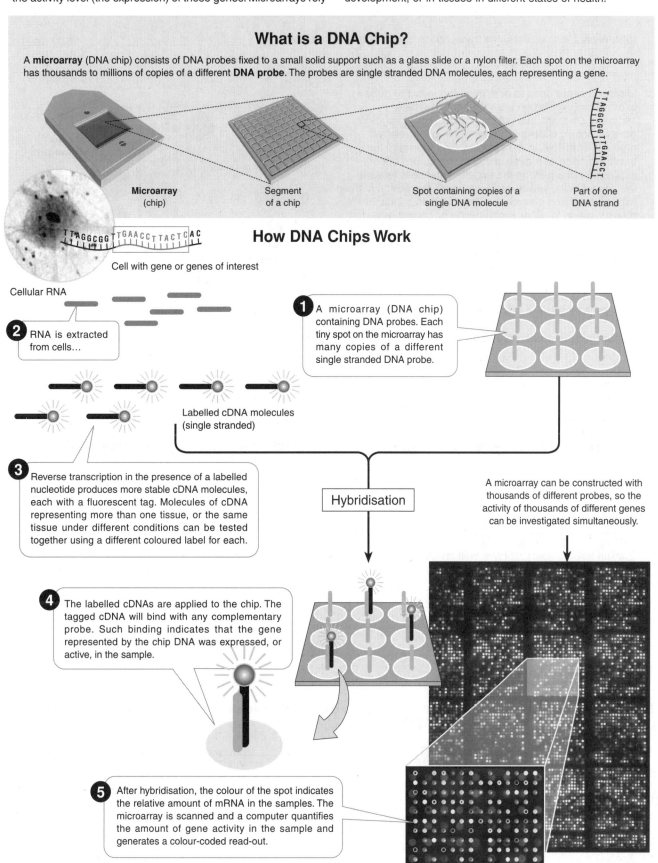

Cell with gene or genes of interest

Cellular RNA

2 RNA is extracted from cells…

1 A microarray (DNA chip) containing DNA probes. Each tiny spot on the microarray has many copies of a different single stranded DNA probe.

Labelled cDNA molecules (single stranded)

3 Reverse transcription in the presence of a labelled nucleotide produces more stable cDNA molecules, each with a fluorescent tag. Molecules of cDNA representing more than one tissue, or the same tissue under different conditions can be tested together using a different coloured label for each.

Hybridisation

A microarray can be constructed with thousands of different probes, so the activity of thousands of different genes can be investigated simultaneously.

4 The labelled cDNAs are applied to the chip. The tagged cDNA will bind with any complementary probe. Such binding indicates that the gene represented by the chip DNA was expressed, or active, in the sample.

5 After hybridisation, the colour of the spot indicates the relative amount of mRNA in the samples. The microarray is scanned and a computer quantifies the amount of gene activity in the sample and generates a colour-coded read-out.

Gene Technology

Related activities: Gene Cloning Using Plasmids, Genetically Modified Plants
Web links: Genomics, DNA Microarray, Review of Gene Technology

RA 3

1. Describe one purpose of microarrays: _____

_____

_____

2. (a) Identify the basic principle by which microarrays work: _____

_____

_____

(b) Identify the role of reverse transcription in microarray technology: _____

_____

3. Microarrays are used to determine the levels of gene expression (expression analysis). In one type of microarray, hybridisation of the red (experimental) and green (control) cDNAs is proportional to the relative amounts of mRNA in the samples. Red indicates the overexpression of a gene and green indicates under-expression of a gene in the experimental cells relative the control cells, yellow indicates equal expression in the experimental and control cells, and no colour indicates no expression in either experimental or control cells. In an experiment, cDNA derived from a strain of antibiotic resistant bacteria (experimental cells) was labelled with a red fluorescent tag and cDNA derived from a a non-resistant strain of the same bacterium (control cells) was labelled with a green fluorescent tag. The cDNAs were mixed and hybridised to a chip containing spots of DNA from genes 1-25. The results are shown on the right.

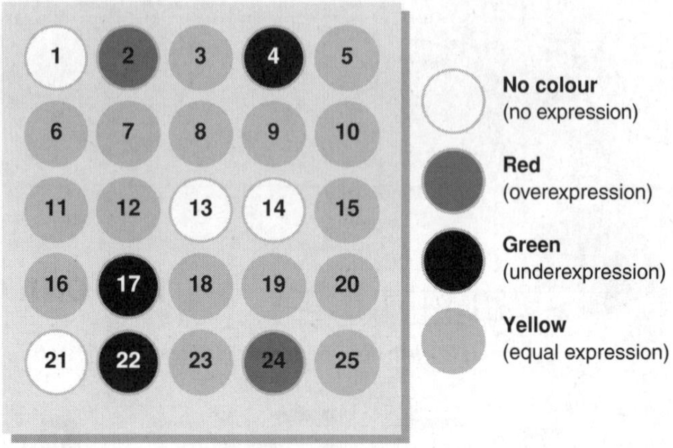

(a) Discuss the conclusions you could make about which genes might be implicated in antibiotic resistance in this case:

_____

_____

_____

(b) Suggest how this information could be used to design new antibiotics that are less vulnerable to resistance:

_____

_____

_____

4. Explain how microarrays have built on earlier DNA probe technology and describe the advantages they offer in studies of gene expression:

_____

_____

_____

_____

5. Microarrays are frequently used in diagnostic medicine to compare gene expression in cancerous and non-cancerous tissue. Suggest how this information could be used:

_____

_____

_____

_____

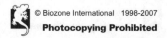

Investigating Genetic Biodiversity

PCR and **DNA sequencing** can be used in the assessment of **genetic biodiversity**. From a conservation point of view, large amounts of genetic variation within a species may be indicative of a greater ability to adapt to environmental change (e.g. changes in climate). The amount of variation between populations of a species is of particular interest. Sometimes the genetic variation found between populations is enough to warrant separating them into two or more '**morphologically cryptic**' species (containing populations that are identical in appearance, but different genetically). **Springtails** are abundant arthropods, closely related to insects, which live in soil throughout the world. One particular species, *Gomphiocephalus hodgsoni*, is the largest year-round inhabitant of the Antarctic continent. It is

being studied in an area of Antarctica known as the Dry Valleys, particularly in Taylor Valley. This region is largely ice-free, and the springtails survive in moist habitats such as at the edges of lakes and glacial streams. Springtails collected throughout Taylor Valley appear to be morphologically identical. However, after DNA analysis of a gene from springtail **mitochondrial DNA**, significant genetic biodiversity has been found between populations. This may indicate the presence of more than one species. As climate change and the presence of humans affect the habitat of Taylor Valley over time, it is important to understand and monitor the genetic structure of the springtail populations in order to ensure that biodiversity is conserved.

The **springtail** *Gomphiocephalus hodgsoni* (above) is a small arthropod, just over 1 mm long. Liam Nolan investigated the genetic relatedness of populations in and around Taylor Valley in Antarctica.

Taylor Valley, one of the Dry Valleys in Antarctica, is clear of snow much of the year. The ephemeral stream is ideal springtail habitat.

The Process of DNA Analysis of Two Springtails (A and B) is illustrated below:

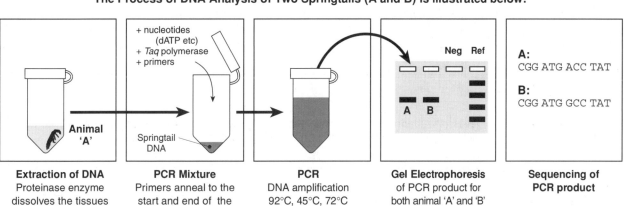

A:
CGG ATG ACC TAT

B:
CGG ATG GCC TAT

Extraction of DNA	**PCR Mixture**	**PCR**	**Gel Electrophoresis**	**Sequencing of**
Proteinase enzyme dissolves the tissues of the springtail to release DNA	Primers anneal to the start and end of the gene in the mitochondrial DNA	DNA amplification 92°C, 45°C, 72°C 45 cycles	of PCR product for both animal 'A' and 'B'	**PCR product**

Source: Many thanks to Liam Nolan, teacher at Tauranga Girls' College, for supplying the information for these pages. Liam studied with the **Centre for Biodiversity and Ecology Research** (University of Waikato, Hamilton, New Zealand), whilst the recipient of a study award from the NZ Ministry of Education.

Conditions in Antarctica are harsh, even at the best of times. Members of the research group shared a tent at their camp in Taylor Valley, set aside as a field laboratory. Despite overnight temperatures well below freezing, the tent often became very hot during the day as the mid-summer sun heated it for most of the 24 hour cycle.

Gene Technology

Related activities: Gel Electrophoresis, PCR, DNA Sequencing, The Genetic Code

ERA 3

Scientific expeditions into the field in Antarctica are fraught with logistical problems. Apart from making sure that sophisticated scientific equipment functions properly in freezing temperatures, just getting the equipment from Scott Base to the field station is difficult, requiring the use of helicopters.

Scott Base is the centre for research by New Zealand scientists. They work mostly during the summer months, when there is perpetual daylight. There are facilities for carrying out some lab work, as well as recreational facilities for the expedition members.

1. Explain why a **proteinase** enzyme is helpful in the extraction of DNA from springtails:

_____

_____

2. (a) Describe the function of *Taq* **polymerase** in **PCR**: _____

_____

(b) Explain why nucleotides are added to the PCR mixture: _____

_____

(c) Explain the effect of different temperatures (used in PCR) on the DNA and primers:

_____

_____

_____

3. (a) The **electrophoresis gel** is also loaded with a known '**negative**'; a substance that will produce a definite negative result, for comparison with samples A and B. Describe what would be put into the negative well:

_____

_____

(b) A **reference**, which contains a mixture of DNA segments of known length, is also loaded onto the gel. Explain why such fragments are added into the reference well:

_____

_____

_____

4. (a) The given DNA sequences (on the previous page) are taken from two different individuals. Describe how the two sequences differ:

_____

(b) Mutations (changes in DNA) are most frequently found at the third base of a codon. Refer to the *mRNA-amino acid table* earlier in the workbook and discuss the effect of this change in the DNA sequence:

_____

_____

_____

DNA Profiling Using PCR

In chromosomes, some of the DNA contains simple, repetitive sequences. These *noncoding* nucleotide sequences repeat themselves over and over again and are found scattered throughout the genome. Some repeating sequences are short (2-6 base pairs) called **microsatellites** or **short tandem repeats** (STRs) and can repeat up to 100 times. The human genome has numerous different microsatellites. Equivalent sequences in different people vary considerably in the numbers of the repeating unit. This phenomenon has been used to develop **DNA profiling**, which identifies the natural variations found in every person's DNA. Identifying such differences in the DNA of individuals is a useful tool for forensic investigations.

The laboratory responsible for forensic DNA testing in the UK is the Forensic Science Service (FSS). The FSS targets 10 STR sites; enough to guarantee that the odds of someone else sharing the same result are extremely unlikely; about one in a thousand million (a billion). The FSS is also responsible for compiling the National DNA Database of samples taken from convicted criminals or criminal suspects. These may be used to solve previously unsolved crimes, as well as to assist in future investigations. DNA profiling can also be used for investigating genetic relatedness (e.g. paternity cases, checking the pedigrees of bloodstock), or for searching for the presence of a particular gene (e.g. genetic screening for diseases).

Microsatellites (Short Tandem Repeats)

Microsatellites consist of a variable number of tandem repeats of a 2 to 6 base pair sequence. In the example below it is a two base sequence (CA) that is repeated.

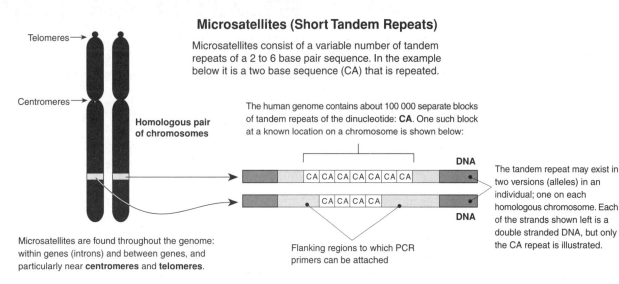

The human genome contains about 100 000 separate blocks of tandem repeats of the dinucleotide: **CA**. One such block at a known location on a chromosome is shown below:

The tandem repeat may exist in two versions (alleles) in an individual; one on each homologous chromosome. Each of the strands shown left is a double stranded DNA, but only the CA repeat is illustrated.

Microsatellites are found throughout the genome: within genes (introns) and between genes, and particularly near **centromeres** and **telomeres**.

Flanking regions to which PCR primers can be attached

How short tandem repeats are used in DNA profiling

This diagram shows how three people can have quite different microsatellite arrangements at the same point (locus) in their DNA. Each will produce a different DNA profile using gel electrophoresis:

1 Extract DNA from sample

A sample collected from the tissue of a living or dead organism is treated with chemicals and enzymes to extract the DNA, which is separated and purified.

2 Amplify microsatellite using PCR

Specific primers (arrowed) that attach to the flanking regions (light grey) either side of the microsatellite are used to make large quantities of the microsatellite and flanking regions sequence only (no other part of the DNA is amplified/replicated).

3 Visualise fragments on a gel

The fragments are separated by length, using **gel electrophoresis**. DNA, which is negatively charged, moves toward the positive terminal. The smaller fragments travel faster than larger ones.

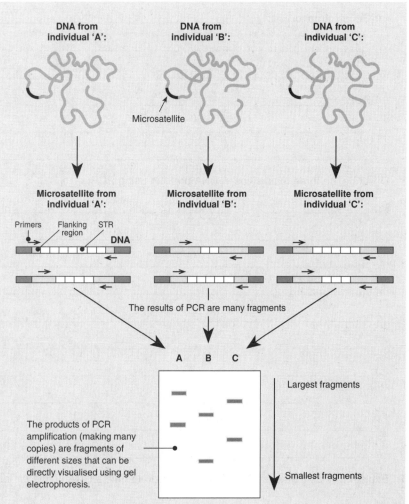

The products of PCR amplification (making many copies) are fragments of different sizes that can be directly visualised using gel electrophoresis.

The results of PCR are many fragments

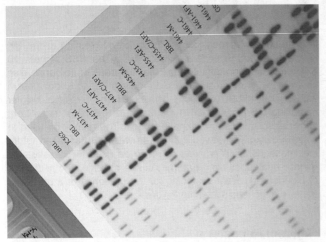

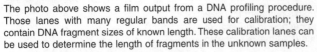

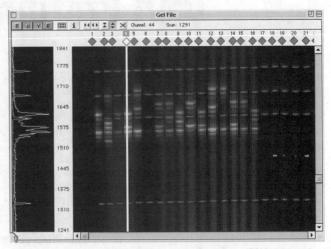

The photo above shows a film output from a DNA profiling procedure. Those lanes with many regular bands are used for calibration; they contain DNA fragment sizes of known length. These calibration lanes can be used to determine the length of fragments in the unknown samples.

DNA profiling can be automated in the same way as DNA sequencing. Computer software is able to display the results of many samples that are run at the same time. In the photo above, the sample in lane 4 has been selected. It displays fragments of different length on the left of the screen.

1. Describe the properties of **short tandem repeats** that are important to the application of **DNA profiling** technology:

_____

_____

_____

_____

_____

2. Explain the role of each of the following techniques in the process of DNA profiling:

(a) Gel electrophoresis: _____

_____

_____

(b) PCR: _____

_____

_____

3. Describe the three main steps in DNA profiling using PCR:

(a) _____

_____

_____

(b) _____

_____

_____

(c) _____

_____

_____

_____

4. Explain why as many as 10 STR sites are used to gain a DNA profile for forensic evidence: _____

_____

DNA Profiling Using Probes

Although DNA profiling using PCR is becoming increasingly the dominant procedure, the older technology of using DNA probes is still in use. The probe method uses another type of repeat sequence to that used in profiling with PCR. The repeat sequences are called **minisatellites** or **variable number tandem repeats** (VNTRs), and comprise longer repeating units (a few tens of nucleotides long). Equivalent sequences in different people have

the same core sequence of 10-15 bases (to which a DNA **probe** is attached), but thereafter the patterns vary considerably in length from one person to another. This phenomenon has been used to develop a DNA profiling procedure called the **Southern blotting** method (illustrated below). In humans, the chance that two people will have identical DNA fingerprints is less than one in a billion, making DNA profiling a useful tool for forensic investigations.

Southern Blotting Method

① Extract DNA from sample
A sample of tissue from a living or dead organism is treated with chemicals and enzymes to extract the DNA, which is separated and purified.

② Cut up DNA
Using **restriction enzymes**, the DNA is cut up into thousands of fragments of all different sizes.

③ Separate fragments
The fragments are separated by length, using **gel electrophoresis**. DNA, which is negatively charged, moves toward the positive terminal. The shorter fragments travel faster and further than longer ones.

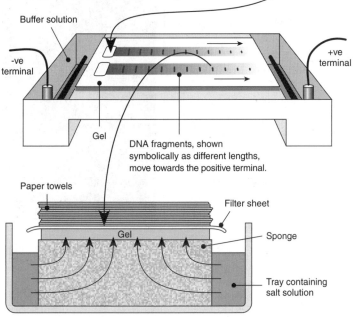

Buffer solution

-ve terminal

+ve terminal

Gel

DNA fragments, shown symbolically as different lengths, move towards the positive terminal.

Paper towels

Filter sheet

Gel

Sponge

Tray containing salt solution

④ Transfer DNA fragments to filter sheet
DNA molecules are split into single strands using alkaline chemicals. The DNA is transferred onto a nitrocellulose filter sheet by pressing it against the gel. The salt solution passes through the gel, carrying the DNA fragments onto the surface of the filter sheet. This is the blot.

A technician carrying out a DNA profiling test of samples taken from the scene of a crime. Such tests are admissible in a court of law as forensic evidence.

Developed film

The resulting DNA profile consists of a 'signature' of bands; each band consisting of thousands of fragments of the same length with probes attached.

⑦ Create autoradiograph
When using radioactive probes, the filter sheet is exposed to X-ray film. The radioactive probes attached to the sorted fragments show up as dark bands on the film. The spacing of these bands is the **DNA profile**, which is used as evidence.

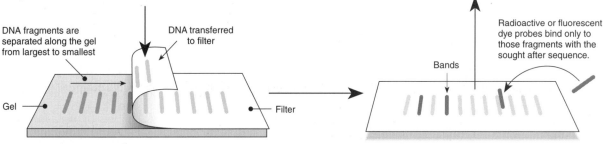

DNA fragments are separated along the gel from largest to smallest

DNA transferred to filter

Radioactive or fluorescent dye probes bind only to those fragments with the sought after sequence.

Bands

Gel

Filter

⑤ Remove filter sheet
The gel with filter sheet still attached is removed and separated. The DNA fragments that have now moved to the filter sheet are in exactly the same position as on the gel.

⑥ Attach radioactively labelled probes
The filter sheet is immersed in a bath with **radioactive probes** (synthetic complementary DNA). Many thousands of these segments bind to the sample DNA fragments where they are localised as bands.

Gene Technology

Related activities: Restriction Enzymes, Gel Electrophoresis, DNA Chips, DNA Profiling Using DNA   **Web links**: Review of Gene Technology

RA 3

188

How DNA probes may be used

Artificially constructed DNA probes work by binding to a specific sequence on DNA that is of interest to the investigator. Gene probes may be used to search for:

- The presence of a specific allele of a gene (e.g. cystic fibrosis gene).

- The approximate location of a gene on a chromosome (i.e. which chromosome and what position on its *p* or *q* arm it binds to).

- The 'genetic fingerprint' of a person to tell them apart from others (e.g. paternity testing, forensic identification of suspects).

How a DNA probe works

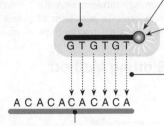

A **DNA probe** is a small fragment of nucleic acid (either cloned or artificially synthesised), that is labelled with an *enzyme*, a *radioactive* tag, or a *fluorescent dye* tag.

Fluorescent dye tag: Shows up as fluorescent bands when gel is exposed to ultraviolet light source.

or

Radioactive tag: Shows up as a dark band when the gel is exposed to photographic film.

Under appropriate conditions, the probe will bind to a complementary DNA sequence by base pairing, identifying the presence and location of the **target DNA** sequence for further analysis.

G T G T G T

A C A C A C A C A C A

Target DNA strand (such as a tandem repeat) with a complementary sequence that is being searched for by the probe.

1. The DNA profile on the right is a hypothetical example of a forensic result where the victim was raped and murdered. There were three suspects in the case. A semen sample was taken from the body of the victim and this was used as the evidence (see arrow on the X-ray film). Two probes were used in this investigation. The three suspects were required to give blood samples and a sample was also taken from the victim.

(a) Identify which of the three suspects was probably the killer: _____

(b) Explain with what degree of certainty do you give this verdict:

_____

_____

(c) Explain why a sample from the **victim** was also taken and analysed:

_____

_____

2. Explain why DNA profiling is a more useful diagnostic tool for **forensic** analysis than simply using **blood types**:

_____

_____

_____

_____

FORENSICS GEL #: 15423   RUN DATE:

EXP TIME: PROBE:

Suspect 1 Suspect 2 Suspect 3 Evidence Victim

3. In some well-known criminal trials in recent years (e.g. the trial of 'O.J. Simpson' for the murder of his wife, USA, 1995) the prosecution cases relied heavily on DNA evidence. Despite providing a DNA profile of the accused that clearly implicated them in the crime, the evidence was successfully challenged by defence counsel on technical grounds (concerning what is called the '**chain of evidence**'). Explain why such DNA evidence has failed to gain a prosecution:

_____

_____

_____

4. Forensic applications of DNA profiling are well known. Briefly describe two other applications of DNA profiling:

(a) _____

_____

(b) _____

_____

Gene Cloning Using Plasmids

Gene cloning is a process of making large quantities of a desired piece of DNA once it has been isolated. The purpose of this process is often to yield large quantities of either an individual gene or its protein product when the gene is expressed. Methods have been developed to insert a DNA fragment of interest (e.g. a human gene for a desired protein) into the DNA of a vector, resulting in a **recombinant DNA molecule** or **molecular clone**. A **vector** is a self-replicating DNA molecule (e.g. plasmid or viral DNA) used to transmit a gene from one organism into another. To be useful, all vectors must be able to replicate inside their host

organism, they must have one or more sites at which a restriction enzyme can cut, and they must have some kind of genetic marker that allows them to be easily identified. Organisms such as bacteria, viruses and yeasts have DNA that behaves in this way. Large quantities of the desired gene can be obtained if the recombinant molecule is allowed to replicate in an appropriate host. The host (e.g. bacterium) may then go on to express the gene and produce the desired protein. Two types of vector are **plasmids** (illustrated below) and **bacteriophages** (viruses that infect bacteria).

Cloning a Human Gene

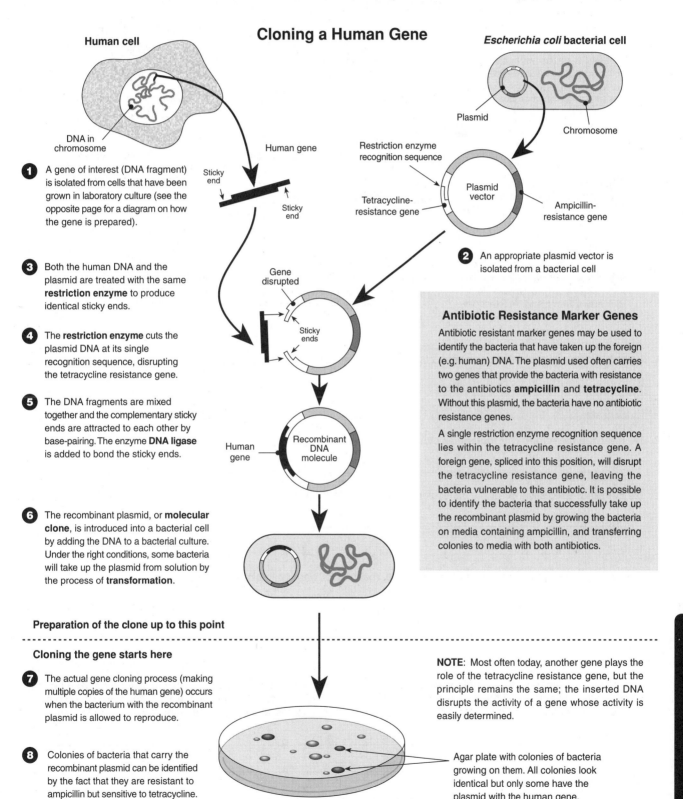

Human cell

DNA in chromosome

1 A gene of interest (DNA fragment) is isolated from cells that have been grown in laboratory culture (see the opposite page for a diagram on how the gene is prepared).

Human gene

Sticky end

Sticky end

Escherichia coli bacterial cell

Plasmid

Chromosome

Restriction enzyme recognition sequence

Tetracycline-resistance gene

Plasmid vector

Ampicillin-resistance gene

2 An appropriate plasmid vector is isolated from a bacterial cell

3 Both the human DNA and the plasmid are treated with the same **restriction enzyme** to produce identical sticky ends.

Gene disrupted

Sticky ends

4 The **restriction enzyme** cuts the plasmid DNA at its single recognition sequence, disrupting the tetracycline resistance gene.

5 The DNA fragments are mixed together and the complementary sticky ends are attracted to each other by base-pairing. The enzyme **DNA ligase** is added to bond the sticky ends.

Human gene

Recombinant DNA molecule

Antibiotic Resistance Marker Genes

Antibiotic resistant marker genes may be used to identify the bacteria that have taken up the foreign (e.g. human) DNA. The plasmid used often carries two genes that provide the bacteria with resistance to the antibiotics **ampicillin** and **tetracycline**. Without this plasmid, the bacteria have no antibiotic resistance genes.

A single restriction enzyme recognition sequence lies within the tetracycline resistance gene. A foreign gene, spliced into this position, will disrupt the tetracycline resistance gene, leaving the bacteria vulnerable to this antibiotic. It is possible to identify the bacteria that successfully take up the recombinant plasmid by growing the bacteria on media containing ampicillin, and transferring colonies to media with both antibiotics.

6 The recombinant plasmid, or **molecular clone**, is introduced into a bacterial cell by adding the DNA to a bacterial culture. Under the right conditions, some bacteria will take up the plasmid from solution by the process of **transformation**.

Preparation of the clone up to this point

- -

Cloning the gene starts here

7 The actual gene cloning process (making multiple copies of the human gene) occurs when the bacterium with the recombinant plasmid is allowed to reproduce.

8 Colonies of bacteria that carry the recombinant plasmid can be identified by the fact that they are resistant to ampicillin but sensitive to tetracycline.

NOTE: Most often today, another gene plays the role of the tetracycline resistance gene, but the principle remains the same; the inserted DNA disrupts the activity of a gene whose activity is easily determined.

Agar plate with colonies of bacteria growing on them. All colonies look identical but only some have the plasmid with the human gene.

Gene Technology

Related activities: Transgenic Organisms, Using Recombinant Bacteria
Web links: Gene Cloning, Review of Gene Technology

RA 3

Preparing a Gene For Cloning

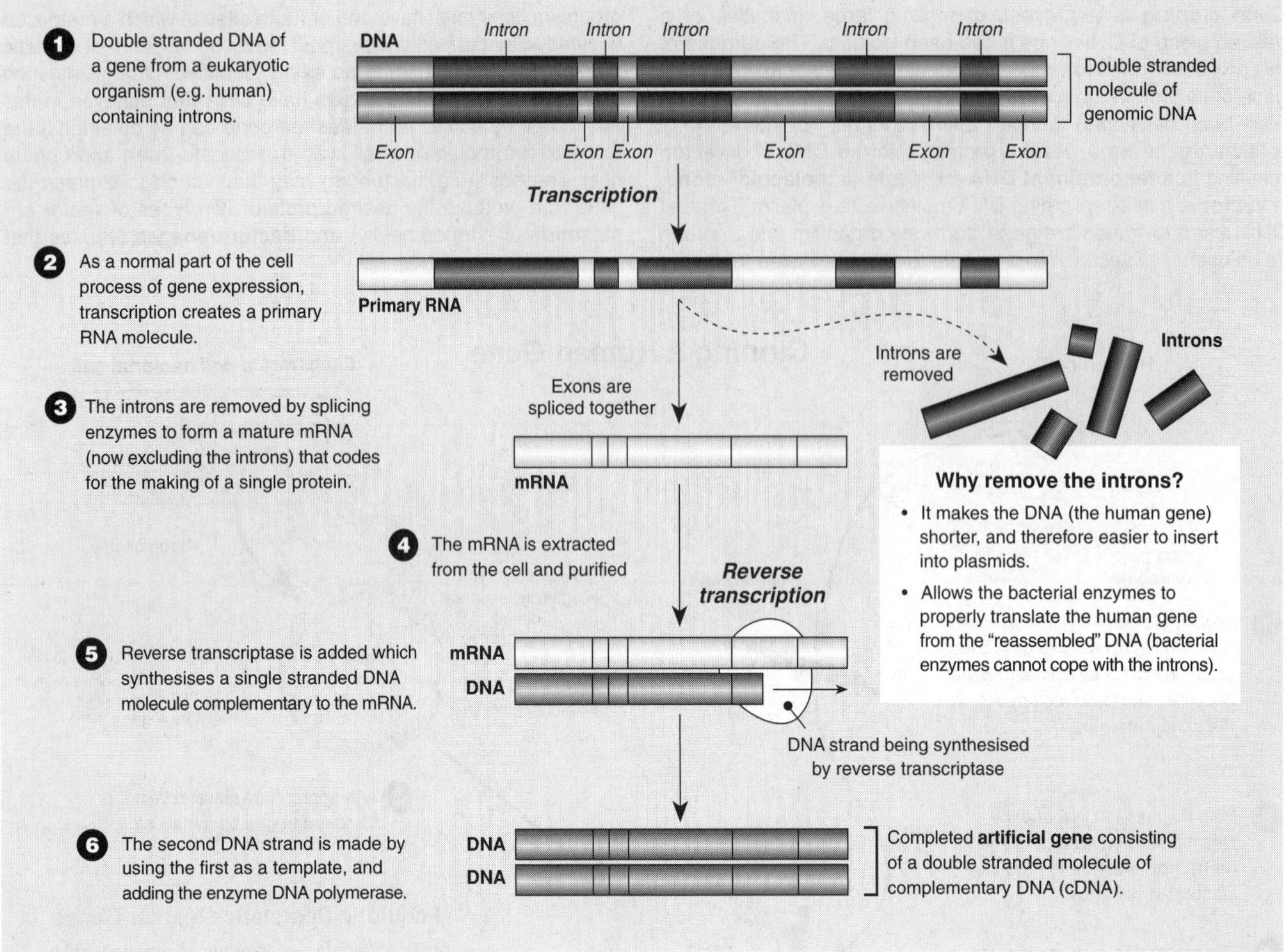

1 Double stranded DNA of a gene from a eukaryotic organism (e.g. human) containing introns.

DNA   Intron   Intron   Intron   Intron   Intron

Double stranded molecule of genomic DNA

Exon   Exon Exon   Exon   Exon   Exon

Transcription

2 As a normal part of the cell process of gene expression, transcription creates a primary RNA molecule.

Primary RNA

3 The introns are removed by splicing enzymes to form a mature mRNA (now excluding the introns) that codes for the making of a single protein.

Exons are spliced together

Introns are removed

Introns

mRNA

Why remove the introns?

- It makes the DNA (the human gene) shorter, and therefore easier to insert into plasmids.

- Allows the bacterial enzymes to properly translate the human gene from the "reassembled" DNA (bacterial enzymes cannot cope with the introns).

4 The mRNA is extracted from the cell and purified

Reverse transcription

5 Reverse transcriptase is added which synthesises a single stranded DNA molecule complementary to the mRNA.

mRNA

DNA

DNA strand being synthesised by reverse transcriptase

6 The second DNA strand is made by using the first as a template, and adding the enzyme DNA polymerase.

DNA
DNA

Completed **artificial gene** consisting of a double stranded molecule of complementary DNA (cDNA).

1. Explain the role of **restriction enzymes** in preparing a clone: _____

_____

_____

2. (a) Describe the nature of a **molecular clone**: _____

_____

(b) Explain the significance of the molecular clone being a self replicating molecule: _____

_____

_____

3. Discuss possible applications of **gene cloning** (i.e. reasons for wanting to clone a gene): _____

_____

_____

_____

4. When cloning a gene using **plasmid vectors**, the bacterial colonies containing recombinant plasmids are mixed up with colonies that have none. All the colonies look identical, but some have received plasmids with the human gene, some without, while others receive no plasmid at all. Explain how the colonies with the recombinant plasmids are identified:

_____

_____

_____

_____

Transgenic Organisms

Transgenesis is concerned with the movement of genes from one species to another. An organism developing from a cell into which foreign DNA has been inserted is called a **transgenic organism**. Transgenic techniques have been applied to plants, animals, and bacteria. They allow direct modification of a genome and enable traits to be introduced that are not naturally present in a species. This technology can be applied to improving crops and livestock, producing human proteins, and treating genetic defects through **gene therapy**. Cloning technology can be used to propagate transgenic organisms so that introduced genes quickly become part of the germ line (and are inherited). Some methods involved in transgenesis are shown below:

Liposomes

Liposomes, small spherical vesicles made of a single membrane, can be made commercially to precise specifications. When they are coated with appropriate surface molecules, they are attracted to specific cell types in the body. DNA carried by the liposome can enter the cell by endocytosis or fusion. They can be used to deliver genes to these cells to correct defective or missing genes, providing gene therapy.

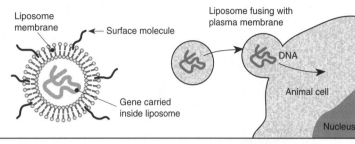

Plasmid Vectors

Plasmids are naturally occurring accessory chromosomes found in bacteria. Plasmids are usually transferred between closely related bacteria by cell-to-cell contact (conjugation). Simple chemical treatments can make mammalian cells, yeast cells and some bacterial cells that do not naturally transfer DNA, take up external, naked DNA. *Agrobacterium tumefaciens* (a bacterium) can insert part of its plasmid directly into plant cells.

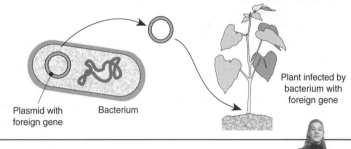

Viral Vectors

Viruses, such as those shown on the right, are well suited for gene therapy. They can accommodate up to 7500 bases of inserted DNA in their protein capsule. When viruses infect and reproduce inside the target cells, they are also spreading the recombinant DNA. They have already been used in several clinical trials of gene therapy for different diseases. A problem with this method involves the host immune reaction to the virus.

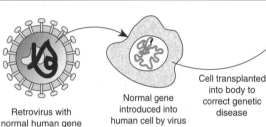

Pronuclear Injection

DNA can be introduced directly into an animal cell by microinjection. Multiple copies of the desired transgene are injected via a glass micropipette into a recently fertilised egg cell, which is then transferred to a surrogate mother. Transgenic mice and livestock are produced in this way, but the process is inefficient: only 2-3% of eggs give rise to transgenic animals and only a proportion of these animals express the added gene adequately.

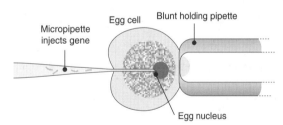

Ballistic DNA Injection

This remarkable way of introducing foreign DNA into living tissue literally shoots it directly into the organism using a "gene gun" (e.g. Helios gene gun made by Bi-Rad). Microscopic particles of gold or tungsten are coated with DNA. They are propelled by a burst of helium into the skin and organs of animals (e.g. rabbit, mouse, pig, fish, etc.) and tissues of intact plants. Some of the cells express the introduced DNA as if it were their own.

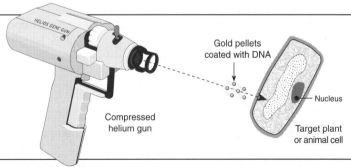

Protoplast Fusion

This process requires the cell walls of plants to be removed by enzymatic digestion. The resulting protoplasts (cells that have lost their cell walls) are then treated with polyethylene glycol which increases their frequency of fusion. In the new hybrid cell, the DNA derived from the two "parent" cells may undergo natural recombination (they may merge).

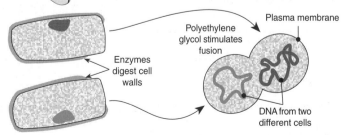

Gene Technology

Related activities: Applications of GMOs, Using Recombinant Bacteria, GM Plants, Vectors for Gene Therapy   **Web links**: Review of Gene Technology

A 3

Creating Transgenic Mice

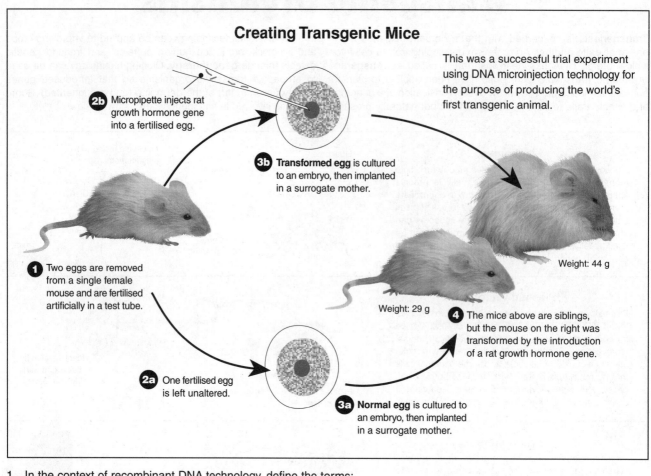

2b Micropipette injects rat growth hormone gene into a fertilised egg.

This was a successful trial experiment using DNA microinjection technology for the purpose of producing the world's first transgenic animal.

3b **Transformed egg** is cultured to an embryo, then implanted in a surrogate mother.

1 Two eggs are removed from a single female mouse and are fertilised artificially in a test tube.

Weight: 44 g

Weight: 29 g

2a One fertilised egg is left unaltered.

4 The mice above are siblings, but the mouse on the right was transformed by the introduction of a rat growth hormone gene.

3a **Normal egg** is cultured to an embryo, then implanted in a surrogate mother.

1. In the context of recombinant DNA technology, define the terms:

   (a) **Transgenesis:** _____

   (b) Foreign DNA: _____

2. Outline the basic principles involved in the production of a **transgenic organism**: _____

   _____

   _____

3. Describe an example of improvement in a commercial crop brought about by the application of transgenic techniques:

   _____

   _____

4. Describe three human needs that have encouraged the development of transgenic techniques:

   (a) _____

   (b) _____

   (c) _____

5. Describe two advantages and one disadvantage of using viruses as vectors for gene delivery:

   (a) Advantages: _____

   _____

   _____

   (b) Disadvantage: _____

6. Explain the purpose behind the transgenic mice experiment (above): _____

   _____

Edible Vaccines

Although still a few years away, the development of edible vaccines produced by transgenic plants using **recombinant DNA technology** will overcome many of the problems faced when using traditional vaccines. Plants engineered to contain the vaccine can be grown locally, in the area where vaccination is required, overcoming the logistic and economic problems of transporting prepared vaccines over long distances. Most importantly, edible vaccines do not require syringes, saving money and eliminating the risk of infection from contaminated needles. One method (below) used to generate edible vaccines relies on the bacterium *Agrobacterium tumefaciens* to deliver the genes for viral or bacterial antigens into plant cells (e.g. potatoes).

Procedure for Making Edible Vaccines

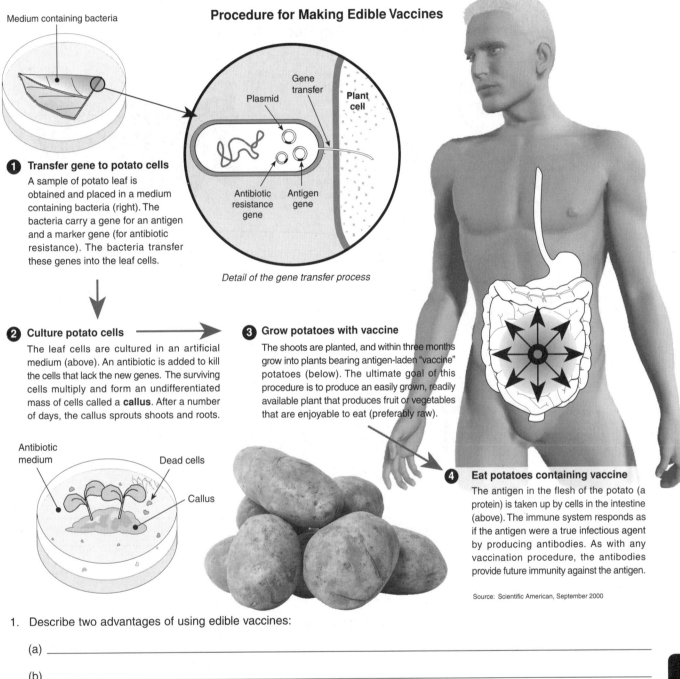

Medium containing bacteria

Plasmid — Gene transfer — **Plant cell**

Antibiotic resistance gene — Antigen gene

Detail of the gene transfer process

1 Transfer gene to potato cells

A sample of potato leaf is obtained and placed in a medium containing bacteria (right). The bacteria carry a gene for an antigen and a marker gene (for antibiotic resistance). The bacteria transfer these genes into the leaf cells.

2 Culture potato cells

The leaf cells are cultured in an artificial medium (above). An antibiotic is added to kill the cells that lack the new genes. The surviving cells multiply and form an undifferentiated mass of cells called a **callus**. After a number of days, the callus sprouts shoots and roots.

Antibiotic medium — Dead cells — Callus

3 Grow potatoes with vaccine

The shoots are planted, and within three months grow into plants bearing antigen-laden "vaccine" potatoes (below). The ultimate goal of this procedure is to produce an easily grown, readily available plant that produces fruit or vegetables that are enjoyable to eat (preferably raw).

4 Eat potatoes containing vaccine

The antigen in the flesh of the potato (a protein) is taken up by cells in the intestine (above). The immune system responds as if the antigen were a true infectious agent by producing antibodies. As with any vaccination procedure, the antibodies provide future immunity against the antigen.

Source: Scientific American, September 2000

1. Describe two advantages of using edible vaccines:

   (a) _____

   (b) _____

2. Describe one disadvantage of using edible vaccines: _____

3. Although potatoes are easy to propagate and are grown in many regions of the world, they are not particularly suitable for use as edible vaccines because cooking denatures the antigenic proteins. Suggest another fruit or vegetable that would be more suitable and explain your answer:

   _____

   _____

4. Explain why a gene for antibiotic resistance is added to the bacterium: _____

   _____

Gene Technology

Related activities: Immunisation, Types of Vaccines

A 2

Using Recombinant Bacteria

In 1990 Pfizer, Inc. produced one of the first two products of recombinant DNA technology to enter the human food supply, the "CHY-MAX" brand of chymosin. This was a protein purified from bacteria that had been given a copy of the chymosin gene from cattle. Traditionally extracted from "chyme" or stomach secretions of suckling calves, chymosin (also called rennin) is an enzyme that digests milk proteins. Chymosin is the active ingredient in rennet, used by cheesemakers to clot milk into curds. CHY-MAX extracted from bacteria grown in a vat is identical in chemical composition to the chymosin extracted from cattle. Pfizer's product quickly won over half the market for rennet because cheesemakers found it to be a cost-effective source of high-quality chymosin in consistent supply. A recombinant form of the fungus, *Mucor*, is also used to manufacture chymosin.

Chymosin Production using Recombinant Bacteria

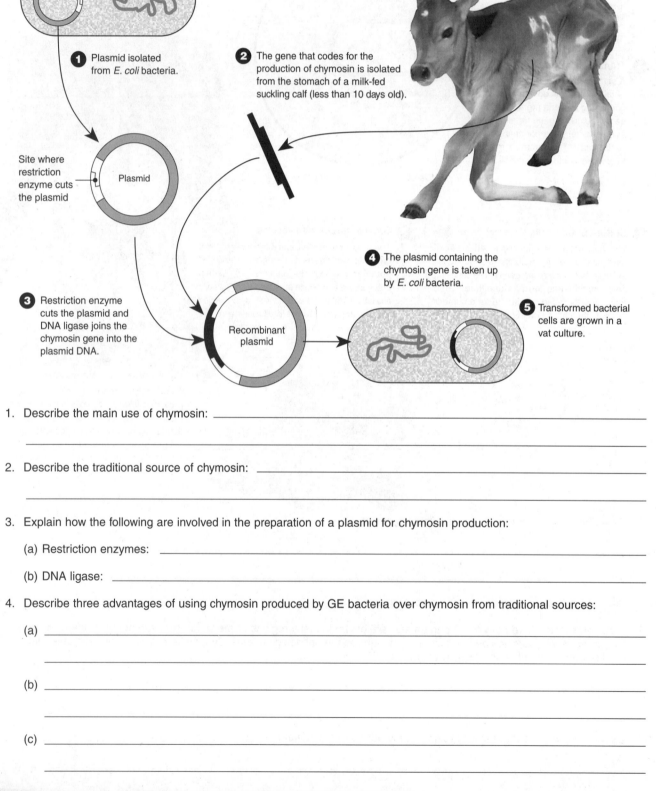

1 Plasmid isolated from *E. coli* bacteria.

2 The gene that codes for the production of chymosin is isolated from the stomach of a milk-fed suckling calf (less than 10 days old).

Site where restriction enzyme cuts the plasmid

Plasmid

3 Restriction enzyme cuts the plasmid and DNA ligase joins the chymosin gene into the plasmid DNA.

Recombinant plasmid

4 The plasmid containing the chymosin gene is taken up by *E. coli* bacteria.

5 Transformed bacterial cells are grown in a vat culture.

1. Describe the main use of chymosin: _____

_____

2. Describe the traditional source of chymosin: _____

_____

3. Explain how the following are involved in the preparation of a plasmid for chymosin production:

   (a) Restriction enzymes: _____

   (b) DNA ligase: _____

4. Describe three advantages of using chymosin produced by GE bacteria over chymosin from traditional sources:

   (a) _____

   _____

   (b) _____

   _____

   (c) _____

   _____

Related activities: Restriction Enzymes, Ligation, Gene Cloning
Using Plasmids, Production of Human Proteins

Genetically Modified Plants

Plants with **novel traits** may be produced by traditional methods, such as accelerated mutagenesis or hybridisation. More recently, recombinant DNA techniques and **marker assisted breeding** have allowed a much more controlled and directed approach to introducing new genetic material into plants. Genomic studies of plants, particularly the major crop plants such as rice and wheat, have enabled scientists to identify the genes for particular traits (below) and apply these new technologies to rapidly develop new, high yielding crop varieties. A large number of plants, including many crop plants, have now been genetically modified using recombinant DNA techniques, and the methodology for

this (called **transformation**) is now well established (see the next page). Scientists are also developing marker assisted breeding technology to move beneficial alleles into modern crop breeding lines through conventional cross breeding. In this method, the allele itself serves as a traceable marker for the trait and seedlings can be scanned for the allele's presence at every round of breeding. This shortens the time it takes to develop a new crop variety. The genetic manipulation of plants through these methods has enabled important agricultural crops to be endowed with new traits that increase yield, improve pest resistance, and reduce the need for agrichemicals.

Matching Traits to Genes in Crop Plants

In crop research, standard mapping techniques can be used to identify the possible location of a gene on a chromosome. Sequencing the DNA in that region enables the gene to then be identified. To find out the gene's function in the plant, scientists can use any one of the techniques described below (A-C).

Ⓐ Database search

To compare a new desirable gene with those already sequenced in other organisms.

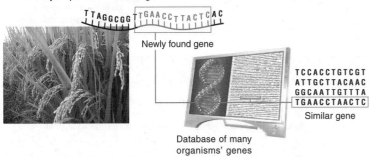

Newly found gene

TCCACCTGTCGT
ATTGCTTACAAC
GGCAATTGTTTA
TGAACCTAACTC

Similar gene

Database of many organisms' genes

The genes responsible for basic cellular activities are often nearly identical in different organisms. A newly found gene can be compared with known genes in existing databases to reveal close matches. 20 000 of the 30 000-50 000 predicted genes in rice have sequence similarity (homology) to previously discovered genes whose function is known.

Ⓑ Expression profile

To determine when the newly found gene is expressed, hence its probable function.

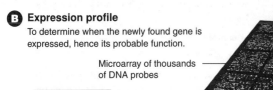

Microarray of thousands of DNA probes

TGAACCTTACTC

Probe matching the newly found gene

A microarray contains thousands of DNA fragments called probes. Each one matches a mRNA, which acts as a signature for gene activity. When plant cell samples are washed across the microarray, any mRNAs present will stick to their matching probes and fluoresce. If a gene is activated (expressed) at one particular stage of plant development, it is assumed to play a role in that stage.

Ⓒ Mutant library

To compare the expression of a gene in a normal and a mutant plant in order to determine the function of the newly found gene.

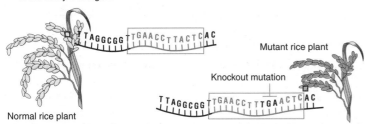

Mutant rice plant

Knockout mutation

Normal rice plant

A small piece of DNA inserted into a gene of interest can "knock out," or silence, that gene in the developing plant. Screening the mutant for differences from normal plants can reveal the gene's usual role.

Desirable Traits

Plant breeders seek to modify traits that lead to increases in yield or improved nutritional value.

Growth
Grain size or number
Size of seed head
Maturation rate

Architecture
Height
Branching
Flowering

Stress tolerance
Drought
Pests and diseases
Herbicides
Intensive fertiliser
application

Nutrient content/quality
Starch
Proteins
Lipids
Vitamins

Predicted Classification of Rice Genes

Rice has a relatively small genome compared with other crop plants (430 million bp compared with 3 billion bp in corn and 16 billion bp in wheat). Because of this, it has been the easiest of all the cereals to work with and is the first to have had its entire genome sequenced. The methods described (left) have been already been used to determine (or predict) the functions of a large fraction of the genes in rice.

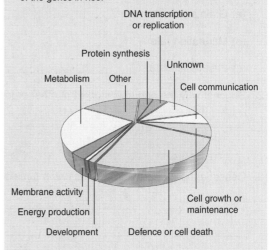

DNA transcription or replication
Protein synthesis
Metabolism
Other
Unknown
Cell communication
Membrane activity
Energy production
Development
Defence or cell death
Cell growth or maintenance

Adapted from: Goff and Salmeron (2004). Back to the future of cereals. Scientific American 291(2), August 2004, pp. 26-33.

Gene Technology

Related activities: Applications of GMOs, DNA Chips
Web links: DNA Microarray

RA 2

Transformation using a *Ti* Plasmid in *Agrobacterium*

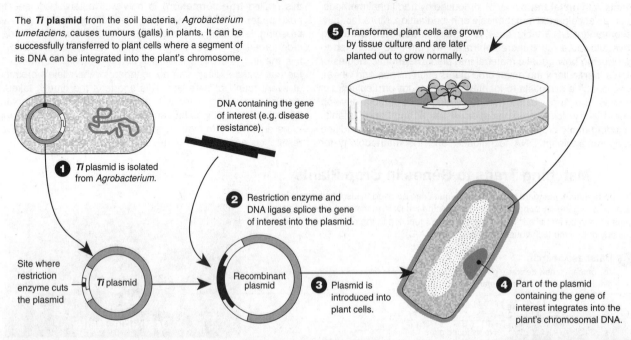

The *Ti* plasmid from the soil bacteria, *Agrobacterium tumefaciens*, causes tumours (galls) in plants. It can be successfully transferred to plant cells where a segment of its DNA can be integrated into the plant's chromosome.

1 *Ti* plasmid is isolated from *Agrobacterium*.

Site where restriction enzyme cuts the plasmid

Ti plasmid

DNA containing the gene of interest (e.g. disease resistance).

2 Restriction enzyme and DNA ligase splice the gene of interest into the plasmid.

Recombinant plasmid

3 Plasmid is introduced into plant cells.

5 Transformed plant cells are grown by tissue culture and are later planted out to grow normally.

4 Part of the plasmid containing the gene of interest integrates into the plant's chromosomal DNA.

Examples of Genetically Modified Plants

Crop	Phenotypic trait altered	Crop	Phenotypic trait altered
Argentine canola	Herbicide tolerance, modified seed fatty acid content (high oleic acid/low linolenic acid expression), pollination control system (male sterility, fertility restoration).	Potato	Resistance to: Colorado potato beetle, leafroll *luteovirus*, potato virus Y.
		Rice	Herbicide resistance, adding provitamin A.
Carnation	Increased shelf-life (delayed senescence), herbicide tolerance, modified flower colour.	Soybean	Herbicide resistance, modified fatty acid content (high oleic acid/low linolenic acid expression), herbicide tolerance.
Chicory	Male sterility, herbicide tolerance.		
Cotton	Herbicide tolerance, resistance to lepidopteran pests (e.g. cotton worm, pink bollworm, tobacco budworm).	Squash	Resistance to infection: cucumber mosaic virus, watermelon mosaic virus, zucchini yellow mosaic virus.
Flax (linseed)	Herbicide tolerance.	Sugar beet	Herbicide tolerance.
Maize	Herbicide tolerance, male sterility, resistance to European corn borer.	Tobacco	Herbicide tolerance.
		Tomato	Increased shelf-life through delayed ripening and delayed softening. Resistance to lepidopteran pests.
Melon	Delayed ripening.		
Papaya	Resistance to infection by papaya ringspot virus.	Wheat	Herbicide tolerance.

1. For each of the following traits, suggest features that could be desirable in terms of increasing yield:

   (a) Grain size or number: _____

   (b) Maturation rate: _____

   (c) Pest resistance: _____

2. Suggest why the genomic studies of other organisms are still useful in terms of identifying gene functions in crop plants:

   _____

   _____

3. Describe the property of *Agrobacterium tumefaciens* that makes it an ideal vector for introducing new genes into plants:

   _____

   _____

4. Suggest why a modified protein content might be desirable in a food crop: _____

   _____

Production of Human Proteins

Transgenic microorganisms are now widely used as **biofactories** for the production of human proteins. These proteins are often used to treat metabolic protein-deficiency disorders. **Type 1 diabetes mellitus** is a metabolic disease caused by a lack of insulin and is treatable only with insulin injection. Before the advent of genetic engineering, insulin was extracted from the pancreatic tissue of pigs or cattle. This method was expensive and problematic in that the insulin caused various side effects and was often contaminated. Since the 1980s, human insulin has been mass

produced using genetically modified (GM) bacteria (*Escherichia coli*) and yeast (*Saccharomyces cerevisiae*). Similar methods are used for the genetic manipulation of both microorganisms, although the size of the bacterial plasmid requires that the human gene be inserted as two, separately expressed, nucleotide sequences (see below). The use of insulin from GM sources has greatly improved the management of Type 1 diabetes, and the range of formulations now available has allowed diabetics to live much more normal lives than previously.

Synthesis of human insulin using recombinant DNA technology

Type I diabetes is treated with regular injections of insulin according to daily needs (right). Since the 1980s, human insulin has been mass produced using genetically modified (GM) microorganisms and marketed under various trade names. Various methodologies are employed to produce the insulin, but all involve inserting a human gene into a plasmid (bacterial or yeast), followed by secretion of a protein product from which the active insulin can be derived.

1 Identify and synthesise the human gene

Insulin is a small, simple protein. It comprises a total of 51 amino acids in two polypeptide chains (A and B). The two chains are linked by disulfide bonds. The nucleotide sequence of the gene for human insulin has been determined from the amino acid sequence. The first step in insulin production is to chemically synthesise the DNA chains that carry the specific nucleotide sequences for the A and B chains of insulin (the A and B 'genes').

2 Insert the synthetic DNA into plasmids

Using a tool kit of restriction enzymes and DNA ligase, the synthetic A and B nucleotide sequences are separately inserted into the gene for the bacterial enzyme, β-galactosidase, which is carried on the bacterial plasmid. In *E. coli*, β-galactosidase controls the transcription of genes. To make the bacteria produce insulin, the insulin gene needs to be tied to the gene for this enzyme.

3 Insert plasmid into the bacterial cell

The recombinant plasmids are then introduced to *E. coli* cells in culture conditions that favour the bacterial uptake of plasmid DNA. In practical terms, the synthesis of human insulin requires millions of copies of bacteria whose plasmid has been combined with the insulin gene. The insulin gene is expressed as it replicates with the β-galactosidase in the cell undergoing mitosis.

4 Make the functional protein

The protein formed consists partly of β-galactosidase, joined either to the A or B chain of insulin. The A and B chains are then extracted from the β-galactosidase fragment and purified. The two chains are then mixed and reconnected in a reaction that forms the disulfide cross bridges and the functional human protein, insulin. The final purified product is made suitable for injection and provided in a number of different formulations.

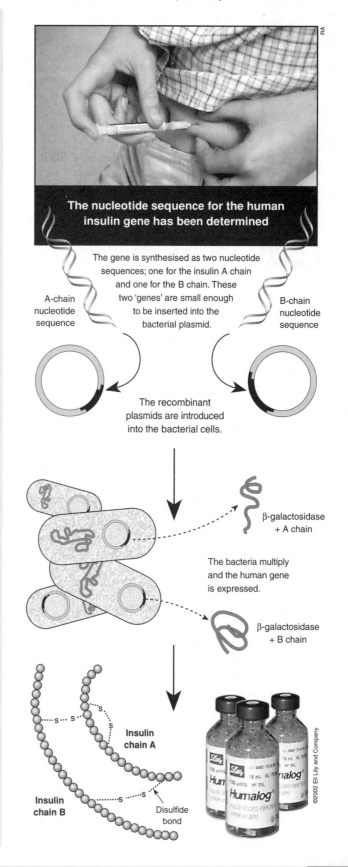

The nucleotide sequence for the human insulin gene has been determined

The gene is synthesised as two nucleotide sequences; one for the insulin A chain and one for the B chain. These two 'genes' are small enough to be inserted into the bacterial plasmid.

A-chain nucleotide sequence

B-chain nucleotide sequence

The recombinant plasmids are introduced into the bacterial cells.

β-galactosidase + A chain

The bacteria multiply and the human gene is expressed.

β-galactosidase + B chain

Insulin chain A

Insulin chain B

Disulfide bond

Gene Technology

©2002 Eli Lily and Company

Related activities: Applications of GMOs, Using Recombinant Bacteria

A 3

Human Proteins Produced Using Genetic Engineering

Human protein and biological role	Traditional production method	Current production
Erythropoetin A hormone, produced by kidneys, which stimulates red blood cell production. Used to treat anaemia in patients with kidney failure.	Not applicable. Previous methods to treat anaemia in patients with kidney failure was through repeated blood transfusions.	Cloned gene grown in hamster ovary cells
Human Growth Hormone Pituitary hormone promoting normal growth in height (deficiency results in dwarfism). Injection used to treat pituitary dwarfism.	Extracted from the pituitary glands of corpses. Many patients developed Creutzfeldt-Jacob disease (CJD) as a result. CJD is a degenerative brain disease, transmitted via infected tissues or their extracts.	Genetically engineered bacteria
Insulin Regulates the uptake of glucose by cells. Used (via injection) in the treatment of Type 1 (insulin-dependent) diabetes mellitus.	Physical extraction from the pancreatic tissue of pigs or cattle. Problems included high cost, sample contamination, and severe side effects.	Genetically engineered bacteria or yeast
Interferon Anti-viral substance produced by virus-infected cells. Used in the treatment of hepatitis B and C, some cancers, and multiple sclerosis.	Not applicable. Relatively recent discovery of the role of these proteins in human physiology.	Genetically engineered bacteria
Factor VIII One of the blood clotting factors normally present in blood. Used in the treatment of haemophilia caused by lack of factor VIII.	Blood donation. Risks of receiving blood contaminated with infective viruses (HIV, hepatitis), despite better screening procedures.	Genetically engineered bacteria

1. Describe the three major problems associated with the traditional method of obtaining insulin to treat diabetes:

   (a) _____

   (b) _____

   (c) _____

2. Explain why the insulin gene is synthesised as two separate A and B chain nucleotide sequences:

   _____

3. Explain why the synthetic nucleotide sequences ('genes') are inserted into the β-galactosidase gene:

   _____

4. Yeast (*Saccharomyces cerevisiae*) is also used in the production of human insulin. It is a eukaryote with a larger plasmid than *E. coli*. Its secretory pathways are more similar to those of humans and β-galactosidase is not involved in gene expression. Predict how these differences might change the procedure for insulin production with respect to:

   (a) Insertion of the gene into the plasmid: _____

   _____

   (b) Secretion and purification of the protein product: _____

   _____

5. Describe the benefits to patients of using GMOs to produce human proteins: _____

   _____

   _____

6. When delivered to a patient, artificially produced human proteins only alleviate disease symptoms; they cannot cure the disease. Describe how this situation might change in the future:

   _____

   _____

   _____

Gene Therapy

Gene therapy refers to the application of gene technology to correct or replace defective genes. It was first envisioned as a treatment, or even a cure, for genetic disorders, but it could also be used to treat a wide range of diseases, including those that resist conventional treatments. Gene therapy may operate by providing a correctly working version of a faulty gene or by adding a **novel gene** to perform a corrective role. In other cases, gene expression may be blocked in order to control cellular (or viral) activity. About two thirds of currently approved gene therapy procedures are targeting cancer, about one quarter aim to treat genetic disorders, such as cystic fibrosis, and the remainder are attempting to provide relief for infectious diseases. Gene therapy requires a **gene delivery system**; a way to transfer the gene to the patient's cells. This may be achieved using a infectious agent such as a virus; a technique called **transfection**. A promising development has been the recent approval for gene therapy to be used in treating tumours in cancer patients. Severe combined immune deficiency syndrome (SCIDS) has also shown improvement after gene therapy. Infants treated for this inherited, normally lethal condition have become healthy young adults (see below). Gene therapy involving **somatic cells** may be therapeutic, but the genetic changes are not inherited. The transfection of **stem cells**, rather than mature somatic cells, achieves a longer persistence of therapy in patients. In the future, the introduction of corrective genes into **germline cells** will enable genetic corrections to be inherited.

Gene Delivery Using Extracted Cells

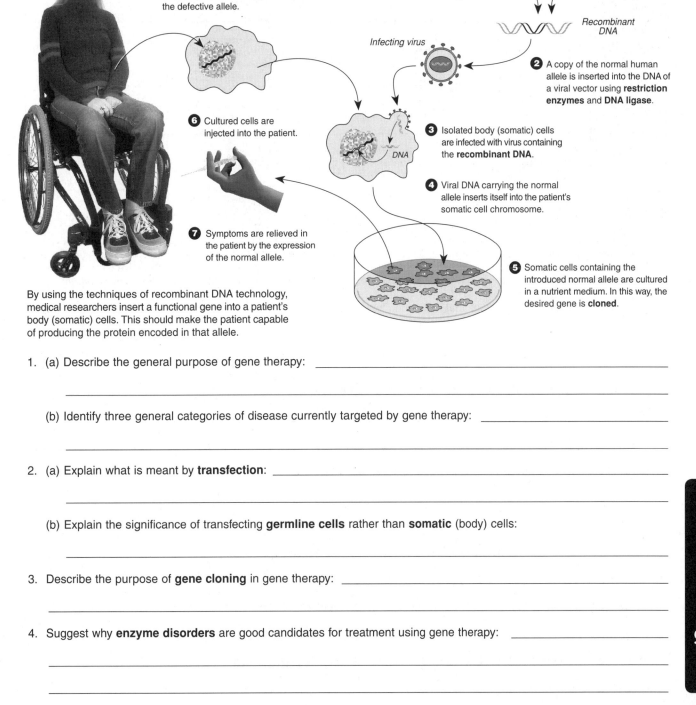

❶ Body cells from patient are isolated. These cells are homozygous for the defective allele.

Viral DNA *Normal human allele*

Recombinant DNA

Infecting virus

❷ A copy of the normal human allele is inserted into the DNA of a viral vector using **restriction enzymes** and **DNA ligase**.

❻ Cultured cells are injected into the patient.

❸ Isolated body (somatic) cells are infected with virus containing the **recombinant DNA**.

DNA

❹ Viral DNA carrying the normal allele inserts itself into the patient's somatic cell chromosome.

❼ Symptoms are relieved in the patient by the expression of the normal allele.

❺ Somatic cells containing the introduced normal allele are cultured in a nutrient medium. In this way, the desired gene is **cloned**.

By using the techniques of recombinant DNA technology, medical researchers insert a functional gene into a patient's body (somatic) cells. This should make the patient capable of producing the protein encoded in that allele.

1. (a) Describe the general purpose of gene therapy: _____

_____

(b) Identify three general categories of disease currently targeted by gene therapy: _____

_____

2. (a) Explain what is meant by **transfection**: _____

_____

(b) Explain the significance of transfecting **germline cells** rather than **somatic** (body) cells: _____

_____

3. Describe the purpose of **gene cloning** in gene therapy: _____

_____

4. Suggest why **enzyme disorders** are good candidates for treatment using gene therapy: _____

_____

_____

Gene Technology

Vectors for Gene Therapy

Gene therapy usually requires a **vector** (carrier) to introduce the DNA. The majority of approved clinical gene therapy protocols (63%) employ **retroviral vectors** to deliver the selected gene to the target cells, although there is considerable risk in using these vectors (below). Other widely used vectors include adenoviral vectors (16%), and liposomes (13%). The remaining 8% employ a variety of vector systems, the majority of which include injection of naked plasmid DNA.

Vectors That Can Be Used For Gene Therapy

	Retrovirus	Adenovirus	Liposome	Naked DNA
Insert size:	8000 bases	8000 bases	>20 000 bases	>20 000 bases
Integration:	Yes	No	No	No
***In vivo* delivery:**	Poor	High	Variable	Poor
Advantages	• Integrate genes into the chromosomes of the human host cell. • Offers chance for long-term stability.	• Modified for gene therapy, they infect human cells and express the normal gene. • Most do not cause disease. • Have a large capacity to carry foreign genes.	• Liposomes seek out target cells using sugars in their membranes that are recognised by cell receptors. • Have no viral genes that may cause disease.	• Have no viral genes that may cause disease. • Expected to be useful for vaccination.
Disadvantages	• Many infect only cells that are dividing. • Genes integrate randomly into chromosomes, so might disrupt useful genes in the host cell.	• Viruses may have poor survival due to attack by the host's immune system. • Genes may function only sporadically because they are not integrated into host cell's chromosome.	• Less efficient than viruses at transferring genes into cells, but recent work on using sugars to aid targeting have improved success rate.	• Unstable in most tissues of the body. • Inefficient at gene transfer.

In the table above, the following terms are defined as follows: **Naked DNA**: the genes are applied by ballistic injection (firing using a gene gun) or by regular hypodermic injection of plasmid DNA. **Insert size**: size of gene that can be inserted into the vector. **Integration**: whether or not the gene is integrated into the host DNA (chromosomes). ***In vivo* delivery**: ability to transfer a gene directly into a patient.

1. (a) Describe the features of viruses that make them well suited as **vectors** for gene therapy: _____

   _____

   _____

   (b) Identify two problems with using viral vectors for gene therapy: _____

   _____

   _____

2. (a) Suggest why it may be beneficial for a (therapeutic) gene to integrate into the patient's chromosome:

   _____

   _____

   (b) Explain why this has the potential to cause problems for the patient: _____

   _____

3. (a) Suggest why naked DNA is likely to be unstable within a patient's tissues: _____

   _____

   (b) Suggest why enclosing the DNA within liposomes might provide greater stability: _____

   _____

Related activities: Gene Therapy, Gene Delivery Systems
Web links: Gene Therapy Primer

Gene Delivery Systems

The mapping of the human genome has improved the feasibility of gene therapy as a option for treating an increasingly wide range of diseases, but it remains technically difficult to deliver genes successfully to a patient. Even after a gene has been identified, cloned, and transferred to a patient, it must be expressed normally. To date, the success of gene therapy has been generally poor, and improvements have been short-lived or counteracted by adverse side effects. Inserted genes may reach only about 1% of target cells and those that reach their destination may work inefficiently and produce too little protein, too slowly to be of benefit. In addition, many patients react immunologically to the vectors used in gene transfer. Much of the current research is focussed on improving the efficiency of gene transfer and expression. One of the first gene therapy trials was for **cystic fibrosis** (CF). CF was an obvious candidate for gene therapy because, in most cases, the disease is caused by a single, known gene mutation. However, despite its early promise, gene therapy for this disease has been disappointing (below).

Gene Therapy as a Potential Treatment for Cystic Fibrosis (CF)

In cystic fibrosis, a gene mutation causes the body to produce an abnormally thick, sticky mucus that accumulates in the lungs and intestines. The identification and isolation of the CF gene in 1989 meant that scientists could look for ways in which to correct the genetic defect rather than just treating the symptoms using traditional therapies.

In trials, normal genes were isolated and inserted into patients using vectors such as **adenoviruses** and **liposomes**.

In order to prevent the progressive and ultimately lethal lung damage, the main target of CF gene therapy is the lung. The viral vector was piped directly into the lung, whereas the liposomes were inhaled in a spray formulation. The results of these trials were disappointing; on average, there was only a 25% correction, the effects were short lived, and the benefits were quickly reversed. Alarmingly, the adenovirus used in one of the trials led to the death of one patient.

Source: Cystic Fibrosis Trust, UK.

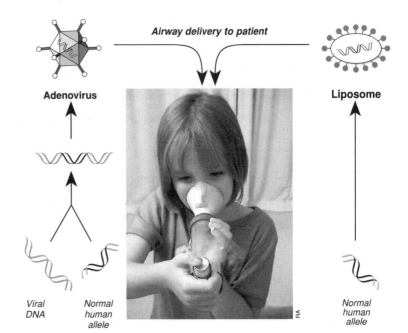

Airway delivery to patient

Adenovirus | **Liposome**

Viral DNA | Normal human allele | Normal human allele

An **adenovirus** that normally causes colds is genetically modified to make it safe and to carry the normal (unmutated) CFTR ('cystic fibrosis') gene.

Liposomes are tiny fat globules. Normal CF genes are enclosed in liposomes, which fuse with plasma membranes and deliver the genes into the cells.

Gene Delivery Systems Used In Human Patients

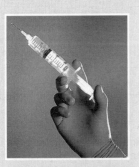

Hypodermic needle injection

- Injection of the vectors directly into the bloodstream or other organs of the patient. Vectors injected into the blood travel throughout the body and may be taken up by the target cells.

- Injections of plasmid DNA into thymus, skin, cardiac muscle and skeletal muscle have already proved successful in non-human trials (mice and primates).

Aerosol

- Aerosols and nebulisers offer an effective spread and efficient delivery of the vector to the site of certain target cells (especially in the respiratory tract).

- Used in trials of gene therapy for cystic fibrosis, but effective only on epithelial cells that can be reached by the aerosol.

Ballistic DNA injection is also called microprojectile gene transfer, the gene-gun, or particle bombardment method.

Ballistic DNA injection

- Plasmid DNA encoding the gene of interest is coated onto microbeads, and these are 'fired' at the target cells using gas pressure or a high voltage discharge.

- Used to transfer genes to a wide variety of cell lines (*ex vivo*) or directly into surgically exposed tissue (*in vivo*).

- May be used in DNA-based vaccines to prevent infectious diseases or cancer.

- Allows delivery of precise DNA dosages. However, genes delivered by this method are expressed transiently and there is considerable cell damage at the centre of the discharge site.

An incubator for culturing cell lines (ex vivo).

©1999 University of Kansas Office of University Relations

Gene delivery to extracted cells and cell culture

- Target cells are isolated from tissue. Non-specific gene delivery is applied to the total cell population or as a microinjection of DNA into the nucleus of a single cell.

- Cells that have taken up the normal allele are cultured outside the body (*ex vivo*) and re-injected into the patient.

- The expression of the normal allele relieves symptoms of the disease.

Gene Technology

Related activities: Gene Therapy, Vectors for Gene Therapy

RA 2

1. A great deal of current research is being devoted to discovering a gene therapy solution to treat **cystic fibrosis** (CF):

   (a) Describe the symptoms of CF: _____

   _____

   _____

   (b) Explain why this genetic disease has been so eagerly targeted by gene therapy researchers: _____

   _____

   _____

   _____

   _____

   (c) Outline some of the problems so far encountered with gene therapy for CF: _____

   _____

   _____

   _____

   _____

   _____

2. Identify two vectors for introducing healthy CFTR genes into CF patients. For each vector, outline how it might be delivered to the patient and describe potential problems with its use:

   (a) Vector 1: _____

   Delivery: _____

   Problems: _____

   _____

   _____

   (b) Vector 2: _____

   Delivery: _____

   Problems: _____

   _____

   _____

3. Changes made to chromosomes as a result of gene therapy involving somatic cells are not inherited. Germ-line gene therapy has the potential to cure disease, but the risks and benefits are still not clear. For each of the points outlined below, evaluate the risk of germ-line gene therapy relative to somatic cell gene therapy and explain your answer:

   (a) Chance of interfering with an essential gene function: _____

   _____

   _____

   _____

   (b) Misuse of the therapy to selectively alter phenotype: _____

   _____

   _____

   _____

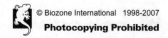

The Ethics of GMO Technology

The risks associated with using **genetically modified organisms** (GMOs) have been the subject of much debate in recent times. Most experts agree that, provided GMOs are tested properly, the health risks to individuals should be minimal from plant products, although minor problems will occur. Health risks from animal GMOs are potentially more serious, especially when the animals are for human consumption. The potential benefits to be gained from the use of GMOs creates enormous pressure to apply the existing technology. However, there are many concerns, including the environmental and socio-economic effects, and problems of unregulated use. There is also concern about the environmental and economic costs of possible GMO accidents. GMO research is being driven by heavy investment on the part of biotechnology companies seeking new applications for GMOs. Currently a matter of great concern to consumers is the adequacy of government regulations for the labelling of food products with GMO content. This may have important trade implications for countries exporting and importing GMO produce.

Important points about GMOs

1. The foreign or altered DNA is in every cell of the genetically modified animal or plant.

2. The mRNA is only expressed in specific tissues.

3. The foreign protein is only expressed in those tissues but it may circulate (e.g. hormone in the bloodstream) or be secreted (e.g. milk).

4. In animals, the transgene is only likely to be transmitted from parent to offspring (but the use of viral vectors may provide a mechanism for accidental transfer of the transgene between unrelated animals).

5. In plants, transmission of the transgene in GMOs is possible by pollen, cuttings, and seeds (even between species).

6. If we eat the animal or plant proper, we will also be eating DNA. The DNA will remain "intact" if raw, but "degraded" if cooked (remember that we eat DNA in our regular food every day).

7. Non-transgenic food products may be processed using genetically modified bacteria or yeast, and cells containing their DNA may be in the food product.

8. A transgenic product (e.g. a protein, polypeptide or a carbohydrate) may be in the GMO, but not in the portions sold to the consumer.

Potential effects of GMOs

1. Increase food production.

2. Decrease use of pesticides, herbicides and animal remedies.

3. Improve the health of the human population and the medicines used to achieve it.

4. May result in transgenic products which may be harmful to some (e.g. new proteins causing allergies).

5. May have little real economic benefit to farmers (and the consumer) when increased production (as little as 10%) is weighed against cost, capital, competition.

6. May result in transgenes spreading uncontrollably into other species: plants, indigenous species, animals, and humans.

7. Concerns that the release of GMOs into the environment may be irreversible.

8. Release of GMOs into the environment may create an evolutionary or ecological "timebomb".

9. Crippling economic sanctions resulting from a consumer backlash against GMO foods and products.

10. May make the animals that are genetically modified unhealthy (animal welfare and ethical issues).

11. May cause the emergence of pest, insect, or microbial resistance to traditional control methods.

12. May create a monopoly and dependence of developing countries on companies who are seeking to control the world's commercial seed supply with "terminator seeds" (that produce plants that cannot themselves seed).

The use of GMOs: some potential problems, safeguards, and solutions

Issue	Problem	Safeguard or solution
Accidental release of GMOs into the environment	Recombinant DNA may be taken up by non-target, organisms. e.g. *weeds may take up a gene for herbicide resistance*. These unintended GMOs may have the potential to become pests or cause disease.	Rigorous standards of control, produced and policed by the United Kingdom Genetic Manipulation Advisory Group. GMOs may have specific genes deleted so that their growth requirements can only be met under particular laboratory environments.
A new gene or genes may disrupt normal gene function	In humans, gene disruption may trigger cancer. In animals, successful transformation and expression of the desired gene is frequently very low.	Future developments in producing transgenic livestock involve the combination of genetic engineering, cloning, and screening so that only successfully transformed cells are used to produce organisms.
Targeted use of transgenic organisms in the environment	Once their desired function in the environment, e.g. environmental clean-up, has been completed, they may be undesirable invaders in the ecosystem	Organisms can be engineered to contain "suicide genes" or inherent metabolic deficiencies so that they do not survive for long in the new environment after completion of their task.
Use of antibiotic resistant genes as markers to identify transgenic organisms in culture	Spread of antibiotic resistance amongst non-target organisms. It has been shown that gut bacteria can take up genes for antibiotic resistance from ingested food products (e.g. wheat and soy products).	None, although alternative methods, such as gene probes, can be used to identify transformed cells. Better food labelling helps consumers identify foods made from GMOs but, even with this precaution, the problem has not been adequately addressed.

1. Suggest why genetically modified (GM) plants are thought to pose a greater environmental threat than GM animals:

_____

_____

_____

Gene Technology

Related activities: Applications of GMOs, Genetically Modified Plants, Production of Human Proteins

RA 2

2. Describe an advantage and a problem with the use of genetically engineered herbicide resistant crop plants:

(a) Advantage: _____

_____

(b) Problem: _____

_____

3. Describe an advantage and a problem with using tropical crops genetically engineered to grow in cold regions:

(a) Advantage: _____

_____

(b) Problem: _____

_____

4. Describe an advantage and a problem with using crops that are genetically engineered to grow in marginal habitats (for example, in very saline or poorly aerated soils):

(a) Advantage: _____

_____

(b) Problem: _____

_____

5. Describe two uses of transgenic animals within the livestock industry:

(a) _____

(b) _____

6. Recently, Britain banned the import of a genetically engineered, pest resistant corn variety containing marker genes for ampicillin antibiotic resistance. Suggest why there was concern over using such marker genes:

_____

_____

7. Many agricultural applications of DNA technology make use of transgenic bacteria which infect plants and express a foreign gene. Explain one advantage of each of the following applications of genetic engineering to crop biology:

(a) Development of nitrogen-fixing *Rhizobium* bacteria that can colonise non-legumes such as corn and wheat:

_____

(b) Addition of transgenic *Pseudomonas flourescens* bacteria into seeds (bacterium produces a pathogen-killing toxin):

_____

8. Some of the public's fears and concerns about genetically modified food stem from moral or religious convictions, while others have a biological basis and are related to the potential biological threat posed by GMOs.

(a) Conduct a class discussion or debate to identify these fears and concerns, and briefly list them below:

_____

_____

_____

(b) Identify which of those you have listed above pose a real biological threat: _____

_____

_____

_____

Gas Exchange

AQA-A	AQA-B	SNAB	Edexcel	OCR
Complete:	Complete:	Complete:	Complete:	Complete:
1-3, 5-7, 15-16, 23, 25, 27 (a-b), (d-f), 28-33	1-17, 21-24, 26, 27 (a-b), (d-f), 28-37	1-8, 15-17, 24-27 (AS) 28-37(A2)	1-7, 9-17, 19-20, 26-33	1-3, 5-7, 15-16, 25-26, 32-33 Extension: 24, 27-31

Learning Objectives

☐ 1. Compile your own glossary from the **KEY WORDS** displayed in **bold type** in the learning objectives below.

The Need for Gas Exchange *(pages 207, 211-212)*

☐ 2. Recognise that organisms need to exchange materials with their environment: **respiratory gases**, nutrients, and excretory products.

☐ 3. Distinguish between **cellular respiration** and **gas exchange**. Explain how cellular respiration creates a constant demand for **oxygen** and a need to eliminate **carbon dioxide** gas.

☐ 4. Understand that the physical properties of an environment place particular constraints on the type of gas exchange system that can be used. Outline the **physical characteristics** of marine, freshwater, and terrestrial environments. Explain briefly how the structural features of organisms relate to the environment in which they are found.

☐ 5. Identify the process by which gases are exchanged across gas exchange surfaces. Describe the essential features of gas exchange surfaces. With reference to **Fick's law** explain the significance of these features.

☐ 6. Describe the relationship between an organism's size and its surface area (the **surface area: volume ratio** or **SA:V**). Explain the significance of this relationship to the exchange of gases with the environment.

☐ 7. Recognise that the development of gas exchange systems in larger organisms is an adaptation to facilitate adequate rates of gas exchange.

☐ 8. Explain the significance of the SA:V relationship to the exchange of heat with the environment. Recognise that changes in body shape in larger organisms facilitate appropriate heat exchanges with the environment.

Gas Exchange in Plants *(pages 208-210)*

☐ 9. Understand that plant cells, like animal cells, respire (see #2-3). List the gases that plants exchange with the environment and identify the processes involved in using and producing these gases. Explain how this situation differs from that in animals.

☐ 10. Describe the structure, location, adaptations, and function of the gas exchange surfaces and related structures in dicotyledonous plant leaves (**mesophyll** and **stomata**). Identify the process by which gases move into and out of plants and comment on the link between gas exchange and incidental water loss.

☐ 11. Draw a labelled diagram of the external and internal structure of a dicot leaf, illustrating the structure and arrangement of stomata and **guard cells**, and their relationship to the internal (mesophyll) tissue.

☐ 12. Describe the structure and role of **lenticels** in gas exchange in woody plants.

☐ 13. Recognise **stomata** as the primary structures regulating the movement of gases to and from the gas exchange surfaces in plants. Identify the different conditions under which the stomata open and close. Describe the role of guard cells in stomatal function, including the mechanism of stomatal opening and closing (ion changes and consequent turgor changes).

☐ 14. Describe and explain the reasons for different arrangements of stomata, e.g. in **xerophytes** and **mesophytes**, and terrestrial and aquatic plants.

Gas Exchange in Animals *(pages 211, 221, 225)*

☐ 15. Recall the essential features of a gas exchange surface. Describe how the gas exchange surfaces of animals are maintained in a functional state.

☐ 16. Describe the functional role of circulatory fluids and their associated **respiratory pigments** in transporting respiratory gases in different animal taxa.

☐ 17. Explain what is meant by **ventilation** of the gas exchange surface. Recognise the need for ventilation mechanisms in animals and explain how the ventilation mechanism is related to the organism's environment.

☐ 18. Describe the structure and function of the tracheal system in insects, including the role of the **spiracles**.

☐ 19. Understand how gas exchange in achieved in a protozoan (e.g. *Paramecium* or *Amoeba*).

Gas exchange in freshwater *(page 222)*

☐ 20. Understand that species are adapted to survive in particular environments. Describe structural and physiological adaptations in invertebrates to varying oxygen levels in freshwater. Examples include **respiratory pigments**, the presence and structure of external gills, and adaptations for air breathing.

Gas exchange in bony fish *(pages 223-224)*

☐ 21. Describe the structure, location, adaptations, and function of the gas exchange surfaces and related structures in bony fish (**gill lamellae** and **filaments**).

☐ 22. Explain how gases are exchanged between the water and the blood. Explain the role of **countercurrent exchange** in fish **gills** in facilitating efficient gas exchange. Comment on the oxygen extraction rates achieved by gills (vs the rates achieved by lungs in air).

☐ 23. Describe ventilation in bony fish.

Gas exchange in humans *(pages 213-216, 220)*
Humans are provided as the mammalian example

☐ 24. Describe the structure, location, adaptations, and function of the gas exchange surfaces and related structures in humans (**trachea**, **bronchi**, **bronchioles**, **lungs**, and **alveoli**).

25. Describe the distribution of the following tissues and cells in the **trachea**, **bronchi**, and **bronchioles**: **cartilage**, **ciliated epithelium**, **goblet cells**, and **smooth muscle cells**. Describe the function of the **cartilage**, **cilia**, **goblet cells**, **smooth muscle**, and **elastic fibres** in the gas exchange system.

26. Recognise the relationship between gas exchange surfaces (alveoli) and the blood vessels in the lung tissue. Draw a simple diagram of an **alveolus** (air sac) to illustrate the movement of O_2 and CO_2, into and out of the blood in the surrounding capillary.

27. Recall the structure of the thorax in humans and describe the mechanism of ventilation (**breathing**). Include reference to the following:
    (a) The role of **surfactants** in lung function.
    (b) The role of the **diaphragm** and **intercostal muscles** in changing the air pressure in the lungs.
    (c) The role of the **pleural membranes** in breathing.
    (d) The distinction between **inspiration** (inhalation) as an active process and **expiration** (exhalation) as a passive process (during normal, quiet breathing).
    (e) The difference between quiet and forced breathing.
    (f) The composition of inhaled and exhaled air.

The Control of Breathing (pages 215-16, 219-20)

28. Explain how basic rhythm of breathing is controlled through the activity of the **respiratory centre** in the medulla and its output via the **phrenic nerves** and the **intercostal nerves**.

29. Explain the role of the **stretch receptors** and the **vagus nerve** in ending inspiration during normal breathing. Identify this control as the **inflation reflex**.

30. Identify influences on the respiratory centre and comment on how these reflect changes in the body's demand for oxygen. Include reference to the activity of the **carotid** and **aortic bodies** (chemoreceptors in the carotid arteries and the aorta).

31. Distinguish between **involuntary** and **voluntary control** of breathing.

32. Explain how ventilation is measured in humans using a **spirometer**. Define the terms: **tidal volume, vital capacity, residual volume, dead space air**.

33. Explain how the breathing (ventilation) rate and **pulmonary ventilation** (PV) rate are calculated and expressed. Provide some typical values for **breathing rate, tidal volume**, and **PV**. Describe how each of these is affected by strenuous exercise.

Energy and Exercise (pages 217-218)

34. Identify sources of energy for muscle contraction, distinguishing between the immediate energy source (**ATP**) and those that yield ATP after oxidative breakdown (**glucose, glycogen, triglycerides**). Explain the role of glycogen and **creatine phosphate** in storing and releasing energy for muscle contraction.

35. With respect to the energy yield and the waste products produced, compare **aerobic** and **anaerobic respiration** as sources of ATP for muscle contraction.

36. Explain what is meant by **muscle fatigue** and relate it to the increase in **blood lactate** levels and decreased pH. Explain how these physiological changes provide the stimulus for increased breathing (and heart) rates.

37. Explain what is meant by **oxygen debt**. Describe the ultimate fate of blood lactate and explain how the oxygen debt is repaid after intense exercise. If required, explain the relationship between VO_2max, **anaerobic threshold**, and oxygen debt.

See the 'Textbook Reference Grid' on pages 8-9 for textbook page references relating to material in this topic.

Supplementary Texts

See pages 5-6 for additional details of these texts:

■ Adds, J. *et al.*, 2004. **Exchange & Transport, Energy & Ecosystems** (NelsonThornes), pp. 2-26.

■ Clegg, C.J., 1998. **Mammals: Structure and Function** (John Murray), pp. 24-31.

See page 7 for details of publishers of periodicals:

STUDENT'S REFERENCE

Animal gas exchange & energy supply

■ **Lungs and the Control of Breathing** Bio. Sci. Rev. 14(4) April 2002, pp. 2-5. *The mechanisms, control, and measurement of breathing. This article includes good, clear diagrams and useful summaries of the important points.*

■ **Gas Exchange in the Lungs** Bio. Sci. Rev. 16(1) Sept. 2003, pp. 36-38. *The structure and function of the alveoli of the lungs, with an account of respiratory problems and diseases such as respiratory distress syndrome and emphysema.*

■ **Gas Laws** Biol. Sci. Rev., 11(1) Sept. 1998, pp. 14-17. *The significance of the gas laws to gas exchange and diffusion of gases within tissues.*

■ **Countercurrent Exchange Mechanisms** Biol. Sci. Rev., 9(1) Sept. 1996, pp. 2-6. *Countercurrent multipliers in biological systems (includes fish gills).*

■ **A Breath of Fresh Air** Biol. Sci. Rev., 7(5) May 1995, pp. 22-25. *Breathing, including the biochemistry of gas exchange, oxygen dissociation curves and homeostatic control of breathing.*

■ **Red Blood Cells** Bio. Sci. Rev. 11(2) Nov. 1998, pp. 2-4. *The structure and function of red blood cells, including details of oxygen transport.*

■ **Marathon Runners: Born or Bred** Biol. Sci. Rev., 17(1) Sept. 2004, pp. 10-13. *The physiology of endurance running, with reference to ATP production through the oxidation of carbohydrate and fat, and how training increases VO_2max.*

■ **Lactic Acid** Biol. Sci. Rev., 18(2) Nov. 2005, pp. 6-9. *Lactic acid: its production as a result of anaerobic metabolism and its surprising role as an important source of energy for working muscles.*

■ **Creatine: Performance Enhancer** Biol. Sci. Rev., 12(3) January 2000, pp. 23-24. *Creatine and its role in the energy metabolism of muscles.*

The effect of pollutants and disease

■ **Air Pollution and Asthma** Biol. Sci. Rev., 9(4) March 1997, pp. 32-36. *The link between air pollution and respiratory disorders such as asthma.*

■ **Dust to Dust** New Scientist, 21 Sept. 2002 (Inside Science). *A supplement that concentrates on dust pollution, but also examines the impact of this pollutant on respiratory health.*

■ **Environmental Lung Disease** New Scientist, 23 September 1995 (Inside Science). *Excellent supplement on lung disorders, with good diagrams illustrating lung functioning and gas transport.*

Plant gas exchange and water loss

■ **Plants, Water and Climate** New Scientist, 25 February 1989 (Inside Science). *Important aspects of plant transport: osmosis and turgor, transport from the root to the leaf, transpiration, and stomata.*

■ **Plants in the Greenhouse World** New Scientist, 6 May 1989 (Inside Science). *Covers photosynthesis in plants, and how growth, stomatal opening, photosynthesis, and respiration are affected by water availability.*

See pages 10-11 for details of how to access **Bio Links** from our web site: **www.biozone.co.uk**. From Bio Links, access sites under the topics:

GENERAL BIOLOGY ONLINE RESOURCES
• Biology I interactive animations • Instructional multimedia, University of Alberta ... *and others* > **Online Textbooks and Lecture Notes**: • Human biology help • Learn.co.uk • S-Cool! A level biology revision guide ... *and others* > **Glossaries**: Animal anatomy glossary... *and others*

ANIMAL BIOLOGY: • Anatomy and physiology • Human physiology lecture notes ... *and others* > **Gas Exchange**: • Gas exchange • Lesson 11: The respiratory system • Respiration in aquatic insects • Respiratory system • Respiratory system: Chpt 41 • Tracheal breathing > **Support & Movement**: • Energy production during physical activity • Energy systems Part I ... *and others*

PLANT BIOLOGY: • Plant biology for non-science majors ... *and others* > **Structure and Function**: • Angiosperm structure and function tutorials • Plant structure ... *and others* > **Nutrition and Gas Exchange**: • Gas exchange in plants

Introduction to Gas Exchange

Living cells require energy for the activities of life. Energy is released in cells by the breakdown of sugars and other substances in the metabolic process called **cellular respiration**. As a consequence of this process, gases need to be exchanged between the respiring cells and the environment. In most organisms (with the exception of some bacterial groups) these gases are carbon dioxide (CO_2) and oxygen (O_2). The diagram below illustrates this process for an animal. Plant cells also respire, but their gas exchange budget is different because they also produce O_2 and consume CO_2 in photosynthesis.

The Need for Gas Exchange

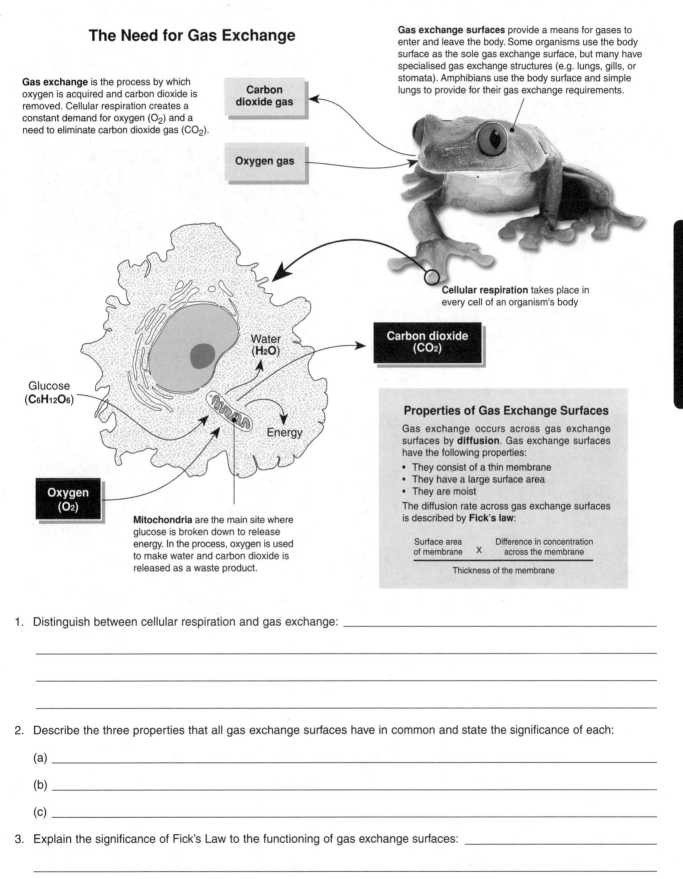

Gas exchange is the process by which oxygen is acquired and carbon dioxide is removed. Cellular respiration creates a constant demand for oxygen (O_2) and a need to eliminate carbon dioxide gas (CO_2).

Carbon dioxide gas

Oxygen gas

Gas exchange surfaces provide a means for gases to enter and leave the body. Some organisms use the body surface as the sole gas exchange surface, but many have specialised gas exchange structures (e.g. lungs, gills, or stomata). Amphibians use the body surface and simple lungs to provide for their gas exchange requirements.

Cellular respiration takes place in every cell of an organism's body

Water (H_2O)

Carbon dioxide (CO_2)

Glucose ($C_6H_{12}O_6$)

Energy

Oxygen (O_2)

Mitochondria are the main site where glucose is broken down to release energy. In the process, oxygen is used to make water and carbon dioxide is released as a waste product.

Properties of Gas Exchange Surfaces

Gas exchange occurs across gas exchange surfaces by **diffusion**. Gas exchange surfaces have the following properties:

- They consist of a thin membrane
- They have a large surface area
- They are moist

The diffusion rate across gas exchange surfaces is described by **Fick's law**:

$$\frac{\text{Surface area of membrane} \times \text{Difference in concentration across the membrane}}{\text{Thickness of the membrane}}$$

Gas Exchange

1. Distinguish between cellular respiration and gas exchange: _____

_____

_____

_____

2. Describe the three properties that all gas exchange surfaces have in common and state the significance of each:

(a) _____

(b) _____

(c) _____

3. Explain the significance of Fick's Law to the functioning of gas exchange surfaces: _____

_____

_____

Related activities: Diffusion, Surface Area and Volume

A 1

Gas Exchange in Plants

Respiring tissues require oxygen, and the photosynthetic tissues of plants also require carbon dioxide in order to produce the sugars needed for their growth and maintenance. The principal gas exchange organs in plants are the leaves, and sometimes the stems. In most plants, the exchange of gases directly across the leaf surface is prevented by the waterproof, waxy cuticle layer. Instead, access to the respiring cells is by means of **stomata**, which are tiny pores in the leaf surface. The plant has to balance its need for carbon dioxide (keeping stomata open) against its need to reduce water loss (stomata closed).

Terrestrial Environment

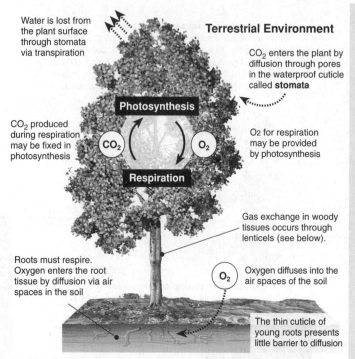

Water is lost from the plant surface through stomata via transpiration

CO_2 enters the plant by diffusion through pores in the waterproof cuticle called **stomata**

CO_2 produced during respiration may be fixed in photosynthesis

Photosynthesis

CO_2 — O_2

Respiration

O_2 for respiration may be provided by photosynthesis

Gas exchange in woody tissues occurs through lenticels (see below).

Roots must respire. Oxygen enters the root tissue by diffusion via air spaces in the soil

Oxygen diffuses into the air spaces of the soil

The thin cuticle of young roots presents little barrier to diffusion

Most gas exchange in plants occurs through the leaves, but some also occurs through the stems and the roots. The shape and structure of leaves (very thin with a high surface area) assists gas exchange by diffusion.

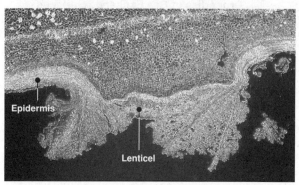

Epidermis

Lenticel

In woody plants, the wood prevents gas exchange. A lenticel is a small area in the bark where the loosely arranged cells allow entry and exit of gases into the stem tissue underneath.

Aquatic Environment

The aquatic environment presents special problems for plants. Water loss is not a problem, but CO_2 availability is often very limited because most of the dissolved CO_2 is present in the form of bicarbonate ions, which is not directly available to plants. Maximising uptake of gaseous CO_2 by reducing barriers to diffusion is therefore important.

Absorption of CO_2 by direct diffusion

Gas exchange through stomata on the upper surface

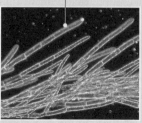

Algae lack stomata but achieve adequate gas exchange through simple diffusion into the cells.

Floating leaves, such as the water lilies above, generally lack stomata on their lower surface.

With the exception of liverworts, all terrestrial plants and most aquatic plants have stomata to provide for gas exchange. CO_2 uptake is aided in submerged plants because they have little or no cuticle to form a barrier to diffusion of gases. The few submerged aquatics that lack stomata altogether rely only on diffusion through the epidermis. Most aquatic plants also have air spaces in their spongy tissues (which also assist buoyancy).

Transitional Environment

The pencil-like breathing roots of mangroves extend 25-30 cm above the surface of the mud

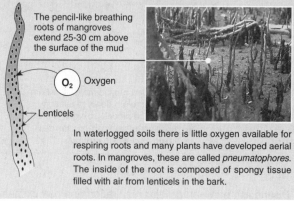

O_2 Oxygen

Lenticels

In waterlogged soils there is little oxygen available for respiring roots and many plants have developed aerial roots. In mangroves, these are called *pneumatophores*. The inside of the root is composed of spongy tissue filled with air from lenticels in the bark.

1. Name the gas produced by cellular respiration that is also a raw material for photosynthesis: _____

2. Describe the role of lenticels in plant gas exchange: _____

   _____

3. Identify two properties of leaves that assist gas exchange: _____

4. With respect to gas exchange and water balance, describe the most important considerations for:

   (a) Terrestrial plants: _____

   (b) Aquatic plants: _____

5. Describe an adaptation for gas exchange in the following plants:

   (a) A submerged aquatic angiosperm: _____

   (b) A mangrove in a salty mudflat: _____

Stomata and Gas Exchange

The leaf epidermis of angiosperms is covered with tiny pores, called **stomata**. Angiosperms have many air spaces between the cells of the stems, leaves, and roots. These air spaces are continuous and gases are able to move freely through them and into the plant's cells via the stomata. Each stoma is bounded by

two **guard cells**, which together regulate the entry and exit of gases and water vapour. Although stomata permit gas exchange between the air and the photosynthetic cells inside the leaf, they are also the major routes for water loss through transpiration.

Gas Exchanges and the Function of Stomata

Gases enter and leave the leaf by way of stomata. Inside the leaf (as illustrated by a dicot, right), the large air spaces and loose arrangement of the spongy mesophyll facilitate the diffusion of gases and provide a large surface area for gas exchanges.

Respiring plant cells use oxygen (O_2) and produce carbon dioxide (CO_2). These gases move in and out of the plant and through the air spaces by diffusion.

When the plant is photosynthesising, the situation is more complex. Overall there is a net consumption of CO_2 and a net production of oxygen. The fixation of CO_2 maintains a gradient in CO_2 concentration between the inside of the leaf and the atmosphere. Oxygen is produced in excess of respiratory needs and diffuses out of the leaf. These **net** exchanges are indicated by the arrows on the diagram.

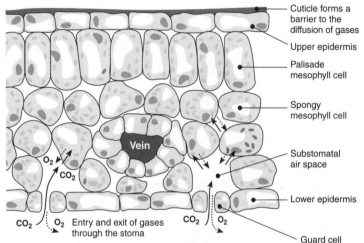

Cuticle forms a barrier to the diffusion of gases
Upper epidermis
Palisade mesophyll cell
Spongy mesophyll cell
Substomatal air space
Lower epidermis
Guard cell

Entry and exit of gases through the stoma

Net gas exchanges in a photosynthesising dicot leaf

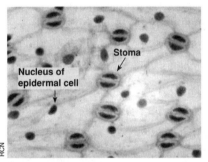

A surface view of the leaf epidermis of a dicot (above) illustrating the density and scattered arrangement of stomata. In dicots, stomata are usually present only on the lower leaf surface.

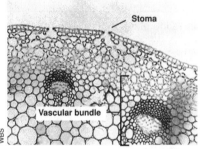

The stems of some plants (e.g. the buttercup above) are photosynthetic. Gas exchange between the stem tissues and the environment occurs through stomata in the outer epidermis.

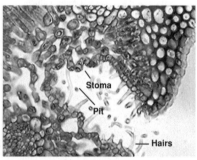

Oleander (above) is a xerophyte with many water conserving features. The stomata are in pits on the leaf underside. The pits restrict water loss to a greater extent than they reduce CO_2 uptake.

The cycle of opening and closing of stomata

The opening and closing of stomata shows a daily cycle that is largely determined by the hours of light and dark.

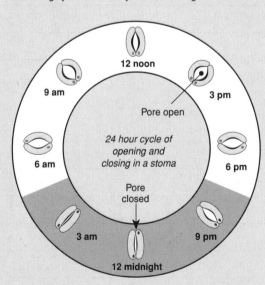

12 noon
9 am
3 pm
Pore open
6 am
24 hour cycle of opening and closing in a stoma
6 pm
Pore closed
3 am
9 pm
12 midnight

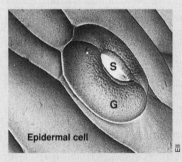

The image left shows a scanning electron micrograph (SEM) of a single stoma from the leaf epidermis of a dicot.

Note the guard cells (G), which are swollen tight and open the pore (S) to allow gas exchange between the leaf tissue and the environment.

Epidermal cell

Factors influencing stomatal opening

Stomata	Guard cells	Daylight	CO_2	Soil water
Open	Turgid	Light	Low	High
Closed	Flaccid	Dark	High	Low

The opening and closing of stomata depends on environmental factors, the most important being light, carbon dioxide concentration in the leaf tissue, and water supply. Stomata tend to open during daylight in response to light, and close at night (left and above). Low CO_2 levels also promote stomatal opening. Conditions that induce water stress cause the stomata close, regardless of light or CO_2 level.

Related activities: Plant Cell Specialisation, Gas Exchange in Plants
Web links: Gas Exchange and Stomata

The guard cells on each side of a stoma control the diameter of the pore by changing shape. When the guard cells take up water by osmosis they swell and become turgid, making the pore wider. When the guard cells lose water, they become flaccid, and the pore closes up. By this mechanism a plant can control the amount of gas entering, or water leaving, the plant. The changes in turgor pressure that open and close the pore result mainly from the reversible uptake and loss of potassium ions (and thus water) by the guard cells.

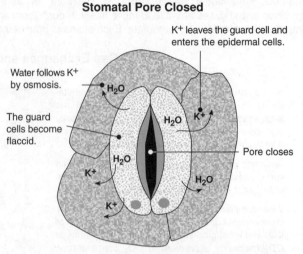

Stomatal Pore Open

K+ enters the guard cells from the epidermal cells (active transport coupled to a proton pump).

Water follows K+ by osmosis.

H_2O

K^+

H_2O

K^+

Guard cell swells and becomes turgid.

Thickened ventral wall

Pore opens

K^+

K^+

H_2O

H_2O

Nucleus of guard cell

ψguard cell < ψepidermal cell: water enters the guard cells

Stomata open when the guard cells actively take up K+ from the neighbouring epidermal cells. The ion uptake causes the water potential (ψ) to become more negative in the guard cells. As a consequence, water is taken up by the cells and they swell and become turgid. The walls of the guard cells are thickened more on the inside surface (the ventral wall) than the outside wall, so that when the cells swell they buckle outward, opening the pore.

Stomatal Pore Closed

K+ leaves the guard cell and enters the epidermal cells.

Water follows K+ by osmosis.

H_2O

H_2O

K^+

The guard cells become flaccid.

H_2O

Pore closes

K^+

H_2O

K^+

ψepidermal cell < ψguard cell: water leaves the guard cells

Stomata close when K+ leaves the guard cells. The loss causes the water potential (ψ) to become less negative in the guard cells, and more negative in the epidermal cells. As a consequence, water is lost by osmosis and the cells sag together and close the pore. The K+ movements in and out of the guard cells are thought to be triggered by blue-light receptors in the plasma membrane, which activate the active transport mechanisms involved.

1. With respect to a mesophytic, terrestrial flowering plant:

   (a) Describe the **net** gas exchanges between the air and the cells of the mesophyll in the dark (no photosynthesis):

   _____

   (b) Explain how this situation changes when a plant is photosynthesising: _____

   _____

   _____

2. Identify two ways in which the continuous air spaces through the plant facilitate gas exchange:

   (a) _____

   (b) _____

3. Outline the role of stomata in gas exchange in an angiosperm: _____

   _____

   _____

4. Summarise the mechanism by which the guard cells bring about:

   (a) Stomatal opening: _____

   _____

   _____

   _____

   (b) Stomatal closure: _____

   _____

   _____

   _____

Gas Exchange in Animals

The way in which gas exchange is achieved is influenced by the animal's general body form and by the environment in which the animal lives. Small, aquatic organisms such as sponges, flatworms and cnidarians, require no specialised respiratory structures. Gases are exchanged between the surrounding water (or moist environment) and the body's cells by diffusion directly across the organism's surface. Larger animals require specialised gas exchange systems. The complexity of these is related to the efficiency of gas exchange required, which is determined by the oxygen demands of the organism.

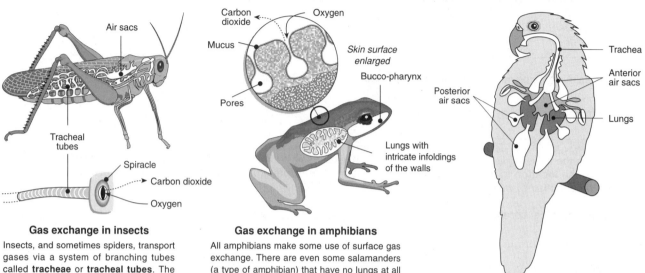

Gas exchange in insects

Insects, and sometimes spiders, transport gases via a system of branching tubes called **tracheae** or **tracheal tubes**. The gases move by diffusion across the moist lining directly to and from the tissues. The end of each tube contains a small amount of fluid which regulates the movement of gases by changing the surface area of air in contact with the cells.

Gas exchange in amphibians

All amphibians make some use of surface gas exchange. There are even some salamanders (a type of amphibian) that have no lungs at all and rely completely on surface gas exchange. This is only possible if the surface is kept moist by secretions from mucous glands. Frogs carry out gas exchange through the skin and in the lungs. At times of inactivity, the skin alone is a sufficient surface with either water or air.

Gas exchange in birds

A bird has air sacs in addition to lungs. The air sacs function in ventilating the lungs, where gas exchange takes place. Together, the anterior and posterior air sacs function as bellows that keep air flowing through the lungs continuously and in one direction.

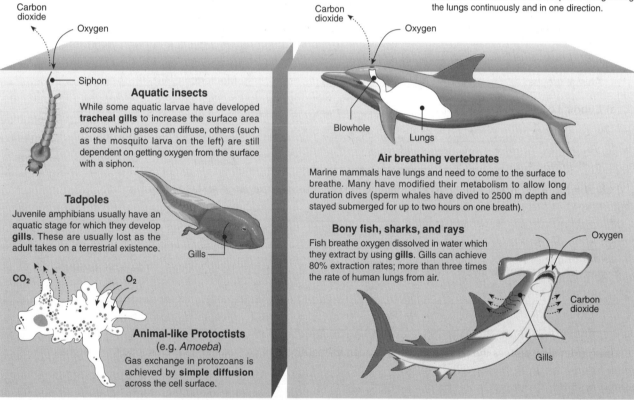

Aquatic insects

While some aquatic larvae have developed **tracheal gills** to increase the surface area across which gases can diffuse, others (such as the mosquito larva on the left) are still dependent on getting oxygen from the surface with a siphon.

Tadpoles

Juvenile amphibians usually have an aquatic stage for which they develop **gills**. These are usually lost as the adult takes on a terrestrial existence.

Animal-like Protoctists
(e.g. *Amoeba*)

Gas exchange in protozoans is achieved by **simple diffusion** across the cell surface.

Air breathing vertebrates

Marine mammals have lungs and need to come to the surface to breathe. Many have modified their metabolism to allow long duration dives (sperm whales have dived to 2500 m depth and stayed submerged for up to two hours on one breath).

Bony fish, sharks, and rays

Fish breathe oxygen dissolved in water which they extract by using **gills**. Gills can achieve 80% extraction rates; more than three times the rate of human lungs from air.

Jellyfish increase their surface area for gas exchange by having ruffles.

Nudibranch snails have elaborate exposed gills to assist gas exchange.

Some salamanders have no lungs and breathe solely through their skin.

Tube worms carry out gas exchange with feathery extensions in the water.

Related activities: Gas Exchange in Insects, Gas Exchange in Freshwater, Gas Exchange in Fish

RA 2

Gas Exchange

1. Suggest two reasons for the development of gas exchange structures and systems in animals:

   (a) _____

   (b) _____

2. (a) Explain why the air sacs of birds provide more efficient use of the air taken in with each breath:

   _____

   _____

   (b) Explain why birds require such an efficient method of gas exchange: _____

   _____

   _____

3. Complete the following list as a summary of the main features of the respiratory structures found in animals. Briefly describe the **location in the body** of each system, name the animal group or groups that use each system, and state in which medium (air or water) each system is used:

   (a) **Body surface**: Location in the body: _____

   _____

   Animal groups: _____ Medium: _____

   (b) **Tracheal tubes**: Location in the body: _____

   _____

   Animal groups: _____ Medium: _____

   (c) **Gills**: Location in the body: _____

   _____

   Animal groups: _____ Medium: _____

   (d) **Lungs**: Location in the body: _____

   _____

   Animal groups: _____ Medium: _____

4. Describe two ways in which air breathers manage to keep their gas exchange surfaces moist:

   (a) _____

   (b) _____

5. Explain why organisms with gills are at risk when their water is polluted by large amounts of organic material:

   _____

   _____

6. Using examples, discuss the relationship between an animal's type of gas exchange system and its environment:

   _____

   _____

   _____

   _____

   _____

   _____

   _____

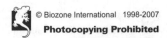

The Human Respiratory System

Lungs are internal sac-like organs found in most amphibians, and all reptiles, birds, and mammals. The paired lungs of mammals are connected to the outside air by way of a system of tubular passageways: the trachea, bronchi, and bronchioles. Ciliated, mucus secreting epithelium lines this system of tubules, trapping and removing dust and pathogens before they reach the gas exchange surfaces. Each lung is divided into a number of lobes, each receiving its own bronchus. Each bronchus divides many times, terminating in the respiratory bronchioles from which arise 2-11 alveolar ducts and numerous **alveoli** (air sacs). These provide a very large surface area (70 m²) for the exchange of respiratory gases by diffusion between the alveoli and the blood in the capillaries. The details of this exchange across the **respiratory membrane** are described opposite.

Morphology of the Respiratory System

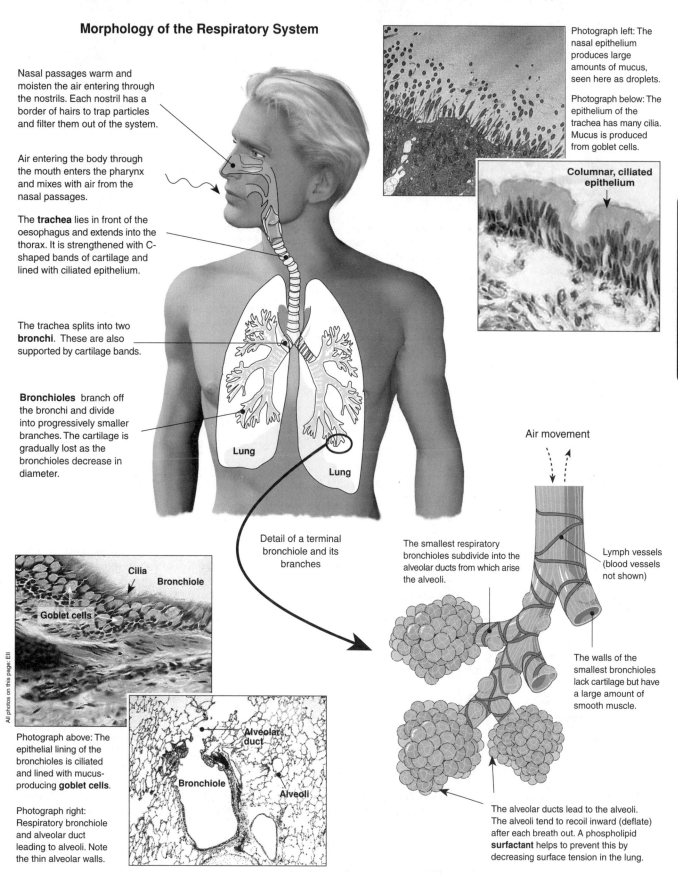

Nasal passages warm and moisten the air entering through the nostrils. Each nostril has a border of hairs to trap particles and filter them out of the system.

Air entering the body through the mouth enters the pharynx and mixes with air from the nasal passages.

The **trachea** lies in front of the oesophagus and extends into the thorax. It is strengthened with C-shaped bands of cartilage and lined with ciliated epithelium.

The trachea splits into two **bronchi**. These are also supported by cartilage bands.

Bronchioles branch off the bronchi and divide into progressively smaller branches. The cartilage is gradually lost as the bronchioles decrease in diameter.

Lung

Lung

Photograph left: The nasal epithelium produces large amounts of mucus, seen here as droplets.

Photograph below: The epithelium of the trachea has many cilia. Mucus is produced from goblet cells.

Columnar, ciliated epithelium

Gas Exchange

Cilia

Bronchiole

Goblet cells

Detail of a terminal bronchiole and its branches

Air movement

The smallest respiratory bronchioles subdivide into the alveolar ducts from which arise the alveoli.

Lymph vessels (blood vessels not shown)

The walls of the smallest bronchioles lack cartilage but have a large amount of smooth muscle.

Photograph above: The epithelial lining of the bronchioles is ciliated and lined with mucus-producing **goblet cells**.

Photograph right: Respiratory bronchiole and alveolar duct leading to alveoli. Note the thin alveolar walls.

Alveolar duct

Bronchiole

Alveoli

The alveolar ducts lead to the alveoli. The alveoli tend to recoil inward (deflate) after each breath out. A phospholipid **surfactant** helps to prevent this by decreasing surface tension in the lung.

All photos on this page: EII

Related activities: Gas Transport in Humans, Breathing in Humans, Review of Lung Function

RA 2

214

An Alveolus

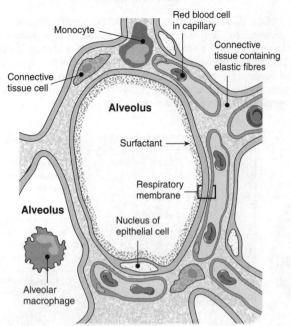

The diagram above illustrates the physical arrangement of the alveoli to the capillaries through which the blood moves. Phagocytic monocytes and macrophages are also present to protect the lung tissue. Elastic connective tissue gives the alveoli their ability to expand and recoil.

The Respiratory Membrane

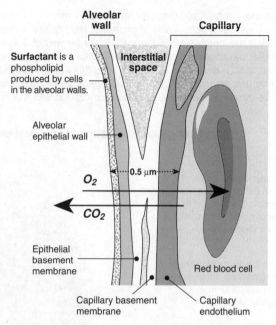

The **respiratory membrane** is the term for the layered junction between the alveolar epithelial cells, the endothelial cells of the capillary, and their associated basement membranes (thin, collagenous layers that underlie the epithelial tissues). Gases move freely across this membrane.

1. (a) Explain how the basic structure of the human respiratory system provides such a large area for gas exchange:

_____

_____

(b) Identify the general region of the lung where exchange of gases takes place: _____

2. Describe the structure and purpose of the respiratory membrane: _____

_____

_____

3. Describe the role of the surfactant in the alveoli: _____

_____

4. Using the information above and opposite, complete the table below summarising the **histology of the respiratory pathway**. Name each numbered region and use a tick or cross to indicate the presence or absence of particular tissues.

	Region	Cartilage	Ciliated epithelium	Goblet cells (mucus)	Smooth muscle	Connective tissue
1						✓
2						
3		gradually lost				
4	Alveolar duct		✗	✗		
5					very little	

5. Babies born prematurely are often deficient in surfactant. This causes respiratory distress syndrome; a condition where breathing is very difficult. From what you know about the role of surfactant, explain the symptoms of this syndrome:

_____

_____

Breathing in Humans

In mammals, the mechanism of breathing (ventilation) provides a continual supply of fresh air to the lungs and helps to maintain a large diffusion gradient for respiratory gases across the gas exchange surface. Oxygen must be delivered regularly to supply the needs of respiring cells. Similarly, carbon dioxide, which is produced as a result of cellular metabolism, must be quickly eliminated from the body. Adequate lung ventilation is essential to these exchanges. The cardiovascular system participates by transporting respiratory gases to and from the cells of the body. The volume of gases exchanged during breathing varies according to the physiological demands placed on the body (e.g. by exercise). These changes can be measured using spirometry.

Inspiration (inhalation or breathing in)

During quiet breathing, inspiration is achieved by increasing the space (therefore decreasing the pressure) inside the lungs. Air then flows into the lungs to fill the space. Inspiration is always an active process involving muscle contraction.

1a External intercostal muscles contract causing the ribcage to expand and move up

1b Diaphragm contracts and drops downwards

2 Thoracic volume increases, lungs expand, and the pressure inside the lungs decreases

3 Air flows into the lungs in response to the pressure gradient

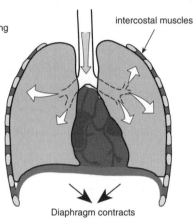

intercostal muscles

Diaphragm contracts

Expiration (exhalation or breathing out)

During quiet breathing, expiration is achieved passively by decreasing the space (thus increasing the pressure) inside the lungs. Air then flows passively out of the lungs to equalize with the air pressure. In active breathing, muscle contraction is involved in bringing about both inspiration and expiration.

1 In **quiet breathing**, external intercostal muscles and diaphragm relax. Elasticity of the lung tissue causes recoil.

In **forced breathing**, the internal intercostals and abdominal muscles also contract to increase the force of the expiration

2 Thoracic volume decreases and the pressure inside the lungs increases

3 Air flows passively out of the lungs in response to the pressure gradient

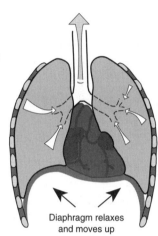

Diaphragm relaxes and moves up

Gas Exchange

Using spirometry to determine changes in lung volume

The apparatus used to measure the amount of air exchanged during breathing and the rate of breathing is a **spirometer** (also called a respirometer). A simple spirometer consists of a weighted drum, containing oxygen or air, inverted over a chamber of water. A tube connects the air-filled chamber with the subject's mouth, and soda lime in the system absorbs the carbon dioxide breathed out. Breathing results in a trace called a spirogram, from which lung volumes can be measured directly.

During inspiration
Air is removed from the chamber, the drum sinks, and an upward deflection is recorded on the paper on the rotating drum.

During expiration
Air is added to the chamber, the drum rises, and a downward deflection is recorded.

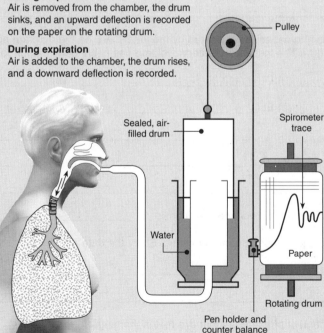

Sealed, air-filled drum

Pulley

Spirometer trace

Water

Paper

Pen holder and counter balance

Rotating drum

Lung Volumes and Capacities

The air in the lungs can be divided into volumes. Lung capacities are combinations of volumes.

Description of volume	Vol / dm³
Tidal volume (TV) Volume of air breathed in and out in a single breath	0.5
Inspiratory reserve volume (IRV) Volume breathed in by a maximum inspiration at the end of a normal inspiration	3.3
Expiratory reserve volume (ERV) Volume breathed out by a maximum effort at the end of a normal expiration	1.0
Residual volume (RV) Volume of air remaining in the lungs at the end of a maximum expiration	1.2

Description of capacity	
Inspiratory capacity (IC) = TV + IRV Volume breathed in by a maximum inspiration at the end of a normal expiration	3.8
Vital capacity (VC) = IRV + TV + ERV Volume breathed in by a maximum inspiration following a maximum expiration	4.8
Total lung capacity (TLC) = VC + RV The total volume of the lungs. Only a fraction of TLC is used in normal breathing	6.0

Only about 70% of the air that is inhaled reaches the alveoli. The rest remains in the air spaces of the nose, throat, larynx, trachea and bronchi. This air is unavailable for gas exchange and is called the **dead air volume (dead space air).**

Related activities: The Human Respiratory System, Energy and Exercise
Web links: Effects of Training, Respiratory Basics Learning Activity

DA 2

Measuring Changes in Lung Volume

Changes in lung volume can be measured using spirometry (see opposite). Total adult lung volume varies between 4 and 6 litres (dm^3) (it is greater in males). The **vital capacity** is somewhat less than this because of the residual volume of air that remains in the lungs even after expiration. The exchange between fresh air and the residual volume is a slow process and the composition of gases in the lungs remains relatively constant (table, right). Once measured, the **tidal volume** can be used to calculate the pulmonary ventilation rate or **PV**: the amount of air exchanged with the environment per minute. During exercise, the breathing rate, tidal volume, and PV increase up to a maximum (as indicated below).

Respiratory gas	Approximate percentages of O_2 and CO_2		
	Inhaled air	Air in lungs	Exhaled air
O_2	21.0	13.8	16.4
CO_2	0.04	5.5	3.6

Above: The percentages of respiratory gases in air (by volume) during normal breathing. The percentage volume of oxygen in the alveolar air (in the lung) is lower than that in the exhaled air because of the influence of the dead air volume in the airways (air unavailable for gas exchange).

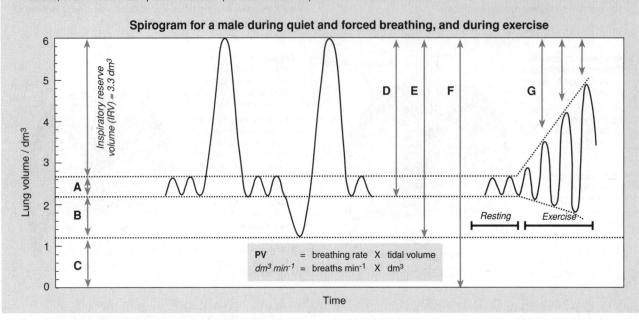

Spirogram for a male during quiet and forced breathing, and during exercise

$$PV = \text{breathing rate} \times \text{tidal volume}$$
$$dm^3\ min^{-1} = \text{breaths min}^{-1} \times dm^3$$

1. (a) Briefly outline the sequence of events involved in quiet breathing: _____

_____

_____

(b) Explain the essential difference between this and the situation during heavy exercise or forced breathing:

_____

_____

2. Using the definitions given opposite, identify the volumes and capacities indicated by the letters **A-F** on the diagram of a spirogram above. For each, indicate the volume (vol) in dm^3. The inspiratory reserve volume has been identified for you:

(a) A: _____ Vol: _____ (d) D: _____ Vol: _____

(b) B: _____ Vol: _____ (e) E: _____ Vol: _____

(c) C: _____ Vol: _____ (f) F: _____ Vol: _____

3. Explain what is happening in the sequence indicated by the letter **G**: _____

_____

4. Calculate PV when breathing rate is 15 breaths per minute and tidal volume is 4.0 dm^3: _____

5. The table above gives approximate percentages for respiratory gases during breathing. Study the data and then:

(a) Calculate the difference in CO_2 between inhaled and exhaled air: _____

(b) Explain where this 'extra' CO_2 comes from: _____

(c) Explain why the dead air volume raises the oxygen content of exhaled air above that in the lungs: _____

_____

Energy and Exercise

Exercise places an immediate demand on the body's energy supply systems. During exercise, the metabolic rate of the muscles increases by up to 20 times and the body's systems must respond appropriately to maintain homeostasis. The ability to exercise for any given length of time depends on maintaining adequate supplies of ATP to the muscles. There are three energy systems operating to do this: the ATP-CP system, the glycolytic system, and the oxidative system. The ultimate sources of energy for ATP generation in muscle via these systems are glucose, and stores of glycogen and triglycerides. Prolonged intense exercise utilises the oxidative system, and relies on a constant supply of oxygen to the tissues. The **VO2** is the amount of oxygen (expressed as a volume) used by muscles during a specified interval for cell metabolism and energy production. **VO2max** is the maximum volume of oxygen that can be delivered and used per minute and therefore represents an individual's upper limit of aerobic metabolism. VO2max is used as a measure of fitness, and is high in trained athletes. At some percentage of VO2max (the **anaerobic threshold**) the body is unable to meet its energy demands aerobically and an **oxygen debt** is incurred.

The ATP-CP System

The simplest of the energy systems is the **ATP-CP system**. CP or **creatine phosphate** is a high energy compound that stores energy sufficient for brief periods of muscular effort. Energy released from the breakdown of CP is not used directly to accomplish cellular work. Instead it rebuilds ATP to maintain a relatively constant supply. This process is anaerobic, occurs very rapidly, and is accomplished without any special structures in the cell. CP levels decline steadily as it is used to replenish depleted ATP levels. The ability of the ATP-CP system to maintain energy levels is limited to 3-15 seconds during an all out sprint. Beyond this, the muscle must rely on other processes for ATP generation.

CP provides enough energy to fuel about 10 s of maximum effort (e.g. a 100 m race).

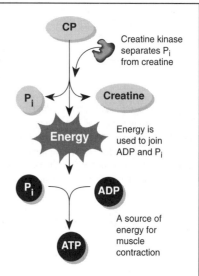

The Glycolytic System

ATP can also be provided by glycolysis: the first phase of cellular respiration. The ATP yield from glycolysis is low (only net 2ATP per molecule of glucose), but it produces ATP rapidly and does not require oxygen. The fuel for the glycolytic system is glucose in the blood, or glycogen, which is stored in the muscle or liver and broken down to glucose-6-phosphate. Glycolysis provides ATP for exercise for just a few minutes. Its main limitation is that it causes lactic acid ($C_3H_6O_8$) to accumulate in the tissues. Indirectly, it is the accumulation of lactic acid that gives the feeling of muscle fatigue. The lactic acid must transported to the liver and respired aerobically. The extra oxygen needed for this is the **oxygen debt**.

Rugby and other field sports demand brief intense efforts with recovery in-between.

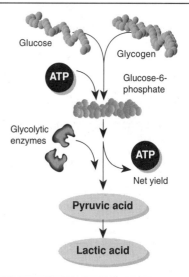

The Oxidative System

In the oxidative system, glucose is completely broken down to yield (about) 36 molecules of ATP. This process uses oxygen and takes place within the mitochondria. Aerobic metabolism has a high energy yield and is the primary method of energy production during sustained high activity. It is reliant on a continued supply of oxygen and therefore on the body s ability to deliver oxygen to the muscles. The fuels for aerobic respiration are glucose, stored glycogen, or stored **triglycerides**. Triglycerides provide free fatty acids, which are oxidised in the mitochondria by the successive removal of two-carbon fragments (a process called β-oxidation). These two carbon units enter the Krebs cycle as acetyl coenzyme A (acetyl CoA).

Prolonged aerobic effort (e.g. distance running) requires a sustained ATP supply.

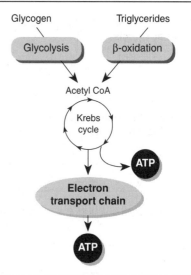

Oxygen Uptake during Exercise and Recovery

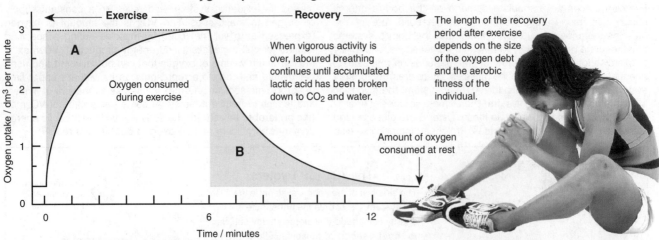

The graph above illustrates the principle of oxygen debt. In the graph, the energy demands of aerobic exercise require 3 dm³ of oxygen per minute. The rate of oxygen uptake increases immediately exercise starts, but the full requirement is not met until six minutes later. The **oxygen deficit** is the amount of oxygen needed (for aerobic energy supply) but not supplied by breathing. During the first six minutes, the energy is supplied largely from anaerobic pathways: the ATP-CP and glycolytic systems (opposite). After exercise, the oxygen uptake per minute does not drop immediately to its resting level. Extra oxygen is taken in despite the drop in energy demand (the **oxygen debt**). The oxygen debt is used to replace oxygen reserves in the body, restore creatine phosphate, and break down the lactic acid (through various intermediates) to CO_2 and water.

1. Explain why the supply of energy through the glycolytic system is limited: _____

_____

_____

2. Summarise the features of the three energy systems in the table below:

	ATP-CP system	Glycolytic system	Oxidative system
ATP supplied by:			
Duration of ATP supply:			

3. Study the graph and explanatory paragraph above, then identify and describe what is represented by:

   (a) The shaded region **A**: _____

   _____

   (b) The shaded region **B**: _____

   _____

4. With respect to the graph above, explain why the rate of oxygen uptake does not immediately return to its resting level after exercise stops:

_____

_____

5. The rate of oxygen uptake increases immediately exercise starts. Explain how the oxygen supply from outside the body to the cells is increased during exercise:

_____

_____

6. Lactic acid levels in the **blood** continue to rise for a time after exercise has stopped. Explain why this occurs:

_____

_____

Control of Breathing

The basic rhythm of breathing is controlled by the **respiratory centre**, a cluster of neurones located in the medulla oblongata. This rhythm is adjusted in response to the physical and chemical changes that occur when we carry out different activities.

Although the control of breathing is involuntary, we can exert some degree of conscious control over it. The diagram below illustrates how breathing is regulated by these voluntary and involuntary controls.

The Control of Breathing

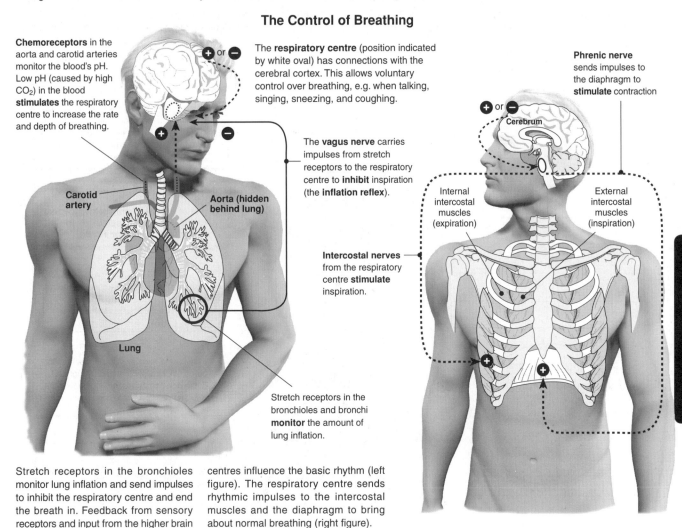

Chemoreceptors in the aorta and carotid arteries monitor the blood's pH. Low pH (caused by high CO_2) in the blood **stimulates** the respiratory centre to increase the rate and depth of breathing.

The **respiratory centre** (position indicated by white oval) has connections with the cerebral cortex. This allows voluntary control over breathing, e.g. when talking, singing, sneezing, and coughing.

Phrenic nerve sends impulses to the diaphragm to **stimulate** contraction

The **vagus nerve** carries impulses from stretch receptors to the respiratory centre to **inhibit** inspiration (the **inflation reflex**).

Cerebrum

Carotid artery

Aorta (hidden behind lung)

Internal intercostal muscles (expiration)

External intercostal muscles (inspiration)

Intercostal nerves from the respiratory centre **stimulate** inspiration.

Lung

Stretch receptors in the bronchioles and bronchi **monitor** the amount of lung inflation.

Stretch receptors in the bronchioles monitor lung inflation and send impulses to inhibit the respiratory centre and end the breath in. Feedback from sensory receptors and input from the higher brain centres influence the basic rhythm (left figure). The respiratory centre sends rhythmic impulses to the intercostal muscles and the diaphragm to bring about normal breathing (right figure).

1. Explain how the basic rhythm of breathing is controlled: _____

_____

2. Describe the role of each of the following in the regulation of breathing:

   (a) Phrenic nerve: _____

   (b) Intercostal nerves: _____

   (c) Vagus nerve: _____

   (d) Inflation reflex: _____

3. (a) Describe the effect of low blood pH on the rate and depth of breathing: _____

   _____

   (b) Explain how this effect is mediated: _____

   _____

   (c) Suggest why blood pH is a good mechanism by which to regulate breathing rate: _____

   _____

   _____

Related activities: Gas Transport in Humans, Review of Lung Function

A 2

Gas Exchange

Review of Lung Function

The respiratory system in humans and other air breathing vertebrates includes the lungs and the system of tubes through which the air reaches them. Breathing (ventilation) provides a continual supply of fresh air to the lungs and helps to maintain a large diffusion gradient for respiratory gases across the gas exchange surface. The basic rhythm of breathing is controlled by the respiratory centre in the medulla of the hindbrain. The volume of gases exchanged during breathing varies according to the physiological demands placed on the body. These changes can be measured using spirometry. The following activity summarises the key features of respiratory system structure and function. The stimulus material can be found in earlier exercises in this topic.

Components of the respiratory system

(a)

(b)

(c)

(d)

(e)

(f)

(g)

The control of breathing

(i) .... controls the rate and depth of breathing. It also has connections with the cerebral cortex that allow voluntary control over breathing (e.g. when talking, singing, sneezing, and coughing).

(ii) .... carries impulses from stretch receptors to the respiratory centre to **inhibit** inspiration (the **inflation reflex**).

(iii) .... from the respiratory centre, **stimulate** inspiration.

(iv) .... in the aorta and carotid arteries, monitor blood pH. Low pH (caused by high CO_2) in the blood stimulates an increase in the rate and depth of breathing.

(v) .... in the bronchioles and bronchi, **monitor** the amount of lung inflation.

(vi) .... sends impulses to the diaphragm to **stimulate** contraction.

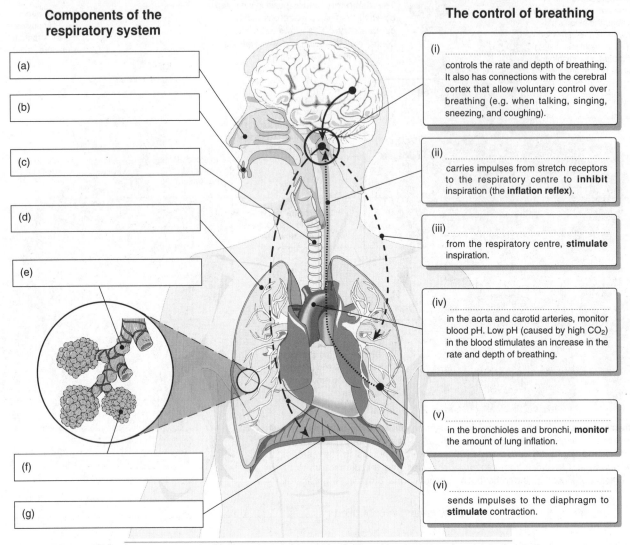

1. On the diagram above, label the components of the respiratory system (a-g) and the components that control the rate of breathing (i - vi).

2. Identify the volumes and capacities indicated by the letters **A - E** on the diagram of a spirogram below.

A = ...

B = ...

C = ...

D = ...

E = ...

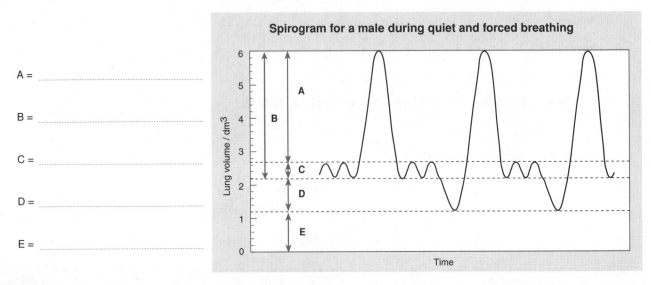

Spirogram for a male during quiet and forced breathing

Related activities: The Human Respiratory System, Breathing in Humans, Control of Breathing, Gas Transport in Humans

Gas Exchange in Insects

One advantage of gas exchange for terrestrial animals is that oxygen is proportionately more abundant in air than in water. However, terrestrial life also presents certain problems: body water can be lost easily through any exposed surface that is moist, thin, permeable, and vascular enough to serve as a respiratory membrane. Most insects are small terrestrial animals with a large surface area to volume ratio. Although they are highly susceptible to drying out, they are covered by a hard exoskeleton with a waxy outer layer that minimises water loss. Tracheal systems are the most common gas exchange organs

of terrestrial arthropods, including insects. Most body segments have paired apertures called spiracles in the lateral body wall through which air enters. Filtering devices in the spiracles prevent small particles from clogging the system, and valves control the degree to which the spiracles are open. In small insects, diffusion is the only mechanism needed to exchange gases, because it occurs so rapidly through the air-filled tubules. Larger, more active insects, such as locusts (below) have a tracheal system which includes air sacs that can be compressed and expanded to assist in moving air through the tubules.

Insect Tracheal Tubes

Insects, and some spiders, transport gases via a system of branching tubes called tracheae or tracheal tubes. The gases move by diffusion across the moist lining directly to and from the tissues. The end of each tube contains a small amount of fluid in which the respiratory gases are dissolved. The fluid is drawn into the muscle tissues during their contraction, and is released back into the tracheole when the muscle rests. Insects ventilate their tracheal system by making rhythmic body movements to help move the air in and out of the tracheae.

Spiracle openings on the abdomen

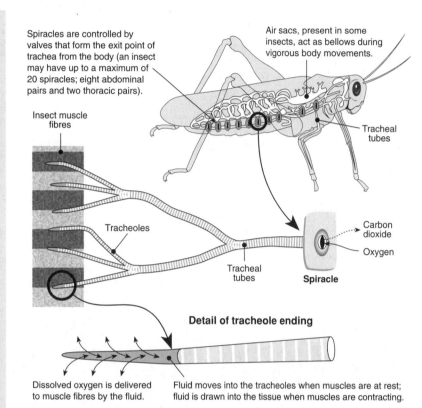

Spiracles are controlled by valves that form the exit point of trachea from the body (an insect may have up to a maximum of 20 spiracles; eight abdominal pairs and two thoracic pairs).

Air sacs, present in some insects, act as bellows during vigorous body movements.

Insect muscle fibres

Tracheal tubes

Tracheoles

Carbon dioxide

Oxygen

Tracheal tubes

Spiracle

Detail of tracheole ending

Dissolved oxygen is delivered to muscle fibres by the fluid.

Fluid moves into the tracheoles when muscles are at rest; fluid is drawn into the tissue when muscles are contracting.

Gas Exchange

1. Explain how oxygen and carbon dioxide are exchanged between the air and tissues at the end of tracheoles in insects:

_____

_____

_____

_____

2. Valves in the spiracles can regulate the amount of air entering the tracheal system. Suggest a reason for this adaptation:

_____

_____

3. Explain how ventilation is achieved in a terrestrial insect: _____

_____

_____

4. Even though most insects are small, they have evolved an efficient and highly developed gas exchange system that is independent of diffusion across the body surface. Suggest why this is the case:

_____

_____

_____

Related activities: Diffusion, Surface Area and Volume, Gas Exchange in Animals, Gas Exchange in Freshwater

RA 2

Gas Exchange in Freshwater

The availability of oxygen in water is very low relative to air: oxygen diffuses into water only very slowly and it is not very soluble (unlike CO_2). Moreover, as water temperature increases, the amount of oxygen that can be dissolved decreases. Despite these constraints, many invertebrate phyla, including the molluscs, annelids, and arthropods, have freshwater representatives. The majority of aquatic invertebrates are insects. As is the case in terrestrial insects, gases move to and from the tissues via the tracheae: the network of air-filled tubes that forms the insect respiratory system. What varies is the method by which oxygen enters this system. Like many aquatic invertebrates, aquatic insect larvae rely on **diffusion** across the body surface, with or without gills. Adult insects carry air with them when submerged. The air may be carried as a distinct bubble beneath the wings, or stay trapped by regions of unwettable (hydrofuge) hairs. A thin film of air trapped by hairs is called a **plastron**. It provides a source of oxygen and acts as a non-compressible diffusion gill, into which oxygen can diffuse from the water.

Gas Exchange in Aquatic Invertebrates

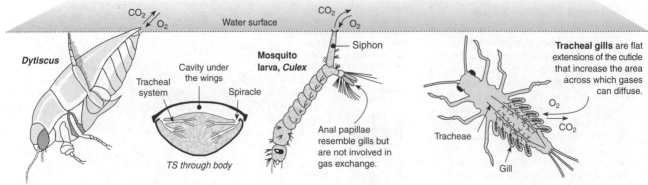

Surface air breathers

The **diving beetle**, *Dytiscus*, traps air from the surface beneath its wings where it forms a compressible gill. The spiracles open into the air space and lead to the tracheal tubes. As the submerged insect respires, the oxygen is gradually used up and the bubble decreases in size. A **mosquito larva** penetrates the water surface with a siphon extending from a spiracle at the tip of the abdomen. The larva hangs at the surface while gas exchange occurs by diffusion.

Tracheal gills

In the larvae of many aquatic insects, gas exchange occurs by diffusion across the body surface. This is enhanced by the presence of **tracheal gills** which may account for 20-70% of O_2 uptake depending on their surface area.

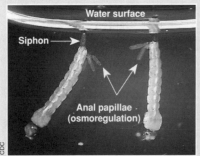

Gas exchange in mosquito larvae occurs with the air and is independent of O_2 content of the water.

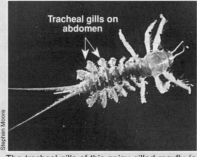

The tracheal gills of this spiny gilled mayfly (a very active species), are located on the abdomen.

Hydrophilid beetles use hydrofuge hairs to trap a film of air against the spiracles (a plastron).

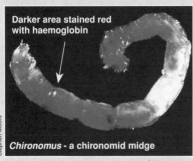

The blood of a few insect larvae, e.g. *Chironomus*, contains the O_2-carrying pigment **haemoglobin**, which allows them to survive when O_2 levels fall.

Anisops carries only a small air mass when diving but can exploit oxygen-poor waters because it has large haemoglobin-filled cells in its abdomen.

The tracheal gills of this damselfly larva are located at the tip of the abdomen (arrows). Like other insects with gills they are intolerant of low oxygen.

1. Giving an example for each, briefly describe two structural adaptations of freshwater invertebrates for gas exchange:

   (a) _____

   (b) _____

2. Describe one physiological adaptation of freshwater invertebrates for gas exchange: _____

_____

Related activities: Diffusion, Gas Exchange in Insects

Gas Exchange in Fish

Fish obtain the oxygen they need from the water by means of gills: membranous structures supported by cartilaginous or bony struts. Gill surfaces are very large and as water flows over the gill surface, respiratory gases are exchanged between the blood and the water. The percentage of dissolved oxygen in a volume of water is much less than in the same volume of air; air is 21%

oxygen while in water dissolved oxygen is about 1% by volume. High rates of oxygen extraction from the water, as achieved by gills, are therefore a necessary requirement for active organisms in an aquatic environment. In fish, ventilation of the gill surfaces to facilitate gas exchange is achieved by actively pumping water across the gill or swimming continuously with the mouth open.

Bony fish have four pairs of gills, each supported by a bony arch. The operculum (gill cover) is important in ventilation of the gills.

Cartilaginous fish have five or six pairs of gills. Water is drawn in via the mouth and spiracle and exits via the gill slits (there is no operculum).

Fish Gills

The gills of fish have a great many folds, which are supported and kept apart from each other by the water. This gives them a high surface area for gas exchange. The outer surface of the gill is in contact with the water, and blood flows in vessels inside the gill. Gas exchange occurs by diffusion between the water and blood across the gill membrane and capillaries. The operculum (gill cover) permits exit of water and acts as a pump, drawing water past the gill filaments. Fish gills are very efficient and can achieve an 80% extraction rate of oxygen from water; over three times the rate of human lungs from air.

Operculum (gill cover)

Circulation and Gas Exchange in Fish

Fish and other vertebrates have a **closed circulatory system** where the blood is entirely contained within vessels. Fish have a **single circuit system;** the blood goes directly to the body from the gills (the gas exchange surface) and only flows once through the heart in each circulation of the

body. The blood loses pressure when passing through the gills and, on leaving them, flows at low pressure around the body before returning to the heart. The gas exchange and circulatory systems are closely linked because the blood has a role in the transport of respiratory gases around the body.

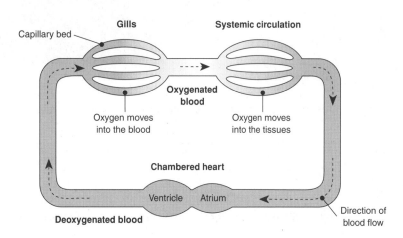

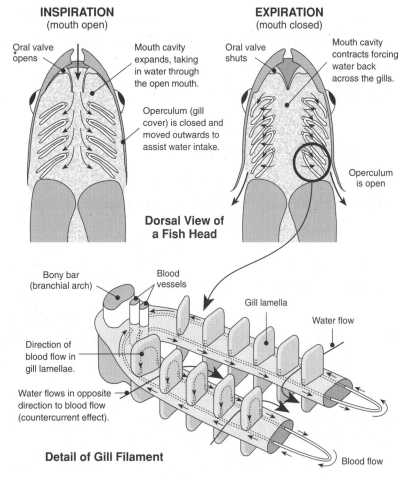

Detail of Gill Filament

Source: C.J. Clegg & D.G. McKean (1994)

Gas Exchange

Related activities: Gas Exchange in Insects, Gas Exchange in Freshwater

RA 2

The structure of fish gills and their physical arrangement in relation to the blood flow ensure that gas exchange rates are maximised. A constant stream of oxygen-rich water flows over the gill filaments in the **opposite** direction to the direction of blood flow through the gills. This is termed **countercurrent flow** (below, left). Blood flowing through the gill capillaries therefore encounters water of increasing oxygen content. In this way, the concentration gradient (for oxygen uptake) across the gill is maintained across the entire distance of the gill lamella. A parallel current flow would not achieve the same oxygen extraction rates because the concentrations across the gill would quickly equalise (below, right).

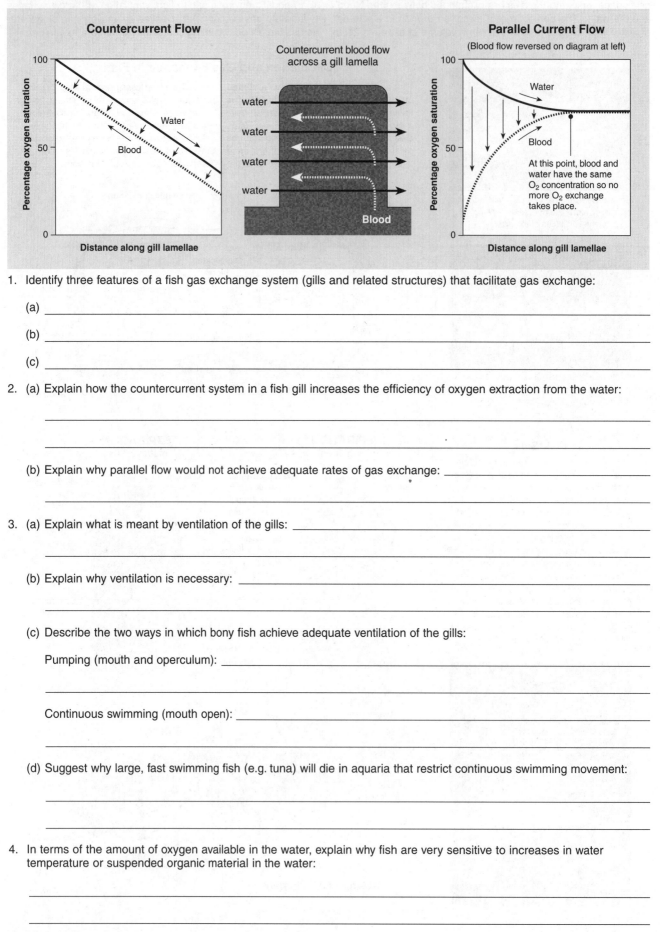

Countercurrent Flow

Percentage oxygen saturation

Water

Blood

Distance along gill lamellae

Countercurrent blood flow
across a gill lamella

water

water

water

water

Blood

Parallel Current Flow
(Blood flow reversed on diagram at left)

Percentage oxygen saturation

Water

Blood

At this point, blood and water have the same O_2 concentration so no more O_2 exchange takes place.

Distance along gill lamellae

1. Identify three features of a fish gas exchange system (gills and related structures) that facilitate gas exchange:

    (a) _____

    (b) _____

    (c) _____

2. (a) Explain how the countercurrent system in a fish gill increases the efficiency of oxygen extraction from the water:

    _____

    _____

    (b) Explain why parallel flow would not achieve adequate rates of gas exchange: _____

    _____

3. (a) Explain what is meant by ventilation of the gills: _____

    _____

    (b) Explain why ventilation is necessary: _____

    _____

    (c) Describe the two ways in which bony fish achieve adequate ventilation of the gills:

    Pumping (mouth and operculum): _____

    _____

    Continuous swimming (mouth open): _____

    _____

    (d) Suggest why large, fast swimming fish (e.g. tuna) will die in aquaria that restrict continuous swimming movement:

    _____

    _____

4. In terms of the amount of oxygen available in the water, explain why fish are very sensitive to increases in water temperature or suspended organic material in the water:

    _____

    _____

Respiratory Pigments

Regardless of the gas exchange system present, the amount of oxygen that can be carried in solution in the blood is small. The efficiency of gas exchange in animals is enhanced by the presence of **respiratory pigments**. All respiratory pigments consist of proteins complexed with iron or copper. They combine reversibly with oxygen and greatly increase the capacity of blood to transport oxygen and deliver it to the tissues. For example, the amount of oxygen dissolved in the plasma in mammals is only about 2 cm³ O_2 per litre. However the amount carried bound to haemoglobin is 100 times this. Haemoglobin is the most widely distributed respiratory pigment and is characteristic of all vertebrates and many invertebrate taxa. Other respiratory pigments include chlorocruorin, haemocyanin, and haemerythrin. Note that the precise structure and carrying capacity of any one particular pigment type varies between taxa (see the range of haemoglobins in the table below).

Respiratory Pigments

Respiratory pigments are coloured proteins capable of combining reversibly with oxygen, hence increasing the amount of oxygen that can be carried by the blood. Pigments typical of representative taxa are listed below. Note that the polychaetes are very variable in terms of the pigment possessed.

Taxon	Oxygen capacity / cm³ O_2 per 100 cm³ blood	Pigment
Oligochaetes	1 - 10	Haemoglobin
Polychaetes	1 - 10	Haemoglobin, chlorocruorin, or haemerythrin
Crustaceans	1 - 6	Haemocyanin
Molluscs	1 - 6	Haemocyanin
Fishes	2 - 4	Haemoglobin
Reptiles	7 - 12	Haemoglobin
Birds	20 - 25	Haemoglobin
Mammals	15 - 30	Haemoglobin

Mammalian Haemoglobin

Haemoglobin is a globular protein consisting of 574 amino acids arranged in four polypeptide sub-units: two identical **beta chains** and two identical **alpha chains**. The four sub-units are held together as a functional unit by bonds. Each sub-unit has an iron-containing haem group at its centre and binds one molecule of oxygen.

Chemical formula:
$$C_{3032}H_{4816}O_{872}N_{780}S_8Fe_4$$

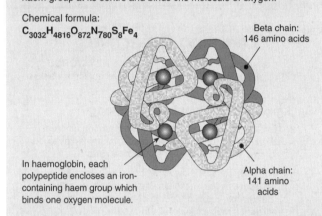

Beta chain: 146 amino acids

In haemoglobin, each polypeptide encloses an iron-containing haem group which binds one oxygen molecule.

Alpha chain: 141 amino acids

Gas Exchange

Aquatic polychaete fanworms e.g. *Sabella*, possess **chlorocruorin**.

Oligochaete annelids, such as earthworms, have **haemoglobin**.

Aquatic crustaceans e.g. crabs, possess **haemocyanin** pigment.

Vertebrates such as this fish have **haemoglobin** pigment.

Cephalopod molluscs such as *Nautilus* contain **haemocyanin**.

Birds, being vertebrates contain the pigment **haemoglobin**.

Many large active polychaetes, e.g. *Nereis*, contain **haemoglobin**.

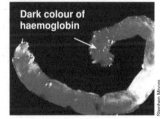

Dark colour of haemoglobin

Chironomus is one of only two insect genera to contain a pigment.

1. (a) Explain how respiratory pigments increase the carrying capacity of the blood: _____

_____

(b) Identify which feature of a respiratory pigment determines its oxygen carrying capacity: _____

_____

2. With reference to haemoglobin, suggest how oxygen carrying capacity is related to metabolic activity: _____

_____

_____

3. Suggest why larger molecular weight respiratory pigments are carried dissolved in the plasma rather than within cells:

_____

Related activities: Gas Transport in Humans

RA 2

Transport Systems

AQA-A	AQA-B	SNAB	Edexcel	OCR
Complete:	Complete:	Complete:	Complete:	Complete:
1-6, 8-12, 14, 19-20, 22-24, 26-27	1-6, 8-10, 12, 14-17, 19-20, 22-23, 28, 31-37, 39-41	1-12, 19-23, 28-41 extension as required	1-6, 8-12, 14-17, 19-20, 22, 28-29, 31-41	1-9, 11-12, 14-30, 32-37, 39-41

Learning Objectives

☐ 1. Compile your own glossary from the **KEY WORDS** displayed in **bold type** in the learning objectives below.

Background and Required Knowledge

☐ 2. Explain the need for **transport systems** in different organisms (e.g. multicellular plants, animals) in relation to size and **surface area to volume ratio**.

☐ 3. With respect to the movement of substances in transport systems, explain what is meant by **mass (bulk) flow**. Explain the role of mass flow in the efficient supply of materials to tissues.

☐ 4. Recognise the relationship between the transport systems of larger organisms and their specialised exchange systems.

Transport in Mammals (Human)   *(page 228)*

☐ 5. Identify the main components and functions of animal transport systems. Distinguish between open circulatory systems and **closed circulatory systems**.

☐ 6. Using a simple diagram, describe the **closed, double circulatory system** of a mammal, identifying: **carotid arteries**, **heart** and associated vessels, and **liver** and **kidneys** and associated vessels. Indicate the direction of blood flow, and the relative oxygen content of the blood at different points. Distinguish between **pulmonary circulation** and the **systemic circulation**.

Blood vessels and body fluids   *(pages 229-235)*

☐ 7. Recognise the structure of **arteries**, **veins**, and **capillaries** using a light microscope.

☐ 8. Draw labelled diagrams to describe and contrast the structure of **arteries**, **arterioles**, **veins**, and **capillaries** in humans. Relate the structure of each type of blood vessel to its specific function in the circulatory system.

☐ 9. Explain the importance of **capillaries**. Draw a diagram to show the relative positions of blood vessels in a capillary network and their relationship to the **lymphatic vessels**. Distinguish between **blood**, **lymph**, **plasma**, and **tissue fluid**.

☐ 10. Describe the formation of **tissue fluid** and explain how and where it is returned to the blood circulatory system.

☐ 11. Describe the nature and/or composition of **blood** including reference to the role of each of the following:

Non-cellular components: **plasma** (water, mineral ions, blood proteins, hormones, nutrients, urea, vitamins).

Cellular components: **erythrocytes**, **leucocytes** (**lymphocytes**, **monocytes**, **granulocytes**), **platelets**.

☐ 12. Identify the main substances transported by the blood and the sites at which exchanges occur.

☐ 13. EXTENSION: Identify problems associated with the supply and transfusion of blood. Identify the need for an effective blood substitute and describe the problems associated with producing **artificial blood**.

Gas transport   *(pages 225, 233-234, 236-238)*

☐ 14. Describe the structure of **erythrocytes** relating their structure to their transport function. Describe the role of **respiratory pigments** (**myoglobin** and **haemoglobin**) in the transport and delivery of oxygen to the tissues.

☐ 15. Explain the ways in which CO_2 is carried in the blood (including the role of haemoglobin).

☐ 16. Describe the transport (including loading/unloading) of oxygen in relation to the **oxygen-haemoglobin** (O_2-Hb) **dissociation curve**. Compare the oxygen affinities and dissociation curves of adult and **foetal haemoglobin** and explain the significance of these differences.

☐ 17. Describe the effect of pH (CO_2 level) on the oxygen-haemoglobin dissociation curve (the **Bohr effect**) and explain its significance.

☐ 18. Explain the short and long term effects of **high altitude** on human physiology, including changes in blood composition, capillary density, and breathing and heart rates. Comment on the role of these changes in maintaining adequate rates of exchange at altitude.

Heart structure and function   *(pages 239-244)*

☐ 19. Describe the internal and external gross structure of the **heart** in relation to its function. On diagrams identify: **atria**, **ventricles**, **atrioventricular valves**, and **semilunar valves**, as well the major vessels (**aorta**, **vena cava**, **pulmonary artery** and **vein**) and the coronary circulation. Relate the differences in the thickness of the heart chambers to their functions.

☐ 20. Describe the **cardiac cycle**, relating stages in the cycle (**atrial systole**, **ventricular systole**, and **diastole**) to the maintenance of blood flow through the heart. Describe the changes in pressure and volume, and associated valve movements during the cycle.

☐ 21. Explain the terms **systolic** and **diastolic blood pressure**. Describe typical values of these in the normal range and in a person with **hypertension**.

☐ 22. Explain what is meant by the **myogenic stimulation** of the heart. Describe how the heart beat is initiated and maintained, identifying the role of the following: the **sinoatrial node** (SAN), the **atrioventricular node** (AVN), the **bundle of His**, and the Purkinje fibres. Relate the activity of the SAN to the **intrinsic heart rate**.

☐ 23. Describe the extrinsic regulation of **heart rate** through **autonomic nerves** (vagus and cardiac nerves). Identify the role of the **medulla**, **baroreceptors** (pressure receptors), and **chemoreceptors** in the response of the heart to changing demands (e.g. exercise).

The physiology of exercise (pages 245-246)

☐ 24. Explain how **pulse** and **pulse rate** relate to heart rate. Explain the significance of resting pulse rate in relation to physical **fitness**.

☐ 25. Investigate the effects of exercise on the body. List measurements that could be made to test fitness.

☐ 26. Define the term: **cardiac output** and explain how it is calculated. Explain how **heart rate**, **stroke volume**, and cardiac output change with **aerobic exercise**.

☐ 27. Discuss the short and long term physiological effects of exercise, including: lactate production, changes in blood flow, and adaptations of the musculoskeletal and cardiovascular systems to regular exercise.

Transport in Flowering Plants (page 247)

☐ 28. Relate the presence of structural tissues in plants to the presence of an organised transport system.

Transport tissues (pages 248-251)

☐ 29. Describe the composition and function of the transport tissues in angiosperms: **xylem** (**vessels**, **tracheids**, fibres, xylem parenchyma) and **phloem** (**companion cells**, **sieve elements**, fibres, phloem parenchyma).

☐ 30. Using labelled diagrams, describe the distribution of **xylem** and **phloem** in a dicotyledonous **root**, **stem** and **leaf**. Define the term: **vascular bundle**.

☐ 31. Using a labelled diagram, describe the structure of a dicot **primary root**, identifying the distribution and adaptations for function of the **root hairs**, **endodermis**, **xylem**, and **phloem**.

Transport mechanisms (pages 252-259)

☐ 32. Describe the mechanism and pathways for water uptake in plant roots. Include reference to the role of **osmosis**, gradients in **water potential**, and the **symplastic**, **apoplastic**, and **vacuolar pathways** through the root. Explain the role of the **endodermis** in the movement of water into the **symplast**.

☐ 33. Describe the ways in which mineral uptake occurs in plant roots (passive and active transport mechanisms).

☐ 34. Define the terms **transpiration** and **transpiration stream**. Recognise transpiration as an inevitable consequence of gas exchange and explain the role of **stomata** in these processes. Identify two benefits of transpiration to plants.

☐ 35. Draw a labelled diagram to show the transpiration stream in a flowering plant. Describe how water and dissolved minerals are moved up the plant from the roots to the leaves. Explain the roles of **cohesion-tension** (capillary action), **root pressure**, and **transpiration pull** in the movement of water up the plant, identifying the relative importance of each.

☐ 36. Explain the effect of humidity, light, air movement, temperature, and water availability on transpiration rate. Describe how the factors affecting transpiration could be investigated experimentally.

☐ 37. Understand that species are adapted to survive in particular environmental conditions. Describe structural and/or physiological adaptations in **xerophytes**. Explain how these adaptations reduce transpiration rate and thereby enhance survival in dry conditions.

☐ 38. Describe structural adaptations of **hydrophytes** with respect to their survival in an aquatic habitat.

☐ 39. Explain **translocation**, identifying it as an **active** (energy requiring) process. Draw a labelled diagram to show the movement of dissolved food molecules (especially sucrose) in the phloem. Identify **sources** and **sinks** in the transport of sucrose.

☐ 40. Describe the **mass flow (pressure-flow) hypothesis** for the mechanism of translocation in plants. Evaluate the evidence for and against the mass flow hypothesis.

☐ 41. Interpret and evaluate the evidence for the occurrence and rate of ion and solute transport in plants.

See the 'Textbook Reference Grid' on pages 8-9 for textbook page references relating to material in this topic.

Supplementary Texts
See pages 5-6 for additional details of these texts:

■ Adds, J. *et al.*, 2004. **Exchange & Transport, Energy & Ecosystems** (NelsonThornes), chpt. 2

■ Clegg, C.J., 1998. **Mammals: Structure and Function** (John Murray), pp. 30-38.

See page 7 for details of publishers of periodicals:

STUDENT'S REFERENCE

Animal circulatory systems & exercise

■ **Keeping Pace - Cardiac Muscle and Heartbeat** Biol. Sci. Rev., 19(3), Feb. 2007, pp. 21-24. *Cardiac muscle cells can generate electrical activity like nerve impulses, and these impulses produce a smooth contraction of the muscle.*

■ **Red Blood Cells** Bio. Sci. Rev. 11(2) Nov. 1998, pp. 2-4. *The structure and function of erythrocytes and their role in oxygen transport.*

■ **Blood Pressure** Biol. Sci. Rev., 12(5) May 2000, pp. 9-12. *Blood pressure: its control, measurement, and significance to diagnosis.*

■ **Foetal Haemoglobin** Biol. Sci. Rev., 16(1) Sept. 2003, pp. 15-17. *The complex structure of haemoglobin molecules: the molecule in red blood cells that delivers oxygen to the tissues.*

■ **Platelets** Biol. Sci. Rev., 13(1), Sept. 2000, pp. 32-35. *The mechanism of blood clotting and the central role of platelets in this process.*

■ **A Fair Exchange** Biol. Sci. Rev., 13(1), Sept. 2000, pp. 2-5. *Formation and reabsorption of tissue fluid (includes disorders of fluid balance).*

■ **A Breath of Fresh Air** Biol. Sci. Rev., 7(5) May 1995, pp. 22-25. *Includes the transport of oxygen, and a description of oxygen dissociation curves.*

■ **ECGs: Getting to the Heart of the Matter** Biol. Sci. Rev., 10(1) Sept. 1997, pp. 21-24. *Monitoring the electrical activity of the heart, the cardiac cycle and medical diagnosis of heart disease.*

■ **Humans with Altitude** New Scientist, 2 Nov. 2002, pp. 36-39. *The short term adjustments and (evolutionary) adaptations of those living at altitude.*

■ **Mountaineering and its Influence on Human Physiology** Biol. Sci. Rev., 8(4) March 1996, pp. 19-24. *The effects of high altitude on body chemistry and the adaptations that are made.*

■ **The Heart** Bio. Sci. Rev. 18(2) Nov. 2005, pp. 34-37. *The structure and physiology of the heart.*

■ **Marathon Runners: Born or Bred** Biol. Sci. Rev., 17(1) Sept. 2004, pp. 10-13. *A comprehensive account of the physiology of endurance running.*

■ **Venous Disease** Biol. Sci. Rev., 19(3), Feb. 2007, pp. 15-17. *This occurs when damage to the deep veins and their valves puts superficial veins under even more pressure.*

Plant transport systems

■ **How Trees Lift Water** Biol. Sci. Rev., 18(1), Sept. 2005, pp. 33-37. *An excellent account of the cohesion-tension mechanism by which plants move water through their tissues against gravity.*

■ **High Tension** Biol. Sci. Rev., 13(1), Sept. 2000, pp. 14-18. *An excellent account of the mechanisms by which plants transport water and solutes.*

See pages 10-11 for details of how to access **Bio Links** from our web site: **www.biozone.co.uk**. From Bio Links, access sites under the topics:

GENERAL BIOLOGY ONLINE RESOURCES
• AP Interactive animation • Biology I interactive animations • Instructional multimedia, University of Alberta ... *and others* > **Online Textbooks and Lecture Notes:** • S-Cool! A level biology revision guide ... *and others* > **Glossaries:** Glossary of the heart ... *and others* **ANIMAL BIOLOGY:** • Anatomy and physiology • Human physiology lecture notes ... *and others* > **Circulatory System:** • Cardiology compass • How the heart works • The circulatory system • The matter of the human heart ... *and others*

PLANT BIOLOGY: • Kimball's plant biology lecture notes • Plant biology for non-science majors • Plant physiology links ... *and others* > **Structure and Function:** • Angiosperm structure and function tutorials • Plant structure ... *and others* > **Support and Transport:** • Plant structure and growth • Plant transport lecture

Software and video resources for this topic are provided on the Teacher Resource CD-ROM

Mammalian Transport

Animal cells require a constant supply of nutrients and oxygen, and continuous removal of wastes. Simple, small organisms achieve this through simple diffusion across moist body surfaces. Larger, more complex organisms require a circulatory system to transport materials because diffusion is too inefficient and slow to supply all the cells of the body adequately. Circulatory systems transport materials, but also help to maintain fluid balance, regulate body temperature, and assist in defending the body against pathogens. The blood vessels form a vast network of tubes that carry blood away from the heart, transport it to the tissues, and then return it to the heart. The arteries, arterioles, capillaries, venules, and veins are organised into specific routes to circulate blood throughout the body. The figure below shows some of the **circulatory routes** through which the blood travels. The **pulmonary system** (or circulation) carries blood between the heart and lungs, and the **systemic system** (circulation) carries blood between the heart and the rest of the body. Two important subdivisions of the systemic circuit are the coronary (cardiac) circulation, which supplies the heart muscle, and the **hepatic portal circulation**, which runs from the gut to the liver.

Schematic Overview of the Human Circulatory System

Deoxygenated blood (coloured grey below) travels to the right side of the heart via the vena cavae. The heart pumps the deoxygenated blood to the lungs where it releases carbon dioxide and receives oxygen. The oxygenated blood (coloured white below) travels via the pulmonary vein back to the heart from where it is pumped to all parts of the body. The **venous system** (figure, left) returns blood from the capillaries to the heart. The **arterial system** (figure right) carries blood from the heart to the capillaries. **Portal systems** carry blood between two capillary beds.

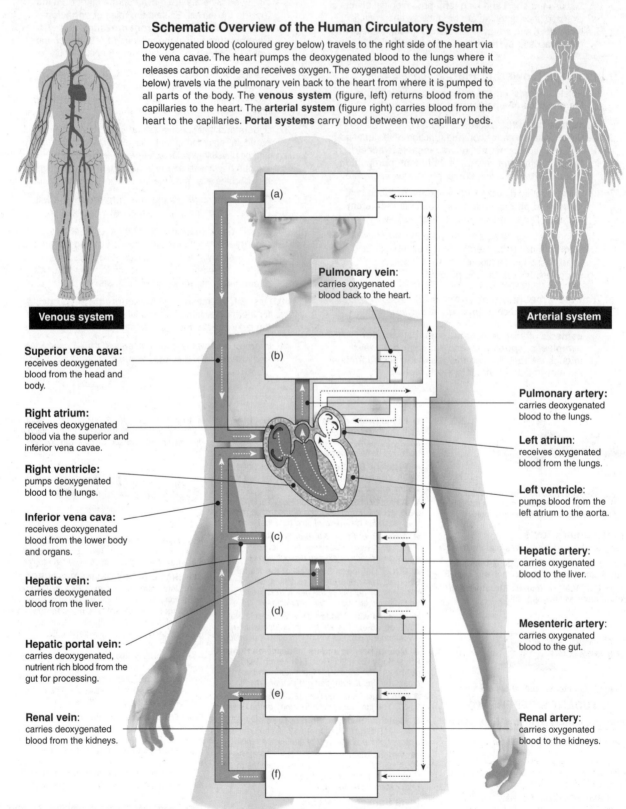

Venous system

Superior vena cava: receives deoxygenated blood from the head and body.

Right atrium: receives deoxygenated blood via the superior and inferior vena cavae.

Right ventricle: pumps deoxygenated blood to the lungs.

Inferior vena cava: receives deoxygenated blood from the lower body and organs.

Hepatic vein: carries deoxygenated blood from the liver.

Hepatic portal vein: carries deoxygenated, nutrient rich blood from the gut for processing.

Renal vein: carries deoxygenated blood from the kidneys.

Pulmonary vein: carries oxygenated blood back to the heart.

Arterial system

Pulmonary artery: carries deoxygenated blood to the lungs.

Left atrium: receives oxygenated blood from the lungs.

Left ventricle: pumps blood from the left atrium to the aorta.

Hepatic artery: carries oxygenated blood to the liver.

Mesenteric artery: carries oxygenated blood to the gut.

Renal artery: carries oxygenated blood to the kidneys.

1. Complete the diagram above by labelling the boxes with the organs or structures they represent.

Related activities: The Human Heart

Arteries

In vertebrates, arteries are the blood vessels that carry blood away from the heart to the capillaries within the tissues. The large arteries that leave the heart divide into medium-sized (distributing) arteries. Within the tissues and organs, these distribution arteries branch to form very small vessels called **arterioles**, which deliver blood to capillaries. Arterioles lack the thick layers of arteries and consist only of an endothelial layer wrapped by a few smooth muscle fibres at intervals along their length. Resistance to blood flow is altered by contraction (**vasoconstriction**) or relaxation (**vasodilation**) of the blood vessel walls, especially in the arterioles. Vasoconstriction increases resistance and leads to an increase in blood pressure whereas vasodilation has the opposite effect. This mechanism is important in regulating the blood flow into tissues.

Arteries

Arteries have an elastic, stretchy structure that gives them the ability to withstand the high pressure of blood being pumped from the heart. At the same time, they help to maintain pressure by having some contractile ability themselves (a feature of the central muscle layer). Arteries nearer the heart have more elastic tissue, giving greater resistance to the higher blood pressures of the blood leaving the left ventricle. Arteries further from the heart have more muscle to help them maintain blood pressure. Between heartbeats, the arteries undergo elastic recoil and contract. This tends to smooth out the flow of blood through the vessel.

Arteries comprise three main regions (right):

1. A thin inner layer of epithelial cells called the **endothelium** lines the artery.

2. A central layer (the **tunica media**) of elastic tissue and smooth muscle that can stretch and contract.

3. An outer connective tissue layer (the **tunica externa**) has a lot of elastic tissue.

(a)

(b)

(c)

(d)

Artery Structure

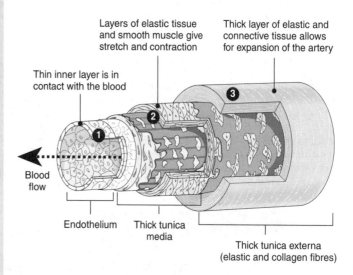

Layers of elastic tissue and smooth muscle give stretch and contraction

Thick layer of elastic and connective tissue allows for expansion of the artery

Thin inner layer is in contact with the blood

Blood flow

Endothelium

Thick tunica media

Thick tunica externa (elastic and collagen fibres)

Cross section through a large artery

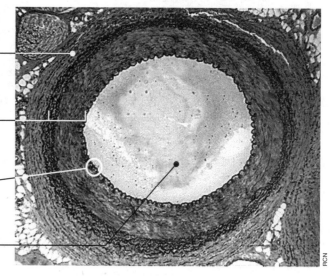

RCN

1. Using the diagram to help you, label the photograph (a)-(d) of the cross section through an artery (above).

2. (a) Explain why the walls of arteries need to be thick with a lot of elastic tissue: _____

   _____

   (b) Explain why arterioles lack this elastic tissue layer: _____

   _____

3. Explain the purpose of the smooth muscle in the artery walls: _____

   _____

4. (a) Describe the effect of vasodilation on the diameter of an arteriole: _____

   (b) Describe the effect of vasodilation on blood pressure: _____

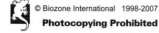
Related activities: Veins, Capillaries and Tissue Fluid
Web links: Review of Blood Vessels

A 1

Transport Systems

Veins

Veins are the blood vessels that return blood to the heart from the tissues. The smallest veins (**venules**) return blood from the capillary beds to the larger veins. Veins and their branches contain about 59% of the blood in the body. The structural differences between veins and arteries are mainly associated with differences in the relative thickness of the vessel layers and the diameter of the lumen. These, in turn, are related to the vessel's functional role.

Veins

When several capillaries unite, they form small veins called **venules**. The venules collect the blood from capillaries and drain it into **veins**. Veins are made up of essentially the same three layers as arteries but they have less elastic and muscle tissue and a larger **lumen**. The venules closest to the capillaries consist of an **endothelium** and a tunica externa of connective tissue. As the venules approach the veins, they also contain the tunica media characteristic of veins (right). Although veins are less elastic than arteries, they can still expand enough to adapt to changes in the pressure and volume of the blood passing through them. Blood flowing in the veins has lost a lot of pressure because it has passed through the narrow capillary vessels. The low pressure in veins means that many veins, especially those in the limbs, need to have valves to prevent backflow of the blood as it returns to the heart.

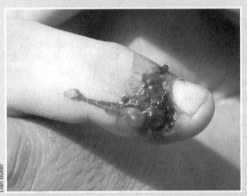

If a vein is cut, as is shown in this severe finger wound, the blood oozes out slowly in an even flow, and usually clots quickly as it leaves. In contrast, arterial blood spurts rapidly and requires pressure to staunch the flow.

Vein Structure

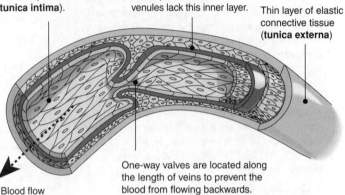

Inner thin layer of simple squamous epithelium lines the vein (**endothelium** or **tunica intima**).

Central thin layer of elastic and muscle tissue (**tunica media**). The smaller venules lack this inner layer.

Thin layer of elastic connective tissue (**tunica externa**)

One-way valves are located along the length of veins to prevent the blood from flowing backwards.

Blood flow

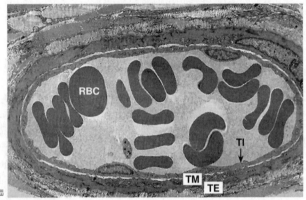

Above: TEM of a vein showing red blood cells (RBC) in the lumen, and the tunica intima (TI), tunica media (TM), and tunica externa (TE).

1. Contrast the structure of veins and arteries for each of the following properties:

    (a) Thickness of muscle and elastic tissue: _____

    _____

    (b) Size of the lumen (inside of the vessel): _____

    _____

2. With respect to their functional roles, give a reason for the differences you have described above: _____

    _____

    _____

3. Explain the role of the valves in assisting the veins to return blood back to the heart: _____

    _____

4. Blood oozes from a venous wound, rather than spurting as it does from an arterial wound. Account for this difference:

    _____

    _____

    _____

Capillaries and Tissue Fluid

In vertebrates, capillaries are very small vessels that connect arterial and venous circulation and allow efficient exchange of nutrients and wastes between the blood and tissues. Capillaries form networks or beds and are abundant where metabolic rates are high. Fluid that leaks out of the capillaries has an essential role in bathing the tissues. The movement of fluid into and out of capillaries depends on the balance between the blood (hydrostatic) pressure (HP) and the solute potential (ψs) at each end of a capillary bed. Not all the fluid is returned to the capillaries and this extra fluid must be returned to the general circulation. This is the role of the **lymphatic system**; a system of vessels that parallels the system of arteries and veins. The lymphatic system also has a role in internal defence, and in transporting lipids absorbed from the digestive tract. Note: A version of this activity (without reference to solute potential terminology), is available on the web and the Teacher Resource CD-ROM.

Exchanges in Capillaries

Blood passes from the arterioles into capillaries: small blood vessels with a diameter of just 4-10 µm. Red blood cells are 7-8 µm and only just squeeze through. The only tissue present is an **endothelium** of squamous epithelial cells. Capillaries form networks of vessels that penetrate all parts of the body. They are so numerous that no cell is more than 25 µm from any capillary. It is in the capillaries that the exchange of materials between the body cells and the blood takes place. Blood pressure causes fluid to leak from capillaries through small gaps where the endothelial cells join. This fluid bathes the tissues, supplying nutrients and oxygen, and removing wastes (right). The density of capillaries in a tissue is an indication of that tissue's metabolic activity. For example, cardiac muscle relies heavily on oxidative metabolism. It has a high demand for blood flow and is well supplied with capillaries. Smooth muscle is far less active than cardiac muscle, relies more on anaerobic metabolism, and does not require such an extensive blood supply.

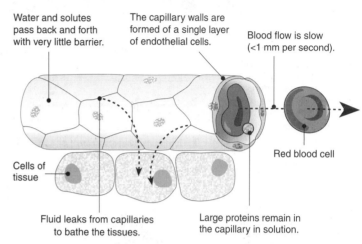

Water and solutes pass back and forth with very little barrier.

The capillary walls are formed of a single layer of endothelial cells.

Blood flow is slow (<1 mm per second).

Red blood cell

Cells of tissue

Fluid leaks from capillaries to bathe the tissues.

Large proteins remain in the capillary in solution.

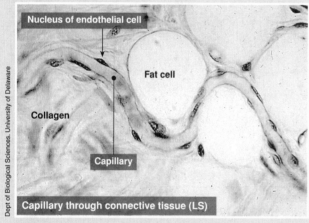

Nucleus of endothelial cell

Fat cell

Collagen

Capillary

Dept of Biological Sciences. University of Delaware

Capillary through connective tissue (LS)

Capillaries are found near almost every cell in the body. In many places, the capillaries form extensive branching networks. In most tissues, blood normally flows through only a small portion of a capillary network when the metabolic demands of the tissue are low. When the tissue becomes active, the entire capillary network fills with blood.

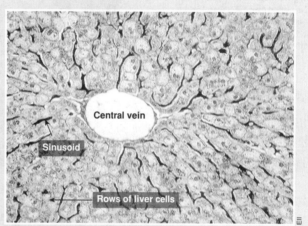

Central vein

Sinusoid

Rows of liver cells

Microscopic blood vessels in some dense organs, such as the liver (above), are called **sinusoids**. They are wider than capillaries and follow a more convoluted path through the tissue. Instead of the usual endothelial lining, they are lined with phagocytic cells. Like capillaries, sinusoids transport blood from arterioles to venules.

1. Describe the structure of a capillary, contrasting it with the structure of a vein and an artery:

_____

_____

_____

_____

2. Sinusoids provide a functional replacement for capillaries in some organs:

(a) Describe how sinusoids differ structurally from capillaries: _____

_____

(b) Describe in what way capillaries and sinusoids are similar: _____

_____

Related activities: The Lymphatic System, Arteries, Veins
Web links: Review of Blood Vessels, Capillaries and Tissue Fluid

RA 2

The Formation of Tissue Fluid

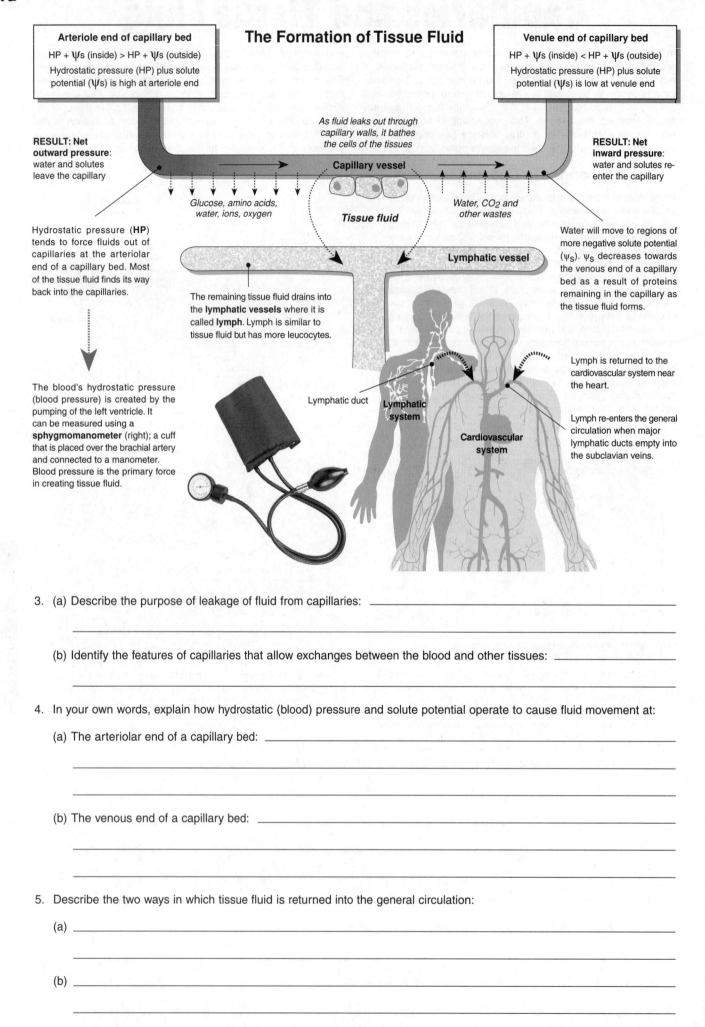

Arteriole end of capillary bed

HP + Ψs (inside) > HP + Ψs (outside)

Hydrostatic pressure (HP) plus solute potential (Ψs) is high at arteriole end

Venule end of capillary bed

HP + Ψs (inside) < HP + Ψs (outside)

Hydrostatic pressure (HP) plus solute potential (Ψs) is low at venule end

RESULT: Net outward pressure: water and solutes leave the capillary

As fluid leaks out through capillary walls, it bathes the cells of the tissues

Capillary vessel

RESULT: Net inward pressure: water and solutes re-enter the capillary

Glucose, amino acids, water, ions, oxygen

Tissue fluid

Water, CO_2 and other wastes

Hydrostatic pressure (**HP**) tends to force fluids out of capillaries at the arteriolar end of a capillary bed. Most of the tissue fluid finds its way back into the capillaries.

The remaining tissue fluid drains into the **lymphatic vessels** where it is called **lymph**. Lymph is similar to tissue fluid but has more leucocytes.

Lymphatic vessel

Water will move to regions of more negative solute potential (ψ_S). ψ_S decreases towards the venous end of a capillary bed as a result of proteins remaining in the capillary as the tissue fluid forms.

The blood's hydrostatic pressure (blood pressure) is created by the pumping of the left ventricle. It can be measured using a **sphygmomanometer** (right); a cuff that is placed over the brachial artery and connected to a manometer. Blood pressure is the primary force in creating tissue fluid.

Lymphatic duct

Lymphatic system

Cardiovascular system

Lymph is returned to the cardiovascular system near the heart.

Lymph re-enters the general circulation when major lymphatic ducts empty into the subclavian veins.

3. (a) Describe the purpose of leakage of fluid from capillaries: _____

_____

(b) Identify the features of capillaries that allow exchanges between the blood and other tissues: _____

_____

4. In your own words, explain how hydrostatic (blood) pressure and solute potential operate to cause fluid movement at:

(a) The arteriolar end of a capillary bed: _____

_____

_____

(b) The venous end of a capillary bed: _____

_____

_____

5. Describe the two ways in which tissue fluid is returned into the general circulation:

(a) _____

_____

(b) _____

_____

Blood

Blood makes up about 8% of body weight. Blood is a complex liquid tissue comprising cellular components suspended in plasma. If a blood sample is taken, the cells can be separated from the plasma by centrifugation. The cells (formed elements) settle as a dense red pellet below the transparent, straw-coloured plasma. Blood performs many functions: it transports nutrients, respiratory gases, hormones, and wastes; it has a role in thermoregulation through the distribution of heat; it defends against infection; and its ability to clot protects against blood loss. The examination of blood is also useful in diagnosing disease. The cellular components of blood are normally present in particular specified ratios. A change in the morphology, type, or proportion of different blood cells can therefore be used to indicate a specific disorder or infection (right).

Non-Cellular Blood Components

The non-cellular blood components form the plasma. Plasma is a watery matrix of ions and proteins and makes up 50-60% of the total blood volume.

Water
The main constituent of blood and lymph.
Role: Transports dissolved substances. Provides body cells with water. Distributes heat and has a central role in thermoregulation. Regulation of water content helps to regulate blood pressure and volume.

Mineral ions
Sodium, bicarbonate, magnesium, potassium, calcium, chloride.
Role: Osmotic balance, pH buffering, and regulation of membrane permeability. They also have a variety of other functions, e.g. Ca^{2+} is involved in blood clotting.

Plasma proteins
7-9% of the plasma volume.
Serum albumin
Role: Osmotic balance and pH buffering, Ca^{2+} transport.
Fibrinogen and prothrombin
Role: Take part in blood clotting.
Immunoglobulins
Role: Antibodies involved in the immune response.
α-globulins
Role: Bind/transport hormones, lipids, fat soluble vitamins.
β-globulins
Role: Bind/transport iron, cholesterol, fat soluble vitamins.
Enzymes
Role: Take part in and regulate metabolic activities.

Substances transported by non-cellular components
Products of digestion
Examples: sugars, fatty acids, glycerol, and amino acids.
Excretory products
Example: urea
Hormones and vitamins
Examples: insulin, sex hormones, vitamins A and B_{12}.
Importance: These substances occur at varying levels in the blood. They are transported to and from the cells dissolved in the plasma or bound to plasma proteins.

Cellular Blood Components

The cellular components of the blood (also called the formed elements) float in the plasma and make up 40-50% of the total blood volume.

Erythrocytes (red blood cells or RBCs)
5-6 million per mm^3 blood; 38-48% of total blood volume.
Role: RBCs transport oxygen (O_2) and a small amount of carbon dioxide (CO_2). The oxygen is carried bound to haemoglobin (Hb) in the cells. Each Hb molecule can bind four molecules of oxygen.

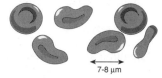

7-8 μm

Platelets

2 μm
Small, membrane bound cell fragments derived from bone marrow cells; about 1/4 the size of RBCs.
0.25 million per mm^3 blood.
Role: To start the blood clotting process.

Leucocytes (white blood cells)
5-10 000 per mm^3 blood
2-3% of total blood volume.
Role: Involved in internal defence. There are several types of white blood cells (see below).

Lymphocytes
T and B cells.
24% of the white cell count.
Role: Antibody production and cell mediated immunity.

Neutrophils

Phagocytes.
70% of the white cell count.
Role: Engulf foreign material.

Eosinophils

Rare leucocytes; normally 1.5% of the white cell count.
Role: Mediate allergic responses such as hayfever and asthma.

Basophils

Rare leucocytes; normally 0.5% of the white cell count.
Role: Produce heparin (an anti-clotting protein), and histamine. Involved in inflammation.

Transport Systems

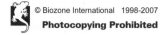
Related activities: Gas Transport in Humans, Blood Clotting and Defence, The Body's Defences

A 2

The Examination of Blood

Different types of microscopy give different information about blood. A SEM (right) shows the detailed external morphology of the blood cells. A fixed smear of a blood sample viewed with a light microscope (far right) can be used to identify the different blood cell types present, and their ratio to each other. Determining the types and proportions of different white blood cells in blood is called a **differential white blood cell count**. Elevated counts of particular cell types indicate allergy or infection.

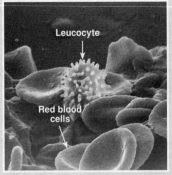

SEM of red blood cells and a leucocyte.

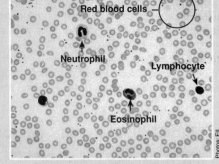

Light microscope view of a fixed blood smear.

1. For each of the following blood functions, identify the component(s) of the blood responsible and state how the function is carried out (the mode of action). The first one is done for you:

   (a) **Temperature regulation**. *Blood component involved:* Water component of the plasma

   Mode of action: Water absorbs heat and dissipates it from sites of production (e.g. organs)

   (b) **Protection against disease**. *Blood component:* _____

   Mode of action: _____

   (c) **Communication between cells, tissues, and organs**. *Blood component:* _____

   Mode of action: _____

   (d) **Oxygen transport**. *Blood component:* _____

   Mode of action: _____

   (e) **CO$_2$ transport**. *Blood components:* _____

   Mode of action: _____

   (f) **Buffer against pH changes**. *Blood components:* _____

   Mode of action: _____

   (g) **Nutrient supply**. *Blood component:* _____

   Mode of action: _____

   (h) **Tissue repair**. *Blood components:* _____

   Mode of action: _____

   (i) **Transport of hormones, lipids, and fat soluble vitamins**. *Blood component:* _____

   Mode of action: _____

2. Identify a feature that distinguishes red and white blood cells: _____

3. Explain two physiological advantages of red blood cell structure (lacking nucleus and mitochondria):

   (a) _____

   (b) _____

4. Suggest what each of the following results from a differential white blood cell count would suggest:

   (a) Elevated levels of eosinophils (above the normal range): _____

   (b) Elevated levels of neutrophils (above the normal range): _____

   (c) Elevated levels of basophils (above the normal range): _____

   (d) Elevated levels of lymphocytes (above the normal range): _____

The Search for Blood Substitutes

Blood's essential homeostatic role is evident when considering the problems encountered when large volumes of blood are lost. Transfusion of whole blood (see photograph below) or plasma is an essential part of many medical procedures, e.g. after trauma or surgery, or as a regular part of the treatment for some disorders (e.g. thalassaemia). This makes blood a valuable commodity. A blood supply relies on blood donations, but as the demand for blood increases, the availability of donors continues to decline. This decline is partly due to more stringent screening of donors for diseases such as HIV/AIDS, hepatitis, and variant CJD. The inadequacy of blood supplies has made the search for a safe, effective blood substitute the focus of much research. Despite some possibilities, no currently available substitute reproduces all of blood's many homeostatic functions.

Essential criteria for a successful blood substitute

- The substitute should be non-toxic and free from diseases.

- It should work for all blood types.

- It should not cause an immune response.

- It should remain in circulation until the blood volume is restored and then it should be safely excreted.

- It must be easily transported and suitable for storage under normal refrigeration.

- It should have a long shelf life.

- It should perform some or all of blood tasks.

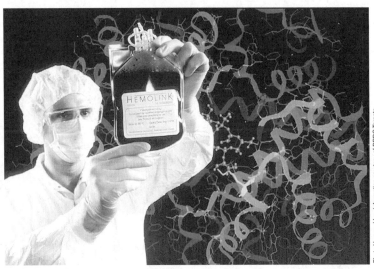

A shortfall in blood supplies, greater demand, and public fear of contaminated blood, have increased the need for a safe, effective blood substitute. Such a substitute must fulfil strict criteria (above).

A researcher displays a haemoglobin based artificial blood product, developed by Defence R&D Canada, Toronto and now produced under license by Hemosol Inc. Human testing and marketing has now progressed successfully into advanced trials. A human haemoglobin molecule is pictured in the background. Photo with permission from Hemosol inc.

Chemical based

These rely on synthetic oxygen-carrying compounds called **perfluorocarbons** (PFCs). PFCs are able to dissolve large quantities of gases. They do not dissolve freely in the plasma, so they must be emulsified with an agent that enables them to be dispersed in the blood.

Advantages: PFCs can transport a lot of oxygen, and transfer gases quickly.

Disadvantages: May result in oxygen accumulation in the tissues, which can lead to damage.

Examples: Oxygent™: Produced in commercial quantities using PFC emulsion technology; Perflubon (a PFC), water, a surfactant, and salts, homogenized into a stable, biologically compatible emulsion.

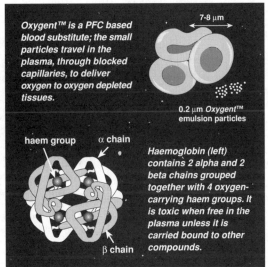

Oxygent™ is a PFC based blood substitute; the small particles travel in the plasma, through blocked capillaries, to deliver oxygen to oxygen depleted tissues.

7-8 µm

0.2 µm *Oxygent™* emulsion particles

haem group   α chain

β chain

Haemoglobin (left) contains 2 alpha and 2 beta chains grouped together with 4 oxygen-carrying haem groups. It is toxic when free in the plasma unless it is carried bound to other compounds.

Haemoglobin based

These rely on haemoglobin (Hb), modified by joining it to a polymer (polyethylene glycol) to make it larger.

Advantages: Modified haemoglobin should better be able to approximate the various properties of blood.

Disadvantages: Hb is toxic unless carried within RBCs; it requires modification before it can be safely transported free in the plasma. Substitutes made from human Hb use outdated blood as the Hb source. Bovine Hb may transmit diseases (e.g. BSE).

Examples: Hemolink™, a modified human Hb produced by Hemosol Inc. in California. Research is focused on developing cell culture lines with the ability to produce Hb.

1. Describe two essential features of a successful blood substitute, identifying briefly why the feature is important:

    (a) _____

    (b) _____

2. Identify the two classes of artificial blood substitutes: _____

3. Discuss the advantages and risks associated with the use of blood substitutes: _____

_____

_____

_____

_____

_____

Related activities: Blood

A 2

The Effects of High Altitude

The air at high altitudes contains less oxygen than the air at sea level. Air pressure decreases with altitude so the pressure (therefore amount) of oxygen in the air also decreases. Sudden exposure to an altitude of 2000 m would make you breathless on exertion and above 7000 m most people would become unconscious. The effects of altitude on physiology are related to this lower oxygen availability. Humans and other animals can make some physiological adjustments to life at altitude; this is called acclimatisation. Some of the changes to the cardiovascular and respiratory systems to high altitude are outlined below.

Mountain Sickness

Altitude sickness or mountain sickness is usually a mild illness associated with trekking to altitudes of 5000 metres or so. Common symptoms include headache, insomnia, poor appetite and nausea, vomiting, dizziness, tiredness, coughing, and breathlessness. The best way to avoid mountain sickness is to ascend to altitude slowly (no more than 300 m per day above 3000 m). Continuing to ascend with mountain sickness can result in more serious illnesses: accumulation of fluid on the brain (cerebral oedema) and accumulation of fluid in the lungs (pulmonary oedema). These complications can be fatal if not treated with oxygen and a rapid descent to lower altitude.

Physiological Adjustment to Altitude

Effect	Minutes	Days	Weeks
Increased heart rate	←——————→		
Increased breathing	←——————→		
Concentration of blood		←——→	
Increased red blood cell production			←——————→
Increased capillary density			←——→

The human body can make adjustments to life at altitude. Some of these changes take place almost immediately: breathing and heart rates increase. Other adjustments may take weeks (see above). These responses are all aimed at improving the rate of supply of oxygen to the body's tissues. When more permanent adjustments to physiology are made (increased blood cells and capillary networks) heart and breathing rates can return to normal.

People who live permanently at high altitude, e.g. Tibetans, Nepalese, and Peruvian Indians, have physiologies adapted (genetically, through evolution) to high altitude. Their blood volumes and red blood cell counts are high, and they can carry heavy loads effortlessly despite a small build. In addition, their metabolism uses oxygen very efficiently.

Llamas, vicunas, and Bactrian camels are well suited to high altitude life. Vicunas and llamas, which live in the Andes, have high blood cell counts and their red blood cells live almost twice as long as those in humans. Their haemoglobin also picks up and offloads oxygen more efficiently than the haemoglobin of most mammals.

1. (a) Describe the general effects of high altitude on the body: _____

_____

(b) Name the general term given to describe these effects: _____

2. (a) Identify one short term physiological adaptation that humans make to high altitude: _____

_____

(b) Explain how this adaptation helps to increase the amount of oxygen the body receives: _____

_____

3. (a) Describe one longer term adaptation that humans can make to living at high altitude: _____

_____

(b) Explain how this adaptation helps to increase the amount of oxygen the body receives: _____

_____

Related activities: Blood, Gas Exchange in Humans

Gas Transport in Humans

The transport of respiratory gases around the body is the role of the blood and its respiratory pigments. Oxygen is transported throughout the body chemically bound to the respiratory pigment **haemoglobin** inside the red blood cells. In the muscles, oxygen from haemoglobin is transferred to and retained by **myoglobin**, a molecule that is chemically similar to haemoglobin except that it consists of only one haem-globin unit. Myoglobin has a greater affinity for oxygen than haemoglobin and acts as an oxygen store within muscles, releasing the oxygen during periods of prolonged or extreme muscular activity. If the myoglobin store is exhausted, the muscles are forced into oxygen debt and must respire anaerobically. The waste product of this, lactic acid, accumulates in the muscle and is transported (as lactate) to the liver where it is metabolised under aerobic conditions.

Gas Exchange and Transport

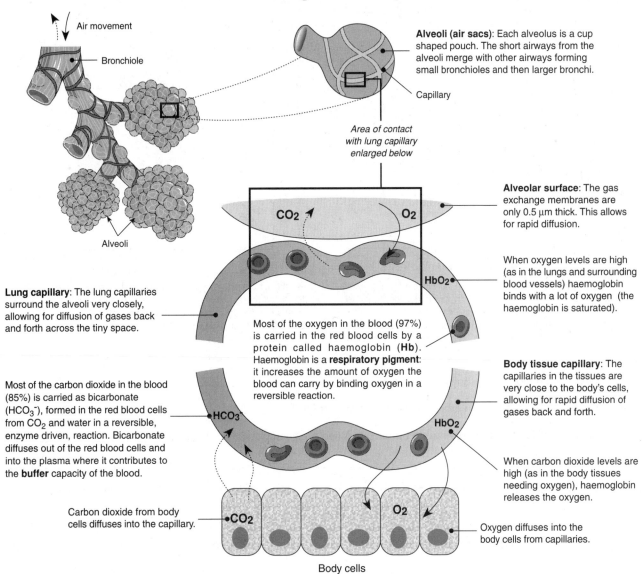

Alveoli (air sacs): Each alveolus is a cup shaped pouch. The short airways from the alveoli merge with other airways forming small bronchioles and then larger bronchi.

Capillary

Air movement

Bronchiole

Alveoli

Area of contact with lung capillary enlarged below

Alveolar surface: The gas exchange membranes are only 0.5 μm thick. This allows for rapid diffusion.

CO_2 O_2

When oxygen levels are high (as in the lungs and surrounding blood vessels) haemoglobin binds with a lot of oxygen (the haemoglobin is saturated).

HbO_2

Lung capillary: The lung capillaries surround the alveoli very closely, allowing for diffusion of gases back and forth across the tiny space.

Most of the oxygen in the blood (97%) is carried in the red blood cells by a protein called haemoglobin (**Hb**). Haemoglobin is a **respiratory pigment**: it increases the amount of oxygen the blood can carry by binding oxygen in a reversible reaction.

Most of the carbon dioxide in the blood (85%) is carried as bicarbonate (HCO_3^-), formed in the red blood cells from CO_2 and water in a reversible, enzyme driven, reaction. Bicarbonate diffuses out of the red blood cells and into the plasma where it contributes to the **buffer** capacity of the blood.

HCO_3^-

HbO_2

Body tissue capillary: The capillaries in the tissues are very close to the body's cells, allowing for rapid diffusion of gases back and forth.

When carbon dioxide levels are high (as in the body tissues needing oxygen), haemoglobin releases the oxygen.

Carbon dioxide from body cells diffuses into the capillary.

CO_2 O_2

Oxygen diffuses into the body cells from capillaries.

Body cells

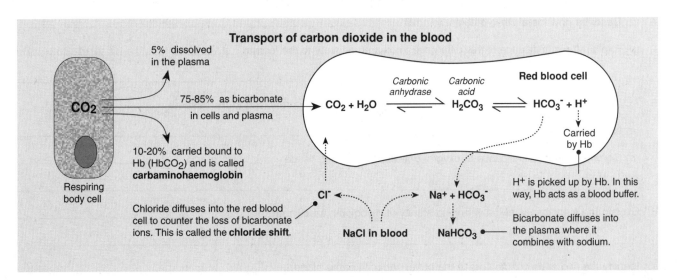

Transport of carbon dioxide in the blood

5% dissolved in the plasma

75-85% as bicarbonate in cells and plasma

CO_2

Respiring body cell

10-20% carried bound to Hb ($HbCO_2$) and is called **carbaminohaemoglobin**

Chloride diffuses into the red blood cell to counter the loss of bicarbonate ions. This is called the **chloride shift**.

Carbonic anhydrase   *Carbonic acid*   **Red blood cell**

$CO_2 + H_2O \rightleftharpoons H_2CO_3 \rightleftharpoons HCO_3^- + H^+$

Carried by Hb

Cl^- $Na^+ + HCO_3^-$

NaCl in blood $NaHCO_3$

H^+ is picked up by Hb. In this way, Hb acts as a blood buffer.

Bicarbonate diffuses into the plasma where it combines with sodium.

Related activities: The Human Respiratory System, Respiratory Pigments

A 2

Oxygen does not easily dissolve in blood, but is carried in chemical combination with haemoglobin (Hb) in red blood cells. The most important factor determining how much oxygen is carried by Hb is the level of oxygen in the blood. The greater the oxygen tension, the more oxygen will combine with Hb. This relationship can be illustrated with an oxygen-haemoglobin dissociation curve as shown below (Fig. 1). In the lung capillaries, (high O_2), a lot of oxygen is picked up and bound by Hb. In the tissues, (low O_2), oxygen is released. In skeletal muscle, myoglobin picks up oxygen from haemoglobin and therefore serves as an oxygen store when oxygen tensions begin to fall. The release of oxygen is enhanced by the **Bohr effect** (Fig. 2).

Respiratory Pigments and the Transport of Oxygen

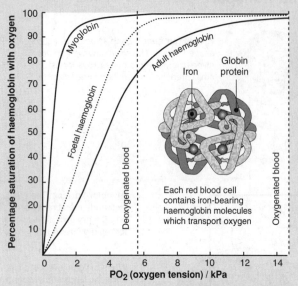

Fig. 1: Dissociation curves for haemoglobin and myoglobin at normal body temperature for foetal and adult human blood.

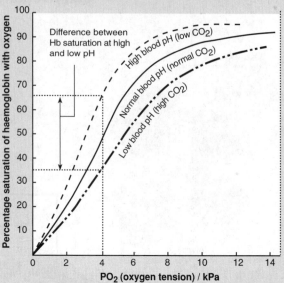

Fig. 2: Oxygen-haemoglobin dissociation curves for human blood at normal body temperature at different blood pH.

As oxygen level increases, more oxygen combines with haemoglobin (Hb). Hb saturation remains high, even at low oxygen tensions. Foetal Hb has a high affinity for oxygen and carries 20-30% more than maternal Hb. Myoglobin in skeletal muscle has a very high affinity for oxygen and will take up oxygen from haemoglobin in the blood.

As pH increases (lower CO_2), more oxygen combines with Hb. As the blood pH decreases (higher CO_2), Hb binds less oxygen and releases more to the tissues (**the Bohr effect**). The difference between Hb saturation at high and low pH represents the amount of oxygen released to the tissues.

1. (a) Identify two regions in the body where oxygen levels are very high: _____

   (b) Identify two regions where carbon dioxide levels are very high: _____

2. Explain the significance of the **reversible binding** reaction of haemoglobin (Hb) to oxygen: _____

   _____

3. (a) Haemoglobin saturation is affected by the oxygen level in the blood. Describe the nature of this relationship:

   _____

   (b) Comment on the significance of this relationship to oxygen delivery to the tissues: _____

   _____

4. (a) Describe how foetal Hb is different to adult Hb: _____

   (b) Explain the significance of this difference to oxygen delivery to the foetus: _____

   _____

5. At low blood pH, less oxygen is bound by haemoglobin and more is released to the tissues:

   (a) Name this effect: _____

   (b) Comment on its significance to oxygen delivery to respiring tissue: _____

   _____

6. Explain the significance of the very high affinity of myoglobin for oxygen: _____

   _____

7. Identify the two main contributors to the buffer capacity of the blood: _____

The Human Heart

The heart is the centre of the human cardiovascular system. It is a hollow, muscular organ, weighing on average 342 grams. Each day it beats over 100 000 times to pump 3780 litres of blood through 100 000 kilometres of blood vessels. It comprises a system of four muscular chambers (two **atria** and two **ventricles**) that alternately fill and empty of blood, acting as a double pump.

The left side pumps blood to the body tissues and the right side pumps blood to the lungs. The heart lies between the lungs, to the left of the body's midline, and it is surrounded by a double layered **pericardium** of tough fibrous connective tissue. The pericardium prevents overdistension of the heart and anchors the heart within the **mediastinum**.

Human Heart Structure

(sectioned, anterior view)

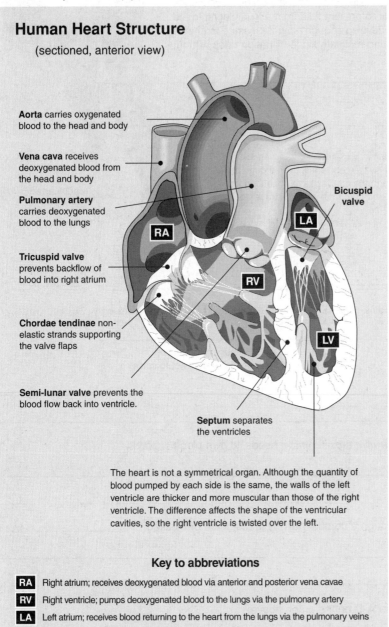

Aorta carries oxygenated blood to the head and body

Vena cava receives deoxygenated blood from the head and body

Pulmonary artery carries deoxygenated blood to the lungs

Tricuspid valve prevents backflow of blood into right atrium

Chordae tendinae non-elastic strands supporting the valve flaps

Semi-lunar valve prevents the blood flow back into ventricle.

Bicuspid valve

Septum separates the ventricles

The heart is not a symmetrical organ. Although the quantity of blood pumped by each side is the same, the walls of the left ventricle are thicker and more muscular than those of the right ventricle. The difference affects the shape of the ventricular cavities, so the right ventricle is twisted over the left.

Key to abbreviations

RA Right atrium; receives deoxygenated blood via anterior and posterior vena cavae

RV Right ventricle; pumps deoxygenated blood to the lungs via the pulmonary artery

LA Left atrium; receives blood returning to the heart from the lungs via the pulmonary veins

LV Left ventricle; pumps oxygenated blood to the head and body via the aorta

Top view of a heart in section, showing valves

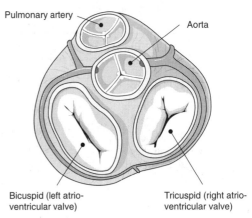

Pulmonary artery

Aorta

Bicuspid (left atrio-ventricular valve)

Tricuspid (right atrio-ventricular valve)

Posterior view of heart

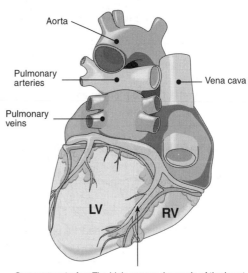

Aorta

Pulmonary arteries

Pulmonary veins

Vena cava

LV

RV

Coronary arteries: The high oxygen demands of the heart muscle are met by a dense capillary network. Coronary arteries arise from the aorta and spread over the surface of the heart supplying the cardiac muscle with oxygenated blood. Deoxygenated blood is collected by cardiac veins and returned to the right atrium via a large coronary sinus.

1. In the schematic diagram of the heart, below, label the four chambers and the main vessels entering and leaving them. The arrows indicate the direction of blood flow. Use large coloured circles to mark the position of each of the four valves.

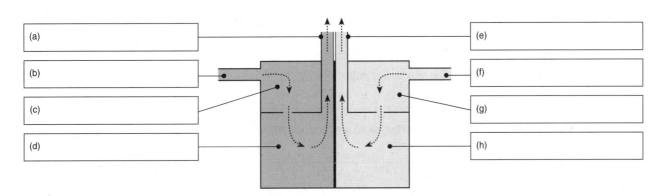

(a)

(b)

(c)

(d)

(e)

(f)

(g)

(h)

Related activities: Review of the Human Heart, Cardiovascular Disease
Web links: Anatomy of the Heart

RA 2

Transport Systems

Pressure Changes and the Asymmetry of the Heart

aorta, 100 mg Hg

The heart is not a symmetrical organ. The left ventricle and its associated arteries are thicker and more muscular than the corresponding structures on the right side. This asymmetry is related to the necessary pressure differences between the pulmonary (lung) and systemic (body) circulations (not to the distance over which the blood is pumped per se). The graph below shows changes blood pressure in each of the major blood vessel types in the systemic and pulmonary circuits (the horizontal distance not to scale). The pulmonary circuit must operate at a much lower pressure than the systemic circuit to prevent fluid from accumulating in the alveoli of the lungs. The left side of the heart must develop enough "spare" pressure to enable increased blood flow to the muscles of the body and maintain kidney filtration rates without decreasing the blood supply to the brain.

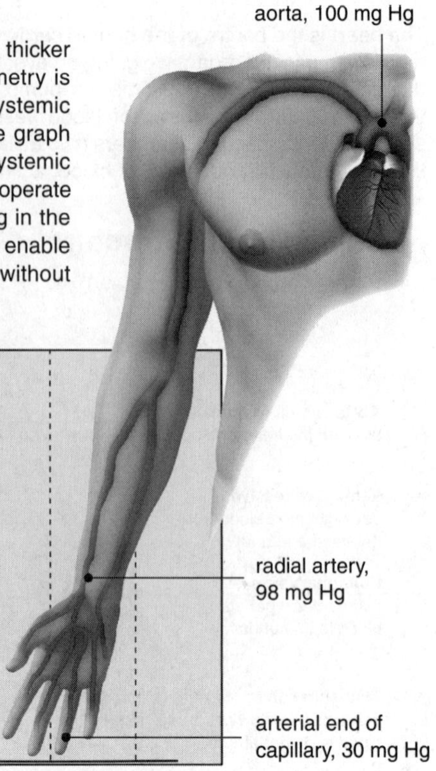

Blood pressure during contraction (systole)

Blood pressure during contraction (diastole)

The greatest fall in pressure occurs when the blood moves into the capillaries, even though the distance through the capillaries represents only a tiny proportion of the total distance travelled.

radial artery, 98 mg Hg

arterial end of capillary, 30 mg Hg

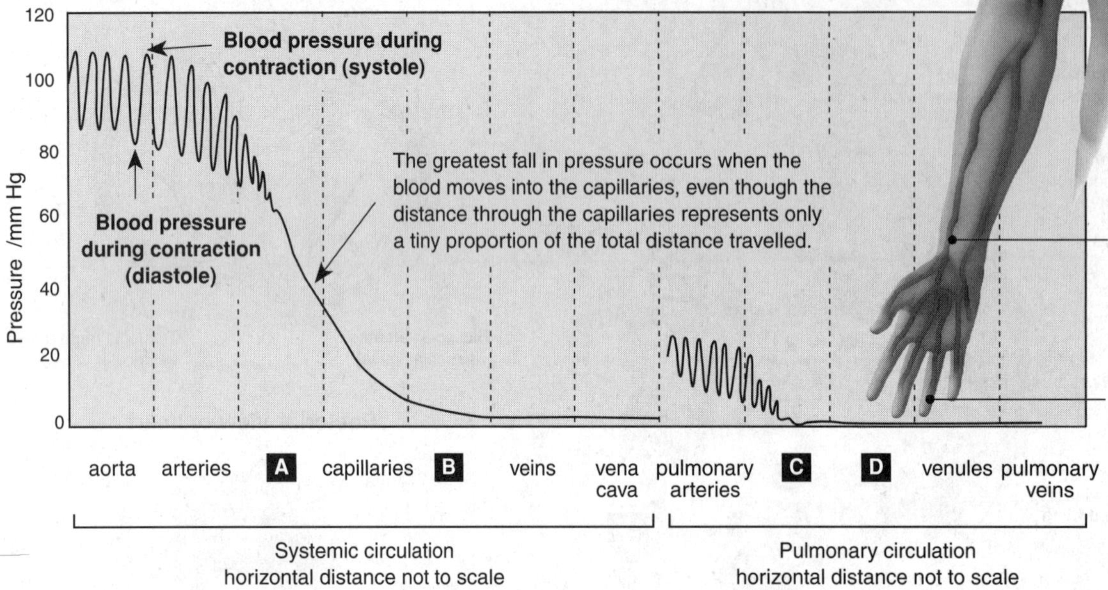

Pressure /mm Hg

120 · 100 · 80 · 60 · 40 · 20 · 0

aorta arteries **A** capillaries **B** veins vena cava pulmonary arteries **C** **D** venules pulmonary veins

Systemic circulation
horizontal distance not to scale

Pulmonary circulation
horizontal distance not to scale

2. Explain the purpose of the valves in the heart: _____

_____

3. The heart is full of blood. Suggest two reasons why, despite this, it needs its own blood supply:

(a) _____

(b) _____

4. Predict the effect on the heart if blood flow through a coronary artery is restricted or blocked: _____

_____

_____

5. Identify the vessels corresponding to the letters **A-D** on the graph above:

A: _____ B: _____ C: _____ D: _____

6. (a) Find out what is meant by the pulse pressure and explain how it is calculated: _____

_____

(b) Predict what happens to the pulse pressure between the aorta and the capillaries: _____

_____

7. (a) Explain what you are recording when you take a pulse: _____

_____

(b) Name a place where pulse rate could best be taken and briefly explain why: _____

_____

_____

Control of Heart Activity

When removed from the body the cardiac muscle continues to beat. Therefore, the origin of the heartbeat is **myogenic**: the contractions arise as an intrinsic property of the cardiac muscle itself. The heartbeat is regulated by a special conduction system consisting of the pacemaker (**sinoatrial node**) and specialised conduction fibres called **Purkinje fibres**. The pacemaker sets a basic rhythm for the heart, but this rate is influenced by the cardiovascular control centre in the medulla in response to sensory information from pressure receptors in the walls of the heart and blood vessels, and by higher brain functions. Changing the rate and force of heart contraction is the main mechanism for controlling cardiac output in order to meet changing demands.

Generation of the Heartbeat

The basic rhythmic heartbeat is **myogenic**. The nodal cells (SAN and atrioventricular node) spontaneously generate rhythmic action potentials without neural stimulation. The normal resting rate of self-excitation of the SAN is about 50 beats per minute.

The amount of blood ejected from the left ventricle per minute is called the **cardiac output**. It is determined by the **stroke volume** (the volume of blood ejected with each contraction) and the **heart rate** (number of heart beats per minute).

> **Cardiac output**
> = **stroke volume** x **heart rate**

Cardiac muscle responds to stretching by contracting more strongly. The greater the blood volume entering the ventricle, the greater the force of contraction. This relationship is known as **Starling's Law.**

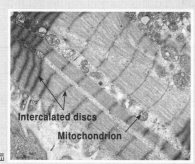

A TEM photo of cardiac muscle showing branched fibres (muscle cells). Each muscle fibre has one or two nuclei and many large mitochondria. **Intercalated discs** are specialised electrical junctions that separate the cells and allow the rapid spread of impulses through the heart muscle.

Sinoatrial node (SAN) is also called the **pacemaker**. It is a mass of specialised muscle cells near the opening of the superior vena cava. The pacemaker initiates the cardiac cycle, spontaneously generating action potentials that cause the atria to contract. The SAN sets the basic pace of the heart rate, although this rate is influenced by hormones and impulses from the autonomic nervous system.

Atrioventricular node (AVN) at the base of the atrium briefly delays the impulse to allow time for the atrial contraction to finish before the ventricles contract.

Bundle of His (atrioventricular bundle) containing Purkinje tissue. A tract of conducting fibres that distribute the action potentials over the ventricles causing ventricular contraction.

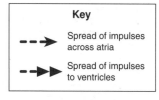

Key	
– – –▸	Spread of impulses across atria
– –▸▸	Spread of impulses to ventricles

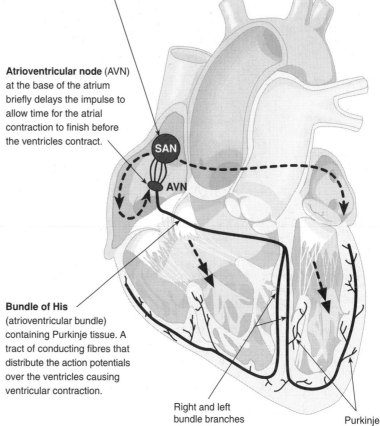

Right and left bundle branches

Purkinje fibres

Transport Systems

1. Identify the role of each of the following in heart activity:

   (a) The sinoatrial node: _____

   (b) The atrioventricular node: _____

   (c) The bundle of His: _____

2. Explain the significance of the delay in impulse conduction at the AVN: _____

   _____

3. (a) Calculate the cardiac output when stroke volume is 70 cm³ and the heart rate is 70 beats per minute:

   _____

   (b) Trained endurance athletes have a very high cardiac output. Suggest how this is achieved: _____

   _____

Autonomic Nervous System
Control of Heartbeat

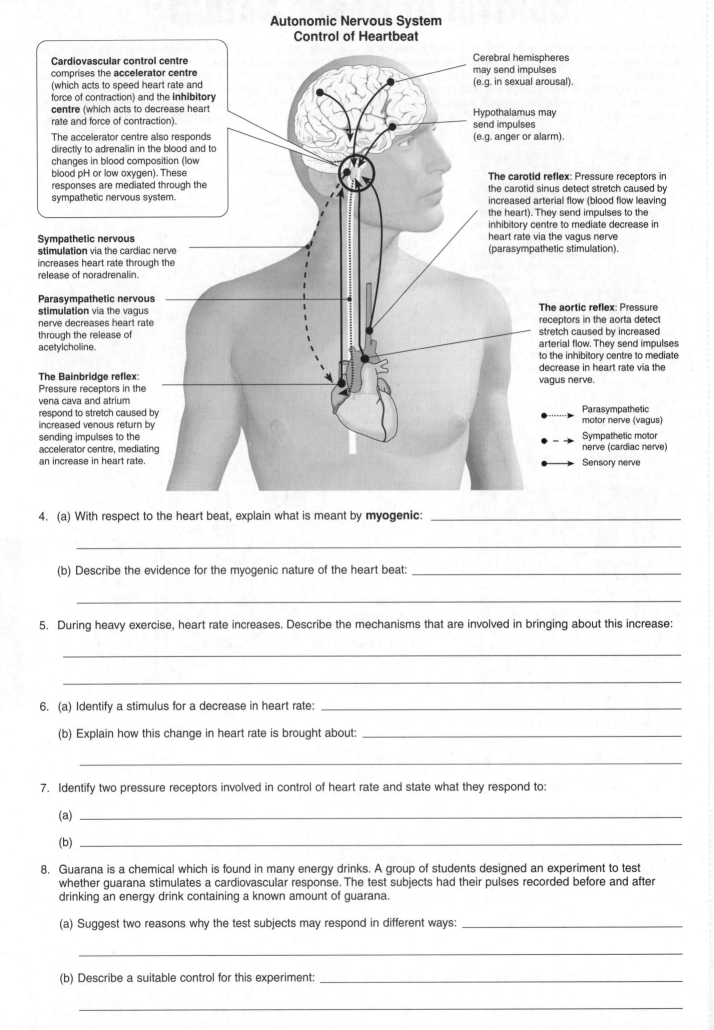

Cardiovascular control centre comprises the **accelerator centre** (which acts to speed heart rate and force of contraction) and the **inhibitory centre** (which acts to decrease heart rate and force of contraction).

The accelerator centre also responds directly to adrenalin in the blood and to changes in blood composition (low blood pH or low oxygen). These responses are mediated through the sympathetic nervous system.

Sympathetic nervous stimulation via the cardiac nerve increases heart rate through the release of noradrenalin.

Parasympathetic nervous stimulation via the vagus nerve decreases heart rate through the release of acetylcholine.

The Bainbridge reflex: Pressure receptors in the vena cava and atrium respond to stretch caused by increased venous return by sending impulses to the accelerator centre, mediating an increase in heart rate.

Cerebral hemispheres may send impulses (e.g. in sexual arousal).

Hypothalamus may send impulses (e.g. anger or alarm).

The carotid reflex: Pressure receptors in the carotid sinus detect stretch caused by increased arterial flow (blood flow leaving the heart). They send impulses to the inhibitory centre to mediate decrease in heart rate via the vagus nerve (parasympathetic stimulation).

The aortic reflex: Pressure receptors in the aorta detect stretch caused by increased arterial flow. They send impulses to the inhibitory centre to mediate decrease in heart rate via the vagus nerve.

●┈┈► Parasympathetic motor nerve (vagus)

●- -► Sympathetic motor nerve (cardiac nerve)

●—► Sensory nerve

4. (a) With respect to the heart beat, explain what is meant by **myogenic**: _____

_____

(b) Describe the evidence for the myogenic nature of the heart beat: _____

_____

5. During heavy exercise, heart rate increases. Describe the mechanisms that are involved in bringing about this increase:

_____

_____

6. (a) Identify a stimulus for a decrease in heart rate: _____

(b) Explain how this change in heart rate is brought about: _____

_____

7. Identify two pressure receptors involved in control of heart rate and state what they respond to:

(a) _____

(b) _____

8. Guarana is a chemical which is found in many energy drinks. A group of students designed an experiment to test whether guarana stimulates a cardiovascular response. The test subjects had their pulses recorded before and after drinking an energy drink containing a known amount of guarana.

(a) Suggest two reasons why the test subjects may respond in different ways: _____

_____

(b) Describe a suitable control for this experiment: _____

_____

The Cardiac Cycle

The **cardiac cycle** refers to the sequence of events of a heartbeat The pumping of the heart consists of alternate contractions (**systole**) and relaxations (**diastole**). During a complete cycle, each chamber undergoes a systole and a diastole. For a heart beating at 75 beats per minute, one cardiac cycle lasts about 0.8 seconds. Pressure changes within the heart's chambers generated by the cycle of contraction and relaxation are responsible for blood movement and cause the heart valves to open and close, preventing the backflow of blood. The noise of the blood when the valves open and close produces the heartbeat sound (**lubb-dupp**).

The Cardiac Cycle

The **pulse** results from the rhythmic expansion of the arteries as the blood spurts from the left ventricle. Pulse rate therefore corresponds to heart rate.

Stage 1: Atrial systole and ventricular filling The ventricles relax and blood flows into them from the atria. Note that 70% of the blood from the atria flows passively into the ventricles. It is during the last third of ventricular filling that the atria contract.

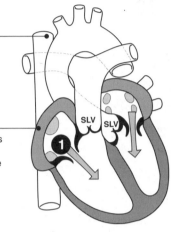

Heart during ventricular filling

Stage 2: Ventricular systole The atria relax, the ventricles contract, and blood is pumped from the ventricles into the aorta and the pulmonary artery. The start of ventricular contraction coincides with the first heart sound.

Stage 3: (not shown) There is a short period of atrial and ventricular relaxation (diastole). Semilunar valves (**SLV**) close to prevent backflow into the ventricles (see diagram, left). The cycle begins again.

Atrio-ventricular valves closed

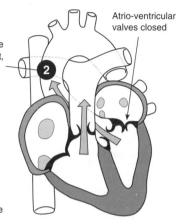

Heart during ventricular contraction

The Cardiac Cycle and the ECG

The electrical impulses transmitted through the heart generate electrical currents that can be detected by placing metal electrodes on the body's surface. They can be recorded on a heart monitor as a trace, called an **electrocardiogram** or ECG. The ECG pattern is the result of the different impulses produced at each phase of the **cardiac cycle**. A normal ECG (below) shows a regular repeating pattern of electrical pulses. Each wave of electrical activity brings about a corresponding contraction in the part of the heart receiving the electrical impulse. Each part of the ECG is given a letter according to an international code (below). An ECG provides a useful method of monitoring changes in heart rate and activity and detection of heart disorders.

The QRS complex: This corresponds to the spread of the impulse through the ventricles, which contract.

The T wave: This signals recovery of the electrical activity of the ventricles, which are relaxed.

The P wave: This represents the spread of the impulse from the pacemaker through the atria, which then contract.

The interval between successive beats allows the heart rate to be calculated.

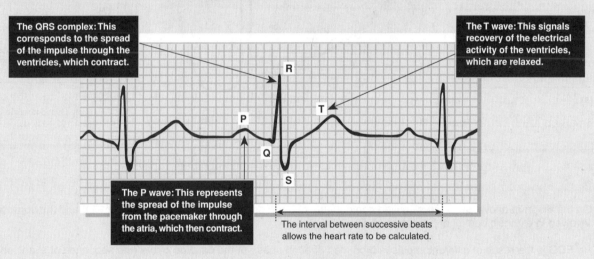

1. Identify each of the following phases of an ECG by its international code:

   (a) Excitation of the ventricles and ventricular systole: _____

   (b) Electrical recovery of the ventricles and ventricular diastole: _____

   (c) Excitation of the atria and atrial systole: _____

2. Suggest the physiological reason for the period of electrical recovery experienced each cycle (the T wave):

   _____

   _____

   _____

Related activities: The Human Heart, Review of the Human Heart, Correcting Heart Problems   **Web links**: Electrocardiogram

RA 2

Transport Systems

Review of the Human Heart

Large, complex organisms require a circulatory system to transport materials because diffusion is too inefficient and slow to supply all the cells of the body adequately. The circulatory system in humans transports nutrients, respiratory gases, wastes, and hormones, aids in regulating body temperature and maintaining fluid balance, and has a role in internal defence. All circulatory systems comprise a network of vessels, a circulatory fluid (blood), and a heart. This activity summarises key features of the structure and function of the human heart. The information for this activity can be found in the pages earlier in this topic.

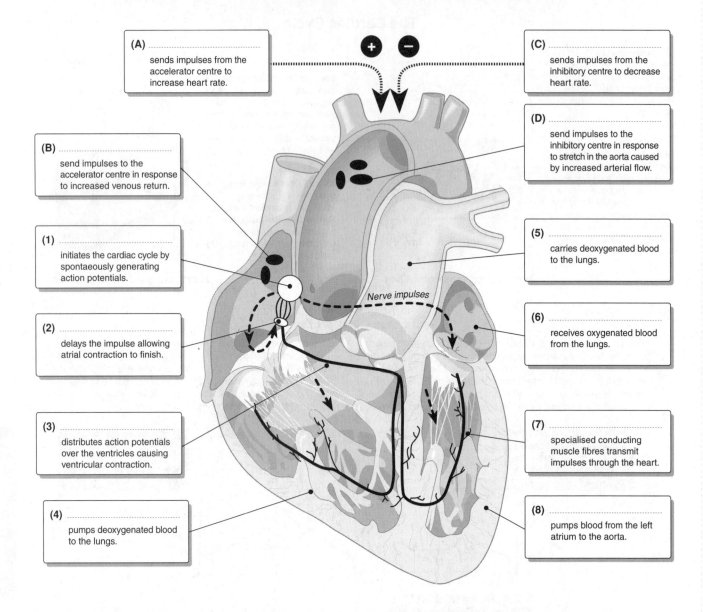

(A) ....
sends impulses from the accelerator centre to increase heart rate.

(C) ....
sends impulses from the inhibitory centre to decrease heart rate.

(B) ....
send impulses to the accelerator centre in response to increased venous return.

(D) ....
send impulses to the inhibitory centre in response to stretch in the aorta caused by increased arterial flow.

(1) ....
initiates the cardiac cycle by spontaeously generating action potentials.

(5) ....
carries deoxygenated blood to the lungs.

(2) ....
delays the impulse allowing atrial contraction to finish.

(6) ....
receives oxygenated blood from the lungs.

(3) ....
distributes action potentials over the ventricles causing ventricular contraction.

(7) ....
specialised conducting muscle fibres transmit impulses through the heart.

(4) ....
pumps deoxygenated blood to the lungs.

(8) ....
pumps blood from the left atrium to the aorta.

Nerve impulses

1. On the diagram above, label the identified components of heart structure and intrinsic control (**1-8**), and the components involved in extrinsic control of heart rate (**A-D**).

2. An **ECG** is the result of different impulses produced at each phase of the **cardiac cycle** (the sequence of events in a heartbeat). For each electrical event indicated in the ECG below, describe the corresponding event in the cardiac cycle:

   A --
   The spread of the impulse from the pacemaker (sinoatrial node) through the atria.

   B --
   The spread of the impulse through the ventricles.

   C --
   Recovery of the electrical activity of the ventricles.

   Electrical activity in the heart

3. Describe one treatment that may be indicated when heart rhythm is erratic or too slow: _____

_____

Exercise and Blood Flow

Exercise promotes health by improving the rate of blood flow back to the heart (venous return). This is achieved by strengthening all types of muscle and by increasing the efficiency of the heart. During exercise blood flow to different parts of the body changes in order to cope with the extra demands of the muscles, the heart and the lungs.

1. The following table gives data for the **rate** of blood flow to various parts of the body at rest and during strenuous exercise. **Calculate** the **percentage** of the total blood flow that each organ or tissue receives under each regime of activity.

Organ or tissue	At rest		Strenuous exercise	
	$cm^3 min^{-1}$	% of total	$cm^3 min^{-1}$	% of total
Brain	700	14	750	4.2
Heart	200		750	
Lung tissue	100		200	
Kidneys	1100		600	
Liver	1350		600	
Skeletal muscles	750		12 500	
Bone	250		250	
Skin	300		1900	
Thyroid gland	50		50	
Adrenal glands	25		25	
Other tissue	175		175	
TOTAL	5000	**100**	17 800	**100**

2. Explain how the body increases the rate of blood flow during exercise: _____

_____

_____

3. (a) State approximately how many times the total rate of blood flow increases between rest and exercise: _____

(b) Explain why the increase is necessary: _____

_____

_____

4. (a) Identify which organs or tissues show no change in the rate of blood flow with exercise: _____

_____

(b) Explain why this is the case: _____

_____

_____

5. (a) Identify which organs or tissues show the most change in the rate of blood flow with exercise: _____

_____

(b) Explain why this is the case: _____

_____

_____

_____

Related activities: Energy and Exercise, The Health Benefits of Exercise
Web links: Effects of Training

Transport Systems

DA 2

Endurance refers to the ability of the muscles and the cardiovascular and respiratory systems to carry out exercise. Muscular endurance allows sprinters to run fast for a short time or body builders and weight lifters to lift an immense weight and hold it for a few seconds. Cardiovascular and respiratory endurance refer to the body as a whole: the ability to endure a high level of activity over a prolonged period. This type of endurance is seen in marathon runners, and long distance swimmers and cyclists. Different sports ("short burst sports" compared with endurance type sports) require different training methods and the physiologies (muscle bulk and cardiovascular fitness) of the athletes can be quite different.

The human heart and circulatory system make a number of adjustments in response to aerobic or endurance training. These include:

- **Heart size**: Increases. The left ventricle wall becomes thicker and its chamber bigger.

- **Heart rate**: Heart rate (at rest and during exercise) decreases markedly from non-trained people.

- **Recovery**: Recovery after exercise (of breathing and heart rate) is faster in trained athletes.

- **Stroke volume**: The volume of blood pumped with each heart beat increases with endurance training.

- **Blood volume**: Endurance training increases blood volume (the amount of blood in the body).

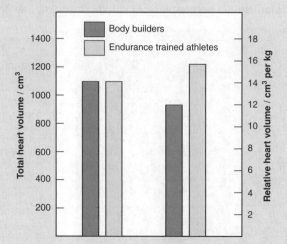

Difference in heart size of highly trained body builders and endurance athletes. Total heart volume is compared to heart volume as related to body weight. Average weights as follows: Body builders = 90.1 kg. Endurance athletes = 68.7 kg.

Weightlifters have good muscular endurance; they lift extremely heavy weights and hold them for a short time. Typical sports with high muscular endurance but lower cardiovascular endurance are sprinting, weight lifting, body building, boxing and wrestling.

Distance runners have very good cardiovascular and respiratory endurance; they sustain high intensity exercise for a long time. Typical sports needing cardiovascular endurance are distance running, cycling, and swimming (triathletes combine all three).

6. Suggest a reason why heart size increases with cardiovascular endurance activity: _____

_____

7. In the graph above right, explain why the relative heart volume of endurance athletes is greater than that of body builders, even though their total heart volumes are the same:

_____

8. Heart stroke volume increases with endurance training. Explain how this increases the efficiency of the heart as a pump:

_____

9. Resting heart rates are much lower in trained athletes compared with non-active people. Explain the health benefits of a lower resting heart rate:

_____

_____

Transport in Plants

The support and transport systems in plants are closely linked; many of the same tissues are involved in both systems. Primitive plants (e.g. mosses and liverworts) are small and low growing, and have no need for support and transport systems. If a plant is to grow to any size, it must have ways to hold itself up against gravity and to move materials around its body. The body of a flowering plant has three parts: **roots** anchor the plant and absorb nutrients from the soil, **leaves** produce sugars by photosynthesis, and **stems** link the roots to the leaves and provide support for the leaves and reproductive structures. Vascular tissues (xylem and phloem) link all plant parts so that water, minerals, and manufactured food can be transported between different regions. All plants rely on fluid pressure within their cells (turgor) to give some support to their structure.

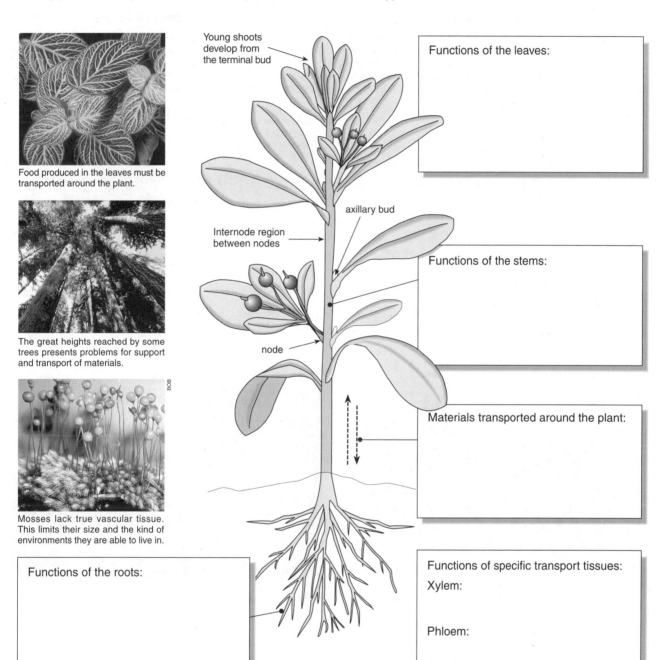

Food produced in the leaves must be transported around the plant.

The great heights reached by some trees presents problems for support and transport of materials.

Mosses lack true vascular tissue. This limits their size and the kind of environments they are able to live in.

Young shoots develop from the terminal bud

axillary bud

Internode region between nodes

node

Functions of the leaves:

Functions of the stems:

Materials transported around the plant:

Functions of specific transport tissues:
Xylem:

Phloem:

Functions of the roots:

Transport Systems

1. In the boxes provided in the diagram above:

   (a) List the main functions of the leaves, roots and stems (remember that the leaves themselves have leaf veins).

   (b) List the materials that are transported around the plant body.

   (c) Describe the functions of the transport tissues: xylem and phloem.

2. Name the solvent for all the materials that are transported around the plant: _____

3. State what processes are involved in the transport of sap in the following tissues:

   (a) The xylem: _____

   (b) The phloem: _____

Related activities: Stem Structure, Xylem, Phloem, Root structure, Uptake at the Root, Translocation

RA 1

Stem Structure

The stems of most plants are the primary organs for supporting the plant. Stems have distinct points, called **nodes**, at which leaves and buds attach. The region of the stem between two nodes is called the **internode** (see previous page). Regardless of their shape or location, all stems can be distinguished as such by the presence of nodes and internodes. Stems, like most parts of the plant, contain vascular tissues. These take the form of bundles containing the xylem and phloem and strengthening fibres. The arrangement of these bundles in the stem depends on the plant type (e.g. monocot or dicot). The growth that leads to the young, flexible stem is called **primary growth**. The increase in the girth (diameter) of the stem is the result of **secondary growth** and is caused by the production of wood. All plants have primary growth but only some plants show secondary growth.

Dicot Stem Structure

In dicots, each vascular bundle contains **xylem** (to the inside) and **phloem** (to the outside). Between the phloem and the xylem is the **vascular cambium**; a layer of cells that divide to produce the thickening of the stem. The middle of the stem, called the **pith**, is filled with thin-walled parenchyma cells. The vascular bundles in dicots are arranged in an orderly way around the periphery of the stem (below).

Monocot Stem Structure

The main features of monocot stem structure are illustrated below. The ground tissue of the stem comprises large parenchyma cells (there is no distinction between cortex and pith). Note how the vascular bundles are scattered randomly through the stem. Contrast this with the orderly arrangement of the vascular bundles in the dicot stem.

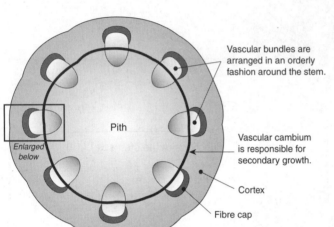

Vascular bundles are arranged in an orderly fashion around the stem.

Pith

Enlarged below

Vascular cambium is responsible for secondary growth.

Cortex

Fibre cap

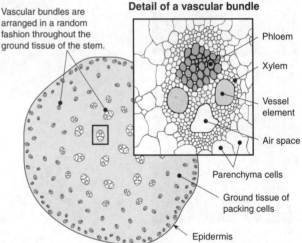

Vascular bundles are arranged in a random fashion throughout the ground tissue of the stem.

Detail of a vascular bundle

Phloem

Xylem

Vessel element

Air space

Parenchyma cells

Ground tissue of packing cells

Epidermis

Cross section through a typical dicot stem

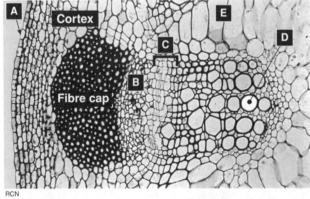

A

Cortex

E

C

D

B

Fibre cap

RCN

Cross section through a corn stem

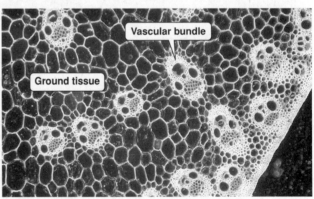

Vascular bundle

Ground tissue

1. Use the information provided to identify the structures labelled **A-E** in the photograph of the dicot stem above:

    (a) A: _____ (b) B: _____ (c) C: _____

    (d) D: _____ (e) E: _____

2. Identify the feature that distinguishes stems from other parts of the plant: _____

    _____

3. (a) Identify a distinguishing feature of stem structure in dicots: _____

    (b) Contrast the arrangement of the vascular bundles in monocots and dicots: _____

    _____

    _____

4. Describe the role of the vascular cambium: _____

    _____

Related activities: Support in Plants, Xylem, Phloem

Translocation

Phloem transports the organic products of photosynthesis (sugars) through the plant in a process called **translocation**. In angiosperms, the sugar moves through the sieve elements, which are arranged end-to-end and perforated with sieve plates. Apart from water, phloem sap comprises mainly sucrose (up to 30%). It may also contain minerals, hormones, and amino acids, in transit around the plant. Movement of sap in the phloem is from a **source** (a plant organ where sugar is made or mobilised) to a **sink** (a plant organ where sugar is stored or used). Loading sucrose into the phloem at a source involves energy expenditure; it is slowed or stopped by high temperatures or respiratory inhibitors. In some plants, unloading the sucrose at the sinks also requires energy, although in others, diffusion alone is sufficient to move sucrose from the phloem into the cells of the sink organ.

Transport in the Phloem by Pressure-Flow

Phloem sap moves from source (region where sugar is produced or mobilised) to sink (region where sugar is used or stored) at rates as great as 100 m h^{-1}: too fast to be accounted for by cytoplasmic streaming. The most acceptable model for phloem movement is the **pressure-flow** (bulk flow) hypothesis. Phloem sap moves by bulk flow, which creates a pressure (hence the term "pressure-flow"). The key elements in this model are outlined below and in steps 1-4 right. For simplicity, the cells that lie between the source or sink cells and the phloem sieve-tube have been omitted.

1 Loading sugar into the phloem from a source (e.g. leaf cell) increases the solute concentration (decreases the water potential, ψ) inside the sieve-tube cells. This causes the sieve-tubes to take up water from the surrounding tissues by osmosis.

2 The water absorption creates a hydrostatic pressure that forces the sap to move along the tube (bulk flow), just as pressure pushes water through a hose.

3 The gradient of pressure in the sieve tube is reinforced by the active unloading of sugar and consequent loss of water by osmosis at the sink (e.g. root cell).

4 Xylem recycles the water from sink to source.

Measuring Phloem Flow

Experiments investigating flow of phloem often use aphids. Aphids feed on phloem sap (left) and act as natural **phloem probes**. When the mouthparts (stylet) of an aphid penetrate a sieve-tube cell, the pressure in the sieve-tube force-feeds the aphid. While the aphid feeds, it can be severed from its stylet, which remains in place in the phloem. The stylet serves as a tiny tap that exudes sap. Using different aphids, the rate of flow of this sap can be measured at different locations on the plant.

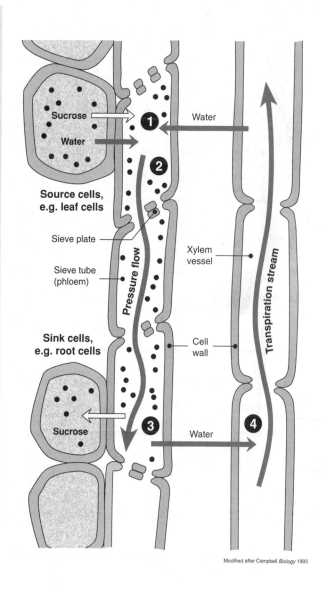

Modified after Campbell *Biology* 1993

Transport Systems

1. (a) Explain what is meant by '**source to sink**' flow in phloem transport: _____

    _____

    (b) Name the usual **source** and **sink** in a growing plant:

    Source: _____   Sink: _____

    (c) Name another possible **source** region in the plant and state when it might be important: _____

    _____

    (d) Name another possible **sink** region in the plant and state when it might be important: _____

    _____

2. Explain why energy is required for translocation and where it is used: _____

    _____

Related activities: Xylem, Phloem, Active and Passive Transport
Web links: Translocation, Sucrose Transport

RA 3

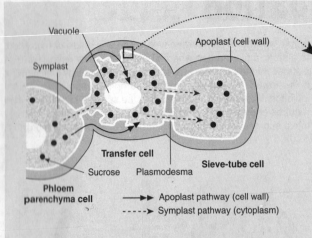

Coupled Transport of Sucrose

High H+ concentration   Apoplast (cell wall)

Sucrose

Proton pump

Diffusion of hydrogen ions

Coupled transport

Plasma membrane

Carrier protein

Membrane protein (symport)

ATP   ADP + P_i

Symplast of transfer cell

Vacuole

Apoplast (cell wall)

Symplast

Transfer cell

Sieve-tube cell

Sucrose   Plasmodesma

Phloem parenchyma cell

➤➤ Apoplast pathway (cell wall)
----➤ Symplast pathway (cytoplasm)

Loading Sucrose into the Phloem

Sugar (sucrose) can travel to the phloem sieve-tubes through both apoplastic and symplastic pathways. It is loaded into the phloem sieve-tube cells via modified companion cells, called **transfer cells** (above). Loading sucrose into the phloem requires active transport. Using a **coupled transport** (secondary pump) mechanism (right), transfer cells expend energy to accumulate the sucrose. The sucrose then passes into the sieve tube through plasmodesmata. The transfer cells have wall ingrowths that increase surface area for the transport of solutes. Using this mechanism, some plants can accumulate sucrose in the phloem to 2-3 times the concentration in the mesophyll.

Above: Proton pumps generate a hydrogen ion gradient across the membrane of the transfer cell. This process requires expenditure of energy. The gradient is then used to drive the transport of sucrose, by coupling the sucrose transport to the diffusion of H+ back into the cell.

3. your own words, describe what is meant by the following:

Translocation: _____

_____

Pressure-flow movement of phloem: _____

_____

(c) upled transport of sucrose: _____

4. Brie explain why water follows the sucrose as the sucrose is loaded into the phloem sieve-tube cell:

_____

_____

5. Expla the role of the companion (transfer) cell in the loading of sucrose into the phloem: _____

_____

_____

6. Contra th omposition of phloem sap and xylem sap (see the activities on xylem and phloem if you need help):

_____

_____

7. Expla why it necessary for phloem to be alive to be functional, whereas xylem can function as a dead tissue:

_____

_____

8. The e plate repr esents a significant barrier to effective mass flow of phloem sap. Suggest why the presence of the sie plate is often ited as evidence against the pressure-flow model for phloem transport:

_____

_____

_____

Adaptations of Xerophytes

Without sufficient water plant cells lose **turgor** and the tissue wilts. If a plant passes its **permanent wilting point** it will die. Water is lost from the plant by **transpiration**: the loss of water vapour, primarily through the stomata. Water balance is not a problem for aquatic plants; they allow water to flow in by osmosis until the cell wall stops further expansion. Plants

adapted to dry conditions are called **xerophytes** and they show structural (xeromorphic) and physiological adaptations for water conservation. Some of these are outlined below. Halophytes (salt tolerant plants) and alpine species may also show xeromorphic features in response to the scarcity of obtainable water and high transpirational losses in these environments.

Tropical Forest Plant

Rain is channelled by funnel shaped leaves.

Loss of water by transpiration.

Shallow fibrous root system.

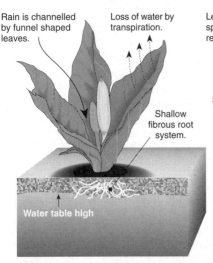

Water table high

Tropical plants live in areas of often high rainfall. There is also a corresponding high transpiration rate. Water availability is not a problem in this environment.

Dry Desert Plant

Leaves modified into spines or hairs to reduce water loss.

Surface area reduced by producing a squat, rounded plant shape.

Shallow, but extensive fibrous root system.

Stem becomes the major photosynthetic organ, plus a reservoir for water storage.

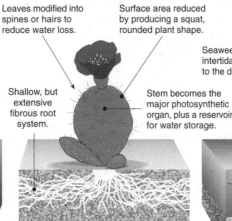

Water table low

Desert plants e.g. cacti, cope with low rainfall and high transpiration rates. Plants develop strategies to reduce water loss, store water, and access available water supplies.

Ocean Margin Plant

Mangrove trees take in brackish water, excreting the salt through glands in the leaves.

Seaweeds growing in the intertidal zone tolerate exposure to the drying air every 12 hours.

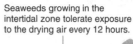
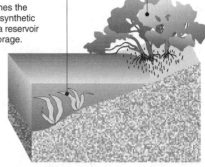

Land plants that colonise the shoreline (e.g. mangroves) must cope with high salt content in the water. Seaweeds below low tide do not have a water balance problem.

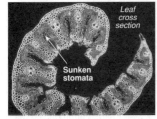

Leaf cross section

Sunken stomata

Grasses living in dry areas curl their leaves and have sunken stomata.

Mosses are poor at obtaining and storing water, restricting distribution.

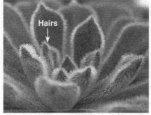

Hairs

Hairs on leaves trap air close to the surface, reducing transpiration rate.

Water droplets

Excess water is forced from leaves (guttation) during high humidity.

Transport Systems

Methods of water conservation in various plant species		
Adaptation for water conservation	**Effect of adaptation**	**Example**
Thick, waxy cuticle to stems and leaves	Reduces water loss through the cuticle.	*Pinus* sp. ivy (*Hedera*), sea holly (*Eryngium*), prickly pear (*Opuntia*).
Reduced number of stomata	Reduces the number of pores through which water loss can occur.	Prickly pear (*Opuntia*), *Nerium* sp.
Stomata sunken in pits, grooves, or depressions Leaf surface covered with fine hairs Massing of leaves into a rosette at ground level	Moist air is trapped close to the area of water loss, reducing the diffusion gradient and therefore the rate of water loss.	**Sunken stomata**: *Pinus* sp., *Hakea* sp. **Hairy leaves**: lamb's ear. **Leaf rosettes**: dandelion (*Taraxacum*), daisy.
Stomata closed during the light, open at night	CAM metabolism: CO_2 is fixed during the night, water loss in the day is minimized.	**CAM plants**, e.g. American aloe, pineapple, *Kalanchoe*, *Yucca*.
Leaves reduced to scales, stem photosynthetic Leaves curled, rolled, or folded when flaccid	Reduction in surface area from which transpiration can occur.	**Leaf scales**: broom (*Cytisus*). **Rolled leaf**: marram grass (*Ammophila*), *Erica* sp.
Fleshy or succulent stems Fleshy or succulent leaves	When readily available, water is stored in the tissues for times of low availability.	**Fleshy stems**: *Opuntia*, candle plant (*Kleinia*). **Fleshy leaves**: *Bryophyllum*.
Deep root system below the water table	Roots tap into the lower water table.	Acacias, oleander.
Shallow root system absorbing surface moisture	Roots absorb overnight condensation.	Most cacti

Related activities: Transpiration, Adaptations of Hydrophytes

A 1

Adaptations in halophytes and drought tolerant plants

Ice plant (*Carpobrotus*): The leaves of many desert and beach dwelling plants are fleshy or succulent. The leaves are triangular in cross section and crammed with water storage cells. The water is stored after rain for use in dry periods. The shallow root system is able to take up water from the soil surface, taking advantage of any overnight condensation.

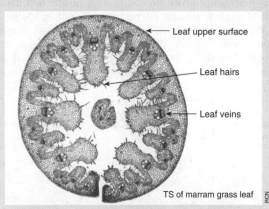

Leaf upper surface

Leaf hairs

Leaf veins

TS of marram grass leaf

Marram grass (*Ammophila*): The long, wiry leaf blades of this beach grass are curled downwards with the stomata on the inside. This protects them against drying out by providing a moist microclimate around the stomata. Plants adapted to high altitude often have similar adaptations.

Ball cactus (*Echinocactus grusonii*): In cacti, the leaves are modified into long, thin spines which project outward from the thick fleshy stem (see close-up above right). This reduces the surface area over which water loss can occur. The stem takes over the role of producing the food for the plant and also stores water during rainy periods for use during drought. As in succulents like ice plant, the root system in cacti is shallow to take advantage of surface water appearing as a result of overnight condensation.

1. Explain the purpose of **xeromorphic** adaptations: _____

_____

2. Describe three xeromorphic adaptations of plants:

   (a) _____

   (b) _____

   (c) _____

3. Describe a physiological mechanism by which plants can reduce water loss during the daylight hours:

_____

_____

4. Explain why creating a moist microenvironment around the areas of water loss reduces transpiration rate:

_____

_____

5. Explain why seashore plants (halophytes) exhibit many desert-dwelling adaptations: _____

_____

_____

Adaptations of Hydrophytes

Hydrophytes are a group of plants that have adapted to living either partially or fully submerged in water. Survival in water poses different problems to those faced by terrestrial plants. Hydrophytes have a reduced root system, a feature that is often related to the relatively high concentration of nutrients in the sediment and the plant's ability to remove nitrogen and phosphorus directly from the water. The leaves of submerged plants are thin to increase the surface area of photosynthetic tissue and reduce internal shading. Hydrophytes typically have no cuticle (waterproof covering) or the cuticle is very thin. This enables the plant ability to absorb minerals and gases directly from the water. In addition, being supported by the water, they require very little in the way of structural support tissue.

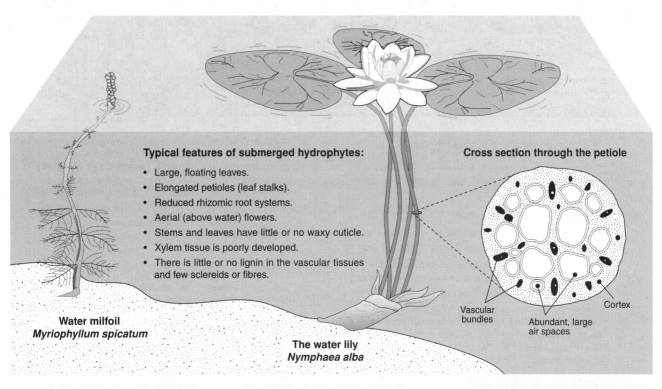

Typical features of submerged hydrophytes:

- Large, floating leaves.
- Elongated petioles (leaf stalks).
- Reduced rhizomic root systems.
- Aerial (above water) flowers.
- Stems and leaves have little or no waxy cuticle.
- Xylem tissue is poorly developed.
- There is little or no lignin in the vascular tissues and few sclereids or fibres.

Cross section through the petiole

Vascular bundles
Cortex
Abundant, large air spaces

Water milfoil
Myriophyllum spicatum

The water lily
Nymphaea alba

Myriophyllum's submerged leaves are well spaced and taper towards the surface to assist with gas exchange and distribution of sunlight.

The floating leaves of water lilies (*Nymphaea*) have a high density of stomata on the upper leaf surface so they are not blocked by water.

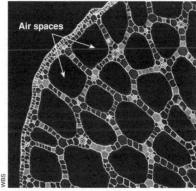

Air spaces

Cross section through *Potamogeton*, showing massive air spaces which assist with flotation and gas exchange.

Transport Systems

1. Explain how the following adaptations assist hydrophytes to survive in an aquatic environment:

   (a) Large air spaces within the plants tissues: _____

   _____

   (b) Thin cuticle: _____

   _____

   (c) High stomatal densities on the upper leaf surface: _____

   _____

2. Explain why hydrophytic plants have retained an aerial (above water) flowering system: _____

   _____

Related activities: Adaptations of Xerophytes

A 2

Defence and the Immune System

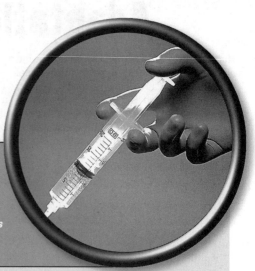

AQA-A	AQA-B	SNAB	Edexcel	OCR
Complete: 1-6, 9-32 Some numbers extension as appropriate	Not applicable in the AS course	Complete: 1-, 7-23, 25-32 (A2)	Not applicable in the AS course	Complete: 1-35 Some numbers extension as appropriate

Learning Objectives

☐ 1. Compile your own glossary from the **KEY WORDS** displayed in **bold type** in the learning objectives below.

Recognising Self and Non-self *(pages 262-263)*

☐ 2. Explain how a body is able to distinguish between self and non-self and comment on the importance of this.

☐ 3. Appreciate the nature of **major histocompatibility complex (MHC)** and its role in self-recognition and in determining tissue compatibility in transplant recipients.

☐ 4. Explain the basis of the **Rh** and **ABO blood group systems** in humans. Explain what is meant by **agglutination** and how this reaction forms the basis of blood grouping. Explain the consequences of blood type incompatibility in **blood transfusions**.

☐ 5. Appreciate that self-recognition poses problems for tissue and organ transplants. Explain the physiological basis of transplant rejection and suggest how it may be avoided. Identify the problems associated with finding compatible tissue and organ donors and suggest how this problem may be solved in the future.

Defence Mechanisms *(page 264)*

☐ 6. Describe the role of **blood clotting** in the resistance of the body to infection by sealing off damage and restricting invasion of the tissues by microorganisms.

Non-specific defences *(pages 265-269)*

☐ 7. Explain what is meant by a **non-specific defence mechanism**. Distinguish between first and second lines of defence. Describe the nature and role of each of the following in protecting against pathogens:

Preventing pathogen entry
- Skin (including sweat and sebum production)
- Mucus-secreting and ciliated membranes
- Body secretions (tears, urine, saliva, gastric juice)

Non-specific defence after pathogen entry
- Natural anti-bacterial and anti-viral proteins such as **interferon** and **complement**
- The **inflammatory response**, **fever**, and cell death
- **Phagocytosis**

☐ 8. Recognise the term phagocyte as referring to any of a number of phagocytic leucocytes (e.g. macrophages).

Specific defences *(pages 265, 270, 275)*

☐ 9. Identify the role of **specific resistance** in body's resistance to infection. Contrast specific and non-specific defences in terms of time for activation and specificity towards a pathogen.

☐ 10. Explain what is meant by an **immune response**. Explain how the immune response involves recognition and response to foreign material. Explain the significance of the immune system having both **specificity** and **memory**. Providing examples, distinguish between **naturally acquired** and **artificially acquired immunity** and between active and passive immunity. Compare the duration of the immunity gained by active and passive means.

☐ 11. Recognise the role of the **lymphatic system** in the production and transport of leucocytes.

The Immune System *(pages 271-274, 281-282)*

☐ 12. Distinguish between: **cell-mediated immunity** and **humoral (antibody-mediated) immunity**.

☐ 13. Recall that other types of white blood cells are involved in non-specific defence mechanisms.

☐ 14. Explain the role of the **thymus** in the immune response. Describe the nature, origin, and role of **macrophages** (a type of phagocyte). Appreciate the role of macrophages in processing and presenting foreign antigens and in stimulating lymphocyte activity.

☐ 15. Explain the origin and maturation of **B lymphocytes** (cells) and **T lymphocytes** (cells). Describe and distinguish between the activities of the B and T lymphocytes in the immune response.

☐ 16. Appreciate the significance of the **clonal selection theory** to the understanding of immune system function. Explain how the immune system is able to respond to the large and unpredictable range of potential antigens in the environment.

☐ 17. Appreciate that **self-tolerance** occurs during development as a result of the selective destruction of B cells that react to self-antigens.

Cell-mediated immunity

☐ 18. T cells are responsible for **cell-mediated immunity**. Describe how T cells recognise **specific** foreign antigens. Describe the functional roles of named T cells, including the **cytotoxic** (killer) **T cells** (T_C) and the **helper T cells** (T_H). Identify the organisms against which these T cells act.

☐ 19. Appreciate the role of T lymphocytes in the rejection of transplanted tissues and organs.

Humoral immunity

☐ 20. Describe how B cells bring about **humoral** (antibody-mediated) **immunity**. Identify the organisms that are the main targets for the humoral response.

☐ 21. Describe and contrast the functional roles of **plasma cells** and **memory cells** and explain the basis for **immunological memory**. Discuss the role of immunological memory in long term immunity (ability to respond quickly to previously encountered antigens).

☐ 22. Name some common **antigens** (**immunoglobulins**) and explain their role in provoking a specific immune response. Describe the structure of an **antibody**, identifying the constant and variable regions, and the antigen binding site. Relate the structure of antibodies to their function.

☐ 23. Describe the methods by which antibodies inactivate antigens and facilitate their destruction.

☐ 24. Describe the production and application of **monoclonal antibodies** in medical diagnosis and treatment.

Vaccines and Immunisation *(pages 275, 277-280)*

☐ 25. Recognise that immunisation provides **artificially acquired immunity**. Recall the difference between **passive** and **active immunity**.

☐ 26. Describe what is meant by a **primary** and a **secondary response** to infection. Explain the role of these responses and the immune system memory in the success of vaccines against specific pathogens.

☐ 27. Appreciate that **immunisation** involves the production of immunity by artificial means and that **vaccination** usually refers to immunisation by inoculation. Know that these terms are frequently used synonymously.

☐ 28. Explain the role of **vaccination** programmes in preventing disease. Discuss the role of aggressive vaccination programmes in the eradication (or near-eradication) of some (named) infectious diseases.

☐ 29. Explain the biological and sociological reasons why vaccination has been successful in eradicating some diseases (e.g. smallpox) but not other diseases such as measles, malaria, or cholera.

☐ 30. Outline the vaccination schedule for the UK, identifying critical times for vaccination against specific diseases. Comment on the role of effective vaccination programmes in public health and the incidence of infectious disease in the UK.

☐ 31. Describe the principles involved in the production of vaccines. Giving examples, explain how vaccines are administered. Distinguish between **subunit** and **whole-agent vaccines** and between **inactivated** (dead) and **live** (attenuated) **vaccines**. Contrast the risks and benefits associated with live and dead vaccines.

☐ 32. Evaluate the risks associated with immunisation. Compare these risks with the risks associated with contracting the disease itself.

Hypersensitivity Reactions *(page 276 and see the TRC: Allergies and Hypersensitivity)*

NOTE: The study of autoimmune disorders provides an ideal context for this topic, introducing ideas relevant to organ transplant technology and tissue rejection.

☐ 33. Explain what is meant by an **autoimmune disease** and provide examples. Define the terms: **allergy**, **allergen**, **hypersensitivity**, **sensitised**. Name some of the common triggers for allergies in susceptible people.

☐ 34. With reference to **asthma** and **hayfever**, outline the role of the immune system in allergic reactions. Include reference to the role of **histamine** in these allergies.

☐ 35. Provide examples of hypersensitivity reactions that differ in their speed of onset (rapid vs delayed).

See the 'Textbook Reference Grid' on pages 8-9 for textbook page references relating to material in this topic.

Supplementary Texts

See pages 5-7 for additional details of these texts:

■ Clegg, C.J., 1998. **Mammals: Structure and Function** (John Murray), pp. 40-41.

■ Freeland, P., 1999. **Microbes, Medicine and Commerce** (Hodder & Stoughton), pp. 92-99.

■ Fullick, A., 1998. **Human Health and Disease** (Heinemann), pp. 27-36.

■ Hudson, T. & K. Mannion, 2001. **Microbes and Disease** (Collins), pp. 70-86.

See page 7 for details of publishers of periodicals:

STUDENT'S REFERENCE

■ **Skin, Scabs and Scars** Biol. Sci. Rev., 17(3) Feb. 2005, pp. 2-6. *The many roles of skin, including its importance in wound healing and the processes involved in its repair when damaged.*

■ **Antibodies** Biol. Sci. Rev., 11(3) Jan. 1999, pp. 34-35. *The structure and function of antibodies: their roles and how they can be used in medicne.*

■ **Monoclonals as Medicines** Biol. Sci. Rev., 18(4) April 2006, pp. 38-40. *The use of monoclonal antibodies in therapeutic and diagnostic medicine.*

■ **Anaphylactic Shock** Biol. Sci. Rev., 19(2) Nov. 2006, pp. 11-13. *An account of anaphylactic shock, a severe allergic reaction caused by a massive overreaction of the body's immune system.*

■ **Inflammation** Biol. Sci. Rev., 17(1) Sept. 2004, pp. 18-20. *The role of this nonspecific defence response to tissue injury and infection. The processes involved in inflammation are discussed.*

■ **Lymphocytes - The Heart of the Immune System** Biol. Sci. Rev., 12(1) Sept. 1999, pp. 32-35. *An excellent account of the role of the various lymphocytes in the immune response.*

■ **Fanning the Flames** New Scientist, 22 May 2004, pp. 40-43. *Inflammation is one of the first lines of internal defence, but it has been implicated in a host of disparate diseases.*

■ **Fight For Your Life** Biol. Sci. Rev., 18(1) Sept. 2005, pp. 2-6. *Internal defence: pathogen recognition, the immune response, and the nature of adaptive and maladaptive immune reactions.*

■ **Immunotherapy** Biol. Sci. Rev., 15(1), Sept. 2002, pp. 39-41. *Medical research is uncovering ways in which our immune system can be used in developing vaccines for cancer.*

■ **A Jab in Time** Biol. Sci. Rev., 9(4) March 1997, pp. 17-20. *Infection and transmission of disease and the use of vaccination to combat diseases.*

■ **Let Them Eat Dirt** New Scientist, 18 July 1998, pp. 26-31. *It seems that normal immune function requires some early exposure to microorganisms.*

■ **Intestinal Worms - Can They Keep You Healthy?** Biol. Sci. Rev., 19(2) Nov. 2006, pp. 2-6. *Having intestinal worms appears to suppress inappropriate allergic responses.*

■ **Beware! Allergens** New Scientist (Inside Science), 22 January 2000. *The allergic response: sensitisation and the role of the immune system.*

■ **Misery for all Seasons** National Geographic, 209(5) May 2006, pp. 116-135. *The causes, effects, and prevention of common allergies.*

TEACHER'S REFERENCE

■ **Life, Death, and the Immune System** Scientific American, Sept. 1993. *An entire special issue on human infection, immune system, and disease.*

■ **Immunity's Early-warning System** Scientific American, Jan. 2005, pp. 24-31. *The immune*

response is mediated by a family of molecules made by defensive cells. When they detect an invader, they trigger the production of signalling proteins that initiate an immune response.

■ **Edible Vaccines** Scientific American, Sept. 2000, pp. 48-53. *Vaccines in food may be the way of future immunisation programmes.*

■ **Genetic Vaccines** Scientific American, July 1999, pp. 34-41. *This excellent article includes a description of how the vaccines work and a table of specific diseases treatable by this method.*

■ **Disarming Flu Viruses** Scientific American, January 1999, pp. 56-65. *The influenza virus, its life cycle, and vaccine development for its control.*

■ **The Long Arm of the Immune System** Sci. American, Nov. 2002, pp. 34-41. *The role of dendritic cells, a class of leucocytes with a role in activating the immune system (good extension).*

■ **Taming Lupus** Scientific American, March 2005, pp. 58-65. *An account of the autoimmune disorder, lupus: its causes, pathways to disease, triggers for disease onset, and possible treatments.*

■ **Filthy Friends** New Scientist, 16 April 2005, pp. 34-39. *Early contact with a range of harmless microbes is important in reducing the risk of allergy.*

See pages 10-11 for details of how to access **Bio Links** from our web site: **www.biozone.co.uk**. From Bio Links, access sites under the topics:

GENERAL BIOLOGY ONLINE RESOURCES > Online Textbooks and Lecture Notes: • S-Cool! A level biology revision guide ... *and others*

ANIMAL BIOLOGY: • Anatomy and physiology • Human physiology lecture notes ... *and others*

HEALTH & DISEASE > Defence and the Immune System: • Blood group antigens • Inducible defences against pathogens • Microbiology and immunology • Primary immunodeficiency diseases • The immune system: An overview • Understanding the immune system ... *and others*

Defence and the Immune System

Targets for Defence

In order for the body to present an effective defence against pathogens, it must first be able to recognise its own tissues (self) and ignore the body's normal microflora (e.g. the bacteria of the skin and gastrointestinal tract). In addition, the body needs to be able to deal with abnormal cells which, if not eliminated, may become cancerous. Failure of self/non-self recognition can lead to autoimmune disorders, in which the immune system mistakenly attacks its own tissues. The body's ability to recognise its own molecules has implications for procedures such as tissue grafts, organ transplants, and blood transfusions. Incompatible tissues (identified as foreign) are attacked by the body's immune system (**rejected**). Even a healthy pregnancy involves suppression of specific features of the self recognition system, allowing the mother to tolerate a nine month gestation with the foetus.

The Body's Natural Microbiota

After birth, normal and characteristic microbial populations begin to establish themselves on and in the body. A typical human body contains 1×10^{13} body cells, yet harbours 1×10^{14} bacterial cells. These microorganisms establish more or less permanent residence but, under normal conditions, do not cause disease. In fact, this normal microflora can benefit the host by preventing the overgrowth of harmful pathogens. They are not found throughout the entire body, but are located in certain regions.

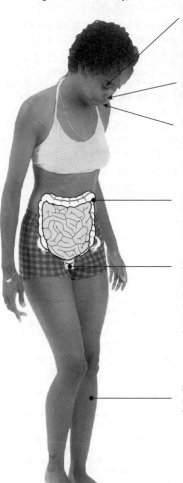

Eyes: The conjuctiva, a continuation of the skin or mucous membrane, contains a similar microbiota to the skin.

Nose and throat: Harbours a variety of microorganisms, e.g. *Staphylococcus spp.*

Mouth: Supports a large and diverse microbiota. It is an ideal microbial environment; high in moisture, warmth, and nutrient availability.

Large intestine: Contains the body's largest resident population of microbes because of its available moisture and nutrients.

Urinary and genital systems: The lower urethra in both sexes has a resident population; the vagina has a particular acid-tolerant population of microbes because of the low pH nature of its secretions.

Skin: Skin secretions prevent most of the microbes on the skin from becoming residents.

Distinguishing Self from Non-Self

The human immune system achieves self-recognition through the **major histocompatibility complex** (MHC). This is a cluster of tightly linked genes on chromosome 6 in humans. These genes code for protein molecules (MHC antigens) that are attached to the surface of body cells. They are used by the immune system to recognise its own or foreign material. **Class I MHC** antigens are located on the surface of virtually all human cells, but **Class II MHC** antigens are restricted to macrophages and the antibody-producing B-lymphocytes.

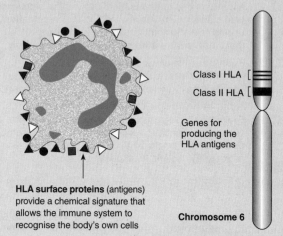

Class I HLA [

Class II HLA [

Genes for producing the HLA antigens

Chromosome 6

HLA surface proteins (antigens) provide a chemical signature that allows the immune system to recognise the body's own cells

Tissue Transplants

The MHC is responsible for the rejection of tissue grafts and organ transplants. Foreign MHC molecules are antigenic, causing the immune system to respond in the following way:

- T cells directly lyse the foreign cells

- Macrophages are activated by T cells and engulf foreign cells

- Antibodies are released that attack the foreign cell

- The complement system injures blood vessels supplying the graft or transplanted organ

To minimise this rejection, attempts are made to match the MHC of the organ donor to that of the recipient as closely as possible.

1. Explain why it is healthy to have a natural population of microbes on and inside the body: _____

_____

2. (a) Explain the nature and purpose of the **major histocompatibility complex** (MHC): _____

_____

_____

_____

(b) Explain the importance of such a self-recognition system: _____

_____

3. Name two situations when the body's recognition of 'self' is undesirable: _____

Related activities: The Body's Defences, The Immune system, Autoimmune Disease

Blood Group Antigens

Blood groups classify blood according to the different marker proteins on the surface of red blood cells (RBCs). These marker proteins act as **antigens** and affect the ability of RBCs to provoke an immune response. The **ABO blood group** is the most important blood typing system in medical practice, because of the presence of anti-A and anti-B antibodies in nearly all people who lack the corresponding red cell antigens (these antibodies are carried in the plasma and are present at birth). If a patient is to receive blood from a blood donor, that blood must be compatible otherwise the red blood cells of the donated blood will clump together (agglutinate), break apart, and block capillaries. There is a small margin of safety in certain blood group combinations, because the volume of donated blood is usually relatively small and the donor's antibodies are quickly diluted in the plasma. In practice, blood is carefully matched, not only for ABO types, but for other types as well. Although human RBCs have more than 500 known antigens, fewer than 30 (in 9 blood groups) are regularly tested for when blood is donated for transfusion. The blood groups involved are: *ABO, Rh, MNS, P, Lewis, Lutheran, Kell, Duffy,* and *Kidd.* The ABO and rhesus (Rh) are the best known. Although blood typing has important applications in medicine, it can also be used to rule out individuals in cases of crime (or paternity) and establish a list of potential suspects (or fathers).

	Blood type A	Blood type B	Blood type AB	Blood type O
Antigens present on the **red blood cells**	antigen *A*	antigen *B*	antigens *A* and *B*	Neither antigen *A* nor *B*
Anti-bodies present in the **plasma**	Contains **anti-B** antibodies; but no antibodies that would attack its own antigen *A*	Contains **anti-A** antibodies; but no antibodies that would attack its own antigen *B*	Contains neither **anti-A** nor **anti-B** antibodies	Contains both **anti-A** and **anti-B** antibodies

Blood type	Frequency in UK *Rh⁺*	*Rh⁻*	Antigen	Antibody	Can donate blood to:	Can receive blood from:
A	36%	7%	*A*	*anti-B*	*A, AB*	*A, O*
B	8%	1%				
AB	2%	1%				
O	38%	7%				

1. Complete the table above to show the antibodies and antigens in each blood group, and donor/recipient blood types:

2. In a hypothetical murder case, blood from both the victim and the murderer was left at the scene. There were five suspects under investigation:

   (a) Describe what blood typing could establish about the guilt or innocence of the suspects: _____
   _____

   (b) Identify what a blood typing could not establish: _____
   _____

   (c) Suggest how the murderer's identity could be firmly established (assuming that s/he was one of the five suspects):
   _____

   (d) Explain why blood typing is not used forensically to any great extent: _____
   _____

3. Explain why the discovery of the ABO system was such a significant medical breakthrough: _____
   _____

Defence and the Immune System

Related activities: Blood
Web links: Blood Typing Game

A 2

Blood Clotting and Defence

Apart from its transport role, **blood** has a role in the body's defence against infection and **haemostasis** (the prevention of bleeding and maintenance of blood volume). The tearing or puncturing of a blood vessel initiates **clotting**. Clotting is normally a rapid process that seals off the tear, preventing blood loss and the invasion of bacteria into the site. Clot formation is triggered by the release of clotting factors from the damaged cells at the site of the tear or puncture. A hardened clot forms a scab, which acts to prevent further blood loss and acts as a mechanical barrier to the entry of pathogens.

Blood Clotting

1 Injury to the lining of a blood vessels exposes collagen fibres to the blood. Platelets stick to the collagen fibres.

3 Platelets clump together. The platelet plug forms an emergency protection against blood loss.

When tissue is wounded, the blood quickly coagulates to prevent further blood loss and maintain the integrity of the circulatory system. For external wounds, clotting also prevents the entry of pathogens. Blood clotting involves a cascade of reactions involving at least twelve clotting factors in the blood. The end result is the formation of an insoluble network of fibres, which traps red blood cells and seals the wound.

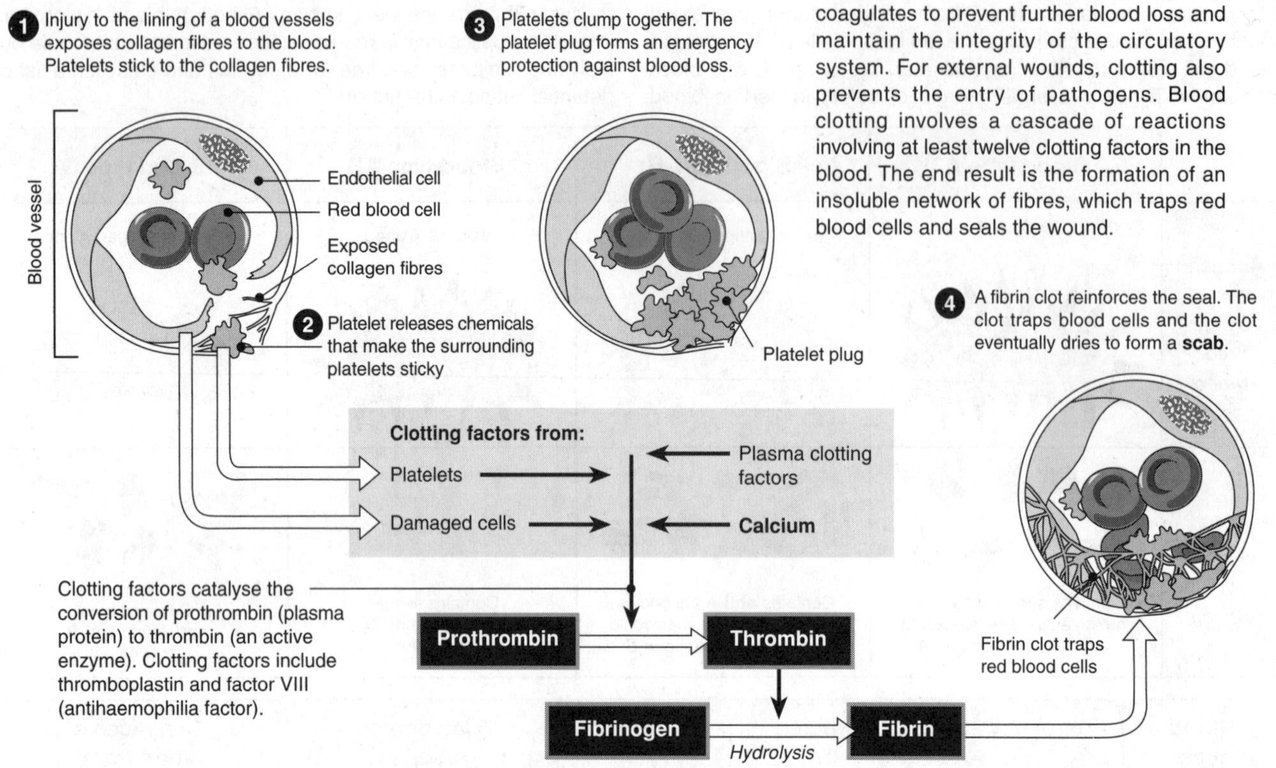

Blood vessel

Endothelial cell
Red blood cell

Exposed collagen fibres

2 Platelet releases chemicals that make the surrounding platelets sticky

Platelet plug

4 A fibrin clot reinforces the seal. The clot traps blood cells and the clot eventually dries to form a **scab**.

Clotting factors from:

Platelets ⟶ ⟵ Plasma clotting factors

Damaged cells ⟶ ⟵ **Calcium**

Clotting factors catalyse the conversion of prothrombin (plasma protein) to thrombin (an active enzyme). Clotting factors include thromboplastin and factor VIII (antihaemophilia factor).

Fibrin clot traps red blood cells

Prothrombin ⟹ **Thrombin**

Fibrinogen ⟶ **Fibrin**
Hydrolysis

1. Explain two roles of the blood clotting system in internal defence and haemostasis:

   (a) _____

   (b) _____

2. Explain the role of each of the following in the sequence of events leading to a blood clot:

   (a) Injury: _____

   (b) Release of chemicals from platelets: _____

   _____

   (c) Clumping of platelets at the wound site: _____

   _____

   (d) Formation of a fibrin clot: _____

   _____

3. (a) Explain the role of clotting factors in the blood in formation of the clot: _____

   _____

   (b) Explain why these clotting factors are not normally present in the plasma: _____

   _____

4. (a) Name one inherited disease caused by the absence of a clotting factor: _____

   (b) Name the clotting factor involved: _____

Related activities: Proteins, Enzymes, Blood
Web links: Haemostasis

The Body's Defences

If microorganisms never encountered resistance from our body defences, we would be constantly ill and would eventually die of various diseases. Fortunately, in most cases our defences prevent this from happening. Some of these defences are designed to keep microorganisms from entering the body. Other defences remove the microorganisms if they manage to get inside. Further defences attack the microorganisms if they remain inside the body. The ability to ward off disease through the various defence mechanisms is called **resistance**. The lack of resistance, or vulnerability to disease, is known as **susceptibility**. One form of defence is referred to as **non-specific resistance**, and includes defences that protect us from any invading pathogen. This includes a first line of defence such as the physical barriers to infection (skin and mucous membranes) and a second line of defence (phagocytes, inflammation, fever, and antimicrobial substances). **Specific resistance** is a third line of defence that forms the **immune response** and targets specific pathogens. Specialised cells of the immune system, called lymphocytes, produce specific proteins called antibodies which are produced against specific antigens.

1st Line of Defence

The skin provides a formidable physical barrier to the entry of pathogens. Healthy skin is rarely penetrated by microorganisms. Certain chemical secretions are produced by skin that inhibit growth of bacteria and fungi. Tears, mucus and saliva also help to wash bacteria away.

2nd Line of Defence

A range of defence mechanisms operate inside the body to inhibit or destroy pathogens. These responses react to the presence of any pathogen, regardless of which species it is. White blood cells are involved in most of these responses.

3rd Line of Defence

Once the pathogen has been *identified* by the immune system, a specific response from white blood cells called lymphocytes occurs. These coordinate a range of specific responses to the pathogen.

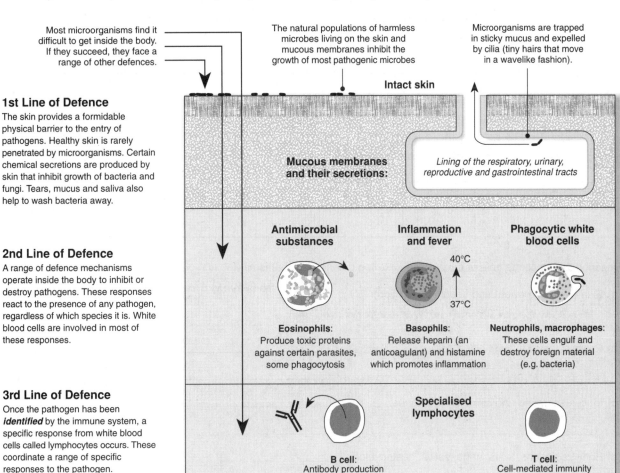

Most microorganisms find it difficult to get inside the body. If they succeed, they face a range of other defences.

The natural populations of harmless microbes living on the skin and mucous membranes inhibit the growth of most pathogenic microbes

Microorganisms are trapped in sticky mucus and expelled by cilia (tiny hairs that move in a wavelike fashion).

Intact skin

Mucous membranes and their secretions:

Lining of the respiratory, urinary, reproductive and gastrointestinal tracts

Antimicrobial substances

Eosinophils: Produce toxic proteins against certain parasites, some phagocytosis

Inflammation and fever

40°C

37°C

Basophils: Release heparin (an anticoagulant) and histamine which promotes inflammation

Phagocytic white blood cells

Neutrophils, macrophages: These cells engulf and destroy foreign material (e.g. bacteria)

Specialised lymphocytes

B cell: Antibody production

T cell: Cell-mediated immunity

1. Compare and contrast the type of response against pathogens carried out by each of the three levels of defence:

_____

_____

_____

_____

_____

_____

_____

_____

_____

_____

_____

Related activities: Targets for Defence, The Action of Phagocytes, Inflammation, Fever, The Immune System, Antibodies   **Web links**: Immunoanimations

RA 2

Defence and the Immune System

2. Distinguish between specific and non-specific resistance: _____

_____

_____

_____

_____

3. Describe features of the different types of white blood cells and explain how these relate to their role in the second line of defence:

_____

_____

_____

_____

_____

_____

_____

_____

_____

_____

4. Describe the functional role of each of the following defence mechanisms (the first one has been completed for you):

(a) Skin (including sweat and sebum production): _Skin helps to prevent direct entry of pathogens into the body. Sebum slows growth of bacteria and fungi._

(b) Phagocytosis by white blood cells: _____

_____

(c) Mucus-secreting and ciliated membranes: _____

_____

(d) Body secretions: tears, urine, saliva, gastric juice: _____

_____

(e) Natural antimicrobial proteins (e.g. interferon): _____

_____

(f) Antibody production: _____

_____

(g) Fever: _____

_____

(h) Cell-mediated immunity: _____

_____

(i) The inflammatory response: _____

_____

5. Infection with HIV results in the progressive destruction of T lymphocytes. Suggest why this leads to an increasing number of opportunistic infections in AIDS sufferers:

_____

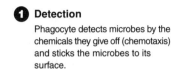

The Action of Phagocytes

Human cells that ingest microbes and digest them by the process of **phagocytosis** are called **phagocytes**. All are types of white blood cells. During many kinds of infections, especially bacterial infections, the total number of white blood cells increases by two to four times the normal number. The ratio of various white blood cell types changes during the course of an infection.

How a Phagocyte Destroys Microbes

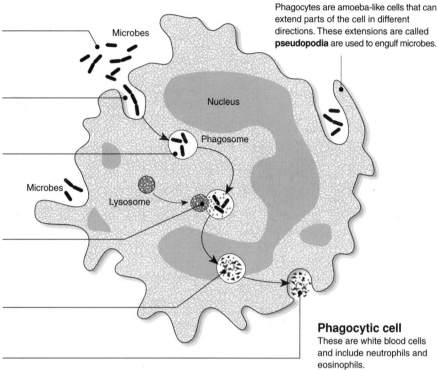

1 Detection

Phagocyte detects microbes by the chemicals they give off (chemotaxis) and sticks the microbes to its surface.

2 Ingestion

The microbe is engulfed by the phagocyte wrapping pseudopodia around it to form a vesicle.

3 Phagosome forms

A phagosome (phagocytic vesicle) is formed, which encloses the microbes in a membrane.

4 Fusion with lysosome

Phagosome fuses with a lysosome (which contains powerful enzymes that can digest the microbe).

5 Digestion

The microbes are broken down by enzymes into their chemical constituents.

6 Discharge

Indigestible material is discharged from the phagocyte cell.

Phagocytes are amoeba-like cells that can extend parts of the cell in different directions. These extensions are called **pseudopodia** are used to engulf microbes.

Phagocytic cell

These are white blood cells and include neutrophils and eosinophils.

The Interaction of Microbes and Phagocytes

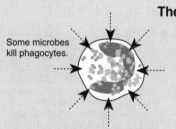

Some microbes kill phagocytes.

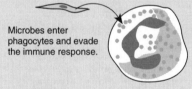

Microbes enter phagocytes and evade the immune response.

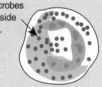

Dormant microbes may hide inside phagocytes.

Some microbes kill phagocytes

Some microbes produce toxins that can actually kill phagocytes, e.g. toxin-producing staphylococci and the dental plaque-forming bacteria *Actinobacillus*.

Microbes evade immune system

Some microbes can evade the immune system by entering phagocytes. The microbes prevent fusion of the lysosome with the phagosome and multiply inside the phagocyte, almost filling it. Examples include *Chlamydia*, *Mycobacterium tuberculosis*, *Shigella*, and malarial parasites.

Dormant microbes hide inside

Some microbes can remain dormant inside the phagocyte for months or years at a time. Examples include the microbes that cause brucellosis and tularemia.

1. Identify the white blood cells capable of phagocytosis: _____

_____

2. Describe how a blood sample from a patient may be used to determine whether they have a microbial infection (without looking for the microbes themselves):

_____

_____

3. Explain how some microbes are able to overcome phagocytic cells and use them to their advantage: _____

_____

_____

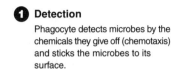
Defence and the Immune System

Related activities: The Body's Defences, Blood

RA 2

Inflammation

Damage to the body's tissues can be caused by physical agents (e.g. sharp objects, heat, radiant energy, or electricity), microbial infection, or chemical agents (e.g. gases, acids and bases). The damage triggers a defensive response called **inflammation**. It is usually characterised by four symptoms: pain, redness, heat and swelling. The inflammatory response is beneficial and has the following functions: (1) to destroy the cause of the infection and remove it and its products from the body; (2) if this fails, to limit the effects on the body by confining the infection to a small area; (3) replacing or repairing tissue damaged by the infection. The process of inflammation can be divided into three distinct stages. These are described below.

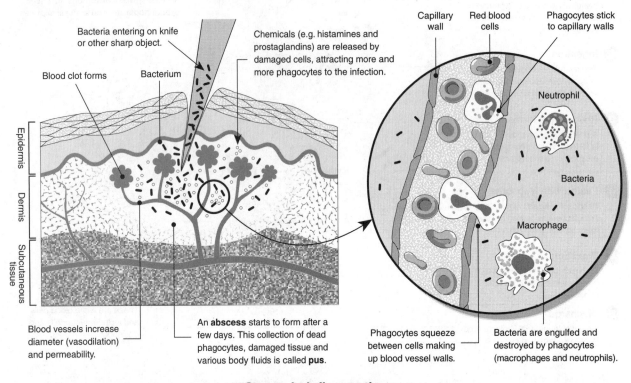

Bacteria entering on knife or other sharp object.

Blood clot forms

Bacterium

Chemicals (e.g. histamines and prostaglandins) are released by damaged cells, attracting more and more phagocytes to the infection.

Capillary wall

Red blood cells

Phagocytes stick to capillary walls

Neutrophil

Bacteria

Macrophage

Epidermis

Dermis

Subcutaneous tissue

Blood vessels increase diameter (vasodilation) and permeability.

An **abscess** starts to form after a few days. This collection of dead phagocytes, damaged tissue and various body fluids is called **pus**.

Phagocytes squeeze between cells making up blood vessel walls.

Bacteria are engulfed and destroyed by phagocytes (macrophages and neutrophils).

Stages in inflammation

Increased diameter and permeability of blood vessels	**Phagocyte migration and phagocytosis**	**Tissue repair**
Blood vessels increase their diameter and permeability in the area of damage. This increases blood flow to the area and allows defensive substances to leak into tissue spaces.	Within one hour of injury, phagocytes appear on the scene. They squeeze between cells of blood vessel walls to reach the damaged area where they destroy invading microbes.	Functioning cells or supporting connective cells create new tissue to replace dead or damaged cells. Some tissue regenerates easily (skin) while others do not at all (cardiac muscle).

1. Outline the three stages of inflammation and identify the beneficial role of each stage:

   (a) _____

   _____

   (b) _____

   _____

   (c) _____

   _____

2. Identify two features of phagocytes important in the response to microbial invasion: _____

   _____

3. State the role of histamines and prostaglandins in inflammation: _____

4. Explain why pus forms at the site of infection: _____

   _____

A 1

Related activities: The Body's Defences, The Action of Phagocytes

Fever

To a point, fever is beneficial, because it assists a number of the defence processes. The release of the protein **interleukin-1** helps to reset the thermostat of the body to a higher level, and increases production of **T cells** (lymphocytes). High body temperature also intensifies the effect of **interferon** (an antiviral protein) and may inhibit the growth of some bacteria and viruses. Because high temperatures speed up the body's **metabolic** **reactions**, it may promote more rapid tissue repair. Fever also increases heart rate so that white blood cells are delivered to sites of infection more rapidly. The normal body temperature range for most people is 36.2 to 37.2°C. Fevers of less than 40°C do not need treatment for **hyperthermia**, but excessive fever requires prompt attention (particularly in children). Death usually results if body temperature rises to 44.4 to 45.5°C.

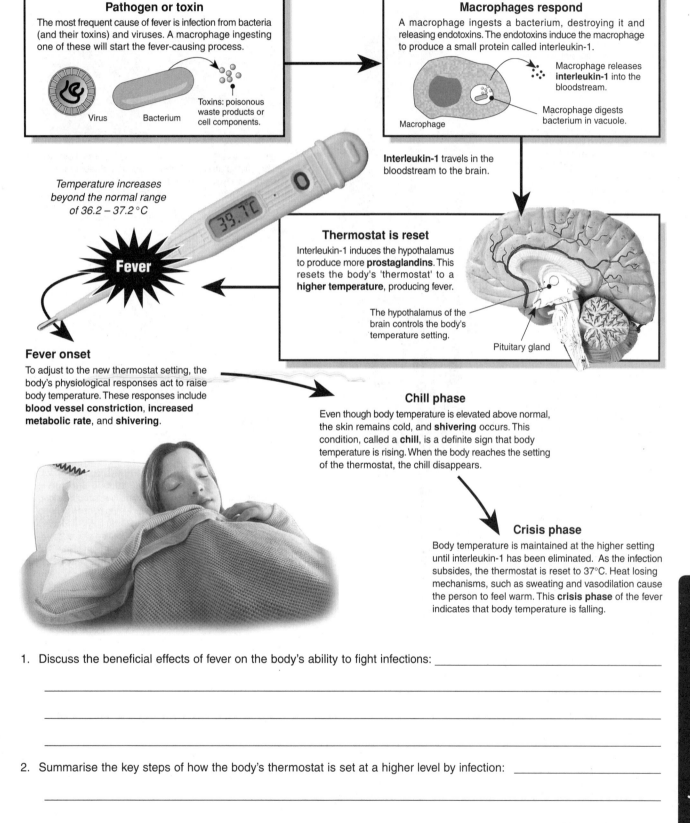

Pathogen or toxin
The most frequent cause of fever is infection from bacteria (and their toxins) and viruses. A macrophage ingesting one of these will start the fever-causing process.

Virus   Bacterium

Toxins: poisonous waste products or cell components.

Macrophages respond
A macrophage ingests a bacterium, destroying it and releasing endotoxins. The endotoxins induce the macrophage to produce a small protein called interleukin-1.

Macrophage releases **interleukin-1** into the bloodstream.

Macrophage digests bacterium in vacuole.

Macrophage

Interleukin-1 travels in the bloodstream to the brain.

Temperature increases beyond the normal range of 36.2 – 37.2 °C

Fever

Thermostat is reset
Interleukin-1 induces the hypothalamus to produce more **prostaglandins**. This resets the body's 'thermostat' to a **higher temperature**, producing fever.

The hypothalamus of the brain controls the body's temperature setting.

Pituitary gland

Fever onset
To adjust to the new thermostat setting, the body's physiological responses act to raise body temperature. These responses include **blood vessel constriction, increased metabolic rate**, and **shivering**.

Chill phase
Even though body temperature is elevated above normal, the skin remains cold, and **shivering** occurs. This condition, called a **chill**, is a definite sign that body temperature is rising. When the body reaches the setting of the thermostat, the chill disappears.

Crisis phase
Body temperature is maintained at the higher setting until interleukin-1 has been eliminated. As the infection subsides, the thermostat is reset to 37°C. Heat losing mechanisms, such as sweating and vasodilation cause the person to feel warm. This **crisis phase** of the fever indicates that body temperature is falling.

1. Discuss the beneficial effects of fever on the body's ability to fight infections: _____

_____

_____

_____

2. Summarise the key steps of how the body's thermostat is set at a higher level by infection: _____

_____

_____

_____

Defence and the Immune System

Related activities: Bacterial Diseases, The Body's Defences, The Action of Phagocytes

A 2

The Lymphatic System

Fluid leaks out from capillaries and forms the tissue fluid, which is similar in composition to plasma but lacks large proteins. This fluid bathes the tissues, supplying them with nutrients and oxygen, and removing wastes. Some of the tissue fluid returns directly into the capillaries, but some drains back into the blood circulation through a network of lymph vessels. This fluid, called **lymph**, is similar to tissue fluid, but contains more leucocytes. Apart from its circulatory role, the lymphatic system also has an important function in the immune response. Lymph nodes are the primary sites where the destruction of pathogens and other foreign substances occurs. A lymph node that is fighting an infection becomes swollen and hard as the lymph cells reproduce rapidly to increase their numbers. The thymus, spleen, and bone marrow also contribute leucocytes to the lymphatic and circulatory systems.

Tonsils: Tonsils (and adenoids) comprise a collection of large lymphatic nodules at the back of the throat. They produce lymphocytes and antibodies and are well-placed to protect against invasion of pathogens.

Thymus gland: The thymus is a two-lobed organ located close to the heart. It is prominent in infants and diminishes after puberty to a fraction of its original size. Its role in immunity is to help produce **T cells** that destroy invading microbes directly or indirectly by producing various substances.

Spleen: The oval spleen is the largest mass of lymphatic tissue in the body, measuring about 12 cm in length. It stores and releases blood in case of demand (e.g. in cases of bleeding), produces mature **B cells**, and destroys bacteria by phagocytosis.

Bone marrow: Bone marrow produces red blood cells and many kinds of leucocytes: monocytes (and macrophages), neutrophils, eosinophils, basophils, and lymphocytes (B cells and T cells).

Lymphatic vessels: When tissue fluid is picked up by lymph capillaries, it is called **lymph**. The lymph is passed along lymphatic vessels to a series of lymph nodes. These vessels contain one-way valves that move the lymph in the direction of the heart until it is reintroduced to the blood at the subclavian veins.

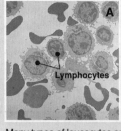
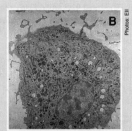

Lymphocytes

Many types of leucocytes are involved in internal defence. The photos above illustrate examples of leucocytes. **A** shows a cluster of **lymphocytes**. B shows a single **macrophage**: large, phagocytic cells that develop from monocytes and move from the blood to reside in many organs and tissues, including the spleen and lymph nodes.

Lymph node

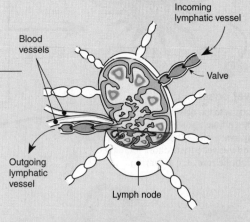

Lymph nodes are oval or bean-shaped structures, scattered throughout the body, usually in groups, along the length of lymphatic vessels. As lymph passes through the nodes, it filters foreign particles (including pathogens) by trapping them in fibres. Lymph nodes are also a "store" of **lymphocytes**, which may circulate to other parts of the body. Once trapped, macrophages destroy the foreign substances by phagocytosis. T cells may destroy them by releasing various products, and/or B cells may release antibodies that destroy them.

1. Briefly describe the composition of lymph: _____

_____

2. Discuss the various roles of lymph: _____

_____

_____

3. Describe one role of each of the following in the lymphatic system:

   (a) Lymph nodes: _____

   (b) Bone marrow: _____

RA 2   **Related activities**: Capillaries and Tissue Fluid, The Immune System

The Immune System

The efficient internal defence provided by the immune system is based on its ability to respond specifically against a foreign substance and its ability to hold a memory of this response. There are two main components of the immune system: the humoral and the cell-mediated responses. They work separately and together to protect us from disease. The **humoral immune response** is associated with the serum (non-cellular part of the blood) and involves the action of **antibodies** secreted by B cell lymphocytes. Antibodies are found in extracellular fluids including lymph, plasma, and mucus secretions. The humoral response protects the body against circulating viruses, and bacteria and their toxins. The **cell-mediated immune response** is associated with the production of specialised lymphocytes called **T cells**. It is most effective against bacteria and viruses located within host cells, as well as against parasitic protozoa, fungi, and worms. This system is also an important defence against cancer, and is responsible for the rejection of transplanted tissue. Both B and T cells develop from stem cells located in the liver of foetuses and the bone marrow of adults. T cells complete their development in the thymus, whilst the B cells mature in the bone marrow.

Lymphocytes and their Functions

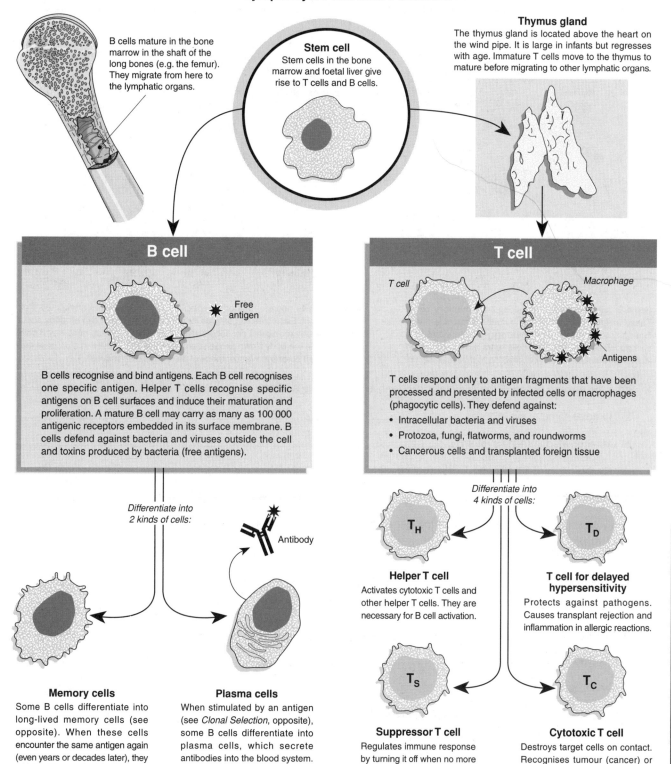

B cells mature in the bone marrow in the shaft of the long bones (e.g. the femur). They migrate from here to the lymphatic organs.

Stem cell
Stem cells in the bone marrow and foetal liver give rise to T cells and B cells.

Thymus gland
The thymus gland is located above the heart on the wind pipe. It is large in infants but regresses with age. Immature T cells move to the thymus to mature before migrating to other lymphatic organs.

B cell

Free antigen

B cells recognise and bind antigens. Each B cell recognises one specific antigen. Helper T cells recognise specific antigens on B cell surfaces and induce their maturation and proliferation. A mature B cell may carry as many as 100 000 antigenic receptors embedded in its surface membrane. B cells defend against bacteria and viruses outside the cell and toxins produced by bacteria (free antigens).

T cell

T cell   Macrophage

Antigens

T cells respond only to antigen fragments that have been processed and presented by infected cells or macrophages (phagocytic cells). They defend against:
- Intracellular bacteria and viruses
- Protozoa, fungi, flatworms, and roundworms
- Cancerous cells and transplanted foreign tissue

Differentiate into 2 kinds of cells:

Antibody

Differentiate into 4 kinds of cells:

T_H

T_D

Helper T cell
Activates cytotoxic T cells and other helper T cells. They are necessary for B cell activation.

T cell for delayed hypersensitivity
Protects against pathogens. Causes transplant rejection and inflammation in allergic reactions.

T_S

T_C

Memory cells
Some B cells differentiate into long-lived memory cells (see opposite). When these cells encounter the same antigen again (even years or decades later), they rapidly differentiate into antibody-producing plasma cells.

Plasma cells
When stimulated by an antigen (see *Clonal Selection*, opposite), some B cells differentiate into plasma cells, which secrete antibodies into the blood system. The antibodies then inactivate the circulating antigens.

Suppressor T cell
Regulates immune response by turning it off when no more antigen is present.

Cytotoxic T cell
Destroys target cells on contact. Recognises tumour (cancer) or virus infected cells by their surface (antigens and MHC markers).

Related activities: The Lymphatic System, Antibodies, Autoimmune Diseases
Web links: Introducing...Specific Immunity, The Immune System Overview

A 2

Defence and the Immune System

The immune system has the ability to respond to the large and unpredictable range of potential antigens encountered in the environment. The diagram below explains how this ability is based on **clonal selection** after antigen exposure. The example illustrated is for B cell lymphocytes. In the same way, a T cell stimulated by a specific antigen will multiply and develop into different types of T cells. Clonal selection and differentiation of lymphocytes provide the basis for **immunological memory**.

Five (a-e) of the many, randomly generated B cells. Each one can recognise only one specific antigen.

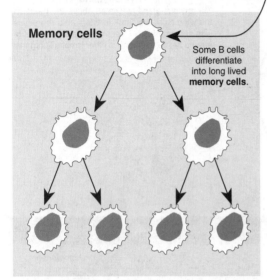

This B cell encounters and binds an antigen. It is then stimulated to proliferate.

Clonal Selection Theory

During development, millions of randomly generated B cells are formed. These are able to recognise many different antigens, including those never before encountered. Each B cell has one specific type of antigenic receptor on its surface whose shape is identical to the antibodies that the cell can make. The receptor will react only to a single antigen. When a B cell encounters its specific antigen, it responds by proliferating into a large clone of cells, all with the same genetic material and the same kind of antibody. This is called **clonal selection** because the antigen selects the B cells that will proliferate.

Memory cells

Some B cells differentiate into long lived **memory cells**.

Some B cells differentiate into **plasma cells**.

Antibodies inactivate antigens

Plasma cells

Some B cells differentiate into long lived **memory cells**. These are retained in the lymph nodes to provide future immunity (**immunological memory**). In the event of a second infection, B-memory cells react more quickly and vigorously than the initial B-cell reaction to the first infection.

Plasma cells secrete antibodies specific to the antigen that stimulated their development. Each plasma cell lives for only a few days, but can produce about 2000 antibody molecules per second. Note that during development, any B cells that react to the body's own antigens are selectively destroyed in a process that leads to **self tolerance** (acceptance of the body's own tissues).

1. State the general action of the two major divisions in the immune system:

   (a) Humoral immune system: _____

   (b) Cell-mediated immune system: _____

2. Identify the origin of B cells and T cells (before maturing): _____

3. (a) Identify where B cells mature: _____ (b) Identify where T cells mature: _____

4. Briefly describe the function of each of the following cells in the immune system response:

   (a) Memory cells: _____

   (b) Plasma cells: _____

   (c) Helper T cells: _____

   (d) Suppressor T cells: _____

   (e) Delayed hypersensitivity T cells: _____

   (f) Cytotoxic T cells: _____

5. Briefly explain the basis of **immunological memory**: _____

   _____

   _____

   _____

Antibodies

Antibodies and antigens play key roles in the response of the immune system. Antigens are foreign molecules that are able to bind to antibodies (or T cell receptors) and provoke a specific immune response. Antigens include potentially damaging microbes and their toxins (see below) as well as substances such as pollen grains, blood cell surface molecules, and the surface proteins on transplanted tissues. **Antibodies** (also called immunoglobulins) are proteins that are made in response to antigens. They are secreted into the plasma where they circulate and can recognise, bind to, and help to destroy antigens. There are five classes of **immunoglobulins**. Each plays a different role in the immune response (including destroying protozoan parasites, enhancing phagocytosis, protecting mucous surfaces, and neutralising toxins and viruses). The human body can produce an estimated 100 million antibodies, recognising many different antigens, including those it has never encountered. Each type of antibody is highly specific to only one particular antigen. The ability of the immune system to recognise and ignore the antigenic properties of its own tissues occurs early in development and is called **self-tolerance**. Exceptions occur when the immune system malfunctions and the body attacks its own tissues, causing an **autoimmune disorder**.

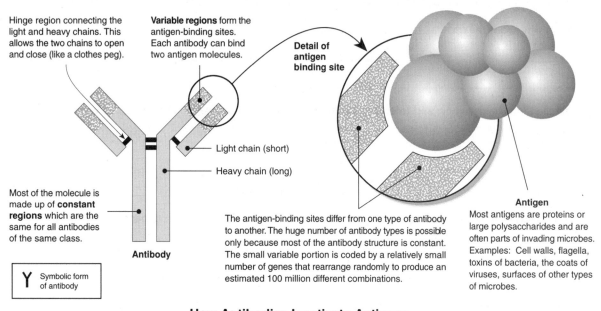

Hinge region connecting the light and heavy chains. This allows the two chains to open and close (like a clothes peg).

Variable regions form the antigen-binding sites. Each antibody can bind two antigen molecules.

Detail of antigen binding site

Light chain (short)

Heavy chain (long)

Most of the molecule is made up of **constant regions** which are the same for all antibodies of the same class.

Antibody

Y Symbolic form of antibody

The antigen-binding sites differ from one type of antibody to another. The huge number of antibody types is possible only because most of the antibody structure is constant. The small variable portion is coded by a relatively small number of genes that rearrange randomly to produce an estimated 100 million different combinations.

Antigen
Most antigens are proteins or large polysaccharides and are often parts of invading microbes. Examples: Cell walls, flagella, toxins of bacteria, the coats of viruses, surfaces of other types of microbes.

How Antibodies Inactivate Antigens

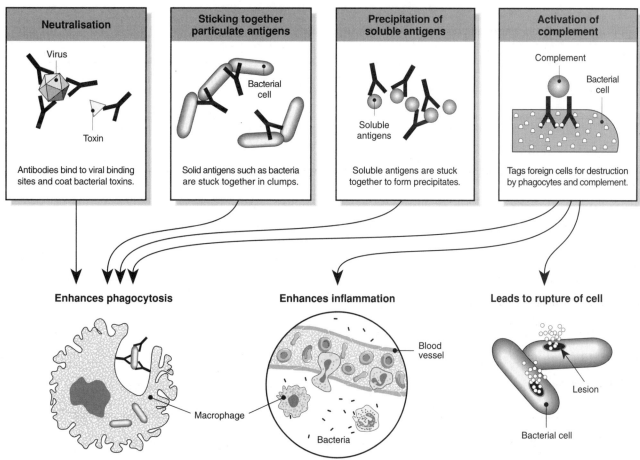

Neutralisation	Sticking together particulate antigens	Precipitation of soluble antigens	Activation of complement
Virus Toxin Antibodies bind to viral binding sites and coat bacterial toxins.	Bacterial cell Solid antigens such as bacteria are stuck together in clumps.	Soluble antigens Soluble antigens are stuck together to form precipitates.	Complement Bacterial cell Tags foreign cells for destruction by phagocytes and complement.

Enhances phagocytosis

Macrophage

Enhances inflammation

Blood vessel

Bacteria

Leads to rupture of cell

Lesion

Bacterial cell

Related activities: Targets for Defence, The Immune System, Autoimmune Diseases, Acquired Immunity, Immunisation

RA 2

Defence and the Immune System

1. Distinguish between an antibody and an antigen: _____

_____

_____

_____

_____

_____

2. It is necessary for the immune system to clearly distinguish the body's own cells and proteins from foreign ones.

(a) Explain why this is the case: _____

_____

_____

(b) In simple terms, explain how **self tolerance** develops (see the activity *The Immune System* if you need help):

_____

_____

(c) Name the type of disorder that results when this recognition system fails: _____

(d) Describe two examples of disorders that are caused in this way, identifying what happens in each case:

_____

_____

_____

_____

3. Discuss the ways in which antibodies work to inactivate antigens: _____

_____

_____

_____

_____

_____

_____

_____

_____

_____

4. Explain how antibody activity enhances or leads to:

(a) Phagocytosis: _____

_____

(b) Inflammation: _____

_____

(c) Bacterial cell lysis: _____

_____

Acquired Immunity

We have natural or **innate resistance** to certain illnesses; examples include most diseases of other animal species. **Acquired immunity** refers to the protection an animal develops against certain types of microbes or foreign substances. Immunity can be acquired either passively or actively and is developed during an individual's lifetime. **Active immunity** develops when a person is exposed to microorganisms or foreign substances and the immune system responds. **Passive immunity** is acquired when antibodies are transferred from one person to another. Recipients do not make the antibodies themselves and the effect lasts only as long as the antibodies are present, usually several weeks or months. Immunity may also be **naturally acquired**, through natural exposure to microbes, or **artificially acquired** as a result of medical treatment.

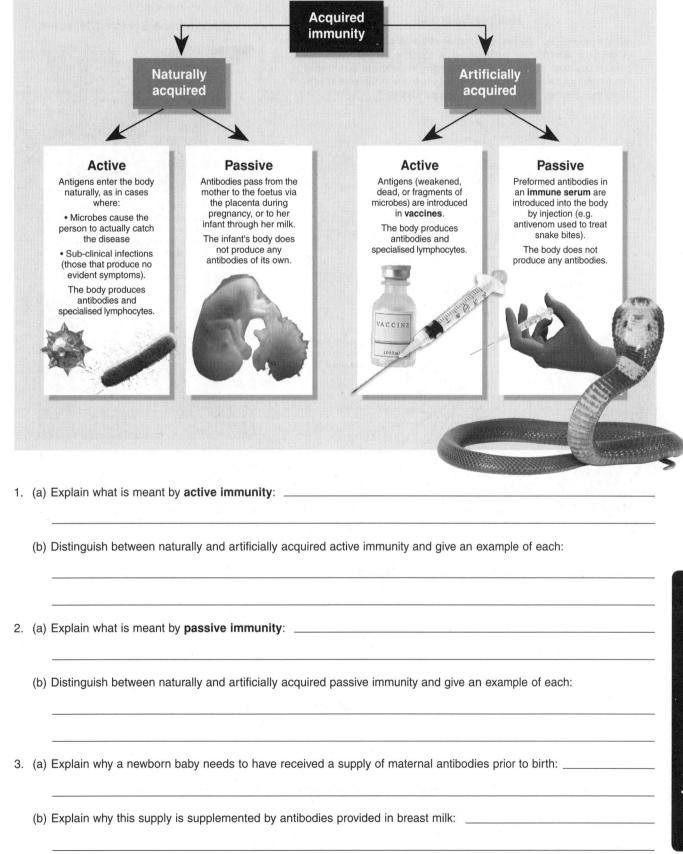

Acquired immunity

Naturally acquired

Artificially acquired

Active
Antigens enter the body naturally, as in cases where:

• Microbes cause the person to actually catch the disease

• Sub-clinical infections (those that produce no evident symptoms).

The body produces antibodies and specialised lymphocytes.

Passive
Antibodies pass from the mother to the foetus via the placenta during pregnancy, or to her infant through her milk.

The infant's body does not produce any antibodies of its own.

Active
Antigens (weakened, dead, or fragments of microbes) are introduced in **vaccines**.

The body produces antibodies and specialised lymphocytes.

Passive
Preformed antibodies in an **immune serum** are introduced into the body by injection (e.g. antivenom used to treat snake bites).

The body does not produce any antibodies.

1. (a) Explain what is meant by **active immunity**: _____

_____

(b) Distinguish between naturally and artificially acquired active immunity and give an example of each:

_____

_____

2. (a) Explain what is meant by **passive immunity**: _____

_____

(b) Distinguish between naturally and artificially acquired passive immunity and give an example of each:

_____

_____

3. (a) Explain why a newborn baby needs to have received a supply of maternal antibodies prior to birth: _____

_____

(b) Explain why this supply is supplemented by antibodies provided in breast milk: _____

_____

Defence and the Immune System

Related activities: Immunisation

A 2

Autoimmune Diseases

Any of numerous disorders, including **rheumatoid arthritis**, insulin dependent **diabetes mellitus**, and **multiple sclerosis**, are caused by an individual's immune system reaction to their own cells or tissues. The immune system normally distinguishes self from non-self. Some lymphocytes are capable of reacting against self, but these are generally suppressed. **Autoimmune diseases** occur when there is some interruption of the normal control process, allowing lymphocytes to escape from suppression, or when there is an alteration in some body tissue so that it is no longer recognised as self. The exact mechanisms behind autoimmune malfunctions are not fully understood but pathogens or drugs may play a role in triggering an autoimmune response in someone who already has a genetic predisposition. The reactions are similar to those that occur in allergies, except that in autoimmune disorders, the hypersensitivity response is to the body itself, rather than to an outside substance.

Multiple Sclerosis

MS is a progressive inflammatory disease of the central nervous system in which scattered patches of **myelin** (white matter) in the brain and spinal cord are destroyed. Myelin is the fatty connective tissue sheath surrounding conducting axons and its destruction results in the symptoms of MS: numbness, tingling, muscle weakness and **paralysis**.

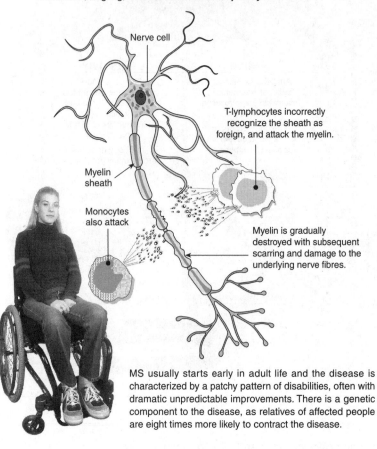

Nerve cell

T-lymphocytes incorrectly recognize the sheath as foreign, and attack the myelin.

Myelin sheath

Monocytes also attack

Myelin is gradually destroyed with subsequent scarring and damage to the underlying nerve fibres.

MS usually starts early in adult life and the disease is characterized by a patchy pattern of disabilities, often with dramatic unpredictable improvements. There is a genetic component to the disease, as relatives of affected people are eight times more likely to contract the disease.

Other Immune System Disorders

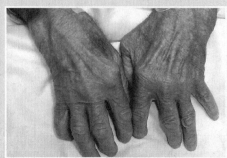

UCSD School of Medicine: Charles Goldberg

Rheumatoid arthritis is a type of joint inflammation, usually in the hands and feet, which results in destruction of cartilage and painful, swollen joints. The disease often begins in adulthood, but can also occur in children or the elderly. Rheumatoid arthritis affects more women than men and is treated with anti-inflammatory and immunosuppressant drugs, and physiotherapy.

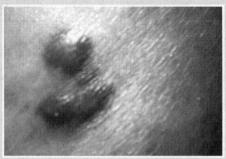

CDC

Lacking a sufficient immune response is called **immune deficiency**, and may be either **congenital** (present at birth) or **acquired** as a result of drugs, cancer, or infectious agents (e.g. HIV infection). HIV causes AIDS, which results in a steady destruction of the immune system. Sufferers then succumb to opportunistic infections and rare cancers such as Kaposi's sarcoma (above).

1. Explain the basis of the following autoimmune diseases:

   (a) Multiple sclerosis: _____

   _____

   (b) Rheumatoid arthritis: _____

   _____

2. Suggest why autoimmune diseases are difficult to treat effectively: _____

   _____

   _____

3. Explain why sufferers of immune deficiencies, such as AIDS, develop a range of debilitating infections:

   _____

   _____

Related activities: The Immune System, HIV and AIDS

Immunisation

A vaccine is a suspension of microorganisms (or pieces of them) that protects against disease by stimulating the production of antibodies and inducing **immunity**. **Vaccination** (often used synonymously with **immunisation**) is a procedure that provides **artificially acquired active immunity** in the recipient. A concerted vaccination campaign led to the eradication (in 1977) of **smallpox**, the only disease to have been eradicated in this way. Once eradicated, a pathogen is no longer present in the environment and vaccination is no longer necessary. Features of smallpox made it particularly suitable for complete eradication. It was a very recognisable and visible disease, with no long-

term, human carriers and no non-human carriers. In addition, people who had not been vaccinated against the disease were identifiable by the absence of a vaccination scar on the upper arm. Disease control (as opposed to eradication) does not necessarily require that everyone be immune. **Herd immunity**, where most of the population is immune, limits outbreaks to sporadic cases because there are too few susceptible individuals to support an epidemic. Vaccination provides effective control over many common bacterial and viral diseases. Viral diseases in particular are best prevented with vaccination, as they cannot be effectively treated once contracted.

Primary and Secondary Responses to Antigens

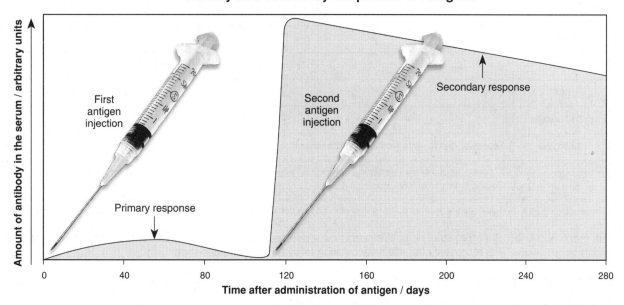

First antigen injection

Second antigen injection

Secondary response

Primary response

Amount of antibody in the serum / arbitrary units

Time after administration of antigen / days

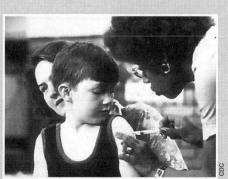

Vaccines to protect against common diseases are administered at various stages during childhood according to an immunisation schedule.

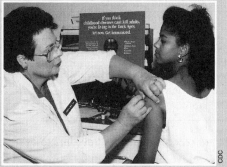

While most vaccinations are given in childhood, adults may be vaccinated against specific diseases (e.g. tuberculosis) if they are in a high risk group or if they are travelling to a region in the world where a disease is prevalent.

Selected Vaccines Used To Prevent Diseases In Humans		
Disease	**Type of vaccine**	**Recommendation**
Diphtheria	Purified diphtheria toxoid	From early childhood and every 10 years for adults
Meningococcal meningitis	Purified polysaccharide of *Neisseria menigitidis*	For people with substantial risk of infection
Whooping cough	Killed cells or fragments of *Bordetella pertussis*	Children prior to school age
Tetanus	Purified tetanus toxoid	14-16 year olds with booster every 10 years
Meningitis caused by *Haemophilus influenzae* b	Polysaccharide from virus conjugated with protein to enhance effectiveness	Early childhood
Influenza	Killed virus (vaccines using genetically engineered antigenic fragments are also being developed)	For chronically ill people, especially with respiratory diseases, or for healthy people over 65 years of age
Measles	Attenuated virus	Early childhood
Mumps	Attenuated virus	Early childhood
Rubella	Attenuated virus	Early childhood; for females of child-bearing age who are not pregnant
Polio	Attenuated or killed virus (enhanced potency type)	Early childhood
Hepatitis B	Antigenic fragments of virus	Early childhood

Defence and the Immune System

Related activities: Acquired Immunity, Types of Vaccine, Bacterial Diseases, Viral Diseases

RDA 2

1. The table below provides a list of the vaccines used in the standard vaccination schedule for children and young adults in the United Kingdom. Additional vaccinations are available for those at high risk of contracting certain diseases.

   (a) List the diseases that each vaccine protects against.

   (b) Consult your family doctor, medical centre or other medical authority to determine the ages that each vaccine should be administered. Place a tick (✔) in each age column as appropriate (the last one has been done for you).

Vaccination Schedule Available to Children in the United Kingdom								
Vaccine	Diseases protected from	Age in months				Age in years		
		2	3	4	12-15	3-5	10-14	13-18
DTP (Triple antigen)								
Hib vaccine*								
OPV (Sabin vaccine)								
MMR								
BCG								
DT booster								
Td booster	Tetanus, diphtheria (low strength dose)							✔

Vaccination schedules are also available *for high risk groups* for the following diseases:
anthrax, hepatitis A, hepatitis B, influenza, pneumococcal disease, typhoid, varicella (chickenpox), and yellow fever.

* Depending on an individual's vaccine tolerance, the Hib vaccine may be conjugated with the DTP vaccine or given as a separate vaccination

2. The graph at the top of the previous page illustrates how a person reacts to the injection of the same antibody on two separate occasions. This represents the initial vaccination followed by a booster shot.

   (a) State over what time period the antigen levels were monitored: _____

   (b) State what happens to the antibody levels after the first injection: _____

   _____

   (c) State what happens to the antibody levels after the booster shot: _____

   _____

   (d) Explain why the second injection has a markedly different effect: _____

   _____

3. The whole question of whether young children should be immunised has been a point of hot debate with some parents. The parents that do not want their children immunised have strongly held reasons for doing so. In a balanced way, explore the arguments for and against childhood immunisation:

   (a) State clearly the benefits from childhood immunisation: _____

   _____

   _____

   (b) Explain why some parents are concerned about immunising their children: _____

   _____

   _____

4. Consult your family doctor or medical centre and list three vaccinations that are recommended for travellers to overseas destinations with high risk of infectious disease:

   (a) Country/region: _____ Vaccine required: _____

   (b) Country/region: _____ Vaccine required: _____

   (c) Country/region: _____ Vaccine required: _____

Types of Vaccine

There are two basic types of vaccine: subunit vaccines and whole-agent vaccines. **Whole-agent vaccines** contain complete nonvirulent microbes, either **inactivated** (killed), or alive but **attenuated** (weakened). Attenuated viruses make very effective vaccines and often provide life-long immunity without the need for booster immunisations. Killed viruses are less effective and many vaccines of this sort have now been replaced by newer subunit vaccines. **Subunit vaccines** contain only the parts of the pathogen that induce the immune response. They are safer than attenuated vaccines because they cannot reproduce in the recipient, and they produce fewer adverse effects because they contain little or no extra material. Subunit vaccines can be made

using a variety of methods, including cell fragmentation (*acellular vaccines*), inactivation of toxins (*toxoids*), genetic engineering (*recombinant vaccines*), and combination with antigenic proteins (*conjugated vaccines*). In all cases, the subunit vaccine loses its ability to cause disease but retains its antigenic properties so that it is still effective in inducing an immune response. Some of the most promising types of vaccine under development are the DNA vaccines, consisting of naked DNA which is injected into the body and produces an antigenic protein. The safety of DNA vaccines is uncertain but they show promise for use against rapidly mutating viruses such as influenza and HIV.

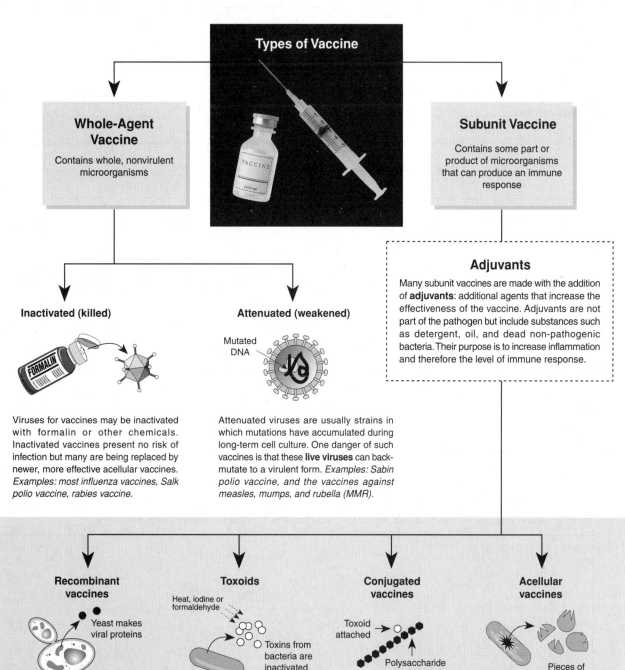

Types of Vaccine

Whole-Agent Vaccine

Contains whole, nonvirulent microorganisms

Subunit Vaccine

Contains some part or product of microorganisms that can produce an immune response

Adjuvants

Many subunit vaccines are made with the addition of **adjuvants**: additional agents that increase the effectiveness of the vaccine. Adjuvants are not part of the pathogen but include substances such as detergent, oil, and dead non-pathogenic bacteria. Their purpose is to increase inflammation and therefore the level of immune response.

Inactivated (killed)

Viruses for vaccines may be inactivated with formalin or other chemicals. Inactivated vaccines present no risk of infection but many are being replaced by newer, more effective acellular vaccines. *Examples: most influenza vaccines, Salk polio vaccine, rabies vaccine.*

Attenuated (weakened)

Mutated DNA

Attenuated viruses are usually strains in which mutations have accumulated during long-term cell culture. One danger of such vaccines is that these **live viruses** can back-mutate to a virulent form. *Examples: Sabin polio vaccine, and the vaccines against measles, mumps, and rubella (MMR).*

Recombinant vaccines

Yeast makes viral proteins

Recombinant sub-unit vaccines can be made using genetic engineering techniques, where non-pathogenic microbes (yeast and bacteria) are programmed to make a desired antigenic fraction. *Example: hepatitis B vaccine.*

Toxoids

Heat, iodine or formaldehyde

Toxins from bacteria are inactivated

Toxoids are bacterial toxins that have been inactivated by heat or chemicals. When injected, the toxoid stimulates the production of antitoxins (antibodies) that neutralise any circulating toxin. *Examples: diphtheria vaccine, tetanus vaccine.*

Conjugated vaccines

Toxoid attached

Polysaccharide from pathogen

Some pathogens produce poly-saccharide capsules that are poorly antigenic, especially in young children. To enhance their effectiveness, they are combined with proteins such as toxoids from other pathogens. *Example: vaccine against Haemophilus influenzae b.*

Acellular vaccines

Pieces of bacterial cells

Involves the fragmentation of a conventional whole-agent vaccine and collecting only those portions that contain the desired antigens. Because the complete cells are not used, infection is not possible. *Examples: newer whooping cough and typhoid vaccines.*

Defence and the Immune System

Related activities: Immunisation, Edible Vaccines, The Structure of Viruses

RA 3

1. Describe briefly how each of the following types of vaccine are made and name an example of each:

(a) Whole-agent vaccine: _____

_____

(b) Subunit vaccine: _____

_____

(c) Inactivated vaccine: _____

_____

(d) Attenuated vaccine: _____

_____

(e) Recombinant vaccine: _____

_____

(f) Toxoid vaccine: _____

_____

(g) Conjugated vaccine: _____

_____

(h) Acellular vaccine: _____

_____

2. **Attenuated viruses** provide long term immunity to their recipients and generally do not require booster shots. Suggest a possible reason why attenuated viruses provide such effective long-term immunity when inactivated viruses do not:

_____

_____

3. Bearing in mind the structure of viruses, explain why heat cannot be used to kill viruses to make **inactivated vaccines**:

_____

_____

4. (a) Vaccines may now be produced using **recombinant DNA technology**. Describe an advantage of creating vaccines using these methods:

_____

(b) Draw a simple diagram to illustrate the use of the recombinant method to manufacture a vaccine:

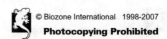

Monoclonal Antibodies

A **monoclonal antibody** is an artificially produced antibody that binds to and inactivates only one specific protein (antigen). Monoclonal antibodies are produced in the laboratory by stimulating the production of B-lymphocytes in mice injected with the antigen. These B-lymphocytes produce an antibody against the antigen. When isolated and made to fuse with immortal tumour cells, they can be cultured indefinitely in a suitable growing medium (as shown below). Monoclonal antibodies are useful for three reasons: they are totally uniform (i.e. clones), they can be produced in very large quantities at low cost, and they are highly specific. The uses of antibodies produced by this method range from diagnostic tools, to treatments for infections and cancer, and prevention of tissue rejection in transplant patients. Many of the diagnostic tests, e.g. for some sexually transmitted or parasitic infections, previously required relatively difficult culturing or microscopic methods for diagnosis. In addition, newer diagnostic test using monoclonal antibodies are easier to interpret and often require fewer highly trained personnel.

Making Monoclonal Antibodies

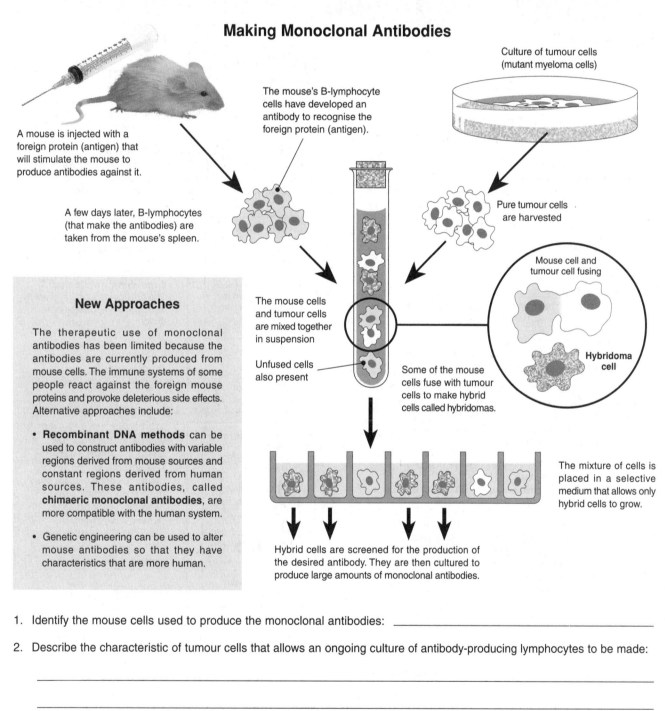

A mouse is injected with a foreign protein (antigen) that will stimulate the mouse to produce antibodies against it.

A few days later, B-lymphocytes (that make the antibodies) are taken from the mouse's spleen.

The mouse's B-lymphocyte cells have developed an antibody to recognise the foreign protein (antigen).

Culture of tumour cells (mutant myeloma cells)

Pure tumour cells are harvested

Mouse cell and tumour cell fusing

Hybridoma cell

The mouse cells and tumour cells are mixed together in suspension

Unfused cells also present

Some of the mouse cells fuse with tumour cells to make hybrid cells called hybridomas.

New Approaches

The therapeutic use of monoclonal antibodies has been limited because the antibodies are currently produced from mouse cells. The immune systems of some people react against the foreign mouse proteins and provoke deleterious side effects. Alternative approaches include:

- **Recombinant DNA methods** can be used to construct antibodies with variable regions derived from mouse sources and constant regions derived from human sources. These antibodies, called **chimaeric monoclonal antibodies**, are more compatible with the human system.

- Genetic engineering can be used to alter mouse antibodies so that they have characteristics that are more human.

The mixture of cells is placed in a selective medium that allows only hybrid cells to grow.

Hybrid cells are screened for the production of the desired antibody. They are then cultured to produce large amounts of monoclonal antibodies.

1. Identify the mouse cells used to produce the monoclonal antibodies: _____

2. Describe the characteristic of tumour cells that allows an ongoing culture of antibody-producing lymphocytes to be made:

_____

_____

3. Compare the method of producing monoclonal antibodies using mice with the alternative methods now available:

_____

_____

_____

_____

Related activities: Antibodies

RA 2

Defence and the Immune System

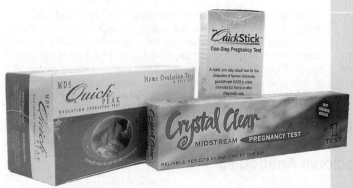

Detecting Pregnancy using Monoclonal Antibodies

When a woman becomes pregnant, a hormone called **human chorionic gonadotropin** (HCG) is released from the placenta. HCG accumulates in the bloodstream and is excreted in the urine. HCG is a glycoprotein, which means antibodies can be produced against it and used in simple test kits (below) to determine if a woman is pregnant. Monoclonal antibodies are also used in other home testing kits, such as those for detecting ovulation time (far left).

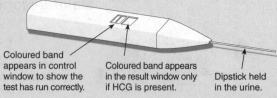

Coloured band appears in control window to show the test has run correctly.

Coloured band appears in the result window only if HCG is present.

Dipstick held in the urine.

How home pregnancy detection kits work

The test area of the dipstick (below) contains two types of antibodies: free monoclonal antibodies and capture monoclonal antibodies, bound to the substrate in the test window.

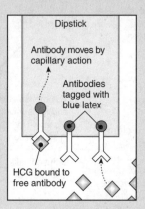

Dipstick

Antibody moves by capillary action

Antibodies tagged with blue latex

HCG bound to free antibody

The free antibodies are specific for HCG and are colour-labelled. HCG in the urine of a pregnant woman binds to the free antibodies on the surface of the dipstick. The antibodies then travel up the dipstick by capillary action.

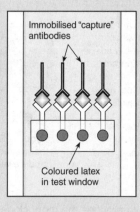

Immobilised "capture" antibodies

Coloured latex in test window

The capture antibodies are specific for the HCG-free antibody complex. The HCG-free antibody complexes travelling up the dipstick are bound by the immobilised **"capture" antibodies**, forming a sandwich. The colour labelled antibodies then create a visible colour change in the test window.

Other Applications of Monoclonal Antibodies

Diagnostic uses

• Detecting the presence of pathogens such as *Chlamydia* and streptococcal bacteria, distinguishing between *Herpesvirus* I and II, and diagnosing AIDS.

• Measuring protein, toxin, or drug levels in serum.

• Blood and tissue typing.

• Detection of antibiotic residues in milk.

Therapeutic uses

• Neutralising endotoxins produced by bacteria in blood infections.

• Used to prevent organ rejection, e.g. in kidney transplants, by interfering with the T cells involved with the rejection of transplanted tissue.

• Used in the treatment of some auto-immune disorders such as rheumatoid arthritis and allergic asthma. The monoclonal antibodies bind to and inactivate factors involved in the cascade leading to the inflammatory response.

• Immunodetection and immunotherapy of cancer. Newer methods specifically target the cell membranes of tumour cells, shrinking solid tumours without harmful side effects.

• Inhibition of platelet clumping, which is used to prevent reclogging of coronary arteries in patients who have undergone angioplasty. The monoclonal antibodies bind to the receptors on the platelet surface that are normally linked by fibrinogen during the clotting process.

4. For each of the following applications, suggest why an antibody-based test or therapy is so valuable:

(a) Detection of toxins or bacteria in perishable foods: _____

_____

_____

(b) Detection of pregnancy without a doctor's prescription: _____

_____

(c) Targeted treatment of tumours in cancer patients: _____

_____

Aspects of Human Health

AQA-A	AQA-B	SNAB	Edexcel	OCR
Not applicable to the AS biology course	Not applicable to the AS course	Complete: 1, 15-18, 20-30	Not applicable to the AS course	Complete: 1-6, 7, 9-14(a)-(d), 15-16, 19-20, 23-26

Learning Objectives

☐ 1. Compile your own glossary from the **KEY WORDS** displayed in **bold type** in the learning objectives below.

The Nature of Disease

Classification of disease *(pages 285, 310)*

☐ 2. Define the terms **disease**, **infection**, **symptom**. Explain clearly what is meant by **health**. Distinguish between **acute** and **chronic diseases**.

☐ 3. Giving an example of each, explain what is meant by the following categories of disease: **infectious**, **non-infectious**, **deficiency**, **inherited** (genetic), **mental**, **degenerative**, **social**, and **self-inflicted**. Understand that some diseases fall into more than one category. Recognise **physical diseases** as all diseases except mental disorders with no apparent physical cause.

Patterns of disease *(pages 286-288)*

☐ 4. Explain patterns of disease distribution: **pandemic**, **epidemic**, and **endemic disease**. Provide examples to clearly illustrate these different patterns.

☐ 5. Distinguish between **aetiology** and **epidemiology**. Explain the role health statistics (gathered from epidemiological studies) in the prediction and management of disease outbreaks. Include reference to **prevalence**, **incidence**, **morbidity**, and **mortality**.

☐ 6. Describe and explain differences in the standards of health in developed and developing countries.

Detecting and treating disease *(pages 85, 144, 289-290, 294-295, 297-298, 303-306, 333-336 and see the TRC: Prenatal Diagnosis of Disease, Genetic Counselling)*

☐ 7. Appreciate the significance of the **Human Genome Project** to the detection (and treatment) of human disease and the maintenance of health.

☐ 8. Discuss the technologies available for detecting and diagnosing medical disorders. Include reference to any of the following: **X-ray imaging** and **radionuclide scanning**, computer imaging techniques such as **MRI** and **CT scanning**, **endoscopy**, **electrocardiography**, enzyme-based **biosensors**.

☐ 9. Understand the role of each of the following in treating and/or preventing disease as appropriate to your chosen case studies: **surgery**, **antibiotics**, therapeutic **drugs** (other than antibiotics), **diet**, and **exercise** (particularly sustained aerobic exercise or **training**).

Non-infectious Diseases *(pages 285, 297-298, 305)*

☐ 10. Recall what is meant by a **non-infectious disease** and recognise different categories of non-infectious disease. Understand that non-infectious diseases often result from the combined effects of environmental, hereditary, and biological factors.

☐ 11. Discuss the role of diet and **exercise** in the prevention of some lifestyle diseases (e.g. **obesity**, **cardiovascular disease**, and **hypertension**).

Diet and its role in disease *(pages 296-300)*

☐ 12. Describe the concept of a **balanced diet**, recognising its components in terms of adequate intake and functions of **protein** (including **essential amino acids**), **fats** (including **essential fatty acids**), **carbohydrates**, **vitamins** (including A and D), and **minerals**.

☐ 13. Discuss the energy and nutrient requirements of people with reference to gender, age, activity level, pregnancy, and lactation. Explain what is meant by a dietary reference value (DRV) and describe the different ways in which DRVs are used.

☐ 14. Distinguish between **starvation** and **malnutrition**. Describe the causes and consequences of malnutrition with reference to some or all of the following:
  (a) Energy and protein deficiency
  (b) **Anorexia nervosa** and/or bulimia nervosa
  (c) **Obesity** and/or excessive intake of fat and salt
  (d) Deficiency of vitamins A and D
  (e) Deficiency of vitamin C and mineral ions

☐ 15. Discuss the possible links between diet and **coronary heart disease** (also called coronary artery disease).

Cardiovascular disease *(pages 264, 291, 301-304)*

☐ 16. Recognise the term **cardiovascular disease** (CVD), as a broad term encompassing a variety of diseases. Identify CVDs associated with a poor diet and lifestyle, and those that are congenital.

☐ 17. Describe the **blood clotting** process and identify its role in cardiovascular disease.

☐ 18. Describe the features of some cardiovascular diseases and disorders as follows:
  (a) **Atheroma** (in this context, synonymous with **atherosclerosis**) and its link with increased risk of **aneurysm** and **coronary thrombosis**.
  (b) **Hypertension**.
  (c) **Myocardial infarction** (heart attack). Describe risk factors in the development of cardiovascular disease (also see #24-25)

☐ 19. Describe the **epidemiology** of cardiovascular diseases, particularly coronary heart disease. Relate their global pattern of occurrence to lifestyle factors.

☐ 20. Describe techniques for the treatment of coronary heart disease, including **coronary bypass surgery**, **heart transplant**, and **angioplasty**. Describe the problems of maintaining heart health after such treatments.

Smoking and disease *(pages 291-292)*

☐ 21. Identify some of the harmful constituents of cigarette smoke and explain the role of tobacco as a cause of preventable disease.

☐ 22. Describe the effects of the **tars** and **carcinogens** in tobacco smoke on the gas exchange system.

☐ 23. Describe the symptoms of the diseases associated with tobacco smoking: **lung cancer**, **chronic bronchitis**, and **emphysema**.

☐ 24. Describe the effects of **nicotine** and **carbon monoxide** on the cardiovascular system. Include reference to the development and symptoms of **coronary heart disease**, **atherosclerosis**, and **stroke**.

☐ 25. Discuss the ways in which smoking may affect the risk of developing cardiovascular disease (also see #18).

☐ 26. Evaluate the epidemiological and experimental evidence linking cigarette smoking to the incidence of disease and early death.

Cancers *(pages 159, 291-295)*

☐ 27. Define the terms: **cancer**, **tumour**, and **carcinogen**. List some of the known causes of cancers. Recognise the involvement of environmental, hereditary, and/or biological factors in the development of cancers.

☐ 28. Describe tumour growth and explain how cancers spread (undergo **metastasis**). Identify why some cancers spread more rapidly than others. Distinguish between **benign** and **malignant tumours**.

☐ 29. Describe the cause, development, **symptoms**, **diagnosis**, treatment, and **prognosis** for a named cancer, e.g. **lung cancer** or **malignant skin cancer**.

☐ 30. Consider the effectiveness of treatments generally available for cancer. Discuss the role of early detection as an aid to more effective cancer control.

Degenerative diseases *(page 307)*

☐ 31. Identify the physiological basis of **ageing**. Describe measures to delay the onset of degenerative disease and evaluate their effectiveness.

☐ 32. Describe some of the **degenerative diseases** of ageing, including their symptoms and physiological basis. Include reference to any of the following:
(a) **Alzheimer's disease (senile dementia)**.
(b) **Osteoarthritis**.
(c) **Osteoporosis**.
(d) **Cataracts**.

 See the 'Textbook Reference Grid' on pages 8-9 for textbook page references relating to material in this topic.

Supplementary Texts

See pages 5-6 for additional details of these texts:

■ Fullick, A., 1998. **Human Health and Disease** (Heinemann), chpt. 1, 3-6 as required.

■ Murray, P. & N. Owens, 2001. **Behaviour and Populations** (Collins), chpt 8.

See page 7 for details of publishers of periodicals:

STUDENT'S REFERENCE

■ **What is Cancer?** Biol. Sci. Rev., 11(1) Sept. 1998, pp. 38-41. *The cellular basis of cancer, with a look at some new ways to combat the disease.*

■ **Cancer: What is it and how is it Treated?** Biol. Sci. Rev., 16(1) Sept. 2003, pp. 26-30. *A definition of cancer, with an explanation of its genetic basis, and a list of types. Methods of treatment and their physiological action are discussed.*

■ **Coronary Heart Disease** Biol. Sci. Rev., 18(1) Sept. 2005, pp. 21-24. *An account of cardiovascular disease, including risk factors and treatments.*

■ **Heart Disease and Cholesterol** Biol. Sci. Rev., 13(2) Nov. 2000, pp. 2-5. *The links between dietary fat, cholesterol level, and heart disease.*

■ **Smoking** Biol. Sci. Rev., 10(1) Sept. 1997, pp. 14-16. *Smoking related diseases and the effects of tobacco smoking on human physiology.*

■ **Why are we so Fat?** National Geographic, 206(2), August 2004, pp. 46-61. *A comprehensive account of the obesity in America and around the world. Includes a summary of health problems associated with obesity.*

■ **Diabetes** Biol. Sci. Rev., 15(2) November 2002, pp. 30-35. *The nature of Type I diabetes: symptoms, complications, and control of the disease. This account includes details of the structure of the endocrine portion of the pancreas.*

■ **Obesity: Size Matters** Biol. Sci. Rev., 18(4) April 2006, pp. 10-13. *An account of obesity and the health issues surrounding it.*

■ **Leptin** Biol. Sci. Rev., 15(3), Feb. 2003, pp. 30-32. *The role of the hormone leptin in regulating body mass and controlling obesity.*

■ **Lactose Intolerance** Biol. Sci. Rev., 17(3), Feb. 2005, pp. 28-31. *This account describes the nature of lactose intolerance (the inability to digest milk or milk products). Rather than an allergy, this disorder is a physiological response following a genetically programmed loss of the enzymes lactase.*

■ **Obesity: A Weighty Problem** Biol. Sci. Rev., 10(1) Sept. 1997, pp. 17-20. *Human diet, the energy intake equation, and an examination of the genetic and environmental causes of obesity.*

■ **The Good, the Fad and the Unhealthy** New Scientist, 27 Sept. 2006, pp. 42-49. *The facts, the myths and the downright lies of nutrition.*

■ **Eating Disorders: Myths and Misconceptions** Biol. Sci. Rev., 9(5) May 1997, pp. 25-27. *The causes and treatments of eating disorders.*

■ **Vital Vitamins** Biol. Sci. Rev., 11(5) May 1999, pp. 32-35. *The role of dietary vitamins, including the details of diseases caused by vitamin deficiencies.*

■ **Rebuilding the Food Pyramid** Scientific American, January 2003, pp. 52-59. *A major revision of the basic nutritional guidelines provided for consumers and health professionals. A critique of dietary information and an analysis of what we should be eating now (a good topic for debate).*

■ **Food Glorious Food** New Scientist, 18 Oct. 1997, (Inside Science). *Protective and high risk foods, the role of carbohydrates and fibre and aspects of diet-related health and disease.*

■ **The Biology of Ageing** Biol. Sci. Rev., 10(3) January 1998, pp. 18-21. *Ageing and degenerative disease (includes Alzheimer's and its pathology).*

■ **Unravelling the Mysteries of Human Ageing** Biol. Sci. Rev., 14(3) February 2002, pp. 33-37. *The physiology of human ageing and an account of age related diseases and disabilities.*

TEACHER'S REFERENCE

■ **Obesity: An Overblown Epidemic?** Scientific American, June 2005, pp. 48-55. *Arguments for and against the conventional wisdom linking obesity to poorer health and increased incidence of disease.*

■ **Dark Angel** New Scientist, 18 Dec. 2004, pp. 38-41. *An account of the p53 gene and the role of its expressed protein in the prevention and triggering of cancers.*

■ **The Cancer Revolution** New Scientist, 23 August 2003, pp. 36-39. *The use of DNA microarrays to identify the genes responsible for causing cancer. Gene activity signatures could then be used to predict whether a tumour is likely to spread to other parts of the body.*

■ **What You Need to Know About Cancer** SPECIAL ISSUE: Scientific American, Sept. 1996, whole issue. *Thorough coverage of the causes of cancer, its prevention, detection, and therapies.*

■ **Untangling the Roots of Cancer** New Scientist, July 2003, pp. 48-57. *How do cells become malignant? This article includes a diagram to explain theories of cancer development.*

■ **Atherosclerosis: The New View** Scientific American, May 2002, pp. 28-37. *The latest views on the pathological development and rupture of plaques in atherosclerosis. An excellent account.*

■ **How to Defy Death** New Scientist, 25 March 2000, pp. 20-23. *Theories on how diet can promote longevity: eating less may slow cellular damage.*

■ **Piecing Together Alzheimer's** Sci. American, Dec. 2000, pp. 52-59. *An excellent account of the physiology and pathology of this common disease.*

■ **Public Health in Transition** Sci. American, Sept. 2005, pp. 70-77. *Why chronic disorders such as heart disease and diabetes are now universal.*

See pages 10-11 for details of how to access **Bio Links** from our web site: **www.biozone.co.uk**. From Bio Links, access sites under the topics:

GENERAL BIOLOGY ONLINE RESOURCES
• Biology I interactive animations • Instructional multimedia, University of Alberta … *and others* > **Online Textbooks and Lecture Notes:** • S-Cool! A level biology revision guide … *and others* > **Glossaries:** Health glossary … *and others*

HEALTH & DISEASE: • WHO/OMS: Health topics • NIH: Science education > **Non-infectious Diseases:** • Frequently asked questions about diabetes • Oncolink • Cancer Group Institute • Chemicals and human health • Your genes: your health • Heart disease • Cancer Research UK • NCI's Cancernet • Smoking and your digestive system … *and others* > **Human Health Issues:** • British Nutrition Foundation • Eating disorders • Food safety & nutrition info • The effects of drugs on the human body … *and others*

Presentation MEDIA to support this topic:

HEALTH & DISEASE:
• **Non-infectious Disease**

Health vs Disease

Disease is more difficult to define than **health**, which is described as a state of complete physical, mental, and social well-being. A disease is usually associated with particular **symptoms** that help to define and diagnose it. The term **disease** is used to describe a condition whereby part or all of an organism's normal physiological function is upset. All diseases, with the exception of some mental diseases, can be classified as **physical diseases** (i.e. diseases that cause permanent or temporary damage to the body). Physical diseases can be subdivided into two major groups: **infectious diseases** caused by an infectious agent (**pathogen**) and **non-infectious diseases** (most of which are better described as disorders). Non-infectious diseases are often not clearly the result of any single factor, but they can be further categorised into major subgroups according to their principal cause (outlined below). However, many diseases fall into more than one category, e.g. Alzheimer's disease and some cancers.

The Nature of Disease

Infectious Diseases
Infectious diseases are diseases that are caused by pathogens and which can be transmitted from one person to another. Most, although not all, pathogens are microorganisms, and they fall into five main categories: viruses, bacteria, fungi, protozoans, and multicellular parasites.

Mental Disorders
The term mental disorder encompasses a range of diseases that affect a person's thoughts, memory, emotions, and personal behaviour. Examples include Alzheimer's, schizophrenia, and depression.

Deficiency Diseases
Deficiency diseases are non-infectious diseases caused by an inadequate or unbalanced diet, or by over eating. Examples include obesity, rickets, scurvy, marasmus, and kwashiorkor.

Degenerative Diseases
Degenerative diseases are non-infectious diseases caused by ageing and the inability of the body to carry out effective repairs and regeneration. Examples include osteoarthritis, Alzheimer's disease, and many cancers.

Social Diseases
Social diseases include a wide range of disorders that are influenced by living conditions and personal behaviour. They may or may not be caused by an infectious agent. Examples include obesity, sexually transmitted diseases, and lung cancer and emphysema due to smoking.

Inherited Diseases
Some diseases result from inherited malfunctions in a body system and have no external cause. Defective genes may cause the failure of a body system throughout a person's life, or the onset of disease may occur later in life. Examples include cystic fibrosis, multiple sclerosis, Alzheimer's, and Huntington's disease.

Down syndrome is a congenital disease caused by having three copies of chromosome 21.

Smoking is a common social behaviour that causes lung cancer, chronic bronchitis, and emphysema.

Mental diseases encompass a range of often unrelated disorders involving disturbances to personality.

Asthma is a common, non-infectious respiratory disease with a number of underlying causes.

1. Discuss the differences between health and disease: _____

_____

_____

_____

2. Using illustrative examples, suggest why many diseases fall into more than one disease category:

_____

_____

Related activities: Diseases Caused by Smoking, Dietary Disorders, Deficiency Diseases, Cardiovascular Disease, Ageing & Human Health

A 2

The Role of Health Statistics

Health is difficult to define and to measure, and most of the information about the state of health of a nation's population comes from studying disease. **Epidemiology** is the study of the occurrence and the spread of disease. The **health statistics** collected by epidemiologists are used by health authorities to identify patterns of disease in their country. These patterns, including the **incidence** and **prevalence** of a disease are important in planning health services and investigating causes of disease. Health statistics enable the effectiveness of health policies and practices, such as vaccination programmes, to be monitored. The World Health Organisation (WHO) gathers data on an international basis to identify global patterns.

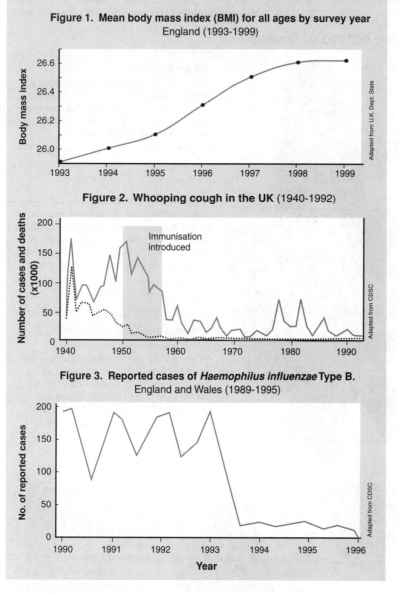

Figure 1. Mean body mass index (BMI) for all ages by survey year
England (1993-1999)

Adapted from U.K. Dept. Stats

Figure 2. Whooping cough in the UK (1940-1992)

Immunisation introduced

Adapted from CDSC

Figure 3. Reported cases of *Haemophilus influenzae* **Type B.**
England and Wales (1989-1995)

Adapted from CDSC

The causes of illness and death for people in developing countries are very different from those in affluent societies.

Figure 4. The causes of death in developed and developing countries, 1998

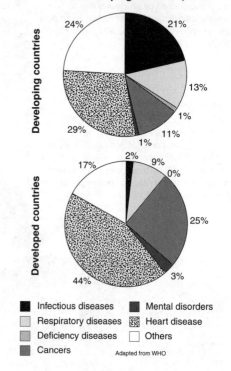

Developing countries

Developed countries

■ Infectious diseases   ■ Mental disorders
☐ Respiratory diseases   ▨ Heart disease
▨ Deficiency diseases   ☐ Others
■ Cancers

Adapted from WHO

1. Explain the contribution of epidemiologists to monitoring public health: _____

_____

2. Describe the trend in BMI between 1993 and 1999 (Figure 1): _____

_____

3. (a) Suggest a probable reason for the pattern of reported cases of *Haemophilus influenzae* (Figure 3) prior to 1993:

_____

(b) Suggest a possible cause for the decline in the incidence of *Haemophilius influenzae* after 1993: _____

_____

4. (a) Identify a difference between the cause of death between developed and developing countries: _____

_____

(b) Suggest a reason for this difference: _____

Patterns of Disease

Diseases present in low levels of a population at any time are known as **endemic** diseases. Occasionally there may be a sudden increase in the **prevalence** of a particular disease. On a local level this is known as an **outbreak**. Such an increase in prevalence on a national scale is called an **epidemic**. An epidemic occurs when an infectious disease spreads rapidly through a population and affects large numbers of people. One example is influenza, epidemics of which are relatively common and occur every two to three years. On rare occasions an epidemic disease will spread to other countries throughout the world. This is known as a **pandemic**. Examples of diseases that are known to have caused pandemics are bubonic plague, cholera, tuberculosis, HIV/AIDS, and influenza. **Epidemiologists** gather data on the number of infected people (**morbidity**) and the number of people that have died (**mortality**) within a population. These data help to establish the **incidence** (number of new cases per unit time) and **prevalence** (number of infected people expressed as a proportion of the population) of the disease in the population at any given time. **Aetiology** is the study of the cause of a disease. It can assist in pinpointing the origin of new diseases, such as the respiratory disease SARS (see the next page), as they arise in populations.

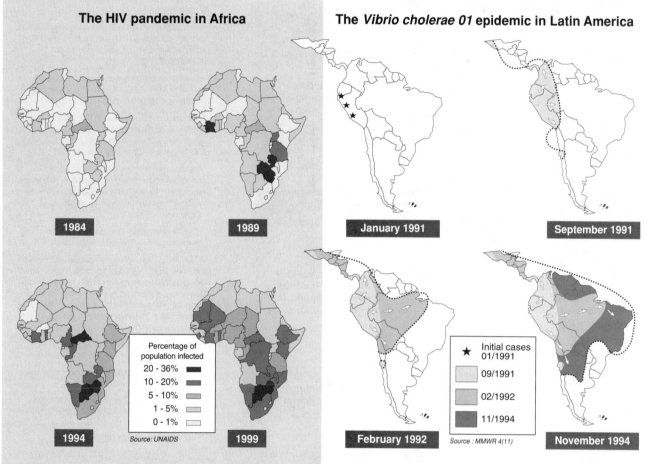

The HIV pandemic in Africa

1984

1989

Percentage of
population infected

20 - 36%
10 - 20%
5 - 10%
1 - 5%
0 - 1%

1994   *Source: UNAIDS*

1999

The *Vibrio cholerae 01* epidemic in Latin America

January 1991

September 1991

★ Initial cases
01/1991
09/1991
02/1992
11/1994

February 1992   *Source : MMWR 4(11)*

November 1994

The figure above shows the spread of HIV through Africa as part of the current global pandemic. More than 36 million people are infected with HIV worldwide and 70% of those infected live in sub-Saharan Africa. In this region, seven countries have an adult prevalence of 20% or higher, including Botswana where 36% of the population is infected.

Cholera had not been reported in Latin America for over a century before the initial outbreaks occurred in January, 1991. Cholera is transmitted through ingestion of food and beverages contaminated with faeces, or by bathing in faecally contaminated water. By the time the epidemic began to subside in 1994, more than 1 million cases and nearly 10 000 deaths had been reported. Death rates were high as a result of inadequate provision for oral rehydration.

1. Using examples, distinguish between different patterns of disease (epidemic, pandemic, and endemic disease):

_____

_____

_____

_____

_____

2. Suggest why it is important to establish the **incidence** of a disease when it begins to spread through a community:

_____

_____

Related activities: Cholera, Epidemiology of AIDS, Emerging Diseases

The Initial Spread of SARS in Toronto, Canada
(February – April, 2003)

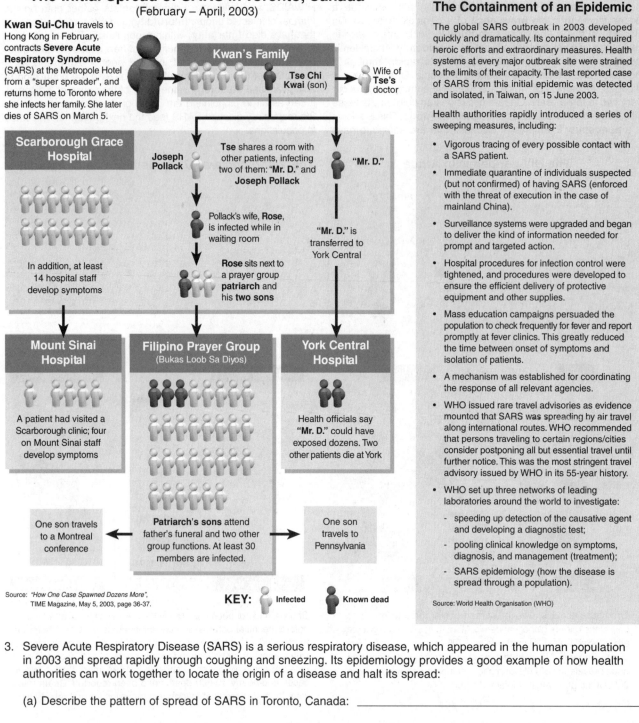

Kwan Sui-Chu travels to Hong Kong in February, contracts **Severe Acute Respiratory Syndrome** (SARS) at the Metropole Hotel from a "super spreader", and returns home to Toronto where she infects her family. She later dies of SARS on March 5.

Kwan's Family

Tse Chi Kwai (son) → Wife of **Tse's** doctor

Scarborough Grace Hospital

Joseph Pollack

Tse shares a room with other patients, infecting two of them: "**Mr. D.**" and **Joseph Pollack**

"**Mr. D.**"

In addition, at least 14 hospital staff develop symptoms

Pollack's wife, **Rose**, is infected while in waiting room

Rose sits next to a prayer group **patriarch** and his **two sons**

"**Mr. D.**" is transferred to York Central

Mount Sinai Hospital

A patient had visited a Scarborough clinic; four on Mount Sinai staff develop symptoms

Filipino Prayer Group (Bukas Loob Sa Diyos)

York Central Hospital

Health officials say "**Mr. D.**" could have exposed dozens. Two other patients die at York

One son travels to a Montreal conference

Patriarch's sons attend father's funeral and two other group functions. At least 30 members are infected.

One son travels to Pennsylvania

Source: "How One Case Spawned Dozens More", TIME Magazine, May 5, 2003, page 36-37.

KEY: Infected   Known dead

The Containment of an Epidemic

The global SARS outbreak in 2003 developed quickly and dramatically. Its containment required heroic efforts and extraordinary measures. Health systems at every major outbreak site were strained to the limits of their capacity. The last reported case of SARS from this initial epidemic was detected and isolated, in Taiwan, on 15 June 2003.

Health authorities rapidly introduced a series of sweeping measures, including:

- Vigorous tracing of every possible contact with a SARS patient.

- Immediate quarantine of individuals suspected (but not confirmed) of having SARS (enforced with the threat of execution in the case of mainland China).

- Surveillance systems were upgraded and began to deliver the kind of information needed for prompt and targeted action.

- Hospital procedures for infection control were tightened, and procedures were developed to ensure the efficient delivery of protective equipment and other supplies.

- Mass education campaigns persuaded the population to check frequently for fever and report promptly at fever clinics. This greatly reduced the time between onset of symptoms and isolation of patients.

- A mechanism was established for coordinating the response of all relevant agencies.

- WHO issued rare travel advisories as evidence mounted that SARS was spreading by air travel along international routes. WHO recommended that persons traveling to certain regions/cities consider postponing all but essential travel until further notice. This was the most stringent travel advisory issued by WHO in its 55-year history.

- WHO set up three networks of leading laboratories around the world to investigate:
  - speeding up detection of the causative agent and developing a diagnostic test;
  - pooling clinical knowledge on symptoms, diagnosis, and management (treatment);
  - SARS epidemiology (how the disease is spread through a population).

Source: World Health Organisation (WHO)

---

3. Severe Acute Respiratory Disease (SARS) is a serious respiratory disease, which appeared in the human population in 2003 and spread rapidly through coughing and sneezing. Its epidemiology provides a good example of how health authorities can work together to locate the origin of a disease and halt its spread:

(a) Describe the pattern of spread of SARS in Toronto, Canada: _____

_____

(b) Describe the particular features of disease control that were important in containing the spread of SARS:

_____

_____

(c) Identify which aspect of modern life contributed to the rapid global spread of SARS: _____

_____

4. Suggest why aetiology is important when controlling an outbreak of a new disease: _____

_____

_____

Diagnosing Medical Problems

The proper and prompt treatment of disease requires accurate, rapid diagnosis. Some diagnostic techniques, such as CT and MRI scans (below), are very sophisticated, while others (e.g. blood and glucose tests using biosensors) are less complicated.

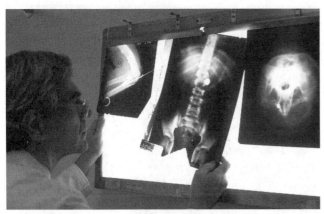

X-ray imaging

X-rays are a form of electromagnetic radiation that can pass through tissues and expose photographic film. The X-rays are absorbed by dense body tissues (e.g. bone) which appear as white areas, but they pass easily through less dense tissues (e.g. muscle), which appear dark. X-rays are used to identify fractures or abnormalities in bone. X-ray technology is also used in conjunction with computer imaging techniques (see below).

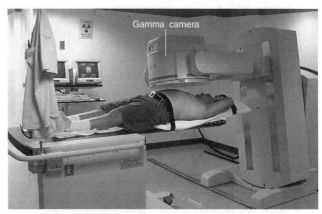

Gamma camera

Radionuclide scanning

Radionuclide scanning involves introducing a radioactive substance (the radionuclide) into the body, where it is taken up in different amounts by different tissues (e.g. radioactive iodine is taken up preferentially by the thyroid). The radiation emitted by the tissues that take up the radionuclide is detected by a gamma camera. Radionuclide scanning provides better detail of function than other techniques, but gives less anatomical detail.

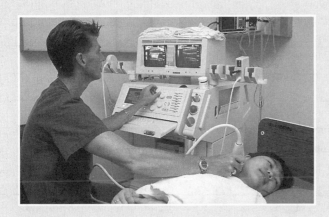

Diagnostic uses of ultrasound

Ultrasound is a diagnostic tool used to visualise internal structures without surgery or X-rays. Ultrasound imaging is based on the fact that tissues of different densities reflect sound waves differently. Sound waves are directed towards a structure (e.g. uterus, heart, kidney, liver) and the reflected sound waves are recorded. An image of the internal structures is analysed by computer and displayed on a screen.

Echocardiography uses ultrasound to investigate heart disorders such as congenital heart disease and valve disorders. The liver and other abdominal organs can also be viewed with ultrasound for diagnosis of disorders such as cirrhosis, cysts, blockages, and tumours. Ultrasound scans of the uterus are commonly used during pregnancy to indicate placental position and aspects of foetal growth and development. This information aids better pregnancy management.

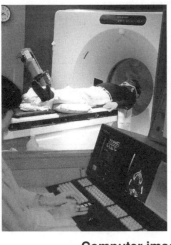

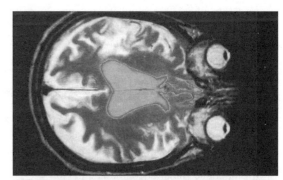

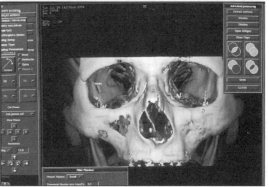

Computer imaging techniques

Computers are used extensively to examine the soft tissues of the body for diagnostic purposes. The photos directly above show **magnetic resonance imaging** (MRI), which uses computer analysis of high frequency radio waves to map out variations in tissue density, especially of the central nervous system (above, far right). In **computerised tomography** (CT) scans, a series of X-rays is made through an organ and the picture from each X-ray slice is reconstructed (using computer software) into a 3-D image (e.g. the skull, right). Such images can be used to detect abnormalities such as tumours.

Related activities: Cancer, Breast Cancer, Cardiovascular Disease
Web links: Genetic Counselling, Prenatal Diagnosis of Disease

RA 2

Endoscopy

An **endoscope** is an illuminated tube comprising fibre-optic cables with lenses attached. Endoscopy can be used for a visual inspection of the inside of organs (or any body cavity) to look for blockages or damage. Endoscopes can also be fitted with devices to remove foreign objects, temporarily stop bleeding, remove tissue samples (biopsy), and remove polyps or growths.

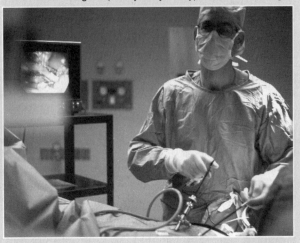

Laparoscopy is the endoscopic examination of the organs in the abdominal cavity, and is used during simple surgical operations (e.g. tubal ligation). Endoscopic examination of the stomach is called gastroscopy.

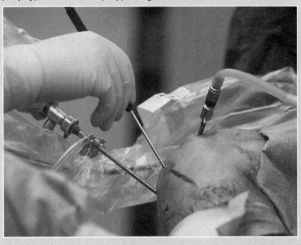

Arthroscopy is used for inspecting joints, usually knee joints (above), while the patient is under a general anaesthetic. Using very small incisions, damaged cartilage can be removed from the joint using other instruments.

1. Explain how radionuclide scanning differs from X-rays: _____

_____

_____

2. (a) Describe the benefits of using ultrasound over X-rays: _____

_____

_____

(b) Echocardiography was the first medical application of ultrasound. Describe how it could be used in detecting cardiovascular disease:

_____

_____

(c) Explain how ultrasound can be used in conjunction with mammography in detecting breast cancer:

_____

_____

3. Describe the basic principle of the scanning technology behind each of the following computer imaging techniques:

(a) Computerised Tomography (CT): _____

_____

(b) Magnetic Resonance Imaging (MRI): _____

_____

4. Describe the benefits of using computer imaging techniques such as MRI or CT: _____

_____

_____

5. Describe the benefits of endoscopy over conventional open surgery: _____

_____

_____

Diseases Caused by Smoking

Tobacco smoking has only recently been accepted as a major health hazard, despite its practice in developed countries for more than 400 years, and much longer elsewhere. Cigarettes became popular at the end of World War I because they were cheap, convenient, and easier to smoke than pipes and cigars. They remain popular for the further reason that they are more addictive than other forms of tobacco. The milder smoke can be more readily inhaled, allowing **nicotine** (a powerful addictive poison) to be quickly absorbed into the bloodstream. **Lung cancer** is the most widely known and most harmful effect of smoking. Tobacco smoking is also directly associated with coronary artery disease, emphysema, chronic bronchitis, peripheral vascular disease, and stroke. Despite recent indications that mortality due to smoking may be declining in the UK, one third of all deaths from cancer, including around 80% of lung cancer deaths, are linked to this cause. The damaging components of cigarette smoke include tar, carbon monoxide, nitrogen dioxide, and nitric oxide. Many of these harmful chemicals occur in greater concentrations in sidestream smoke (**passive smoking**) than in mainstream smoke (inhaled) due to the presence of a filter in the cigarette.

Long term effects of tobacco smoking

Smoking damages the arteries of the brain and may result in a **stroke**.

All forms of tobacco-smoking increase the risk of **mouth cancer**, **lip cancer**, and **cancer of the throat** (pharynx).

Lung cancer is the best known harmful effect of smoking.

In a young man who smokes 20 cigarettes a day, the risk of **coronary artery disease** is increased by about three times over that of a nonsmoker.

Smoking leads to severe constriction of the arteries supplying blood to the extremities and leads to **peripheral vascular disease**.

Short term effects of tobacco smoking

- Reduction in capacity of the lungs.
- Increase in muscle tension and a decrease in steadiness of the hands.
- Raised blood pressure (10-30 points).
- Very sharp rise in carbon monoxide levels in the lungs contributing to breathlessness.
- Increase in pulse rate by up to 20 beats per minute.
- Surface blood vessel constriction drops skin temperature by up to 5°C.
- Dulling of appetite as well as the sense of smell and taste.

How smoking damages the lungs

Non-smoker

Normal alveoli arrangement

Thin layer of mucus

Cilia

Cells lining airways

Smoker

Coalesced alveoli

Extra mucus produced

Smoke particles

Cancerous cell

Smoke particles indirectly destroy the walls of the lung's alveoli.

Cavities lined by heavy black tar deposits.

SPECIMEN A-73-309   DATE

Gross pathology of lung tissue from a patient with emphysema. Tobacco tar deposits can be seen. Tar contains at least 17 known carcinogens.

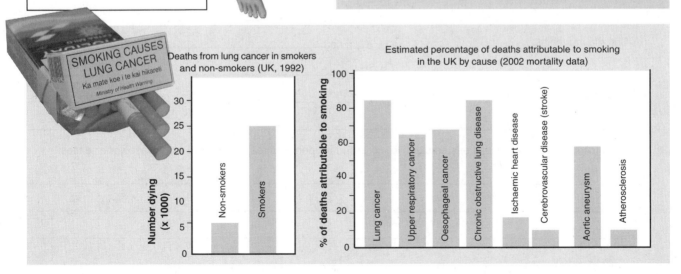

SMOKING CAUSES LUNG CANCER
Ka mate koe i te kai hikareti
Ministry of Health Warning

Deaths from lung cancer in smokers and non-smokers (UK, 1992)

Number dying (x 1000): Non-smokers, Smokers

Estimated percentage of deaths attributable to smoking in the UK by cause (2002 mortality data)

% of deaths attributable to smoking: Lung cancer, Upper respiratory cancer, Oesophageal cancer, Chronic obstructive lung disease, Ischaemic heart disease, Cerebrovascular disease (stroke), Aortic aneurysm, Atherosclerosis

Related activities: Cancer, Cardiovascular Disease

Components of Cigarette Smoke

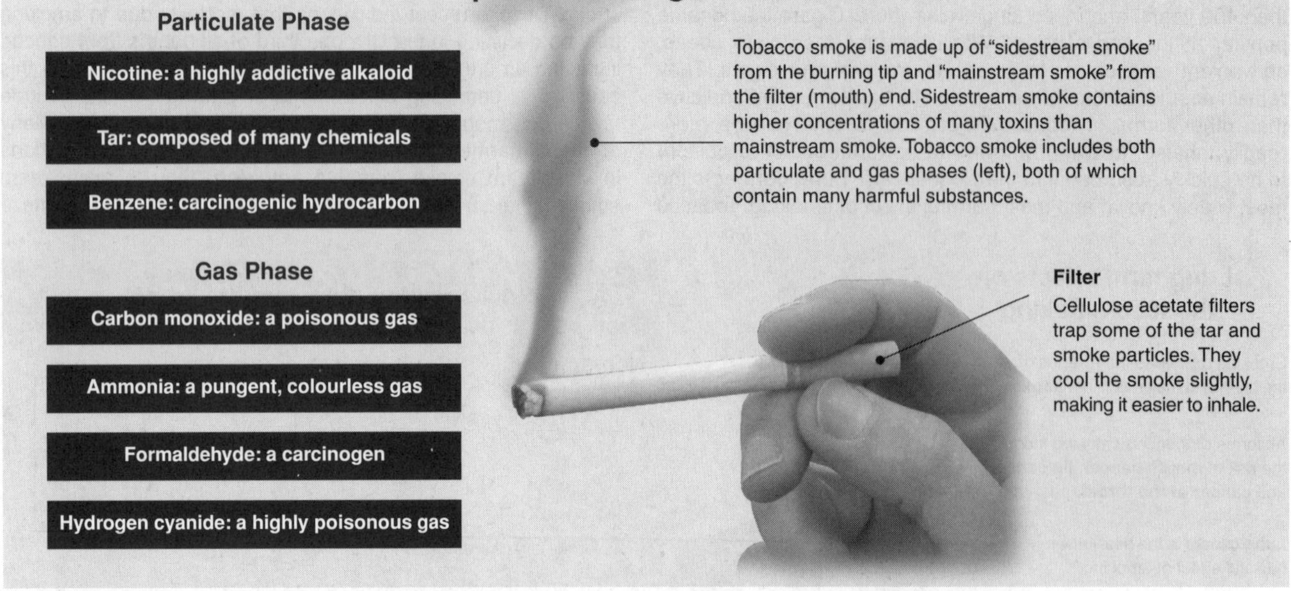

Particulate Phase

Nicotine: a highly addictive alkaloid

Tar: composed of many chemicals

Benzene: carcinogenic hydrocarbon

Gas Phase

Carbon monoxide: a poisonous gas

Ammonia: a pungent, colourless gas

Formaldehyde: a carcinogen

Hydrogen cyanide: a highly poisonous gas

Tobacco smoke is made up of "sidestream smoke" from the burning tip and "mainstream smoke" from the filter (mouth) end. Sidestream smoke contains higher concentrations of many toxins than mainstream smoke. Tobacco smoke includes both particulate and gas phases (left), both of which contain many harmful substances.

Filter
Cellulose acetate filters trap some of the tar and smoke particles. They cool the smoke slightly, making it easier to inhale.

1. Discuss the physical changes to the lung that result from long-term smoking:

2. Determine the physiological effect of each of the following constituents of tobacco smoke when inhaled:

    (a) Tar:

    (b) Nicotine:

    (c) Carbon monoxide:

3. Describe the symptoms of the following diseases associated with long-term smoking:

    (a) Emphysema:

    (b) Chronic bronchitis:

    (c) Lung cancer:

4. Evaluate the evidence linking cigarette smoking to increased incidence of respiratory and cardiovascular diseases:

Cancer

Cancer is a term describing a large group of diseases characterised by the progressive and uncontrolled growth of abnormal cells. Cancer is not a new disease, nor is it restricted just to humans. Most other animals suffer from cancer; evidence of it has even been found in the fossilised bones of dinosaurs. There is no single cause for all the forms of cancer; environmental, genetic, and biological factors may all be involved. Although the incidence of cancer has apparently increased in more recent times, this may simply reflect our increased life spans, as the incidence of many cancers increases with age. In 2005, cancers accounted for 26% of all deaths in the UK, making cancer the leading cause of mortality after cardiovascular disease. Of all cancer deaths, nearly half are caused by just four cancers (lung, bowel, breast, and prostate).

Features of Cancer Cells

The bloated, lumpy shape is readily distinguishable from a healthy cell, which has a flat, scaly appearance.

Metabolism may be deranged and the cell ceases to function.

Cancerous cells lose their attachments to neighbouring cells.

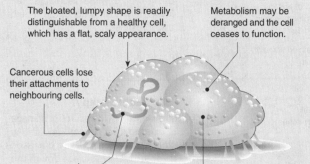

Cancer cells may have unusual numbers of chromosomes.

Cancer cells can go on dividing indefinitely, if they have a continual supply of nutrients, and are said to be immortal.

The diagram *above* shows a single **lung cell** that has become cancerous. It no longer carries out the role of a lung cell, and instead takes on a parasitic 'lifestyle', taking from the body what it needs in the way of nutrients and contributing nothing in return. The rate of cell division is greater than in normal cells in the same tissue because there is no *resting phase* between divisions.

Common Cancers

Skin cancer (melanoma): Cancerous tumours usually develop on skin exposed to **UV light**, but can occur anywhere on the body. Melanomas generally develop from an existing mole, which may enlarge, become lumpy, bleed, change colour, or develop a spreading black edge (as shown below). Melanomas are highly **malignant** and often spread to other parts of the body.

Lung cancer: Lung cancer is one of the most common of all malignant tumours and 98% of all cases are associated with cigarette smoking. Symptoms of lung cancer include coughing up blood, chest pain, breathlessness, and headache if the tumour has metastasised to the brain. These symptoms are generally caused by the tumour impairing lung function.

A melanoma with the characteristic spreading black edge.

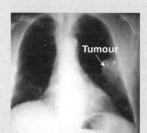

Chest X-ray showing a large, dense mass indicating the presence of a tumour.

Stages in the Formation of Cancer

The growth of a cancer begins when the genes controlling cell growth and multiplication (**oncogenes**) are transformed by agents known as **carcinogens**. Most well studied is the p53 gene which normally acts to prevent cell division in damaged cells. Scientists have found that the p53 gene is altered in 40% of all cancers. Once a cell is transformed into a tumour-forming type (**malignant**), the change in its oncogenes is passed on to all offspring cells:

Cancer cells ignore density-dependent inhibition and continue to multiply even after contacting one another, piling up until the nutrient supply becomes limiting.

1. Benign tumour cells
Defects (mutations) in one or two controlling genes cause the formation of a benign tumour. This is a localised population of proliferating cells where formation of new cells is matched by cell death.

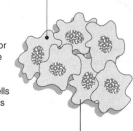

2. Malignant tumour cells
More mutations may cause the cells to become malignant. These cells stop producing a chemical that prevents blood vessels from forming. New capillaries grow into the tumour, providing it with nutrients.

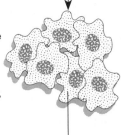

3. Metastasis
The new capillaries also provide a route for the malignant cells to break away from the tumour and travel to other parts of the body where they start new cancers.

Malignant cells break away from tumour mass and travel to other parts of the body either through the **blood system** or **lymphatic system**.

1. Describe briefly the following stages of a developing cancer:

(a) Benign tumour: _____

(b) Malignant tumour: _____

© Biozone International 1998-2007
Photocopying Prohibited

Related activities: The Genetic Origins of Cancer, Diseases Caused by Smoking, Breast Cancer, Diagnosing Medical Problems

A 2

Cancer Symptoms

The symptoms produced by different kinds of cancers depends on the site of growth, the tissue of origin, and the extent of the growth. Symptoms may be a direct feature of the growth (e.g. lumps), bleeding or disruption of the function of the organ affected.

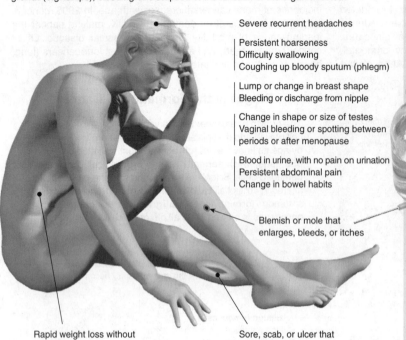

Severe recurrent headaches

Persistent hoarseness
Difficulty swallowing
Coughing up bloody sputum (phlegm)

Lump or change in breast shape
Bleeding or discharge from nipple

Change in shape or size of testes
Vaginal bleeding or spotting between periods or after menopause

Blood in urine, with no pain on urination
Persistent abdominal pain
Change in bowel habits

Blemish or mole that enlarges, bleeds, or itches

Rapid weight loss without an apparent cause

Sore, scab, or ulcer that fails to heal within 3 weeks

Treatment of Cancer

Chemotherapy

Chemotherapy is the treatment of cancer by drugs that act selectively on the cancer cells. Anticancer drugs act either by destroying tumour cells or stopping them from multiplying. Unfortunately, the drugs used in these treatments may also have substantial effects on normal tissue. Chemotherapeutic drugs act on all rapidly dividing cells, not just tumour cells. They may cause destruction of white blood cells, hair loss, sterility, and affect the mouth and intestines.

Radiotherapy

Ionising radiation, normally a source of damage to DNA, is used to treat cancer tumours. As the radiation passes through the diseased tissue, it destroys or slows down the development of abnormal cells. Provided the correct dosage of radiation is given, normal cells suffer very little, and there is no long-term damage. Side effects are usually short-lived and involve minor burning of the skin or some localised hair loss.

(c) Metastasis: _____

_____

2. Explain how the following treatments work to destroy cancerous tumours (while leaving healthy tissue less affected):

   (a) Chemotherapy: _____

   _____

   _____

   (b) Radiotherapy: _____

   _____

   _____

3. (a) Describe some of the unwanted (harmful) side effects of these two treatments (above): _____

   _____

   _____

   (b) Explain why these side effects happen: _____

   _____

4. List the probable causes and characteristic symptoms associated with the following types of cancer:

   (a) Causes of skin cancer: _____

   Symptoms: _____

   _____

   (b) Causes of lung cancer: _____

   Symptoms: _____

   _____

Breast Cancer

Breast cancer is by far the most common cancer in women, with more than 44 000 new cases in the UK in 2003. More than 25% of all female cancers occur in the breast, and the incidence increases with age, with 80% of cases occurring in post menopausal women. Fewer than 1% of breast cancer cases occur in men. Female sex hormones are implicated in the development of many breast cancers. The incidence of the disease is higher in women who began menstruation early and/or whose menopause was late. Women who have no children or who had their first child when they were in their late 20s or 30s (or older) are also at higher risk. There is also a definite **familial** (heredity) factor in many cases. A high fat diet is also implicated. In Japan, where a low fat diet is typical, the disease is rare. Yet Japanese women living in the United States and eating a higher-fat American diet have the same rate of breast cancer as American women generally.

Characteristics of breast cancer

The incidence of breast cancer increases with age; it is almost unknown before age 25 but the incidence rises sharply in women aged 25-44. Most deaths from breast cancer occur because the disease has already spread beyond the breast when first detected.

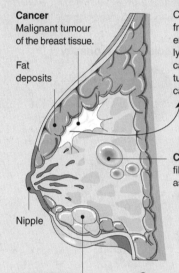

Cancer
Malignant tumour of the breast tissue.

Fat deposits

Cancer cells may detach from the tumour mass and enter the blood vessels and lymph ducts where they can form secondary tumours. This process is called **metastasis**.

Cysts, which are fluid-filled sacs, are not associated with cancer.

Nipple

Fibroadenoma
One of a number of common benign tumours.

Cross-section through a female breast, showing the various types of tissue masses present.

Breast self examination

Regular self-examinations to detect lumps in the breast tissue are recommended (left). Regular breast self examination may be the first step in detecting abnormal changes in the breast tissue.

Mammography

Mammography, which involves a breast X-ray, can detect tumours less than 15 mm in diameter (too small to be detected by a physical breast exam).

In mammography, the breast is compressed between the X-ray plate below and a plastic cover screen above. Several views are then taken.

A **biopsy** is performed if there is a chance that a lump may be malignant. A sample of the affected tissue is taken with a hollow needle and examined under a microscope. If cancerous cells are present, X-rays, ultrasound scanning, and blood tests can determine if the disease has spread to other parts of the body, such as the bones or the liver. Treatment may then follow.

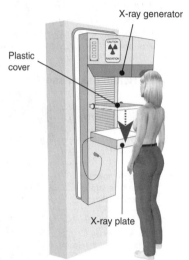

X-ray generator

Plastic cover

X-ray plate

Treatment

Surgical removal of the tumour achieves a cure (as defined by survival for 20 years after treatment) in one third of women with early breast cancer. Studies have shown that survival is not improved by extensive surgery such as radical mastectomy (1). Less radical procedures (2 and 3) are now frequently recommended, combined with **radiotherapy** or **anticancer drugs**, such as *tamoxifen*.

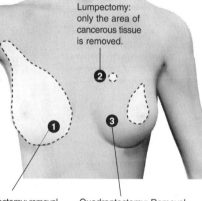

Lumpectomy: only the area of cancerous tissue is removed.

Radical mastectomy: removal of the entire breast, chest muscle, associated lymph nodes, and fat and skin.

Quadrantectomy: Removal of the tumour plus a wedge of surrounding tissue.

1. Describe three factors associated with increased risk of developing breast cancer and suggest why they increase risk:

_____

_____

2. Suggest in what way breast self examination may be deficient in detecting early breast cancers: _____

_____

3. Describe a possible treatment for early breast cancer involving a small isolated tumour: _____

_____

4. State the evidence for a link between diet and increased risk of developing breast cancer: _____

_____

_____

Related activities: Cancer

A 2

Dietary Disorders

Most forms of malnutrition in western societies are the result of poorly balanced nutrient intakes rather than a lack of food *per se*. Dietary disorders may arise as a result of overeating (**obesity**), insufficient food intake (**anorexia nervosa**), or abnormally erratic eating habits (**bulimia nervosa**). Other health problems typically prevalent in western societies, including **cardiovascular diseases**, have been associated to varying degrees with the consumption of highly processed foods, high in cholesterol and saturated fats. Low fibre intake is a factor in the development of **colon cancer**, while high salt intake may lead to **hypertension**.

Anorexia Nervosa

An eating disorder characterised by an intense fear of being fat, severe weight loss, and a wilful avoidance of food. Clinically, anorexics are below 75% of the weight expected for their height and age. Anorexia most often affects teenage girls and young adult women (approximately 5% of sufferers are male). The exact cause of this form of self-starvation is not known, but research suggests that it is caused when emotional distress interacts with a physiological imbalance in a vulnerable individual. Anorexia is quite distinct from **bulimia**. Bulimics generally binge eat, and then purge their stomachs, rather than avoiding food altogether.

Obesity

Obesity is the most common form of malnutrition in affluent societies. It is a condition where there is too much body fat (not the same as being overweight). In Britain 20-30% of all adults are obese. Some genetic and hormonal causes are known, although obesity is a result of energy intake (eating) exceeding the **net energy expenditure**. Dieting is often ineffective for long-term weight loss because once normal eating is resumed the body responds by storing more fat in fat cells. Obesity increases the incidence of hypertension (high blood pressure), stroke, coronary artery disease, and Type 2 (adult onset) diabetes mellitus.

Health risks associated with anorexia nervosa

Health risks associated with obesity

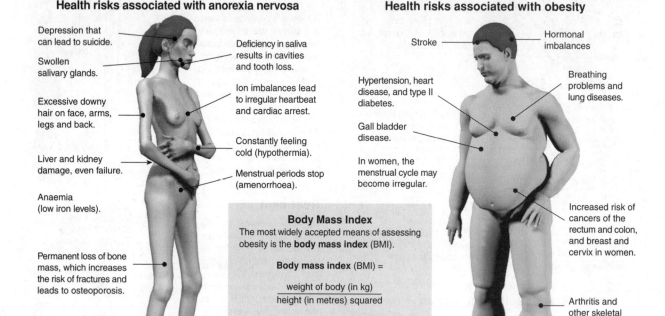

Body Mass Index
The most widely accepted means of assessing obesity is the **body mass index** (BMI).

Body mass index (BMI) =

$$\frac{\text{weight of body (in kg)}}{\text{height (in metres) squared}}$$

A BMI of: 17 to 20 = underweight
20 to 25 = normal weight
25 to 30 = overweight
over 30 = obesity

1. Describe the two basic energy factors that determine how a person's weight will change:

_____

2. Using the BMI, calculate the minimum and maximum weight at which a 1.85 m tall man would be considered:

(a) Overweight: _____   (c) Obese: _____

(b) Normal weight: _____   (d) Underweight: _____

3. State the possible health consequences of the following aspects of a diet:

(a) High salt consumption: _____

(b) Low fibre content: _____

(c) High cholesterol content: _____

4. Describe the key differences between anorexia nervosa and bulimia nervosa: _____

_____

_____

Related activities: A Balanced Diet, Deficiency Diseases, The Health Benefits of Exercise

A Balanced Diet

Nutrients are required for metabolism, tissue growth and repair, and as an energy source. Good nutrition (provided by a **balanced diet**) is recognised as a key factor in good health. Conversely poor nutrition (malnutrition) may cause ill-health or **deficiency diseases**. A diet refers to the quantity and nature of the food eaten. While not all foods contain all the representative nutrients, we can obtain the required balance of different nutrients by eating a wide variety of foods. In a recent overhaul of previous dietary recommendations, the health benefits of monounsaturated fats (such as olive and canola oils), fish oils, and whole grains have been recognised, and people are being urged to reduce their consumption of highly processed foods and saturated (rather than total) fat. Those on diets that restrict certain food groups (e.g. vegans) must take care to balance their intake of foods to ensure an adequate supply of protein and other nutrients (e.g. iron and B vitamins). **Reference Nutrient Intakes** (RNIs) (see the next page) provide nutritional guidelines for different sectors of the population in the UK. RNIs help to define the upper and lower limits of adequate nutrient intake for most people, but they are not recommendations for intakes by individuals.

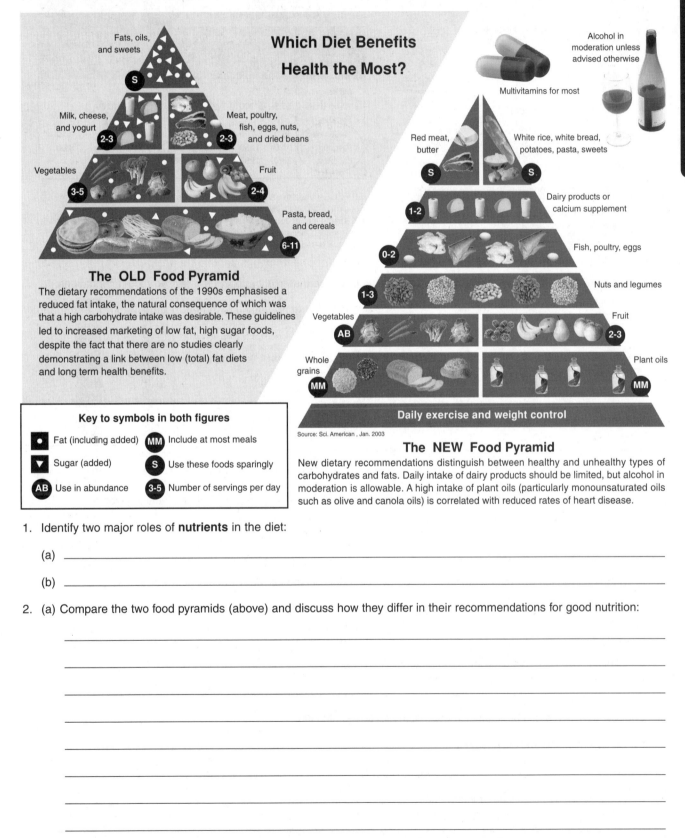

Which Diet Benefits Health the Most?

Source: Sci. American , Jan. 2003

The OLD Food Pyramid

The dietary recommendations of the 1990s emphasised a reduced fat intake, the natural consequence of which was that a high carbohydrate intake was desirable. These guidelines led to increased marketing of low fat, high sugar foods, despite the fact that there are no studies clearly demonstrating a link between low (total) fat diets and long term health benefits.

The NEW Food Pyramid

New dietary recommendations distinguish between healthy and unhealthy types of carbohydrates and fats. Daily intake of dairy products should be limited, but alcohol in moderation is allowable. A high intake of plant oils (particularly monounsaturated oils such as olive and canola oils) is correlated with reduced rates of heart disease.

Key to symbols in both figures

- ● Fat (including added)
- ▼ Sugar (added)
- **AB** Use in abundance
- **MM** Include at most meals
- **S** Use these foods sparingly
- **3-5** Number of servings per day

1. Identify two major roles of **nutrients** in the diet:

   (a) _____

   (b) _____

2. (a) Compare the two food pyramids (above) and discuss how they differ in their recommendations for good nutrition:

   _____

   _____

   _____

   _____

   _____

   _____

   _____

   _____

Nutritional Guidelines in the UK

In the UK, Dietary Reference Values (DRVs) provide guidelines for nutrient and energy intake for particular groups of the population. In a population, it is assumed that the nutritional requirements of the population as a whole are represented by a normal, bell-shaped, curve (below). DRVs collectively encompass RNIs, LRNIs, and EARs, and replace the earlier Recommended Daily Amounts (RDAs), which *recommended* nutrient intakes for particular groups in the population, including those with very high needs.

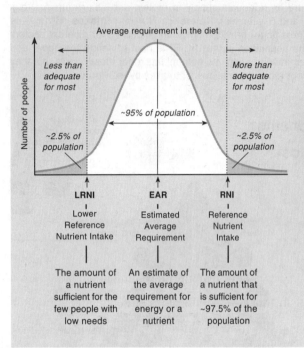

The amount of a nutrient sufficient for the few people with low needs (LRNI – Lower Reference Nutrient Intake). An estimate of the average requirement for energy or a nutrient (EAR – Estimated Average Requirement). The amount of a nutrient that is sufficient for ~97.5% of the population (RNI – Reference Nutrient Intake).

Table 1 (below): Estimated Average Requirements (EAR) for energy, and Reference Nutrient Intakes (RNIs) for selected nutrients, for UK males and females aged 19-50 years (per day).

Source: Dept of Health. Dietary Reference Values for Food Energy and Nutrients for the UK, 1991.

| Age range | Reference Nutrient Intakes (RNIs) | | | | | EARs | |
	Protein (g)	Calcium (mg)	Iron (mg)	Folate (μg)	Vit.C (mg)	EAR (MJ) Males	Females
Males							
19-50 years	55.5	700	8.7	700	40	10.60	
Females							
19-50 years	45.0	700	14.8	600	40		8.10
Pregnant	51.0	1250	14.8	700	50		8.90
Lactating	56.0	1250	14.8	950	70		10.20

DRVs have been set for population groups within the UK, taking into account age and gender. Only a portion of the table is shown here.

RNIs are provided for each constituent of a balanced diet

EARs for energy are based on the present lifestyles and activity levels of the UK population.

(b) Based on the information on the graph (right), state the evidence that might support the revised recommendations:

_____

_____

_____

_____

_____

_____

_____

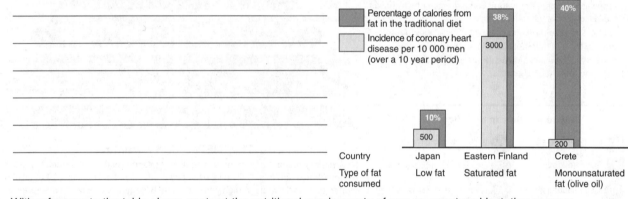

Legend:
- Percentage of calories from fat in the traditional diet
- Incidence of coronary heart disease per 10 000 men (over a 10 year period)

Country	Japan	Eastern Finland	Crete
	10% / 500	38% / 3000	40% / 200
Type of fat consumed	Low fat	Saturated fat	Monounsaturated fat (olive oil)

3. With reference to the table above, contrast the nutritional requirements of non-pregnant and lactating women:

_____

_____

4. (a) Suggest in which way the older RDAs could have been misleading for many people: _____

_____

_____

(b) Explain how the DRVs differ from the older RDAs: _____

_____

5. Suggest how **DRVs** can be applied in each of the following situations:

(a) Dietary planning and assessment: _____

_____

(b) Food labelling and consumer information: _____

_____

Deficiency Diseases

Malnutrition is the general term for nutritional disorders resulting from not having enough food (starvation), not enough of the right food (deficiency), or too much food (obesity). Children under 5 are the most at risk from starvation and deficiency diseases because they are growing rapidly and are more susceptible to disease. Malnutrition is a key factor in the deaths of 6 million children each year and, in developing countries, dietary deficiencies are a major problem. In these countries, malnutrition usually presents as **marasmus** or **kwashiorkor** (energy and protein deficiencies).

Specific vitamin and mineral deficiencies (below and following page) in adults are associated with specific disorders, e.g. **beriberi** (vitamin B$_1$), **scurvy** (vitamin C), **rickets** (vitamin D), **pellagra** (niacin), or **anaemia** (iron). Vitamin deficiencies in childhood result in chronic, lifelong disorders. Deficiency diseases are rare in developed countries. People who do suffer from some form of dietary deficiency are either alcoholics, people with intestinal disorders that prevent proper nutrient uptake, or people with very restricted diets (e.g. vegans).

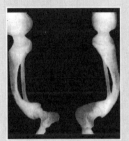

Vitamin D Deficiency
Lack of vitamin D in children produces the disease rickets. In adults a similar disease is called osteomalacia. Suffers typically show skeletal deformities (e.g. bowed legs, left) because inadequate amounts of calcium and phosphorus are incorporated into the bones. Vitamin D is produced by the skin when exposed to sunlight and it is vital for the absorption of calcium from the diet.

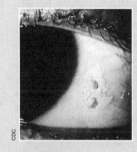

Vitamin A Deficiency
Vitamin A (found in animal livers, eggs, and dairy products) is essential for the production of light-absorbing pigments in the eye and for the formation of cell structures. Symptoms of deficiency include loss of night vision, inflammation of the eye, **keratomalacia** (damage to the cornea), and the appearance of **Bitots spots**, evident as foamy, opaque patches on the white of the eye (refer to photo).

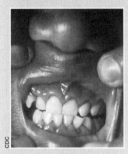

Vitamin C Deficiency
Vitamin C deficiency causes a disease known as scurvy. It is now rare in developed countries because of increased consumption of fresh fruit and vegetables. Inadequate vitamin C intake disturbs the body's normal production of collagen, a protein in connective tissue that holds body structures together. This results in poor wound healing, rupture of small blood vessels (visible bleeding in the skin), swollen gums, and loose teeth.

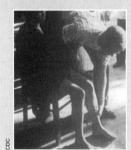

Vitamin B$_1$ Deficiency
Vitamin B$_1$ (thiamine) is required for respiratory metabolism, and nerve and muscle function. Lack of thiamine causes the metabolic disorder, **beriberi**, which occurs predominantly in underfed populations, or in breast fed babies whose mother is on a restrictive diet. Symptoms of beriberi include nerve degeneration, heart failure, and oedema (swelling caused by fluid accumulation). Without medical treatment, sufferers will die.

Kwashiorkor
A severe type of protein-energy deficiency in young children (1-3 years old), occurring mainly in poor rural areas in the tropics. Kwashiorkor occurs when a child is suddenly weaned on to a diet that is low in calories, protein, and certain essential micronutrients. The problem is often made worse by a poor appetite due to illnesses such as measles. Children have stunted growth, oedema (accumulation of fluid in the tissues), and are inactive, apathetic and weak. Resistance against infection is lost, which may be fatal.

Marasmus
Marasmus is the most common form of deficiency disease. It is a severe form of protein and energy malnutrition that usually occurs in famine or starvation conditions. Children suffering from marasmus are stunted and extremely emaciated. They have loose folds of skin on the limbs and buttocks, due to the loss of fat and muscle tissue. Unlike kwashiorkor sufferers, marasmus does not cause the bloated and elongated abdomen. However sufferers have no resistance to disease and common infections are typically fatal.

1. Distinguish between **malnutrition** and **starvation**:

_____

_____

_____

_____

2. For each of the following vitamins, identify the natural sources of the vitamin, its function, and effect of deficiency:

   (a) Vitamin A: _____

      Function: _____

      Deficiency: _____

   (b) Vitamin B$_1$: _____

      Function: _____

      Deficiency: _____

Related activities: Dietary Disorders, A Balanced Diet

RA 2

Common Mineral Deficiencies

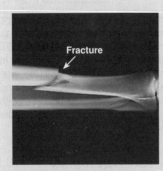

Calcium Deficiency

Calcium is required for enzyme function, formation of bones and teeth, blood clotting, and muscular contraction. Calcium deficiency causes poor bone growth and structure, increasing the tendency of bones to fracture and break. It also results in muscular spasms and poor blood clotting ability.

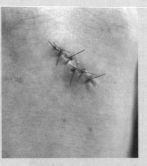

Zinc Deficiency

Zinc is found in red meat, poultry, fish, whole grain cereals and breads, legumes, and nuts. It is important for enzyme activity, production of insulin, making of sperm, and perception of taste. A deficiency in zinc causes growth retardation, a delay in puberty, muscular weakness, dry skin, and a delay in wound healing.

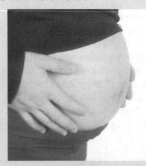

Iron Deficiency

Anaemia results from lower than normal levels of haemoglobin in red blood cells. Iron from the diet is required to produce haemoglobin. People most at risk include women during **pregnancy** and those with an inadequate dietary intake. Symptoms include fatigue, fainting, breathlessness, and heart palpitations.

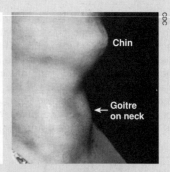

Iodine Deficiency

Iodine is essential for the production of thyroid hormones. These hormones control the rate of metabolism, growth, and development. Shortage of iodine in the diet may lead to **goitre** (thyroid enlargement as shown above). Iodine deficiency is also responsible for some cases of thyroid underactivity (**hypothyroidism**).

(c) Vitamin C: _____

   Function: _____

   Deficiency: _____

(d) Vitamin D: _____

   Function: _____

   Deficiency: _____

3. Suggest why young children, pregnant women, and athletes are among the most susceptible to dietary deficiencies:

   _____

   _____

   _____

4. Explain why a lack of iron leads to the symptoms of anaemia (fatigue and breathlessness): _____

   _____

   _____

5. Suggest why a zinc deficiency is associated with muscular weakness and a delay in puberty: _____

   _____

   _____

6. Using the example of **iodine**, explain how artificial dietary supplementation can be achieved and discuss its benefits:

   _____

   _____

7. Explain why people suffering from nutritional deficiencies have a poor resistance to disease: _____

   _____

   _____

   _____

   _____

Cardiovascular Disease

Cardiovascular disease (CVD) is a term describing all diseases involving the heart and blood vessels. It includes coronary heart disease (CHD), atherosclerosis, hypertension (high blood pressure), peripheral vascular disease, stroke, and congenital heart disorders. CVD is responsible for 20% of all deaths worldwide and is the principal cause of deaths in developed countries. In the UK, deaths due to CVD have been declining since the 1970s due to better prevention and treatment. Despite this, CVD is still the leading cause of mortality, and accounted for 37% of all deaths in 2004. The continued prevalence of CVD is of considerable public health concern, particularly as many of the **risk factors** involved, such as cigarette smoking, obesity, and high blood cholesterol, are controllable. Uncontrollable risk factors include advancing age, gender, and heredity.

Aspects of Human Health

Cardiovascular Diseases

Atherosclerosis: Atherosclerosis (sometimes called hardening of the arteries or ischaemic heart disease), is a disease of the arteries caused by **atheroma** (deposits of fats and cholesterol) on the inner walls of the arteries. The lining of the arteries degenerates due to the accumulation of fat and plaques. Atheroma eventually restricts blood flow through the arteries and increases the risk of blood clot formation (**thrombosis**). Complications arising as a result of atherosclerosis include heart attack (**infarction**), stroke and gangrene.

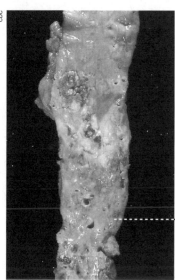

This aorta has been opened lengthwise to reveal the inner surface studded with the lesions of atherosclerosis.

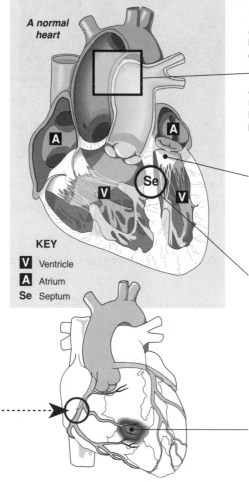

A normal heart

KEY

V Ventricle
A Atrium
Se Septum

Restricted supply of blood to heart muscle resulting in myocardial infarction

Aortic aneurysm: A ballooning and weakening of the wall of the aorta.

Aneurysms usually result from generalised heart disease and high blood pressure.

Valve defects: Unusual heart sounds (murmurs) can result when a valve (often the mitral valve) does not close properly, allowing blood to bubble back into the atria. Valve defects may be congenital (present at birth) but they can also occur as a result of rheumatic fever.

Septal defects: These hole-in-the-heart congenital defects occur where the dividing wall (**septum**) between the left and right sides of the heart is not closed. These defects may occur between the atria or the ventricles, and are sometimes combined with valve problems.

Myocardial infarction (*heart attack*): Occurs when an area of the heart is deprived of blood supply resulting in tissue damage or death. It is the major cause of death in developed countries. Symptoms of infarction include a sudden onset of chest pain, breathlessness, nausea, and cold clammy skin. Damage to the heart may be so severe that it leads to heart failure and even death (myocardial infarction is fatal within 20 days in 40 to 50% of all cases).

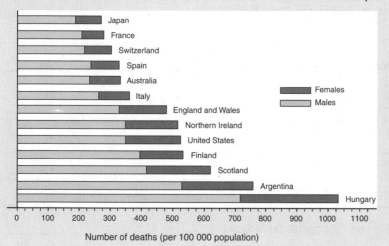

Deaths rates from CVD for males and females from selected countries (2001)

Japan
France
Switzerland
Spain
Australia
Italy
England and Wales
Northern Ireland
United States
Finland
Scotland
Argentina
Hungary

Females
Males

Number of deaths (per 100 000 population)

The graph shows the death rate (per 100 000 population) attributable to cardiovascular disease (CVD) in both men and women in selected countries. Data are current to 2001. The rate of CVD is lowest in Japan and France and high in Eastern Europe.

There are many suggested causes for these differences. One study by the World Health Organisation (WHO) stated that variation between countries can be primarily attributed to diet (i.e. saturated fat, salt, vitamin and antioxidant content). The WHO study also found strong north-south gradients in both fruit and vegetable consumption between countries. For example, people in England consumed twice as much fruit and one third more vegetables than those living in Northern Ireland.

Source for data and graph: WHO

Related activities: The Human Heart, Correcting Heart Problems, The Health Benefits of Exercise

RDA 3

Diagnosing Cardiovascular Disease

Cardiovascular disease is suspected in people who experience breathlessness, chest pain, or palpitations during exercise, particularly if they also fall into a high-risk category (see table, far right).

Diagnosis of *coronary artery disease* and *angina pectoris* can be made from the results of a **cardiac exercise tolerance test**. During the test, the patient (photo, right) is attached to an electrocardiograph (ECG) machine, which records the electrical activity of the heart during exercise on a treadmill. Angina (chest pain caused by insufficient blood supply to the heart) is confirmed when there are specific changes in the ECG wave patterns as the intensity of exercise is increased.

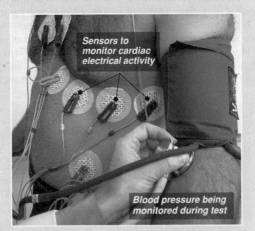

Sensors to monitor cardiac electrical activity

Blood pressure being monitored during test

Risk factors for CVD

- High blood pressure
- Cigarette smoking
- High blood cholesterol
- Obesity
- Type II diabetes mellitus
- High achiever personality
- Environmental stress
- Sedentary lifestyle

Controllable risk factors in the development of cardiovascular disease are listed above. The risks associated with any genetic predisposition to CVD are not included in the list.

1. Explain briefly how atherosclerosis leads to death of heart tissue and a heart attack (infarct): _____

_____

_____

2. Mortality attributable to CVD is declining, despite its increasing prevalence. Suggest why: _____

_____

3. (a) From the graph on the previous page, determine the proportion of CVD deaths occurring in females and males in England and Wales:

Females: _____   Males: _____

(b) Suggest a possible reason for this difference: _____

_____

4. Suggest possible alternative reasons, other than diet, for the global distribution of CVD: _____

_____

_____

_____

5. (a) Distinguish between controllable and uncontrollable risk factors in the development of CVD: _____

_____

_____

(b) Suggest why some of the controllable risk factors often occur together: _____

_____

(c) Explain why patients with several risk factors have a much higher risk of developing CVD: _____

_____

6. (a) Choose one of the controllable risk factors listed above, and describe its role in the development of CVD:

_____

_____

_____

(b) Suggest how the risk (of CVD) presented by this factor could be reduced: _____

_____

Correcting Heart Problems

Over the last decade the death rates from CVD have slowly declined, despite an increase in its prevalence. This reduction in mortality has been achieved partly through better management and treatment of the disease. Medical technology now provides the means to correct many heart problems, even if only temporarily. Some symptoms of CVD, arising as a result of blockages to the coronary arteries, are now commonly treated using techniques such as coronary bypass surgery and angioplasty. Other cardiac disorders, such as disorders of heartbeat, are frequently treated using cardiac pacemakers. Valve defects, which are often congenital, can be successfully corrected with surgical valve replacement. The latest technology, still in its trial phase, involves non-surgical replacement of aortic valves. The procedure, known as percutaneous (through the skin) heart valve replacement, will greatly reduce the trauma associated with correcting these particular heart disorders.

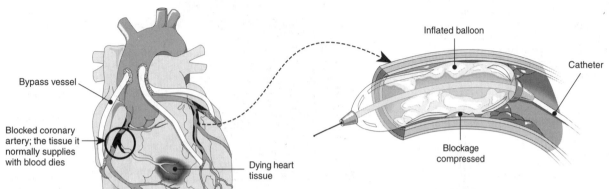

Coronary Bypass Surgery

Commonly used surgery to bypass blocked coronary arteries with blood vessels from elsewhere in the body (e.g. leg vein or mammary artery). Sometimes, double or triple bypasses are performed.

Angioplasty

Angioplasty is an alternative procedure used for some patients with coronary artery disease. A balloon tipped catheter is placed via the aorta into the coronary artery. The balloon is inflated to reduce the blockage of the artery and later removed. Heparin (an anticlotting agent) is given to prevent the formation of blood clots. The death rate from complications is about 1%.

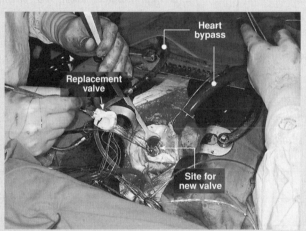

The photograph above shows a valve replacement operation in progress. The valve can be seen threaded up and ready for placement. Two large tubes bypass the heart so that circulation to the lungs and rest of the body is maintained during the operation.

Replacement Heart Valves

Tissue valve *Ball valve* *Disc valve*

Artificial valves can be of two types: **biological (tissue) valves** and **synthetic valves**. Tissue valves are usually made of animal tissue such as pig tissue. They do not last long (7-10 years) but there are fewer problems with blood clotting and tissue rejection. For these reasons, they are often used in older patients who would not need another replacement in their lifetime. Synthetic ball or disc valves are constructed from non-biological materials. Such valves last a long time but tend to create blood clots (raising the risk of stroke). Used on younger patients, they must take long-term anti-clotting drugs.

1. Explain why patients who have undergone coronary bypass surgery or angioplasty require careful supervision of their diet and lifestyle following the operation, even though their problem has been alleviated:

_____

_____

2. (a) State the type of valve that would be used for an elderly patient needing a valve replacement: _____

   (b) Explain the reasons for your answer: _____

   _____

3. Explain the problems associated with the use of each type of replacement valve:

   (a) Tissue valves: _____

   (b) Synthetic valves: _____

Related activities: Cardiovascular Disease, The Human Heart, Control of Heart Activity, The Cardiac Cycle

RA 2

Cardiac Pacemakers

A cardiac pacemaker is sometimes required to maintain an effective heart rate in cases where the heart beats irregularly or too slowly (as in the case of heart block, see the lower trace, right). Pacemakers provide regular electrical stimulation of the heart muscle so that it contracts and relaxes with a normal rhythm. They stand by until the heart rate falls below a pre-set rate. **Temporary pacemakers** are often used after cardiac surgery or heart attacks, while **permanent pacemakers** are required for patients with ongoing problems. Pacemakers allow a normal (even strenuous) lifestyle.

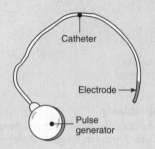

Both permanent and temporary pacemakers consist of a **pulse generator** and a catheter (flexible wire) with electrodes that deliver the stimulus to the heart muscle. The pulse generator contains a small battery and an electronic system to monitor heart activity.

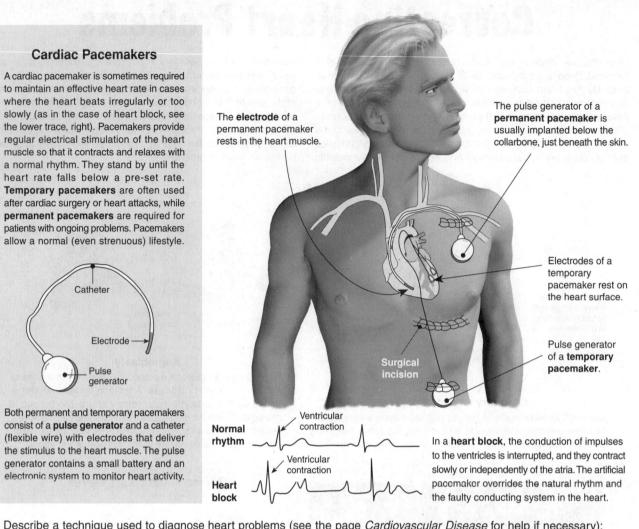

The **electrode** of a permanent pacemaker rests in the heart muscle.

The pulse generator of a **permanent pacemaker** is usually implanted below the collarbone, just beneath the skin.

Electrodes of a temporary pacemaker rest on the heart surface.

Pulse generator of a **temporary pacemaker**.

Surgical incision

Normal rhythm — Ventricular contraction

Heart block — Ventricular contraction

In a **heart block**, the conduction of impulses to the ventricles is interrupted, and they contract slowly or independently of the atria. The artificial pacemaker overrides the natural rhythm and the faulty conducting system in the heart.

4. Describe a technique used to diagnose heart problems (see the page *Cardiovascular Disease* for help if necessary):

_____

_____

5. Describe two modern techniques for treating the effects of atherosclerosis in the coronary arteries:

(a) _____

_____

(b) _____

_____

6. (a) Suggest a possible surgical correction in the case of complete, non-recoverable heart failure: _____

_____

(b) Identify problems with this treatment option: _____

_____

7. Explain why it is necessary for the heart to receive regular electrical stimulation: _____

_____

_____

8. (a) Describe the purpose of a cardiac pacemaker, explaining how it achieves its effect: _____

_____

(b) Explain why a temporary pacemaker is often useful for a short time after cardiac surgery: _____

_____

The Health Benefits of Exercise

Regular exercise helps protect against a range of health problems, improves mood, and assists in managing stress. Exercise promotes health by improving the rate of blood flow back to the heart (**venous return**). This is achieved by strengthening all types of muscle and by increasing the efficiency of the heart. During exercise blood flow to different parts of the body changes in order to cope with the extra demands of the muscles, the heart and the lungs. Over time, regular exercise leads to greater **endurance**, and improves the body's ability to respond to everyday demands of physical activity.

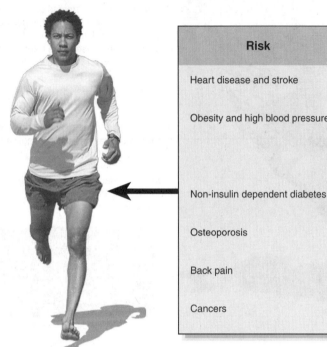

Risk	Specific Health Benefits of Exercise
Heart disease and stroke	Strengthens heart muscle, lowers blood pressure, improves blood flow, and increases the heart's working capacity.
Obesity and high blood pressure	Exercise reduces body fat by building or preserving muscle mass and improving the body's ability to use calories. Combined with proper nutrition, exercise controls weight and prevents obesity, which is associated with many diseases, including high blood pressure (hypertension).
Non-insulin dependent diabetes	Weight loss associated with exercise prevents and controls adult onset diabetes mellitus.
Osteoporosis	Regular weight bearing exercise promotes bone formation and prevents age-related bone loss.
Back pain	Helps to prevent back pain by increasing muscle strength and endurance, and improving flexibility and posture.
Cancers	Exercise lowers the risk of breast and colon cancers.

Regular, moderate exercise promotes psychological well-being, improves immune function, reduces muscular and mental tension, and increases concentration and energy levels.

Strength and resistance exercises, often with machines or weights, are an important component of physiotherapy for people recovering from trauma or illness.

Exercise is a social activity for many, providing a reason for regular social contact. Exercise also increases self-esteem and confidence, and reduces feelings of anxiety and depression.

A basic level of fitness is essential for maintaining muscular strength and flexibility into old age. Without it, people lose the ability to do everyday activities such as housework or lifting.

1. (a) Explain how the body increases the rate of blood flow during exercise: _____

   _____

   (b) Describe the physiological effects of this when exercise is performed on a regular basis: _____

   _____

   (c) Explain how these changes benefit health in the long term: _____

   _____

   _____

   _____

Exercise and the Pulmonary and Cardiovascular Systems

The body has an immediate response to exercise but also, over time, responds to the stress of repeated exercise (which is called training) by adapting and improving its capacity for exercise and the efficiency with which it performs. Many of the health benefits of exercise stem from this improved efficiency, which means the body works with less effort during everyday activity.

Cardiovascular Performance

Heart rate: Heart rate increases during exercise but aerobic training leads to a lower steady state heart rate overall for any given level of work.

Stroke volume (the amount of blood pumped with each beat) increases with regular aerobic activity. This is related to an increased heart capacity, an increase in the heart's force of contraction, and an increase in venous return.

The increase in stroke volume results in an increased **cardiac output**.

In response to training, the **resting systolic blood pressure** (a measure of how much the heart is relaxing between beats) is lowered.

Blood flow changes during exercise so that more blood is diverted to working muscles and less is delivered to the gut.

Ventilation Rate

The rate and depth of breathing increases during exercise. Training improves the efficiency of lung ventilation so for any given exercise level, the effort associated with breathing is reduced.

Overall result:
Improved exchange of gases. For any given exercise level, breathing takes less effort.

Overall result:
The increased demands of exercise are met more efficiently. Everyday activity requires less effort.

2. Describe the health benefits of each of the following effects of regular exercise. For each one, explain the physiological mechanisms behind the health benefits:

(a) Increase in stroke volume and cardiac output: _____

_____

_____

(b) Increased ventilation efficiency: _____

_____

_____

(c) Increase in lean muscle mass and decreased body fat: _____

_____

_____

(d) Increased muscular strength and endurance: _____

_____

_____

(e) Maintenance of stable, healthy body weight: _____

_____

_____

3. Suggest why irregular or very low intensity exercise does not provide the health benefits of regular activity:

_____

_____

_____

Ageing and Human Health

After physical maturity is attained the body undergoes **degenerative changes** known as senescence or ageing. Ageing is a progressive failure of the body's homeostatic responses, occurring as a result of cells dying and renewal rates slowing or stopping. It is a general response, producing observable changes in structure and physiology; there is a decline in skeletal and muscular strength, and reduced immune function. Ageing increases susceptibility to stress and disease, and disease and ageing often accelerate together.

Aspects of Human Health

Osteoarthritis of the knee joint

Osteoarthritis is a common degenerative disease aggravated by mechanical stress on bone joints. It is characterised by the degeneration of cartilage and the formation of osteophytes (bony outgrowths at the joint). This leads to pain, stiffness, inflammation, and full or partial loss of joint function. Osteoarthritis occurs in almost all people over the age of 60 and affects three times as many women as men. Weight bearing joints such as those in the knee, foot, hips, and spine are most commonly affected. Currently there is no cure for osteoarthritis, although symptoms can be relieved by painkillers and anti-inflammatory drugs.

Loss of lubricating fluid and cartilage

Osteophytes

Age Related Changes

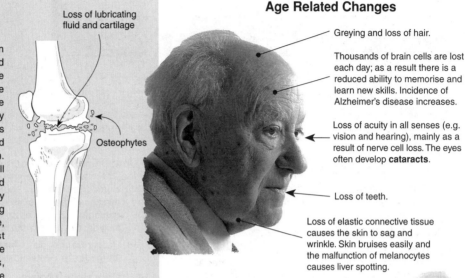

Greying and loss of hair.

Thousands of brain cells are lost each day; as a result there is a reduced ability to memorise and learn new skills. Incidence of Alzheimer's disease increases.

Loss of acuity in all senses (e.g. vision and hearing), mainly as a result of nerve cell loss. The eyes often develop **cataracts**.

Loss of teeth.

Loss of elastic connective tissue causes the skin to sag and wrinkle. Skin bruises easily and the malfunction of melanocytes causes liver spotting.

Osteoporosis of the spine

Osteoporosis is an age-related disorder where bone mass decreases, and there is a loss of height and an increased tendency for bones to break (fracture). Women are at greater risk of developing the disease than men because their skeletons are lighter and their oestrogen levels fall after menopause (oestrogen provides some protection against bone loss). Younger women with low hormone levels and/or low body weight are also affected. Osteoporosis affects the whole skeleton, but especially the spine, hips, and legs.

Loss of height

Hunching of spine

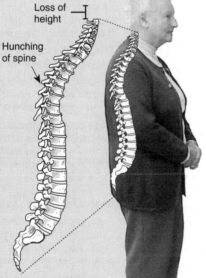

- Several cell types, including neurones, and skeletal and cardiac muscle cells cannot be replaced.
- Metabolic rate decreases. Digestive and kidney function declines.
- The arteries develop deposits associated with atherosclerosis.
- Muscle and bone mass decrease and fat deposits increase. There is a loss of height.
- Arthritis and other joint problems occur, particularly in the hands, feet, hips, elbows, and knees.
- Fertility declines. In women this happens with menopause, usually at about 45-55 years of age. In men, fertility declines more slowly.
- Cancers increase, e.g. prostate cancer in men, and breast and cervical cancer in women.

1. Briefly explain what causes ageing of the body, carefully relating the physiological changes to the observable effects:

_____

_____

2. Suggest how weight-bearing exercise could delay the onset of ageing: _____

_____

3. Name and describe a degenerative disease or disorder, including reference to symptoms and physiological causes:

_____

_____

_____

_____

Infectious Disease

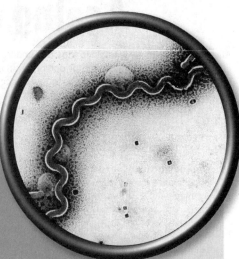

AQA-A	AQA-B	SNAB	Edexcel	OCR
Not applicable to the AS biology course	Not applicable to the AS course	Complete: 1-2, 4, 10-12, 22-26 (A2)	Not applicable to the AS biology course	Complete: 1-2, 4, 10-17, 19-21, 24-28, 30-31 Extension as appropriate

Learning Objectives

☐ 1. Compile your own glossary from the **KEY WORDS** displayed in **bold type** in the learning objectives below.

Nature of Infectious Disease *(pages 310-312)*

☐ 2. Recall the difference between **infectious disease** and **non-infectious disease**. Define the terms **pathogen** and **infection**. Identify pathogens in different taxa including the bacteria, viruses, fungi, and protoctists.

☐ 3. Describe the modes of **transmission** for some named infectious diseases. Identify the role of better hygiene and sanitation in controlling some infectious diseases.

☐ 4. Appreciate the significance of increasing drug resistance to the effective control of infectious disease. Describe causes of drug resistance in malaria, tuberculosis, or HIV and suggest how the problem might feasibly be tackled.

Bacterial Diseases *(pages 313-317, 333-336)*

☐ 5. Recognise that bacteria are widespread and only a small proportion ever cause disease. Identify the ways in which pathogenic bacteria cause disease. Explain how new strains of pathogenic bacteria can arise.

☐ 6. Giving examples, explain the ways in which bacterial diseases are transmitted. Relate the type and incidence of bacterial disease to the prevailing social conditions.

☐ 7. Describe factors affecting bacterial **pathogenicity**, including: features of the cell wall and capsule, **toxin** production, **infectivity**, and **invasiveness**.

☐ 8. Distinguish between different types of bacterial toxins and their actions: **exotoxins** (e.g. *Staphylococcus*) and **endotoxins** (e.g. *Salmonella*). Recognise **enterotoxins** as exotoxins that affect the gastrointestinal tract.

☐ 9. With reference to **disinfectants**, **antiseptics**, and **antibiotics**, explain how bacterial diseases are controlled and treated. Describe the role of antibiotics in medicine and identify problems with their use.

Case study: tuberculosis (TB)

☐ 10. Describe the causes and modes of transmission of TB. Recognise TB as a **reemerging disease**. Assess the global importance of TB and understand its history in the human population, including reference to its prevalence, decline, and reemergence.

☐ 11. Discuss the factors important in the prevalence of TB in a population. Explain what is meant by the term **carrier** and explain the role of carriers in the spread of TB.

☐ 12. Explain the role of **antibiotics** in the treatment of TB. Discuss the difficulties associated with the treatment of TB (including the importance of bacterial resistance to antibiotics). Describe the roles of social, economic, and biological factors in the control and prevention of TB.

Contamination of food and water

☐ 13. Describe the involvement of inadequate provision of clean drinking water, poor sanitation, and/or poor food hygiene in the transmission of food and water borne pathogens. Examples spread by the **faecal-oral route** include: *Salmonella*, *Vibrio cholerae*, and *E. coli*.

☐ 14. Recognise the role of **faecal coliforms** as indicators for the faecal contamination of water supplies.

Case study: cholera

☐ 15. Describe the agent involved and modes of transmission of **cholera**. Assess the past and current global importance of cholera and relate its distribution to factors such as levels of sanitation and general poverty.

☐ 16. Describe the roles of social, economic, and biological factors in the control and prevention of cholera.

☐ 17. Describe the treatment for cholera (both mild and severe cases) and comment on the importance of prompt and adequate provision of this treatment.

Case study: bacterial food poisoning

☐ 18. Describe the cause and transmission of **salmonellosis** or **staphylococcal food poisoning**. Identify factors governing the occurrence, prevention, and severity of these diseases.

Protozoan Diseases *(pages 318-319)*

☐ 19. Describe examples of diseases caused by protozoans. Understand that many pathogenic protozoans are highly specialised parasites with part of their life cycle occurring within a human.

Case study: malaria

☐ 20. Describe the agent involved and modes of transmission of **malaria**. Evaluate the global importance of malaria and describe factors in its distribution.

☐ 21. Describe the roles of social, economic, and biological factors in the treatment, control, and prevention of malaria. Comment on the adequacy of these methods with reference to the difficulties associated with developing drugs against protozoans.

Viral Diseases *(pages 321-328, 333)*

☐ 22. Define the terms **viral disease**, **virus**, **viroid**, **retrovirus**. Identify features that make viruses such host-specific pathogens. Using a named example or examples, describe how viral diseases are transmitted, and how they infect a host and cause disease.

☐ 23. Identify some viral diseases of global importance today and the causative agent in each case. Using examples, identify the role of **vaccination** in the past and present control of viral diseases.

Case study: HIV/AIDS

☐ 24. Describe the agent involved and modes of transmission of **HIV/AIDS**. Assess its global (including economic) importance and describe factors in its distribution.

25. Identify stages in the development of an HIV infection, including the effect of HIV on the immune system. Explain why AIDS is termed a **syndrome**.

26. Describe social, economic, and biological factors in the treatment, control, and prevention of HIV/AIDS.

Emerging Diseases *(pages 329-330, 331-332)*

27. Distinguish between **emerging** and **reemerging diseases** and give examples. Describe factors in the emergence, spread, and **virulence** of such diseases.

28. Describe the nature of infectious **prions** and explain how they cause disease. Give examples of prion diseases, their mode of transmission, the time period for development of symptoms, and the mortality.

Multicellular Pathogens *(page 320)*

*Insects and other arthropods are major vectors of disease. They are often **ectoparasites**, carrying pathogens (e.g. viruses) and transmitting them via their mouthparts.*

29. Describe the disease caused by one or more of the following. Include reference to the pathogen/parasite and its mode of transmission and life cycle:
   - Flatworms, e.g. the cestode **hydatid tapeworm** and the trematode, *Schistosoma*.
   - Roundworms, e.g. *Ascaris*, hookworm, and the nematodes that cause trichinosis and elephantiasis.

30. Describe an example of an insect-carried infection of humans. Name some **ectoparasites** and the conditions or diseases for which they are responsible.

Pathogens and Immunity *(pages 267, 324)*

31. Describe how some pathogens (including intracellular parasites such as HIV) manage to evade the normal immune response of an organism through **immune suppression**. Using examples, explain other ways in which parasites may avoid detection by the immune system and invade a host, e.g. by shedding their protein coat. Appreciate that this makes it difficult to develop vaccines against the pathogen involved.

See the 'Textbook Reference Grid' on pages 8-9 for textbook page references relating to material in this topic.

Supplementary Texts

See pages 5-6 for additional details of these texts:

■ Clegg, C.J., 2002. **Microbes in Action**, (John Murray), chpt 1-5, and chpt 10.

■ Freeland, P., 1999. **Microbes, Medicine and Commerce** (Hodder & Stoughton), pp. 37-42, 102-108.

■ Fullick, A., 1998. **Human Health and Disease** (Heinemann), chpt. 2.

■ Hudson, T. & K. Mannion, 2001. **Microbes and Disease** (Collins), pp. 48-69.

■ Murray, P. & N. Owens, 2001. **Behaviour and Populations** (Collins), chpt. 7.

See page 7 for details of publishers of periodicals:

STUDENT'S REFERENCE

■ **War on Disease** National Geographic, 201(2) February 2002, pp. 4-31. *An excellent account on the global importance of a range of infectious diseases. A great overview for students & teachers.*

■ **Rules of Contagion** New Scientist, 28 Oct. 2006, pp. 44-47. *The different levels of virulence of infectious diseases and which are the most deadly.*

■ **March of the Superbugs** New Scientist (Inside Science),19 July 2003. *It now seems widespread resistance is making antibiotics worthless. This account describes how resistance arises and how it spread through bacterial populations.*

■ **Viral Plagues** Biol. Sci. Rev., 17(3) Feb. 2005, pp. 37-41. *The nature of viruses and viral transmission, how viral infections are diagnosed, and what we can do to combat them.*

■ **Hide and Seek** Biol. Sci. Rev., 18(2) Nov. 2005, pp. 30-33. *Trypanosome infection and how these parasites avoid detection by the immune system.*

Presentation MEDIA to support this topic:

HEALTH & DISEASE:
• **Infectious Disease**

■ **Chasing the Superbugs** Biol. Sci. Rev., 18(4) April 2006, pp. 21-27. *Gene transfer and its implications to multi-drug resistance in bacteria.*

■ **Tracking the Next Killer Flu** National Geographic, 208(4) Oct. 2005, pp. 4-31. *Discussion on flu viruses and how they spread.*

■ **Preparing for a Pandemic** Scientific American, Nov. 2005, pp. 22-31. *A predicted global epidemic caused by some newly evolved strain of influenza may be temporarily contained with antiviral drugs.*

■ **Koch's Postulates** Biol. Sci. Rev., 15(3) February 2003, pp. 24-25. *Koch's postulates and the diagnosis of infectious disease.*

■ **Food / How Safe?** National Geographic, May 2002, pp. 2-31. *An excellent account of the issue of food safety and bacterial contamination of food.*

■ **Finding and Improving Antibiotics** Biol. Sci. Rev. 12(1) Sept. 1999, pp. 36-38. *Antibiotics, their production & testing, and the search for new drugs.*

HIV/AIDS and prions

■ **Opportunistic Infections and AIDS** Biol. Sci. Rev., 14 (4) April 2002, pp. 21-24. *An account of the suite of infections characterising AIDS (good).*

■ **Search for a Cure** National Geographic, 201(2) February 2002, pp. 32-43. *An account of the status of the AIDS epidemic and the measures to stop it.*

■ **Global BSE Crisis: Special Report** New Scientist, 7 August 2004, pp. 32-41. *A series of short articles examining the current state of the BSE epidemic: threats to humans and known and likely distributions of the disease globally.*

TB, malaria, food & water-borne disease

■ **Schistosomiasis** Biol. Sci. Rev., 16(3) Feb. 2004, pp. 21-25. *An account of the life cycle and reproductive biology of the schistosome fluke.*

■ ***Campylobacter jejuni*** Biol. Sci. Rev., 15(1) Sept. 2002, pp. 26-28. *An account of the diseases caused by Campylobacter, an increasingly common contaminant. Preventative measures are discussed.*

■ **Campylobacter ...on the Run!** Biol. Sci. Rev., 19(3) Feb. 2007, pp. 7-9. *A look at the physical characteristics of this food-contaminating bacterium.*

■ **The White Plague** New Scientist (Inside Science), 9 Nov. 2002. *The causes and nature of TB, its global incidence, and a discussion of the implications of drug resistance to TB treatment.*

■ **Tuberculosis** Biol. Sci. Rev., 14(1) Sept. 2001, pp. 30-33. *Despite vaccination, TB has become more common recently. Why has it returned?*

■ **Malaria** Biol. Sci. Rev., 15(1) Sept. 2002, pp. 29-33. *An account of the world's most important parasitic infection of humans. The parasite's life cycle, disease symptoms, control and prevention, and future treatment options are all discussed.*

■ **Beating the Bloodsuckers** Biol. Sci. Rev., 16(3) Feb. 2004, pp. 31-35. *The global distribution of malaria, the current state of malaria research,* *and an account of the biology of the Plasmodium parasite and the body's immune response to it.*

■ **Will there ever be a Malaria Vaccine?** Biol. Sci. Rev., 19(1), Sept. 2006, pp. 24-28. *An outline of the categories of malarial vaccine development.*

TEACHER'S REFERENCE

■ **Positive Progress** New Scientist, 8 Feb. 2003, pp. 33-45. *A series of articles focusing on current issues in HIV research: why some individuals do not contract AIDS, the latest in vaccine development, and new measures against infection.*

■ **An Endangered Species in the Stomach** Sci. American, Feb. 2005, pp. 24-31. *Studies of Helicobacter pylori may lead to better treatments and understanding of other bacteria.*

■ **Capturing a Killer Flu Virus** Scientific American, Jan. 2005, pp. 48-57. *The origin of the killer flu virus remains unsolved even after the virus's genes have been analysed.*

■ **HIV: Vaccines out of Africa** Biologist, 48(2) April 2002. *Vaccination programmes have been successful in wiping out some viral diseases, but they are often difficult to construct. AIDS is proving the famous case to illustrate this difficulty.*

■ **Breeding Snail Fever** Scientific American, July 2005, pp. 12-13. *Construction of the Three Gorges dam has encouraged the spread of schistosomiasis.*

■ **New Medicines for the Developing World** Biol. Sci. Rev. 14 (1) Sept. 2001, pp. 22-26. *The politics of treating disease in the developing world: why is there little incentive to develop programmes to prevent and treat some diseases?*

See pages 10-11 for details of how to access **Bio Links** from our web site: **www.biozone.co.uk**. From Bio Links, access sites under the topics:

GENERAL BIOLOGY ONLINE RESOURCES
• Biology I interactive animations • Instructional multimedia, University of Alberta ... *and others* >
Online Textbooks and Lecture Notes: • S-Cool! A level biology revision guide Learn.co.uk ... *and others* > **Glossaries**: • Health glossary

HEALTH & DISEASE: • CDC disease links • WHO/OMS: health > **Infectious Diseases**: • Centers for Disease Control and Prevention (CDC) • Cholera and epidemic dysentery • Disease-causing bacteria • HIV Insite: gateway to AIDS knowledge • Koch's postulates • Prion diseases • PHLS: Disease facts ... *and many others*

> **Prevention and Treatment**: • Antimicrobial agents • Inducible defences against pathogens • Monoclonal antibodies ... *and others*

Infection and Disease

The term disease often refers to **infectious disease**; disease caused by an infectious agent or **pathogen**. In 1861, **Louis Pasteur** demonstrated experimentally that microorganisms can be present in non-living matter and can contaminate seemingly sterile solutions. He also showed conclusively that microbes can be destroyed by heat; a discovery that formed the basis of modern-day **aseptic technique**. The development of the germ theory of disease followed Pasteur's discoveries and, in 1876-1877, **Robert Koch** established a sequence of experimental steps (now known as **Koch's postulates**) for directly relating a specific microbe to a specific disease. During the past 100 years, the postulates have been invaluable in determining the specific agents of many diseases.

Infectious Disease

Pathogens and Parasites

Pathogens are organisms that cause disease. Some pathogens are also (intra- or extracellular) parasites and seek to exploit the rich food resources of the host and use the host's tissues as incubators for their own reproduction. The invasion of the body by pathogens is called **infection**. Pathogens can be classified as microorganisms (bacteria, fungi, and viruses) or macroorganisms (i.e. organisms visible to the naked eye, such as worms, ticks, and mites). Macroorganisms can cause disease as a direct result of their activity, or they can serve as **vectors** for the transmission of other infectious agents.

Robert Koch

In 1876-1877, the German physician Robert Koch demonstrated that a specific infectious disease (anthrax) was caused by a specific micro-organism (*Bacillus anthracis*). From his work he devised what are now known as **Koch's postulates**.

Koch's postulates

1. The same pathogen must be present in every case of the disease.

2. The pathogen must be isolated from the diseased host and grown in pure culture.

3. The pathogen from the pure culture must cause the disease when it is introduced by inoculation into a healthy, but susceptible organism (usually animal).

4. The pathogen must be isolated from the inoculated animal and be shown to be the original organism.

Exceptions to Koch's Postulates

- Some bacteria and viruses cannot be grown on artificial media (they multiply only within cells).

- Some pathogens cause several disease conditions (e.g. *Mycobacterium tuberculosis*, *Streptococcus pyogenes*).

Types of Pathogens

Bacteria: All bacteria are prokaryotes, but they are diverse in both their structure and metabolism. Bacteria are categorised according to the properties of their cell walls and characteristics such as cell shape and arrangements, oxygen requirement, and motility. Many bacteria are useful, but the relatively few species that are pathogenic are responsible for enormous social and economic cost.

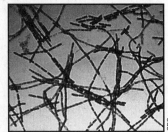

Bacillus anthracis: the rod-shaped bacterial pathogen that causes anthrax

Eukaryotic pathogens: Eukaryotic pathogens (fungi, algae, protozoa, and parasitic worms) include the pathogens responsible for malaria and schistosomiasis. Many are highly specialised parasites with a number of hosts. Serious fungal diseases are also more prevalent now than in the past, affecting those with compromised immune systems, such as AIDS patients.

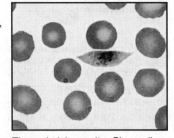

The malarial parasite, *Plasmodium*, seen in a red blood cell smear.

Viral pathogens: Viruses are responsible for many of the everyday diseases with which we are familiar (e.g. the common cold), as well as rather more alarming and dangerous diseases, such as Ebola. Viruses were first distinguished from other pathogens because of their small size and because they are obligate intracellular parasites and need living host cells in order to multiply.

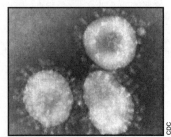

The *Coronavirus* responsible for the 2003 global epidemic of SARS.

1. Using a named example, explain what is meant by a **pathogen**: _____

_____

2. Explain the contribution of Robert Koch to the **aetiology** of disease: _____

_____

_____

_____

3. Suggest why diseases caused by **intracellular protozoan parasites** can be particularly difficult to control and treat:

_____

_____

_____

_____

Related activities: Health vs Disease, Transmission of Disease
Web links: Forensic Entomology

Transmission of Disease

The human body, like that of other large animals, is under constant attack by a wide range of potential parasites and pathogens. Once inside us, these organisms seek to reproduce and exploit us for food. Pathogens may be transferred from one individual to another by a number of methods (below). The transmission of infectious diseases can be virtually eliminated by observing appropriate personal hygiene procedures, and by chlorinating drinking water and providing adequate sanitation.

Portals of Entry

Respiratory tract
The mouth and nose are major entry points for pathogens, particularly airborne viruses, which are inhaled from other people's expelled mucus.

Examples: diphtheria, meningococcal meningitis, tuberculosis, whooping cough, influenza, measles, German measles (rubella), chickenpox.

Gastrointestinal tract
The mouth is one of the few openings where we deliberately place foreign substances into our body. Food is often contaminated with microorganisms, but most of these are destroyed in the stomach.

Examples: cholera, typhoid fever, mumps, hepatitis A, poliomyelitis, bacillary dysentery, salmonellosis.

Breaking the skin surface
The skin provides an effective barrier to the entry of most pathogens. However, a cut or abrasion will allow easy entry for pathogens. Some parasites and pathogens have adaptive features that allow them to penetrate the skin surface.

Examples: tetanus, gas gangrene, bubonic plague, hepatitis B, rabies, malaria, leptospirosis, and HIV.

Urinogenital openings
The urinogenital openings provide entry points for the pathogens responsible for sexually transmitted infections (STIs) and other opportunistic infections (i.e. thrush).

Examples: gonorrhoea, syphilis, HIV, and *E. coli* (a cause of urinary tract infections).

The Body Under Assault

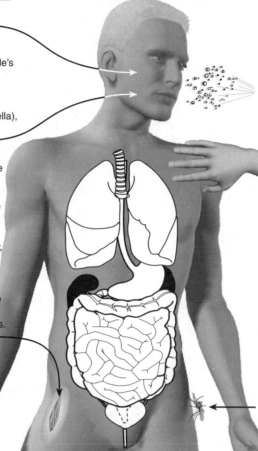

Modes of Transmission

Contact transmission
The agent of disease may occur by contact with other infected humans or animals:

Droplet transmission: Mucus droplets are discharged into the air by coughing, sneezing, laughing, or talking within a radius of 1 m.

Direct contact: Direct transmission of an agent by physical contact between its source and a potential host. Includes touching, kissing, and sexual intercourse. May be person to person, or between humans and other animals.

Indirect contact: Includes touching objects that have been in contact with the source of infection. Examples include: eating utensils, drinking cups, bedding, toys, money, and used syringes.

Vehicle transmission
Agents of disease may be transmitted by a medium such as food, blood, water, intravenous fluids (e.g. drugs), and air. Airborne transmission refers to the spread of fungal spores, some viruses, and bacteria that are transported on dust particles.

Animal Vectors
Some pathogens are transmitted between hosts by other animals. Bites from arthropods (e.g. mosquitoes, ticks, fleas, and lice) and mammals (e.g. rodents) may introduce pathogens, while flies can carry pathogens on their feet. In 1897, **Ronald Ross** identified the *Anopheles* mosquito as the vector for malaria. He was the first to implicate insects in the transmission of disease.

Infectious Disease

1. State how pathogens benefit from invading a host: _____

_____

2. Describe two personal hygiene practices that would minimise the risk of transmitting an infectious disease:

   (a) _____

   (b) _____

3. Identify the common **mode of transmission** and the **portal of entry** for the following pathogens:

   (a) Protozoan causing malaria: _____

   (b) Tetanus bacteria: _____

   (c) Cholera bacteria: _____

   (d) Common cold virus: _____

   (e) Tuberculosis bacteria: _____

   (f) HIV (AIDS) virus: _____

   (g) Gonorrhoea bacteria: _____

Related activities: Bacterial Diseases, Viral Diseases, The Control of Disease

RA 2

Resistance in Pathogens

Many pathogens are effectively controlled by the use of drugs and vaccines, but the emergence of drug resistant pathogens is increasingly undermining the ability to treat and control killer diseases such as HIV/AIDS, tuberculosis, and malaria. Methicillin resistant strains of the common bacterium *Staphylococcus aureus* (MRSA) have acquired genes encoding antibiotic resistance to all penicillins, including **methicillin** and other narrow-spectrum pencillin-type drugs. Such strains, called "superbugs", were discovered in the UK in 1961 and are now widespread, and the infections they cause are exceedingly difficult to treat. High mutation rates and short generation times in viral, bacterial, and protozoan pathogens have contributed to the rapid spread of drug resistance through populations. This is well documented for malaria (below), TB, and HIV/AIDS. Rapid evolution in pathogens is exacerbated too by the strong selection pressure created by the wide use and misuse of antimicrobial drugs, the poor quality of available drugs, and poor patient compliance. The most successful treatment for several diseases, including HIV/AIDS and TB appears to be a multi-pronged attack using a cocktail of drugs to target the pathogen at many stages.

Global Spread of Chloroquine Resistance

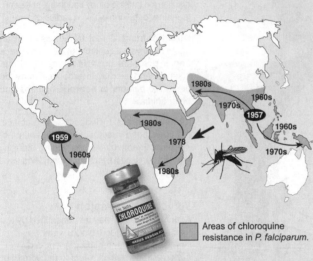

Areas of chloroquine resistance in *P. falciparum*.

Malaria in humans is caused by various species of *Plasmodium*, a protozoan parasite transmitted by *Anopheles* mosquitoes. The inexpensive antimalarial drug **chloroquine** was used successfully to treat malaria for many years, but its effectiveness has declined since resistance to the drug was first recorded in the 1960s. Chloroquine resistance has spread steadily (above) and now two of the four *Plasmodium* species, *P. falciparum* and *P. vivax* are chloroquine-resistant. *P. falciparum* alone accounts for 80% of all human malarial infections and 90% of the deaths, so this rise in resistance is of global concern. New anti-malarial drugs have been developed, but are expensive and often have undesirable side effects. Resistance to even these newer drugs is already evident, especially in *P. falciparum*, although this species is currently still susceptible to artemisinin, a derivative of the medicinal herb *Artemisia annua*.

Drug Resistance in HIV

Strains of drug-resistant HIV arise when the virus mutates during replication. Resistance may develop as a result of a single mutation, or through a step-wise accumulation of specific mutations. These mutations may alter drug binding capacity or increase viral fitness, or they may be naturally occurring polymorphisms (which occur in untreated patients). Drug resistance is likely to develop in patients who do not follow their treatment schedule closely, as the virus has an opportunity to adapt more readily to a "non-lethal" drug dose. The best practice for managing the HIV virus is to treat it with a cocktail of anti-retroviral drugs with different actions to minimise the number of viruses in the body. This minimises the replication rate, and also the chance of a drug resistant mutation being produced.

Anti-HIV drug

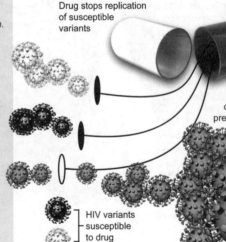

Drug stops replication of susceptible variants

Resistant variant replicates and comes to predominate

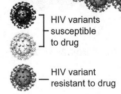

HIV variants susceptible to drug

HIV variant resistant to drug

1. Describe factors contributing to the rapid spread of drug resistance in pathogens:

_____

_____

2. With reference to a specific example, explain how drug resistance arises in a pathogen population:

_____

_____

_____

3. Suggest how health authorities could target multiple drug resistance in common pathogens: _____

_____

_____

_____

Related activities: Tuberculosis, Malaria, HIV and AIDS, Antimicrobial Drugs

Bacterial Diseases

Of the many species of bacteria that exist in the world, relatively few cause disease in humans, other animals, plants or any other organisms. The diagram below shows four adaptive features that help bacteria infect host tissue and cause disease. Bacteria infect a host to exploit the food potential of the host's body tissues. The fact that this exploitation causes disease is not in the interest of the bacteria; a healthy host is better than a sick one. Some well-known human diseases caused by bacteria are illustrated in the diagram below. The natural reservoir (source of infection) of a disease varies from species to species, ranging from humans, insects, and other animals, to sewage and contaminated water.

Bacterial Infection

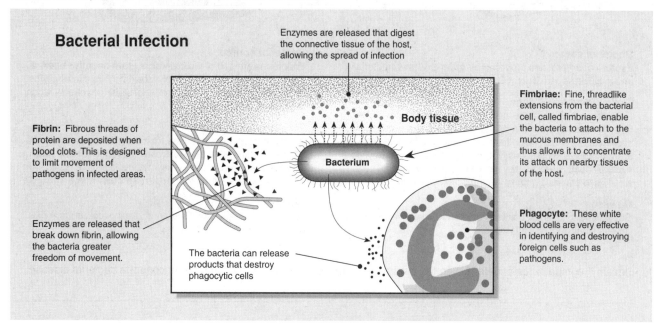

Enzymes are released that digest the connective tissue of the host, allowing the spread of infection

Body tissue

Fibrin: Fibrous threads of protein are deposited when blood clots. This is designed to limit movement of pathogens in infected areas.

Enzymes are released that break down fibrin, allowing the bacteria greater freedom of movement.

Bacterium

The bacteria can release products that destroy phagocytic cells

Fimbriae: Fine, threadlike extensions from the bacterial cell, called fimbriae, enable the bacteria to attach to the mucous membranes and thus allows it to concentrate its attack on nearby tissues of the host.

Phagocyte: These white blood cells are very effective in identifying and destroying foreign cells such as pathogens.

Infectious Disease

Examples of Bacterial Diseases

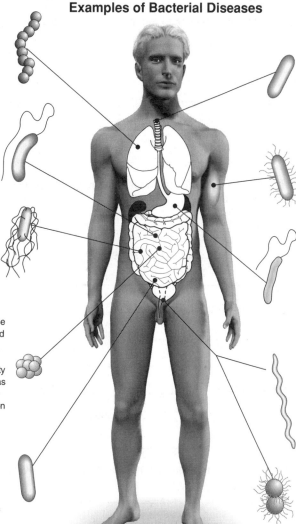

Streptococcus bacteria
These bacteria can cause scarlet fever, sore throats (pharyngitis) and a form of pneumonia. They exist as chains or in pairs. They cause more illness than any other group of bacteria.

Vibrio cholerae
These bacteria cause cholera, a disease common in Asia, caused by a temporary lapse in sanitation (where drinking water is contaminated with human waste).

Salmonella bacteria
This group is not divided up into species, but comprises over 2000 varieties (called *serovars*). They cause gastrointestinal diseases such as typhoid.

Staphylococcus aureus
This bacterium inhabits noses, the surface of skin, and is also found growing in cured meats such as ham. One of the most common causes of food poisoning, it produces many toxins that increase its ability to invade the body or damage tissue. It has the ability to develop antibiotic resistance very quickly and for this reason is a common problem in hospitals.

Enterobacter cloacae
This bacterium can cause urinary tract infections and is widely distributed in humans and animals, as well as in water, sewage and soil. It is a common source of hospital-acquired infection.

Hemophilus influenzae
Despite its name, this bacterium does not cause influenza. This organism inhabits the mucous membranes of the upper respiratory tract and mouth. It causes the most common form of meningitis in young children and is a frequent cause of earaches. It can also cause epiglottitis, bronchitis and pneumonia.

Yersinia pestis
This bacterium caused the Black Death or the bubonic plague of medieval Europe. Fleas from urban rats and ground squirrels transmit the bacteria among animals and to humans. Direct contact with animals and respiratory droplets from infected people can be involved in transmission.

Helicobacter pylori
H. pylori is a helical bacterium that infects various regions of the stomach and duodenum. *Helicobacter* spp. are the only know microbes to thrive in the highly acidic environment of the stomach and are responsible for many cases of peptic and duodenal ulcers as well as gastritis.

Treponema pallidum
This spirochaete bacterium causes syphilis and is transmitted through sexual intercourse. The helical shape allows it to move by a corkscrew rotation.

Neisseria gonorrheae
This bacterium causes the sexually transmitted disease gonorrhea. The fimbriae enable the organism to attach to the mucous membranes of the vagina and urethra of the penis.

Related activities: TB, Foodborne Disease, Cholera, Antimicrobial Drugs
Web links: Microbiology in Motion

RA 2

Properties of Exotoxins

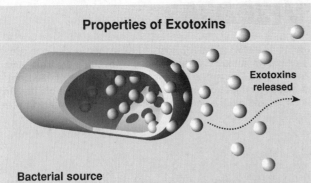

Exotoxins released

Bacterial source
Exotoxins are proteins produced by **gram-positive** bacteria and released as part of normal bacterial growth and metabolism.

Toxicity and lethal dose
Exotoxins are amongst the most toxic compounds known. Due to their solubility they can diffuse easily into the circulatory system and are then easily transported around the body. They are unstable and can usually (but not always) be destroyed easily by heat. However, they have a high infectivity and a very small dose causes symptoms in the infected person.

Diseases
Gas gangrene, tetanus, botulism, diphtheria, scarlet fever, and various staphylococcal infections.

Properties of Endotoxins

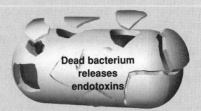

Dead bacterium releases endotoxins

Bacterial source
Endotoxins are part of the cell wall of **gram-negative** bacteria. They are composed primarily of lipids (in contrast to exotoxins, which are proteins). Endotoxins exert their effect only when the bacteria die.

Toxicity and lethal dose
Although endotoxins are less toxic than exotoxins, they are heat stable and withstand autoclaving (121°C for one hour). The dose required to produce symptoms is relatively high, but the immune system cannot neutralise them with antitoxins.

Diseases
Typhoid fever, urinary tract infections, meningococcal meningitis, and *Salmonella* food poisoning.

1. Explain the importance of determining the natural reservoir of infection when attempting to control a bacterial disease:

   _____

   _____

2. Distinguish between exotoxins and endotoxins, identifying the role of each in disease: _____

   _____

   _____

3. Evaluate the evidence for the link between *Helicobacter pylori* infection and the incidence of peptic ulcers:

   _____

   _____

4. Summarise important features of each of the following bacterial pathogens. For disease symptoms, consult a textbook, the internet, a good dictionary, or an encyclopedia:

   (a) *Salmonella* bacteria cause the disease: _____

   Natural reservoir: _____ Symptoms: _____

   _____

   (b) *Clostridium botulinum* causes the disease: _____

   Natural reservoir: _____ Symptoms: _____

   _____

   (c) *Staphylococcus aureus* causes the disease: _____

   Natural reservoir: _____ Symptoms: _____

   _____

5. Identify three common features of the three bacterial pathogens identified in the previous question:

   (a) _____

   (b) _____

   (c) _____

Tuberculosis

Tuberculosis (TB) is a contagious disease caused by the *Mycobacterium tuberculosis* bacterium (**MTB**). The breakdown in health services in some countries, the spread of HIV/AIDS, and the emergence of **multidrug-resistant TB** are contributing to the increasingly harmful impact of this disease. In 1993, the World Health Organisation (WHO) responded to the growing pandemic and declared TB a global emergency. By 1998, the WHO estimated that about a third of the world's population were already infected with MTB. They estimate that 8 million new cases are added annually and that TB causes about 2 million deaths each year (note that in the figures below, only **notified cases** are reported). If controls are not strengthened, it is anticipated that between 2002 and 2020, approximately 1000 million people will be newly infected, over 150 million people will get sick, and 36 million will die from TB.

Infection and Transmission

TB is a contagious disease, and is spread through the air when infectious people cough, sneeze, talk, or spit. A person needs only to inhale a small number of MTB to be infected.

Left untreated, each person with active TB will infect on average between 10 and 15 people every year. People infected with MTB will not necessarily get sick with the disease; the immune system 'walls off' the MTB which can lie dormant for years, protected by a thick waxy coat. When the immune system is weakened, the chance of getting sick (showing symptoms) is greater.

Symptoms

TB usually affects the lungs, but it can also affect other parts of the body, such as the brain, the kidneys, and the spine.

The general symptoms of TB disease include weakness and nausea, weight loss, fever, and night sweats. The symptoms of TB of the lungs include coughing, chest pain, and coughing up blood. The bacteria can spread from the bronchioles to other body systems, where the symptoms depend on the part of the body that is affected.

Treatment

TB is treated with an aggressive antibiotic regime. Since the early 1990s, the WHO has recommended the DOTS (Directly Observed Therapy, Short-course) strategy to control TB worldwide. This programme improves the proportion of patients successfully completing therapy (taking their full course of antibiotics). Proper completion of treatment is the most effective way in which to combat increasing drug resistance.

The Pathogenesis of Tuberculosis
The series below illustrates stages in MTB infection.

MTB enter the lung and are ingested by macrophages (phagocytic white blood cells).

The multiplying bacteria cause the macrophages to swell and rupture. The newly released bacilli infect other macrophages. At this stage a tubercle may form and the disease may lie dormant.

Eventually the tubercle ruptures, allowing bacilli to spill into the bronchiole. The bacilli can now be transmitted when the infected person coughs.

Estimated TB Incidence Rates in 2006 (cases per 100 000)

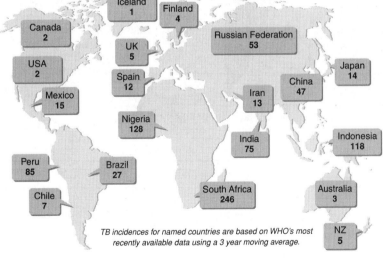

TB incidences for named countries are based on WHO's most recently available data using a 3 year moving average.

1. Identify the pathogen that causes tuberculosis (TB): _____

2. Explain how MTB may exist in a dormant state in a person for many years without causing disease symptoms:

3. State how TB is transmitted between people: _____

4. Suggest how some strains of MTB have acquired **multi-drug resistance**: _____

Foodborne Disease

Foodborne disease is caused by consuming contaminated foods or beverages. More than 250 food and waterborne diseases have been identified. The symptoms and severity of these vary according to the infectious agent, although diarrhoea and vomiting are two universal symptoms. Food poisoning is a term used for any gastrointestinal illness with sudden onset, usually accompanied by stomach pain, diarrhoea, and vomiting, and caused by eating **contaminated food**. It is a common cause of **gastroenteritis** (inflammation of the stomach and intestines). In 2005, there were an estimated 79 000 foodborne illnesses in the UK alone, although about 20% of these were acquired abroad. Such illnesses usually result from food contaminated with viruses, or bacteria or their toxins. They may also result from contamination of food or water by chemicals such as nitrates.

Common Sources of Bacterial Food Poisoning

Salmonella Infections

Most serotypes of *Salmonella* bacteria are pathogenic. **Endotoxins** released from dead bacteria are a likely (but not proven) cause of the symptoms associated with infection.

Salmonella enteritidis can spread to humans via a variety of foods of animal origin (especially poultry products) and is the cause of **salmonellosis** (*Salmonella* food poisoning). Typical symptoms include fever, accompanied by diarrhoea and abdominal cramps.

Salmonella typhi is a highly pathogenic *Salmonella* serotype and causes the life threatening disease, **typhoid fever**. *S.typhi* lives in humans and is shed in the faeces. Transmission occurs through the ingestion of food or drink that has been handled by a person shedding the bacterium, or when water used to prepare of wash food is contaminated with sewage containing the pathogen. Recovered patients can become carriers and continue to shed the bacteria and spread infection. Typhoid fever is common in most regions of the world except in industrialised nations such as the USA, Canada, and western Europe.

Faecal contamination of the hands at meal times is a common cause of gastroenteritis.

Sharing food and utensils may transmit foodborne pathogens between individuals.

Inadequate supply of clean drinking water is a major problem in many parts of the world.

E. coli Gastroenteritis

Escherichia coli is the most common form of infantile and travellers' diarrhoea in developing countries. *E. coli* is the most abundant microbe in the intestinal tract and is normally harmless. However, certain strains are pathogenic and have specialised fimbriae allowing them to bind to the intestinal epithelial cells. They also release **exotoxins** which cause the production of copious watery diarrhoea and symptoms similar to mild cholera. *E. coli* infection is caused by poor sanitation and can be very difficult to avoid in developing countries.

Staphylococcus aureus

S. aureus is a normal inhabitant of human nasal passages. From here, it can contaminate the hands, where it may cause skin lesions and/or contaminate food. Contaminated food held at room temperature will rapidly produce a population of about 1 million bacteria per gram of food and enough **exotoxin** to cause illness. Unusually, the toxin is heat stable and can survive up to 30 minutes of boiling. Reheating the contaminated food may destroy the bacteria but not the toxin itself.

1. Describe three ways in which food can become contaminated by *E. coli*: _____

_____

_____

2. Describe why food poisoning is more prevalent in developing countries than in developed countries: _____

_____

_____

3. Outline the basic precautions that should be taken with drinking water when travelling to developing countries:

_____

_____

4. (a) Describe the symptoms of salmonellosis: _____

_____

(b) Identify the method of transmission of this disease: _____

5. Explain why reheating food will still cause food poisoning if the food is contaminated with *Staphylococcus aureus*:

_____

Related activities: The Control of Disease

Cholera

Cholera is an acute intestinal infection caused by the bacterium *Vibrio cholerae*. The disease has a short incubation period, from one to five days. The bacterium produces an enterotoxin that causes a copious, painless, watery diarrhoea that can quickly lead to severe dehydration and death if treatment is not promptly given. Most people infected with *V. cholerae* do not become ill, although the bacterium is present in their faeces for 7-14 days. When cholera appears in a community it is essential to take measures against its spread. These include: **hygienic disposal of human faeces**, provision of an adequate supply of **safe drinking water**, **safe food handling and preparation** (e.g. preventing contamination of food and cooking food thoroughly), and **effective general hygiene** (e.g. hand washing with soap). Cholera has reemerged as a global health threat after virtually disappearing from the Americas and most of Africa and Europe for more than a century. Originally restricted to the Indian subcontinent, cholera spread to Europe in 1817 in the first of seven pandemics. The current pandemic (below) shows signs of slowly abating, although under-reporting is a problem.

Symptoms

More than 90% of cases are of mild or moderate severity and are difficult to distinguish from other types of acute diarrhoea. Less than 10% of ill people develop typical cholera with signs of moderate or severe dehydration.

Treatment

Most cases of diarrhoea can be treated by giving a solution of oral rehydration salts. During an epidemic, 80-90% of diarrhoea patients can be treated by oral rehydration alone, but patients who become severely dehydrated must be given intravenous fluids. In severe cases, antibiotics can reduce the volume and duration of diarrhoea and reduce the presence of *V. cholerae* in the faeces.

Transmission

Cholera is spread by contaminated water and food. Sudden large outbreaks are usually caused by a contaminated water supply. *Vibrio cholerae* is often found in the aquatic environment and is part of the normal flora of brackish water and estuaries. Human beings are also one of the reservoirs of the pathogenic form of *Vibrio cholerae*.

The Cholera Pandemic: Reported Cases and Deaths (2005)

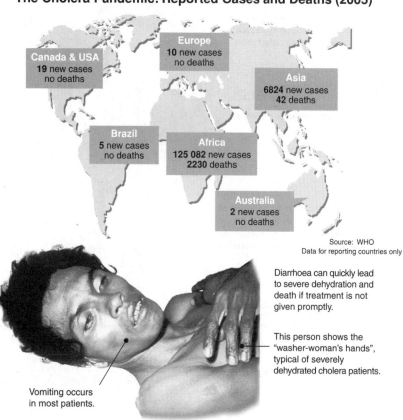

Europe
10 new cases
no deaths

Canada & USA
19 new cases
no deaths

Asia
6824 new cases
42 deaths

Brazil
5 new cases
no deaths

Africa
125 082 new cases
2230 deaths

Australia
2 new cases
no deaths

Source: WHO
Data for reporting countries only

Diarrhoea can quickly lead to severe dehydration and death if treatment is not given promptly.

This person shows the "washer-woman's hands", typical of severely dehydrated cholera patients.

Vomiting occurs in most patients.

Infectious Disease

1. Identify the pathogen that causes cholera: _____

2. Describe the symptoms of cholera and explain why these symptoms are so dangerous if not treated quickly:

_____

_____

_____

3. State how cholera is transmitted between people: _____

_____

4. Describe the effective treatment of cholera at the following stages in the progression of the disease:

(a) Mild onset of dehydration: _____

(b) Severe symptoms: _____

5. Identify the risk factors associated with the incidence of cholera and relate these to social and economic conditions:

_____

_____

_____

Protozoan Diseases

Protozoa are one-celled, eukaryotic organisms that belong to the Kingdom Protoctista. Among the protozoans, there are many variations on cell structure. While most inhabit water and soil habitats, some are part of the natural microbiota of animals (i.e. they are microorganisms that live on or in animals). Relatively few of the nearly 20 000 species of protozoans cause disease; those that do are often highly specialised, intracellular parasites with complex life cycles involving one or more hosts. Under certain adverse conditions, some protozoans produce a protective capsule called a **cyst**. A cyst allows the protozoan to survive conditions unsuitable for survival. For specialised parasitic species, this includes survival for periods outside a host.

AMOEBAE

Amoebae move by extending projections of their cytoplasm. Several pathogenic amoebae infect humans and feed mainly on red blood cells. *Entamoeba* is transmitted through ingestion of cysts that are passed in the faeces. People become infected with *Naegleria* while swimming, when the waterborne cysts pass across mucous membranes and infect blood, brain, and spinal cord.

Pathogen	Disease
Naegleria fowleri	Microencephalitis
Entamoeba histolytica	Amoebic dysentery

APICOMPLEXA

These protozoans are not mobile and tend to be intracellular parasites. They use special enzymes to penetrate the host's tissues. They have complex life cycles involving transmission between several host species.

Pathogen	Disease	Host species
Plasmodium vivax	Malaria	*Anopheles* mosquito
Toxoplasma gondii	Toxoplasmosis	Cats
Pneumocystis carinii	Pneumonia	Humans

MICROSPORA

This unusual group of protozoans lack mitochondria and live as intracellular parasites (within cells). They were first reported to cause human diseases in 1984.

Pathogen	Disease
Nosema	Chronic diarrhoea, kerato-conjunctivitis (in AIDS patients)

FLAGELLATES

Flagellates are usually spindle-shaped, with flagella projecting from the front end. The whiplike motion of the flagella pulls the cells through their environment. *Giardia* is found in the small intestine of mammals. It is passed in the faeces and survives in the environment as a cyst until ingested by the next host. *Trichinomas* moves using an undulating membrane. It is unable to form a cyst and must be transferred directly from host to host quickly (e.g. during sexual intercourse or via toilet facilities or towels). Various *Trypanosoma* species, which cause African sleeping sickness, are spread by the tsetse fly.

Pathogen	Disease
Giardia lamblia	Giardia enteritis
Trichinomas vaginalis	Urethritis, vaginitis
Trypanosoma (in tsetse fly vector)	Sleeping sickness (African trypanosomiasis)

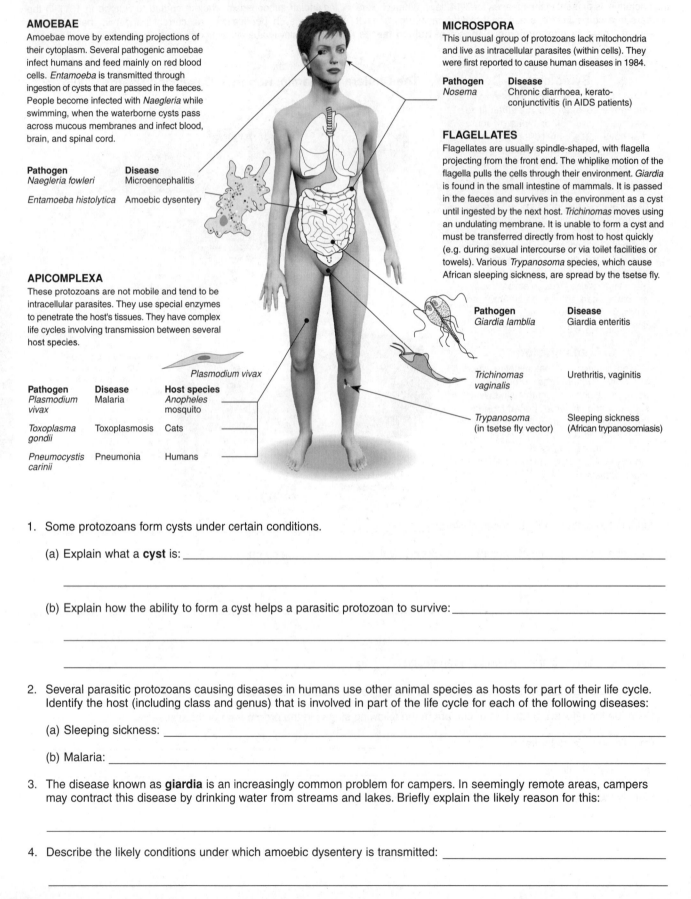

Plasmodium vivax

1. Some protozoans form cysts under certain conditions.

   (a) Explain what a **cyst** is: _____

   _____

   (b) Explain how the ability to form a cyst helps a parasitic protozoan to survive: _____

   _____

   _____

2. Several parasitic protozoans causing diseases in humans use other animal species as hosts for part of their life cycle. Identify the host (including class and genus) that is involved in part of the life cycle for each of the following diseases:

   (a) Sleeping sickness: _____

   (b) Malaria: _____

3. The disease known as **giardia** is an increasingly common problem for campers. In seemingly remote areas, campers may contract this disease by drinking water from streams and lakes. Briefly explain the likely reason for this:

   _____

4. Describe the likely conditions under which amoebic dysentery is transmitted: _____

   _____

Related activities: Malaria
Web links: Animations for Parasitism

Malaria

Malaria is a serious parasitic disease, spread by bites of **Anopheles mosquitoes**, affecting up to 300 million people in the tropics each year. The parasites responsible for malaria are protozoa known as **plasmodia**. Four species can cause the disease in humans. Each spends part of its life cycle in humans and part in *Anopheles* mosquitoes. Even people who take antimalarial drugs and precautions against being bitten may contract malaria. Malaria, especially *falciparum* malaria, is often a medical emergency that requires hospitalisation. Treatment involves the use of antimalarial drugs and, in severe cases, blood

transfusions may be necessary. Symptoms, which appear one to two weeks after being bitten, include headache, shaking, chills, and fever. *Falciparum* malaria is more severe, with high fever, coma, and convulsions, and it can be fatal within a few days of the first symptoms. These more severe symptoms result from this plasmodium's ability to infect all ages of red blood cells (whereas other species attack only young or old cells). Destruction of a greater proportion of blood cells results in *haemolytic anaemia*. The infected blood cells become sticky and block blood vessels to vital organs such as the kidneys and the brain.

Malaria

Malaria occurs in over 100 countries and territories. More than 40% of the people in the world are at risk. Large areas of Central and South America, Hispaniola (Haiti and the Dominican Republic), Africa, the Indian subcontinent, Southeast Asia, the Middle East, and Oceania are considered malaria-risk areas (an area of the world that has malaria).

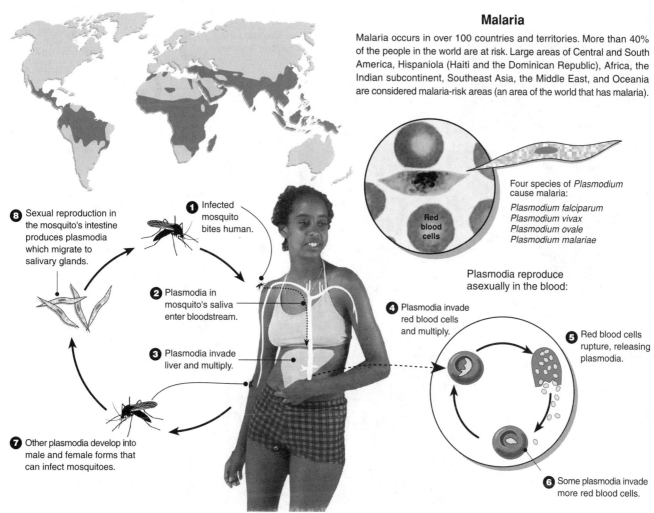

Infectious Disease

1. Explain how a plasmodium parasite enters the body: _____

2. Suggest a way in which villagers could reduce the occurrence of malaria carrying mosquitoes in their immediate area: _____

3. (a) Describe the symptoms of a malaria attack: _____

(b) Explain why the symptoms of *falciparum* malaria are more severe than other forms of malaria: _____

4. Global warming is expected to increase the geographical area of malaria infection. Explain why this is expected: _____

Related activities: The Control of Disease
Web links: Malaria Animation

RA 2

The Schistosoma Parasite

Some **endoparasites**, such as flatworms and roundworms, cause disease directly and are highly specialised to live inside their hosts. Schistosomes, or blood flukes, are specialised parasitic **trematode flatworms** of the genus *Schistosoma*. They are found as adults in the blood vessels of their mammalian hosts and cause the disease **schistosomiasis**, one of the most widespread and devastating parasitic diseases of humans. It is endemic in 74 developing countries with more than 80% of infected people living in sub-Saharan Africa. Unlike most other flukes, schistosomes have separate sexes, and the female and male remain clasped together for their entire reproductive life. Transmission of the *Schistosoma* parasite occurs in freshwater when intermediate snail hosts release infective larval forms of the parasite (cercariae). In intestinal schistosomiasis, there is progressive enlargement of the spleen and liver, and intestinal damage and bleeding. The disease has a low fatality rate, but a high morbidity. Sufferers become severely weakened and liver, spleen, and kidney function become impaired.

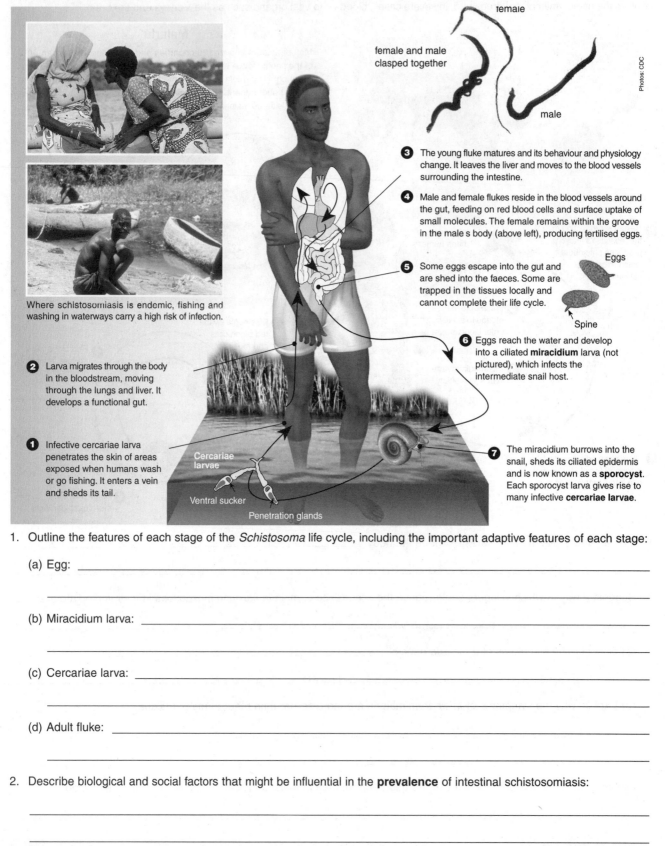

Where schistosomiasis is endemic, fishing and washing in waterways carry a high risk of infection.

female and male clasped together

female

male

Photos: CDC

❸ The young fluke matures and its behaviour and physiology change. It leaves the liver and moves to the blood vessels surrounding the intestine.

❹ Male and female flukes reside in the blood vessels around the gut, feeding on red blood cells and surface uptake of small molecules. The female remains within the groove in the male s body (above left), producing fertilised eggs.

❺ Some eggs escape into the gut and are shed into the faeces. Some are trapped in the tissues locally and cannot complete their life cycle.

Eggs

Spine

❻ Eggs reach the water and develop into a ciliated **miracidium** larva (not pictured), which infects the intermediate snail host.

❷ Larva migrates through the body in the bloodstream, moving through the lungs and liver. It develops a functional gut.

❶ Infective cercariae larva penetrates the skin of areas exposed when humans wash or go fishing. It enters a vein and sheds its tail.

Cercariae larvae

Ventral sucker

Penetration glands

❼ The miracidium burrows into the snail, sheds its ciliated epidermis and is now known as a **sporocyst**. Each sporocyst larva gives rise to many infective **cercariae larvae**.

1. Outline the features of each stage of the *Schistosoma* life cycle, including the important adaptive features of each stage:

   (a) Egg: _____

   _____

   (b) Miracidium larva: _____

   _____

   (c) Cercariae larva: _____

   _____

   (d) Adult fluke: _____

   _____

2. Describe biological and social factors that might be influential in the **prevalence** of intestinal schistosomiasis:

   _____

   _____

Viral Diseases

Some crop and livestock diseases, and many diseases of humans are caused by viruses (see below and the next page). Most viruses are able to infect specific types of cells of only one host species. The particular **host range** is determined by the virus's requirements for its specific attachment to the host cell and the availability, within the host, of the cellular factors needed for viral multiplication. For animal viruses, the receptor sites are on the plasma membranes of the host cells. Antiviral drugs are difficult to design because they must kill the virus without killing the host cells. Moreover, viruses cannot be attacked when in an inert state.

Antiviral drugs work by preventing entry of the virus into the host cell or by interfering with their replication. There are only a few antiviral drugs currently in use (e.g. ribavirin to combat influenza, acyclovir to combat herpes, AZT and protease inhibitors to combat HIV/AIDS). Immunisation is still regarded as the most effective way in which to control viral disease. However immunisation against viruses does not necessarily provide lifelong immunity. New viral strains develop as preexisting strains acquire mutations. These mutations allow the viruses to change their surface proteins and thus evade detection by the host's immune system.

Types of Viruses Affecting Humans

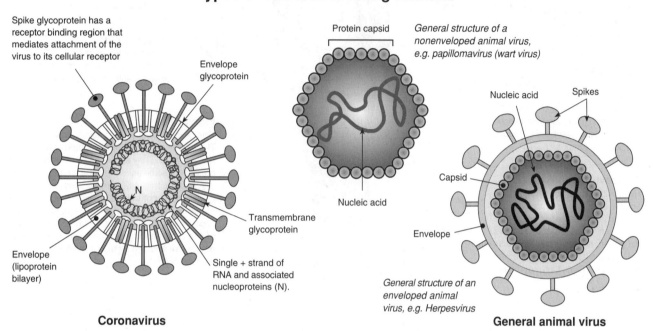

Spike glycoprotein has a receptor binding region that mediates attachment of the virus to its cellular receptor

Envelope glycoprotein

N

Envelope (lipoprotein bilayer)

Transmembrane glycoprotein

Single + strand of RNA and associated nucleoproteins (N).

Coronavirus

Protein capsid

General structure of a nonenveloped animal virus, e.g. papillomavirus (wart virus)

Nucleic acid

Nucleic acid

Spikes

Capsid

Envelope

General structure of an enveloped animal virus, e.g. Herpesvirus

General animal virus

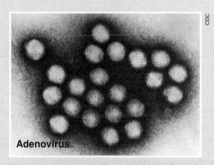

Adenovirus

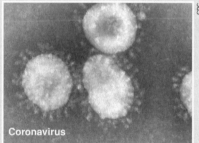

Coronavirus

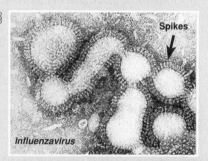

Spikes

Influenzavirus

Adenoviruses are medium-sized (90-100 nm), nonenveloped viruses containing double-stranded DNA. They most commonly cause respiratory illness and are unusually stable to chemical or physical agents, allowing for prolonged survival outside of the body.

Coronaviruses primarily infect the upper respiratory and gastrointestinal tracts of birds and mammals, including humans. Their name derives from the crown or corona of spikes and they have the largest genome of any of the single stranded RNA viruses.

In some viruses, the capsid is covered by an **envelope**, which protects the virus from the host's nuclease enzymes. Spikes on the envelope provide a binding site for attachment to the host. *Influenzavirus* is an enveloped virus with many glycoprotein spikes.

1. Summarise important features of each of the following viral pathogens. For disease symptoms, consult a textbook, the internet, a good dictionary, or an encyclopedia:

(a) HIV causes the disease: _____

Natural reservoir: _____ Symptoms: _____

_____

_____

(b) Coronaviruses cause: _____

Natural reservoir: _____ Symptoms: _____

Related activities: Virus Structures, HIV and AIDS, Animal Virus Replication
Web links: Viral Infection

RA 2

Human Viral Pathogens

HIV (*Lentivirus*)
The human immunodeficiency virus (HIV) causes AIDS. AIDS is a complex assortment of secondary infections that result after HIV has severely weakened the body's immune system.

Hepatitis viruses
The viruses responsible for hepatitis A, B, and C are not related and are from different viral families. Symptoms include liver damage.

Papillomavirus
This virus causes the formation of warts in humans. Some strains may also transform cells and have been implicated in causing cervical cancer. Host cells may reproduce rapidly, resulting in a tumour.

Herpesviruses
Nearly 100 herpesviruses are known. Types found in humans include those that cause cold sores, chickenpox, shingles, infectious mononucleosis, and genital herpes. They have also been linked to a type of human cancer called Burkitt's lymphoma.

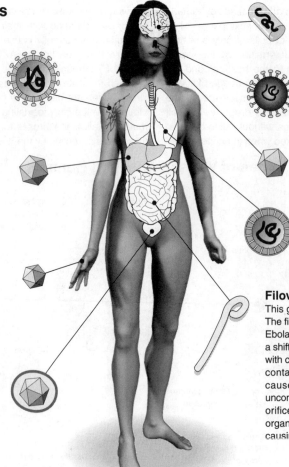

Lyssavirus
This bullet-shaped virus causes rabies and is usually contracted from a bite by a rabid dog or fox.

Coronaviruses
Associated with upper respiratory infections and responsible for 15-20% of colds. A coronavirus is responsible for the disease SARS.

Rhinoviruses
More than 100 rhinoviruses exist and are the most common cause of colds.

Influenzavirus
This virus causes influenza (the flu) in humans. The ability of this virus to rapidly mutate results in many strains.

Filoviruses
This group of viruses is relatively newly emerged. The filoviruses include the dangerous Marburg and Ebola viruses. They appear to have recently made a shift from some animal into the human population with catastrophic results. Filoviruses are spread by contact with contaminated blood or tissue and cause a severe form of haemorrhagic fever; uncontrolled bleeding occurs from just about every orifice of the body. Eventually, all internal body organs are affected by massive internal bleeding, causing death.

(c) *Influenzavirus* causes the disease: _____

　　　Natural reservoir: _____ Symptoms: _____

　　　_____

(d) Filoviruses cause: _____

　　　Natural reservoir: _____ Symptoms: _____

　　　_____

2. Describe the basis of viral host specificity and explain why viruses generally show a very narrow host range:

_____

_____

3. In view of your answer above, explain why it is not uncommon for viruses to cross the species barrier to infect another host type. Provide an example to illustrate your answer:

_____

_____

_____

4. Giving an example, explain why it is difficult to develop suitable long term vaccines against some viruses:

_____

_____

_____

HIV and AIDS

AIDS (acquired immune deficiency syndrome) first appeared in the news in 1981, with cases being reported in Los Angeles, in the United States. By 1983, the pathogen causing the disease had been identified as a retrovirus that selectively infects **helper T cells**. The disease causes a massive deficiency in the immune system due to infection with **HIV** (human immunodeficiency virus). HIV is a retrovirus (RNA, not DNA) and is able to splice its genes into the host cell's chromosome. As yet, there is no cure or vaccine, and the disease has taken the form of a **pandemic**, spreading to all parts of the globe and killing more than a million people each year. It has now been established that HIV arose by the recombination of two simian viruses. It has probably been endemic in some central African regions for decades, as HIV has been found in blood samples from several African nations from as early as 1959. HIV's mode of infection is described on the next page and its origin and prevalence are covered in the next activity.

Capsid
Protein coat that protects the nucleic acids (RNA) within.

Viral envelope
A piece of the cell membrane budded off from the last human host cell.

Nucleic acid
Two identical strands of RNA contain the genetic blueprint for making more HIV viruses.

Reverse transcriptase
Two copies of this important enzyme convert the RNA into DNA once inside a host cell.

Surface proteins
These spikes allow HIV to attach to receptors on the host cells (T cells and macrophages).

The structure of HIV

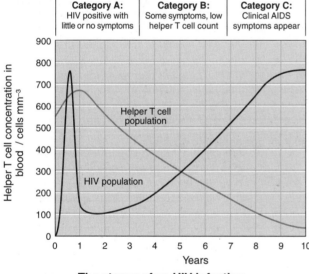

Category A: HIV positive with little or no symptoms	Category B: Some symptoms, low helper T cell count	Category C: Clinical AIDS symptoms appear

Helper T cell population

HIV population

Helper T cell concentration in blood / cells mm⁻³

Years

The stages of an HIV infection

AIDS is actually only the end stage of an HIV infection. Shortly after the initial infection, HIV antibodies appear within the blood. The progress of infection has three clinical categories shown on the graph above.

HIV/AIDS

Individuals affected by the human immunodeficiency virus (HIV) may have no symptoms, while medical examination may detect swollen lymph glands. Others may experience a short-lived illness when they first become infected (resembling infectious mononucleosis). The range of symptoms resulting from HIV infection is huge, and is not the result of the HIV infection directly. The symptoms arise from an onslaught of secondary infections that gain a foothold in the body due to the suppressed immune system (due to the few helper T cells). These infections are from normally rare fungal, viral, and bacterial sources. Full blown AIDS can also feature some rare forms of cancer. Some symptoms are listed below:

Fever, lymphoma (cancer) and toxoplasmosis of the brain, dementia.

Eye infections (*Cytomegalovirus*).

Skin inflammation (dermatitis) particularly affecting the face.

Oral thrush (*Candida albicans*) of the oesophagus, bronchi, and lungs.

A variety of opportunistic infections, including: chronic or persistent *Herpes simplex*, tuberculosis (TB), pneumocystis pneumonia, shingles, shigellosis and salmonellosis.

Diarrhoea caused by *Isospora* or *Cryptosporidium*.

Marked weight loss.

A number of autoimmune diseases, especially destruction of platelets.

Kaposi's sarcoma: a highly aggressive malignant skin tumour consisting of blue-red nodules, usually start at the feet and ankles, spreading to the rest of the body later, including respiratory and gastrointestinal tracts.

Infectious Disease

1. Explain why the HIV virus has such a devastating effect on the human body's ability to fight disease:

_____

_____

_____

2. Consult the graph above showing the stages of HIV infection (remember, HIV infects and destroys helper T cells).

   (a) Describe how the virus population changes with the progression of the disease: _____

   _____

   _____

Related activities: AIDS Epidemiology, Replication in Animal Viruses
Web links: HIV Interactive Animation

DA 2

Transmission, Diagnosis, Treatment, and Prevention of HIV

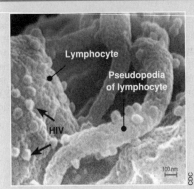

A SEM shows spherical HIV-1 virions on the surface of a human lymphocyte.

Lymphocyte

Pseudopodia of lymphocyte

HIV

100 nm

CDC

HIV is easily transmitted between intravenous drug users who share needles.

Modes of Transmission

1. HIV is transmitted in blood, vaginal secretions, semen, breast milk, and across the placenta.

2. In developed countries, blood transfusions are no longer a likely source of infection because blood is tested for HIV antibodies.

3. Historically, transmission of HIV in developed countries has been primarily through intravenous drug use and homosexual activity, but heterosexual transmission is increasing.

4. Transmission via heterosexual activity is important in Asia and Africa.

Treatment and Prevention

HIV's ability to destroy, evade, and hide inside cells of the human immune system make it difficult to treat. Research into conventional and extremely unconventional approaches to vaccination and chemotherapy is taking place. The first chemotherapy drug to show promise was AZT, which is a nucleotide analogue that inhibits reverse transcriptase. Protease inhibitors (Saquinavir, Ritonavir, Indinavir) are drugs that work by blocking the HIV protease. Once this is blocked, HIV makes copies of itself that cannot infect other cells. These drugs seem to be less toxic and to have less severe side effects than other anti-AIDS drugs. Subunit vaccines are being tested that use HIV glycoproteins inserted into other viruses.

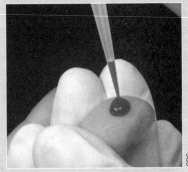

Diagnosis of HIV is possible using a simple antibody-based test on a blood sample.

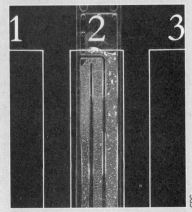

1   2   3

CDC

A positive HIV rapid test result shows clumping (aggregation) where HIV antibodies have reacted with HIV protein-coated latex beads.

(b) Describe how the helper T cells respond to the infection: _____

_____

_____

3. Describe three common ways in which HIV can be transmitted from one person to another: _____

_____

_____

4. Explain what is meant by the term **HIV positive**: _____

_____

5. In the years immediately following the discovery of the HIV pathogen, there was a sudden appearance of AIDS cases amongst **haemophiliacs** (people with an inherited blood disorder). State why this group was being infected with HIV:

_____

_____

6. Explain why it has been so difficult to develop a **vaccine** for HIV: _____

_____

_____

7. In a rare number of cases, people who have been HIV positive for many years still have no apparent symptoms. Explain the significance of this observation and its likely potential in the search for a cure for AIDS:

_____

_____

_____

Epidemiology of AIDS

In many urban centres of sub-Saharan Africa, Latin America, and the Caribbean, AIDS has already become the leading cause of death for both men and women aged 15 to 49 years. AIDS kills people in their most productive years and ranks as the leading cause of potential healthy life-years lost in sub-Saharan Africa. Within the next decade, crude death rates in some countries will more than double, and infant and child mortality rates will increase markedly. Perhaps the most significant impact will be seen in projected life expectancies due to the increased mortality of young adults. The AIDS pandemic has lowered the estimated world population level for the year 2050 from 9.4 billion to 8.9 billion, mostly caused by the massive toll of AIDS in Africa.

Regional HIV Statistics and Figures, December 2006

North America
People living with HIV / AIDS¶:	1.4 million
Adult prevalence rate*:	0.8%
People newly infected with HIV:	43 000
Deaths of people from AIDS:	18 000
Main modes of transmission**:	MSM, IDU, Hetero

Western & Central Europe
People living with HIV / AIDS¶:	740 000
Adult prevalence rate*:	0.3%
People newly infected with HIV:	22 000
Deaths of people from AIDS:	12 000
Main modes of transmission**:	Hetero, MSM, IDU

Eastern Europe & Central Asia
People living with HIV / AIDS¶:	1.7 million
Adult prevalence rate*:	0.9%
People newly infected with HIV:	270 000
Deaths of people from AIDS:	84 000
Main modes of transmission**:	IDU, Hetero

Caribbean
People living with HIV / AIDS¶:	250 000
Adult prevalence rate*:	1.2%
People newly infected with HIV:	27 000
Deaths of people from AIDS:	19 000
Main modes of transmission**:	Hetero, MSM, IDU

Latin America
People living with HIV / AIDS¶:	1.7 million
Adult prevalence rate*:	0.5%
People newly infected with HIV:	140 000
Deaths of people from AIDS:	65 000
Main modes of transmission**:	Hetero, MSM, IDU

North Africa and Middle East
People living with HIV / AIDS¶:	460 000
Adult prevalence rate*:	0.2%
People newly infected with HIV:	68 000
Deaths of people from AIDS:	36 000
Main modes of transmission**:	Hetero, IDU, MSM

Sub-Saharan Africa
People living with HIV / AIDS¶:	24.7 million
Adult prevalence rate*:	5.9%
People newly infected with HIV:	2.8 million
Deaths of people from AIDS:	2.1 million
Main modes of transmission**:	Hetero

Oceania
People living with HIV / AIDS¶:	81 000
Adult prevalence rate*:	0.4%
People newly infected with HIV:	7100
Deaths of people from AIDS:	4000
Main modes of transmission**:	MSM, Hetero, IDU

South & South East Asia
People living with HIV / AIDS¶:	7.8 million
Adult prevalence rate*:	0.6%
People newly infected with HIV:	860 000
Deaths of people from AIDS:	590 000
Main modes of transmission**:	Hetero, IDU

East Asia
People living with HIV / AIDS¶:	750 000
Adult prevalence rate*:	0.1%
People newly infected with HIV:	100 000
Deaths of people from AIDS:	43 000
Main modes of transmission**:	IDU, Hetero, MSM

Estimated percentage of adults (15-49) living with HIV/AIDS

■	>15%
■	5 – 15%
□	0 – 5%

Source: UNAIDS, WHO

* The proportion of adults (15 to 49 years of age) living with HIV/AIDS in 2004   ¶ People includes adults & children
** Modes of transmission: **Hetero**: heterosexual sex; **IDU**: injecting drug use; **MSM**: sex between men

The origins of HIV

AIDS researchers have confirmed that the two strains of HIV each originated from cross-species transmission (**zoonosis**) from other primates. HIV-1, responsible for the global pandemic, arose as a result of recombination between two separate strains of simian immunodeficiency virus (SIV) in infected **common chimpanzees** in west-central Africa. HIV-2 is less virulent than HIV-1 and, until recently, was restricted to West Africa. It originated from a strain of SIV found in **sooty mangabey** monkeys in that region. The killing of primates as "bushmeat" for human consumption allows the virus to transmit to human hunters when they handle infected carcasses with cuts or other open wounds on their hands. Such cross-species transmissions could be happening every day.

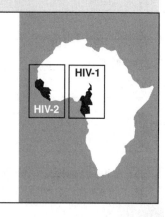

Infectious Disease

Related activities: HIV and AIDS, The Control of Disease

DA 2

Factors in the spread of HIV

Epidemiologists cannot predict with certainty how rapidly a given epidemic will expand or when it will peak, although short term predictions can be made on the basis of trends in HIV spread and information on risk behaviour. Fortunately, there is strong evidence showing that countries will ultimately reduce their new infections if they carry out effective prevention programmes encouraging abstinence, or fidelity and safer sex. A crucial factor is promoting the acceptance and use of condoms, both the traditional kind and the female condom. Condoms are protective irrespective of age, the scope of sexual networks, or the presence of other sexually transmitted infections. There is evidence from around the world that many factors play a role in starting a sexually transmitted HIV epidemic or driving it to higher levels. Some of these risk factors are listed below.

In many African communities, men travel from rural settlements into the cities in search of work. These men often develop sexual networks while they are away and bring HIV with them when they return.

Social and behavioural risk factors
- Little or no condom use.
- Large proportion of the adult population with multiple partners.
- Overlapping (as opposed to serial) sexual partnerships. Individuals are highly infectious when they first acquire HIV and are more likely to infect any concurrent partners.
- Large sexual networks which are often seen in individuals who move back and forth between home and a far off work place.
- Women's economic dependence on marriage or prostitution, robbing them of control over the circumstances or safety of sex.

Biological risk factors
- High rates of sexually transmitted infections, especially those causing genital ulcers.
- Low rates of male circumcision (for poorly understood reasons, circumcised males have a reduced risk of contracting HIV).
- High viral load (HIV levels in the blood is typically highest when a person is first infected and again in the late stages of illness).

1. Comment on the social, economic, and biological factors involved in the prevalence of HIV in many of the **rural** communities of sub-Saharan Africa:

_____

_____

_____

_____

2. Describe the effects of AIDS on the countries of sub-Saharan Africa with respect to the following:

   (a) Age structure of their populations: _____

   _____

   (b) Their local economies: _____

   _____

3. Effective antiviral therapies have reduced deaths from HIV/AIDS in developed countries. Suggest why a similar reduction has not occurred in the countries of sub-Saharan Africa:

_____

_____

4. Briefly state the origin of the two main strains of HIV:

   HIV-1: _____

   _____

   HIV-2 _____

   _____

5. Using the information provided on the previous page and your own graph paper, plot a column graph of the number of people living with HIV/AIDS for each region. Staple the completed graph into this workbook.

Replication in Animal Viruses

Animal viruses are more complex and varied in structure than the viruses that infect bacteria. Likewise, animal host cells are more diverse in structure and metabolism than bacterial cells. Consequently, animal viruses exhibit a number of different mechanisms for **replicating**, i.e. entering a host cell and producing and releasing new virions. Enveloped viruses bud out from the host cell, whereas those without an envelope are released by rupture of the cell membrane. Three processes (attachment, penetration, and uncoating) are shared by both DNA- and RNA containing animal viruses but the methods

of biosynthesis vary between these two major groups. Generally, DNA viruses replicate their DNA in the nucleus of the host cell using viral enzymes, and synthesise their capsid and other proteins in the cytoplasm using the host cell's enzymes. This is outlined below for a typical enveloped DNA virus. RNA viruses are more variable in their methods of biosynthesis. The example on the next page describes replication in the retrovirus HIV, where the virus uses its own reverse transcriptase to synthesise viral DNA and produce **latent proviruses** or active, mature retroviruses.

Entry of an Enveloped Virus into a Cell

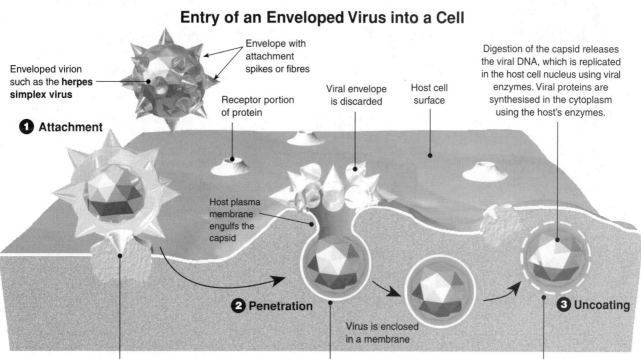

Enveloped virion such as the **herpes simplex virus**

Envelope with attachment spikes or fibres

Receptor portion of protein

Viral envelope is discarded

Host cell surface

Digestion of the capsid releases the viral DNA, which is replicated in the host cell nucleus using viral enzymes. Viral proteins are synthesised in the cytoplasm using the host's enzymes.

1 Attachment

Host plasma membrane engulfs the capsid

2 Penetration

Virus is enclosed in a membrane

3 Uncoating

Infectious Disease

When a viral particle encounters the cell surface, it attaches to the **receptor sites** of proteins on the cell's plasma membrane.

Once the viral particle is attached, the host cell begins to engulf the virus by **endocytosis**. This is the cell's usual response to foreign particles.

The nucleic acid core is uncoated and the **biosynthesis** of new viruses begins. Mature virions are released by budding from the host cell.

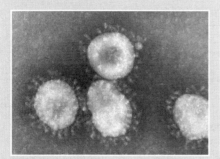

Coronaviruses are irregularly shaped viruses associated with upper respiratory infections and SARS. The envelope bears distinctive projections.

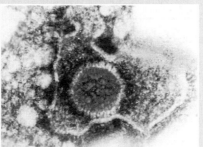

Herpesviruses are medium-sized enveloped viruses that cause various diseases including fever blisters, chickenpox, shingles, and herpes.

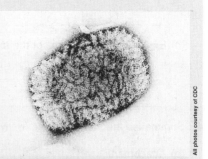

This *Vaccinia* virus belongs to the family of pox viruses; large (200-350 nm), enveloped DNA viruses that cause diseases such as smallpox.

1. Describe the purpose of the glycoprotein spikes found on some enveloped viruses: _____

_____

2. (a) Explain the significance of endocytosis to the entry of an enveloped virus into an animal cell: _____

_____

_____

   (b) State where an enveloped virus replicates its viral DNA: _____

   (c) State where an enveloped virus synthesises its proteins: _____

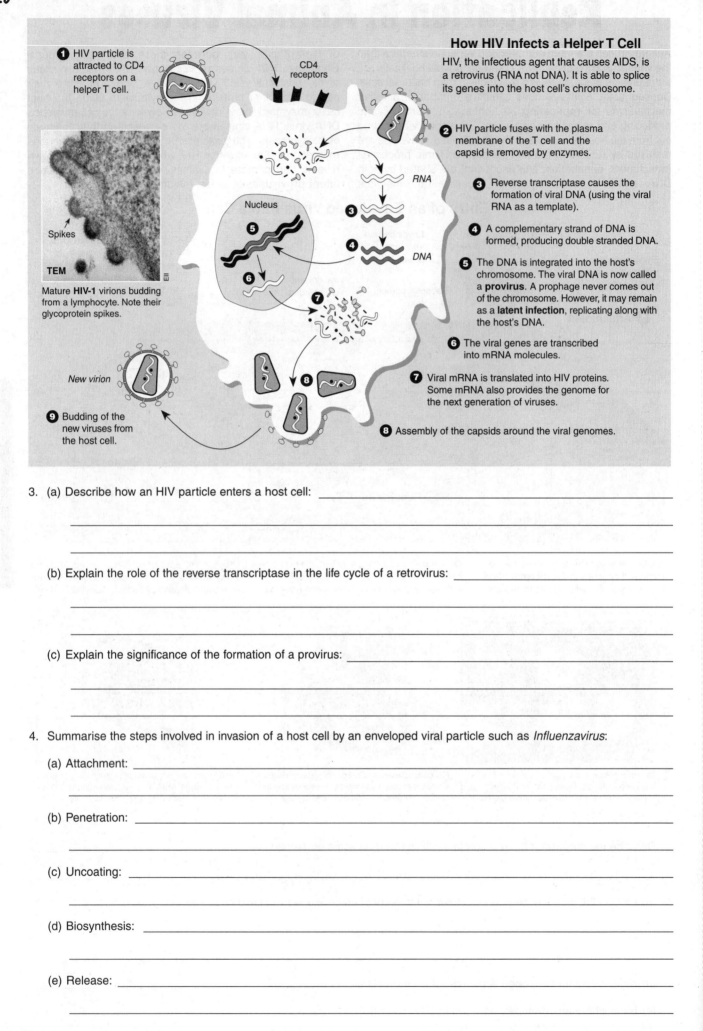

How HIV Infects a Helper T Cell

HIV, the infectious agent that causes AIDS, is a retrovirus (RNA not DNA). It is able to splice its genes into the host cell's chromosome.

1 HIV particle is attracted to CD4 receptors on a helper T cell.

CD4 receptors

2 HIV particle fuses with the plasma membrane of the T cell and the capsid is removed by enzymes.

RNA

3 Reverse transcriptase causes the formation of viral DNA (using the viral RNA as a template).

4 A complementary strand of DNA is formed, producing double stranded DNA.

Nucleus

5 The DNA is integrated into the host's chromosome. The viral DNA is now called a **provirus**. A prophage never comes out of the chromosome. However, it may remain as a **latent infection**, replicating along with the host's DNA.

DNA

6 The viral genes are transcribed into mRNA molecules.

7 Viral mRNA is translated into HIV proteins. Some mRNA also provides the genome for the next generation of viruses.

Spikes

TEM

Mature **HIV-1** virions budding from a lymphocyte. Note their glycoprotein spikes.

New virion

9 Budding of the new viruses from the host cell.

8 Assembly of the capsids around the viral genomes.

3. (a) Describe how an HIV particle enters a host cell: _____

_____

_____

(b) Explain the role of the reverse transcriptase in the life cycle of a retrovirus: _____

_____

_____

(c) Explain the significance of the formation of a provirus: _____

_____

_____

4. Summarise the steps involved in invasion of a host cell by an enveloped viral particle such as *Influenzavirus*:

(a) Attachment: _____

_____

(b) Penetration: _____

_____

(c) Uncoating: _____

_____

(d) Biosynthesis: _____

_____

(e) Release: _____

_____

Emerging Diseases

Emerging diseases are so named because they are diseases with no previous history in the human population. Often, as with HIV/AIDS and avian influenza (H5N1), they are **zoonoses** (animal diseases that cross to humans). Zoonoses are capable of causing highly lethal **pandemics** (world-wide epidemics) amongst an unprepared population. The increasing incidence of **multiple drug resistance** in pathogens (including those that cause tuberculosis, malaria, pneumonia, gonorrhoea, and cholera) has lead to the **re-emergence** of diseases that were

previously thought to be largely under control. Food-borne diseases, such as *Campylobacter*, are also on the rise, despite improvements in hygiene. Even diseases once thought to be non-infectious (e.g. stomach ulcers and cervical cancer) are now known to be linked to infectious agents. In the 1940s, many common and lethal diseases (e.g. scarlet fever and diphtheria) were conquered using antibiotics. It is now evident that antibiotics are not only losing their power, they are encouraging the emergence of deadly and untreatable infections.

E. coli 0157:H7

A highly pathogenic strain of *Escherichia coli*, *E.coli* O157:H7 (below), causes bloody diarrhoea, sweating, vomiting, and sometimes death. Past sources of contamination include meats (Scotland) and apple juice (western US). Several deaths in New York and Canada were caused by outbreaks in 1999-2000. The numbers in the name refer to specific markers on the surface which distinguish the strains.

SEM: 6836x

BSE and CJD

Investigation into the appearance of a new form of **Creutzfeldt-Jakob Disease** (vCJD) in Britain in 1994-1995 established a link with **Mad Cow Disease** or BSE (**bovine spongiform encephalopathy**). This **prion** disease is spread through the consumption of contaminated beef.

Avian influenza A (H5N1)

In January 2004, a new strain of 'bird flu' (H5N1) spread rapidly through 8 Asian countries. Outbreaks occurred again in 2005, each time with high human mortality. It is now continuing its spread through Africa and Europe. Avian flu mutates rapidly and crosses species barriers with apparently little difficulty. These features make it a serious public health threat. The **H5N1 virus** is pictured right. At this magnification, the stippled appearance of the protein coat encasing the virion can easily be seen.

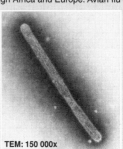

TEM: 150 000x

Resistant Tuberculosis

The reappearance of TB as a virulent disease is the result of an increasing multi-drug resistance to antibiotics and fewer people being immunised.

Hantavirus

An outbreak in Argentina of *hantavirus pulmonary syndrome* in 1996 caused 9 deaths from 17 cases. The source of infection was contact with rodent feces. A recent outbreak in Panama caused 3 deaths.

Severe Acute Respiratory Syndrome

The first case of this respiratory illness was reported 16 November 2002, in China. Initially, epidemiologists thought that people were contracting SARS from infected masked palm civet and racoon-dogs. It is now known that the reservoir for this **coronavirus** is a bat, which passes the infection to other mammals. Once in the human population, SARS spread rapidly through close contact. SARS had a mortality of about 10%, with 50% for people aged 60+.

West Nile Virus

A sometimes fatal encephalitis caused by a flaviviral infection. Most of those infected have no symptoms, but 20% will have some symptoms and a small proportion (less than 1%) will develop severe infection. Symptoms of severe infection include high fever, coma, convulsions, and paralysis. In 2002, there were 277 deaths from West Nile fever in the US, with infection rates concentrated in certain states. The disease is transmitted to humans via **mosquitoes** (below), which are infected with the virus when feeding on bird **reservoir hosts**. Over 110 bird species are known to have been infected with West Nile virus, and bird deaths are closely monitored in the US as indicators of West Nile outbreaks.

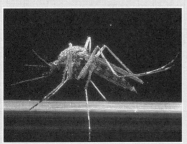

Hemorrhagic Fevers: Ebola & Marburg

Viral hemorrhagic fevers are a group of diseases from four distinct families of viruses. The two best known examples are the filoviruses **Ebola** (below) and **Marburg**. Outbreaks of Ebola have occurred sporadically: in 1976 and 1979, and again in 1995-1996 and 2001-2003. Marburg virus erupted in Angola early in 2005 and was still continuing in May of this year. Mortality was high at 87%, with a total of 276 of 316 reported cases being fatal.

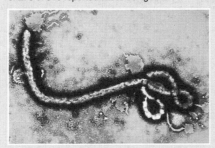

HIV and AIDS

The AIDS pandemic is set to have a lasting effect on the world population. At least two strains are recognized: the deadly **HIV-1 virus** is more widespread than the slightly more benign **HIV-2 strain**. HIV viruses (arrowed) are shown below emerging from a human T cell. HIV is responsible for the massive AIDS pandemic that some claim to be species threatening.

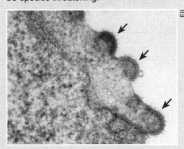

Related activities: Patterns of Disease, HIV and AIDS, The Control of Disease, Antimicrobial Drugs

RA 2

1. Describe the biological and social factors important in the emergence and spread of a named **emerging disease**:

   _____

   _____

   _____

   _____

   _____

2. Explain the role of **zoonoses** in the emergence of new diseases: _____

   _____

   _____

3. Using an example, explain what a **re-emerging disease** is: _____

   _____

   _____

4. Explain how drug resistance in pathogens has led to an increase in the number of re-emerging diseases:

   _____

   _____

   _____

5. Distinguish between an **epidemic** and a **pandemic**: _____

   _____

   _____

6. Describe the biological and social factors involved when diseases spread rapidly through hospitals: _____

   _____

   _____

   _____

7. The Spanish influenza pandemic of 1917-18 was made worse by the return of troops from World War I to their home countries. More than 20 million people died in the pandemic, which had a death rate of about 3%. Explain how this pandemic differed from that of SARS in 2003, in terms of its **global spread** and **death rate**:

   _____

   _____

   _____

8. The next pandemic may well be avian flu. Discuss why this disease poses such a public health threat and describe the precautions necessary in preventing its global spread:

   _____

   _____

   _____

   _____

   _____

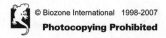

Prion Diseases

Until recently, all pathogens were thought to contain some form of nucleic acid. It now seems possible that a protein alone can be an infectious agent. Called **prions**, they are capable of replication and of causing infection. Prions have been spread by eating contaminated meat and, because they resist normal sterilisation methods, they can be spread on surgical instruments. Prions are produced by mutations in the gene coding for a normal cell protein (PrP). They cause a group of degenerative nervous diseases in mammals called transmissible spongiform encephalopathies (TSE). These include scrapie in sheep, bovine spongiform encephalopathy (**BSE**) in cattle, and variant **Creutzfeldt-Jakob disease** and **kuru** in humans. Different mutations of the PrP gene are thought to be responsible in each case.

Kuru is the condition which first brought prion diseases to prominence in the 1950s. Found in the geographically isolated tribes in the Fore highlands of Papua New Guinea. Researchers discovered that these people were eating the brain tissue of dead relatives for religious reasons. They ground up the brain into a pale grey soup, heated it and ate it. Clinically, the disease resembles CJD.

The Infectious Nature of Prion Proteins

A shape change transforms the harmless protein into its infectious 'prion' form. This shape change may be caused by a point mutation in the gene that codes for it.

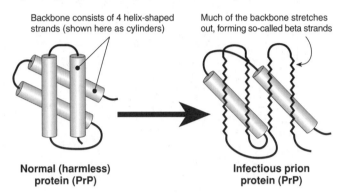

Backbone consists of 4 helix-shaped strands (shown here as cylinders)

Much of the backbone stretches out, forming so-called beta strands

Normal (harmless) protein (PrP)

Infectious prion protein (PrP)

Propagation of the Prion Protein

Infectious protein (prion) has an unusual shape allowing it to bind to the normal form of the protein.

The normal (harmless) protein is converted into the infectious prion form.

The original and newly formed prions attack other normal proteins nearby. Those molecules, in turn, attack other normal molecules, until the prions accumulate to dangerous levels.

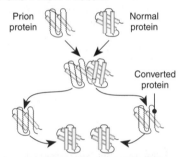

Prion protein

Normal protein

Converted protein

Prion diseases of selected mammals

Mammal	Disease
Sheep	Scrapie
Mink	Transmissible Mink Encephalopathy (TME)
Mule deer, elk	Chronic Wasting Disease (CWD)
Cattle	Bovine Spongiform Encephalopathy (BSE)

Infectious Disease

Prion Diseases of Humans

Disease	Typical symptoms	Acquisition of disease	Distribution	Span of overt illness
Kuru	Loss of coordination, often followed by dementia.	Infection probably through cannibalism (which stopped in 1958).	Known only in highlands of Papua New Guinea; some 2600 cases have been identified since 1957.	Three months to one year
"Classical" **Creutzfeldt-Jakob Disease** (CJD)	Dementia, followed by loss of coordination, although sometimes this sequence is reversed.	Usually unknown (in "sporadic" disease). In 10-15% of cases, inheritance of a mutation in the gene coding for the prion protein. Infection as an accidental consequence of surgery, as well as growth hormone injections, corneal transplants from dead donors (not blood transfusions).	*Sporadic form:* 1 person per million worldwide. *Inherited form:* some 100 extended families have been identified. *Infectious form:* 80 cases from medical procedures (e.g. injection of human growth hormone from pituitary of dead people).	Typically about one year; the range is one month to more than 10 years
Mad Cow Disease or **Variant Creutzfeldt-Jakob Disease** (vCJD)	Dementia, shaky movements, unsteady gait, sudden, jerky, involuntary movements of head, face, or limbs.	Infection by eating beef products from cattle infected with bovine spongiform encephalopathy (BSE).	By June 1999, 43 people had been identified as being infected from BSE cattle in the UK.	Unknown but probably between 2 and 30 years
Gerstmann-Straussler-Scheinker Disease (GSS)	Loss of coordination, often followed by dementia.	Inheritance of a mutation in the gene coding for the prion protein (PrP).	Some 50 extended families have been identified.	Typically about two to six years
Fatal Familial Insomnia	Trouble sleeping and disturbance of the autonomic nervous system, followed by insomnia and dementia.	Inheritance of a mutation in the gene coding for the prion protein (PrP).	Nine extended families have been identified.	Typically about one year

Source: Modified after Scientific American, January 1995, p. 32.

Related activities: Emerging Diseases

DA 2

Reported incidence of scrapie and BSE in the UK

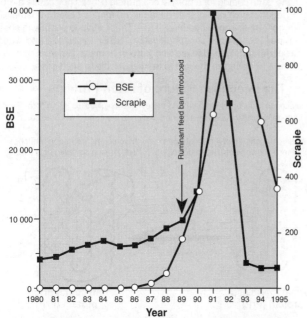

The first cases of Bovine Spongiform Encephalopathy (BSE) were seen at the end of 1986. The disease had spread because meat and bone meal (MBM) rendered from the bodies of infected cows and sheep (infected with a similar disease, scrapie), were used in feeds given to other cattle. On the 18th July 1988, Britain banned ruminant-to-ruminant feeding. By the end of 1998, approximately 170 000 cases had been confirmed and another 100 000 cattle were culled in an attempt to stop the spread of the disease. BSE very nearly destroyed the British beef industry.

Deaths of human prion disease cases in the UK

Year	Sporadic	Iatrogenic	Familial	GSS	vCJD	Total¶
1992	45	2	5	1	-	53
1993	37	4	3	2	-	46
1994	53	1	4	3	-	61
1995	35	4	2	3	3	47
1996	40	4	2	4	10	60
1997	60	6	4	1	10	81
1998	63	3	3	2	18	89
1999	62	6	2	0	15	85
2000	50	1	2	1	28	82
2001	58	4	3	2	20	87
2002	72	0	4	1	17	94
2003	79	5	4	2	18	108
2004	51	2	4	1	9	67
2005	65	3	7	6	5	86
2006	57	1	6	3	5	72
2007*	7	2	0	1	2	12

Source: Department of Health, United Kingdom: www.cjd.ed.ac.uk/figures.htm

Sporadic: Classic CJD cases that appear to occur spontaneously with no definite cause and account for 85% of all cases.

Iatrogenic: Classic CJD cases resulting from a medical procedure. All U.K. cases have resulted from treatment with human derived pituitary growth hormones or from grafts using dura mater (a membrane lining the skull).

Familial: Cases occurring in families associated with mutations in the PrP gene (10-15% of cases).

GSS: *Gertsmann-Straussler-Scheinker syndrome;* an extremely rare inherited autosomal dominant disease that causes shaky movements and terminal dementia.

vCJD: Variant CJD (originally named *new variant* CJD). Hitherto unrecognised variant of CJD discovered in April 1996.

Total¶: Includes all confirmed cases.

* Incomplete data (as to 4 May 2007)

1. Describe the main feature of prions that distinguishes them from other infectious agents: _____

   _____

2. Explain briefly how a prion is able to replicate inside a mammal's body: _____

   _____

   _____

   _____

3. In 1988, the British government introduced a ban on feeding cattle with meat and bone meal.

   (a) Explain the purpose of this ban: _____

   _____

   (b) Suggest why the incidence of **BSE** continued to increase for a number of years after the ban: _____

   _____

   _____

4. State the source of infection for people with **variant CJD**: _____

5. Describe the cultural practice of highland tribes of Papua New Guinea that spread the prion disease known as **kuru**:

   _____

   _____

6. Name a prion disease that affects the following mammals:

   (a) Sheep: _____ (b) Cattle: _____ (c) Humans: _____

7. Identify three medical procedures that have been known to accidentally introduce CJD into patients: _____

   _____

The Control of Disease

Many factors can influence the spread of disease, including the social climate, diet, general health, and access to medical care. Human intervention and modification of behaviour can reduce the transmission rate of some diseases and inhibit their spread. Examples include the use of personal physical barriers, such as condoms, to prevent sexually transmitted infections (STIs), and the use of **quarantine** to ensure that potential carriers of disease are isolated until incubation periods have elapsed. Cleaning up the environment also lowers the incidence of disease by reducing the likelihood that pathogens or their vectors will survive. The effective control of infectious disease depends on knowing the origin of the outbreak (its natural reservoir), its mode of transmission within the population, and the methods that can be feasibly employed to contain it. Diseases are often classified according to how they behave in a given population. Any disease that spreads from one host to another, either directly or indirectly, is said to be a **communicable disease**. Those that are easily spread from one person to another, such as chicken pox or measles, are said to be **contagious**. Such diseases are a threat to **public health** and many must be notified to health authorities. **Noncommunicable diseases** are not spread from one host to another and pose less of a threat to public health. A disease that occurs only occasionally and is usually restricted in its spread is called a **sporadic disease**.

Methods for controlling the spread of disease

Transmission of disease can be prevented or reduced by adopting 'safe' behaviours. Examples include using condoms to reduce the spread of STIs, isolation of people with a specific illness (such as SARS), or establishing quarantine procedures for people who may be infected, but are not yet ill.

The development of effective sanitation, sewage treatment, and treatment of drinking water has virtually eliminated dangerous waterborne diseases from developed countries. These practices disrupt the normal infection cycle of pathogens such as cholera and giardia.

Appropriate personal hygiene practices reduce the risk of infection and transmission. Soap may not destroy the pathogens but washing will dilute and remove them from the skin. Although popular, antibacterial soaps encourage development of strains resistant to antimicrobial agents.

The environment can be made less suitable for the growth and transmission of pathogens. For example, spraying drainage ditches and draining swamps eliminates breeding habitats for mosquitoes carrying diseases such as malaria and dengue fever.

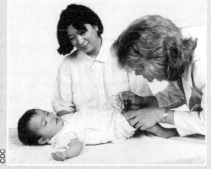

Immunisation schedules form part of public health programmes. If most of the population is immune, 'herd immunity' limits outbreaks to sporadic cases. In such populations there are too few susceptible individuals to support the spread of an epidemic.

Disinfectants and sterilisation techniques, such as autoclaving, destroy pathogenic microbes before they have the opportunity to infect. The use of these techniques in medicine has significantly reduced post operative infections and associated deaths.

1. Distinguish between contagious and non-communicable diseases, providing an example of each:

_____

_____

2. (a) Explain the difference between **isolation** and **quarantine**: _____

_____

_____

_____

Related activities: Patterns of Disease, Immunisation, Antimicrobial Drugs

RA 2

(b) Using the recent example of SARS, explain how isolation and quarantine operate to prevent the spread of disease:

_____

_____

3. Explain how the use of condoms reduces the spread of the human immunodeficiency virus (HIV) that causes AIDS:

_____

_____

4. Explain how the drainage of stagnant water in tropical regions may reduce the incidence of malaria in those countries:

_____

_____

5. Describe how each of the following methods is used to control the **growth** of disease-causing microbes:

(a) Disinfectants: _____

_____

(b) Antiseptics: _____

_____

(c) Heat: _____

_____

(d) Ionising radiation (gamma rays): _____

_____

(e) Desiccation: _____

_____

(f) Cold: _____

_____

6. The **Human Genome Project** (HGP) was launched in 1990 and completed in 2003, two years ahead of schedule. Its achieved aim was to sequence the entire human genome, but much of the research since has focussed on determining the various roles of the (expressed) gene products. It is hoped that a more complete understanding the human genome will revolutionise the treatment and prevention of disease. Briefly discuss how the HGP will facilitate:

(a) Diagnosis of disease: _____

_____

_____

(b) Treatment of disease: _____

_____

7. The first measles vaccine was introduced to Britain in 1964. However, in 1993 there were 9000 cases of measles notified to the health authorities in England and Wales.

(a) Suggest why measles has not been eliminated in Britain: _____

_____

(b) Explain how vaccination interrupts the transmission of measles within a population: _____

_____

_____

Antimicrobial Drugs

Antimicrobial drugs include synthetic (manufactured) **drugs** as well as drugs produced by bacteria and fungi, called **antibiotics**. Antibiotics are produced naturally by these microorganisms as a means of inhibiting competing microbes around them (a form of antibiosis, hence the name antibiotic). The first antibiotic, called penicillin, was discovered in 1928 by Alexander Fleming. Since then, similar inhibitory reactions between colonies growing on solid media have been commonly observed. Antibiotics are actually rather easy to discover, but few of them are of medical or commercial value. Many antibiotics are toxic to humans or lack any advantage over those already in use. More than half of our antibiotics are produced by species of filamentous bacteria that commonly inhabit the soil, called *Streptomyces*. A few antibiotics are produced by bacteria of the genus *Bacillus*. Others are produced by moulds, mostly of the genera *Cephalosporium* and *Penicillium*. Antimicrobial drugs are used in **chemotherapy** programmes to treat infectious diseases. Like disinfectants, these chemicals interfere with the growth of microorganisms (see diagram below). They may either kill microbes directly (**bactericidal**) or prevent them from growing (**bacteriostatic**). To be effective, they must often act inside the host, so their effect on the host's cells and tissues is important. The ideal antimicrobial drug has **selective toxicity**, killing the pathogen without damaging the host. Some antimicrobial drugs have a narrow **spectrum of activity**, and affect only a limited number of microbial types. Others are **broad-spectrum drugs** and affect a large number of microbial species (see the table below). When the identity of a pathogen is not known, a broad-spectrum drug may be prescribed in order to save valuable time. There is a disadvantage with this, because broad spectrum drugs target not just the pathogen, but much of the host's normal microflora also. The normal microbial community usually controls the growth of pathogens and other microbes by competing with them. By selectively removing them with drugs, certain microbes in the community that do not normally cause problems, may flourish and become **opportunistic pathogens**.

How Antimicrobial Drugs Work

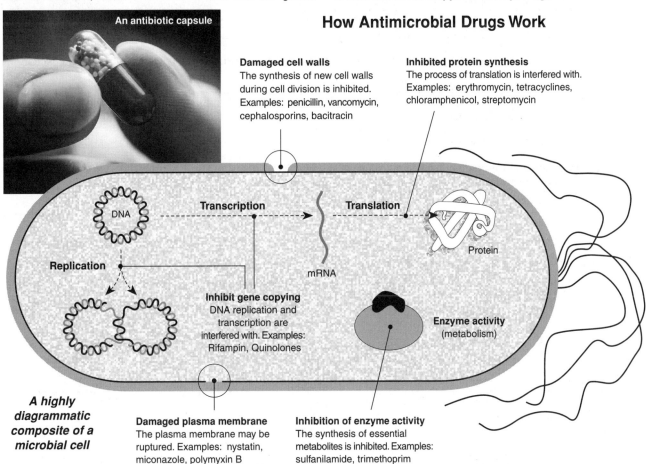

An antibiotic capsule

Damaged cell walls
The synthesis of new cell walls during cell division is inhibited. Examples: penicillin, vancomycin, cephalosporins, bacitracin

Inhibited protein synthesis
The process of translation is interfered with. Examples: erythromycin, tetracyclines, chloramphenicol, streptomycin

Transcription · Translation · DNA · Replication · mRNA · Protein

Inhibit gene copying
DNA replication and transcription are interfered with. Examples: Rifampin, Quinolones

Enzyme activity
(metabolism)

A highly diagrammatic composite of a microbial cell

Damaged plasma membrane
The plasma membrane may be ruptured. Examples: nystatin, miconazole, polymyxin B

Inhibition of enzyme activity
The synthesis of essential metabolites is inhibited. Examples: sulfanilamide, trimethoprim

(side tab) Infectious Disease

Spectrum of antimicrobial activity of a number of chemotherapeutic drugs

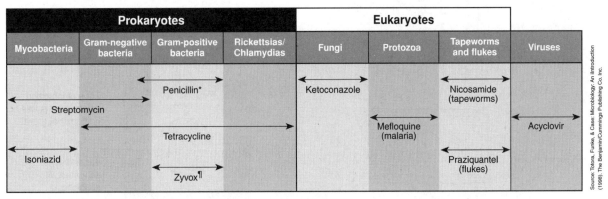

Prokaryotes				Eukaryotes			
Mycobacteria	Gram-negative bacteria	Gram-positive bacteria	Rickettsias/ Chlamydias	Fungi	Protozoa	Tapeworms and flukes	Viruses
		Penicillin*		Ketoconazole		Nicosamide (tapeworms)	
Streptomycin							
	Tetracycline				Mefloquine (malaria)		Acyclovir
Isoniazid						Praziquantel (flukes)	
		Zyvox¶					

Source: Tortora, Funke, & Case: Microbiology: An Introduction (1998); The Benjamin/Cummings Publishing Co. Inc.

* There are some synthetic derivatives of penicillin that act effectively against gram-negative bacteria.

¶ The first new class of antibiotics to be used in 35 years.

1. Discuss the requirements of an "ideal" anti-microbial drug, and explain in what way antibiotics satisfy these requirements:

_____

_____

_____

_____

2. Some bacteria have ways of tolerating treatment by antibiotics, and are termed 'superbugs'.

    (a) Explain what is meant by **antibiotic resistance** in bacteria: _____

_____

_____

    (b) Explain why a course of antibiotics should be finished completely, even when the symptoms of infection have gone:

_____

_____

3. (a) Explain the advantages and disadvantages of using a **broad-spectrum drug** on an unidentified bacterial infection:

_____

_____

    (b) Identify two groups of broad spectrum drugs: _____

4. Although there are a few drugs that have some success in controlling viruses, antibiotics are ineffective. Explain why antibiotics do not work against viruses:

_____

_____

_____

5. Describe four ways in which antimicrobial drugs kill or inhibit the growth of microbes: _____

_____

_____

6. The diagram below shows an experiment investigating the effectiveness of different antibiotics on a pure culture of a single species of bacteria. Giving a reason, state which antibiotic (A-D) is most effective in controlling the bacteria:

_____

_____

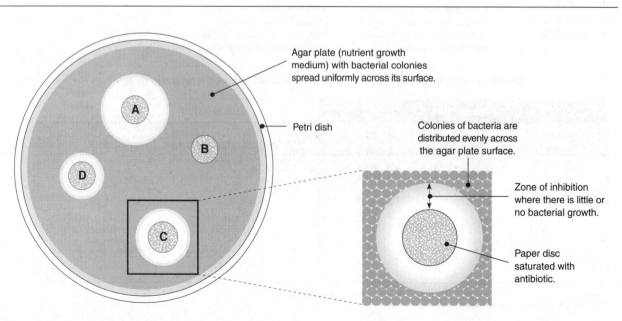

Agar plate (nutrient growth medium) with bacterial colonies spread uniformly across its surface.

Petri dish

Colonies of bacteria are distributed evenly across the agar plate surface.

Zone of inhibition where there is little or no bacterial growth.

Paper disc saturated with antibiotic.

Energy and Ecosystems

AQA-A	AQA-B	SNAB	Edexcel	OCR
Not applicable in the AS course	Not applicable in the AS course	Complete: 1, 25-26 (AS) 1-3, 5-7, 13-21 (A2)	Complete: 1-2, 5-20, 22-28 Extension: 4, 21	Complete: 1-7, 13-19, 27(a)-(b) Extension: 20-23, 27(d)

Learning Objectives

☐ 1. Compile your own glossary from the **KEY WORDS** displayed in **bold type** in the learning objectives below.

Biomes and Ecosystems *(pages 339-340)*

☐ 2. Provide examples of **biosphere**, **ecosystem**, and **community**. Distinguish between **biotic factors** and **abiotic factors**. Explain clearly how a community is different from a **population**.

☐ 3. Recognise major **biomes** on Earth and explain how they are classified according to major vegetation type. Appreciate the influence of latitude and local climate in determining the distribution of world biomes.

☐ 4. Identify the **biotic** and **abiotic** components of a named ecosystem. Describe an example of an ecosystem in the UK with which you are familiar. Include reference to the community (including the predominant **vegetation** type) and the physical factors that determine the characteristics of the ecosystem. Explain how the different parts of an ecosystem influence each other.

Habitat and Niche *(pages 341-350)*

☐ 5. Provide examples of **habitat** and **microhabitat**. List the factors used to describe a habitat. Identify habitat as one of the components of an organism's niche. Understand why particular species have preferences for particular physical environments.

☐ 6. List the factors that are used to describe an **ecological niche** (niche). Describe examples of the niche of a variety of species. Recognise that organisms show **adaptations** for survival in a given niche.

☐ 7. Recognise the constraints that are normally placed on the actual niche occupied by an organism. Distinguish between the **fundamental** and the **realised niche**.

Modes of Nutrition *(pages 351-355)*

☐ 8. Using examples, distinguish between **autotrophic** and chemoheterotrophic (=**heterotrophic**) nutrition. Identify the source of energy and carbon in each case. Describe the general role of **nutrients** in plant and animal nutrition. Describe the three principal modes of heterotrophic nutrition: **parasitic**, **saprophytic** (=**saprobiontic**), and **holozoic**.

☐ 9. Describe the structure and nutrition of a typical **saprobiont** (=**saprophyte** or **saprotroph**) as illustrated by the bread mould *Rhizopus*. Identify the type of food utilised, the nutrients and other growth requirements of the fungus, and the method by which the food is digested and absorbed.

☐ 10. Describe the structure and nutrition of a typical cestode **parasite** as illustrated by the pork tapeworm *Taenia solium*. Identify the type of food utilised, the nutrients and other growth requirements of the **parasite**, and the method by which the food is digested and absorbed.

☐ 11. Explain what is meant by **mutualistic nutrition** as illustrated by the nutritional relationship between:
  • Nitrogen-fixing bacterium *Rhizobium* and members of the Papilionaceae (legumes). Describe how the bacteria infect the root and induce the formation of **nodules**. Identify the role of the nodule in providing the appropriate environment for the bacteria.
  • Cellulose digesting microorganisms and ruminants. Identify the location of the symbiotic bacteria and ciliates in the ruminant gut.
  For each example, identify the nutritional benefits gained by each partner in the relationship.

☐ 12. Classify holozoic animals according to the type of food they take in: e.g. **carnivore**, **omnivore**, **herbivore**. Identify and describe the adaptations of herbivores and carnivores, as illustrated by a named **ruminant** and a named carnivore. Include reference to: the length of the gut, the relative size/capacity of the various regions, the structure of the stomach, the digestive enzymes present, the role of microbial digestion in nutrition and protein intake, and the type and arrangement of teeth (the dentition). In each case, explain the significance of the adaptation with reference to processing the food.

Energy and Trophic Levels

☐ 13. In practical terms, explain what the **laws of thermodynamics** mean with respect to energy conversions in ecosystems. Explain how these laws relate to where organisms get their energy from and what happens to it. Describe the ultimate source of energy for nearly all ecosystems.

☐ 14. Understand the interrelationship between nutrient cycling and energy flow in ecosystems:
  • Energy flows through ecosystems in the high energy chemical bonds within **organic matter**.
  • Nutrients move within and between ecosystems in **biogeochemical cycles** involving exchanges between the atmosphere, the Earth's crust, water, and living organisms.

Trophic relationships *(pages 361-366)*

☐ 15. Recall that green plants absorb light energy from the sun and use it to convert CO_2 and water to glucose and oxygen (in the process of **photosynthesis**).

☐ 16. Describe how the energy flow in ecosystems is described using **trophic levels**. Assign trophic levels to the organisms in a named community.

☐ 17. Identify the relationship between **producers**, **consumers**, **detritivores**, and **decomposers**, and describe the role of each in energy transfer. Recognise the detrital and grazing food chains as major pathways of energy flow through ecosystems.

☐ 18. Describe how energy is transferred between different trophic levels in **food chains** and **food webs**. Describe the **efficiency** of this energy transfer and compare the amount of energy available to each trophic level. Explain what happens to the remaining energy and why energy cannot be recycled.

☐ 19. Construct simple food chains and a food web for a named community. Show how the organisms are interconnected through their feeding relationships. With respect to the nature and function of trophic relationships, understand the term **bioaccumulation**.

Measuring energy flow *(pages 367-370 and the TRC: Uses of Plants)*

☐ 20. Understand how **productivity**, **gross primary production**, and **net primary production** relate to the transfer of energy to the next trophic level.

☐ 21. Explain how the energy flow in an ecosystem can be described quantitatively using an **energy flow diagram**. Include reference to: **trophic levels** (scaled boxes to illustrate relative amounts of energy at each level), direction of energy flow, processes involved in energy transfer, and energy sources and sinks.

Ecological pyramids *(pages 371-372)*

☐ 22. Describe food chains quantitatively using **ecological pyramids**. Explain how these may be based on **numbers**, **biomass**, or **energy**. Identify problems with the use of number pyramids, and explain why pyramids of biomass or energy are usually preferable.

☐ 23. Draw and interpret energy and biomass pyramids for different communities. Describe how biomass and energy change between trophic levels.

Nutrient and Water Cycles *(pages 356-360)*

☐ 24. Recall the features of the **water cycle**. Understand the ways in which water is cycled between various reservoirs and review the processes involved, including: **evaporation**, **condensation**, **precipitation**, **runoff**. Understand how humans intervene in the water cycle.

☐ 25. Using diagrams, describe the stages in the **carbon cycle**, identifying the form of carbon at the different stages, and using arrows to show the direction of nutrient flow and labels to identify the processes involved. Explain the role of microorganisms, carbon sinks, and carbonates in the cycle.

☐ 26. Identify factors influencing the rate at which processes in the cycling of carbon take place. Explain how humans may intervene in the carbon cycle and describe the effects of these interventions.

☐ 27. Describe the stages in the **nitrogen cycle**, identifying the form of nitrogen at the different stages, and using arrows to show the direction of nutrient flow and labels to identify the processes involved. Explain the role of microorganisms in the cycle, as illustrated by:

   (a) **Nitrifying bacteria** (*Nitrosomonas, Nitrobacter*)
   (b) **Nitrogen-fixing bacteria** (*Rhizobium, Azotobacter*)
   (c) **Nitrogen-fixing cyanobacteria**
   (d) **Denitrifying bacteria** (*Pseudomonas, Thiobacillus*).

☐ 28. Explain how humans may intervene in the nitrogen cycle and describe the effects of these interventions.

See the 'Textbook Reference Grid' on pages 8-9 for textbook page references relating to material in this topic.

Supplementary Texts
See page 6 for additional details of this text:

■ Adds, J. *et al*., 2004. **Exchange & Transport, Energy & Ecosystems** (NelsonThornes), chpt. 6 & 7

See page 7 for details of publishers of periodicals:

STUDENT'S REFERENCE

Ecosystems and physical factors

■ **Extreme Olympics** New Scientist, 30 March 2002 (Inside Science). *Extreme ecosystems and the adaptations of the organisms that live in them.*

■ **The Other Side of Eden** Biol. Sci. Rev., 15(3) Feb. 2003, pp. 2-7. *The Eden Project: the collection of artificial ecosystems in Cornwall. Its aims, directions, and its role in the study of ecosystems.*

■ **Big Weather** New Scientist, 22 May 1999 (Inside Science). *Global weather patterns and their role in shaping the ecology of the planet.*

■ **Plants on the Move** New Scientist, 20 March 1999 (Inside Science). *Understanding how plants have coped with past climates could help us to predict how distributions will change in the future.*

Adaptation, habitat, and niche

■ **The Ecological Niche** Biol. Sci. Rev., 12(4), March 2000, pp. 31-35. *An excellent account of*

the niche - an often misunderstood concept that is never-the-less central to ecological theory.

■ **Cave Dwellers: Living without Light** Biol. Sci. Rev., 17(1) Sept. 2004, pp. 38-41. *This account discusses the nature of cave ecosystems and the adaptations of the organisms that live there.*

■ **Biodiversity and Ecosystems** Biol. Sci. Rev., 11(4), March 1999, pp. 18-23. *Species richness and the breadth and overlap of niches. An account of how biodiversity influences ecosystem dynamics.*

■ **Wild in the City** New Scientist, 29 Oct. 2005, pp. 32-38. *The world's expanding cities and towns are providing niches for many wild species. The resulting efforts to make urban areas more wildlife friendly is good news but poses a challenge. Luring animals into urban environments could expose them to hazards they are ill-equipped to handle.*

Energy flow and nutrient cycles

■ **Ecosystems** Biol. Sci. Rev., 9(4) March 1997, pp. 9-14. *Ecosystems: food chains & webs, nutrient cycles & energy flows, and ecological pyramids.*

■ **Dung Beetles: Nature's Recyclers** Biol. Sci. Rev., 14(4) April 2002, pp. 31-33. *The ecological role of dung beetles in the recycling of nutrients.*

■ **Fish Predation** Biol. Sci. Rev., 14(1) Sept. 2001, pp. 10-14. *Some fish species in freshwater systems in the UK are important top predators and can heavily influence ecosystem dynamics.*

■ **A Users Guide to the Carbon Cycle** Biol. Sci. Rev., 10(1) Sept. 1997, pp. 10-13. *The carbon cycle: fixation and return to the atmosphere. The intervention of humans in the cycle is discussed.*

■ **The Carbon Cycle** New Scientist, 2 Nov. 1991 (Inside Science). *The role of carbon in ecosystems.*

■ **Ultimate Interface** New Scientist, 14 Nov. 1998 (Inside Science). *Biogeochemical cycles and the role of the soil in cycling processes.*

■ **Something in the Air** New Scientist, 21 Jan. 2006, pp. 40-43. *Scientists believe that nitrogen emissions are an increasingly serious threat to the environment and if ignored, the consequences are likely to be worse than just global warming.*

■ **Capturing Greenhouse Gases** Scientific American, February 2000, pp. 54-61. *An article*

examining human intervention in the carbon cycle. Includes a useful synopsis of carbon transfers.

■ **Microorganisms in Agriculture** Biol. Sci. Rev., 11(5) May 1999, pp. 2-4. *The vital role of microorganisms in the ecology of communities.*

■ **Let's make Nodules** New Scientist, 11 Jan. 1997, pp. 22-25. *Underground, in the dark, there is a subtle chemistry that brings bacteria (Rhizobium) and legumes together for their mutual benefit.*

■ **The Nitrogen Cycle** Biol. Sci. Rev., 13(2) November 2000, pp. 25-27. *An excellent account of the the nitrogen cycle: conversions, role in ecosystems, and the influence of human activity.*

See pages 10-11 for details of how to access **Bio Links** from our web site: **www.biozone.co.uk**. From Bio Links, access sites under the topics:

GENERAL BIOLOGY ONLINE RESOURCES
• Biology I interactive animations • Instructional multimedia, University of Alberta ... *and others* > **Glossaries**: Ecology glossary ... *and others*

ECOLOGY: • EarthTrends: Information portal • Introduction to biogeography and ecology > **Ecosystems:** • What are ecosystems ... *and many other sites related to specific ecosystems of interest* > **Energy Flows and Nutrient Cycles:** • A marine food web • Bioaccumulation • Human alteration of the global nitrogen cycle • Nitrogen: The essential element • The carbon cycle • The nitrogen cycle • The water cycle • Trophic pyramids and food webs

Presentation MEDIA to support this topic:

ECOLOGY
• **Ecological Niche**
• **Communities**

Biomes

Global patterns of vegetation distribution are closely related to climate. **Biomes** are large areas where the vegetation type shares a particular suite of physical requirements. They have characteristic features, but the boundaries between them are not distinct. The same biome may occur in widely separated regions of the world wherever the climatic and soil conditions are similar.

Wherever they occur, mountainous regions are associated with their own altitude adapted vegetation. The rainshadow effect of mountains governs the distribution of deserts in some areas too (e.g. in Chile). Although the classification of biomes may vary slightly, most classifications recognise desert, tundra, grassland and forest types and differentiate them on the basis of latitude.

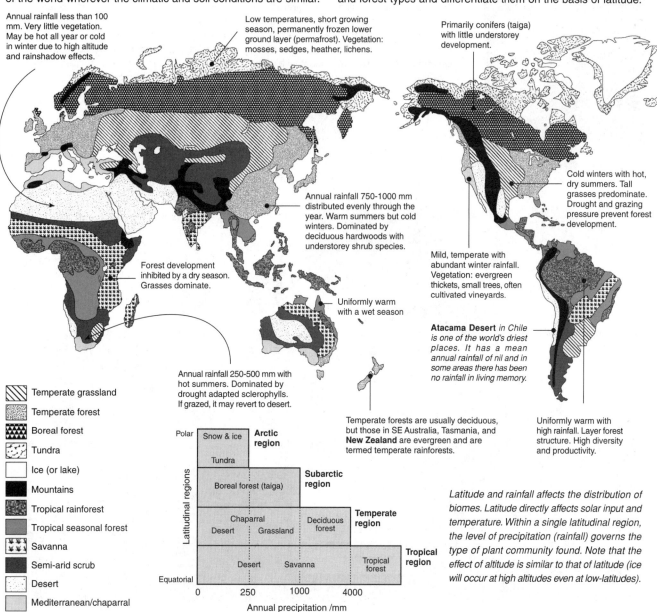

Annual rainfall less than 100 mm. Very little vegetation. May be hot all year or cold in winter due to high altitude and rainshadow effects.

Low temperatures, short growing season, permanently frozen lower ground layer (permafrost). Vegetation: mosses, sedges, heather, lichens.

Primarily conifers (taiga) with little understorey development.

Annual rainfall 750-1000 mm distributed evenly through the year. Warm summers but cold winters. Dominated by deciduous hardwoods with understorey shrub species.

Cold winters with hot, dry summers. Tall grasses predominate. Drought and grazing pressure prevent forest development.

Forest development inhibited by a dry season. Grasses dominate.

Mild, temperate with abundant winter rainfall. Vegetation: evergreen thickets, small trees, often cultivated vineyards.

Uniformly warm with a wet season

Atacama Desert in Chile is one of the world's driest places. It has a mean annual rainfall of nil and in some areas there has been no rainfall in living memory.

Annual rainfall 250-500 mm with hot summers. Dominated by drought adapted sclerophylls. If grazed, it may revert to desert.

Temperate forests are usually deciduous, but those in SE Australia, Tasmania, and **New Zealand** are evergreen and are termed temperate rainforests.

Uniformly warm with high rainfall. Layer forest structure. High diversity and productivity.

Legend:
- Temperate grassland
- Temperate forest
- Boreal forest
- Tundra
- Ice (or lake)
- Mountains
- Tropical rainforest
- Tropical seasonal forest
- Savanna
- Semi-arid scrub
- Desert
- Mediterranean/chaparral

Latitudinal regions			Region
Polar	Snow & ice		**Arctic region**
	Tundra		
	Boreal forest (taiga)		**Subarctic region**
	Chaparral	Deciduous forest	**Temperate region**
	Desert	Grassland	
Equatorial	Desert	Savanna	Tropical forest	**Tropical region**

Annual precipitation /mm: 0   250   1000   4000

Latitude and rainfall affects the distribution of biomes. Latitude directly affects solar input and temperature. Within a single latitudinal region, the level of precipitation (rainfall) governs the type of plant community found. Note that the effect of altitude is similar to that of latitude (ice will occur at high altitudes even at low-latitudes).

Energy and Ecosystems

1. Suggest what abiotic factor(s) limit the northern extent of boreal forest: _____

_____

2. Grasslands have about half the productivity of tropical rainforests, yet this is achieved with less than a tenth of the biomass; grasslands are more productive per unit of biomass. Suggest how this greater efficiency is achieved:

_____

_____

_____

3. Suggest a reason for the distribution of deserts and semi-desert areas in northern parts of Asia and in the west of North and South America (away from equatorial regions):

_____

_____

Related activities: Physical Factors and Gradients
Web links: The World's Biomes

A 2

Components of an Ecosystem

The concept of the ecosystem was developed to describe the way groups of organisms are predictably found together in their physical environment. A community comprises all the organisms within an ecosystem. Both physical (abiotic) and biotic factors affect the organisms in a community, influencing their distribution and their survival, growth, and reproduction.

The Biosphere

The **biosphere** containing all the Earth's living organisms amounts to a narrow belt around the Earth extending from the bottom of the oceans to the upper atmosphere. Broad scale life-zones or **biomes** are evident within the biosphere, characterised according to the predominant vegetation. Within these biomes, **ecosystems** form natural units comprising the non-living, physical environment (the soil, atmosphere, and water) and the **community** (all the populations of different species living and interacting in a particular area).

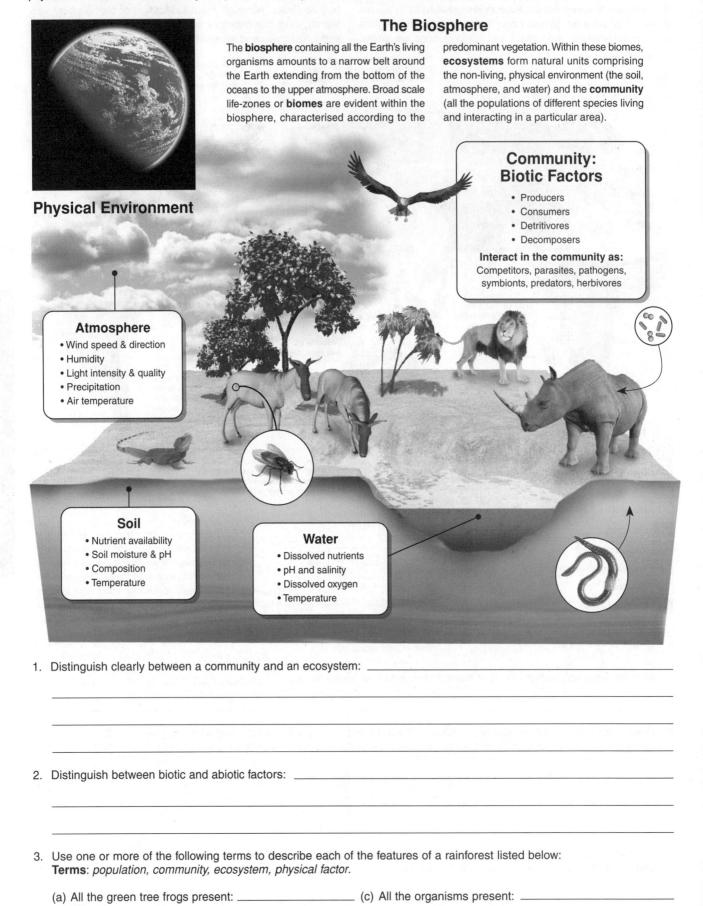

Physical Environment

Community: Biotic Factors
- Producers
- Consumers
- Detritivores
- Decomposers

Interact in the community as:
Competitors, parasites, pathogens, symbionts, predators, herbivores

Atmosphere
- Wind speed & direction
- Humidity
- Light intensity & quality
- Precipitation
- Air temperature

Soil
- Nutrient availability
- Soil moisture & pH
- Composition
- Temperature

Water
- Dissolved nutrients
- pH and salinity
- Dissolved oxygen
- Temperature

1. Distinguish clearly between a community and an ecosystem: _____

_____

_____

_____

2. Distinguish between biotic and abiotic factors: _____

_____

_____

3. Use one or more of the following terms to describe each of the features of a rainforest listed below:
   Terms: *population, community, ecosystem, physical factor.*

   (a) All the green tree frogs present: _____ (c) All the organisms present: _____

   (b) The entire forest: _____ (d) The humidity: _____

A 1   **Related activities**: Biomes

Physical Factors and Gradients

Gradients in abiotic factors are found in almost every environment; they influence habitats and microclimates, and determine patterns of species distribution. This activity, covering the next four pages, examines the physical gradients and microclimates that might typically be found in four, very different environments. Note that **dataloggers** (pictured right), are being increasingly used to gather such data. The principles of their use are covered in the topic *Practical Ecology*, in Advanced Biology A2.

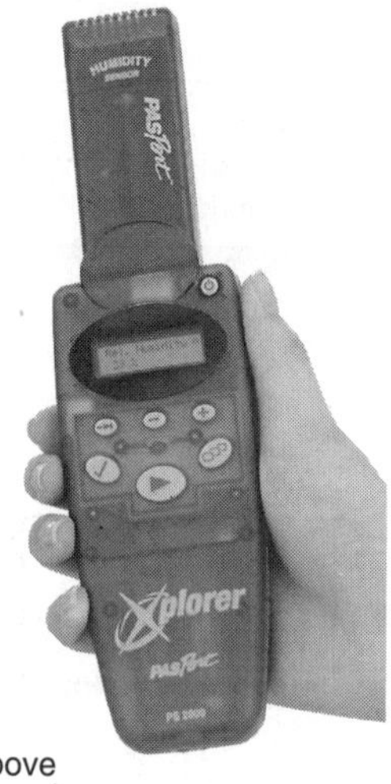

A Desert Environment

Desert environments experience extremes in temperature and humidity, but they are not uniform with respect to these factors. This diagram illustrates hypothetical values for temperature and humidity for some of the microclimates found in a desert environment at midday.

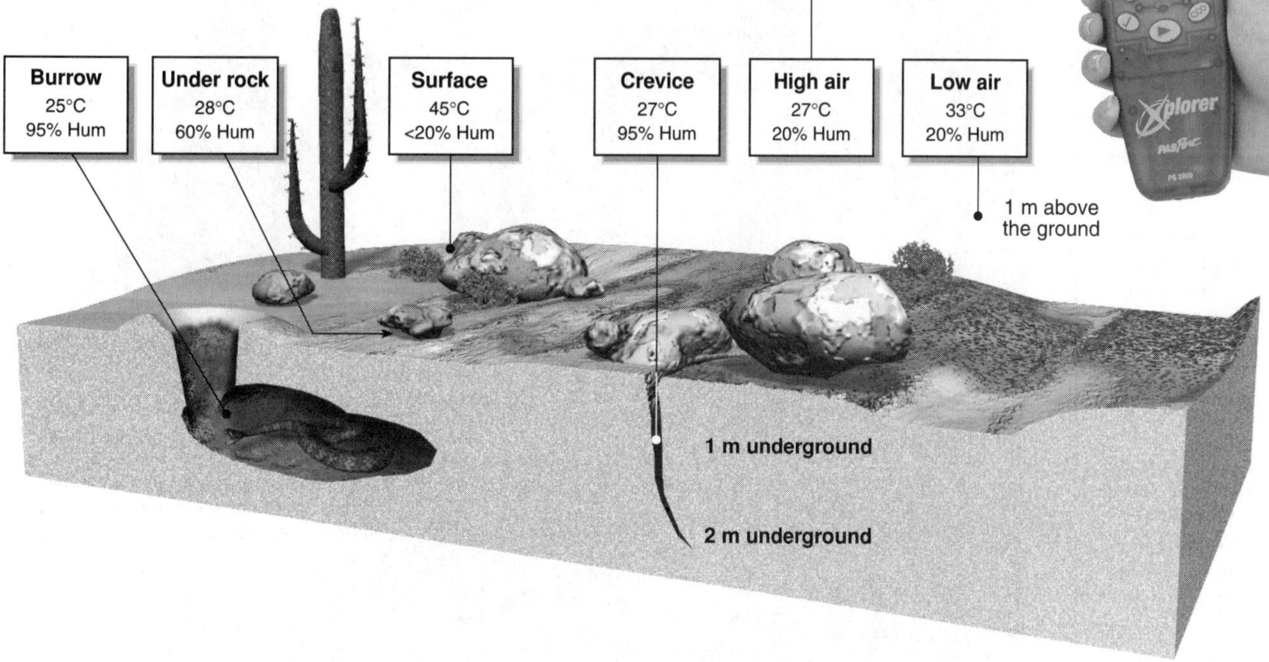

300 m altitude

Burrow	**Under rock**	**Surface**	**Crevice**	**High air**	**Low air**
25°C	28°C	45°C	27°C	27°C	33°C
95% Hum	60% Hum	<20% Hum	95% Hum	20% Hum	20% Hum

1 m above the ground

1 m underground

2 m underground

Energy and Ecosystems

1. Distinguish between **climate** and **microclimate**: _____

_____

_____

2. Study the diagram above and describe the general conditions where high humidity is found: _____

_____

_____

3. Identify the three microclimates that a land animal might exploit to avoid the extreme high temperatures of midday:

_____

_____

4. Describe the likely consequences for an animal that was unable to find a suitable microclimate to escape midday sun:

_____

_____

5. Describe the advantage of high humidity to the survival of most land animals: _____

_____

_____

6. Describe the likely changes to the temperature and relative humidity that occur during the night: _____

_____

_____

Related activities: Habitats

DA 2

Physical Factors in a Tropical Rainforest

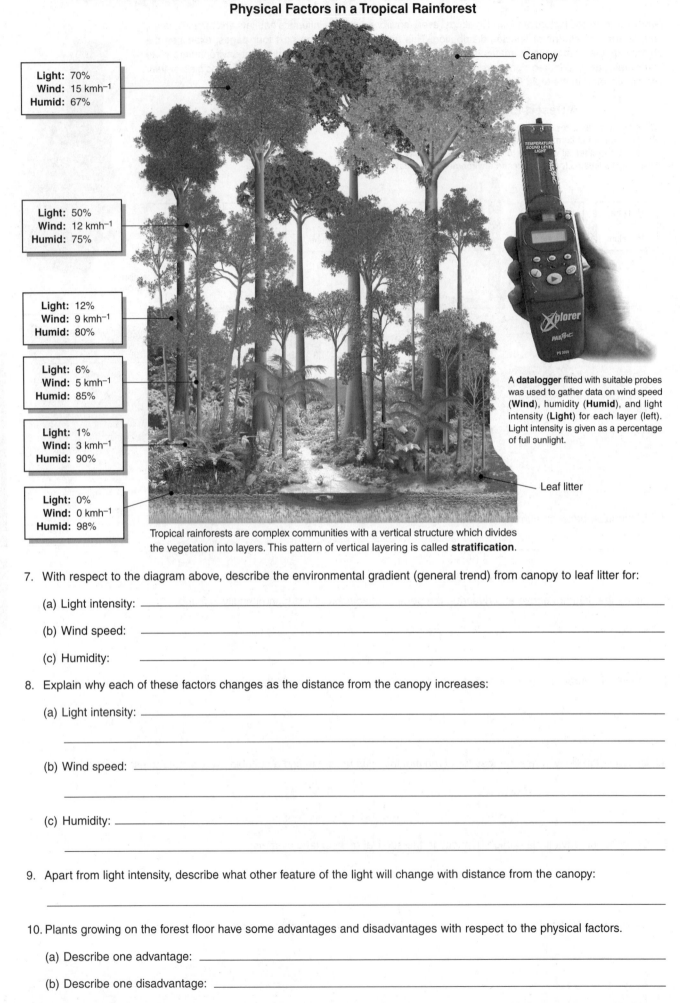

Light: 70%
Wind: 15 kmh^{-1}
Humid: 67%

Light: 50%
Wind: 12 kmh^{-1}
Humid: 75%

Light: 12%
Wind: 9 kmh^{-1}
Humid: 80%

Light: 6%
Wind: 5 kmh^{-1}
Humid: 85%

Light: 1%
Wind: 3 kmh^{-1}
Humid: 90%

Light: 0%
Wind: 0 kmh^{-1}
Humid: 98%

Canopy

A **datalogger** fitted with suitable probes was used to gather data on wind speed (**Wind**), humidity (**Humid**), and light intensity (**Light**) for each layer (left). Light intensity is given as a percentage of full sunlight.

Leaf litter

Tropical rainforests are complex communities with a vertical structure which divides the vegetation into layers. This pattern of vertical layering is called **stratification**.

7. With respect to the diagram above, describe the environmental gradient (general trend) from canopy to leaf litter for:

(a) Light intensity: _____

(b) Wind speed: _____

(c) Humidity: _____

8. Explain why each of these factors changes as the distance from the canopy increases:

(a) Light intensity: _____

_____

(b) Wind speed: _____

_____

(c) Humidity: _____

_____

9. Apart from light intensity, describe what other feature of the light will change with distance from the canopy:

_____

10. Plants growing on the forest floor have some advantages and disadvantages with respect to the physical factors.

(a) Describe one advantage: _____

(b) Describe one disadvantage: _____

Physical Factors at Low Tide on a Rock Platform

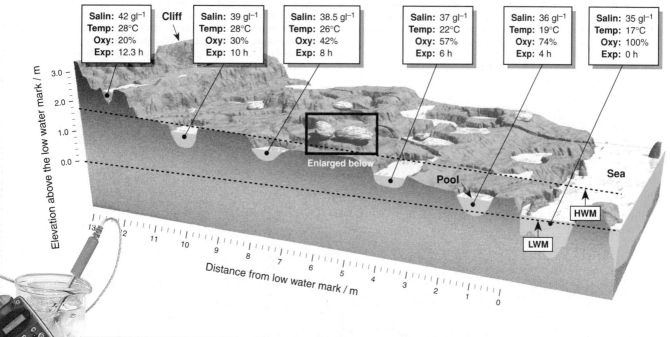

| Salin: 42 gl⁻¹ | Salin: 39 gl⁻¹ | Salin: 38.5 gl⁻¹ | Salin: 37 gl⁻¹ | Salin: 36 gl⁻¹ | Salin: 35 gl⁻¹ |

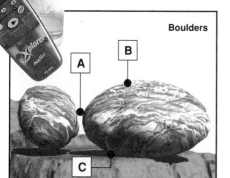

The diagram above shows a profile of a rock platform at low tide. The **high water mark** (HWM) shown here is the average height the spring tide rises to. In reality, the high tide level will vary with the phases of the moon (i.e. spring tides and neap tides). The **low water mark** (LWM) is an average level subject to the same variations due to the lunar cycle. The rock pools vary in size, depth, and position on the platform. They are isolated at different elevations, trapping water from the ocean for periods of time up to 12.3 h duration (a full tidal cycle is about 12 h 20m). Pools near the HWM are exposed for longer periods of time than those near the LWM. The difference in exposure times results in some of the physical factors exhibiting a **gradient**; the factor's value gradually changes over distance. Physical factors sampled in the pools include salinity, or the amount of dissolved salts (g) per litre (**Salin**), temperature (**Temp**), dissolved oxygen compared to that of open ocean water (**Oxy**), and exposure, or the amount of time isolated from the ocean water (**Exp**).

11. Describe the environmental gradient (general trend) from the low water mark (LWM) to the high water mark (HWM) for:

   (a) Salinity: _____

   (b) Temperature: _____

   (c) Dissolved oxygen: _____

   (d) Exposure: _____

12. Rock pools above the normal high water mark (HWM), such as the uppermost pool in the diagram above, can have wide extremes of salinity. Explain the conditions under which these pools might have either:

   (a) Very low salinity: _____

   _____

   (b) Very high salinity: _____

   _____

13. (a) The inset diagram (above, left) is an enlarged view of two boulders on the rock platform. Describe how the physical factors listed below might differ at each of the labelled points **A**, **B**, and **C**:

   Mechanical force of wave action: _____

   _____

   Surface temperature when exposed: _____

   _____

   (b) State the term given to these localised variations in physical conditions: _____

Physical Factors in a Kettle Hole Lake in Summer

Kettle hole lakes are formed from the flooded holes remaining in the depressions left by ice after the retreat of glaciers. They are common in Britain around Shropshire and are usually relatively shallow. Occasionally they may be deep enough to develop temporary, but relatively stable, temperature gradients from top to bottom (below). Small lakes are relatively closed systems and events in them are independent of those in other nearby lakes, where quite different water quality may be found. The physical factors are not constant throughout the water in the lake. Surface water and water near the margins can have quite different values for such factors as water temperature (**Temp**), dissolved oxygen (**Oxygen**) measured in milligrams per litre (mg l^{-1}), and light penetration (**Light**) indicated here as a percentage of the light striking the surface.

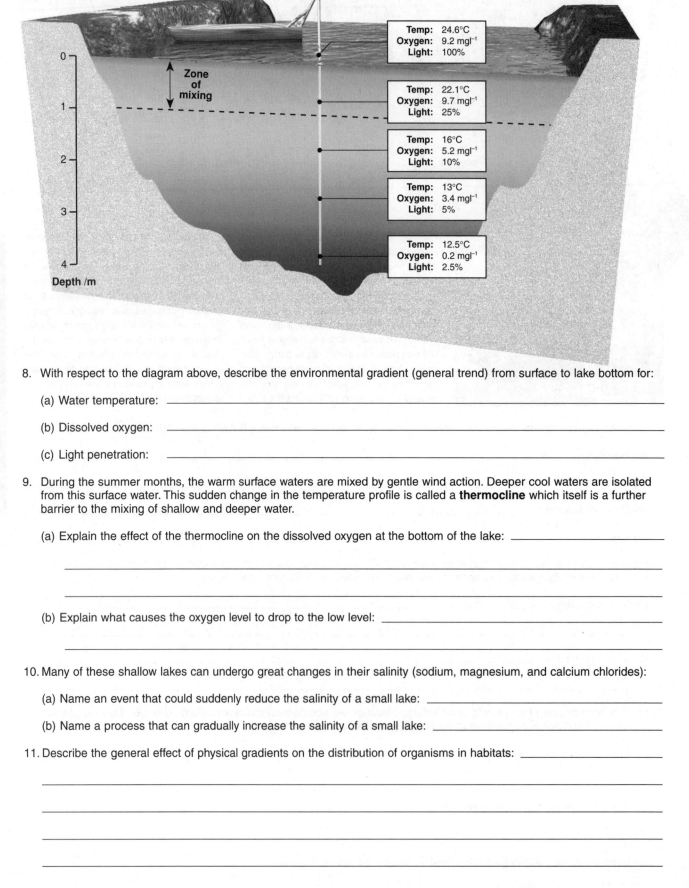

8. With respect to the diagram above, describe the environmental gradient (general trend) from surface to lake bottom for:

   (a) Water temperature: _____

   (b) Dissolved oxygen: _____

   (c) Light penetration: _____

9. During the summer months, the warm surface waters are mixed by gentle wind action. Deeper cool waters are isolated from this surface water. This sudden change in the temperature profile is called a **thermocline** which itself is a further barrier to the mixing of shallow and deeper water.

   (a) Explain the effect of the thermocline on the dissolved oxygen at the bottom of the lake: _____

   _____

   _____

   (b) Explain what causes the oxygen level to drop to the low level: _____

   _____

10. Many of these shallow lakes can undergo great changes in their salinity (sodium, magnesium, and calcium chlorides):

    (a) Name an event that could suddenly reduce the salinity of a small lake: _____

    (b) Name a process that can gradually increase the salinity of a small lake: _____

11. Describe the general effect of physical gradients on the distribution of organisms in habitats: _____

    _____

    _____

    _____

Habitats

The environment in which an organism lives (including all the physical and biotic factors) is termed its **habitat**. For each of the organisms below, briefly describe their habitat (an example is provided). As well as describing the general environment (e.g. river, swamp), include detail about the biotic and abiotic factors in the habitat which enable the organism to thrive.

Jew's ear fungus: *Auricularia auricula*

1. General habitat of the Jew's ear fungus: _Woodland, especially on elder_

   (a) Biotic factors: _Source of live and/or dead wood (usually elder) from which to obtain its nutrition_

   (b) Abiotic factors: _Autumnal: needs cooler temperatures, high moisture levels in the soil and high humidity_

Oystercatcher: *Haemotopus ostralegus*

2. General habitat of the oystercatcher: _____

   (a) Biotic factors: _____

   (b) Abiotic factors: _____

Red deer: *Cervus elaphus*

3. General habitat of red deer: _____

   (a) Biotic factors: _____

   (b) Abiotic factors: _____

Hawthorn: *Crataegus monogyna*

4. General habitat of hawthorn: _____

   (a) Biotic factors: _____

   (b) Abiotic factors: _____

Paper wasp: *Polistes*

5. General habitat of the paper wasp: _____

   (a) Biotic factors: _____

   (b) Abiotic factors: _____

Sea thrift: *Armeria vulgaris*

6. General habitat of sea thrift: _____

   (a) Biotic factors: _____

   (b) Abiotic factors: _____

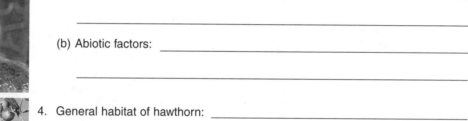

Energy and Ecosystems

Related activities: Components of an Ecosystem

RA 2

Law of Tolerances

The **law of tolerances** states that: *For each abiotic factor, an organism has a range of tolerances within which it can survive. Toward the upper and lower extremes of this tolerance range, that abiotic factor tends to limit the organism's ability to survive.* The wider an organism's tolerance range for a given abiotic factor (e.g. temperature, pH, salinity, turbidity, humidity, water pressure, light intensity), the more likely it is that the organism will be able to survive variations in that factor. Species **dispersal** is also strongly influenced by **tolerance range**. The wider the tolerance range of a species, the more widely dispersed the organism is likely to be. As well as a tolerance range, organisms have a narrower **optimum range** within which they function best. This may vary from one stage of an organism's development to another or from one season to another. Every species has its own optimum range. Organisms will usually be most abundant where the abiotic factors are closest to the optimum range.

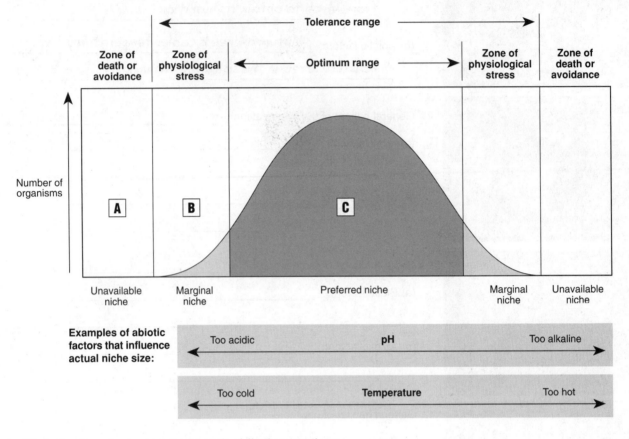

1. Study the diagram above and answer the following questions:

   (a) State the range in the diagram which contains the greatest number of organisms: _____

   _____

   (b) Explain why this is the case: _____

   _____

2. Organism C is occupying its preferred niche, in terms of physical factors. Explain what you would think would be the greatest constraint on organism C's growth and reproduction, within its preferred niche:

   _____

   _____

3. Organism B is occupying an area outside its preferred niche. Describe some probable stresses on B in this area:

   _____

   _____

   _____

4. Organism A has been forced, by crowding, to occupy an area completely unlike its preferred niche. Explain the likely result of organism A being forced into this area:

   _____

   _____

Related activities: Physical Factors and Gradients, Ecological Niche

Ecological Niche

The concept of the ecological niche has been variously described as an organism's 'job' or 'profession'. This is rather too simplistic for senior biology level. The **ecological niche** is better described as the functional position of an organism in its environment, comprising its habitat and the resources it obtains there, and the periods of time during which it is active. The diagram below illustrates the components that together define the niche of any organism. The full range of environmental conditions (biological and physical) under which an organism can exist describes its **fundamental niche**. As a result of pressure from, and interactions with, other organisms (e.g. superior competitors) species are usually forced to occupy a niche that is narrower than this and to which they are most highly adapted. This is termed the **realised niche**.

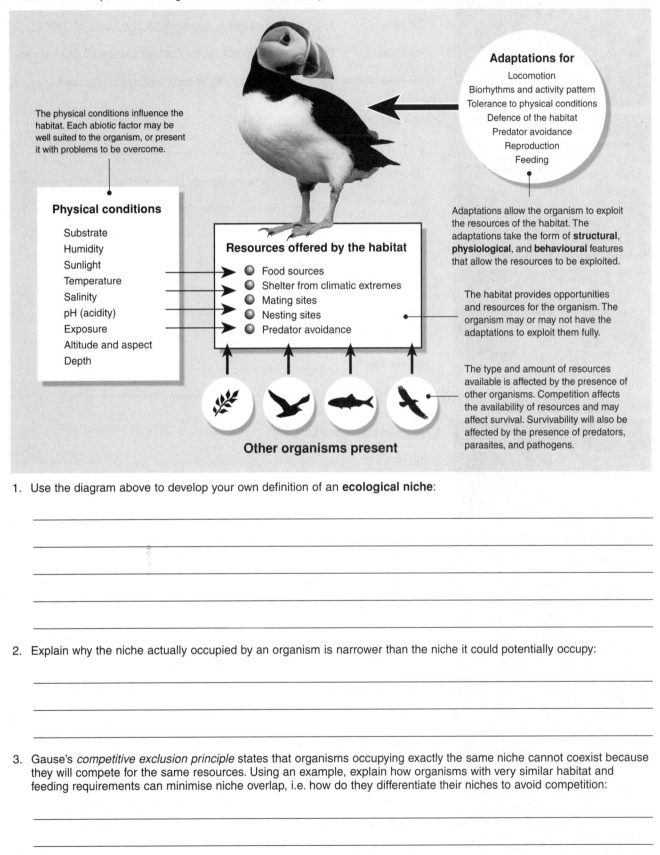

The physical conditions influence the habitat. Each abiotic factor may be well suited to the organism, or present it with problems to be overcome.

Adaptations for
Locomotion
Biorhythms and activity pattern
Tolerance to physical conditions
Defence of the habitat
Predator avoidance
Reproduction
Feeding

Adaptations allow the organism to exploit the resources of the habitat. The adaptations take the form of **structural**, **physiological**, and **behavioural** features that allow the resources to be exploited.

Physical conditions

Substrate
Humidity
Sunlight
Temperature
Salinity
pH (acidity)
Exposure
Altitude and aspect
Depth

Resources offered by the habitat
- Food sources
- Shelter from climatic extremes
- Mating sites
- Nesting sites
- Predator avoidance

The habitat provides opportunities and resources for the organism. The organism may or may not have the adaptations to exploit them fully.

The type and amount of resources available is affected by the presence of other organisms. Competition affects the availability of resources and may affect survival. Survivability will also be affected by the presence of predators, parasites, and pathogens.

Other organisms present

Energy and Ecosystems

1. Use the diagram above to develop your own definition of an **ecological niche**:

_____

_____

_____

_____

2. Explain why the niche actually occupied by an organism is narrower than the niche it could potentially occupy:

_____

_____

_____

3. Gause's *competitive exclusion principle* states that organisms occupying exactly the same niche cannot coexist because they will compete for the same resources. Using an example, explain how organisms with very similar habitat and feeding requirements can minimise niche overlap, i.e. how do they differentiate their niches to avoid competition:

_____

_____

_____

Related activities: Physical Factors and Gradients, Habitats, Law of Tolerances, Adaptations to Niche

A 2

Ecological Niches

The concept of an organism's **ecological niche** is fundamental to understanding ecology. To fully describe a niche, take note of an organism's: trophic level, mode of feeding, activity periods, habitat and the resources exploited within it, as well as the adaptive features they possess to exploit them. Describe the **niche** for each of the following organisms:

Honey fungus: *Armillaria*

1. Niche of the honey fungus:

   (a) Nutrition: <u>Parasitic of many trees, using extracellular digestion.</u>

   (b) Activity: <u>Fruiting bodies grow in clumps at the foot of trees.</u>

   (c) Habitat: <u>Found in most forest types. Pest in commercial plantations.</u>

   (d) Adaptations: <u>Spreads vigorously by spores and root-like cords.</u>

Sea star: *Astropecten*

2. Niche of the sea star:

   (a) Nutrition: _____

   (b) Activity: _____

   (c) Habitat: _____

   (d) Adaptations: _____

Hedgehog: *Erinaceus europeus*

3. Niche of the hedgehog:

   (a) Nutrition: _____

   (b) Activity: _____

   (c) Habitat: _____

   (d) Adaptations: _____

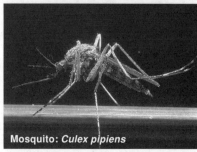

Mosquito: *Culex pipiens*

4. Niche of the mosquito:

   (a) Nutrition: _____

   (b) Activity: _____

   (c) Habitat: _____

   (d) Adaptations: _____

Pheasant: *Phasianus colchicus*

5. Niche of the pheasant:

   (a) Nutrition: _____

   (b) Activity: _____

   (c) Habitat: _____

   (d) Adaptations: _____

Grey squirrel: *Sciurus carolinensis*

6. Niche of the grey squirrel:

   (a) Nutrition: _____

   (b) Activity: _____

   (c) Habitat: _____

   (d) Adaptations: _____

Related activities: Habitats, Ecological Niche, Adaptations to Niche, Modes of Nutrition

Adaptations to Niche

The adaptive features that evolve in species are the result of selection pressures on them through the course of their evolution. These features enable an organism to function most effectively in its niche, enhancing its exploitation of its environment and therefore its survival. The examples below illustrate some of the adaptations of two species: a British placental mammal and a migratory Arctic bird. Note that adaptations may be associated with an animal's structure (morphology), its internal physiology, or its behaviour.

Northern or Common Mole
(Talpa europaea)

Head-body length: 113-159 mm, tail length: 25-40 mm, weight range: 70-130 g.

Mole hill

Lining of dry grass

Adult

Young

Moles (photos above) spend most of the time underground and are rarely seen at the surface. Mole hills are the piles of soil excavated from the tunnels and pushed to the surface. The cutaway view above shows a section of tunnels and a nest chamber. Nests are used for sleeping and raising young. They are dug out within the tunnel system and lined with dry plant material.

The northern (common) mole is a widespread insectivore found throughout most of Britain and Europe, apart from Ireland. They are found in most habitats but are less common in coniferous forest, moorland, and sand dunes, where their prey (earthworms and insect larvae) are rare. They are well adapted to life underground and burrow extensively, using enlarged forefeet for digging. Their small size, tubular body shape, and heavily buttressed head and neck are typical of burrowing species.

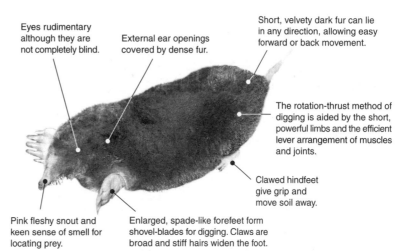

Eyes rudimentary although they are not completely blind.

External ear openings covered by dense fur.

Short, velvety dark fur can lie in any direction, allowing easy forward or back movement.

The rotation-thrust method of digging is aided by the short, powerful limbs and the efficient lever arrangement of muscles and joints.

Clawed hindfeet give grip and move soil away.

Pink fleshy snout and keen sense of smell for locating prey.

Enlarged, spade-like forefeet form shovel-blades for digging. Claws are broad and stiff hairs widen the foot.

Habitat and ecology: Moles spend most of their lives in underground tunnels. Surface tunnels occur where their prey is concentrated at the surface (e.g. land under cultivation). Deeper, permanent tunnels form a complex network used repeatedly for feeding and nesting, sometimes for several generations. **Senses and behaviour**: Keen sense of smell but almost blind. Both sexes are solitary and territorial except during breeding. Life span about 3 years. Moles are prey for owls, buzzards, stoats, cats, and dogs. Their activities aerate the soil and they control many soil pests. Despite this, they are regularly trapped and poisoned as pests.

Snow Bunting
(Plectrophenax nivalis)

The snow bunting is a small ground feeding bird that lives and breeds in the Arctic and sub-Arctic islands. Although migratory, snow buntings do not move to traditional winter homes but prefer winter habitats that resemble their Arctic breeding grounds, such as bleak shores or open fields of northern Britain and the eastern United States.

Snow buntings have the unique ability to moult very rapidly after breeding. During the warmer months, the buntings are a brown colour, changing to white in winter (right). They must complete this colour change quickly, so that they have a new set of feathers before the onset of winter and before migration. In order to achieve this, snow buntings lose as many as four or five of their main flight wing feathers at once, as opposed to most birds, which lose only one or two.

Very few small birds breed in the Arctic, because most small birds lose more heat than larger ones. In addition, birds that breed in the brief Arctic summer must migrate before the onset of winter, often travelling over large expanses of water. Large, long winged birds are better able to do this. However, the snow bunting is superbly adapted to survive in the extreme cold of the Arctic region.

White feathers are hollow and filled with air, which acts as an insulator. In the dark coloured feathers the internal spaces are filled with pigmented cells.

Less heat is lost from white plumage compared to dark plumage.

Snow buntings, on average, lay one or two more eggs than equivalent species further south. They are able to rear more young because the continuous daylight and the abundance of insects at high latitudes enables them to feed their chicks around the clock.

During snow storms or periods of high wind, snow buntings will burrow into snowdrifts for shelter.

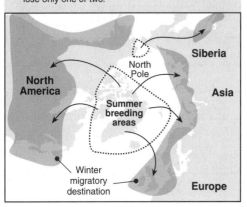

Siberia

North Pole

North America

Asia

Summer breeding areas

Winter migratory destination

Europe

Habitat and ecology: Widespread throughout Arctic and sub-Arctic Islands. Active throughout the day and night, resting for only 2-3 hours in any 24 hour period. Snow buntings may migrate up to 6000 km but are always found at high latitudes. **Reproduction and behaviour**: The nest, which is concealed amongst stones, is made from dead grass, moss, and lichen. The male bird feeds his mate during the incubation period and helps to feed the young.

Energy and Ecosystems

Related activities: Ecological Niches

RA 2

1. Describe a structural, physiological, and behavioural adaptation of the **common mole**, explaining how each adaptation assists survival:

   (a) Structural adaptation: _____

   _____

   (b) Physiological adaptation: _____

   _____

   (c) Behavioural adaptation: _____

   _____

2. Describe a structural, physiological, and behavioural adaptation of the **snow bunting**, explaining how each adaptation assists survival:

   (a) Structural adaptation: _____

   _____

   (b) Physiological adaptation: _____

   _____

   (c) Behavioural adaptation: _____

   _____

3. The rabbit is a colonial mammal which lives underground in warrens (burrow systems) and feeds on grasses, cereal crops, roots, and young trees. Rabbits are a hugely successful species worldwide and often reach plague proportions. Through discussion, or your own knowledge and research, describe **six adaptations** of rabbits, identifying them as structural (S), physiological (P), or behavioural (B). The examples below are typical:

   Structural: Widely spaced eyes gives wide field of vision for surveillance and detection of danger.

   Physiological: High reproductive rate; short gestation and high fertility aids rapid population increases when food is available.

   Behavioural: Freeze behaviour when startled reduces the possibility of detection by wandering predators.

   (a) _____

   (b) _____

   (c) _____

   (d) _____

   (e) _____

   (f) _____

4. Examples of adaptations are listed below. Identify them as predominantly structural, physiological, and/or behavioural:

   (a) Relationship of body size and shape to latitude (tropical or Arctic): _____

   (b) The production of concentrated urine in desert dwelling mammals: _____

   (c) The summer and winter migratory patterns in birds and mammals: _____

   (d) The C4 photosynthetic pathway and CAM metabolism of plants: _____

   (e) The thick leaves and sunken stomata of desert plants: _____

   (f) Hibernation or torpor in small mammals over winter: _____

   (g) Basking in lizards and snakes: _____

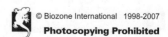

Modes of Nutrition

The way in which living organisms obtain their source of energy and carbon is termed their nutritional mode. There is a great diversity in nutritional modes amongst different phyla, with the prokaryotes (bacteria) showing the greatest variety in terms of the range of organic and inorganic compounds used as energy sources. The diagram below illustrates the classification of nutritional modes in living organisms. The diagram simplifies the real situation and concentrates on the diversity within eukaryotic groups. Aspects of nutrition in a typical saprotroph and a specialised mammalian parasite are described later in this topic.

Nutritional Patterns in Organisms

Living organisms can be classified according to their source of energy and carbon. According to their **energy source**, organisms are classified as either **phototrophs** (using light as their main energy source) or **chemotrophs** (using inorganic or organic compounds for energy). As a **carbon source**, **autotrophs** (*self-feeders*) use carbon dioxide, and **heterotrophs** (*feeders on others*) need an organic carbon source. Most organisms are either photoautotrophs, chemoautotrophs, or chemoheterotrophs. Prokaryotes show a huge variety of nutritional modes. Many are photo- or chemoautotrophs (chemosynthetic) but a large number are chemoheterotrophs (as are animals and fungi). For many, the energy and carbon source is glucose.

Heterotrophic Nutrition (Chemoheterotrophs*)

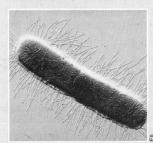

Most of the bacteria with which we are familiar are chemoheterotrophs.

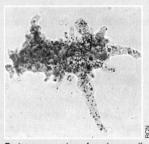

Protozoans, such as *Amoeba*, engulf food particles by phagocytosis.

* A few bacterial groups are photoheterotrophic.

Autotrophic Nutrition

Photoautotrophs: Photosynthetic bacteria, cyanobacteria, algae, plants.

Chemoautotrophs: Sulfur, iron, hydrogen, and nitrifying bacteria.

Fungi may be saprophytic (see below), parasitic, or mutualistic.

Feeding provides animals with a carbon and energy source: glucose.

Nutritional Modes of Heterotrophs

Heterotrophic organisms feed on organic material in order to obtain the energy and nutrients they require. They depend either directly on other organisms (dead or alive), or their by-products (e.g. faeces, cell walls, or food stores). There are three principal modes of heterotrophic nutrition: saprotrophic, parasitic, and holozoic. Within the animal phyla, holozoic nutrition is the most common nutritional mode.

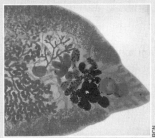

Most fungi and many bacteria are saprophytes (also called saprotrophs). They are decomposer organisms feeding off dead or decaying matter.

Parasites, e.g. flukes, live on or within their host for much or all of their life. Bacteria, fungi, protoctists, and animals all have parasitic representatives.

Holozoic means to feed on solid organic material from the bodies of other organisms. It is the main feeding mode of animals, although a few specialised plants may obtain some nutrients this way. Holozoic animals are classified according to the form of the food they take in: small or large particles, or fluid.

1. Discuss the differences in nutritional mode between photoautotrophs, chemoautotrophs, and chemoheterotrophs:

_____

_____

_____

_____

_____

2. Explain how saprotrophs differ from parasites: _____

_____

Related activities: Saprophytic Nutrition, Parasitic Nutrition, Mutualistic Nutrition, Ruminants and Carnivores

A 2

Energy and Ecosystems

Saprophytic Nutrition

All fungi lack chlorophyll and are **heterotrophic**, absorbing nutrients by direct absorption from the substrate. Many are **saprophytic** (also called saprobiontic or saprotrophic), feeding on dead organic matter, although some are parasitic or live in a relationship with another organism (mutualistic). Parasitic fungi are common plant pathogens, invading plant tissues through stomata, wounds, or by penetrating the epidermis. Mutualistic fungi are very important: they form lichens in association with algae or cyanobacteria, and the mutualistic mycorrhizal associations between fungi and plant roots are essential to the health of many forest plants. Saprophytic fungi, together with bacteria, are the major decomposers of the biosphere. They contribute to decay and therefore to nutrient recycling. Like all fungi, the body is composed of rapidly growing filaments called **hyphae**, which are usually divided by incomplete compartments called **septa**. The hyphae together form a large mass called a **mycelium** (the feeding body of the fungus). The familiar mushroom-like structures that we see are the above-ground reproductive bodies that arise from the main mycelium. The nutrition of a typical saprophyte, *Rhizopus*, is outlined below.

Bread Mould (*Rhizopus*)

Saprophytes grow best in dark, moist environments, but are found wherever organic material is available. *Rhizopus* is a common fungus, found on damp, stale bread and rotting fruit. Unlike many fungi, *Rhizopus* has hyphae that are undivided by septa.

Sporangium (fruiting body)

Stolons: hyphae growing horizontally on the substrate

Hyphal tip enlarged right

Rhizoids: hyphae that anchor stolons to the substrate

The entire tangled aggregation of hyphae is termed the **mycelium**

Rhizopus mycelium

Saprophytic Nutrition in Bread Mould (*Rhizopus*)

Nutrients required by most saprophytes

An organic carbon source, e.g. starch, cellulose, glucose.

A source of nitrogen

Growth factors such as vitamins

Some ions, e.g. magnesium, phosphorus, trace elements

Hypha

Transport

Cell wall

Products absorbed

Enzymatic digestion

Excess nutrients are stored as glycogen within **vacuoles** in the mycelium.

Sugars
Fatty acids
Glycerol
Amino acids

Digestion occurs outside the fungal body. The small molecules are then absorbed by the hyphae across the chitinous cell wall and the plasma membrane and are transported to all parts of the fungus.

Enzymes secreted from the hyphal tip digest the complex carbohydrate, proteins, and fats in the substrate.

The environmental requirements of fungi are met by the substrate on which they are growing:

- Temperature between 5° and 25°C
- Water (the fungal body is about 90% water)
- Oxygen (very few fungi are anaerobic)
- Neutral to slightly acid pH (pH 5.6-7) .

1. (a) Clearly describe the structure of the feeding body of a saprophytic fungus: _____

_____

(b) Explain why a moist environment is essential for fungal growth: _____

2. Identify four nutrients required by a saprophytic fungus:

(a) _____   (c) _____

(b) _____   (d) _____

3. State where these nutrients come from: _____

_____

4. Describe the way in which a saprophytic fungus obtains its nutrients: _____

_____

_____

5. Contrast digestion and absorption in a saprophytic fungus and a holozoic animal: _____

_____

_____

Related activities: Modes of Nutrition

Parasitic Nutrition

Parasitism is the most common of all symbiotic relationships. Here the host is always harmed by the presence of the parasite but is usually not killed. The main benefit derived by the parasite is obtaining nutrition, but there may be secondary advantages, such as protection. Many animal groups have members that have adopted a **parasitic** lifestyle, although parasites occur more commonly in particular taxa. Insects, some annelids (e.g. leeches), and flatworms have many parasitic representatives, and two classes of flatworms are entirely parasitic. Animal parasites are highly specialised carnivores, feeding off the body fluids or skin of host species. Parasites that attach to the outside of a host are called **ectoparasites** and have mouthparts specialised for piercing and sucking blood or tissue fluids. Those that live within the body of the host are called **endoparasites**. They may obtain nutrients by sucking or absorb simple food compounds directly from the host, as in the case of the pork tapeworm shown below. All 3400 or so species of tapeworm are endoparasites and the majority are adapted for living in the guts of vertebrates. In all species, a primary host and one or more intermediate hosts are required to complete the life cycle.

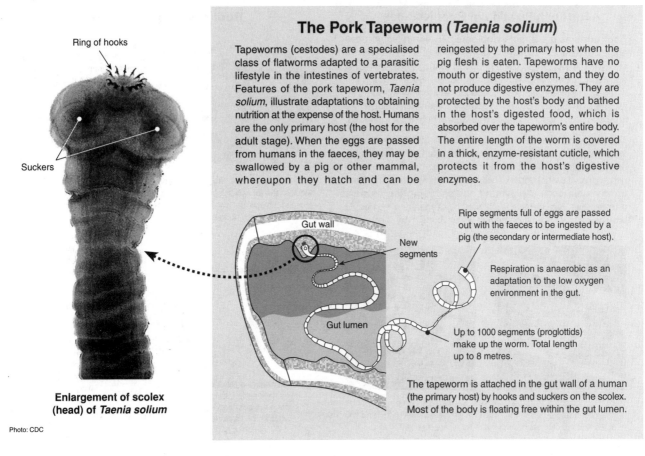

The Pork Tapeworm (*Taenia solium*)

Tapeworms (cestodes) are a specialised class of flatworms adapted to a parasitic lifestyle in the intestines of vertebrates. Features of the pork tapeworm, *Taenia solium*, illustrate adaptations to obtaining nutrition at the expense of the host. Humans are the only primary host (the host for the adult stage). When the eggs are passed from humans in the faeces, they may be swallowed by a pig or other mammal, whereupon they hatch and can be reingested by the primary host when the pig flesh is eaten. Tapeworms have no mouth or digestive system, and they do not produce digestive enzymes. They are protected by the host's body and bathed in the host's digested food, which is absorbed over the tapeworm's entire body. The entire length of the worm is covered in a thick, enzyme-resistant cuticle, which protects it from the host's digestive enzymes.

Ring of hooks

Suckers

Enlargement of scolex (head) of *Taenia solium*

Photo: CDC

Gut wall

Gut lumen

New segments

Ripe segments full of eggs are passed out with the faeces to be ingested by a pig (the secondary or intermediate host).

Respiration is anaerobic as an adaptation to the low oxygen environment in the gut.

Up to 1000 segments (proglottids) make up the worm. Total length up to 8 metres.

The tapeworm is attached in the gut wall of a human (the primary host) by hooks and suckers on the scolex. Most of the body is floating free within the gut lumen.

Energy and Ecosystems

1. Describe the way in which the pork tapeworm obtains its required nutrition: _____

_____

2. Briefly describe four adaptations of the pork tapeworm for its parasitic lifestyle (include two nutritional adaptations):

   (a) _____

   (b) _____

   (c) _____

   (d) _____

3. (a) Explain what is meant by a primary host: _____

   (b) Explain what is meant by an intermediate host: _____

   (c) Name the primary host for the pork tapeworm: _____

   (d) Name an intermediate host for the pork tapeworm: _____

4. Identify a similarity between the nutrition of a tapeworm and the nutrition of a saprophytic fungus (see previous page):

_____

5. Name another animal parasite and give its primary host: _____

Related activities: Saprophytic Nutrition, The Schistosoma Parasite

RA 2

Mutualistic Nutrition

Although nitrogen is an abundant element, making up about 80% of the Earth's atmosphere, biologically available nitrogen compounds are relatively scarce. Atmospheric nitrogen (N_2) is stable, and a lot of energy is required to break the dinitrogen bond and form organic compounds. However, many prokaryotes are able to do this, and plants that can use bacteria to fix nitrogen have a great nutritional advantage. Much of the nitrogen available to plants is supplied by nitrogen fixing bacteria. These bacteria reduce atmospheric nitrogen to ammonium ions, combining them with organic acids to produce amino acids. The amino acids provide a nitrogen supply to plants. Nitrogen fixation in plants occurs within **root nodules**; unique associations or **symbioses** between plants and nitrogen fixing bacteria. The presence of nodules allows plants to grow successfully, even when soil nitrate is low. When the plant dies, the nitrogen is returned to the soil through decomposition. For this reason, nitrogen fixing plants (particularly legumes) are important in soil management, and promote natural soil fertility when used in crop rotations.

Nitrogen Fixation in Root Nodules

Root nodules are a root **symbiosis** between a higher plant and a bacterium. The bacteria fix atmospheric nitrogen and are extremely important to the nutrition of many plants, including the economically important legume family. Root nodules are extensions of the root tissue caused by entry of a bacterium. In legumes, this bacterium is *Rhizobium*. Other bacterial genera are involved in the root nodule symbioses in non-legume species.

The bacteria in these symbioses live in the nodule where they fix atmospheric nitrogen and provide the plant with most, or all, of its nitrogen requirements. In return, they have access to a rich supply of carbohydrate. The fixation of atmospheric nitrogen to ammonia occurs within the nodule, using the enzyme **nitrogenase**. Nitrogenase is inhibited by oxygen and the nodule provides a low O_2 environment in which fixation can occur.

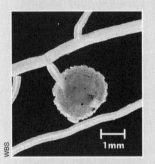

Two examples of legume nodules caused by *Rhizobium*. The photographs above show the size of a single nodule (left), and the nodules forming clusters around the roots of *Acacia* (right).

Root Nodules in Legumes

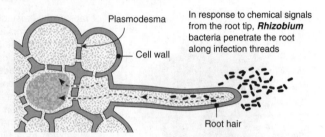

In response to chemical signals from the root tip, *Rhizobium* bacteria penetrate the root along infection threads

After infecting a root, the bacteria produce a hormone-like chemical, which induces the formation of the enlarged nodule. *Rhizobium* bacteria are free living in the soil, but adopt a large bacteroid morphology when they invade a root and induce nodule formation.

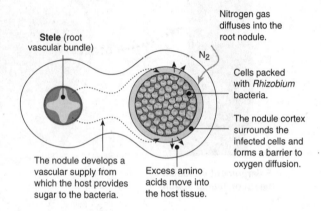

1. Explain the term **symbiosis** in relation to plants and nitrogen fixing bacteria: _____

_____

2. Root nodules are a mutualistic relationship between a bacterium and a plant. Explain the benefits of the relationship to:

(a) The plant: _____

_____

(b) The bacterium: _____

_____

3. Identify the bacterial genus involved in root nodule formation in legumes: _____

4. Explain the purpose of the following features of a root nodule:

(a) The nodule cortex: _____

(b) The vascular supply to the nodule: _____

5. Identify two examples of leguminous plants: _____

6. Identify the stimulus for the formation of the enlarged nodule: _____

_____

Ruminants and Carnivores

Among animals, bulky, high fibre diets are harder to digest than diets containing very little plant material. Herbivores consume large quantities of plant cellulose but, like all mammals, are unable to produce the enzyme *cellulase* to hydrolyse it. Instead, they depend on symbiotic microorganisms to digest the cellulose for them. Food must remain in the digestive tract for a long time for this to occur and thus herbivores tend to have long guts with large capacity chambers. The microbial digestion of cellulose may take place in the stomach (foregut fermentation) or the colon and caecum (hindgut fermentation). In ruminant herbivores, such as deer, sheep, cattle, and goats, the stomach is greatly expanded into chambers to facilitate this. In addition, the partially digested cud is regurgitated, rechewed, and reswallowed several times to increase the effectiveness of cellulose digestion.

Ruminant herbivore: Cattle (*Bos taurus*)

Ruminants are specialised herbivores with teeth specialised for chewing and grinding. The ruminant stomach is divided into a series of large chambers which slow the passage of food and allow time for bacteria and ciliates to act on the cellulose in the plant material. This mutualistic relationship provides the microbes with a warm, oxygen free, nutrient rich environment. In return, ruminants derive much of their energy from the volatile fatty acids produced by the bacterial digestion of cellulose.

Carnivore: Lion (*Panthera leo*)

The teeth and guts of carnivores are superbly adapted for eating animal flesh. The canine and incisor teeth are specialised to bite down and cut, while the carnassials are enlarged, lengthened, and positioned to act as shears to slice through flesh. The stomach is single chambered and its secretions are highly acidic. As meat is easier to digest than cellulose, the guts of carnivores are comparatively more uniform and shorter than those of herbivores. The hind gut is short and caeca are small or absent.

Dental adaptations

Adaptations of the gut

Flow of food in the stomach

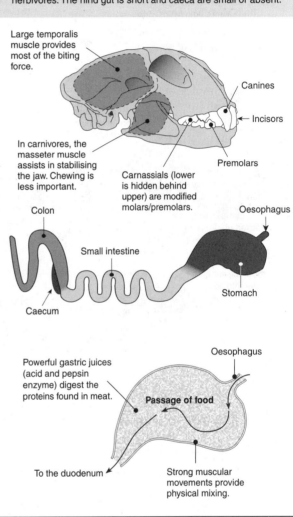

Energy and Ecosystems

1. Describe the benefits of the mutualistic relationship between ruminants and their rumen microorganisms to:

    (a) The ruminant: _____

    (b) The microorganisms: _____

2. Explain why carnivore guts are simpler in their overall structure than ruminant guts: _____

    _____

    _____

3. Identify a structural difference between carnivores and ruminant herbivores with respect to:

    (a) The teeth: _____

    (b) The gut: _____

Related activities: Mutualistic Nutrition, Carbohydrates, Proteins

RA 2

The Water Cycle

The hydrologic cycle (water cycle), collects, purifies, and distributes the Earth's fixed supply of water. The main processes in this water recycling are described below. Besides replenishing inland water supplies, rainwater causes erosion and is a major medium for transporting dissolved nutrients within and among ecosystems. On a global scale, evaporation (conversion of water to gaseous water vapour) exceeds precipitation (rain, snow etc.) over the oceans. This results in a net movement of water vapour (carried by winds) over the land. On land, precipitation exceeds evaporation. Some of this precipitation becomes locked up in snow and ice, for varying lengths of time. Most forms surface and groundwater systems that flow back to the sea, completing the major part of the cycle. Living organisms, particularly plants, participate to varying degrees in the water cycle. Over the sea, most of the water vapour is due to evaporation alone. However on land, about 90% of the vapour results from plant transpiration. Animals (particularly humans) intervene in the cycle by utilising the resource for their own needs.

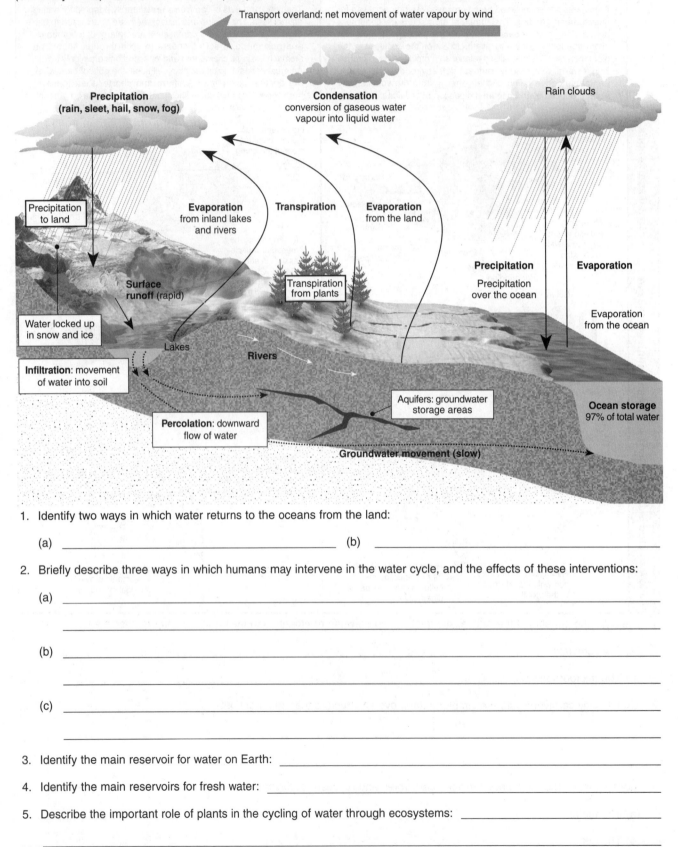

1. Identify two ways in which water returns to the oceans from the land:

   (a) _____ (b) _____

2. Briefly describe three ways in which humans may intervene in the water cycle, and the effects of these interventions:

   (a) _____

   _____

   (b) _____

   _____

   (c) _____

   _____

3. Identify the main reservoir for water on Earth: _____

4. Identify the main reservoirs for fresh water: _____

5. Describe the important role of plants in the cycling of water through ecosystems: _____

   _____

Related activities: The Biochemical Nature of the Cell, Transpiration

The Carbon Cycle

Carbon is an essential element in living systems, providing the chemical framework to form the molecules that make up living organisms (e.g. proteins, carbohydrates, fats, and nucleic acids). Carbon also makes up approximately 0.03% of the atmosphere as the gas carbon dioxide (CO_2), and it is present in the ocean as carbonate and bicarbonate, and in rocks such as limestone. Carbon cycles between the living (biotic) and non-living (abiotic)

environment: it is fixed in the process of photosynthesis and returned to the atmosphere in respiration. Carbon may remain locked up in biotic or abiotic systems for long periods of time as, for example, in the wood of trees or in fossil fuels such as coal or oil. Human activity has disturbed the balance of the carbon cycle (the global carbon budget) through activities such as combustion (e.g. the burning of wood and **fossil fuels**) and deforestation.

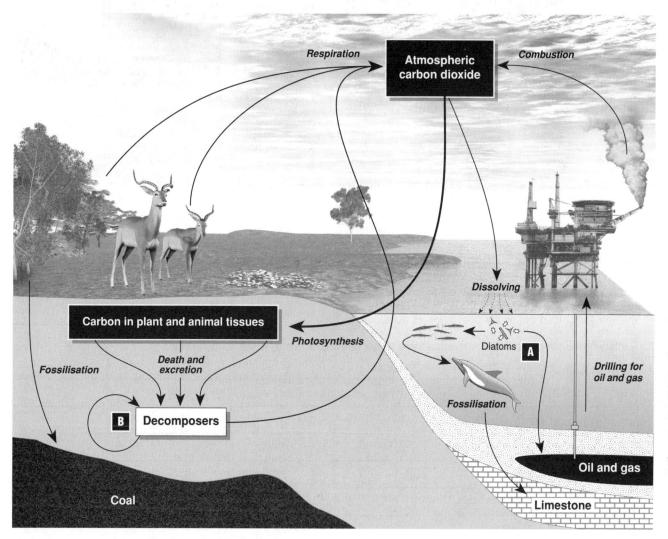

Energy and Ecosystems

1. In the diagram above, add arrows and labels to show the following activities:

(a) Dissolving of limestone by acid rain
(b) Release of carbon from the marine food chain
(c) Mining and burning of coal
(d) Burning of plant material.

2. Describe the **biological origin** of the following geological deposits:

(a) Coal: _____

(b) Oil: _____

(c) Limestone: _____

3. Describe the two processes that release carbon into the atmosphere: _____

_____

_____

4. Name the four geological reservoirs (sinks), in the diagram above, that can act as a source of carbon:

(a) _____ (c) _____

(b) _____ (d) _____

Related activities: Organic Molecules, Gas Exchange in Plants, Gas Exchange in Animals

A 2

Termite mound in rainforest

Dung beetle on cow pat

Bracket fungus on tree trunk

Termites: These insects play an important role in nutrient recycling. With the aid of symbiotic protozoans and bacteria in their guts, they can digest the tough cellulose of woody tissues in trees. Termites fulfill a vital function in breaking down the endless rain of debris in tropical rainforests.

Dung beetles: Beetles play a major role in the decomposition of animal dung. Some beetles merely eat the dung, but true dung beetles, such as the scarabs and *Geotrupes*, bury the dung and lay their eggs in it to provide food for the beetle grubs during their development.

Fungi: Together with decomposing bacteria, fungi perform an important role in breaking down dead plant matter in the leaf litter of forests. Some mycorrhizal fungi have been found to link up to the root systems of trees where an exchange of nutrients occurs (a mutualistic relationship).

5. Explain what would happen to the carbon cycle if there were no decomposers present in an ecosystem:

6. Study the diagram on the previous page and identify the processes represented at the points labelled [**A**] and [**B**]:

(a) Process carried out by the diatoms at label **A**:

(b) Process carried out by the decomposers at label **B**:

7. Explain how each of the three organisms listed below has a role to play in the carbon cycle:

(a) Dung beetles:

(b) Termites:

(c) Fungi:

8. In natural circumstances, accumulated reserves of carbon such as peat, coal and oil represent a **sink** or natural diversion from the cycle. Eventually the carbon in these sinks returns to the cycle through the action of geological processes which return deposits to the surface for oxidation.

(a) Describe what effect human activity is having on the amount of carbon stored in sinks:

(b) Explain two global effects arising from this activity:

(c) Suggest what could be done to prevent or alleviate these effects:

The Nitrogen Cycle

Nitrogen is a crucial element for all living things, forming an essential part of the structure of proteins and nucleic acids. The Earth's atmosphere is about 80% nitrogen gas (N_2), but molecular nitrogen is so stable that it is only rarely available directly to organisms and is often in short supply in biological systems. Bacteria play an important role in transferring nitrogen between the biotic and abiotic environments. Some bacteria are able to fix atmospheric nitrogen, while others convert ammonia to nitrate and thus make it available for incorporation into plant and animal tissues. Nitrogen-fixing bacteria are found living freely in the soil *(Azotobacter)* and living symbiotically with some plants in root nodules *(Rhizobium)*. Lightning discharges also cause the oxidation of nitrogen gas to nitrate which ends up in the soil. Denitrifying bacteria reverse this activity and return fixed nitrogen to the atmosphere. Humans intervene in the nitrogen cycle by producing, and applying to the land, large amounts of nitrogen fertiliser. Some applied fertiliser is from organic sources (e.g. green crops and manures) but much is inorganic, produced from atmospheric nitrogen using an energy-expensive industrial process. Overuse of nitrogen fertilisers may lead to pollution of water supplies, particularly where land clearance increases the amount of leaching and runoff into ground and surface waters.

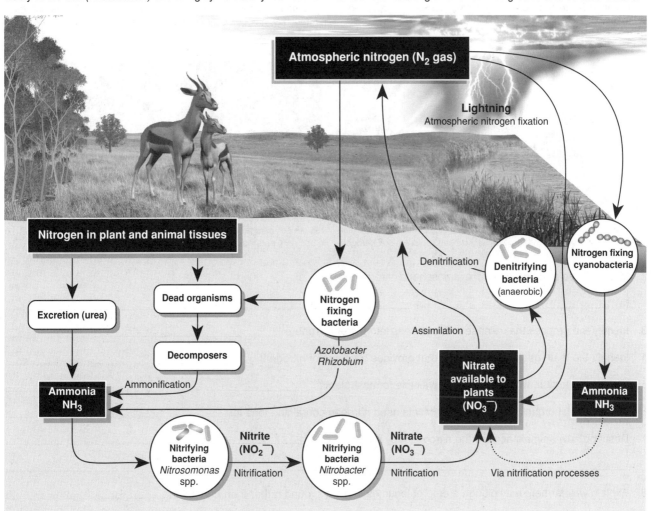

Energy and Ecosystems

1. Describe five instances in the nitrogen cycle where **bacterial** action is important. Include the name of each of the processes and the changes to the form of nitrogen involved:

   (a) _____

   _____

   (b) _____

   _____

   (c) _____

   _____

   (d) _____

   _____

   (e) _____

   _____

Related activities: Mutualistic Nutrition, Amino Acids, Proteins
Web links: Nitrogen Cycle Animation

RA 3

Human Intervention in the Nitrogen Cycle

Until about sixty years ago, microbial nitrogen fixation was the only mechanism by which nitrogen could be made available to plants. However, during WW II, Fritz Haber developed the **Haber process** whereby nitrogen and hydrogen gas are combined to form gaseous ammonia. The ammonia is converted into ammonium salts and sold as inorganic fertiliser. Its application has revolutionised agriculture by increasing crop yields.

As well as adding nitrogen fertilisers to the land, humans use anaerobic bacteria to break down livestock wastes and release NH_3 into the soil. They also intervene in the nitrogen cycle by discharging **effluent** into waterways. Nitrogen is removed from the land through burning, which releases nitrogen oxides into the atmosphere. It is also lost by mining, harvesting crops, and irrigation, which leaches nitrate ions from the soil.

Crop Rotation

Crop rotation is an agricultural practice in which different crops are cultivated in succession on the same area of land over a period of time. Its purpose is to maintain soil fertility and reduce the adverse effects of pests. Legumes, such as peas and beans, are important in the rotation as they restore nitrogen to the soil. Some crops, like potatoes, suppress weeds and improve soil structure. Other crops that may be included in a typical rotation are wheat, barley, and squash. Different crops have different soil requirements and benefits, so changing crops from year to year minimises deficiencies and allows the soil to replenish.

A typical rotation is of three to five years with plants in different rotations being chosen from different families for their specific contributions to pest management and aspects of soil quality (such as nitrogen content and structure).

Humans may intervene in the nitrogen cycle by applying manure (left), which restores soil nitrogen, and by harvesting crop biomass, which removes material that would potentially rot and replenish soil nitrogen.

Legumes, such as soy beans (above, left) are used in crop rotations to restore soil nitrogen. Alternating between fibrous-rooted and deep-rooted crops (e.g. potatoes) improves soil structure.

2. Identify three processes that **fix** atmospheric nitrogen:

   (a) _____ (b) _____ (c) _____

3. Identify the process that releases nitrogen gas into the atmosphere: _____

4. Identify the main geological reservoir that provides a source of nitrogen: _____

5. Identify the form in which nitrogen is available to most plants: _____

6. Identify a vital organic compound that plants need nitrogen containing ions for: _____

7. Describe how animals acquire the nitrogen they need: _____

   _____

8. Explain why farmers may plough a crop of legumes into the ground rather than harvest it: _____

   _____

9. Describe five ways in which humans may intervene in the nitrogen cycle and the effects of these interventions:

   (a) _____

   _____

   (b) _____

   _____

   (c) _____

   _____

   (d) _____

   _____

   (e) _____

   _____

Energy in Ecosystems

An ecosystem is a natural unit of living (biotic) components, together with all the non-living (abiotic) components with which they interact. Two processes central to ecosystem function are **energy flow** and **chemical cycling**. The mitochondria of eukaryotic cells use the organic products of photosynthesis as fuel for cellular respiration. Respiration generates ATP; an energy currency for cellular work. Cellular work generates heat which is lost from the system. The waste products of cellular respiration are used as the raw materials for photosynthesis (see diagram below). Chemical elements such as nitrogen, phosphorus, and carbon are cycled between the biotic and abiotic components of the ecosystem. Energy, unlike matter, cannot be recycled. Ecosystems must receive a constant input of new energy from an outside source. In most cases, this is the sun.

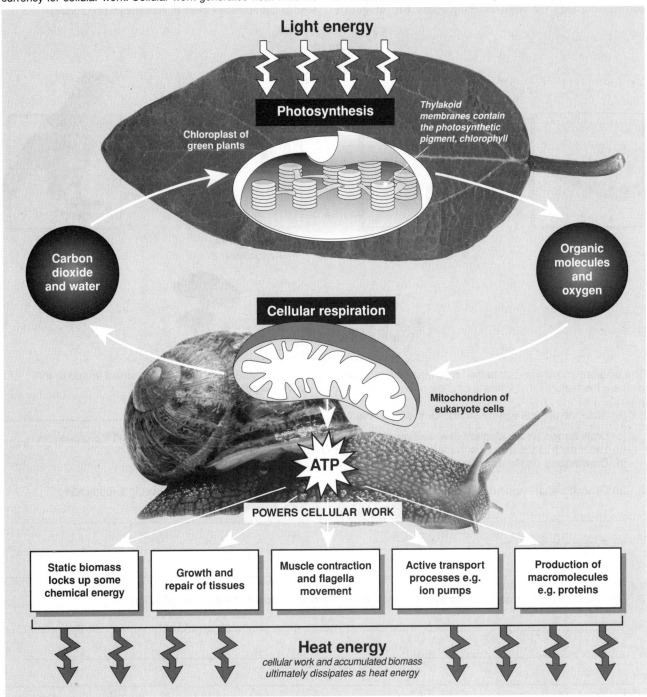

1. Write a word equation for each of the following processes. Include the energy source, raw materials, and waste products:

    (a) Photosynthesis: _____

    (b) Respiration: _____

2. Explain why ecosystems require a constant input of energy from an external source: _____

    _____

3. With respect to cycling of matter, explain the relationship between photosynthesis and respiration: _____

    _____

Energy and Ecosystems

Food Chains

Every ecosystem has a **trophic structure**: a hierarchy of feeding relationships that determines the pathways for energy flow and nutrient cycling. Species are divided into trophic levels on the basis of their sources of nutrition. The first trophic level (**producers**), ultimately supports all other levels. The consumers are those that rely on producers for their energy. Consumers are ranked according to the trophic level they occupy (first order, second order, etc.). The sequence of organisms, each of which is a source of food for the next, is called a **food chain**. Food chains commonly have four links but seldom more than six. Those organisms whose food is obtained through the same number of links belong to the same trophic level. Note that some consumers (particularly "top" carnivores and omnivores) may feed at several different trophic levels, and many primary consumers eat many plant species. The different food chains in an ecosystem therefore tend to form complex webs of interactions (food webs).

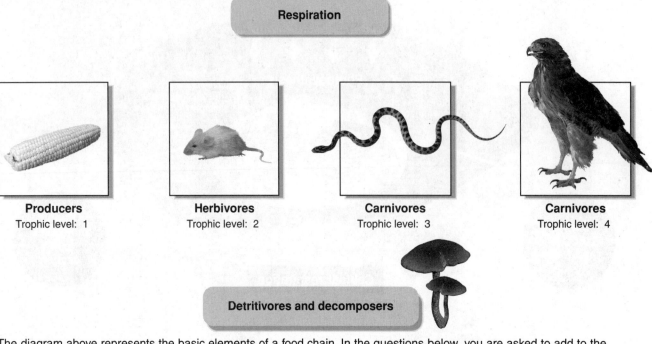

Respiration

Producers	Herbivores	Carnivores	Carnivores
Trophic level: 1	Trophic level: 2	Trophic level: 3	Trophic level: 4

Detritivores and decomposers

The diagram above represents the basic elements of a food chain. In the questions below, you are asked to add to the diagram the features that indicate the flow of energy through the community of organisms.

1. (a) State the original energy source for this food chain: _____

   (b) Draw arrows on the diagram to show how the energy flows from the original energy source to all the organisms.
   (c) Label each of the arrows with the process that carries out this transfer of energy.
   (d) Draw arrows on the diagram to show how the energy is lost by way of respiration.

2. (a) Describe what happens to the **amount** of energy available to each successive trophic level in a food chain:

   _____

   (b) Explain why this is the case: _____

   _____

3. Discuss the trophic structure of ecosystems, including reference to **food chains** and **trophic** levels:

   _____

   _____

   _____

   _____

   _____

   _____

   _____

   _____

4. If the eagle (above) was found to eat both snakes and mice, explain what you could infer about the tropic level(s) it occupied:

   _____

Related activities: Modes of Nutrition, Constructing a Food Web, Energy Inputs and Outputs, Energy Flow in an Ecosystem

Constructing a Food Web

The actual species inhabiting any particular lake may vary depending on locality, but certain types of organisms (as shown below) are typically represented. For the sake of simplicity, only fifteen organisms are represented here. Real lake communities may have hundreds of different species interacting together. The bulk of this species diversity is in the lower trophic levels (producers and invertebrate grazers). Your task is to assemble the organisms below into a food web, in a way that illustrates their trophic status and their relative trophic position(s). The food resource represented by **detritus** is not shown here. Detritus comprises the accumulated debris of dead organisms in varying stages of decay. This debris may arise from within the lake itself or it may be washed in from the surrounding lake margins and streams. The detritus settles through the water column and eventually forms a layer on the lake bottom. It provides a rich food source for any organism that can exploit it.

Feeding Requirements of Lake Organisms

Daphnia
Small freshwater crustacean that forms part of the zooplankton. It feeds on planktonic algae by filtering them from the water with its limbs.

Autotrophic protoctists
e.g. Chlamydomonas, Euglena (pictured)
Two of genera that form the phytoplankton (commonly called algae or "plant plankton").

Asplanchna (planktonic rotifer)
A large, carnivorous rotifer that feeds on protozoa and young zooplankton (e.g. *Daphnia*). Note that most rotifers are small herbivores.

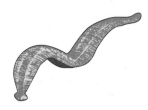

Leech (*Glossiphonia*)
Leeches are fluid feeding predators of smaller invertebrates, including rotifers, small pond snails and worms.

Macrophytes (various species)
A variety of flowering aquatic plants are adapted for being submerged, free-floating, or growing at the lake margin.

Three-spined stickleback (*Gasterosteus*)
A common fish of freshwater ponds and lakes. It feeds mainly on small invertebrates such as *Daphnia* and insect larvae.

Diving beetle (*Dytiscus*)
Diving beetles feed on aquatic insect larvae and adult insects blown into the lake community. The will also eat organic detritus collected from the bottom mud.

Carp (*Cyprinus*)
A heavy bodied freshwater fish that feeds mainly on bottom living insect larvae and snails, but will also take some plant material (not algae).

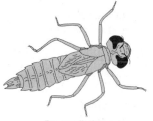

Dragonfly larva
Large aquatic insect larvae that are voracious predators of small invertebrates including *Hydra*, *Daphnia*, other insect larvae, and leeches.

Great pond snail (*Limnaea*)
Omnivorous pond snail, eating both plant and animal material, living or dead, although the main diet is aquatic macrophytes.

Herbivorous water beetles (*e.g. Hydrophilus*)
Feed on water plants, although the young beetle larvae are carnivorous, feeding primarily on small pond snails.

Protozan (*e.g. Paramecium*)
Ciliated protozoa such as *Paramecium* feed primarily on bacteria and microscopic green algae such as *Chlamydomonas*.

Pike (*Esox lucius*)
A top ambush predator of all smaller fish and amphibians, although they are also opportunistic predators of rodents and small birds.

Mosquito larva
(*Culex* spp.)
The larvae of most mosquito species, e.g. *Culex*, feed on planktonic algae before passing through a pupal stage and undergoing metamorphosis into adult mosquitoes.

Hydra
A small carnivorous cnidarian that captures small prey items such as small *Daphnia* and insect larvae using its stinging cells on the tentacles.

Energy and Ecosystems

Related activities: Food Chains, Energy Inputs and Outputs
Web links: Fitting Algae into the Food Web, Marine Food Webs

A 2

Instructions

1. (a) Read the information provided for each species on the previous page, taking note of what it feeds on.

   (b) Identify the **producer** species present, as well as herbivores, carnivores, and omnivores.

   (c) Starting with **producer** species, construct **4** different **food chains** (using their names only) to show the feeding relationships between the organisms (NOTE: some food chains may be shorter than others; some species will be repeated in one or more subsequent food chains). An example of a food chain has already been completed for you.

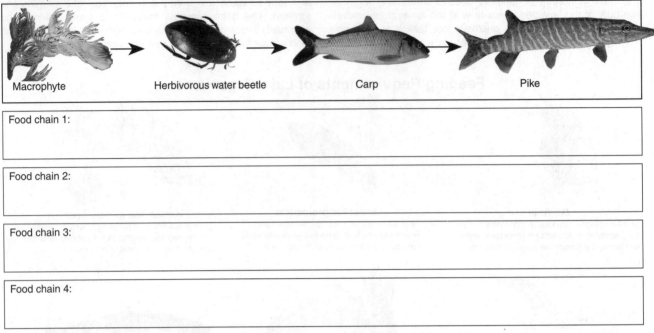

Macrophyte → Herbivorous water beetle → Carp → Pike

Food chain 1:

Food chain 2:

Food chain 3:

Food chain 4:

2. (a) Use the food chains created above to help you to draw up a **food web** for this community. Use the information supplied to draw arrows showing the flow of **energy** between species (only energy **from** the detritus is required).

   (b) Label each species to indicate its position in the food web, i.e. its trophic level (**T1, T2, T3, T4, T5**). Where a species occupies more than one trophic level, indicate this, e.g. **T2/3**:

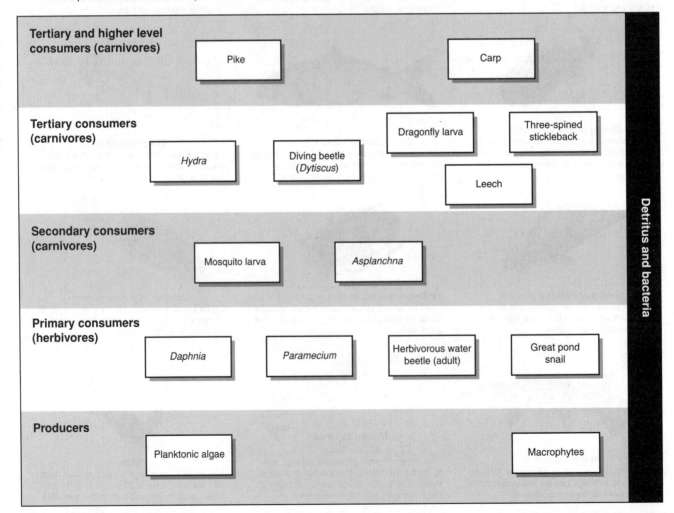

© Biozone International 1998-2007

Photocopying Prohibited

Energy Inputs and Outputs

The way living things obtain their energy can be classified into two categories. The group upon which all others depend is called **producers** or **autotrophs**. They are organisms able to manufacture their food from simple inorganic substances. The **consumers** or **heterotrophs** (comprising the herbivores, carnivores, omnivores, decomposers, and detritivores), feed on

the autotrophs or other heterotrophs to obtain their energy. The energy flow into and out of each trophic level in a food chain can be identified and represented diagrammatically using arrows of different sizes. The sizes of the arrows (see the diagrams below and on the next page) represent different amounts of energy lost from that particular trophic level.

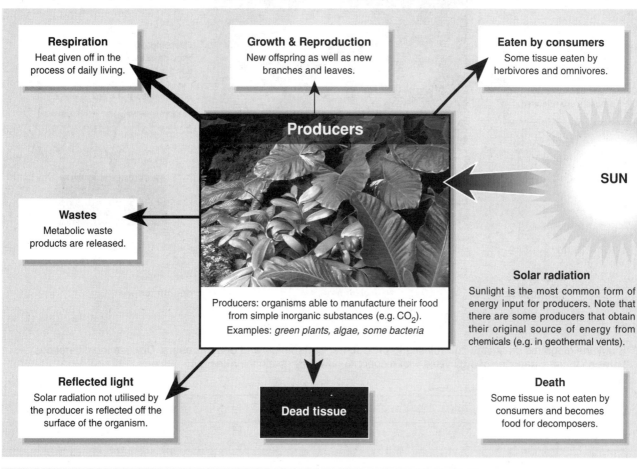

Respiration
Heat given off in the process of daily living.

Growth & Reproduction
New offspring as well as new branches and leaves.

Eaten by consumers
Some tissue eaten by herbivores and omnivores.

Producers

SUN

Wastes
Metabolic waste products are released.

Solar radiation
Sunlight is the most common form of energy input for producers. Note that there are some producers that obtain their original source of energy from chemicals (e.g. in geothermal vents).

Producers: organisms able to manufacture their food from simple inorganic substances (e.g. CO_2).
Examples: *green plants, algae, some bacteria*

Reflected light
Solar radiation not utilised by the producer is reflected off the surface of the organism.

Dead tissue

Death
Some tissue is not eaten by consumers and becomes food for decomposers.

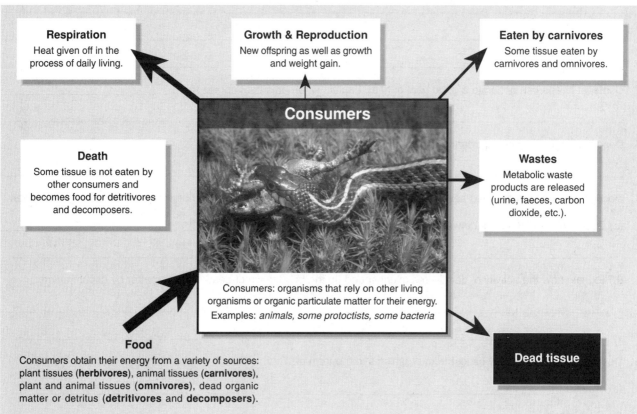

Respiration
Heat given off in the process of daily living.

Growth & Reproduction
New offspring as well as growth and weight gain.

Eaten by carnivores
Some tissue eaten by carnivores and omnivores.

Consumers

Death
Some tissue is not eaten by other consumers and becomes food for detritivores and decomposers.

Wastes
Metabolic waste products are released (urine, faeces, carbon dioxide, etc.).

Consumers: organisms that rely on other living organisms or organic particulate matter for their energy.
Examples: *animals, some protoctists, some bacteria*

Food
Consumers obtain their energy from a variety of sources: plant tissues (**herbivores**), animal tissues (**carnivores**), plant and animal tissues (**omnivores**), dead organic matter or detritus (**detritivores** and **decomposers**).

Dead tissue

Energy and Ecosystems

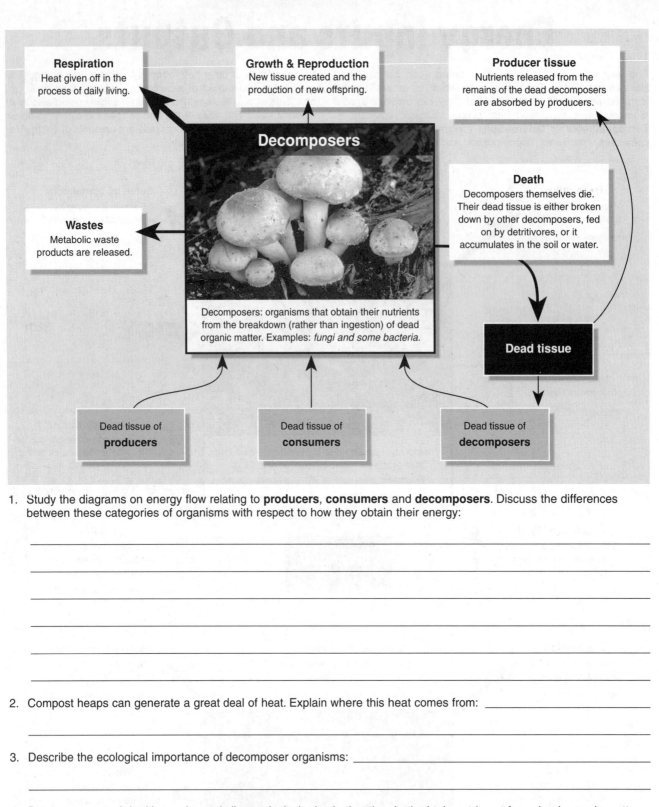

Respiration
Heat given off in the process of daily living.

Growth & Reproduction
New tissue created and the production of new offspring.

Producer tissue
Nutrients released from the remains of the dead decomposers are absorbed by producers.

Decomposers

Death
Decomposers themselves die. Their dead tissue is either broken down by other decomposers, fed on by detritivores, or it accumulates in the soil or water.

Wastes
Metabolic waste products are released.

Decomposers: organisms that obtain their nutrients from the breakdown (rather than ingestion) of dead organic matter. Examples: *fungi and some bacteria*.

Dead tissue

Dead tissue of **producers**

Dead tissue of **consumers**

Dead tissue of **decomposers**

1. Study the diagrams on energy flow relating to **producers**, **consumers** and **decomposers**. Discuss the differences between these categories of organisms with respect to how they obtain their energy:

_____

_____

_____

_____

_____

_____

2. Compost heaps can generate a great deal of heat. Explain where this heat comes from: _____

_____

3. Describe the ecological importance of decomposer organisms: _____

_____

4. Decomposers and detritivores have similar ecological roles in that they both obtain nutriment from dead organic matter.

(a) Describe the differences between decomposers and detritivores: _____

_____

(b) Explain how the activity of detritivores might speed up the breakdown of dead organic matter by decomposers:

_____

_____

5. Describe how energy may be lost from organisms in the form of:

(a) Wastes: _____

(b) Respiration: _____

Primary Productivity

The energy entering ecosystems is fixed by producers in photosynthesis. The rate of photosynthesis is dependent on factors such as temperature and the amount of light, water, and nutrients. The total energy fixed by producers in photosynthesis is referred to as the **gross primary production (GPP)** and is usually expressed as Joules (or kJ) m^{-2}. However, a portion of this energy is required by the plant for respiration. Subtracting respiration from GPP gives the **net primary production (NPP)**. The **rate** of biomass production, or **net primary productivity**, is the biomass produced per area per unit time.

Measuring Productivity

Primary productivity of an ecosystem depends on a number of interrelated factors (light intensity, nutrients, temperature, water, and mineral supplies), making its calculation extremely difficult. Globally, the least productive ecosystems are those that are limited by heat energy and water. The most productive ecosystems are systems with high temperatures, plenty of water, and non-limiting supplies of soil nitrogen. The primary productivity of oceans is lower than that of terrestrial ecosystems because the water reflects (or absorbs) much of the light energy before it reaches and is utilised by producers. The table below compares the difference in the net primary productivity of various ecosystems.

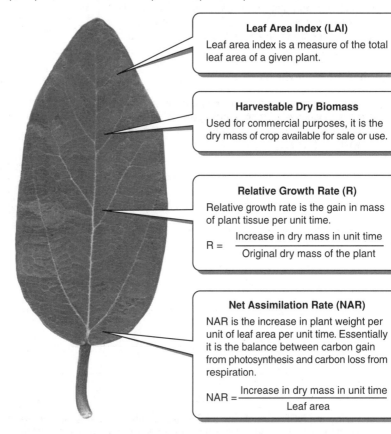

Leaf Area Index (LAI)

Leaf area index is a measure of the total leaf area of a given plant.

Harvestable Dry Biomass

Used for commercial purposes, it is the dry mass of crop available for sale or use.

Relative Growth Rate (R)

Relative growth rate is the gain in mass of plant tissue per unit time.

$$R = \frac{\text{Increase in dry mass in unit time}}{\text{Original dry mass of the plant}}$$

Net Assimilation Rate (NAR)

NAR is the increase in plant weight per unit of leaf area per unit time. Essentially it is the balance between carbon gain from photosynthesis and carbon loss from respiration.

$$NAR = \frac{\text{Increase in dry mass in unit time}}{\text{Leaf area}}$$

Ecosystem Type	Net Primary Productivity	
	kcal m^{-2} y^{-1}	kJ m^{-2} y^{-1}
Tropical rainforest	15 000	63 000
Swamps and marshes	12 000	50 400
Estuaries	9000	37 800
Savanna	3000	12 600
Temperate forest	6000	25 200
Boreal forest	3500	14 700
Temperate grassland	2000	8400
Tundra/cold desert	500	2100
Coastal marine	2500	10 500
Open ocean	800	3360
Desert	< 200	< 840

* Data compiled from a variety of sources.

Net Primary Productivity of Selected Ecosystems (figures are in kJ m^{-2} y^{-1})

< 2500	< 12 500 – 42 000	< 42 000 – 105 000	2500 – 42 000
Arid desert	Temperate forest	Tropical rain forest	Continental shelf waters
Polar tundra and ice desert	Grassland agriculture	Intensive horticulture	Open ocean

1. Briefly describe three factors that may affect the primary productivity of an ecosystem:

   (a) _____

   (b) _____

   (c) _____

2. Explain the difference between **productivity** and **production** in relation to plants: _____

_____

_____

Related activities: Energy Inputs and Outputs, Energy Flow in an Ecosystem
Web links: Uses of Plants

DA 2

Energy and Ecosystems

3. Suggest how the LAI might influence the rate of primary production: _____
_____
_____

4. Using the data table opposite, choose a suitable graph format and plot the differences in the net primary productivity of various ecosystems (use either of the data columns provided, but not both). Use the graph grid provided, right.

5. With reference to the graph:

(a) Suggest why tropical rainforests are among the most productive terrestrial ecosystems, while tundra and desert ecosystems are among the least productive:

_____

_____

_____

_____

_____

(b) Suggest why, amongst aquatic ecosystems, the NPP of the open ocean is low relative to that of coastal systems:

_____

_____

_____

6. Estimating the NPP is relatively simple: all the plant material (including root material) from a measured area (e.g. 1 m^2) is collected and dried (at 105°C) until it reaches a constant mass. This mass, called the **standing crop**, is recorded (in kg m^{-2}). The procedure is repeated after some set time period (e.g. 1 month). The difference between the two calculated masses represents the estimated NPP:

(a) Explain why the plant material was dried before weighing: _____

_____

(b) Define the term **standing crop**: _____

(c) Suggest why this procedure only provides an estimate of NPP: _____

_____

(d) State what extra information would be required in order to express the standing crop value in kJ m^{-2}: _____

_____

(e) Suggest what information would be required in order to calculate the GPP: _____

_____

7. Intensive horticultural systems achieve very high rates of production (about 10X those of subsistence systems).

(a) Outline the means by which these high rates are achieved: _____

_____

(b) Comment on the sustainability of these high rates (summary of a group discussion if you wish):

_____

_____

_____

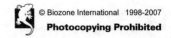

Energy Flow in an Ecosystem

The flow of energy through an ecosystem can be measured and analysed. It provides some idea as to the energy trapped and passed on at each trophic level. Each trophic level in a food chain or web contains a certain amount of biomass: the dry weight of all organic matter contained in its organisms. Energy stored in biomass is transferred from one trophic level to another (by eating, defaecation etc.), with some being lost as low-grade heat energy to the environment in each transfer. Three definitions are useful:

- **Gross primary production**: The total of organic material produced by plants (including that lost to respiration).
- **Net primary production**: The amount of biomass that is available to consumers at subsequent trophic levels.

- **Secondary production**: The amount of biomass at higher trophic levels (consumer production). Production figures are sometimes expressed as rates (productivity).

The percentage of energy transferred from one trophic level to the next varies between 5% and 20% and is called the **ecological efficiency** (efficiency of energy transfer). An average figure of 10% is often used. The path of energy flow in an ecosystem depends on its characteristics. In a tropical forest ecosystem, most of the primary production enters the detrital and decomposer food chains. However, in an ocean ecosystem or an intensively grazed pasture more than half the primary production may enter the grazing food chain.

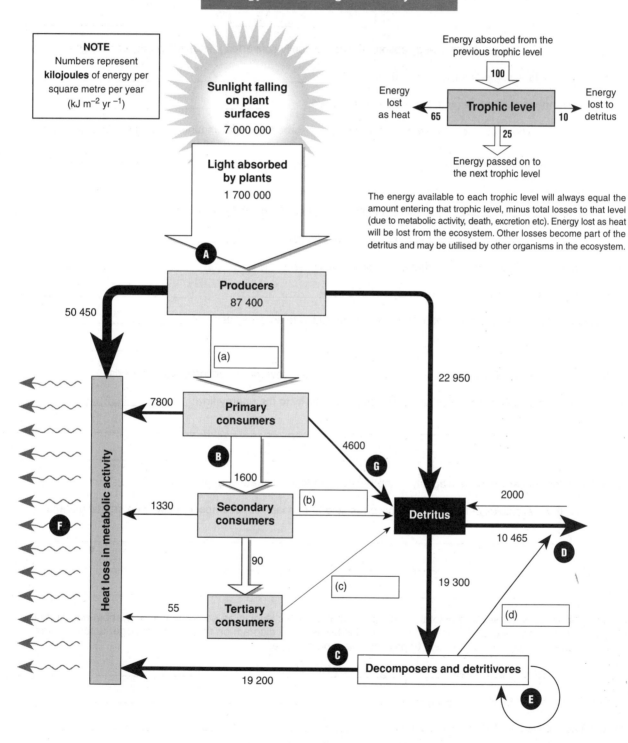

Energy Flow Through an Ecosystem

NOTE
Numbers represent **kilojoules** of energy per square metre per year
$(kJ\ m^{-2}\ yr^{-1})$

Sunlight falling on plant surfaces
7 000 000

Light absorbed by plants
1 700 000

Energy absorbed from the previous trophic level
100

Energy lost as heat 65 | **Trophic level** | 10 Energy lost to detritus

25

Energy passed on to the next trophic level

The energy available to each trophic level will always equal the amount entering that trophic level, minus total losses to that level (due to metabolic activity, death, excretion etc). Energy lost as heat will be lost from the ecosystem. Other losses become part of the detritus and may be utilised by other organisms in the ecosystem.

Producers 87 400

50 450

(a)

22 950

Primary consumers

7800

4600

1600

Secondary consumers

1330

(b)

Detritus

2000

10 465

Tertiary consumers

90

55

(c)

19 300

(d)

Heat loss in metabolic activity

19 200

Decomposers and detritivores

A B C D E F G

Energy and Ecosystems

Related activities: Energy Inputs and Outputs, Primary Productivity, Ecological Pyramids, The Carbon Cycle

RDA 3

1. Study the diagram on the previous page illustrating energy flow through a hypothetical ecosystem. Use the example at the top of the page as a guide to calculate the missing values (a)–(d) in the diagram. Note that the sum of the energy inputs always equals the sum of the energy outputs. Place your answers in the spaces provided on the diagram.

2. Describe the original source of energy that powers this ecosystem: _____

3. Identify the processes that are occurring at the points labelled **A – G** on the diagram on the previous page:

   A. _____   E. _____

   B. _____   F. _____

   C. _____   G. _____

   D. _____

4. (a) Calculate the percentage of light energy falling on the plants that is absorbed at point **A**:

   Light absorbed by plants ÷ sunlight falling on plant surfaces x 100 = _____

   (b) Describe what happens to the light energy that is not absorbed: _____

   _____

5. (a) Calculate the percentage of light energy absorbed that is actually converted (fixed) into producer energy:

   Producers ÷ light absorbed by plants x 100 = _____

   (b) State the **amount** of light energy absorbed that is **not** fixed: _____

   (c) Account for the difference between the amount of energy absorbed and the amount actually fixed by producers:

   _____

   _____

6. Of the total amount of energy **fixed** by producers in this ecosystem (at point **A**) calculate:

   (a) The total amount that ended up as metabolic waste heat (in kJ): _____

   (b) The percentage of the energy fixed that ended up as waste heat: _____

7. (a) State the groups for which detritus is an energy source: _____

   (b) Describe by what means detritus could be removed or added to an ecosystem: _____

   _____

8. In certain conditions, detritus will build up in an environment where few (or no) decomposers can exist.

   (a) Describe the consequences of this lack of decomposer activity to the energy flow: _____

   _____

   _____

   (b) Add an additional arrow to the diagram on the previous page to illustrate your answer.

   (c) Describe three examples of materials that have resulted from a lack of decomposer activity on detrital material:

   _____

   _____

   _____

9. The **ten percent law** states that the total energy content of a trophic level in an ecosystem is only about one-tenth (or 10%) that of the preceding level. For each of the trophic levels in the diagram on the preceding page, determine the amount of energy passed on to the next trophic level as a percentage:

   (a) Producer to primary consumer: _____

   (b) Primary consumer to secondary consumer: _____

   (c) Secondary consumer to tertiary consumer: _____

Ecological Pyramids

The trophic levels of any ecosystem can be arranged in a pyramid shape. The first trophic level is placed at the bottom and subsequent trophic levels are stacked on top in their 'feeding sequence'. Ecological pyramids can illustrate changes in the numbers, biomass (weight), or energy content of organisms at each level. Each of these three kinds of pyramids tell us something different about the flow of energy and materials between one trophic level and the next. The type of pyramid you choose in order to express information about the ecosystem will depend on what particular features of the ecosystem you are interested in and, of course, the type of data you have collected.

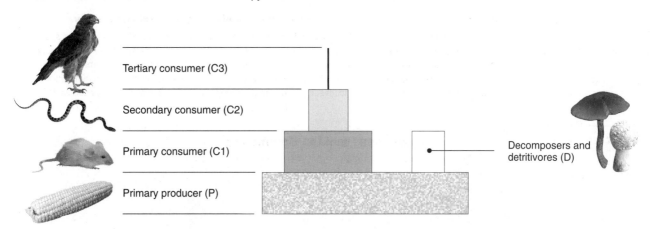

Tertiary consumer (C3)

Secondary consumer (C2)

Primary consumer (C1)

Primary producer (P)

Decomposers and detritivores (D)

The generalised ecological pyramid pictured above shows a conventional pyramid shape, with a large number (or biomass) of producers forming the base for an increasingly small number (or biomass) of consumers. Decomposers are placed at the level of the primary consumers and off to the side. They may obtain energy from many different trophic levels and so do not fit into the conventional pyramid structure. For any particular ecosystem at any one time (e.g. the forest ecosystem below), the shape of this typical pyramid can vary greatly depending on whether the trophic relationships are expressed as numbers, biomass or energy.

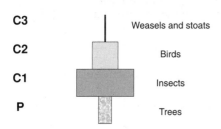

C3   Weasels and stoats
C2   Birds
C1   Insects
P   Trees

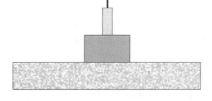

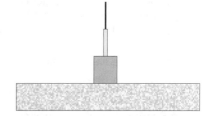

Numbers in a forest community

Pyramids of numbers display the number of individual organisms at each trophic level. The pyramid above has few producers, but they may be of a very large size (e.g. trees). This gives an 'inverted pyramid', although not all pyramids of numbers are like this.

Biomass in a forest community

Biomass pyramids measure the 'weight' of biological material at each trophic level. Water content of organisms varies, so 'dry weight' is often used. Organism size is taken into account, so meaningful comparisons of different trophic levels are possible.

Energy in a forest community

Pyramids of energy are often very similar to biomass pyramids. The energy content at each trophic level is generally comparable to the biomass (i.e. similar amounts of dry biomass tend to have about the same energy content).

1. Describe what the three types of ecological pyramids measure:

   (a) Number pyramid: _____

   (b) Biomass pyramid: _____

   (c) Energy pyramid: _____

2. Explain the advantage of using a biomass or energy pyramid rather than a pyramid of numbers to express the relationship between different trophic levels:

   _____

   _____

   _____

3. Explain why it is possible for the forest ecosystem (on the next page) to have very few producers supporting a large number of consumers:

   _____

   _____

Related activities: Food Chains, Energy Flow in an Ecosystem

DA 2

Energy and Ecosystems

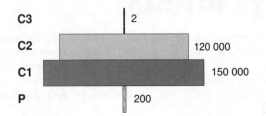

Pyramid of numbers: forest community

In a forest community a few producers may support a large number of consumers. This is due to the large size of the producers; large trees can support many individual consumer organisms. The example above shows the numbers at each trophic level for an oak forest in England, in an area of 10 m².

Pyramid of numbers: grassland community

In a grassland community a large number of producers are required to support a much smaller number of consumers. This is due to the small size of the producers. Grass plants can support only a few individual consumer organisms and take time to recover from grazing pressure. The example above shows the numbers at each trophic level for a derelict grassland area (10 m²) in Michigan, United States.

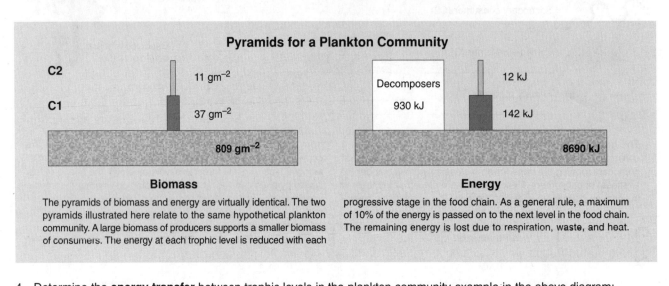

Pyramids for a Plankton Community

Biomass

Energy

The pyramids of biomass and energy are virtually identical. The two pyramids illustrated here relate to the same hypothetical plankton community. A large biomass of producers supports a smaller biomass of consumers. The energy at each trophic level is reduced with each progressive stage in the food chain. As a general rule, a maximum of 10% of the energy is passed on to the next level in the food chain. The remaining energy is lost due to respiration, waste, and heat.

4. Determine the **energy transfer** between trophic levels in the plankton community example in the above diagram:

(a) Between producers and the primary consumers: _____

(b) Between the primary consumers and the secondary consumers: _____

(c) Explain why the energy passed on from the producer to primary consumers is considerably less than the normally expected 10% occurring in most other communities (describe where the rest of the energy was lost to):

_____

_____

(d) After the producers, which trophic group has the greatest energy content: _____

(e) Give a likely explanation why this is the case: _____

_____

_____

An unusual biomass pyramid

The biomass pyramids of some ecosystems appear rather unusual with an inverted shape. The first trophic level has a lower biomass than the second level. What this pyramid does not show is the rate at which the producers (algae) are reproducing in order to support the larger biomass of consumers.

Zooplankton and bottom fauna 21 gm⁻²

Algae 4 gm⁻²

Biomass

5. Give a possible explanation of how a small biomass of producers (algae) can support a larger biomass of consumers (zooplankton):

_____

_____

_____

Sexual Reproduction

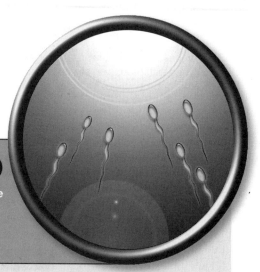

AQA-A	AQA-B	SNAB	Edexcel	OCR
Not applicalble to the AS course	Complete: 1-2, 4, 15	Complete: 1-2, 15	Complete: 1-19	Not applicalble to the AS course

Learning Objectives

☐ 1. Compile your own glossary from the **KEY WORDS** displayed in **bold type** in the learning objectives below.

Principles of Reproduction *(pages 374, 379-380)*

☐ 2. Explain the role of **meiosis** in **gamete formation**, identifying the significance of the reduction division. Explain how **fertilisation** (fusion of the gametes) restores the diploid chromosome number in the zygote.

☐ 3. Understand the behaviour of chromosomes during **meiosis I** and **meiosis II**. Include reference to the formation and significance of **chiasmata**.

☐ 4. Understand that haploid and diploid phases occur in the life cycles of organisms. Interpret **life cycles** of organisms in terms of **mitosis, meiosis, fertilisation,** and **chromosome number**.

Reproduction in Angiosperms *(pages 375-378)*

☐ 5. Using a diagram, identify and describe the structure and function of the principal parts of a typical (i.e. **monoecious**), **insect-pollinated** dicotyledonous **flower**, including: **calyx, corolla, stamens, carpel**.

☐ 6. Using a diagram, describe the structure and function of the principal parts of a typical **wind-pollinated** flower (e.g. a **grass**).

☐ 7. Using diagrams, describe **pollination** and the events leading to **fertilisation**. Include reference to the development of the pollen tube, the role of the **polar nuclei**, and the significance of the **double fertilisation**.

☐ 8. Describe adaptations for **wind pollination** and **insect pollination** and explain their significance.

☐ 9. Explain what is meant by **cross pollination** and explain its significance. Describe mechanisms in angiosperms for ensuring cross pollination: **protandry, protogyny,** and **dioecious flowers**.

Reproduction in Humans *(pages 381-392)*

☐ 10. Using a labelled diagram, identify and describe the structure and function of male and female reproductive systems in humans.

☐ 11. Describe the production of male and female gametes (**spermatogenesis** and **oogenesis**). Explain the role of **hormones** in **gametogenesis** in males and females.

☐ 12. Describe the main features of the human **menstrual cycle** including: the development of the ovarian **follicles** and **corpora lutea**, the cyclical changes to the **uterine endometrium**, and **menstruation**.

☐ 13. Relate the changes in the menstrual cycle to the changes in the hormones regulating the cycle: **progesterone, oestrogen,** follicle stimulating hormone (**FSH**), and luteinising hormone (**LH**).

☐ 14. Describe how male gametes are transferred to the female prior to fertilisation. Explain how fertilisation is dependent on the timing of gamete transfer.

☐ 15. Describe the importance of **fertilisation** and the specialisation of the gametes to their particular functions. If required, describe the events in fertilisation.

☐ 16. Outline the stages in the early development of the **zygote**: cleavage, **implantation**, and foetal growth. In more detail, describe the events in implantation and their significance.

☐ 17. Interpret a diagram of the uterus during **pregnancy**, identifying: **uterus, placenta, umbilical cord, embryonic membranes, amniotic fluid, foetus**.

☐ 18. Describe the structure and function of the **placenta**. Explain how the placenta is maintained during **pregnancy** and describe its functions in relation to the development of the embryo.

☐ 19. Describe the stages of **birth** (parturition) and explain the role of **oxytocin** in this process. Explain the role of **lactation** in the early nutrition of the young. Describe the roles of **prolactin** and **oxytocin** in lactation and explain how these hormones are regulated.

 See the 'Textbook Reference Grid' on pages 8-9 for textbook page references relating to material in this topic.

Supplementary Texts

See pages 5-7 for additional details of these texts:

■ Clegg, C.J., 1998. **Mammals: Structure and Function** (John Murray), pp. 78-86.

■ Murray, P. & N. Owens, 2001. **Behaviour and Populations** (Collins), pp. 28-61.

See page 7 for details of publishers of periodicals:

■ **The Biology of Milk** Biol. Sci. Rev., 16(3) Feb. 2004, pp. 2-6. *The production and composition of milk, its role in mammalian biology, and the physiological processes controlling its release.*

■ **Spermatogenesis** Biol. Sci. Rev., 15(4) April 2003, pp. 10-14. *The process and control of sperm production in humans.*

■ **The Placenta** Biol. Sci. Rev., 12 (4) March 2000, pp. 2-5. *The structure and function of the human placenta (includes prenatal diagnoses).*

See pages 10-11 for details of how to access **Bio Links** from our web site: **www.biozone.co.uk**. From Bio Links, access sites under the topics:

ANIMAL BIOLOGY: > Reproduction and Development: • Learn.co.uk: Reproduction • Menstrual cycle and pregnancy • Hormones of the reproductive system • Reproduction ... *and others*

PLANT BIOLOGY: > Reproduction: • Asexual reproduction biology: Pearson College • Flower structure • Flowers and reproduction

Meiosis

The process of **meiosis** is a special type of cell division concerned with producing sex cells (gametes) for the purpose of sexual reproduction. This cell division occurs in the sex organs of plants and animals. If genetic mistakes (**gene** and **chromosome mutations**) occur here, they will be passed on to the offspring (they will be inherited).

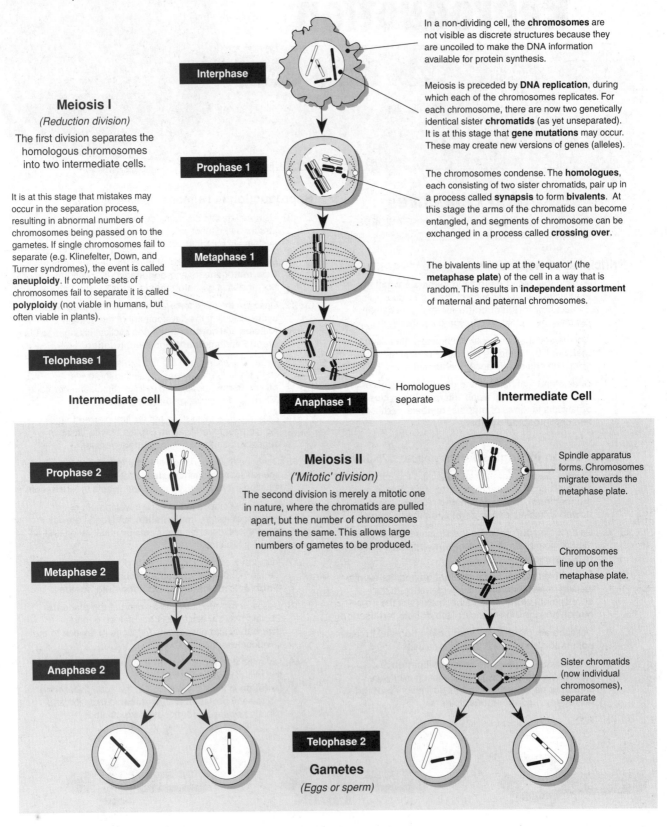

In a non-dividing cell, the **chromosomes** are not visible as discrete structures because they are uncoiled to make the DNA information available for protein synthesis.

Meiosis I
(Reduction division)

The first division separates the homologous chromosomes into two intermediate cells.

It is at this stage that mistakes may occur in the separation process, resulting in abnormal numbers of chromosomes being passed on to the gametes. If single chromosomes fail to separate (e.g. Klinefelter, Down, and Turner syndromes), the event is called **aneuploidy**. If complete sets of chromosomes fail to separate it is called **polyploidy** (not viable in humans, but often viable in plants).

Meiosis is preceded by **DNA replication**, during which each of the chromosomes replicates. For each chromosome, there are now two genetically identical sister **chromatids** (as yet unseparated). It is at this stage that **gene mutations** may occur. These may create new versions of genes (alleles).

The chromosomes condense. The **homologues**, each consisting of two sister chromatids, pair up in a process called **synapsis** to form **bivalents**. At this stage the arms of the chromatids can become entangled, and segments of chromosome can be exchanged in a process called **crossing over**.

The bivalents line up at the 'equator' (the **metaphase plate**) of the cell in a way that is random. This results in **independent assortment** of maternal and paternal chromosomes.

Interphase

Prophase 1

Metaphase 1

Telophase 1

Intermediate cell

Anaphase 1

Homologues separate

Intermediate Cell

Meiosis II
('Mitotic' division)

The second division is merely a mitotic one in nature, where the chromatids are pulled apart, but the number of chromosomes remains the same. This allows large numbers of gametes to be produced.

Prophase 2

Metaphase 2

Anaphase 2

Spindle apparatus forms. Chromosomes migrate towards the metaphase plate.

Chromosomes line up on the metaphase plate.

Sister chromatids (now individual chromosomes), separate

Telophase 2

Gametes
(Eggs or sperm)

1. Describe the behaviour of the chromosomes in the first division of meiosis: _____

   _____

2. Describe the behaviour of the chromosomes in the second division of meiosis: _____

   _____

Related activities: Angiosperm Reproduction, Animal Sexual Reproduction
Web links: Meiosis Tutorial

A 1

The Structure of Flowers

Flowering plants (**angiosperms**) are highly successful organisms. The egg cell is retained within the flower of the parent plant and the male gametes (contained in the **pollen**) must be transferred to it by **pollination** in order for fertilisation to occur. Most angiosperms are **monoecious**, with male and female parts on the same plant. Some of these plants will self-pollinate, but most have mechanisms that make this difficult or impossible. The female and male parts may be physically separated in the flower, or they may mature at different times (in **protandrous** plants the male matures first, whereas in **protogynous** plants the female matures first). **Dioecious plants** avoid this problem by carrying the male and female flowers on separate plants. Different methods of pollination (animal, wind, and water pollination) also help to ensure that **cross-pollination** occurs. Common animal pollinators include insects, bats, birds, and small reptiles. Animals are able to transfer pollen between plants very effectively and often over large distances, so much so that many plants have come to depend on only one or two animal pollinators.

Insect Pollinated Flowers

In most angiosperms the flower has both male and female parts. The flowers are temporary structures, often produced in large numbers. Those that are pollinated by insects typically offer an attraction such as nectar or edible flower parts and their pollen is relatively large and heavy. In general, each flower consists of a stem, bearing sepals, petals, stamens, and carpels. Such flowers may be able to self pollinate although there are often mechanisms to prevent this. In **dioecious** plants, the male and female flowers occur on separate plants and cross pollination is assured.

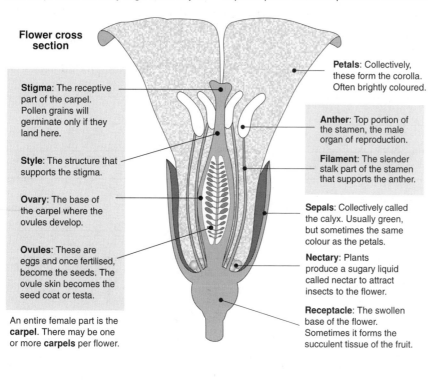

Flower cross section

Stigma: The receptive part of the carpel. Pollen grains will germinate only if they land here.

Style: The structure that supports the stigma.

Ovary: The base of the carpel where the ovules develop.

Ovules: These are eggs and once fertilised, become the seeds. The ovule skin becomes the seed coat or testa.

An entire female part is the **carpel**. There may be one or more **carpels** per flower.

Petals: Collectively, these form the corolla. Often brightly coloured.

Anther: Top portion of the stamen, the male organ of reproduction.

Filament: The slender stalk part of the stamen that supports the anther.

Sepals: Collectively called the calyx. Usually green, but sometimes the same colour as the petals.

Nectary: Plants produce a sugary liquid called nectar to attract insects to the flower.

Receptacle: The swollen base of the flower. Sometimes it forms the succulent tissue of the fruit.

Wind Pollinated Flowers

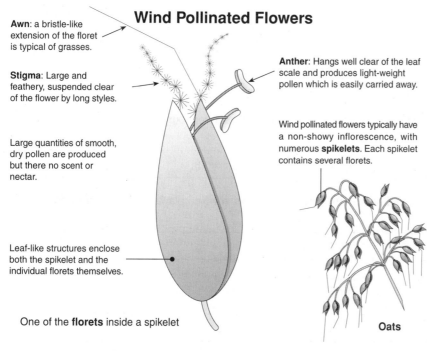

Awn: a bristle-like extension of the floret is typical of grasses.

Stigma: Large and feathery, suspended clear of the flower by long styles.

Large quantities of smooth, dry pollen are produced but there no scent or nectar.

Leaf-like structures enclose both the spikelet and the individual florets themselves.

One of the **florets** inside a spikelet

Anther: Hangs well clear of the leaf scale and produces light-weight pollen which is easily carried away.

Wind pollinated flowers typically have a non-showy inflorescence, with numerous **spikelets**. Each spikelet contains several florets.

Oats

Petals form 'guides' for insects that visit for nectar or pollen. In this way, wandering insects transfer pollen.

Stigma

Anther

Here, the stigma and anthers are separated to reduce self-pollination.

Pollen on bee leg

Pollen can be transported from flower to flower on the hairs of insects.

Most grasses are wind pollinated. The feathery appearance of their flowers is typical of wind pollinated plants.

Sexual Reproduction

Related activities: Angiosperm Reproduction, Pollination and Fertilisation

RA 2

1. Using the diagram on the previous page to help you, identify the parts of the flower labelled (a)-(g) on the diagram below:

Flower cross section

(a)

(b)

(c)

(d)

(e)

(f)

(g)

RCN

2. (a) Name the male structures on a flower: _____

   (b) Name the female structures on a flower: _____

3. Distinguish between **monoecious** and **dioecious** plants and explain how each type of plant avoids self pollination:

   _____

   _____

   _____

   _____

4. Describe two adaptations of insect pollinated flowers:

   (a) _____

   (b) _____

5. Describe two adaptations of wind pollinated flowers:

   (a) _____

   (b) _____

6. Describe one advantage and one cost to the plant of insect pollination:

   (a) Advantage: _____

   (b) Cost: _____

7. Describe two ways in which plants manage to attract animal pollinators:

   (a) _____ (b) _____

8. Contrast the efficiency of wind and animals as pollinating agents, giving a reason for your answer:

   _____

   _____

9. Describe the main the advantage of **cross pollination** and discuss the ways in which plants can ensure this occurs:

   _____

   _____

   _____

   _____

   _____

Angiosperm Reproduction

The primary method of reproduction for flowering plants is by seeds, which develop after fertilisation of the female parts of the flower. Seeds are an advantage to the plant because they contain the protected plant embryo with a store of food. The typical life cycle of a flowering plant (below) involves the formation of gametes (egg and sperm) from the haploid gametophytes, the fertilisation of the egg by a sperm cell to form the zygote, the production of fruit around the seed, and the germination of the seed and its growth by mitosis. The eggs and sperm are housed within the female and male gametophytes (embryo sac and pollen grain respectively). Each mature pollen grain contains two sperm nuclei and each mature embryo sac contains the egg and two polar nuclei. The leafy plant that bears the flowers represents the sporophyte generation of the life cycle.

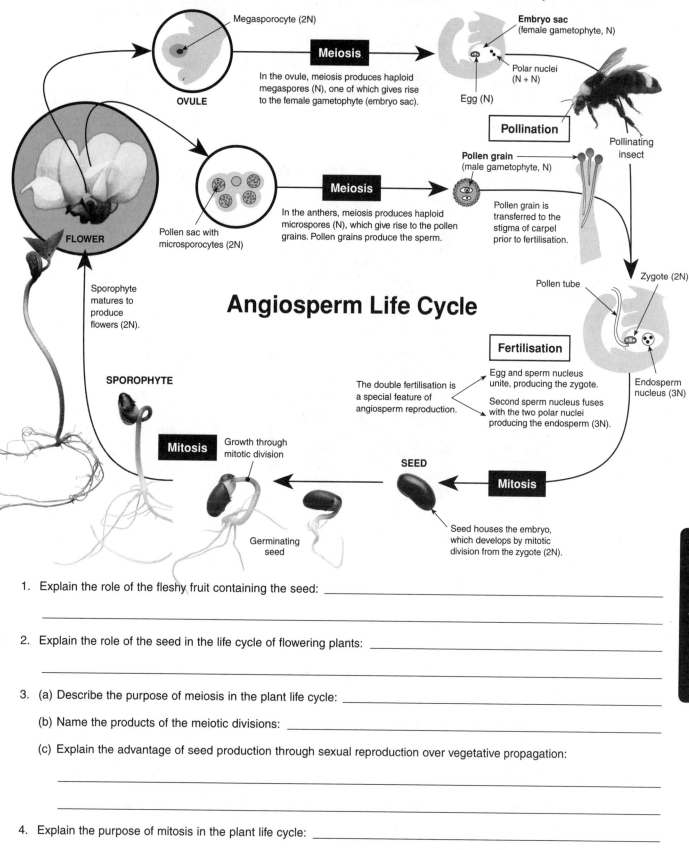

Angiosperm Life Cycle

Megasporocyte (2N)

Meiosis

In the ovule, meiosis produces haploid megaspores (N), one of which gives rise to the female gametophyte (embryo sac).

OVULE

Embryo sac (female gametophyte, N)

Polar nuclei (N + N)

Egg (N)

Pollination

Pollinating insect

FLOWER

Pollen sac with microsporocytes (2N)

Meiosis

In the anthers, meiosis produces haploid microspores (N), which give rise to the pollen grains. Pollen grains produce the sperm.

Pollen grain (male gametophyte, N)

Pollen grain is transferred to the stigma of carpel prior to fertilisation.

Sporophyte matures to produce flowers (2N).

Pollen tube

Zygote (2N)

Fertilisation

The double fertilisation is a special feature of angiosperm reproduction.

Egg and sperm nucleus unite, producing the zygote.

Second sperm nucleus fuses with the two polar nuclei producing the endosperm (3N).

Endosperm nucleus (3N)

SPOROPHYTE

Mitosis

Growth through mitotic division

SEED

Mitosis

Germinating seed

Seed houses the embryo, which develops by mitotic division from the zygote (2N).

1. Explain the role of the fleshy fruit containing the seed: _____

_____

2. Explain the role of the seed in the life cycle of flowering plants: _____

_____

3. (a) Describe the purpose of meiosis in the plant life cycle: _____

    (b) Name the products of the meiotic divisions: _____

    (c) Explain the advantage of seed production through sexual reproduction over vegetative propagation:

    _____

    _____

4. Explain the purpose of mitosis in the plant life cycle: _____

_____

Sexual Reproduction

Related activities: Pollination and Fertilisation
Web links: Life Cycle of an Angiosperm

A 2

Pollination and Fertilisation

Before the egg and sperm can fuse in fertilisation, the pollen (which contains the male gametes) must be transferred from the male anthers to the female stigma in **pollination**. Plants rarely self-pollinate, although they can be made to do so. Most often the stigma of one plant receives pollen from other plants in **cross-pollination**. After pollination, the sperm nuclei can enter the ovule and fertilisation can occur. In angiosperms, there is a double fertilisation: one to produce the embryo and the other to produce the endosperm nucleus. The endosperm nucleus gives rise to the endosperm, the food store for the embryonic plant.

Growth of the pollen tube and double fertilisation

Pollen grains are immature male gametophytes, formed by meiosis in the microspore mother cells within the pollen sac. Pollination is the actual transfer of the pollen from the stamens to the stigma. Pollen grains cannot move independently. They are usually carried by wind (**anemophily**) or animals (**entomophily**). After landing on the sticky stigma, the pollen grain is able to complete development, germinating and growing a pollen tube that extends down to the ovary. Directed by chemicals (usually calcium), the pollen tube enters the ovule through the micropyle, a small gap in the ovule. A **double fertilisation** takes place. One sperm nucleus fuses with the egg to form the zygote. A second sperm nucleus fuses with the two polar nuclei within the embryo sac to produce the endosperm tissue (3n). There are usually many ovules in an ovary, therefore many pollen grains (and fertilisations) are needed before the entire ovary can develop.

Different pollens are variable in shape and pattern, and genera can be easily distinguished on the basis of their distinctive pollen. This feature is exploited in the relatively new field of forensic botany; the tracing of a crime through botanical evidence. The species specific nature of pollen ensures that only genetically compatible plants will be fertilised. Some species, such as *Primula*, produce two pollen types, and this assists in cross pollination between different flower types.

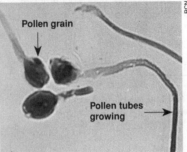
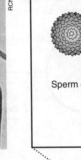

Germinating pollen grains

Pollen grain

Pollen tubes growing

Cell wall composed of extremely hard material called **sporopollenin**

Sperm cells

Tube nucleus

Pollen tube

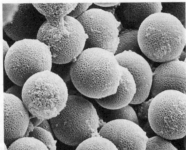

SEM: *Primula* (primrose) pollen

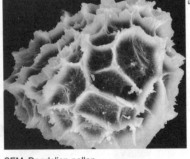

SEM: Dandelion pollen

Germinating pollen grain

Anther with pollen grains in pollen sacs

Pollen tube grows down to ovary guided by chemical cues

Stamen

Ovary wall

Ovule

Embryo sac

Polar nuclei

Egg

Micropyle

Two sperm nuclei

1. Distinguish clearly between **pollination** and **fertilisation**: _____

_____

_____

_____

2. Describe the role of the double fertilisation in angiosperm reproduction: _____

_____

3. Name the main chemical responsible for pollen tube growth: _____

4. Suggest a reason for the great variability seen in the structure of pollen grains: _____

_____

5. Pollen can be used as an indicator of past climates and vegetation. Give two reasons why pollen is well suited to this use:

(a) _____

(b) _____

Related activities: The Structure of Flowers, Angiosperm Reproduction
Web links: Seed Structure, Seed Dispersal

Animal Sexual Reproduction

All types of sexual reproduction involve the production of **gametes** (sex cells), produced by special sex organs called **gonads**. Female gametes (**eggs**) and male gametes (**sperm**) come together in **fertilisation**. Animal sexual reproduction follows one of three main patterns, determined by the location of fertilisation and embryonic development. These patterns are: external fertilisation and development; internal fertilisation followed by external development; internal fertilisation and development. **External fertilisation** is found in many aquatic invertebrates and most fish, where eggs and sperm are released into the surrounding water. Male and female parents usually release their gametes (spawn) at the same time and place in order to increase the chances of successful fertilisation. In other invertebrates, reptiles, sharks, birds, and mammals, sperm is transferred by **copulation**; sperm are transferred directly from the male to inside the female. This **internal fertilisation** increases the chance that the gametes will meet successfully. In birds and most reptiles, one adaptation to life on land has been the evolution of the **amniote egg**: a structure that enables the embryo to complete its development outside the parent surrounded by a protective shell and nourished by a yolk sac. The pattern of internal development in mammals provides the most advantages for the embryo in terms of nourishment and protection during development.

Achieving Fertilisation

Many marine invertebrates release gametes into the sea. Fertilisation and development are external to the parent. *Example: giant clam*

Insects often have elaborate courtship rituals. Fertilisation is internal, but the eggs are laid and develop externally. *Example: dipteran flies*

In amphibians, a prolonged coupling, called amplexus, precedes gamete release and external fertilisation. *Example: frogs*

In birds and reptiles gamete fertilisation is internal but the eggs are laid (usually in nests) and develop externally. *Example: quail*

Mammals exhibit internal fertilisation, a long period of internal development, and often prolonged parental care. *Example: African lions*

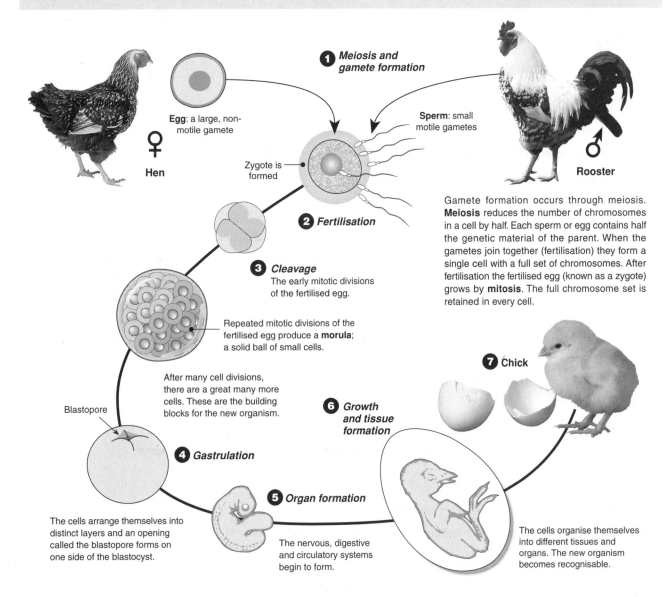

❶ *Meiosis and gamete formation*

Egg: a large, non-motile gamete ♀

Hen

Sperm: small motile gametes ♂

Rooster

Zygote is formed

❷ *Fertilisation*

❸ *Cleavage*
The early mitotic divisions of the fertilised egg.

Repeated mitotic divisions of the fertilised egg produce a **morula**; a solid ball of small cells.

After many cell divisions, there are a great many more cells. These are the building blocks for the new organism.

Blastopore

❹ *Gastrulation*

The cells arrange themselves into distinct layers and an opening called the blastopore forms on one side of the blastocyst.

❺ *Organ formation*

The nervous, digestive and circulatory systems begin to form.

❻ *Growth and tissue formation*

The cells organise themselves into different tissues and organs. The new organism becomes recognisable.

❼ Chick

Gamete formation occurs through meiosis. **Meiosis** reduces the number of chromosomes in a cell by half. Each sperm or egg contains half the genetic material of the parent. When the gametes join together (fertilisation) they form a single cell with a full set of chromosomes. After fertilisation the fertilised egg (known as a zygote) grows by **mitosis**. The full chromosome set is retained in every cell.

Sexual Reproduction

Related activities: Male Reproductive System, Female Reproductive System

A 2

Hermaphroditism

Most animals have separate sexes (individuals are either male or female). However, in some animals both sperm and eggs can be produced in the same individual. Such animals are known as **hermaphrodites**. In earthworms (below), flatworms, and some molluscs (e.g. land snails), both male and female organs are active in the same animal and there is typically a reciprocal transfer of sperm (each receives sperm from the other during copulation). In this type of hermaphroditism, there is no self-fertilisation: a mate is necessary for any fertilisation to occur. However, some specialised hermaphroditic animals, such as parasitic tapeworms, are capable of self-fertilisation.

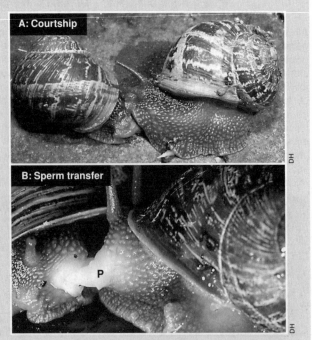

A: Courtship

B: Sperm transfer

Courtship and mating in the snail *Cantareus aspersus* (formerly *Helix aspersa*, above). During an elaborate courtship (A), calcareous darts are fired from the genital opening (behind the tentacle) into the body of the partner. Mating (B) involves reciprocal transfer of sperm via a penis (P).

White patches are sperm being exchanged

The photo above shows two earthworms in a mating clasp. Each worm places its reproductive region (the clitellum) against the reproductive region of the other worm, and sperm are exchanged.

1. Describe one advantage of sexual reproduction: _____

_____

2. Describe one potential disadvantage of sexual reproduction: _____

_____

3. Compare and contrast the key differences between male and female gametes in relation to:

   (a) The size of gametes: _____

   (b) Number of gametes produced: _____

   (c) Motility of gametes: _____

4. Distinguish between **internal** fertilisation and **external fertilisation**, identifying advantages of each strategy:

_____

_____

_____

_____

5. (a) Name an animal group with internal fertilisation but external development: _____

   (b) Name an animal group with internal fertilisation and internal development: _____

   (c) Describe one benefit and one cost involved in providing for internal development of an embryo:

   Benefit: _____

   Cost: _____

6. Explain why each new individual produced from the fusion of the two gametes is unique: _____

_____

_____

Male Reproductive System

The reproductive role of the male is to produce the sperm and deliver them to the female. When a sperm combines with an egg, it contributes half the genetic material of the offspring and, in humans and other mammals, determines its sex. The reproductive structures in human males (shown below) are in many ways typical of other mammals.

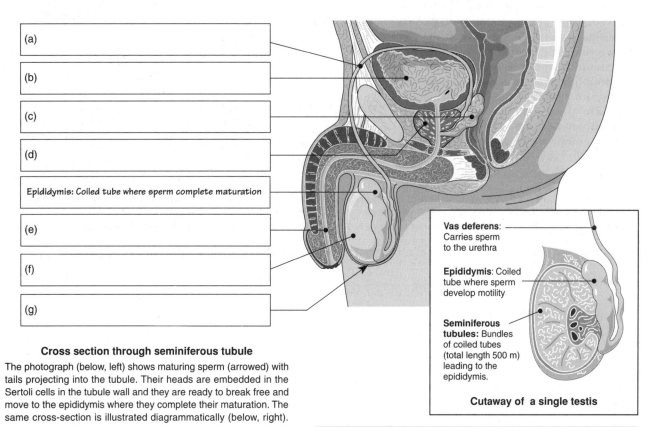

(a)

(b)

(c)

(d)

Epididymis: Coiled tube where sperm complete maturation

(e)

(f)

(g)

Vas deferens: Carries sperm to the urethra

Epididymis: Coiled tube where sperm develop motility

Seminiferous tubules: Bundles of coiled tubes (total length 500 m) leading to the epididymis.

Cutaway of a single testis

Cross section through seminiferous tubule

The photograph (below, left) shows maturing sperm (arrowed) with tails projecting into the tubule. Their heads are embedded in the Sertoli cells in the tubule wall and they are ready to break free and move to the epididymis where they complete their maturation. The same cross-section is illustrated diagrammatically (below, right).

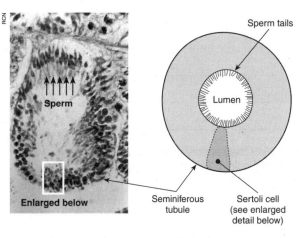

Sperm

Enlarged below

Sperm tails

Lumen

Seminiferous tubule

Sertoli cell (see enlarged detail below)

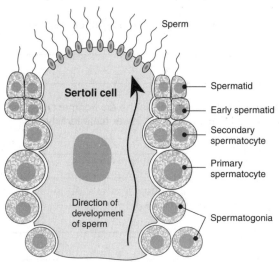

Sperm

Sertoli cell

Direction of development of sperm

Spermatid

Early spermatid

Secondary spermatocyte

Primary spermatocyte

Spermatogonia

Spermatogenesis

Spermatogenesis is the process by which mature spermatozoa (sperm) are produced in the testis. In humans, they are produced at the rate of about 120 million per day. Spermatogenesis is regulated by the hormones **FSH** (from the anterior pituitary) and testosterone (secreted from the testes in response to **ICSH** (LH) from the anterior pituitary). Spermatogonia, in the outer layer of the seminiferous tubules, multiply throughout reproductive life. Some of them divide by meiosis into spermatocytes, which produce spermatids. These are transformed into mature sperm by the process of spermiogenesis in the seminiferous tubules of the testis. Full sperm motility is achieved in the epididymis.

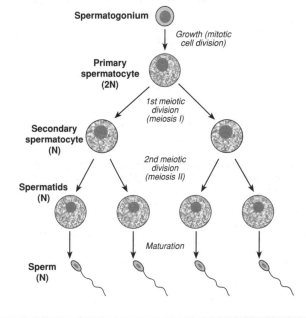

Spermatogonium

Growth (mitotic cell division)

Primary spermatocyte (2N)

1st meiotic division (meiosis I)

Secondary spermatocyte (N)

2nd meiotic division (meiosis II)

Spermatids (N)

Maturation

Sperm (N)

Sexual Reproduction

Related activities: Meiosis

RA 3

Sperm Structure

Mature spermatozoa (sperm) are produced by a process called spermatogenesis in the testes (see description of the process on the previous page). Meiotic division of spermatocytes produces spermatids which then differentiate into mature sperm. Sperm are quite simple in structure; their purpose is to swim to the egg and donate their genetic material. They are composed of three regions: headpiece, midpiece, and tail. Sperm do not live long (only about 48 hours), but they swim quickly and there are so many of them (millions per ejaculation) that some are able to reach the egg to fertilise it.

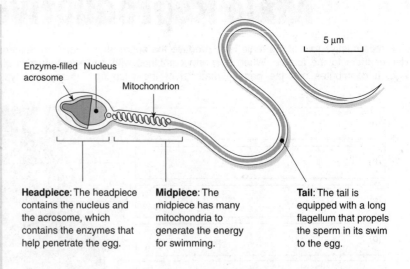

Enzyme-filled acrosome Nucleus Mitochondrion 5 µm

Headpiece: The headpiece contains the nucleus and the acrosome, which contains the enzymes that help penetrate the egg.

Midpiece: The midpiece has many mitochondria to generate the energy for swimming.

Tail: The tail is equipped with a long flagellum that propels the sperm in its swim to the egg.

1. The male human reproductive system and associated structures are shown on the previous page. Using the following word list identify the labelled parts (write your answers in the spaces provided on the diagram).
   Word list: *bladder, scrotal sac, sperm duct (vas deferens), seminal vesicle, testis, urethra, prostate gland*

2. In a short sentence, state the function of each of the structures labelled (a)-(g) in the diagram on the previous page:

   (a) _____

   (b) _____

   (c) _____

   (d) _____

   (e) _____

   (f) _____

   (g) _____

3. (a) Identify the process by which mature sperm are formed: _____

   (b) Identify the hormones regulating this process: _____

   (c) State where most of this process occurs: _____

   (d) State where the process is completed: _____

4. The secretions of the prostate gland (which make up a large proportion of the seminal fluid produced in an ejaculation) are of alkaline pH, while the secretions of the vagina are normally slightly acidic. With this information, explain the role the prostate gland secretions have in maintaining the viability of sperm deposited in the vagina.

   _____

   _____

5. Each ejaculation of a healthy, fertile male contains 100-400 million sperm. Suggest why so many sperm are needed:

   _____

   _____

6. Recently, concern has been expressed about the level of synthetic oestrogen-like chemicals in the environment. Explain the reason for this concern and discuss evidence in support of the claim that these chemicals lower male fertility:

   _____

   _____

   _____

   _____

Female Reproductive System

The female reproductive system in mammals produces eggs, receives the penis and sperm during sexual intercourse, and houses and nourishes the young. Female reproductive systems in mammals are similar in their basic structure (uterus, ovaries etc.) but the shape of the uterus and the form of the placenta during pregnancy vary. The human system is described below.

Oogenesis

Oogenesis is the process by which mature ova (egg cells) are produced by the ovary. Oogonia are formed in the female embryo and undergo repeated mitotic divisions to form the primary oocyte. These remain in prophase of meiosis I throughout childhood. At this stage, all the eggs a female will ever have are present, but they remain in this resting phase until puberty. At puberty, meiosis resumes. Eggs are released, arrested in metaphase of meiosis II. This second division is only completed upon fertilisation.

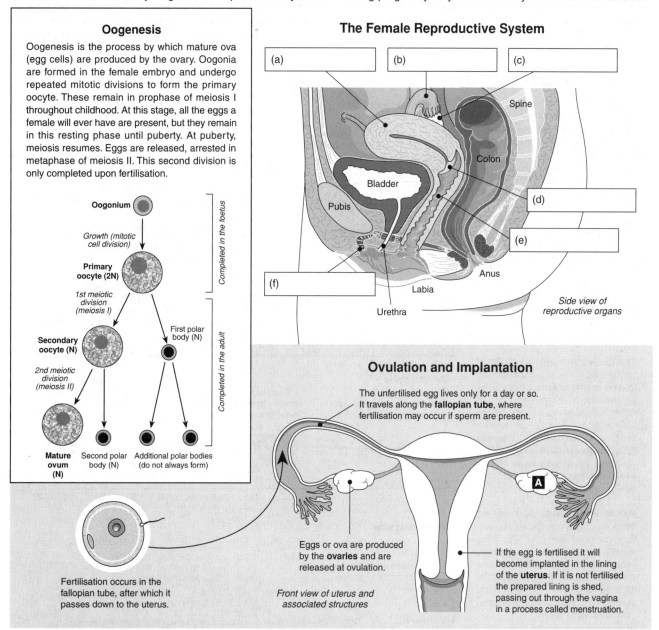

The Female Reproductive System

Side view of reproductive organs

Ovulation and Implantation

The unfertilised egg lives only for a day or so. It travels along the **fallopian tube**, where fertilisation may occur if sperm are present.

Fertilisation occurs in the fallopian tube, after which it passes down to the uterus.

Eggs or ova are produced by the **ovaries** and are released at ovulation.

Front view of uterus and associated structures

If the egg is fertilised it will become implanted in the lining of the **uterus**. If it is not fertilised the prepared lining is shed, passing out through the vagina in a process called menstruation.

1. The female human reproductive system and associated structures are illustrated above. Using the word list, identify the labelled parts. **Word list**: *ovary, uterus (womb), vagina, fallopian tube (oviduct), cervix, clitoris*.

2. In a few words or a short sentence, state the function of each of the structures labelled (a) - (d) in the above diagram:

   (a) _____

   (b) _____

   (c) _____

   (d) _____

3. (a) Name the organ labelled (**A**) in the diagram: _____

   (b) Name the event associated with this organ that occurs every month: _____

   (c) Name the process by which mature ova are produced: _____

4. (a) Name the stage in meiosis at which the oocyte is released from the ovary: _____

   (b) State when in the reproductive process meiosis II is completed: _____

Related activities: Meiosis, The Menstrual Cycle   **RA 2**

Sexual Reproduction

The Menstrual Cycle

In non-primate mammals the reproductive cycle is characterised by a **breeding season** and an **oestrous cycle** (a period of greater sexual receptivity during which ovulation occurs). In contrast, humans and other primates are sexually receptive throughout the year and may mate at any time. Like all placental mammals, their uterine lining thickens in preparation for pregnancy. However, unlike other mammals, primates shed this lining as a discharge through the vagina if fertilisation does not occur. This event, called **menstruation**, characterises the human reproductive or **menstrual cycle**. In human females, the menstrual cycle starts from the first day of bleeding and lasts for about 28 days. It involves a predictable series of changes that occur in response to hormones. The cycle is divided into three phases (see below), defined by the events in each phase.

The Menstrual Cycle

Luteinising hormone (LH) and follicle stimulating hormone (FSH): These hormones from the anterior pituitary have numerous effects. FSH stimulates the development of the ovarian follicles resulting in the release of oestrogen. Oestrogen levels peak, stimulating a surge in LH and triggering ovulation.

Hormone levels: Of the follicles that begin developing in response to FSH, usually only one (the Graafian follicle) becomes dominant. In the first half of the cycle, oestrogen is secreted by this developing Graafian follicle. Later, the Graafian follicle develops into the corpus luteum (below right) which secretes large amounts of progesterone (and smaller amounts of oestrogen).

The corpus luteum: The Graafian follicle continues to grow and then (around day 14) ruptures to release the egg (ovulation). LH causes the ruptured follicle to develop into a corpus luteum (yellow body). The corpus luteum secretes progesterone which promotes full development of the uterine lining, maintains the embryo in the first 12 weeks of pregnancy, and inhibits the development of more follicles.

Menstruation: If fertilisation does not occur, the corpus luteum breaks down. Progesterone secretion declines, causing the uterine lining to be shed (menstruation). If fertilisation occurs, high progesterone levels maintain the thickened uterine lining. The placenta develops and nourishes the embryo completely by 12 weeks.

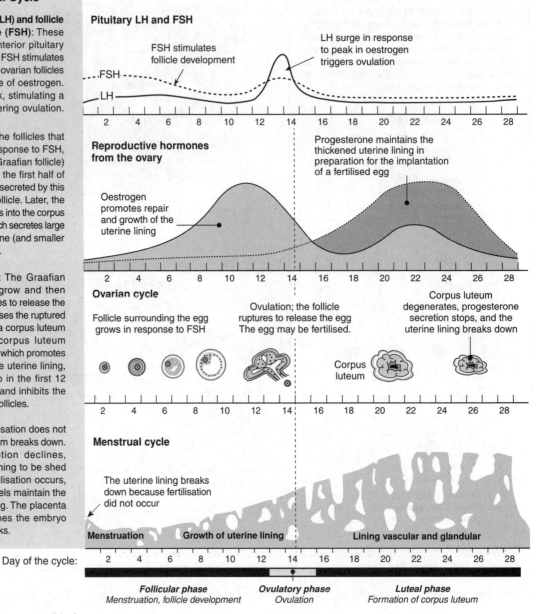

Day of the cycle:

Follicular phase
Menstruation, follicle development

Ovulatory phase
Ovulation

Luteal phase
Formation of corpus luteum

1. Name the hormone responsible for:

   (a) Follicle growth: _____ (b) Ovulation: _____

2. Each month, several ovarian follicles begin development, but only one (the Graafian follicle) develops fully:

   (a) Name the hormone secreted by the developing follicle: _____

   (b) State the role of this hormone during the follicular phase: _____

   (c) Suggest what happens to the follicles that do not continue developing: _____

3. (a) Identify the principal hormone secreted by the corpus luteum: _____

   (b) State the purpose of this hormone: _____

4. State the hormonal trigger for menstruation: _____

Related activities: Control of the Menstrual Cycle
Web links: The Menstrual Cycle Animation

Control of the Menstrual Cycle

The female menstrual cycle is regulated by the interplay of several reproductive hormones. The main control centres for this regulation are the **hypothalamus** and the **anterior pituitary gland**. The hypothalamus secretes GnRH (gonadotrophin releasing hormone), a hormone that is essential for normal gonad function in males and females. GnRH is transported in blood vessels to the anterior pituitary where it brings about the release of two hormones: follicle stimulating hormone (FSH) and luteinising hormone (LH). It is these two hormones that induce the cyclical changes in the ovary and uterus. Regulation of blood hormone levels during the menstrual cycle is achieved through **negative feedback** mechanisms. The exception to this is the mid cycle surge in LH (see previous page) which is induced by the rapid increase in oestrogen secreted by the developing follicle.

Control of the Menstrual Cycle

FSH/LH secretion occurs in response to a hormone signal from the hypothalamus

Key
+ → Stimulation
− ⇢ Inhibition

Hypothalamus
GnRH

Anterior pituitary gland

Oestrogen inhibits FSH secretion (negative feedback)

Progesterone inhibits LH and FSH secretion (negative feedback)

FSH   **LH**

Developing Graafian follicle secretes **oestrogen**

Ovulation/development of corpus luteum which secretes **progesterone**

Oestrogen   **Progesterone**

Repair and growth of the uterine lining

Thickening and maintenance of the uterine lining

GnRH   GnRH

Oestrogen   Progesterone

FSH   LH

Oestrogen   Progesterone

Follicular phase
(First half of the cycle)

Ovulation and luteal phase
(Second half of cycle)

The diagrams above and left summarise the main hormonal controls during the two halves of the menstrual cycle. In the first half of the cycle, FSH stimulates follicle development in the ovary. The developing follicle secretes oestrogen which acts on the uterus and, in the anterior pituitary, inhibits FSH secretion. In the second half of the cycle, LH induces ovulation and development of the corpus luteum. The corpus luteum secretes progesterone which acts on the uterus and also inhibits further secretion of LH (and also FSH).

1. Using the information above and on the previous page, complete the table below summarising the role of hormones in the control of the menstrual cycle. To help you, some of the table has been completed:

Hormone	Site of secretion	Main effects and site of action during the menstrual cycle
GnRH		
		Stimulates the growth of ovarian follicles
LH		
		At high level, stimulates LH surge. Promotes growth and repair of the uterine lining.
Progesterone		

2. Briefly explain the role of negative feedback in the control of hormone levels in the menstrual cycle:

_____

_____

3. **FSH** and **LH** (called ICSH or interstitial cell stimulating hormone in males) also play a central role in male reproduction. Refer to the activity *Male Reproductive System* and state how these two hormones are involved **in male reproduction**:

_____

Sexual Reproduction

Related activities: The Menstrual Cycle, Male Reproductive System
Web links: Contraception, Treating Female Infertility

RA 2

The Placenta

As soon as an embryo embeds in the uterine wall it begins to obtain nutrients from its mother and increase in size. At two months, when the major structures of the adult are established, it is called a foetus. It is entirely dependent on its mother for nutrients, oxygen, and elimination of wastes. The placenta is the specialised organ that performs this role, enabling exchange between foetal and maternal tissues, and allowing a prolonged period of foetal growth and development within the protection of the uterus. The placenta also has an endocrine role, producing hormones that enable the pregnancy to be maintained.

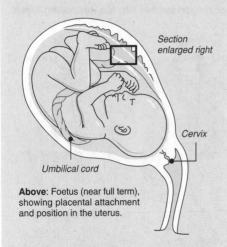

Above: Foetus (near full term), showing placental attachment and position in the uterus.

Below: Photograph shows a 14 week old foetus. Limbs are fully formed, many bones are beginning to ossify, and joints begin to form. Facial features are becoming more fully formed.

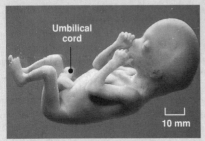

Umbilical cord

10 mm

Schematic diagram showing part of the placenta in section

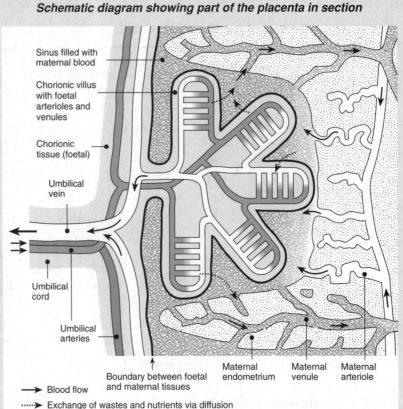

Sinus filled with maternal blood

Chorionic villus with foetal arterioles and venules

Chorionic tissue (foetal)

Umbilical vein

Umbilical cord

Umbilical arteries

Boundary between foetal and maternal tissues

Maternal endometrium

Maternal venule

Maternal arteriole

→ Blood flow

·····➤ Exchange of wastes and nutrients via diffusion

The placenta is a disc-like organ, about the size of a dinner plate and weighing about 1 kg. It develops when fingerlike projections of the foetal chorion (the chorionic villi) grow into the endometrium of the uterus. The villi contain the numerous capillaries connecting the foetal arteries and vein. They continue invading the maternal tissue until they are bathed in the maternal blood sinuses. The maternal and foetal blood vessels are in such close proximity that oxygen and nutrients can diffuse from the maternal blood into the capillaries of the villi. From the villi, the nutrients circulate in the umbilical vein, returning to the foetal heart. Carbon dioxide and other wastes leave the foetus through the umbilical arteries, pass into the capillaries of the villi, and diffuse into the maternal blood. Note that foetal blood and maternal blood do not mix: the exchanges occur via diffusion through thin walled capillaries.

1. In simple terms, explain the basic structure of the human placenta: _____

_____

_____

_____

2. The umbilical cord contains the foetal arteries and vein. Describe the status of the blood in each type of foetal vessel:

   (a) Foetal arteries: Oxygenated and containing nutrients / Deoxygenated and containing nitrogenous wastes (delete one)

   (b) Foetal vein: Oxygenated and containing nutrients / Deoxygenated and containing nitrogenous wastes (delete one)

3. Teratogens are substances that may cause malformations in embryonic development (e.g. nicotine, alcohol):

   (a) Give a general explanation why substances ingested by the mother have the potential to be harmful to the foetus:

   _____

   (b) Explain why cigarette smoking is so harmful to foetal development: _____

   _____

Related activities: Fertilisation and Early Growth

Fertilisation and Early Growth

When an egg cell is released from the ovary it is arrested in metaphase of meiosis II and is termed a secondary oocyte. **Fertilisation** occurs when a sperm penetrates an egg cell at this stage and the sperm and egg nuclei unite to form the zygote. Fertilisation is always regarded as time 0 in a period of gestation (pregnancy) and has five distinct stages (below). After fertilisation, the zygote begins its **development**, i.e. its growth and differentiation into a multicellular organism (see next page).

Fertilisation (Time 0)

The stages in fertilisation are represented below in a numbered sequence (1-5)

1. Capacitation

The surface of the sperm cell undergoes changes that are essential to enabling the acrosome reaction and sperm entry.

2. The Acrosome Reaction

Enzymes from the acrosome (an enzyme-filled bag at the tip of the sperm) are released and digest a pathway through the follicle cells (not shown) and the jelly-like zona pellucida surrounding the egg cell (secondary oocyte).

3. Fusion of Sperm Head

The plasma membranes of the sperm and egg fuse, and the nucleus of the sperm enters the egg cytoplasm. Fusion causes a sudden membrane depolarisation that acts as a "fast block" to further sperm entry. The fusion of the two plasma membranes also triggers the completion of meiosis II in the egg cell and induces the cortical reaction (below).

4. The Cortical Reaction

The fusion of the two plasma membranes induces a permanent change in the egg surface that prevents further sperm entry. Cortical granules in the egg cytoplasm release their contents into the space between the plasma membrane and the vitelline layer. Substances released from the granules raise and harden the vitelline layer to form a slow (permanent) block to further sperm entry.

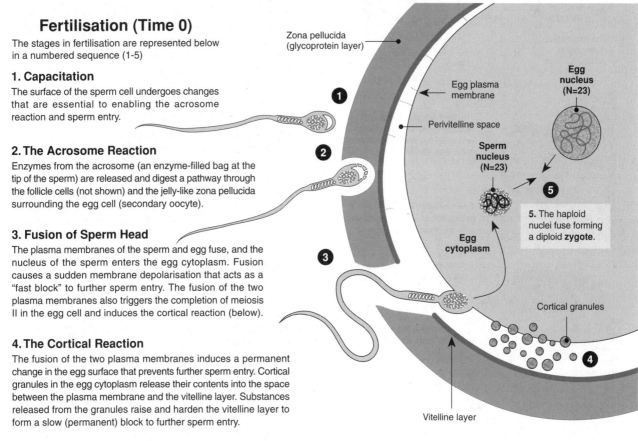

5. The haploid nuclei fuse forming a diploid **zygote**.

1. Briefly describe the significant events (and their importance) occurring at each of the following stages of fertilisation:

    (a) Capacitation: _____

    _____

    (b) The acrosome reaction: _____

    _____

    (c) Fusion of egg and sperm plasma membranes: _____

    _____

    (d) The cortical reaction: _____

    _____

    (e) Fusion of egg and sperm nuclei: _____

    _____

2. Explain the significance of the blocks that prevent entry of more than one sperm into the egg (polyspermy):

    _____

    _____

3. (a) Explain why the egg cell, when released from the ovary, is termed a secondary oocyte: _____

    _____

    (b) State at which stage its meiotic division is completed: _____

Related activities: Female Reproductive System, Male Reproductive System, Meiosis   **Web links**: Fertilisation

A 2

Sexual Reproduction

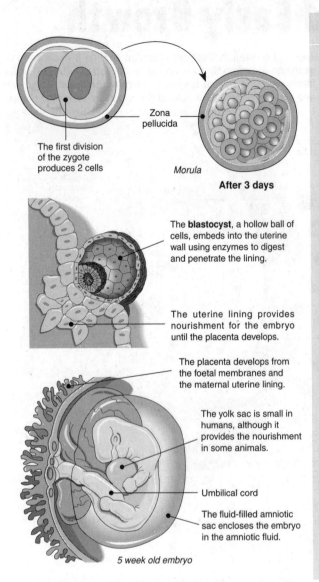

Zona
pellucida

The first division
of the zygote
produces 2 cells

Morula

After 3 days

The **blastocyst**, a hollow ball of
cells, embeds into the uterine
wall using enzymes to digest
and penetrate the lining.

The uterine lining provides
nourishment for the embryo
until the placenta develops.

The placenta develops from
the foetal membranes and
the maternal uterine lining.

The yolk sac is small in
humans, although it
provides the nourishment
in some animals.

Umbilical cord

The fluid-filled amniotic
sac encloses the embryo
in the amniotic fluid.

5 week old embryo

Early Growth and Development

Cleavage and the development of the morula

Immediately after fertilisation, rapid cell division takes place.
These early cell divisions are called **cleavage** and they increase
the number of cells, but not the size of the zygote. The first
cleavage is completed after 36 hours, and each succeeding
division takes less time. After 3 days, successive cleavages have
produced a solid mass of cells called the **morula**, (left) which is
still about the same size as the original zygote.

Implantation of the blastocyst (after 6-8 days)

After several days in the uterus, the morula develops into the
blastocyst. It makes contact with the uterine lining and pushes
deeply into it, ensuring a close maternal-foetal contact. Blood
vessels provide early nourishment as they are opened up by
enzymes secreted by the blastocyst. The embryo produces **HCG**
(human chorionic gonadotropin), which prevents degeneration
of the corpus luteum and signals that the woman is pregnant.

The embryo at 5-8 weeks

Five weeks after fertilisation, the embryo is only 4-5 mm long,
but already the central nervous system has developed and the
heart is beating. The embryonic membranes have formed; the
amnion encloses the embryo in a fluid-filled space, and the allanto-
chorion forms the foetal portion of the placenta. From two months
the embryo is called a foetus. It is still small (30-40 mm long), but
the limbs are well formed and the bones are beginning to harden.
The face has a flat, rather featureless appearance with the eyes
far apart. Foetal movements have begun and brain development
proceeds rapidly. The placenta is well developed, although not
fully functional until 12 weeks. The umbilical cord, containing the
foetal umbilical arteries and vein, connects foetus and mother.

4. State what contribution the sperm and egg cell make to each of the following:

   (a) The nucleus of the zygote: Sperm contribution: _____   Egg contribution: _____

   (b) The cytoplasm of the zygote: Sperm contribution: _____   Egg contribution: _____

5. Explain what is meant by cleavage and comment on its significance to the early development of the embryo:

   _____

   _____

6. (a) Explain the importance of implantation to the early nourishment of the embryo: _____

   _____

   (b) Identify the foetal tissues that contribute to the formation of the placenta: _____

   (c) Suggest a purpose of the amniotic sac and comment on its importance to the developing embryo: _____

   _____

   (d) Suggest why the heart is one of the very first structures to develop in the embryo: _____

   _____

7. State why the foetus is particularly prone to damage from drugs towards the end of the first trimester (2-3 months):

   _____

   _____

The Hormones of Pregnancy

Human reproductive physiology occurs in a cycle (the menstrual cycle) which follows a set pattern and is regulated by the interplay of several hormones. Control of hormone release is brought about through feedback mechanisms: the levels of the female reproductive hormones, oestrogen and progesterone, regulate the secretion of the pituitary hormones that control the ovarian cycle (see earlier pages). Pregnancy interrupts this cycle and maintains the corpus luteum and the placenta as endocrine organs with the specific role of maintaining the developing foetus for the period of its development. During the last month of pregnancy the peptide hormone oxytocin induces the uterine contraction that will expel the baby from the uterus.

Hormonal Changes During Pregnancy, Birth, and Lactation

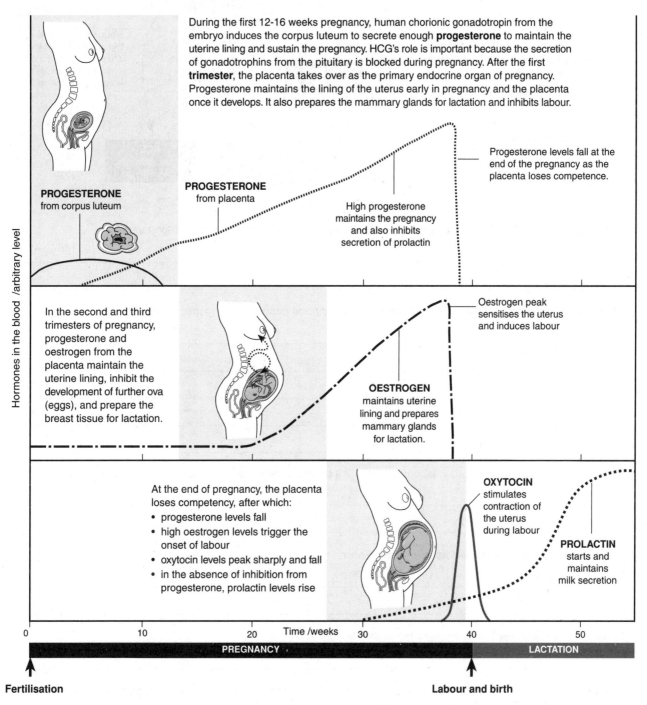

During the first 12-16 weeks pregnancy, human chorionic gonadotropin from the embryo induces the corpus luteum to secrete enough **progesterone** to maintain the uterine lining and sustain the pregnancy. HCG's role is important because the secretion of gonadotrophins from the pituitary is blocked during pregnancy. After the first **trimester**, the placenta takes over as the primary endocrine organ of pregnancy. Progesterone maintains the lining of the uterus early in pregnancy and the placenta once it develops. It also prepares the mammary glands for lactation and inhibits labour.

PROGESTERONE from corpus luteum

PROGESTERONE from placenta

High progesterone maintains the pregnancy and also inhibits secretion of prolactin

Progesterone levels fall at the end of the pregnancy as the placenta loses competence.

In the second and third trimesters of pregnancy, progesterone and oestrogen from the placenta maintain the uterine lining, inhibit the development of further ova (eggs), and prepare the breast tissue for lactation.

OESTROGEN maintains uterine lining and prepares mammary glands for lactation.

Oestrogen peak sensitises the uterus and induces labour

At the end of pregnancy, the placenta loses competency, after which:
• progesterone levels fall
• high oestrogen levels trigger the onset of labour
• oxytocin levels peak sharply and fall
• in the absence of inhibition from progesterone, prolactin levels rise

OXYTOCIN stimulates contraction of the uterus during labour

PROLACTIN starts and maintains milk secretion

Hormones in the blood /arbitrary level

Time /weeks

0   10   20   30   40   50

PREGNANCY   LACTATION

↑ Fertilisation

↑ Labour and birth

Sexual Reproduction

1. (a) Explain why the corpus luteum is the main source of progesterone in early pregnancy: _____

_____

_____

(b) Explain how progesterone secretion from the corpus luteum is maintained: _____

_____

Related activities: The Menstrual Cycle, Control of the Menstrual Cycle, Birth and Lactation

RA 2

Hormones in Pregnancy

HCG (Human chorionic gonadotrophin)
- Secreted first by the developing embryo and later by the placenta
- Maintains the corpus luteum (1st trimester)

Progesterone
- Maintains endometrium
- Inhibits uterine contraction
- Maintains endometrium

Oestrogens
- Maintain endometrium
- Prepare mammary glands for lactation
- Very high levels increase the sensitivity of the uterus to oxytocin

Human placental lactogen (HPL)
- Stimulates breast growth and development

Relaxin
- Produced by the placenta towards the end of the pregnancy
- Relaxes pubic symphysis at birth
- Helps dilate cervix at birth

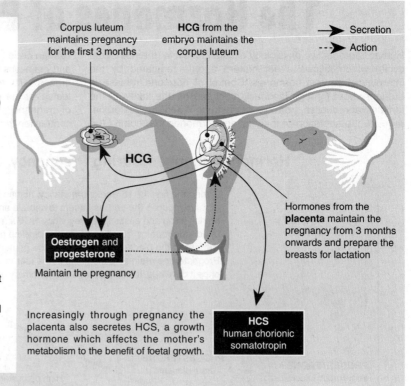

Corpus luteum maintains pregnancy for the first 3 months

HCG from the embryo maintains the corpus luteum

→ Secretion
--→ Action

HCG

Oestrogen and **progesterone**

Maintain the pregnancy

Hormones from the **placenta** maintain the pregnancy from 3 months onwards and prepare the breasts for lactation

Increasingly through pregnancy the placenta also secretes HCS, a growth hormone which affects the mother's metabolism to the benefit of foetal growth.

HCS human chorionic somatotropin

2. Explain why secretion of pituitary gonadotrophins (FSH and LH) is suppressed during pregnancy:

_____

_____

3. Identify two hormones responsible for maintaining pregnancy and describe their respective roles:

(a) _____

_____

(b) _____

_____

_____

4. (a) Identify two hormones involved in labour (onset of the birth process) and describe their role in the process:

_____

_____

(b) Describe two physiological factors in initiating labour: _____

_____

_____

5. Explain why prolactin secretion increases markedly after birth: _____

_____

6. Use your answers from the preceding questions to discuss how pregnancy represents an interruption of the menstrual cycle that is maintained and then ended by a complex interplay of hormones.

_____

_____

_____

_____

_____

Birth and Lactation

A human pregnancy (the period of **gestation**) lasts, on average, about 38 weeks after fertilisation. It ends in labour, the birth of the baby, and expulsion of the placenta. During pregnancy, progesterone maintains the placenta and inhibits contraction of the uterus. At the end of a pregnancy, increasing oestrogen levels overcome the influence of progesterone and labour begins. Prostaglandins, factors released from the placenta, and the physiological state of the baby itself are also involved in triggering the actual timing of labour onset. Labour itself comprises three stages (below), and ends with the delivery of the placenta. After birth, the mother provides nutrition for the infant through **lactation**: the production and release of milk from mammary glands. Breast milk provides infants with a complete, easily digested food for the first 4-6 months of life. All breast milk contains maternal antibodies, which give the infant protection against infection while its own immune system develops.

Birth and the Stages of Labour

Stage 1: Dilation

Duration: 2-20 hours

The time between the onset of labour and complete opening (dilation) of the cervix. The amniotic sac may rupture at this stage, releasing its fluid. The hormone **oxytocin** stimulates the uterine contractions necessary to dilate the cervix and expel the baby. It is these uterine contractions that give the pain of labour, most of which is associated with this first stage.

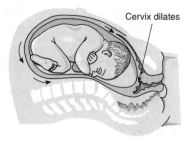
Cervix dilates

Stage 2: Expulsion

Duration: 2-100 minutes

The time from full dilation of the cervix to delivery. Strong, rhythmic contractions of the uterus pass in waves (arrows), and push the baby to the end of the vagina, where the head appears.

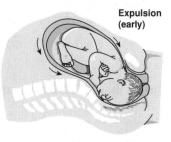
Expulsion (early)

As labour progresses, the time between each contraction shortens. Once the head is delivered, the rest of the body usually follows very rapidly. Delivery completes stage 2.

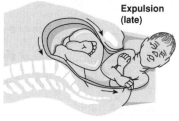
Expulsion (late)

Stage 3: Delivery of placenta

Time: 5-45 minutes after delivery

The third or **placental stage**, refers to the expulsion of the placenta from the uterus. After the placenta is delivered, the placental blood vessels constrict to stop bleeding.

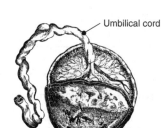
Umbilical cord

Placenta

Delivery of the baby: the end of stage 2

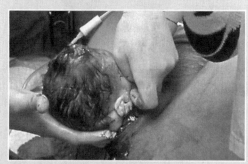
Delivery of the head. This baby is face forward. The more usual position for delivery is face to the back of the mother.

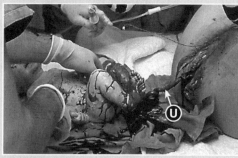
Full delivery of the baby. Note the umbilical cord (U), which supplies oxygen until the baby's breathing begins.

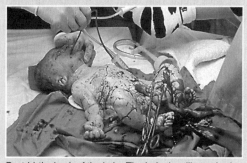
Post-birth check of the baby. The baby is still attached to the placenta and the airways are being cleared of mucus.

Sexual Reproduction

1. Name the three stages of birth, and briefly state the main events occurring in each stage:

    (a) Stage 1: _____

    (b) Stage 2: _____

    (c) Stage 3: _____

2. (a) Name the hormone responsible for triggering the **onset** of labour: _____

    (b) Describe two other factors that might influence the timing of labour onset: _____

    _____

    _____

Related activities: The Hormones of Pregnancy·

A 2

Lactation and its Control

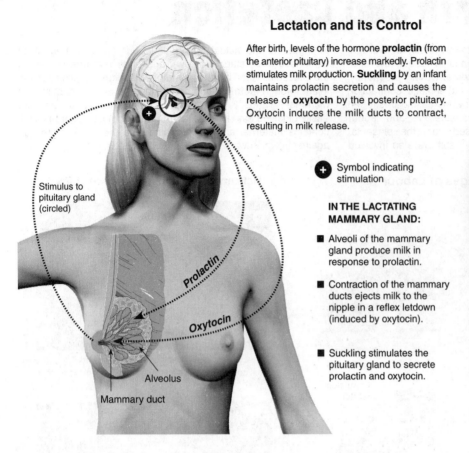

After birth, levels of the hormone **prolactin** (from the anterior pituitary) increase markedly. Prolactin stimulates milk production. **Suckling** by an infant maintains prolactin secretion and causes the release of **oxytocin** by the posterior pituitary. Oxytocin induces the milk ducts to contract, resulting in milk release.

Stimulus to pituitary gland (circled)

Prolactin

Oxytocin

Alveolus

Mammary duct

● **+** Symbol indicating stimulation

IN THE LACTATING MAMMARY GLAND:

■ Alveoli of the mammary gland produce milk in response to prolactin.

■ Contraction of the mammary ducts ejects milk to the nipple in a reflex letdown (induced by oxytocin).

■ Suckling stimulates the pituitary gland to secrete prolactin and oxytocin.

It is essential to establish breast feeding soon after birth, as this is when infants exhibit the strong reflexes that enable them to learn to suckle effectively. The first formed milk, colostrum, has very little sugar, virtually no fat, and is rich in maternal antibodies. Breast milk that is produced later has a higher fat content, and its composition varies as the nutritional needs of the infant change during growth.

3. Explain why the umbilical cord continues to supply blood to the baby for a short time after delivery: _____

4. For each of the following processes, state the primary controlling hormone and its site of production:

(a) Uterine contraction during labour: Hormone: _____ Site of production: _____

(b) Production of milk: Hormone: _____ Site of production: _____

(c) Milk ejection in response to suckling: Hormone: _____ Site of production: _____

5. State which hormone inhibits prolactin secretion during pregnancy: _____

6. Describe two benefits of breast feeding to the health of the infant:

(a) _____

(b) _____

7. (a) Describe the nutritional differences between the first formed milk (colostrum) and the milk that is produced later:

(b) Suggest a reason for these differences: _____

8. Explain why the nutritional composition of breast milk might change during a six-month period of breast feeding:

9. Infants exhibit marked growth spurts at six weeks and three months of age. At these time, their caloric (energy intake) requirements also increase sharply. With reference to what you know about the control of lactation, suggest how a breast-feeding mother could continue to provide for the increased energy requirements of her infant:

Index

Advanced Biology A2

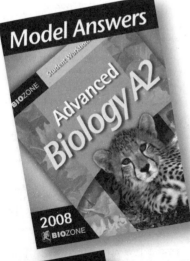

This companion title to Advanced Biology AS provides coverage of the following topics for AQA-A, AQA-B, Edexcel, CIE, OCR & SNAB:

- Cellular Metabolism
- Populations and Interactions
- Practical Ecology
- Sources of Variation
- Inheritance
- Population Genetics and Speciation
- Patterns of Evolution
- Biodiversity and Classification
- Homeostasis
- Muscles and Movement
- Responses and Coordination

Price: £10.95 for student purchase.
This price represents a 35% discount off the RRP.
NOTE: ADD £3.00 for Postage & Packaging.

Model Answers

Model Answers books are available for **both** Advanced Biology AS and Advanced Biology A2. Each provides suggested answers to nearly all of the activities in the workbook.

Price: £4.95 each
NOTE: ADD £1.00 for Postage & Packaging

How to Order

1. Clearly list all titles you want to purchase.
2. Enclose a cheque, including postage and packaging.
3. Include your name, address, and the name of your school.
4. Send to address below:

BIOZONE Learning Media
P.O. Box 23698
Edinburgh, EH5 2WX, UK
Phone: 0131 557 5060
Email: sales@biozone.co.uk

Please do not send cash. Sorry, we do not accept credit cards, nor will we send books without first receiving payment. Your order will be dispatched the same day your payment is received.